ARCHITECTURE
in INDIANAPOLIS

1900–1920

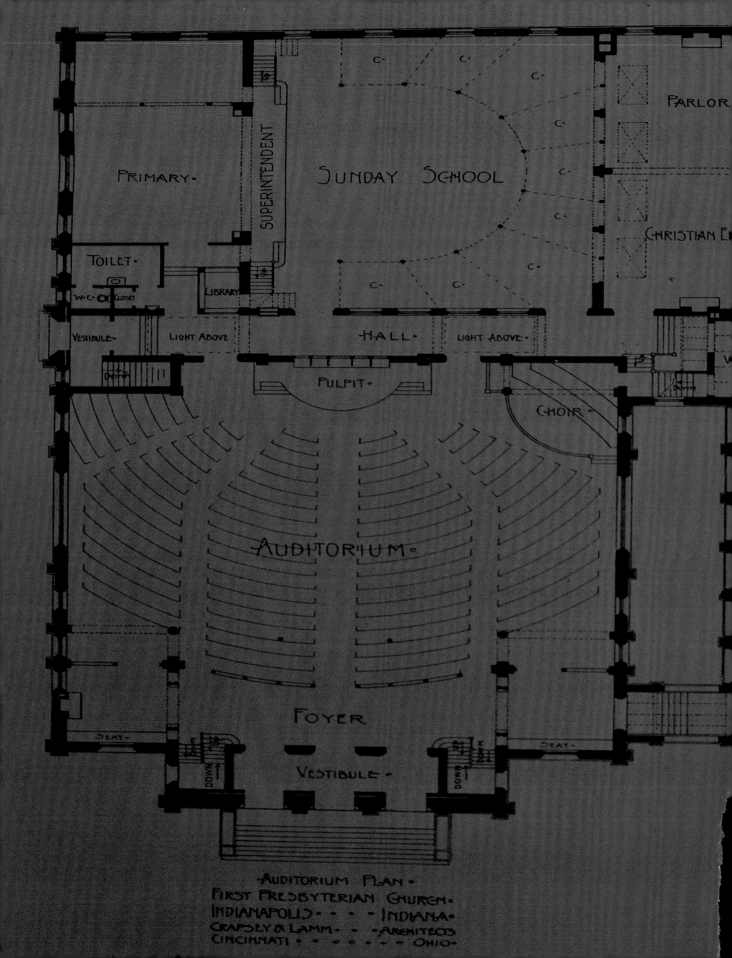

JAMES A. GLASS

ARCHITECTURE *in* INDIANAPOLIS

1900–1920

VOLUME TWO

INDIANA UNIVERSITY PRESS

This book is a publication of

Indiana University Press
Office of Scholarly Publishing
Herman B Wells Library 350
1320 East 10th Street
Bloomington, Indiana 47405 USA

iupress.org

© 2025 by James A. Glass

All rights reserved

No part of this book may be reproduced or utilized in any form or by any means, electronic or mechanical, including photocopying and recording, or by any information storage and retrieval system, without permission in writing from the publisher.

Manufactured in China

First Printing 2025

Cataloging information is available from the Library of Congress.

ISBN 978-0-253-07221-4 (hardback)
ISBN 978-0-253-07223-8 (paperback)
ISBN 978-0-253-07222-1 (web PDF)

For my dad, Robert L. Glass

CONTENTS

Foreword ix
Preface xi
Acknowledgments xiii

Introduction 2
1 | Commercial and Industrial Architecture, 1900–1920 7
2 | Public, Social, and Charitable Architecture, 1900–1920 110
3 | Buildings of Worship, 1900–1920 223
4 | City Mansions and Country Estates, 1900–1920 300
5 | Detached Homes, Doubles, and Apartments, 1900–1920 381
6 | The Development of an Architectural Profession, 1820–1920 471
Epilogue 495

Appendix A: Architectural Glossary 497
Appendix B: Architectural Style Guide 510
Notes 525
Bibliography 565
Index 591

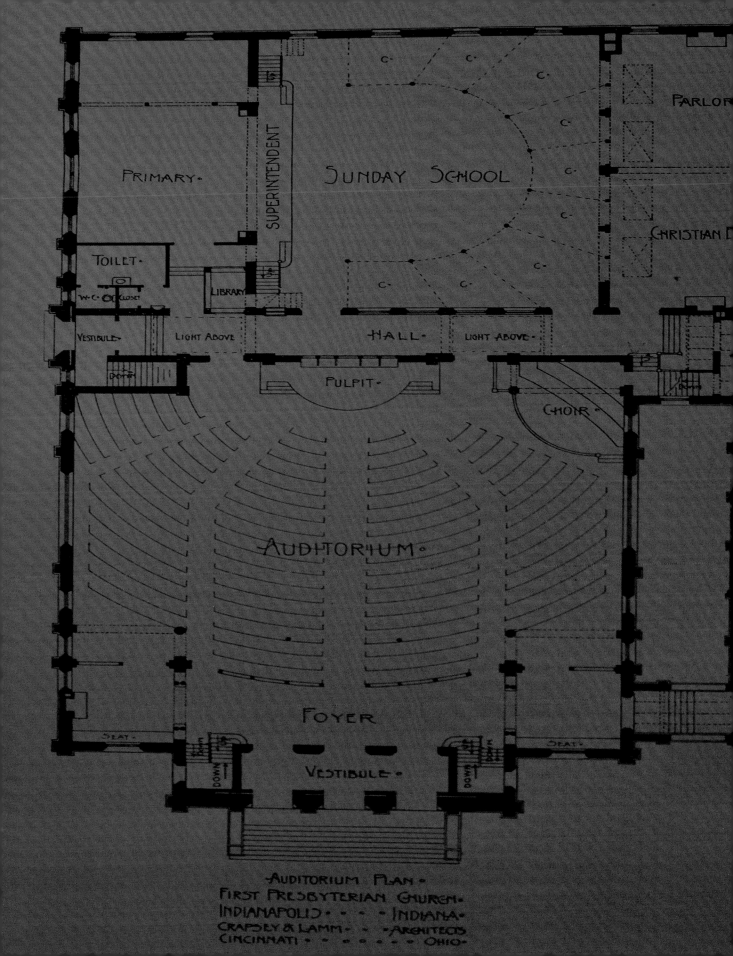

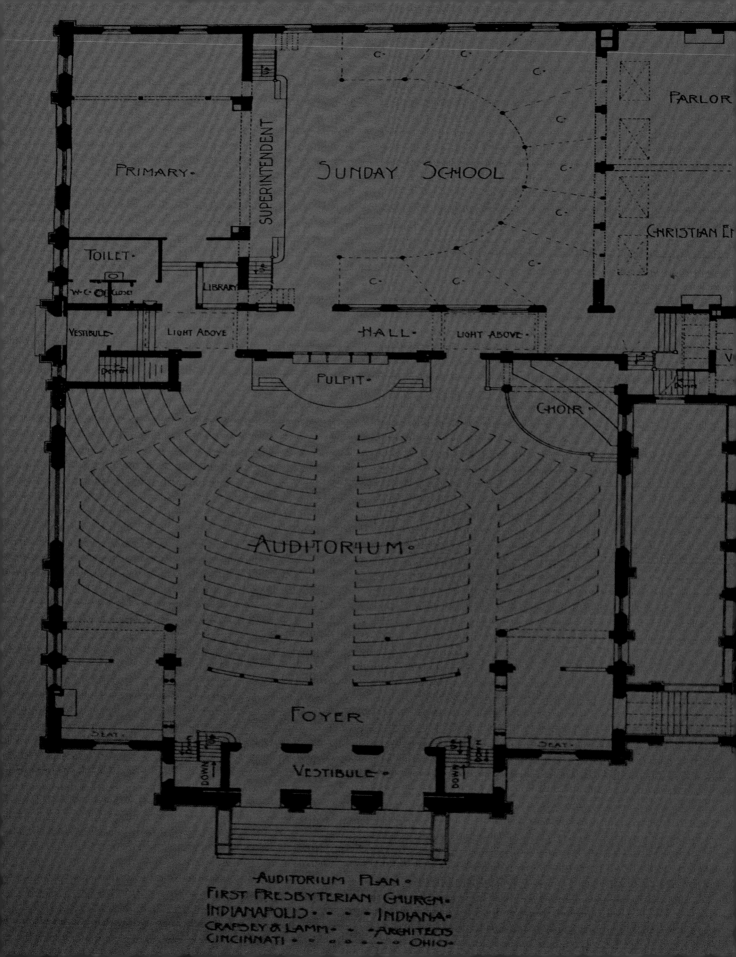

FOREWORD

Given its title, one might logically conclude this is a book about architecture. Indeed, it is, and much more. Together, the two volumes of *Architecture in Indianapolis* are nothing less than the story of a city's remarkable progress over the course of a short one hundred years as revealed in its buildings.

With his comprehensive and detailed analysis of architecture in Indianapolis's first century, Dr. James Glass creates a work that will appeal to scholars, architectural enthusiasts, and historic preservationists alike. While he examines trends in architecture ranging from local to international, Dr. Glass skillfully considers the city's buildings in a broad historical context that includes aesthetics, materials, technologies, and economics. It speaks to what is unique to Indianapolis *and* to what the city's buildings share in common with those elsewhere in the world.

The two volumes of *Architecture in Indianapolis* flow both chronologically and typologically, linking the city's buildings to its growth into a major inland metropolis. The book's discourse on residential, religious, commercial, public, and industrial buildings conveys the dramatic and persistent change the city experienced during its first century.

As he does in his acclaimed architectural history lectures, Dr. Glass drills deep into the elements of architectural design. The detailed, almost granular depiction of these elements, when assembled as a whole, ultimately leads to an understanding of a building's essence, much like observing a pointillist painting up close before viewing it from a distance. Perhaps most revealing of all the chapters in volume 2 is its last, which chronicles the growth of the architecture profession in Indianapolis. This is a profound addition to our knowledge of the practice and the people who constituted the profession and whose talents defined the physical characteristics of the city.

Through this work, we can celebrate the accomplishments of architects and builders who shaped and continually reshaped the city during its first hundred years. I would be remiss, though, in not noting the numerous losses, some truly lamentable, of landmarks featured in this book. I am convinced, however, that this compelling work will increase an appreciation for those historic places that have survived and with that will come a redoubled commitment to preserve them for present and future generations.

Architecture in Indianapolis fills a long-standing void in the history of the city's buildings and the architectural profession. It reflects the perspective of the author, who has dedicated his career to scholarship in the fields of history, architecture, and historic preservation. His thoroughly researched, generously illustrated, definitive treatise on Indianapolis's buildings is a major achievement and a valued addition to the understanding of our heritage.

MARSH DAVIS
President
Indiana Landmarks

PREFACE

I ENTERED THE WORLD OF HISTORIC PRESERVATION AS A HISTORIAN—one who was trained to research and interpret the past through documents and histories. During my seven years on the staff of the Indianapolis Historic Preservation Commission, the first efforts at preservation in the state capital were taking form in such neighborhoods as Lockerbie Square, the Old Northside, Woodruff Place, Fletcher Place, and Chatham Arch. Through my work at the commission, I discovered an affinity for architecture and decided to pursue graduate study in the history of architecture and urban development at Cornell University. My major doctoral field became the history of architecture, and I enjoyed absorbing much of the scholarship to that point on the evolution of architecture and building in the Mediterranean, Europe, and the United States.

My career track led me back in historic preservation at a consulting firm, the Indiana Division of Historic Preservation and Archaeology, and the Graduate Program in Historic Preservation at Ball State University. I retained my interest in architectural history and wrote monthly articles on Indianapolis and Indiana buildings for the *Indianapolis Star*. In 2013, I tried an experiment—organizing a public lecture at which I presented a lecture on Spanish architecture. To my surprise, over one hundred people attended. In succeeding years, I presented similar lectures on architecture in Greece and Turkey, Roman and Renaissance architecture, Chinese architecture, architecture in Mexico, and architecture in London. Attendance continued to grow.

The response suggested to me that there was a ready audience in Indianapolis for the subject of historic architecture. That encouraged me to contemplate a book on architecture in Indianapolis, which I began during the COVID-19 pandemic and continued with the research and writing over three years. In 2021 and 2022,

I tested audience interest in Indianapolis architecture by presenting two public lectures at Indiana Landmarks based on my research and analysis to date. At the second presentation, over four hundred people registered for in-person or online access.

I hope that you, the readers of this book, covering the first decades of the twentieth century, and volume 1, covering the first eighty years of Indianapolis architecture, find the information, interpretations, and images of interest and that you are drawn to see firsthand some of the buildings you encounter.

ACKNOWLEDGMENTS

This book began as a project to mark the bicentennial of Indianapolis and quickly grew in size and scope into a detailed exploration of the history of architecture in the Indiana state capital during the first century of city history. As it has evolved, I have been fortunate to find ready support from many friends and colleagues. Particularly gratifying has been the keen interest and major financial sponsorship of Indiana Landmarks, the state's potent historic preservation advocacy organization. Marsh Davis, president of Landmarks and a friend for many decades, has read the entire manuscript and offered cogent reactions and suggestions. I appreciate those and his very generous foreword.

Other friends have willingly read all the chapters and offered critiques from the point of view of potential readers. In particular, I would like to thank my longtime friends and travel companions Carolyn and Gene Lausch for their thorough annotations in the margins on the coherency of my thoughts and grammar. I also appreciate the critiques and suggestions of Charlie Hyde, president and CEO of the Benjamin Harrison Presidential Site, and his constant encouragement to complete the project. The late Dan Henkel, a friend of thirty-three years, provided an abundance of editorial critiques and counsel on the promotion of the eventual book. Bill Groth, a friend and travel companion, gave a careful eye to my wording and valuable feedback from a lay perspective. Thanks are also due to two wonderful scholars of nineteenth- and early twentieth-century architecture in Indianapolis. James DeGrazia, who has exhaustively researched articles related to architects of the period in city newspapers, has generously shared his research with me. Danita Davis, an authority on architect Louis Gibson and other architects, likewise has shared her knowledge and helped me find rare images. Both also have reviewed the manuscript and offered helpful suggestions. David Baker, long-time administrator of the Indianapolis Historic Preservation Commission, has offered ideas from his perspective on the city's buildings. Jim Vaughn, a historian of the West Baden Springs Hotel, has commented on various aspects. Other readers who have reviewed the unfolding book and provided encouragement include Dr. Tom Greist, Beth Henkel, Dawn Butler Cramer, and Phil Cramer.

In a special category, I would like to thank Dr. Michael Tomlan, professor and director of the Graduate Program in Historic Preservation Planning at Cornell University. He willingly, on short notice and within a tight time frame, reviewed the whole manuscript from the perspective of a senior scholar on American architectural history and provided an abundance of critiques that have saved me from a number of errors and mistakes in interpretation.

Thanks are due in addition to Evan Hale for the attractive location maps and style guide illustrations he produced and refined and to Danita Davis for the meticulous conversion of photos to the format and size needed for publication and for locating hard-to-find historical images. The thorough index for volume 2 is due to the careful efforts of Heidi Winston.

I would further like to acknowledge the resourcefulness and encouragement during my research for both volumes 1 and 2 of the reference staffs of the Indiana State Library and of the Indiana Historical Society Library.

Finally, I would like to thank my father, Robert Glass, for his steadfast support and interest in the book and his sponsorship of a significant portion of the publication costs and Drs. Tom and Anne Greist for their generous donation toward meeting publication expenses. I am also grateful to Indiana University Press for undertaking publication of volumes 1 and 2 and for the staff's careful work in pre-publication, production, and marketing.

Architecture in Indianapolis: 1900–1920 Volume Two received a Historic Preservation Education Grant offered by Indiana Landmarks, Indiana Humanities, and the National Endowment for the Humanities.

ARCHITECTURE
in INDIANAPOLIS

1900–1920

INTRODUCTION

Its founders located Indianapolis, the capital of Indiana, approximately in the center of the new state. The capital's principal planner, Alexander Ralston, is said to have remarked wistfully, "It would make a beautiful city if it were ever built."[1] And indeed, a study of the multitude of buildings constructed along its avenues and streets over the first century of Indianapolis's existence confirms the realization of Ralston's hopes. From the arrival of the first white settlers in 1820 to the aftermath of World War I in 1920, varied and aesthetically pleasing works of architecture represented each epoch in the city's history, designed by an architectural profession that grew in numbers, competence, and maturity.

Together, the two volumes of this book tell the story of the architectural evolution of Indianapolis during its first hundred years and describe a sampling of buildings from each period while highlighting the work and roles of many of the principal architects.

PREVIOUS STUDIES

No architectural history of the state capital has been previously written, nor has one been written about the architecture of the state as a whole. Although the Society of Architectural Historians has sponsored an ambitious program of publishing histories and inventories of architecture for all the states in the country, *Buildings of the United States*, no volume has been projected to date for Indiana.

Within Indianapolis, the first publication to inventory the architecture of all periods and comment on the designs was *Indianapolis Architecture*, published by the Indiana Architectural Foundation in 1975. Its sequel, *Indianapolis*

Architecture: Transformations since 1975, covered works of architecture built between 1975 and 1993. Several excellent histories and inventories of existing buildings have been written about Indianapolis neighborhoods, including *The Main Stem: The History and Architecture of North Meridian Street*, by David J. Bodenhamer, Lamont Hulse, and Elizabeth B. Monroe; *The History and Architecture of Meridian-Kessler* and *Greater Irvington: Architecture, People and Places on the Indianapolis Eastside*, both by Paul C. Diebold; and *Historic Washington Park: An Indianapolis Neighborhood on the National Register of Historic Places*, by Bret Waller and Sheryl Vanderstel.

In 1935, architect-builder Lee Burns produced one of the first works to discuss the lives and works of nineteenth-century architects in Indiana, *Early Architects and Builders of Indiana*. In 1962, Wilbur Peat wrote the first book to study nineteenth-century residential architecture in the state and provide nomenclature for styles, *Indiana Houses of the Nineteenth Century*. Since then, two scholarly and well-illustrated architectural histories of Indiana cities have been published—*The Early Architecture of Madison, Indiana*, by John T. Windle and Robert M. Taylor Jr. (1986), and *Richmond, Indiana: The Physical Development and Aesthetic Heritage to 1920*, by Mary Raddant Tomlan and Michael A. Tomlan (2003). Indiana Landmarks has published several attractive books depicting and commenting on the varied architecture of the state, chief among them *99 Historic Homes of Indiana* of 2002.

Due to growing public interest in old buildings and the emergence of the historic preservation movement, many books and booklets presenting inventories of local historic architecture in Indiana and offering commentaries on styles have appeared. Howard E. Wooden wrote one of the earliest in 1962, *Architectural Heritage of Evansville*, followed by such illuminating works as David Parrish's *Historic Architecture of Lafayette, Indiana* of 1978, David Barksdale and Gregory A. Sekula's *Historic Homes of New Albany, Indiana* of 2015, and a book produced by the Wythongan Valley Preservation Council on *Architectural Styles in Marshall County* (2016). On a regional basis, Ronald E. Schmitt has compiled *Images of Midwestern Architecture: Southern Indiana* and *Images of Midwestern Architecture: Northern Indiana*, containing photos of notable buildings and architectural comments. Volumes emphasizing Modern architecture have been published for both Columbus and New Harmony, Indiana.

The Indiana Division of Historic Preservation and Archaeology and Indiana Landmarks have printed interim reports presenting the results of county surveys of historic sites and structures since the late 1970s, with brief analyses of the architectural styles, building types, and vernacular traditions. As part of the survey program, interim survey reports were published for Indianapolis and Marion County in the 1990s, with separate booklets issued on the nine townships. The focus was on inventorying large numbers of historic properties and providing short overview essays on the history and architectural styles of each township.[2]

THIS BOOK

Indianapolis is worthy of a detailed exploration of its architecture, which produced notable and varied designs reflecting national themes and displaying creative interpretations of styles seen elsewhere. The two volumes of this work endeavor to supply such an exploration with three main audiences in mind: (1) the general reader in central Indiana with an interest in architecture and old buildings, (2) professionals and advocates in the historic preservation fields of Indianapolis and Indiana as a whole, and (3) scholars in the field of architectural history. The general reader can read in detail or skim through the text and examine the illustrations showing the richness of architectural variety that Indianapolis produced. The professionals and advocates can do the same but also deepen their understanding of the significance of particular buildings from the 1820–1920 period. They may use these two books to provide context for evaluating particular structures under threat or interpreting the significance of historic buildings within Indianapolis and Marion County and even outside the county.

Architectural historians, it is hoped, will find that the two volumes together offer a useful case study of American architecture in a leading midwestern city during the formative years of the nineteenth and early twentieth centuries. It is true that the architecture found within each area of Indiana and of the country as a whole has its own personality. Still, many commonalities of design illustrated by buildings in Indianapolis are likely to be observed outside the city.

The chapters in volume 2 describe multiple facets of the story of architecture in Indianapolis during the first twenty years of the twentieth century. The first five chapters discuss particular building types and subtypes, the architectural styles that found favor for each, and the design interpretations that architects produced to satisfy their clients. These five each begin with a brief historical introduction to the building types and subtypes to be discussed and end with a conclusion. The introductions provide economic and social contexts for better understanding the building types and architectural trends in the city. Conclusions recapitulate the principal points. The final chapter treats the evolution of the architectural profession over the whole first century.

Chapter 1 discusses the commercial and industrial architecture of Indianapolis as it became a major midwestern center of steam railroad and electric interurban travel and commerce. Chapter 2 describes some of the principal works of public architecture during the same period, constructed by governments, nonprofit organizations, and charitable institutions. Chapter 3 samples the buildings of worship constructed by Christian and Jewish denominations. Chapter 4 covers examples of the city mansions built in the early twentieth century by wealthy residents, principally along streets of the north side, and describes several country houses and estates constructed by the wealthiest citizens. Chapter 5 discusses all the other house types and styles of the era—business and professional detached houses, middle-class residences, worker's bungalows, doubles for middle-class residents, and apartments for varied income levels. Chapter 6 traces the evolution of the architectural profession in Indianapolis from its beginnings dominated by builders and carpenters to a recognized professional occupation with its own organizations and standards.

In chapters 1–5, photos and drawings illustrate each building discussed, and captions briefly describe the design. The reader may gain a sense of the changes in architecture and what represents each period by simply looking at the illustrations and reading the captions. The text provides a detailed explanation of each building and the intent of the designer. Each of these chapters also includes biographical profiles of the principal architects who practiced during each period—their training and education, the scope of their practice, and the primary buildings they designed.

In order to convey a more complete picture of architecture in the city, volumes 1 and 2 discuss both extant and demolished buildings representing building types and architectural styles and trends. In addition to providing a fuller understanding of city architecture, it is hoped that the inclusion of demolished structures will give readers a sense of the loss through demolition that has occurred, erasing much of the pre-1920 architectural heritage of the city. Those buildings that have been razed are indicated at the beginning of their captions with a plus sign (+). At the end of the caption, the date of demolition and the reason for destruction are given. As will be seen, the three primary reasons for demolition of the vanished buildings all relate to the advent of the automobile: construction of gas stations, parking lots, and auto dealerships.

Volumes 1 and 2 also attempt to shed some light on buildings constructed by and for African American residents of the city during the first hundred years. Relatively little research or writing has previously been done on the architecture of the Black community prior to 1920. This volume discusses several churches constructed by African American congregations, the Robert Gould Shaw School 40 constructed for African American students, a fraternal building erected by Black Pythians, the Senate Avenue YMCA built by the initiative of Black leaders, and a house constructed by African American businesswoman and entrepreneur Madam C. J. Walker.

For nonarchitectural historians, the book includes an architectural glossary (app. A) and an architectural style guide containing drawings illustrating styles and terms associated with them (app. B). For geographic orientation, each chapter includes maps locating most of the buildings discussed in that segment.

The author hopes that this book serves several functions: a history of architecture in a particular place and time, which can be read with reference to the illustrations and architectural profiles; a source that can be sought for its photos and captions to obtain a quick grasp of the architecture and styles; and a reference book, which a reader can use to find information through the index on specific topics.

1 | COMMERCIAL AND INDUSTRIAL ARCHITECTURE

1900–1920

In 1907, the Indianapolis City Directory said with pride that Indianapolis held "the honor of being the largest inland city." It had become known successively as a major railroad center, the heart of the biggest network in the country of electric interurbans, a home to a formidable concentration of commercial activity and manufacturing, and a city of many conventions.[1]

Indianapolis had become a major hub of commercial and industrial activity during the 1880s and 1890s largely because of the crowds of passengers passing through Union Station and the large volume of freight traffic borne by the Belt Railroad around the city. That activity continued after 1900 and grew steadily. During 1906, for example, 60,994 trains passed through Union Station, an increase of 5,200 trains over the previous year. The same year, over a million freight cars transferred from one rail line to another over the Belt Railroad. By 1913, seventeen steam railroad lines connected the state capital with all the major cities in the American Midwest, West, and East.[2] The increasing volume of passenger trains was to bring about a massive track elevation project south of Union Station beginning in 1915 and the construction of a large new concourse and train shed between 1916 and 1922 (see later in this chapter).

The beginning of the twentieth century also saw the advent of an extensive system of electric interurban trains that brought both competition to the steam railroads and an explosion of passenger traffic in and out of Indianapolis. By 1913, the city directory was reporting that during the previous year, thirteen electric interurban systems had carried 6,431,714 passengers in and out of the city.[3] This heavy volume of new passenger traffic to and from the city stimulated commercial businesses and retail trade greatly in the new century, resulting in the construction of a large traction terminal station downtown.

The location of Indianapolis played a significant role in its growth and sustained prosperity. It was situated near the center of population in the United States and, by 1910, was within three hundred miles of one-fourth of the country's population. Indianapolis-made products easily found access to the principal metropolises of the Midwest. The city's own population grew steadily, from 204,518 in 1900 to 291,940 in 1916, and by 1910, the shopping territory of Indianapolis merchants had expanded to include two million people. Residents in this enlarged territory could now make day trips to shop in the state capital via electric and steam railroads.[4]

For two decades after 1900, the local economy saw occasional dips, but the level of prosperity continued upward without additional depressions. The natural gas boom of east-central Indiana (see chap. 7 of vol. 1) ended in 1901 with the exhaustion of most gas wells, but several major industries in Indianapolis and other cities converted to coal or manufactured gas. The other advantages enjoyed by the state capital helped maintain its prosperity. The Panic of 1907 undoubtedly caused some short-term slows in financial and business transactions, but by 1910, the total resources of the city's national banks and trust companies had reached $70 million. After the beginning of World War I in Europe in 1914, industrial production and commercial activity maintained their prewar levels, and some businesses expanded.[5]

In architectural and building terms, the volume of construction for all building types increased steadily between 1900 and the entry of the United States into the war in 1917. During 1906, buildings representing a total cost of $5,530,971 rose in the city, and the municipal government was issuing about three hundred building permits per month. During 1912, the value of buildings constructed rose to $9,150,407 and the value of real estate transfers totaled $23,604,434. The 1913 city directory reported that the downtown now boasted twenty-five modern office buildings from six to sixteen stories high.[6]

Office buildings became one of the principal types of commercial structures that investors built between 1900 and 1917. Owners and architects found models for local office buildings in the many skyscrapers that were rising in the great midwestern metropolis, Chicago. A new building type, the department store, became dominant in downtown retailing. Investors constructed hotels offering a variety of accommodations and varied architectural and artistic quality. The large increases of passenger traffic in and out of the downtown called for the construction of additional new building types—a traction terminal and shed for electric interurbans and an immense concourse at Union Station affording easy access to the elevated steam trains above. More large-scale construction took place when the Big Four Railroad built train repair shops in the new suburb of Beech Grove. Wholesale buildings continued to be erected in the wholesale district, and several reinforced concrete buildings rose there that served printing and engraving companies. A boom in manufacturing stimulated the construction of factories with reinforced concrete frames and immense windows in lieu of the brick walls and heavy wooden structures of factories erected in the 1880s and 1890s. A special impetus to industrial plant design and construction came through the advent of the automobile, which swiftly boosted Indianapolis to the status of the second-largest producer of motorcars in the country by 1916.[7]

The 1900–1920 period saw the continuation of several architectural themes or styles from the previous era for commercial and industrial buildings. Architects and clients continued to favor the Italian Renaissance for office buildings, hotels, and some wholesale and factory structures. A new theme, NeoClassicism, drawn directly from the architecture of the ancient Greeks and Romans and popularized by use in the 1893 Columbian Exposition in Chicago, influenced the design of many private office buildings and public edifices. In one case, the new Union Station concourse of 1916–22, architect William Price anticipated the Art Deco and Moderne styles of the 1920s and 1930s with his abstracted Gothic buttresses and stylized decorative motifs.

COMMERCIAL OFFICE BUILDINGS

As seen in chapter 7 of volume 1, the tall office building, popularly called the skyscraper, took root in the central business district of Indianapolis with construction of the Commercial Club, Majestic Building, Lemcke Building, Stevenson Building, and Law Building during the 1890s. The obvious models for design came from Chicago, a short three-hour train ride from the Indiana state capital. Chicago architects William LeBaron Jenney, Burnham and Root, Adler and Sullivan, and Holabird and Roche devised formulas for structural systems, materials, and exterior composition that local architects used.[8] To a lesser extent, Indianapolis architects incorporated elements from New York skyscrapers, which could be studied via plans and photos in leading architectural periodicals. From both Chicago and New York, local architects derived the tripartite formula described by critic Montgomery Schuyler in which designers organized the stories of tall office buildings into sections corresponding to the capital, shaft, and base of a Classical column.[9]

Newton Claypool Building

In late 1900, Newton Claypool, son of wealthy capitalist Edward Fay Claypool, announced plans to build a large, seven-story office building on the southwest corner of Ohio and Pennsylvania Streets. The younger Claypool retained veteran Indianapolis architect John H. Stem, who designed a square structure with substantial 120-foot frontages on both Pennsylvania and Ohio Streets (fig. 1.1). Like the Stevenson and Law Buildings constructed shortly before, the new structure followed fireproof construction standards, with a steel frame, mottled gray brick exterior walls, and a layer of cement between floors. Stem's exterior treatment was somewhat monotonous, with an unornamented grid of windows in trios separated by plain, flat piers. The architect incorporated Ionic pilasters into the top two stories on both elevations, but the pilasters lacked much definition and did not relieve the monotony. A larger and more projecting cornice might have also countered the predominant verticality of the piers. The architect chose a simple cornice design, supported by brackets and paired with a plain frieze.[10]

The most important element in Stem's Newton Claypool design was his use of a large interior atrium. A pyramidal skylight covered the square space, the bottom of which served as a lobby for the building. Balconies lined each story overlooking the atrium, and the offices in the building—especially equipped for physicians and dentists—opened onto the balconies. Stem specified clay tile and glass partitions for interior walls, marble wainscoting for corridors, and quartered oak for interior finishes. Claypool spent between $200,000 and $250,000 on the building.[11]

Indianapolis Traction Terminal Office Building and Shed

The explosive growth of electric interurbans after 1900 transformed the Indianapolis economy and brought thousands of visitors, customers, and businessmen to the city. By 1905, the state capital was becoming the center of the biggest interurban network in the country. Nearly four hundred electric trains entered the city per day. To handle the traffic in and out of town, in 1902, interurban interests planned the largest traction terminal in the United States on the northwest corner of Market and Illinois Streets. The Schoepf-McGowan financial syndicate

Figure 1.1. A + beside the name of a building indicates that it no longer exists. †Newton Claypool Building, southwest corner, Ohio and Pennsylvania Streets, built in 1900–1901 and designed by John H. Stem, following the tripartite skyscraper formula and detailed with Classical pilasters and Renaissance cornice. View in 1905, emphasizing Ohio Street (north) facade. Demolished in 1980 and replaced in 1986–87 by Bank One (now Salesforce) Tower. Bass Photo Co. Collection, Indiana Historical Society. (Image cropped)

of New York controlled most of the interurban lines in Indiana and many of the local electric streetcar companies. Hugh J. McGowan was the local representative of the syndicate and the principal factor in organizing the Indianapolis Traction Terminal Company. He oversaw the construction of the terminal and an adjacent nine-story office building that would house the headquarters of the principal interurban lines.[12]

COMMERCIAL AND INDUSTRIAL ARCHITECTURE | 11

Figure 1.2. +Indianapolis Traction Terminal office building, northwest corner, Market and Illinois Streets, built 1902–4 and designed by D. H. Burnham and Company of Chicago, using the three-part skyscraper formula and Romanesque details. View in c. 1915–20. Demolished in 1968 and replaced with the Blue Cross-Blue Shield office building. Kingan & Co., Souvenir of Indianapolis (Indianapolis: Kingan & Co., c. 1925).

Figure 1.3. +Traction Terminal train shed, West Market Street. Dismantled and removed in 1968 and replaced with Blue Cross-Blue Shield Building. Max R. Hyman, ed., Hyman's Handbook of Indianapolis (Indianapolis: M. R. Hyman, 1907), 183.

McGowan and his syndicate retained one of the most prominent architects in the Midwest, Daniel H. Burnham of Chicago, to design the new structures. Burnham and his former partner, John Wellborn Root, had helped develop the Chicago-style skyscraper, and Burnham had supervised the design and construction of the 1893 Columbian Exposition in his home city. At the time of the Indianapolis commission, his firm was designing the monumental Union Station in Washington, DC. The interurban syndicate hired a top architect to create a symbol of their new transportation mode.[13]

Burnham and his draftsmen designed an office building that incorporated the Romanesque style in key details (fig. 1.2). They used a reddish-brown brick for the outside curtain walls above the second floor. The designers followed the model of most Chicago and New York office buildings in organizing the exterior of the Traction Terminal office building into a grid of windows, in this case arranged in pairs, separated by prominent piers. The piers rose to form Romanesque arches

ARCHITECT PROFILE

Daniel H. Burnham

Daniel Hudson Burnham (1846–1912) was born in Henderson, New York, and raised in Chicago, where he graduated from Central High School. In his early twenties, he entered the architectural offices first of William LeBaron Jenney and then Peter B. Wight. From Wight, in particular, he learned the basics of design and drafting. In 1873, Burnham and John Wellborn Root formed an architectural partnership that in eighteen years became one of the most successful in Chicago. Burnham had a natural gift for sales, client relations, and drawing floor plans, while Root served as the primary designer for residences and many office buildings. After Root's death in 1891, Burnham operated his own office, eventually styled D. H. Burnham and Company, and built it into one of the largest architectural firms in the country.

Burnham organized and effectively managed his force of draftsmen to produce a steady stream of designs for varied clients throughout the country. He himself was the top executive, while head designers such as Charles Atwood oversaw design development and production of construction documents. The delegation of labor led to staff architects such as Frederick Williamson and Howard White supervising construction on major buildings in Chicago and other cities, such as Indianapolis. The architects derived the compositions and structural systems of the Traction Terminal and Merchants National Bank Buildings in the Indiana state capital from a host of skyscrapers that the Burnham firm designed in Chicago. Burnham's practice extended to department stores, such as Marshall Field and Company in Chicago, and railway stations, such Union Station in Washington, DC, and the Pennsylvania Railroad Station in Richmond, Indiana. Stylistically, he and his staff followed national trends, from Romanesque to Roman Classical.

Burnham also exerted a major influence as a city planner, growing out of his oversight of the Columbian Exposition of 1893 in Chicago. From there, he helped developed plans for Washington, DC, San Francisco, Cleveland, and Chicago itself.

Source: Thomas S. Hines, *Burnham of Chicago: Architect and Planner* (Chicago: University of Chicago Press, 1979), xvii–xxiii, 5–19, 22–25, 92–124, 268–306, 174–196. Source for photo: Ryerson and Burnham Archives, Art Institute of Chicago, n.d. https://artic.contentdm.oclc.org/digital/collection/mqc/id/50370/rec/50, accessed June 26, 2024.

along the ninth floor, leading the eye upward to the projecting, Renaissance-style cornice. The architects enriched the tops of the piers with Corinthian capitals in terra-cotta, which also served as impost blocks for the arches. They gave further attention to the Romanesque theme through a monumental archway framing the Illinois Street entrance. The designers supported the massive arch with Corinthian columns, all in Indiana limestone. The first two stories of the skyscraper, covered with white limestone, contrasted with the upper stories. The building followed fireproof standards, with a steel skeleton and hollow tile interior partitions.[14]

The architects gave the office building a rectangular shape. They attached a two-story segment along the west side to house the terminal waiting room. Adjoining the waiting room, they devised an immense shed to cover the nine interurban tracks (fig. 1.3). Steel trusses formed the structure of the shed, supporting a wooden gable roof with a skylight at the center. Burnham and the contractors pursued construction at a rapid rate and completed the terminal and office building in 1904. The total cost came to about $700,000.[15]

Board of Trade Building

Since the 1870s, the Indianapolis Board of Trade, an association promoting the trade of agricultural products, such as grain and corn, had occupied a building on the corner of Capitol Avenue and Maryland Street. The board watched the business district move to the north and, in 1905, decided to construct a new office building on the southeast corner of Ohio and Meridian, at the other end of the block occupied by the Newton Claypool Building. The building committee interviewed three architectural firms—Brubaker and Eldridge, the new firm of Rubush and Hunter, and a young architect, Clarence Martindale—and selected Henry C. Brubaker and William K. Eldridge. The winning firm had been formed a short time before by Brubaker, an architect, and Eldridge, a civil engineer.[16]

Brubaker and Eldridge had submitted conceptual plans for the new Board of Trade Building as part of the interview. After the selection, the building committee decided to accompany the designers to Chicago and look over several "modern office buildings." Brubaker and Eldridge then incorporated the features found desirable during the trip into their revised plans. The final design involved an eight-story building with a U-shaped plan above the first floor. The U shape created a spacious open court that admitted abundant light into offices located along the core. Eldridge made a particular contribution to the design by devising a reinforced concrete structure for the building, one of the first such structures to be used in an Indianapolis office building. Thereafter, a concrete structure with embedded iron bars for tensile strength began to supersede steel columns and beams as the preferred structural system for most commercial and public buildings.[17]

For the exterior, Brubaker used the tripartite formula of a base section, shaft, and capital (fig. 1.4). He covered the first two stories with Indiana limestone and employed a Renaissance system of Corinthian pilasters, both fluted and smooth, to support an Ionic frieze and projecting cornice with consoles. He constructed the shaft section with red brick curtain walls and added interest by lining the double-hung sash windows with cream terra-cotta blocks. Above the seventh story, a substantial terra-cotta stringcourse separated the shaft from the culminating eighth story, which Brubaker adorned with terra-cotta courses linking the windows and keystones in the window heads. Unlike Stem, with his modest Newton Claypool cornice down the street, Brubaker crowned the Board of Trade Building with a boldly projecting cornice of copper supported by pairs of brackets and intervening consoles. The cornice dominated the building and drew the eye upward.

Figure 1.4. +Indianapolis Board of Trade Building, southeast corner, Ohio and Meridian Streets, built 1905–6 and designed by Brubaker and Eldridge, architects and engineers, using the tripartite "column" skyscraper formula for the facade and drawing from the Italian Renaissance for details. This was one of the first office buildings in Indianapolis with a reinforced concrete structure. View, c. 1907. Demolished in 1981 and replaced by the Bank One (now Salesforce) Tower.
Bass Photo Co. Collection, Indiana Historical Society. (Image cropped)

Knights of Pythias Office Building

The next major office building to appear on the downtown scene was the first of several tall structures built by Indiana's principal fraternal orders. In 1904, the Grand Lodge of the Knights of Pythias of Indiana decided to erect an office building containing their headquarters and an auditorium for statewide meetings. They chose as a location the point formed by Pennsylvania Street and Massachusetts Avenue. The building committee set the maximum price for the building at $350,000 and conducted a national architectural competition to produce the best design. Fourteen firms submitted plans. After reviewing the submissions, the panel chose the design prepared by J. F. Alexander and Son of Lafayette. James F. Alexander had practiced architecture in his home city since 1880 and designed several office buildings there.[18]

The Alexander design called for a flat-iron building to fit the triangular site (fig. 1.5). The architects followed the three-section, "column" formula. They lined the first two stories with Ionic pilasters supporting a frieze and cornice. The pilaster shafts carried rusticated blocks, following a precedent in Italian Renaissance architecture. The building's midsection consisted of eight stories simply detailed with stone ashlar blocks. At the center, along the rounded point of the flat iron, the architects employed oversized stone voussoirs to form flat arches. They gave prominence to the windows on the point at the tenth floor by using round arches for the window heads. The architects covered the top, or "capital," zone along the eleventh floor with smooth ashlar stone highlighted by a cartouche executed by sculptor Alexander Sangernebo at the center. A large projecting cornice supported by boldly scaled consoles dominated the eleven stories and drew the eye upward. The Alexanders provided the standard fireproof structure of the period: a steel skeleton and stone curtain wall backed by brick on the exterior, with tile partitions within.[19]

Inside the tenth floor, they designed a spacious auditorium with a stage and scenery for the state meetings and pageants conducted by the Grand Lodge. The rest of the structure contained offices that brought rental income to the Knights and amortized the debt arising from the construction.[20] The building formed a

Facing, Figure 1.5. +Knights of Pythias office building, 219 North Pennsylvania Street, built in 1905–7 and designed by J. F. Alexander and Son of Lafayette, using the three-part skyscraper formula and Renaissance-style rustication for the limestone facade and pilasters and cornice. View from 1907, Massachusetts Avenue at right. Demolished in 1967 and replaced with the Indiana National Bank Tower. Max R. Hyman, ed., Hyman's Handbook of Indianapolis (Indianapolis: M. R. Hyman, 1907), 45.

notable landmark north of the Circle and became a gateway to Massachusetts Avenue, which was fast becoming a new retail district.

Indianapolis Star Building

In January 1904, fire destroyed the Civil War–era First Baptist Church on the northeast corner of New York and Pennsylvania Streets (see chap. 5 of vol. 1). Nearly three years later, the *Indianapolis Star* newspaper acquired the site and announced plans to construct a building there. Streetcar and interurban magnate George McCulloch had founded the *Star* in 1903, and the newspaper had steadily grown since, absorbing both the Republican *Indianapolis Journal* and the Democratic *Indianapolis Sentinel*. The footprint for the structure had a frontage on Pennsylvania of 60 feet and a depth of 195 feet along New York. It was one of the first commercial buildings to be constructed north of New York in the upper-income residential district that had existed since the Civil War.[21]

The *Star* retained the top local architectural firm Vonnegut and Bohn to design their building. Senior partner Bernard Vonnegut probably served as the designer, although partner Arthur Bohn may have contributed to the result and was involved in supervising construction. A *Star* article on the plans stated that the three-story building would be "in the reserved style of the up-to-date business building." The writer may have meant that Vonnegut's design employed abstract versions of conventional NeoClassical or Renaissance details (fig. 1.6). Vonnegut arranged a separate section for the first story, in which deeply grooved brick joints suggested Renaissance-style rustication. Above a stone stringcourse, he lined the upper stories with substantial brick pilasters, but instead of Classical capitals, he capped them with stone tablets containing sculpted organic details. A more usual cornice lined the top of the third story, above which rose a brick parapet. More of the stone sculptural motifs appeared in a stone surround with which he framed the main entrance on Pennsylvania Street. Alexander Sangernebo carried out the limestone ornamentation of the facade.[22]

Inside, the business offices occupied the first floor and the editorial offices the second. The presses operated on the first floor and in the basement.[23]

Odd Fellows Office Building

About the same time that the *Star* announced its building plans, the Indiana Grand Lodge of the Independent Order of Odd Fellows decided to build the latest tallest office building in the city. The Grand Lodge had previously constructed an

Figure 1.6. +Indianapolis Star Building, northeast corner, New York and Pennsylvania Streets, built in 1906–7 and designed by Bernard Vonnegut of Vonnegut and Bohn using the three-part office building facade formula and Renaissance details. The facade was removed in c. 1970–75 and replaced with a brick veneer and vertical Modern glass panels. The original structure was demolished in 2018 and replaced with the Whit Apartments. Max R. Hyman, ed., Hyman's Handbook of Indianapolis (Indianapolis: M. R. Hyman, 1907), 195.

exotic headquarters on the northeast corner of Pennsylvania and Washington in 1854–55, designed by James Renwick Jr. and Francis Costigan (see chap. 3 of vol. 1). By 1906, the Odd Fellows had experienced a manyfold increase in membership during the golden age of fraternal orders in Indiana. The Grand Lodge also was persuaded, like the Knights of Pythias, that they could recoup their investment over time if they combined several functions: multiple office stories, the lodge headquarters, and an auditorium for statewide Odd Fellow meetings. They therefore announced plans for a fourteen-story structure on an expanded rectangular site at Pennsylvania and Washington.[24]

COMMERCIAL AND INDUSTRIAL ARCHITECTURE | 21

Facing, **Figure 1.7.** Independent Order of Odd Fellows Building, northeast corner, Washington and Pennsylvania Streets, built in 1907–8 and designed by Rubush and Hunter using the tripartite skyscraper formula and Renaissance details. View from c. 1905–10. Postcard in author's collection.

The Odd Fellows retained a local architectural firm that was swiftly claiming major commissions downtown. Preston C. Rubush and Edgar Otis Hunter had formed their partnership in 1904 and rapidly expanded their practice through grandly scaled and appointed designs and cordial relations with clients. For the Odd Fellows Building, they crafted a fireproof structure—with a steel frame and exterior curtain walls fronted with limestone—and followed the three-part formula of base, shaft, and capital for the exterior composition (fig. 1.7). The base section consisted of two stories with a frieze and cornice. The architects placed five limestone-covered piers along the base stories and, in between, metal columns encased in stamped sheet metal with decorative motifs. Next came a transitional third story, with limestone piers dividing trios of windows. For the "shaft" section, from the fourth through twelfth stories, the architects used a common arrangement of regular limestone piers separating trios of windows. The architects specified the use of Chicago windows, in which the central window in each trio was wider than its mates. Above the twelfth story, a projecting cornice/stringcourse ended the shaft section. Above, the "capital" section consisted of giant, two-story arched windows, which lined the outside of the auditorium for Grand Lodge meetings. These Renaissance-style windows, recessed slightly into the facade, were flanked by colossal pilasters with Doric capitals modified by the insertion of decorative shields. Above the windows, the composition terminated with a frieze, a projecting cornice supported by modillions, and a solid parapet styled as a balustrade.[25]

Like Vonnegut and Bohn, Rubush and Hunter used cartouches and foliated elements in stone to decorate their facade. Such features adorned the upper portions of the street-level pilasters and the piers along the twelfth story. Also, the architects capped the twelfth-story details with sculpted goddess heads from classical mythology. In the spandrels between the piers in the shaft section, the designers created sheet-metal coverings with stamped designs. Alexander Sangernebo produced the sculpted elements of the facade. Within the thirteenth story, the architects decorated the 1,300-seat Grand Lodge auditorium and its anteroom with elaborate ornamentation.[26]

The Odd Fellows included retail stores and offices in their skyscraper to generate income to pay the operating expenses for the building, service the debt from constructing the structure, and pay off the principal. The estimated cost of the building and site amounted to about $778,000.[27]

Merchants National Bank Building

In 1865, a group of investors founded Merchants National Bank. Under the management of the three Frenzel brothers—John P., Otto N., and Oscar F.—it grew to become one of the principal financial institutions in the city. In 1907, the bank announced plans to build the tallest skyscraper in the state on the southeast corner of Washington and Meridian, center of the retail and commercial district downtown. To design the tallest building, the Frenzels retained the prestigious Chicago architectural firm D. H. Burnham and Company. The firm returned to the city three years after completing the Traction Terminal office building and shed. The bank acquired the entire rectangular property from Washington south to Pearl Street, but unexpired leases on the north half of the footprint forced it to build the structure in two phases.[28]

The Burnham staff designed the entire office building in 1907 but oversaw the immediate construction of only the first four stories in the south half of the site (fig. 1.8). The initial portion contained the banking room and offices of Merchants National Bank. Architect Fred C. Williamson of Burnham's staff oversaw the completion of the first phase in 1907–8. Three years later, Howard J. White of Burnham and Company supervised the construction of the rest of the building. The designers devised a fireproof structure consisting of a steel frame embedded in concrete. Because of the height of the building, the engineers in the Burnham office set the girders so as to resist heavy wind currents. The exterior curtain walls ranged in thickness from twelve to fifteen inches.[29]

For the outside composition (fig. 1.9), the architects crafted a classic statement of the tripartite skyscraper formula: a limestone-fronted base section consisting of colossal Doric pilasters lining the first two stories and supporting an entablature; a transitional story faced with limestone and punctuated by horizontal banks of windows; a shaft section of red, vitrified Kittanning brick; and a final capital zone of limestone, with regular horizontal bays separated by large sculptures of circular shields superimposed on fasces with bound rods and ax-heads. A projecting cornice supported by modillions capped the facade.[30]

The architects designed a banking room for their clients that still boasts impressive materials and artistic refinement today. A newspaper account described the style of the room thusly: "the general spirit of the interior is that of the ancient Greek modified to meet current conditions." An analysis of the interior design

Left, **Figure 1.8.** Rendering for Merchants National Bank Building on the southeast corner, Washington and Meridian Streets, built in 1907–12 and designed by D. H. Burnham and Company of Chicago using the classic tripartite skyscraper formula and Classical and Renaissance details. *Year Book of the Indiana Chapter A.I.A. and Catalog of the Third Annual Exhibition 1912* (Indianapolis: Indiana Chapter A.I.A., 1912).

Right, **Figure 1.9.** Merchants National Bank (now Barnes and Thornburg) Building in 2023. James Glass.

| *Facing,* **Figure 1.10.** Merchants National Bank banking room in 2014. James Glass.

shows that the Burnham draftsmen freely interpreted the Greek idiom and added original features that drew also from Roman and Renaissance architecture (fig. 1.10). Doric columns with fluted upper shafts and dark-green lower shafts of Georgia marble line the two-story room. Above, a ceiling with deeply recessed Roman coffers covers the center of the space. Egg and dart moldings line the coffers. Between the columns, the architects placed bronze teller's cages decorated with rosettes and shields. Along the sides of the room, they installed a mezzanine level for clerical staff and offices for the bank officers and board of directors. In the basement, customers found the safety deposit department with an immense vault and mahogany-paneled retiring rooms.[31]

Stores occupied the ground floor on Washington Street, and Burnham's designers provided for retail storerooms on the floors immediately above the bank. The rest of the immense building contained 125,000 square feet for offices. The architects specified Alabama marble for seven-foot panels along the corridor walls and black-and-white ceramic floors with Greek borders. Interior finishes were to be imported mahogany, increasingly popular. Interestingly, the architects placed toilet rooms for men and women on a single floor.[32]

Pennway Building

In 1909, Dr. John M. Kitchen decided to construct a building to house the offices of physicians. Eyeing the location picked by the *Indianapolis Star* shortly before for its headquarters, Kitchen purchased the southeast corner of New York and Pennsylvania Streets as his site. He was continuing a trend to locate office structures north of the original business district, which was increasingly viewed as congested. Construction of the four-story building required the demolition of a historic house, the residence once occupied by Civil War governor Oliver P. Morton.[33]

Kitchen hired the architectural firm D. A. Bohlen and Son, and Oscar Bohlen and his staff proceeded to design one of the first commercial buildings in the city with an exterior composed entirely of terra-cotta (figs. 1.11 and 1.12). This material, formed by baking clay in molds and glazing the resulting ceramic forms with varied colors, was rapidly superseding brick and stone as a facade material. Intricate sculptural decorations with eye-catching polychromy could be easily and efficiently produced at a cost significantly less than quarrying limestone and hiring sculptors to carve details in stone. Bohlen chose a cream-colored terra-cotta

Facing top, **Figure 1.11.** Pennway Building, 241 North Pennsylvania Street, built in 1909–10 and designed by Oscar D. Bohlen and D. A. Bohlen and Son, using terra-cotta as veneer for entire facade and Classical and Renaissance motifs. View in 1928. Bass Photo Co. Collection, Indiana Historical Society. (Image cropped)

Facing bottom, **Figure 1.12.** Pennway Building in 2019. James Glass.

for Kitchen's Pennway Building. The architect used the three-part formula for the facade design, with Doric pilasters lining the ground floor, a shaft section consisting of three-story pilasters alternating with pairs of windows, and a capital section composed of an architrave, frieze, and sharply projecting cornice. For decoration, Bohlen created elaborate cartouches along the upper portions of the piers, carrying foliated details and capital *P*'s; a bas-relief organic sculpture in the frieze, and dentils just below the cornice. He arranged the physicians' offices in three-room suites.[34]

Indianapolis News Building

At the same time, the owners of the *Indianapolis News*, the principal evening newspaper, announced plans to build a new office building for their business and editorial operations at 32 West Washington Street, in the heart of the retail district. Delavan Smith and former U.S. vice president Charles W. Fairbanks owned the *News*, and Smith made the business decisions. A native of Chicago, Smith hired a well-known Chicago architect, Jarvis Hunt, as the architect for the new structure. Hunt, nephew of prominent New York architect Richard Morris Hunt, maintained an extensive midwestern practice that included the design of office buildings, railroad stations, and the Great Lakes Naval Station north of Chicago.[35]

On a narrow, thirty-six-foot-wide lot, Hunt devised a striking, Gothic-derived design, all in white, vitrified terra-cotta (fig. 1.13). He followed the three-section formula for office buildings, with a two-story base, a seven-story shaft, and a single story for the top section. Hunt drew primarily from the vocabulary of medieval Gothic cathedrals for the decorative scheme of the facade. He adorned the front of the base section with quatrefoils cut out of a green, sheet-metal framework. He defined the sides of the seven-story section with tall Gothic shafts modeled on those attached to piers in the naves of cathedrals. The shafts culminated in pinnacles above the parapet at the crown of the facade. As elements of horizontality, Hunt provided molded terra-cotta panels below the tenth story and a cornice with a parapet above it.[36]

Facing, **Figure 1.13.** Indianapolis News Building, 32 West Washington Street, built in 1909–10 and designed by Jarvis Hunt of Chicago with terra-cotta facade and Gothic detailing. View in 1910. Bass Photo Co. Collection, Indiana Historical Society. (Image cropped)

The steel frame, encased in the terra-cotta veneer, qualified the building for fireproof status. Hunt finished the interior offices in clay tile and quartered oak. Smith placed the accounting offices on the ground floor and the editorial offices on the seventh through tenth floors. He rented the rest of the floors to the Taylor Carpet Company next door.[37]

Bobbs-Merrill Building

In January 1910, the principal publishing firm of Indianapolis, the Bobbs-Merrill Company, announced plans to build a five-story building for its use on the north side of Vermont Street, facing University Park. The company was known for its stable of well-known authors from Indiana's golden age of literature—Meredith Nicholson, George Ade, and James Whitcomb Riley among them. The *Indianapolis News* reported that the move of Bobbs-Merrill from its previous location on Washington Street to north of the park marked "the forced extension of the business of the city from the congested [commercial] district." The business area of the city was pressing into the previously solidly residential neighborhood north of Vermont Street.[38]

Bobbs-Merrill, led by president William C. Bobbs, vice president John J. Curtis, and secretary and treasurer Charles W. Merrill, hired the architectural firm of Foltz and Parker to design their building. Herbert W. Foltz and Wilson B. Parker had been partners for nearly a decade in Indianapolis, and their previous practice had included many residences, the main YMCA Building (see chap. 2 of this volume), the Southeast Indiana Hospital for the Insane in Madison, the Indianapolis Orphans' Asylum, and several Indianapolis public schools. Their design for the publisher sought, according to the *News*, to obtain "an architectural effect that would make a proper contrast with the architecture of the [newly constructed] First Baptist Church next door and also accord with the landscape in University Park, and thus definitely avoid evidences of ordinary business architecture." A modern eye would judge Foltz and Parker's design (fig. 1.14) as successful in distinguishing itself from the rock-faced stone Romanesque church (see chap. 3 of this volume). The Bobbs-Merrill facade presented a mixture of Italian Renaissance and Georgian details in red brick and limestone. With respect to the park, the

COMMERCIAL AND INDUSTRIAL ARCHITECTURE | 31

Facing, **Figure 1.14.** +Bobbs-Merrill Building, 18 East Vermont Street, built in 1910–11 and designed by Foltz and Parker of Indianapolis with a Georgian and Classical composition for the facade. View in c. 1915. Moved in 1927 to 122 East Michigan Street to make way for the Indiana World War Memorial Plaza. Demolished in c. 1970 to build the Minton-Capehart Building. Bass Photo Co. Collection, Indiana Historical Society. (Image cropped)

designers scaled the Bobbs-Merrill facade to pay deference to the wooded public sanctuary, with its central fountain, lawns, and walks.[39]

The facade composition featured a limestone screen of engaged Tuscan columns with an entablature across the second story of the facade. The columns flanked large arched windows with keystones, and the one-and-a-half-story windows flooded light into the accounting and general offices of the firm on the second floor. Smooth ashlar limestone blocks along the street level contained the recessed entry and five windows and supported the columns above. Above the second-story entablature, the architects used a Georgian formula for stories three and four, with plain colonial-style brick and flat brick arches for windows with sixteen-over-sixteen sashes. They added visual interest to the top floor by lining it with a shallow balcony and balustrade, supported by oversized modillions. Above the fifth story, a plain cornice and frieze provided a further horizontal element to the crown of the composition, surmounted by a simple brick parapet.[40]

The architects ensured that the structure of the Bobbs-Merrill Building, like other major downtown buildings of the period, was fireproof. They employed a steel frame, cement floors and roof, and twelve-inch brick curtain walls on the exterior. They placed a vault under the sidewalk in front of the building to contain the electrotype and stereotype plates from which the clients printed their books. The basement contained the unbound sheets of publications. The street level provided a "counting room" and general offices. The upper three floors housed the editorial and art departments, the editorial department for legal publications, and the library. The Bobbs-Merrill Company invested a total of $100,000 in its new building.[41]

Hume-Mansur Building

The possibilities of terra-cotta as a facade material offering varied forms and textures, decorative possibilities, and colors found its full exploitation in 1911, when construction began on a ten-story office building between the Newton Claypool

Figure 1.15. +Hume-Mansur Building, 23 East Ohio Street, built in 1911–12 and designed by Rubush and Hunter, featured a massive terra-cotta facade with Doric pilasters and cartouches as details. Photo taken in c. 1915. Demolished in 1980 and replaced by Bank One (now Salesforce) Tower. Bass Photo Co. Collection, Indiana Historical Society. (Image cropped)

and Board of Trade Buildings on Ohio Street. Two widows, Mary E. Hume and Hannah A. Mansur, decided to build a $500,000 structure on the sites of their family houses, built in the 1850s and 1860s. To design the Hume-Mansur Building, the women and their representative hired Rubush and Hunter, who by then had served as architects for the Masonic Temple and Indianapolis City Hall (see chap. 2 of this volume). The new structure would be the largest office building in the city and required a massive facade. Rubush and Hunter's design called for the entire face to be covered with white terra-cotta (fig. 1.15). They used the tripartite skyscraper formula of base, shaft, and capital for the composition. Doric pilasters

34 | ARCHITECTURE IN INDIANAPOLIS, 1900–1920

appeared at either end of the first two stories, and plain piers lined the middle of the base section. A simple entablature ran above the second story, marking the transition to the shaft. Gigantic Doric pilasters defined the shaft section, which contained floors three through nine. Above another entablature, the architects adorned the tenth-floor capital section with panels containing decorative cartouches. Over the tenth floor projected a substantial cornice supported by modillions.[42]

Rubush and Hunter provided for a fireproof structure in the new edifice, with a steel frame, cement floors, a cement roof, and hollow-tile and glass partitions on each floor. Two large courts with white glass brick walls provided natural light to the inner offices. Six storerooms lined the street level. Floors two through ten contained offices, with all the suites on the eighth floor equipped for physicians' offices.[43]

On the eleventh floor, Mary Hume and Hannah Mansur decided to build the first roof garden for a downtown building in Indianapolis. Ona Talbot, an impresario of musical concerts and other cultural events, persuaded the owners that a roof garden atop the Hume-Mansur Building could attract large audiences for cultural events. The architects designed a glass-enclosed auditorium along the north side of the roof, adjoined to the south by a segment with an open-air roof. In the auditorium, they included a stage and sufficient space to seat one thousand persons. Unfortunately, Talbot's roof garden enterprise did not succeed financially, and by 1914, the Progressive Club of Indiana had leased the roof garden.[44]

Kahn Office Building

About three years after completion of the Hume-Mansur Building, construction began at 7 North Meridian Street on another commercial building with an elaborate terra-cotta facade. Henry Kahn, head of the Kahn Tailoring Company, decided to build a combination office and retail building at the heart of the central business district. In 1913, he had built one of the largest tailoring factories for individual garment orders in the country at 810 North Capitol Avenue (see later in this chapter). By the beginning of 1915, he was ready to construct an office building that would include the sales offices for his company; rental rooms for tailors and corset and dress makers; and offices for dentists, physicians, and lawyers. Kahn hired the firm of Vonnegut and Bohn to design the Kahn Building, and Arthur Bohn and his new partner, Kurt Vonnegut Sr., proceeded to devise a composition for the facade that used the traditional tripartite skyscraper formula but detailed it in unusual decorative patterns.[45]

ARCHITECT PROFILE

Rubush and Hunter

Preston C. Rubush (1867–1947; *at left*) and Edgar O. Hunter (1873–1949; *at right*) operated one of the most prolific and successful architectural partnerships in Indianapolis history. Between the formation of their firm in 1904 and their retirement in 1939, Rubush and Hunter won commissions to design many of the principal commercial and public buildings in Indianapolis.

Rubush was born in Howard County, Indiana, in 1867 and was educated in the public schools of Indianapolis. His father was a contractor, and Preston learned the trade of a carpenter and cabinetmaker, which later strengthened his regard for construction details as an architect. He took a special course in architecture at the University of Illinois in Champaign-Urbana and worked in the Peoria office of architect James F. Alexander of Lafayette. He then moved to Indianapolis and worked as a draftsman for an architectural office there. In 1893, he formed a partnership with architect John H. Scharn as Scharn and Rubush. Within two years, Rubush's confidence as an architect led him to form his own firm of P. C. Rubush and Company. In 1900, he entered the national architectural competition for the design of the new US Courthouse and Post Office in Indianapolis. Four years later, Preston Rubush formed a partnership with Edgar Hunter.

Hunter was born in Versailles, Indiana, in 1873. His younger brother, Frank B. Hunter, was also an architect. Edgar enrolled and graduated with a degree in architecture from the University of Pennsylvania, one of the top academic programs for architects in the country, with a curriculum based on that of the École des Beaux-Arts in Paris. He made his way to Indianapolis and obtained work as a draftsman for Vonnegut and Bohn.

It appears that Hunter, with his University of Pennsylvania architectural training, was the primary designer of the new firm of Rubush and Hunter. Rubush appears to have been the face of the firm, who solicited businesses and maintained relations with clients. Personalized service to clients and careful supervision of building projects were watchwords of the firm. The partners were tuned to changing stylistic tastes and produced works easily using the language of Classical Greece and Rome, the Renaissance, the Georgian period, Tudor palaces, and the Art Deco era.

Rubush and Hunter enjoyed almost immediate success and within four years had won commissions to design the Masonic Temple, the Independent Order of Odd Fellows office building, the new Indiana School for the Deaf campus, the Indianapolis City Hall, and the Marott Department Store.

In the following decade, the firm designed the Hume-Mansur Building; the Buckingham Apartments; the Fidelity Trust Building; the First Church of Christ, Scientist; the Circle Theater; the Hotel Lincoln; and several imposing residences. Their varied practice continued through the 1920s with the Illinois

Building, the Guaranty Building, the new Columbia Club, the Circle Tower, the Indiana Theater, the Walker Theater, the Architects' and Builders' Building, the American Central Life Insurance Company Building, and the Hollywood Beach Hotel in Florida. During the Depression years, the partners continued a reduced practice, serving as architects for the Art Deco Indianapolis Coca-Cola Bottling Plant and the redesign of the H. P. Wasson and Company department store. Rubush and Hunter's talented chief draftsman, Philip A. Weisenburgh, and their chief of construction, Ernest Werner, took over the company in 1939 and completed some additional commissions in the late 1940s.

Sources: "Preston C. Rubush," in Jacob Piatt Dunn, ed., *Greater Indianapolis: The History, the Industries, the Institutions, and the People of a City of Homes* (Chicago: Lewis, 1910), II:903; "Preston C. Rubush," in Jacob Piatt Dunn, ed., *Indiana and Indianans* (Chicago: American Historical Society, 1919), V:2240–41; "P. C. Rubush Dies in Florida," Indiana Biography Series, 32:7, Indiana State Library; "Edgar O. Hunter," Indiana Biography Series, 34:91, Indiana Division, Indiana State Library; Glory-June Greiff, "Rubush and Hunter," in *Encyclopedia of Indianapolis*, ed. David J. Bodenhamer and Robert G. Barrows, 1208–9 (Indianapolis: Indiana University Press, 1994). Sources for photos: Rubush—*Men of Indiana in Nineteen Hundred and One* (Indianapolis: Benesch, 1901), 138; Hunter—Panoramic photo of architects and possibly some draftspersons at the 1920 Indiana Society of Architects convention in Indianapolis, taken in the Sunken Gardens at Garfield Park, Bass Photo Co. Collection, Indiana Historical Society (image cropped).

Facing, **Figure 1.16.** Kahn Building, 7 North Meridian Street, built in 1915 and designed by Vonnegut and Bohn, who used the three-part Chicago skyscraper formula and clad the whole facade in French gray terra-cotta. View from c. 1916. Bass Photo Co. Collection, Indiana Historical Society. (Image cropped)

The architects clad the piers, cornice, and some horizontal beams of the facade in "French gray terra cotta" (fig. 1.16). For contrast, they used metal with a copper-green color for the storefronts and all the spandrels of the facade. The base section consisted of two floors, with the second floor containing the Kahn sales rooms. They gave the sales rooms extra-tall, Chicago-style windows. The shaft (floors three through nine) carried the eye upward with lofty piers and recessed spandrels. Above the ninth floor, spandrels projected forward to indicate the beginning of the capital section. The architects bestowed on the tenth-floor windows, marking the top story, extra size with segmental arches. A substantial cornice with dentils capped the composition. The molded decorative details on the facade, executed by Alexander Sangernebo, included original cartouches concentrated in the first two stories and along the tenth floor. Inside, multicolored terra-cotta tile decorated the lobby and corridors.[46] The architects produced a lofty visual effect on a narrow, thirty-four-foot-wide lot. The total cost came to about $300,000.[47]

Fletcher Savings and Trust Building

The design of the most substantial office building to take shape in the years between 1910 and 1917 resulted from a national architectural competition that produced an out-of-town winner who was then replaced by a veteran local architectural firm. The Fletcher Savings and Trust Company emerged from the 1912 merger of the Marion and German-American Trust Companies. Immediately, the officers, led by president Evans Woollen Sr. and vice president Albert E. Metzger, made plans to construct a sixteen-story building to house the new firm and advertise its presence and financial resources. They held a national competition in late 1912, and some of the top architects in the country participated—Cass Gilbert, Delano and Aldrich, York and Sawyer, James Gamble Rogers, and Electus D. Litchfield, all from New York. The sole local firms to submit plans out of thirteen entrants were Rubush and Hunter and Vonnegut and Bohn.[48]

The trust company retained an architectural advisor—Dean Warren P. Laird of the School of Architecture at the University of Pennsylvania—who would also serve as one member of the three-judge panel. Shortly before, he had been appointed judge for the competition that the City of Indianapolis held for the City

Hospital campus (see chap. 2 of this volume). The architects competing chose Walter Cook, president of the American Institute of Architects, and H. Warren Magonigle of New York, designer of several notable memorials, as the other jury members. The judges selected Electus Litchfield as the winner of the competition in December 1912. They gave the second, third, and fourth place awards all to New York architects—James Gamble Rogers, York and Sawyer, and Delano and Aldrich. The two local firms did not place in the competition.[49]

Litchfield had been part of a firm that won the competition for the US Courthouse and Post Office in Denver and had placed second in a competition for the design of the US Department of Commerce and Labor Building in Washington, DC. Laird—the architectural advisor—described Litchfield's entry in Indianapolis as projecting the idea "of the place of business of an important commercial institution having offices to let, rather than of an office building, a small portion of which is assigned to the bank." In his design, Litchfield expressed the location of the trust company through a high, two-story colonnade along the principal facade on Market Street. He marked the center of the facade, where the entrance to the bank would be located, with a tall, arched window overlooking the banking room inside. The architect lined the upper three stories with a monumental Renaissance-style arcade.[50]

Litchfield visited the state capital to consult with the trust company officers and board immediately after his selection. Sometime afterward, the board replaced him as the architect for the new building with the local firm of Vonnegut and Bohn.[51]

Vonnegut and Bohn modified some of the details in the Litchfield design but kept much of the initial concept (figs. 1.17 and 1.18). The final result, completed at the beginning of 1915, produced a new skyscraper with a height just under that of the Merchants National Bank Building. The design observed the conventions of tripartite designs. Vonnegut and Bohn organized the rectilinear facades on Market and Pennsylvania Streets into base, shaft, and capital sections, with much of the focus on the first three stories, where the banking rooms and offices of the Fletcher Savings and Trust Company would be located. The building committee selected a flesh-colored granite from Crotch Island, Maine, for the base section and contrasting cream-colored Indiana Bedford limestone for the remaining facade. The architects drew attention to the trust company entrance at the center of the Market Street elevation by flanking the entry with pairs of colossal Ionic columns standing in antis. Between the columns, they marked the entrance proper with a projecting granite pediment. Overhead, they admitted abundant natural light into the banking room within through a bank of windows. Two additional

Left, **Figure 1.17.** Fletcher Savings and Trust Building, 12–50 East Market Street, built in 1913–15 and designed by Vonnegut and Bohn with elements of Renaissance-style design by Electus D. Litchfield of New York. Photo taken in 1920. Bass Photo Co. Collection, Indiana Historical Society. (Image cropped)

Right, **Figure 1.18.** Fletcher Trust Building (adapted as Hilton Garden Inn) in 2023. James Glass.

engaged columns completed the first two stories of the Market Street elevation. The architects continued the rhythm on Pennsylvania Street with Ionic pilasters.[52]

The third story served as a frieze and entablature for the recessed columns below. Above, a Greek key carving in a single granite course marked the transition to the shaft section in limestone, which the designers detailed simply for contrast. They separated the shaft section from the top two stories with projecting

COMMERCIAL AND INDUSTRIAL ARCHITECTURE | 41

balustrades. For contrast with the shaft stories, but to echo the treatment of the entrance, they applied simple Doric pilasters to the top stories. The Italian Renaissance–style cornice effectively capped the composition, supported by large modillions.

A large courtyard on the north and west sides of the footprint admitted light into every office. The building committee chose Mexican mahogany for the wood trim of the banking room and lobby and Tavernale marble for the walls of the trust company suite and elevator hall. The banking room was forty feet high. The total cost of this impressive piece of civic architecture came to $750,000.[53]

RETAIL BUILDINGS

Washington Street was well-established as Indiana's Main Street by the first decade of the twentieth century, and hundreds of retail establishments located on the street to take advantage of the crowds of customers being brought to the center of town by streetcars or electric interurbans. On narrow lots ranging from 20 to 36 feet in width, retailers built or leased buildings that achieved their floor space through multiple stories. Most retail stores specialized in specific categories of goods, but by walking down the street, a customer could find varied merchandise.

Marott's Shoes and McOuat Buildings

Two examples of specialty retail buildings constructed along Washington Street after 1900 still stand at 14–16 and 18–20 East Washington Street (figs. 1.19 and 1.20). Investors Carl Von Hake and the sons of Franklin Vonnegut constructed 18–20 East Washington in 1900. They hired fellow German Americans Vonnegut and Bohn as their architects. The designers took advantage of the new decorative possibilities of terra-cotta and clad the whole facade with a white-colored ceramic veneer. They used Chicago-style ribbon windows for the facade but lined the piers with spiraled moldings and crowned the parapet on top with a field of assorted terra-cotta shields.[54]

The following year, widow Eugenia B. McOuat erected the 14–16 East Washington building as an investment and hired the firm of R. P. Daggett and Company to design it. The architects used a very different aesthetic approach from that used by Vonnegut and Bohn. Robert P. Daggett and partner James B. Lizius designed a seven-story structure with a cast-iron facade and featured rows of ribboned windows separated by substantial horizontal moldings. The windows on five floors were a version of the Chicago window, with double-hung sash openings on either

Left, **Figure 1.19.** McOuat and Marott's Shoes Buildings, 14–16 and 18–20 East Washington Street, in 1902. The Marott's Shoes Building, built in 1900 and designed by Vonnegut and Bohn, was one of the first buildings downtown constructed with a terra-cotta facade. The McOuat Building, built in 1901 and designed by R. P. Daggett and Company, featured a cast-iron facade and a version of the Chicago-style window. Max R. Hyman, ed., *The Journal Handbook of Indianapolis* (Indianapolis: Indianapolis Journal Newspaper, 1902), 371.

Right, **Figure 1.20.** McOuat and Marott's Shoes Buildings, 2023. James Glass.

side of two large, single-pane windows providing continuous natural light on each selling floor. At the street level, the architects contrasted this streamlined, modern treatment with regularly spaced Doric pilasters.[55]

The Badger Furniture Company probably was the first tenant for both buildings. In 1902, it occupied all eight floors in each for its store featuring house furnishings, carpets, and rugs. Later, Marott's Shoes occupied the 18–20 building.[56]

Department Stores

A revolution was coming in retailing, and it reordered shopping in downtown Indianapolis. The modern American department store had first appeared in New York with Alexander Stewart's Marble Palace Store in 1848.[57] In the Midwest, the forerunners of department stores were dry goods merchants, who offered a variety of nonperishable household goods. In Indianapolis, such merchants as Lyman S. Ayres, Hiram P. Wasson, and William H. Block established growing clienteles for their dry goods operations after the Civil War.

An influential department store opened in Chicago during those postwar decades—Marshall Field and Company—and it set the standard for many such establishments in the 1890s and early twentieth century, offering in one colossal building all manner of goods desired by households in Chicago and establishing high standards of service. One of the local dry goods firms, L. S. Ayres and Company, decided to create an Indianapolis version of the Marshall Field's operation in 1905.

L. S. AYRES AND COMPANY DEPARTMENT STORE

The president of the company, Frederic M. Ayres, purchased the Hubbard Block (see chap. 4 of vol. 1) on the southwest corner of Washington and Meridian Streets, which was rapidly becoming the "Crossroads of America," and hired Vonnegut and Bohn to design the first department store building in Indianapolis. Bernard Vonnegut himself probably designed the eight-story structure, construction of

Facing top, **Figure 1.21.** The original section of L. S. Ayres and Company, the first modern department store building in Indianapolis, at One West Washington Street, built in 1905 and designed by Bernard Vonnegut of Vonnegut and Bohn with a grid of windows, piers, and spandrels and spare ornamentation. View in c. 1906–7. Bass Photo Co. Collection, Indiana Historical Society. (Image cropped)

Facing bottom, **Figure 1.22.** Former L. S. Ayres and Company department store with 1914 addition to the west in 2021. James Glass.

which began in 1905 with the erection of a steel skeleton and brick curtain walls on the exterior (figs. 1.21 and 1.22). Vonnegut continued the trend toward simplifying decorative detail that had been taking hold for many downtown buildings since 1900: he chose gray brick, rather than limestone or terra-cotta, for the entire facade and clad the piers and spandrels with it. The architect carried over the three-part formula of skyscrapers for use in a department store. He installed big expanses of plate glass and overhead transoms along the street-level section to display the fashions and other goods visible in the store windows. Above the tall first story, he gave the shaft section a grid of projecting vertical piers and recessed spandrels. Trios of windows appeared between the piers. A prominent stringcourse marked the top story, lined above by a slightly projecting terra-cotta cornice adorned by shields with the letter *A*. Vonnegut was sparing with ornament but judiciously applied it along the cornice and in lions' heads on the corner sculpted by Alexander Sangernebo.[58]

Inside, the architect laid out each floor to serve as a department for a particular type of merchandise. The street-level floor was twenty-two feet high and introduced customers to the store.[59]

MAROTT DEPARTMENT STORE

A year later, a new dry goods competitor presented himself in the person of George J. Marott, a prosperous shoe retailer on Washington Street. In 1906, Marott decided to build his own department store in the 300 block of Massachusetts Avenue, where a satellite shopping district was beginning to take shape, in response to the seven streetcar lines and five interurban lines that ran cars daily past on Massachusetts. Marott hired the firm of Rubush and Hunter to design a five-story department store building with a base section consisting of large store windows and Luxfer light transoms and a streamlined facade with a grid of piers and spandrels (figs. 1.23 and 1.24). The architects omitted a capital section but included a cornice that projected sharply outward. Although the Marott Department Store did not operate long, it helped establish department stores as the future of much of the retailing in the city.[60]

> *Facing top,* **Figure 1.23.** Marott Department Store, 345 Massachusetts Avenue, built in 1906–7 and designed by Rubush and Hunter with a streamlined grid of piers and spandrels for the facade. View from 1909. Max R. Hyman, ed., *Hyman's Handbook of Indianapolis* (Indianapolis: M. R. Hyman, 1909), 226.

> *Facing bottom,* **Figure 1.24.** Former Marott Department Store (now Marott Center). View of facade in 2023. James Glass.

WILLIAM H. BLOCK COMPANY DEPARTMENT STORE

Even though L. S. Ayres and Company seemed to have the upper hand in claiming the department store mantle in the city, an upstart competitor, William H. Block, soon gave them stiff competition. Block, a Jewish immigrant from Austria, had established the William H. Block dry goods store in 1896, leasing a narrow building on Washington Street. By 1911, his store had outgrown its quarters, and the proprietor had incorporated his operation as the William H. Block Company. The president of the new company was ready for his operation to metamorphose into a full-fledged department store with an impressive building to capture the attention and patronage of the public.[61]

Block hired Vonnegut and Bohn, the architects of the Ayres store, as designers for his building, and Arthur Bohn and new partner Kurt Vonnegut Sr. devised an eight-story structure with a sparkling white terra-cotta facade (fig. 1.25). The location was prime: on the southwest corner of Market and Illinois Streets, across the street from the thousands of passengers (and customers) passing through the Traction Terminal for interurbans. Naturally, the architects provided a fireproof structure, with twelve-inch brick curtain walls and tile floors and roof. The exterior formula resembled the facade formula of Ayres—two base stories, five stories in the trunk section, and the eighth story in the capital section. The biggest difference from the earlier store designs came in the pervasive use of terra-cotta, which shone in the sunlight and attracted the eye. Vonnegut and Bohn also introduced terra-cotta ornamentation without Renaissance or Classical precedents, which they were to do again with the Kahn Building in 1915 (see previous section). The designers used shields and foliated devices created by sculptor Alexander Sangernebo to denote the upper part of the base section and the eighth floor. They also gave the latter broad, segmental windows. The steeply projecting cornice with modillions derived from Renaissance sources. As an added accent, Vonnegut and Bohn lined the parapet with light poles on terra-cotta bases.[62]

The William H. Block Company spent $450,000 on its new edifice and gained 210,000 square feet of selling space.[63]

Figure 1.25. William H. Block Company department store, 50 North Illinois Street, built in 1910–11 and designed by Vonnegut and Bohn, using white terra-cotta for the whole facade, with distinctive shields and foliated designs for decoration. View from 1912. *Year Book of the Indiana Chapter A.I.A. and Catalog of the Third Annual Exhibition 1912* (Indianapolis: Indiana Chapter A.I.A., 1912).

ARCHITECT PROFILES

Arthur C. Bohn and Kurt Vonnegut Sr.

After the 1908 death of Bernard Vonnegut, senior partner in the firm of Vonnegut and Bohn, junior partner Arthur Bohn (1861–1948; *on left*) headed the practice. In 1911, architect Kurt Vonnegut Sr. (1884–1956; *on right*), the son of Bernard, and engineer Otto N. Mueller became partners with Bohn in the firm that continued as Vonnegut and Bohn until 1918, when it became Vonnegut, Bohn, and Mueller.

Arthur Bohn was born in Louisville and moved to Indianapolis as a child. There he graduated from a private school and then entered a top architectural office as an apprentice. After saving money, he enrolled in the Royal Polytechnic Institute in Karlsruhe, Germany, where he studied architecture. Subsequently, he took additional studies in an architectural atelier in Paris, where he learned Beaux Arts techniques of drawing and design. He then returned to Indianapolis, where in 1888 he formed a partnership with Bernard Vonnegut, who appears to have served as the primary design partner. After engaging in practice for several years, Bohn returned to Europe for additional study, visiting France, England, Germany, and Italy.

Kurt Vonnegut attended Shortridge High School and completed high school at the American College in France. He then studied architecture at the Massachusetts of Technology (MIT), where he graduated with honors in 1908. Later he completed a Master's degree at MIT and studied a year at the Technical Institute of Berlin.

Both Bohn and Vonnegut were well educated in architecture and had abiding interests in design, so it seems plausible that both contributed to many of the commissions that their firm received between 1911 and Bohn's retirement in 1945.

Vonnegut and Bohn and Vonnegut, Bohn and Mueller designed a variety of large-scale buildings, including the original William H. Block Company department store, the 1914 and 1928–29 additions to the L. S. Ayres and Company department store, the Kahn office and Kahn factory buildings, Hotel Severin, the Fletcher Savings and Trust Company Building, the Meyer-Kiser Bank, the Indiana Bell Company downtown buildings, the Roosevelt Building, and the 1934–36 addition to the William H. Block Company store. They also designed George Washington High School and Public Schools 10, 15, 35, and 45. One of

Bohn's principal projects involved preparing a City Beautiful–style plan for a plaza of state office buildings west of the Statehouse in 1911–12.

After Bohn's retirement, Vonnegut continued to practice in the firm of Vonnegut, Wright, and Porteous. He retired in 1954.

Sources: "Admitted to Firm," *Indianapolis Star*, January 7, 1911, 9; "Arthur Bohn," in Jacob Piatt Dunn, ed., *Indiana and Indianans* (Chicago: American Historical Society, 1919), IV:1796; "Arthur Bohn," in Kin Hubbard, ed., *A Book of Indiana* (Indianapolis: Indiana Biographical Association, 1929), 207, 357; "Arthur Bohn," in Charles Roll, ed., *Indiana: One Hundred and Fifty Years of American Development* (Chicago: Lewis, 1931), 443–44; C. Walter McCarty, ed., *Indiana Today* (New Orleans: James O. Jones, 1942), 235; "Arthur Bohn," *Indianapolis News*, February 24, 1941, Indiana Biography Series, 21:42, Indiana Division, Indiana State Library; "Arthur Bohn," *Indianapolis Times*, January 14, 1948, 4, c. 2; "Kurt Vonnegut League Member Dies," *Construction News*, vol. 22, no. 41 (1956), 8; "Kurt Vonnegut," *Indianapolis Star*, October 2, 1956, 20. Sources for photos: Bohn—McCarty, *Indiana Today*, 235; Vonnegut—painting by artist Clifton Wheeler, courtesy of The Portfolio, Indianapolis.

THE AYRES ADDITION

In 1914, a fire destroyed the 1870s Iron Block to the west of L. S. Ayres and Company, and Frederic Ayres immediately planned an addition that would double the size of his department store building and respond to the competition presented by the new Block's store. Ayres again hired Vonnegut and Bohn, and although Bernard Vonnegut had died, Arthur Bohn and Bernard's son Kurt replicated the elder Vonnegut's design for the addition. For design of the interior features, the Ayres company hired architect C. A. Wheeler, who was in charge of design for the mammoth store of Marshall Field and Company in Chicago. Thus, a direct connection architecturally existed between Field's and Ayres, as witnessed in the redesigned first-floor shopping room, complete with plaster Corinthian columns similar to those designed by D. H. Burnham and Company for the Chicago store.[64]

Specialty Retail Stores

Despite the disruption to sales caused by the department stores, the specialty retail store did not disappear. For example, in the expanding business district north of Ohio Street on Pennsylvania Street, two small buildings rose in 1909, both devoted to music retailing. At 229–31 North Pennsylvania, the Wulschner-Stewart Company constructed a four-story structure containing showrooms to display the firm's pianos and an auditorium for performances (fig. 1.26). R. P. Daggett and Company designed a facade consisting of a white terra-cotta frame for dark-colored rows of windows in metal. The architects ornamented the frame with pilasters, a cornice supported by brackets and dentils, and rusticated joints for the frame around the storefront. A couple of doors north, at 237 North Pennsylvania Street, the Aeolian Company constructed a narrow, four-story building containing music studios and exhibition parlors decorated with elements of French periods of interior design (fig. 1.26). The designers employed some Classical details and a conventional cornice on the terra-cotta facade.[65]

Eight years later, in March 1917, Nicholas Geiger, operator of three confectionaries and cafés downtown, decided to build a freestanding building devoted to his trade. He acquired a site at 36 East Washington Street and hired Herbert L. Bass and Company of Indianapolis as the architects. Bass and his draftsmen designed a four-story building with a mixture of Federal and Renaissance details (figs. 1.27 and 1.28). The architects clad the first two stories in white terra-cotta. They placed a large elliptical fan light from the Federal style over the entrance

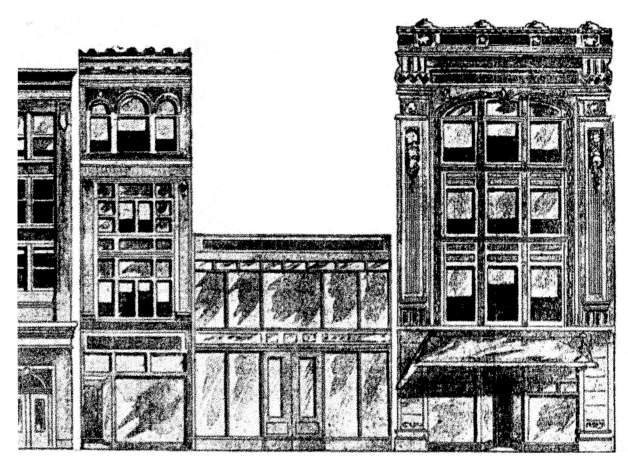

Figure 1.26. 1909 drawings of the facades for the (*left to right*) +Aeolian Building, +Gibson Automotive Building, and +Wulschner-Stewart Building, 229–237 North Pennsylvania Street, all built in 1909. Frank B. Hunter designed the Gibson Building and R. P. Daggett and Company the Wulschner-Stewart Building. The Gibson Building featured a Modern design of plate glass and skeletal framework. The architects of the other two structures clad them in terra-cotta with Classical and Renaissance details. All three buildings were demolished in 1967 to make way for the Indiana National Bank Tower. "New Buildings Are of Artistic Design," *Indianapolis Star*, March 21, 1909, 47.

and flanked the entrance and west side of the building with Corinthian pilasters. The Bass designers used red brick for the third and fourth stories and employed casement windows with transoms and flat brick arches. The architects capped the Geiger Building with a terra-cotta Renaissance cornice and balustrade above.[66]

COMMERCIAL AND INDUSTRIAL ARCHITECTURE | 53

Left, **Figure 1.27.** 1917 rendering by architect Herbert L. Bass and Company of confectionary building erected by Nicholas Geiger at 36 East Washington Street in 1917, with Georgian and Renaissance detailing. "Leonard Geiger Adds New Store," *Indianapolis Star,* March 11, 1917, 8.

Right, **Figure 1.28.** View of Geiger Building seen from the east in 2023. James Glass.

Automotive Showrooms and Service Buildings

Alongside department stores and traditional retail establishments, a powerful new force in transportation-related retailing took shape in the first decade of the twentieth century. Automobiles had appeared in Indianapolis during the 1890s and thereafter steadily became an alternative to streetcars, interurbans, and steam railroads for travel. Showrooms for new automobile model sales and garages for servicing motorcars began to dot the streets of the Mile Square, especially in the residential neighborhoods north of Ohio Street.

In 1909, at the same time that the Wulschner-Stewart and Aeolian Companies were erecting their buildings, the Gibson Automobile Company constructed an auto showroom at 235 North Pennsylvania Street, between the two music retailers (fig. 1.26). The Gibson firm had outgrown its original showroom on Massachusetts Avenue and constructed the new structure adjacent to its first building. Architect Frank B. Hunter of Indianapolis designed a facade for the Gibson Company almost entirely composed of plate glass windows to provide maximum light on the automobiles exhibited within.[67]

During the following years, garages for servicing automobiles and combined sales and service buildings appeared in the midst of the residences north of Ohio Street. Capitol Avenue north of Vermont Street rapidly became known as Auto Row. In 1911, for example, the Globe Realty Company constructed two garage structures for servicing automobiles at 525–37 North Capitol Avenue (fig. 1.29). James A. Allison and Carl G. Fisher, two national leaders of the automobile industry, headed the company. Herbert W. Foltz, their architect, designed two reinforced concrete buildings with nearly identical facades. The compositions featured abundant glazed window space, piers to balance the horizontal lines of windows and stringcourses, and simple cornices.[68]

Three years later, Oliver Williams constructed a substantial four-story building (fig. 1.30) on the site of two houses at the southeast corner of Capitol Avenue and Emmet Street. Auto sales rooms occupied the street level in the new building. Williams intended to lease the upper floors to tenants interested in motorcars or "automobile trucks." To accommodate the weight of vehicles, the architect, J. Edwin Kopf of Indianapolis, specified a reinforced concrete structure. He used steel sashes to afford the maximum window area on each floor. Kopf clad the exterior piers in orange enameled brick and used cream-colored terra-cotta for decorative accents.[69]

In March 1917, Carl Fisher, president of the Indianapolis Motor Speedway, announced construction of another building along Auto Row on Capitol Avenue. The Fisher Automobile Company erected a $90,000 building at 440 North Capitol with a reinforced concrete structure. The architects, D. A. Bohlen and Son, designed a four-story building, three bays wide, with a white enameled brick facade and glazed terra-cotta decorative details (fig. 1.31). On the first floor, the architects arranged for the display of the touring cars and trucks sold by the company. The company devoted the front half of the second floor to sales and displays, while the

Facing top, **Figure 1.29.** +Drawing of Globe Realty Company garages for servicing automobiles, 525–27 and 535–37 North Capitol Avenue, on Indianapolis's new Auto Row. Built in 1911 and designed by Herbert W. Foltz, with reinforced concrete structures and an abundance of windows. This is a 1911 perspective drawing by Foltz. 525–27 was demolished between 1987 and 1990 and 535–37 was demolished in c. the early 1990s, both replaced by parking lots. "Garage Buildings to Be Erected on Capitol Avenue," *Indianapolis Star,* March 27, 1911, 10.

Facing bottom, **Figure 1.30.** Williams Building, 611 North Capitol Avenue, built in 1914 by investor Oliver A. Williams and designed by J. Edwin Kopf of Indianapolis with orange enameled brick for the facade and a reinforced concrete structure to accommodate the weight of automobiles. View in 2021. James Glass.

Above, **Figure 1.31.** 1917 Rendering of +Fisher Automobile Company Building, on the west side of the 400 block of North Capitol Avenue, just south of Michigan Street, built by Carl Fisher and his Fisher Automobile Company and designed by D. A. Bohlen and Son with white enamel brick on the facade and glazed terra-cotta details. Demolished in c. 1995 and replaced by a parking lot. "$90,000 Building for Autos Begun," *Indianapolis Star,* March 24, 1917, 9.

top two floors were to become a "service station" for customer vehicles. Freight elevators made possible the elevation and descent of automobiles.[70]

HOTELS

With the rapid growth of Indianapolis, its continued status as a center for steam railroad passenger travel, and the advent of electric interurban traffic, a new group of hotels took shape in the early years of the twentieth century. These ranged from the grandest and most monumental structures to modest hostelries pitched to the budget commercial traveler.

Claypool Hotel

Without any doubt, the Claypool was most splendid hotel built in Indianapolis during this period or any other. It was the brainchild of veteran hotel operator Henry W. Lawrence, who had previously operated profitably the Spencer House on South Illinois Street, the English Hotel on the Circle, and the historic Bates House at Illinois and Washington Streets. Lawrence saw the possibilities for a grand hotel on the site of the Bates House and in 1899 approached the owner of the Bates, Edward Fay Claypool. He proposed to organize a hotel company that would lease the site from Claypool for ninety-nine years and compensate him for the loss of the Bates House income. Lawrence then sold bonds and raised $750,000 from local investors for preferred stock in the Indiana Hotel Company, which was enough to build the Claypool Hotel. He had previously met Frank M. Andrews, a Dayton architect, and arranged for him to design the hotel and take stock in the company. In 1900, Lawrence and Andrews toured cities in the Northeast to inspect top hotels in New York City, Boston, Albany, and Richmond, looking for features that would enhance their hotel. The architect completed the plans and specifications in 1901, and Lawrence's company awarded the general contract to George B. Swift and Company of Chicago.[71]

When completed in May 1903, the immense, nine-story Claypool Hotel towered over the intersection of Illinois and Washington. The hotel contained 450 rooms, 384 of which were guest rooms. Private baths could be had in 284 rooms. The total investment by the Indiana Hotel Company, including land, building, decorations, furnishings, and equipment, came to $1.5 million.[72]

Andrews designed a monumental rectangular building, with buff brick exterior walls enriched by terra-cotta details (fig. 1.32). He confected a mature Italian

Figure 1.32. +Claypool Hotel exterior, northwest corner, Washington and Illinois Streets, built in 1901–3 and designed by Frank M. Andrews of Dayton, Ohio, with a grand Italian Renaissance facade featuring Corinthian pilasters and Palladian devices. View from c. 1910. Demolished in 1969 after fire damage and replaced by a parking lot. The Embassy Suites hotel now occupies the site. Postcard from author's collection.

Renaissance style, much like what New York architects McKim, Mead, and White had been popularizing for hotels, private clubs, and public buildings. Andrews divided the two facades into the familiar three vertical zones: a two-story base section; a trunk, or shaft, section; and a crowning section of two stories. On the Illinois Street elevation, containing the principal entrance, he marked the entry with a pediment and lined the rest of the second story with loggia-style porches fronted with arches and Corinthian pilasters in cream-colored terra-cotta. At the center of the Washington Street elevation, he used a similar scheme for the second story involving Palladian windows flanked by Corinthian pilasters. The architect drew attention up to the top stories by using colossal Corinthian pilasters and engaged

COMMERCIAL AND INDUSTRIAL ARCHITECTURE | 59

columns grouped symmetrically. The pilasters provided an element of verticality to balance the overall impression of horizontality, imparted by the mass of the building, the entablatures on the facade, and the projecting cornice and balustrade at the top. Andrews used a steel frame, brick curtain exterior walls, and tile floors to assure fireproofing.[73]

Inside, the grand scale continued with the main lobby—a two-story rectangular hall measuring seventy-two by ninety-eight feet and thirty-three feet tall (fig. 1.33). Andrews lined the lobby with sixteen colossal Doric columns having scagliola shafts scored to simulate Siena marble. Overhead, the columns supported

Facing, **Figure 1.33.** +Main lobby of Claypool Hotel in 1924. Colossal Roman-style columns with scagliola shafts lined the space. Bass Photo Co. Collection, Indiana Historical Society. (Image cropped)

Above, **Figure 1.34.** +Main dining room, Claypool Hotel, undated photo. Bass Photo Co. Collection, Indiana Historical Society. (Image cropped)

an entablature ornamented with triglyphs, bas-relief sculptural panels, and large consoles. Above, the ceiling featured plaster-encrusted beams and plaster ornaments. Other major rooms included a dining room on the main floor seating four hundred (fig. 1.34), the Assembly Hall on the eighth and ninth floors seating one

COMMERCIAL AND INDUSTRIAL ARCHITECTURE | 61

Facing, **Figure 1.35.** +Louis XIV parlor, Claypool Hotel, undated photo. Bass Photo Co. Collection, Indiana Historical Society. (Image cropped)

thousand, and the Palm Court on the ninth floor. Andrews devised elegant and exotic interior design schemes for the parlors, writing rooms, grill room, billiard room, and smoking room, invoking the Louis XIV period in France (fig. 1.35), Nuremberg medieval architecture, the French First Empire, and Moorish architecture.[74]

In 1914–15, Henry Lawrence decided to extend the hotel to the west and hired a young Indianapolis architect, William Earl Russ, to design the addition and make some changes to the existing building. Russ redesigned one of the dining rooms as a ballroom, and Lawrence retained the noted Cincinnati interior decorator William F. Behrens to redesign some of the period rooms. Behrens recreated the Peacock Alley of the old Waldorf Astoria hotel in New York and designed a Louis XVI–style interior for one of the redesigned rooms.[75]

Hotel Washington

The demand for hotel rooms in the first decade and a half of the new century brought forth multiple proposals for additional hotels, several of which did not reach construction. Investors sensed a demand for hostelries suitable for all price ranges of customers. Local hotel operator J. Edward Krauss constructed one that fit the medium range. In 1912, he organized the Washington Hotel Company, which he and other investors incorporated with a capitalization of $700,000. Krauss and the incorporators hired the veteran architectural firm of R. P. Daggett and Company, now headed by Robert Frost Daggett, to design what they called "the first skyscraper hotel in Indiana." Daggett created a seventeen-story building plus a basement at 32 East Washington Street, in the heart of the retail and office district. The property had a narrow frontage of 43 feet on Washington, so the architects had to provide the space required by extending the building 120 feet back to the north alley and by going up. They gave the building a steel structural skeleton and exterior curtain walls composed of dark-brown brick. For extra fireproofing, Daggett covered the steel columns with concrete and tile and used tile partition walls. He and his draftsmen created two light courts along the west side of the building to provide natural light to all three hundred rooms.[76]

For the facade composition, the architects relied on the tripartite skyscraper formula—a base section of three stories, encased in Bedford limestone veneer; a

ARCHITECT PROFILE

Frank M. Andrews

Frank Mills Andrews (1867–1948) was born in Des Moines, Iowa, and developed an interest in engineering and architecture. He studied civil engineering at Iowa State College and architecture at Cornell University, where he graduated in 1888. While in college, he worked for William Miller, a prominent architect in Ithaca, New York. He then moved to New York City, where he worked briefly for George B. Post, head of one of the top New York architectural firms. Between 1891 and 1892, he worked for the firm of Jenney and Mundie, headed by Chicago skyscraper pioneer William LeBaron Jenney. While in Chicago, Andrews created a Dutch guild hall design for the Columbian Exposition of 1893.

John Patterson, head of the National Cash Register Company of Dayton, Ohio, observed Andrews's work at the exposition and asked him to come to Dayton to design buildings for his company. Andrews designed many of the structures in the National Cash Register campus, as well as the Conover Building and the expansive Dayton Arcade, the facade of which he modeled on a Renaissance-era Dutch guild hall. He also served as the architect of several homes for wealthy citizens.

As his career blossomed, Andrews made a specialty of hotel design. One of the earliest and most lavish of his hotel projects was the Claypool Hotel of Indianapolis of 1899–1903. Slightly before, Andrews won the commission to design the sumptuous 1900 Columbia Club in the Indiana state capital (see chap. 2 of this volume). His other major hotel projects included Hotel McAlpine of New York (reputedly the tallest in the world in 1909), Hotel Seelbach in Louisville, Hotels Sinclair and Taft in Cincinnati, and the George Washington Hotel in New York. In 1905–9, Andrews won the commission to design the Kentucky State Capitol in Frankfort.

The architect later opened an office in Cincinnati and then moved his practice to New York. During World War I, he expanded the scope of his work to England and other foreign countries. He invested in several of his hotel projects and became very wealthy. Andrews died in 1948 in Brooklyn, New York.

Source: "The Unknown Architect: Frank Mills Andrews," Calvary Cemetery, Dayton, accessed September 21, 2021, http://calvarycemeterydayton.org/the-unknown-architect/. Source for photo: "The Unknown Architect: Frank Mills Andrews." Courtesy of Curt Dalton, Dayton History.

shaft section of brick with limestone lintels for the windows; and a capital section with arched windows on the sixteenth floor and two-story limestone pilasters (figs. 1.36 and 1.37). The designers placed a two-story hotel lobby in the rear half of the ground floor, north of two rooms for retail stores. They finished the lobby walls with marble and gold and the ceiling with ivory-colored plaster. In the basement, they designed a German rathskeller restaurant. On the second floor, they placed parlors for business meetings. The fifteenth floor contained an assembly room seating several hundred people. Krauss described Hotel Washington as "a first-class hotel with reasonable prices."[77]

Hotel Severin

Also in 1912, investors announced plans for a hotel intended to compete for clientele with the Claypool. Henry Severin came from a wealthy German family in Indianapolis and headed Meier, Lewis, and Company, a manufacturing firm. He joined forces with businessmen Harry B. Gates and Richard H. McClellan to build the four-hundred-room Hotel Severin on the southeast corner of Georgia

Left, **Figure 1.36.** 1912 rendering of Hotel Washington, 32 East Washington Street, designed by R. P. Daggett and Company, using tripartite skyscraper formula and Renaissance details. *Year Book of the Indiana Chapter A.I.A. and Catalog of the Third Annual Exhibition 1912* (Indianapolis: Indiana Chapter A.I.A., 1912).

Above, **Figure 1.37.** Former Hotel Washington in 2023. James Glass.

Figure 1.38. Hotel Severin, 31–45 West Georgia Street, was built by the Gates-McClellan Hotel Company in 1912–13 and designed by Vonnegut and Bohn with Italian Renaissance details and a roof garden. View c. 1945–50. Postcard from author's collection.

| Figure 1.39. Former Hotel Severin (now Omni-Severin Hotel) in 2023. James Glass.

and Illinois Streets, just a half block from the thousands of passengers arriving daily at Union Station. Gates and McClellan organized a hotel company and sold stock to local investors. Directors of the new company included automobile entrepreneurs Carl Fisher and James Allison.[78]

The Gates-McClellan Hotel Company hired the firm of Vonnegut and Bohn as architects, and Arthur Bohn and Kurt Vonnegut Sr. designed a twelve-story building with a basement (figs. 1.38 and 1.39). They specified a fireproof structure and exterior curtain walls of red brick and provided for Indiana Bedford limestone details sculpted by Alexander Sangernebo. The architects employed an

68 | ARCHITECTURE IN INDIANAPOLIS, 1900–1920

Italian Renaissance composition for the two facades. Along the first two stories, they arranged an arcade of tall windows framed with rusticated limestone blocks. On the corners of the shaft section, they placed broad limestone quoins. To terminate the facades, they sharply projected a Renaissance-style cornice supported by modillions. The architects drew attention to the twelfth floor by framing the windows with limestone architraves, flanked by lion's head sculptures. Below the twelfth story, the firm placed stone swags composed of their trademark bundles of fruit. Limestone balconies enlivened the long shaft of unornamented brick window surrounds.[79]

In the basement, Vonnegut and Bohn designed a rathskeller restaurant with brown oak wainscoting and columns. On the main floor, they featured a two-story lobby with marble accents and a ballroom with plaster vaults and mini-domes. All four hundred guest rooms included private baths, and some contained shower-baths. On the roof, the architects designed a thirteenth-floor ballroom and roof garden. The hotel opened for business in August 1913.[80]

THEATERS

Another key element of a growing city and an opportunity for commercial success was entertainment, chiefly delivered through theaters. The twentieth century opened with the principal downtown Indianapolis theaters—English's Opera House, Dickson's Grand Opera House, and the Park Theater—continuing to offer a mixture of plays, vaudeville, and occasionally operas. Local investors soon built new theaters to offer competition.

Majestic Theater

In 1907, banker Volney T. Malott constructed a combination hotel and theater at 128–30 South Illinois Street. He retained D. A. Bohlen and Son as his architects, and Oscar Bohlen and his draftsmen designed the seven-story Hotel Edward on Illinois and, behind it, the five-story Majestic Theater. For the auditorium in the theater, the architects devised an elaborate plaster proscenium with concentric arches and two tiers of box seats on either side of the stage (fig. 1.40). Arcades at the rear of the boxes provided access to them. The plaster decorative scheme for the proscenium, arcades, and boxes was a mélange of Italian Baroque and French Rococo. The theater could seat 1,350 patrons, and manager C. O. Brown of the International Theatrical Co. booked vaudeville acts and occasional showings of the new entertainment medium, silent movies.[81]

Colonial Theater

Up the street, in 1909, local investors constructed a building at 240 North Illinois Street that they hoped would draw away the vaudeville audiences of the Majestic and the Grand Opera House. The owners followed Volney Malott's formula of combining a hotel and theater, apparently anticipating some out-of-town patrons booking rooms in the Colonial Hotel and attending performances in the adjacent Colonial Theater. Rubush and Hunter, the architects, employed a rectangular plan for the hotel-theater and provided fireproof construction, with a steel frame and

Facing, **Figure 1.40.** +Stage, proscenium arch, and private boxes of the Majestic Theater, 128–30 South Illinois Street, built by banker Volney T. Malott in combination with Hotel Edward in 1907 and designed by D. A. Bohlen and Son drawing on Italian Baroque and French Rococo decorations for the proscenium arch and boxes. View in 1907. The theater was demolished in c. 1960–61 and replaced by a parking lot. Bass Co. Photo Collection, Indiana Historical Society Library. (Image cropped)

Above, **Figure 1.41.** +Colonial Hotel and Theater, southwest corner, New York and Illinois Streets, built in 1909 and designed by Rubush and Hunter, drawing on Georgian and Classical details for the exterior. View in 1911. Demolished in 1978–79 and replaced by a parking lot. Bass Co. Photo Collection, Indiana Historical Society Library. (Image cropped)

brick exterior curtain walls. They devised a vaguely Georgian/Classical theme for the outside, arranging brick pilasters without capitals along the facade, six-over-six sash windows, and an Ionic frieze and dentil moldings below the cornice (fig. 1.41). For the 1,600-seat theater, the architects designed a heavily ornamented plaster proscenium and provided two balconies. William Morris of the Morris Vaudeville

Circuit of New York leased the theater and assured his Indianapolis patrons that the best in vaudeville performances could be expected at the Colonial, including top star Sophie Tucker and the "Svengalis."[82]

Murat Temple and Theater

Also in 1909, a new theater offering formidable competition to English's Opera House for high-class theatrical fare appeared on the downtown scene. The Indianapolis branch of the Ancient Arabic Order of the Nobles of the Mystic Shrine, popularly known as Shriners, built the exotic and eye-catching Murat Temple at 502 North New Jersey Street (fig. 1.42). They located their building in a residential neighborhood that was beginning to give way to commercial and institutional development along Massachusetts Avenue. A branch of Masonry, the Shriners desired to build a substantial structure that would house a large theater suitable both for their fraternal meetings and for theatrical productions open to the public. As their architect, they hired Oscar Bohlen of D. A. Bohlen and Son, who previously had overseen the rebuilding of English's Opera House in 1897 (see chap. 7 of vol. 1) and more recently had designed the Majestic Theater.

The Shriners also entered into an enviable ten-year lease of the theater to the Lee and Sam Shubert Theatrical Company of New York. The two Shubert brothers running the company in 1909—Lee and Jacob—were well on their way to dominating bookings and theater operations in the whole country.[83]

Oscar Bohlen visited New York to consult with the Shuberts on the design of the Indianapolis theater stage and interior decorations. Lee and Jacob Shubert especially desired to incorporate a revolving stage, one of the latest innovations in New York, at the Murat. With such a stage, half of a circular stage platform could be used for a current act while the other half turned backstage and simultaneously readied for the next act, saving much time during intermissions. Revolving stages then only existed in a couple of theaters, including the New Theater just opened by the Shuberts in New York, and Bohlen visited the New Theater to perfect his understanding of the mechanism.[84]

Facing, **Figure 1.42.** Murat Temple, 502 North New Jersey Street, built in 1909–10 and designed by Oscar Bohlen of D. A. Bohlen and Son, drawing on the designs of Islamic buildings, with a minaret-like tower at the corner, a dome, and striped brick masonry. 2023 view. James Glass.

Bohlen and his staff also studied ancient Islamic architectural designs, probably through illustrations in architectural periodicals, and found some prototypes for the exterior design of the temple. Much of the ritual of the Shriners centered on somewhat fanciful conceptions of the lives and legends of medieval Arabs in the deserts of North Africa and the Middle East, and Bohlen's clients therefore wished their building to reflect Arabic and Islamic culture. For the exterior of the four-story temple, the Bohlen firm followed such Middle Eastern Islamic buildings as the Madrassa and Tomb of Sultan Qayt Bay in Cairo (1472–74), known for its slender minaret with multiple stages, high-profile dome, striped brick masonry, and geometric decorative motifs.[85] Similarly, the architects made an imposing minaret the focal point of the Murat exterior. It soars four stories above a square tower at the southeast corner and transitions to an octagonal shape. The stages of the minaret feature openings with both ogee and pointed arches, all in terra-cotta. Next, a cylindrical brick shaft rises to a flaring battlement and the culminating

Facing, **Figure 1.43.** Detail of terra-cotta decorative elements on the facade combining Classical columns and geometric Islamic-style patterns and designed by sculptor Alexander Sangernebo. 2023 view. James Glass.

Above, **Figure 1.44.** View of the Murat Theater in 1948 showing two tiers of private boxes along the side and a painting of one of the Great Pyramids and the Sphinx near Giza, Egypt. Oscar Bohlen based the design in part on that of the New Theater in New York, built and operated by the Shubert Theatrical Company. Bass Co. Photo Collection, Indiana Historical Society Library. (Image cropped)

spire. To balance the minaret, on the northeast corner of the facade, the architects designed a pumpkin dome in copper with an octagonal drum. They constructed the exterior walls of the Murat with alternating stripes of yellow and brown brick, like the Egyptian prototype.

Working with gifted sculptor Alexander Sangernebo, Bohlen employed cream-colored terra-cotta to carry out the rest of the ornamental program.[86] At the center of the facade, above the entrance, he designed a terra-cotta arcade composed of engaged columns with net capitals that support slightly pointed arches (fig. 1.43). Above, he incorporated courses of geometric figures—diamonds, polygons, circles, and bull's-eyes. Below the arcade, Bohlen devised a large stained-glass lunette, with pointed terra-cotta arch and spandrels above it. He and Sangernebo dematerialized the surfaces of the arch and spandrels with intricate geometric figures, in keeping with the Islamic prohibition of using figural decoration. Another similar terra-cotta arcade adorns the fourth story of the south elevation. Stained glass panes with green, gray, and white patterns enrich rows of windows on both the facade and the south elevation. The architect and sculptor lined the top of the parapet with rows of terra-cotta fleurs-de-lis.

Inside, a lobby and clubrooms originally occupied the east end of the first two floors. The immense theater auditorium filled the rest of the building above the basement, which contained a banquet hall. Large, 112-foot steel trusses supported the roof over the theater, and the designers hung a plaster ceiling for the auditorium from the trusses. To avoid structural posts and blocked views of the stage, the architect and his engineers employed a structure of steel and concrete, which they anchored in the steel frame of the outer walls to support the large balcony. Along the sides of the auditorium in front of the balcony, Bohlen hung rows of descending private boxes with convex exteriors (fig. 1.44). The total seating capacity of the theater was 1,980 people.[87]

For the decorative program of the theater, the architect used a mix of Arabic themes and Classicism. Above the boxes on either side appeared large murals depicting a caravan of desert travelers on camels and a scene near the Great Pyramids and the Sphinx in Egypt. Classical pilasters lined the walls behind the boxes. Overhead, two hundred incandescent lights lit a dome, forty-six feet in diameter, from which hung a chandelier.[88]

In February 1910, Jacob Shubert himself visited the newly completed theater and pronounced it "entirely beyond my expectation" and a great house for grand opera. In fact, several foreign and domestic opera companies did perform in the Murat in its early years, as well as classical and popular musical performers and comedians.[89]

MOVIE THEATERS

Alhambra Theater

The advent of motion pictures transformed the world of theaters. Between 1903 and 1910, twenty-four theaters were built in downtown Indianapolis, many devoted to showing short movies along with other entertainment. After 1910, investors began to build theaters devoted primarily to the exhibition of motion pictures. In 1913, veteran theater managers Fred C. Dickson and Henry M. Talbott organized the Orpheum Amusement Company to build the Alhambra, the first theater in the city to show only movies. They hired a new architect on the scene, Victor E. Winterrowd, to design a two-story fireproof structure at 42–44 West Washington Street. He designed an eye-catching terra-cotta facade in which a canopy projected from the upper portion, adorned with medallions and bas-relief sculptures of human heads (fig. 1.45). Below, dark quatrefoils and diamonds contrasted with a white-colored field. Inside, the architect provided seating for 622 patrons. He installed three operating booths for projection on the second floor and a large pipe organ.[90]

Circle Theater

By 1915, motion pictures in the United States had become an industry of half a billion dollars a year. Up to ten million people annually patronized motion picture theaters. Responding to the demand, movie producers made full-length films with budgets of several hundred thousand dollars. To keep ticket prices low and generate large profits, exhibitors desired large movie houses in which multiple shows could yield high receipts that would pay the rental fees for films and make a profit.[91]

Several downtown merchants and other investors responded to the new economics of motion pictures in 1915, organizing the Monument Realty Company. Investors included A. L. Block, president of L. Strauss & Company men's clothiers; Robert Lieber, a partner in the H. Lieber Company, a manufacturer of picture frames and the operator of an art gallery; Meyer Efroymson of Efroymson and Wolf, operators of the Star Store; Ralph Norwood and Isidore Feibleman of the law firm Bamberger and Feibleman; and an M. Cohn, operator of stores in Denver, Colorado. The company purchased the Wood Livery Stable property in the southeast quadrant of the Circle as the site for the Circle Theater, the first movie palace in Indianapolis. The investors intended the Circle to be the largest theater in the state and a showcase for first-run silent movies.[92]

The company stockholders made several trips to study large motion picture theaters recently completed in major cities of the East and Midwest—Rochester, Buffalo, and Syracuse in New York, as well as New York City and Detroit. They noted appealing features in each and hired the firm of Rubush and Hunter to design the theater. The architects designed a rectangular auditorium and placed it at the rear of the polygonal-shaped property, with the long side of the theater running along Scioto Street to the east and its shorter end, containing the stage, running along Court Street to the south. They ran a two-story wing, containing the entrance and two storerooms, northwest from the auditorium to the Circle.[93]

78 | ARCHITECTURE IN INDIANAPOLIS, 1900–1920

Facing, **Figure 1.45.** +Alhambra Theater, 42–44 West Washington Street, built in 1912 and designed by Victor E. Winterrowd of Indianapolis, with a facade design making use of terra-cotta for canopies, sculptures, and colors. View in 1917. Converted to a restaurant in 1922–23; the exterior was demolished in c. the early 1980s. Bass Co. Photo Collection, Indiana Historical Society Library. (Image cropped)

Above, **Figure 1.46.** Circle Theater, 45 Monument Circle, built in 1916–17 and designed by Rubush and Hunter, drawing on Renaissance details and Classical Greek friezes for a facade of gleaming white terra-cotta. Restored to serve as the home of the Indianapolis Symphony Orchestra in 1982–84. 2021 view. James Glass.

The owners wanted the dignity of a classically themed facade on the Circle, so the architects designed a white terra-cotta front with multiple elements recalling Greek antiquity (fig. 1.46). They suggested a Classical temple front with Doric pilasters that support a frieze with a projecting cornice and a culminating pediment above the cornice. For the frieze, Rubush and Hunter's draftsmen designed fourteen bas-relief figures of musicians and dancing girls, executed in Rookwood

COMMERCIAL AND INDUSTRIAL ARCHITECTURE | 79

tile. Within the tympanum of the pediment, they designed an additional eighteen similar figures. All the figures suggested the sculptures lining the frieze of the Parthenon in Athens. At the center of the second story of the facade, the architects retained a painter to create a mural depicting a rustic Greek scene with dancers.[94]

Inside, Rubush and Hunter created an auditorium seating three thousand people. They provided for two thousand seats on the main floor and one thousand in the large balcony, which they sustained with a forty-thousand-pound steel girder. Although the Circle owners intended the theater to feature movies, they also wished to show live entertainment occasionally. Rubush and Hunter responded

Facing, **Figure 1.47.** Balcony and west wall of the Circle Theater auditorium, the first movie palace in Indianapolis, 1916. Bass Co. Photo Collection, Indiana Historical Society Library. (Image cropped)

Above, **Figure 1.48.** Adam-style bas-relief motifs in the ceiling of the vestibule, Circle Theater, created by sculptor Henry Richard Behrens. 2019 view. James Glass.

by devising a stage with a proscenium arch and a depth of thirty-five feet. The designers also afforded space for the largest theater pipe organ in the state.[95]

The architects devised a decorative program based on the interior design approach of famed eighteenth-century British architect Robert Adam.[96] Just as Adam had designed low-relief, delicate plaster sculptures suggesting motifs from Roman and Italian Renaissance interiors, Rubush and Hunter specified bas-relief plaster figures to cover all the walls and ceilings of the foyer, lobby, and auditorium. Working with sculptor and interior designer Henry Richard Behrens,[97] they interwove griffins, urns, and friezes of dancing maidens and delicately detailed pilasters with

COMMERCIAL AND INDUSTRIAL ARCHITECTURE | 81

endless patterns of arabesques with spiderly, dainty profiles. Above the balcony in the auditorium ceiling, the designers created panels with geometric shapes (fig. 1.47). Each panel contains low-relief plaster sculptures, much as Adam created such patterns for the ceilings of rooms in many of his residential designs. And just as the British architect used multiple colors to maximize the effect of his plaster creations, the architects of the Circle and the sculptor Behrens used rose, ivory, and gray effectively to highlight their details (fig. 1.48).

UNION STATION CONCOURSE AND TRAIN SHED

One of the largest and most costly building and transportation projects of the early twentieth century in Indianapolis came about because of three problems faced by the Indianapolis Union Railway Company and the City of Indianapolis. First, the volume of passengers passing through Union Station had grown substantially, increasing from 125 trains per day in 1894 to about 200 trains per day by 1910. More waiting-room space was needed for passengers and larger facilities to handle baggage, US mail carried on trains, and express package shipping. Second, the multiple tracks running east–west through the existing train shed at Union Station crossed the north–south streets near the station at grade, leading to chronic traffic congestion as trains blocked wagons and the new automobiles attempted to move between the south side and downtown. Finally, within the train shed, passengers found it necessary to walk across the tracks in order to reach their trains, raising safety concerns.[98]

The solution: the Indianapolis Union Railway Company and the City of Indianapolis collaborated on a massive track elevation program that began in 1915 and concluded in 1918, and the railway company built a large new concourse and elevated train shed for Union Station on its own. The company retained the noted architectural firm of Price and McLanahan of Philadelphia to plan the concourse/train shed and presumably much of the track elevation project. The architects had cultivated a close connection to the Pennsylvania Railroad, one of the owners of Union Station, and in the years before the Indianapolis project had designed other train stations and depots in Indiana for the railroad. In addition, William L. Price, the senior partner and chief designer, was familiar with the state capital from having previously served as architect for several large houses in Indianapolis (see chap. 4 of this volume).[99]

The track elevation project, extending eventually from West Street on the west side to Ohio Street on the east, raised the level of the union tracks to the second story and created a large track plaza for passenger and freight trains between

Figure 1.49. Union Station concourse and train shed, showing the facade between Meridian and McCrea Streets. The concourse and shed were built by the Indianapolis Union Railway Company between 1915 and 1922 and designed by Price and McLanahan of Philadelphia using a steel skeleton and reinforced concrete with brick veneer. Note the abstracted Gothic buttresses, Roman thermal windows, and use of colored terra-cotta for details. View in 2023. James Glass.

Meridian and New Jersey Streets. The architects and consulting engineers used concrete as the primary material for the bridges and retaining walls. They used exposed steel columns and beams for the structure of the bridges.[100]

The new train shed, concourse, baggage space, and mail rooms covered seven acres between Meridian Street and Capitol Avenue, dwarfing the 1887–88 Union Station. William Price and C. A. Paquette, the chief engineer for the project, used a combined steel skeleton and reinforced concrete structure for the ground-level facilities and second-floor tracks and an exposed system of steel girders and trusses for the roof structure. Price clad the main facade on the north elevation

COMMERCIAL AND INDUSTRIAL ARCHITECTURE | 83

with buff-colored brick, accented with colored terra-cotta ornamentation. For the three-story section of the shed facade on Louisiana Street between McCrea and Meridian Streets, he employed pavilions at the ends with thermal-style windows derived from Roman imperial baths and cornices with segmental arches (fig. 1.49). The architect marked the piers along the facade between the pavilions with stylized buttresses drawn from Gothic architecture. Above the buttresses, furthering the rhythm, he incorporated abstracted buttress heads into the cornice. Along the two-story facade between Illinois Street and Capitol Avenue, Price continued the treatment of piers as buttresses, with terra-cotta buttress heads and polychromatic decorative pieces created by sculptor Alexander Sangernebo.[101]

In his abstraction of historical details and emphasis on sparely ornamented masses of masonry at Union Station, Price showed his movement away from historical styles, seen previously in Indianapolis with his 1911 design for the Frank H. and Harriet Githens Wheeler mansion (see chap. 4 of this volume), and his embrace of Modern, non-European themes of design.[102]

Over Illinois Street, he employed three large pilasters to front the piers between the openings for the street (fig. 1.50). Price composed the capitals of the green terra-cotta pilasters with stylized foliated motifs modeled and executed by Sangernebo. Above Illinois Street and between the pilasters, he incorporated multipane windows for the second story. Below, he created blind terra-cotta openings with heads of additional multicolored details with foliated elements.[103]

Inside, directly south of the original barrel-vaulted waiting room of Union Station, the architect planned a cross hall that contained a central information desk for directing outgoing passengers (fig. 1.51). South of the hall, he laid out two long concourses leading to six enclosed stairways between them. Passengers could climb each stairway and emerge on the platform of the train they wished to board. Price used a cream-colored terra-cotta tile for the walls and enlivened it with insets of polychromatic terra-cotta pieces probably created by Sangernebo. On the wall behind the information desk, he placed two semicolumns of terra-cotta, with concave capitals incorporating bas-relief flowers in multiple colors (fig. 1.52). The capitals and floral motifs are somewhat Egyptian in style. In the arched frieze above the capitals, the architect created tracery-like panels made up of stylized flower stalks and buds of various sizes and species, all painted in vivid colors. In the cross hall, he installed three shallow barrel vaults of plaster running north and south. A grid of beams covers the center of each vault; on the wall surfaces below the arches of the vaults, Price placed more of the stylized flower stalks and buds seen above the information desk.

Figure 1.50. View of terra-cotta facade of Union Station concourse and train shed above Illinois Street. Note the colossal green pilasters and blind panels with foliated details and multiple colors created by sculptor Alexander Sangernebo. View in 2023. James Glass.

Price's Illinois Street facade design and interior decorative scheme are similar in their abstraction and colors to works of the Art Nouveau movement in Europe at the beginning of the twentieth century but are more stylized.

Price and McLanahan planned baggage-handling rooms in the ground-floor section of the shed east of the passenger concourse and at the far west end. Immediately west of the concourse, they reserved space for the package express and US mail operations.[104]

Facing top, **Figure 1.51.** Union Station cross hall south of 1887 waiting room leading to concourses for track gates, looking west toward the Illinois Street entrance. Architect William Price used terra-cotta for the walls and decorative details. View in 2023. James Glass.

Facing bottom, **Figure 1.52.** In the Union Station cross hall, behind the information desk, polychromatic columns with concave and faceted capitals suggest Egyptian architecture. Above are stylized flower buds and stalks, probably executed by Alexander Sangernebo. Multicolor terra-cotta insets ornament the column shafts and the walls. View in 2023. James Glass.

Although construction on the concourse and train shed began in 1915 and 1916, delays in construction and delivery of building materials during World War I delayed completion until 1922. At that point, five hundred thousand passengers were passing through Union Station each month. The cost of Price's immense shed and concourse came to $2 million.[105]

WHOLESALE BUILDINGS

Closely tied to retail stores, industrial concerns, and the railroads during the first two decades of the new century were wholesale houses—the "middlemen" who obtained refined agricultural products, dry goods, manufactured products, and specialty items from the producers at wholesale prices, packaged them, and sold them to retailers. In Indianapolis, the wholesale district continued to thrive between Washington and South Streets and West and East Streets, as some two hundred wholesale and jobbing houses operated in the city. Many wholesale buildings had been built after the Civil War and continued in use. After 1900, investors and wholesale firms built some new structures in response to growth.[106]

KO-WE-BA Building

An example still stands on the southwest corner of Maryland and Delaware Streets. The Kothe, Wells, and Bauer Company, a wholesale grocer concern, had experienced steady growth since the 1890s, marketing under its popular KO-WE-BA brand. In 1908, the firm hired architects Rubush and Hunter to design a new building especially devised for their business. The architects recommended a traditional structure of wooden joists on all floors, cast-iron columns on the first through third floors, and wooden columns on the top, fourth, floor. The exterior

ARCHITECT PROFILE

William L. Price

William L. Price (1861–1916) was born in Wallingford, Pennsylvania, and educated at Westtown School, near West Chester. He learned carpentry and the building trades while in his teens and was drawn to architecture. He entered the office of Philadelphia architect Addison Hutton and then, with his brother Frank, became a draftsman in architect Frank Furness's office, a few years after noted architect Louis Sullivan worked there. In the Furness office, Price was exposed to the progressive architecture that Frank Furniss created for the wealthy class of Philadelphia. In 1883, the two brothers established their own architectural office and initially designed houses for local developers. By 1891, they established a reputation for well-designed mansions in historical styles. In 1893, William formed his own practice. By the mid-1890s, he became engaged with the social values of the English Arts and Crafts Movement and the American single tax movement, founding Arden, Delaware, as a single tax community and Rose Valley, Pennsylvania, as an Arts and Crafts community. Price designed many of the buildings in both.

In 1903, he formed a partnership with architect and real estate investor M. Hawley McLanahan as Price and McLanahan, and the new firm quickly expanded beyond Philadelphia. Price served as the principal designer. Through connections to the management of the Pennsylvania Railroad, based in Philadelphia, Price and McLanahan soon were designing stations for the railroad west through Ohio and Indiana and into Chicago and Illinois.

In Indiana, the firm designed Pennsylvania Railroad stations in Converse, Hartford City, Ridgeville, Dunkirk, and Fort Wayne and the concourse and train station for Union Station in Indianapolis. Especially with the Fort Wayne station and the Indianapolis project, Price exploited the structural and aesthetic properties of reinforced concrete and experimented with abstracting traditional forms, such as buttresses and thermal windows, as well as using terra-cotta as decorative panels.

In the first decade of the twentieth century, Price capitalized on the plastic qualities of reinforced concrete in designing the exotic Blenheim Hotel and the Moderne Traymore in Atlantic City, New Jersey. He clad the Blenheim (1905–6) with cement stucco and massive terra-cotta ornaments of sea creatures and crowned it with Spanish-style tiled domes and cupolas. The Traymore (1914–15) he made more abstract, with vertical ranks of bays and

horizontal balconies creating an ahistorical order, while the setbacks of the upper stories anticipated the skyscraper forms of the next decade.

He and McLanahan also cultivated a wide range of wealthy clients throughout the eastern United States and the Midwest for the design of mansions. In Indianapolis, they began with the Tudor- and Renaissance-styled home of Frank and Clarissa Lintner Van Camp on North Meridian Street in 1905 and then capped their work in the Indiana capital with an estate for carburetor manufacturer Frank Wheeler and his wife, Harriet, on Cold Spring Road in 1911–12 (see chap. 4 of this volume).

Soon afterward, William Price's health declined, and he died in 1916, with many projects, such as the Indianapolis Union Station concourse and train shed, just beginning construction.

Sources: George E. Thomas, *William L. Price: Arts and Crafts to Modern Design* (New York: Princeton Architectural Press, 2000), 39–45, 67–68, 77–113, 118–38, 159–61, 216–41, and September 19, 2023, communication from George E. Thomas to the author. Source for photo: Courtesy of George E. Thomas, taken by Phillips Studio, Price & McLanahan Archives, George E. Thomas Collection.

Figure 1.53. Former KO-WE-BA Building, southwest corner, Maryland and Delaware Streets, built by the Kothe, Wells and Bauer (KO-WE-BA) wholesale grocers in 1908–9 and designed by Rubush and Hunter with brick load-bearing exterior walls and distinctive stone brackets supporting the cornice. View in 2023. James Glass.

brick walls are load bearing. Rubush and Hunter detailed the exterior simply, with brick piers and spandrels in the upper stories and a sharply projecting cornice supported by carved stone brackets (fig. 1.53). Above the ground floor on the Delaware and Pennsylvania elevations, they ran a stringcourse with stone accents as a second horizontal element. The architects placed the KO-WE-BA offices at the east end of the ground floor and devoted the rest of the building to packaging and storage of the firm's incoming products and outgoing shipments.[107]

Hibben, Hollweg, and Company Building

After the building of the wholesale dry goods firm Hibben, Hollweg and Company burned in 1911, the firm decided to construct a much larger structure. Both of the senior partners, Harold B. Hibben and Louis Hollweg, were veteran wholesalers and believed in the future of the wholesale district. They hired the firm of Vonnegut and Bohn to design the new building, and senior partner Arthur Bohn and junior partner Kurt Vonnegut Sr. devised a handsome six-story building on the northeast corner of Georgia and Meridian Streets (figs. 1.54 and 1.55). The architects used a similar facade composition to that employed by Rubush and Hunter with the KO-WE-BA Building: projecting brick piers balanced by slightly recessed spandrels, a prominent cornice, and a limestone stringcourse above the first story. The architects employed copper shields, a trademark of the late Bernard Vonnegut, as decorative elements below the cornice and constructed the walls of glazed brown brick. The interior structure was again conservative—wooden joists, together with rows of cast-iron columns and steel beams supporting the joists.[108]

Century and John W. Murphy Buildings

A second building type that appeared in the wholesale district was the so-called powerhouse. Investors erected the most substantial of these, the Century Building, in the year of the new century, 1900, on the northwest corner of Maryland and Pennsylvania Streets (fig. 1.56). The owners conceived of a building especially designed for the needs of printing companies, with a structure that could carry heavy loads and a power plant to generate electricity for the operations of tenants. As architects, they hired the local firm of Samuel H. Brubaker and Company, who proceeded to design a seven-story building with a fireproof steel frame and concrete floors and roof. The architects organized the facade on Pennsylvania and the side elevation on Maryland according to the three-part formula used for office buildings. For the base section, the architects drew on both Romanesque and Classical sources for ornamentation—a Romanesque arch and impost blocks for the central entrance and engaged Ionic columns and rectangular Doric pilasters along the storefronts. Above a prominent stringcourse, Brubaker and his staff articulated the shaft section with projecting piers and recessed spandrels. They increased the verticality of the facade by outlining each bank of three windows with an upraised brick molding. A second stringcourse marked the beginning of the top story, above which projected a cornice supported by two types of brackets.[109]

In 1909, the estate of John W. Murphy began construction on another power building at 32–34 East Georgia Street. Samuel Brubaker returned to design a structure similar in concept to the Century Building—intended to accommodate small industrial operations requiring power, such as printing shops. Brubaker devised a seven-story building with a reinforced concrete structure and brick exterior walls (fig. 1.57). He used terra-cotta to "relieve" the simple brick details.[110]

Facing top, **Figure 1.54.** Hibben, Hollweg, and Company Building, 141 South Meridian Street, built by the leading wholesale dry goods firm in 1912–13 and designed by Vonnegut and Bohn with glazed brick exterior and distinctive copper shields below the cornice and limestone sculptures of produce, both of which were used elsewhere by the architectural firm. View in c. 1913–14. Bass Photo Co. Collection, Indiana Historical Society. (Image cropped)

Facing bottom, **Figure 1.55.** Former Hibben, Hollweg, and Company Building in 2021. James Glass.

Above, **Figure 1.56.** The Century Building, 36 South Pennsylvania Street, was built in 1900 and designed by the firm Samuel Brubaker and Company with a heavy steel and reinforced concrete structure for printing companies. The exterior grid pattern with piers and spandrels comes from the tripartite skyscraper formula. Note the Romanesque arch over the entry and the recessed Ionic columns along the ground level. View in 2021. James Glass.

Figure 1.57. John W. Murphy Building, 32–34 East Georgia Street, built in 1909–10 and designed by Samuel Brubaker with a reinforced concrete structure for small industrial firms. He used terra-cotta sparingly for details on the facade. View in 2021. James Glass.

INDUSTRIAL BUILDINGS

Big Four Shops, Beech Grove

One of the largest industrial complexes to be constructed in Marion County before World War II took shape southeast of Indianapolis between 1906 and 1911. The New York Central Railroad, which operated throughout the Northeast and Midwest, constructed shops to repair or reconstruct locomotives, passenger coaches, and freight cars from the entire New York system. In 1906, the Big Four division of the railroad purchased a 640-acre tract for a company town they named Beech Grove and obtained an adjacent tract for the shop buildings.[111] The Big Four hired Indianapolis architect George W. Bunting Jr.[112] to take on the large commission of designing some sixteen buildings. Bunting, who also designed the Big Four shops in Albany, New York, oversaw a force of ten draftsmen in preparing the working drawings and specifications for the final two years of the immense project. He designed at least ten of the buildings with brick load-bearing exterior walls, monitor roofs supported by steel trusses, and concrete floors. These principal buildings, ranging from one to two very tall stories, included the Machine and Erecting Shop; the Coach Shop; the Paint Shop; the Forge Shop; the Boiler Shop; the Tank, Cab, and Pilot Shop (fig. 1.58); the Planing Mill; and the Powerhouse. Bunting designed the Freight Car Shop with a steel frame and brick construction but without a monitor roof. He devised a fireproof, reinforced concrete building with three floors for management offices. The gigantic scale required for operating the complex is indicated by the four and a half acres covered by the Machine and Erecting Shop alone (fig. 1.59).[113]

When completed, the shops employed 3,500 workers, and Beech Grove overnight became a town with a population of three thousand and schools, commercial buildings, and churches subsidized by the real estate subsidiary of the Big Four. The total estimated cost incurred by the railroad in constructing the shops, acquiring the machinery, and developing the real estate at Beech Grove: $7 million.[114]

Automobile Factories

Rail travel seemed supreme in the first decade of the twentieth century, but the new automobile phenomenon captured the public imagination in Indianapolis and across the country in the second decade. Indiana and its capital city had been incubators for the invention of the "horseless carriage" in the 1890s, and in the new century, Indianapolis became a center for manufacturing automobiles. Carl Fisher and his entrepreneurial partners, James Allison, Arthur Newby, and Frank

Above, **Figure 1.58.** Tank, Cab, and Pilot Shop of the Big Four Shops, Beech Grove, Indiana. Built in 1910 by the Big Four division of the New York Central Railroad and designed by George W. Bunting Jr. of Indianapolis. Note the monitor roof and huge sashes of multiple paned glass windows for natural light. Photo taken in c. 1910. Bass Photo Co. Collection, Indiana Historical Society. (Image cropped)

Facing, **Figure 1.59.** Machine and Erecting Shop, Big Four Shops, adapted for use by Amtrak. Built in 1907 and designed by George W. Bunting Jr. View in 2021. James Glass.

Wheeler, cast the spotlight on Indianapolis with their construction of the Indianapolis Motor Speedway in 1909 and promotion of motorcars through the annual 500-Mile Race. They also immersed themselves in nearly every aspect of the automobile manufacturing field—Fisher and Allison making Prest-O-Lite headlights at a factory in their new auto suburb, Speedway City; Newby constructing cars at the National Motor Vehicle Co.; and Wheeler producing carburetors for auto engines.

COLE MOTOR CAR COMPANY FACTORY

Some of the auto manufacturing companies in Indianapolis got their start making buggies and carriages. Joseph J. Cole had founded one such concern. He switched to manufacturing automobiles in 1907. Sales rose rapidly, and in 1911, Cole purchased a tract of land bounded by Washington, Davidson, Market, and Noble (now College Avenue) Streets. He then hired architects Herbert L. Bass and Company to design the first Cole factory building on the southwest corner of Market and Davidson Streets. Bass designed one of the first industrial structures in the city constructed of reinforced concrete. Two rows of concrete columns inside

COMMERCIAL AND INDUSTRIAL ARCHITECTURE | 97

Facing top, **Figure 1.60.** Cole Motor Car Company factory building at 730 East Washington Street, built in 1913 and designed by Herbert L. Bass and Company with a white glazed brick facade with a grid of piers, spandrels, and windows and with limestone accents, including the Cole signature on tablets below the cornice. Photo taken in 1970. Historic American Buildings Survey, Prints & Photographs Division, Library of Congress.

Facing bottom, **Figure 1.61.** Cole Motor Car Company factory building at 730 East Washington Street in 2023, as adapted for use as the Marion County Jail. James Glass.

supported the interior frame of the four-story, rectangular Cole building. On the exterior, Bass exposed the concrete frame on the side elevations and added brick spandrels. He devoted the rest of the wall surface on all four sides to glass windows composed of hundreds of panes set in steel frames.[115]

In 1913, Cole reported that he had enough sale orders to double production, so the Cole Motor Car Company constructed a larger building costing $225,000 to the south of the original structure. Herbert Bass returned as architect and planned an L-shaped building that fronts at 730 East Washington and runs north to Market Street (figs. 1.60 and 1.61). The architect matched the appearance of the 1911 building in the side elevations of the new structure and devised a facade for Washington Street faced with white glazed brick and embellished by buttress-like piers with limestone caps and pilasters. Below the parapet, Bass designed three limestone tablets containing the trademark "Cole" signature. He again used a reinforced concrete structure and installed nearly one thousand sixty-watt lamps to light the factory for a twenty-four-hour-per-day operation. The architect planned the four floors and basement to house most of the manufacturing functions. On the first floor would be the general offices, chassis assembly, and testing. On the second would be chassis painting. On the third floor would be the trimming shop, and on the fourth floor would be the body finishing and engineering departments. Altogether, the two wings of the Cole plant furnished 275,000 square feet of floor space.[116]

After the end of World War I, in 1919, Joseph Cole and the board of the company constructed an additional reinforced concrete building on the north side of Market Street, immediately north of the existing buildings.[117]

NATIONAL MOTOR VEHICLE COMPANY FACTORY

In 1915, the National Motor Vehicle Company announced plans to build a substantial addition to its factory on the southwest corner of Twenty-Second and Yandes

Streets. Arthur C. Newby had founded the company about 1900 after engaging in bicycle chain manufacturing. The new concern became one of the early automobile manufacturers in the city. The company attributed its need for expansion in 1915 to Newby's promotion of National's "Highway" cars at the 1914 500-Mile Race. Orders came in from all over the country, necessitating a doubling of its factory capacity. National Motor Vehicle retained local architect Clarence Martindale in 1915 to design two reinforced concrete buildings—one to face Twenty-Second Street and the other Yandes (fig. 1.62). Along Twenty-Second Street, the architect devised a two-story exterior with twelve-inch brick curtain walls and no ornamentation, relying solely on the articulation of piers and spandrels for details (fig. 1.63). This section contained the general offices of the company on the corner. The wing along Yandes featured broad bays of multipaned industrial windows, set in the brick and concrete framework. Further demand in 1916 caused the firm to build a third wing immediately west of the Yandes Street section.[118]

STUTZ MOTOR CAR COMPANY FACTORY

Harry C. Stutz, a gifted auto engineer and designer, organized the Stutz Motor Car Company in 1913 with business partner Henry Campbell. Within a year, Stutz and Campbell constructed their first four-story factory building on the northwest corner of Tenth Street and Capitol Avenue. It appears that both Rubush and Hunter and D. A. Bohlen and Son worked on the designs of the unfolding Stutz complex. The first building rose in 1914, possibly designed by Oscar Bohlen and his staff. In it, the architects followed the auto industry standard of reinforced concrete structures and clad the exteriors with twelve-inch yellow-brick curtain walls. The first story of the 1914 building received a rusticated look with recessed joints. A concrete cornice projected from the top story along which appeared terra-cotta cartouches inscribed with the capital letter *S*. Inside the first building, the architects arranged for auto frame assembly and company offices on the first floor, auto engine assembly and finishing on the second floor, body painting on

Facing top, **Figure 1.62.** National Motor Vehicle Company factory, southwest corner, Twenty-Second and Yandes Streets, built in 1915 and designed by Clarence Martindale of Indianapolis with two reinforced concrete wings. The wing along Twenty-Second Street was covered with stucco, and both wings featured large expanses of windows. The photo was taken c. 1915–18. Bass Photo Co. Collection, Indiana Historical Society. (Image cropped)

Facing bottom, **Figure 1.63.** View of north wing of National Motor Vehicle Company factory in 2023. James Glass.

Facing top, **Figure 1.64.** Stutz Motor Car Company factory buildings, between Tenth and Eleventh Streets on the west side of Capitol Avenue. The original 1914 building is on the left, next is the building constructed in 1916; the other two were erected in 1919–20. Rubush and Hunter and D. A. Bohlen and Son each designed parts of the complex using reinforced concrete structures. Note the terra-cotta tablets at the corners with the letter S. Now the Stutz Business and Art Center. Photo taken in 2013. James Glass.

Facing bottom, **Figure 1.65.** Interior of Stutz Motor Car Company factory. View within Building B, looking north. Photo taken in 2014. James Glass.

the third floor, and finishing the final cars on the fourth floor. The great success of the company's Stutz Bearcat model necessitated adding an identical building to the north in 1916, definitely designed by the Bohlen firm. In 1919–20, after World War I, the company constructed two more similar structures linked to the prior buildings, probably designed by Rubush and Hunter (figs. 1.64 and 1.65).[119]

Kahn Tailoring Company Factory

A more traditional factory operation required a substantial manufacturing building in 1913, as the Kahn Tailoring Company, founded by Henry Kahn, extended its national network of dealers for its ready-made men's suits and suits to order. Kahn retained Vonnegut and Bohn as architects, and they designed a four-story, fireproof building on the northwest corner of St. Clair Street and Capitol Avenue (fig. 1.66). The architects used a doughnut-shaped plan, with an irregularly shaped courtyard at the center to provide natural light on all four floors. They employed a brick curtain wall for the exterior walls and styled the piers along the quarter-block-long facade and the eastern portions of the side elevations as colossal pilasters. They designed concrete capitals for the pilasters that featured recessed vertical grooves and projecting cylinders, in keeping with Vonnegut and Bohn's recent use of abstract motifs for ornamentation. The capitals support a projecting concrete cornice. At the ends of the facade, the architects inserted pointed parapets faced with tablets bearing sculpted objects. They placed more such sculptures in limestone above the central entrance, linked by a stone frieze and cornice.[120]

Vonnegut and Bohn distributed the functions of the tailoring factory logically on each floor. The first floor contained the company's sample room and shipping department; the second floor the company offices, cutting department, and pressing department; the third floor the sewing department and cloakroom; and the fourth floor the sewing department and lunchroom. As in all these multistory factories, freight elevators moved products from one department to the other.[121]

COMMERCIAL AND INDUSTRIAL ARCHITECTURE | 103

Figure 1.66. Former Kahn Tailoring Company factory building, 810 North Capitol Avenue, built in 1913 and designed by Vonnegut and Bohn. Note trademark shields and limestone sculptures on the facade and along the cornice. The building was rehabilitated for affordable apartments in 2013. Photo taken in 2013. James Glass.

WORLD WAR I

When the United States entered World War I in April 1917, many peacetime building projects stopped. A few private and public buildings under construction continued to be erected, although shortages in materials and labor and increased prices caused delays. Most of the nation's commercial and industrial capacity shifted to producing weapons, ships, munitions, and all manner of goods needed for equipping and supplying the troops. In northeast Marion County, the War Department constructed some temporary wooden buildings at Fort Benjamin Harrison[122] for training the Indiana National Guard, but civilian building ebbed.[123]

After the Allied victory at the end of 1918, the national economy slowly switched back to meet much pent-up consumer demand. In the Indiana state capital, for example, the Cole and Stutz motorcar companies constructed additional factory buildings in 1919, anticipating increased auto sales after the war (see previous discussion). A postwar recession beginning in 1919 deferred the return to prosperity, as the federal government suddenly reduced its huge war expenditures, causing much economic disruption. A boom in building was ahead but only took hold during the 1920s (see epilogue).[124]

CONCLUSION

The twenty years between 1900 and 1920 saw almost continuous expansion of the Indianapolis economy and its commercial and industrial sectors. The enviable location of the state capital as the center of passenger and freight traffic on steam railroads and as the principal hub of the electric interurbans boosted growth in retail, wholesale, and industrial sales and financial transactions.

The most obvious physical manifestation of the growth manifested itself in the construction of skyscraper office buildings in the downtown area. In these structures, investors could obtain a significant square footage on a limited site, keeping down the cost of real estate in a building project. High-speed elevators made high-rise office buildings feasible by rushing tenants and visitors to their destinations. As skyscrapers rose in cities across the country, it became a matter of civic pride for business leaders in Indianapolis and many other communities to point to the number of tall office buildings in their downtowns.

Chicago, the midwestern metropolis, exerted broad influence on the nearby, smaller Hoosier state capital. That influence came to bear particularly in architecture. Chicago had been one of the cradles of skyscraper design in the 1880s and 1890s. Its architects had helped popularize the three-part compositional formula that found its way into most Indianapolis office buildings, department stores, and hotels. Also, the pioneering designs of William LeBaron Jenney in the Home Insurance Building of Chicago and others of the Chicago School of architects paved the way for the construction of tall office buildings by concentrating the structural loads in interior steel frames and allowing designers to convert to thin curtain walls of brick on the exterior and increase space for tenants. The previous technique of building interior structures using heavy timber columns and beams and load-bearing outside walls had restricted the height of commercial buildings.

The impact of Chicago can also be seen in the work of several of its principal architects in Indianapolis from 1900 to 1917. Earlier (see chap. 7 of vol. 1), Henry Ives Cobb, a major figure, had designed the Stevenson Building skyscraper. In the new century, Daniel Burnham and his staff designed the Traction Terminal office building and shed and the Merchants National Bank tower. The allure of Marshall Field and Company's huge department store in Chicago led Frederic Ayres to build the first department store with a layout similar to Field's and later to enlist architect C. A. Wheeler of the Marshall Field's staff to supervise the interior design of L. S. Ayres and Company.

A national trend in architecture, already seen in Indianapolis during the 1890s (see chap. 7 in vol. 1), involved design competitions. Advocated by the American Institute of Architects and favored by many local architects, competitions provided for awarding design commissions based on the merit of designs. Outstanding figures in the architectural field with judicious reputations sat on juries who selected winning designs, and the clients frequently hired an architectural advisor such as Warren P. Laird of the University of Pennsylvania to screen submissions and guide them through the competition process. Competitions found particular favor for public buildings, but private firms also employed them on occasion. One of the complaints heard from Indianapolis architects involved the apparent tendency of jurors to select the designs of nationally known, out-of-town architects. That occurred with several major public buildings, such as the US Courthouse and Post Office and the Indianapolis Public Library (see chap. 2 of this volume) but also, at least initially, the Fletcher Savings and Trust Company competition, in which New York architect Electus Litchfield won the competition.

With respect to stylistic themes, the architects of commercial and industrial buildings in Indianapolis between 1900 and the entry of the United States into World War I in 1917 followed national trends. The Italian Renaissance continued as a preferred source for overall composition and details, and overtly Classical language drawn more directly from the buildings of ancient Rome and Greece became more evident. William Price diverged from the norm in Indianapolis and other major cities when he used abstracted Gothic buttresses and stylized ornament in his Union Station concourse and train shed.

Local architects drew ideas for designs from the photographs and plans published in *Inland Architect*, *American Architect and Building News*, *Architectural Record*, and other architectural periodicals. For major buildings, they often visited other cities to study comparable structures.

Indianapolis architects also closely followed national trends in structural design and fireproofing. After the Civil War, concern grew across the nation about the potential of fires to kill or injure users of buildings, as it became evident that wooden interior structures and flammable partitions entailed little protection from fires. In Chicago, William LeBaron Jenney dramatically reduced fire risk through his use of steel structural frames. Further protections in Chicago came through encasing steel beams and columns with terra-cotta, which reduced the possibility of the steel melting in extreme heat. In Indianapolis, such architects as Bernard

Vonnegut in the Commercial Club Building of 1892–93 and Oscar Bohlen in the Majestic Building of 1894–95 already had incorporated the innovations of Chicago with respect to steel structural frames. By 1900, local architects were following national refinements for what was termed "fireproof construction." In addition to employing a steel skeleton and encasing structural members with terra-cotta, architects often laid concrete floors. Further protection against fires came with the gradual adoption of reinforced concrete structures for all types of commercial and public buildings. The first Indianapolis office building to incorporate a reinforced concrete frame was the Board of Trade Building of Brubaker and Eldridge in 1905–6.

A final new feature in commercial buildings of Indianapolis during the first two decades of the new century came in the form of terra-cotta. This versatile material, capable of mass production, could produce exotic and varied decorative forms in many colors. When used as a veneer for the entire facade of an office building or department store, it dazzled passersby and gained steady favor as an alternative to stone or brick. The best examples came from Rubush and Hunter with their Hume-Mansur Building and Vonnegut and Bohn with the William H. Block Company department store and Kahn office building.

The principal Indianapolis architectural firms designing commercial and industrial buildings during this period were a mixture of well-established practices and newcomers. Veteran architect John H. Stem designed the Newton Claypool Building. Vonnegut and Bohn, led by Bernard Vonnegut and Arthur Bohn and later by Bohn and Kurt Vonnegut Sr., designed several large office buildings, a hotel, and two major department stores. R. P. Daggett and Company, headed after about 1910 by Robert Frost Daggett, designed Hotel Washington and several retail buildings. A new firm, Rubush and Hunter, almost immediately gained sizeable commissions, such as the Odd Fellows Building and the Marott Department Store. Another new arrival, Herbert L. Bass, made his mark with small retail buildings and factory buildings. Other firms occasionally gained large commissions, such as Brubaker and Eldridge, Samuel H. Brubaker, and Clarence Martindale.

Two out-of-town architects from nearby cities designed major Indianapolis buildings: Frank M. Andrews of Cincinnati created the grand Claypool Hotel and, about the same time, the sumptuous new Columbia Club (see chap. 2 of this volume). James F. Alexander of Lafayette won a national competition to design the flat-iron Knights of Pythias office building.

Map 1.1

Buildings from Chapter 1 of Volume 2 plotted on 1914 Sanborn Insurance Map of Mile Square of Indianapolis (Vol. 1) (numbers drawn from figure numbers); + = demolished

- **1** + Newton Claypool Building
- **2** + Indianapolis Traction Terminal Office Building and Shed
- **4** + Indianapolis Board of Trade Building
- **5** + Knights of Pythias Office Building
- **6** + Indianapolis Star Building
- **7** 1907-8 Independent Order of Odd Fellows Building
- **8** Merchants National Bank Building
- **11** Pennway Building
- **13** Indianapolis News Building
- **14** + Bobbs-Merrill Building
- **15** + Hume-Mansur Building
- **16** Kahn [office] Building
- **17** Fletcher Savings and Trust Company Building
- **19** McOuat and Marott's Shoes Buildings
- **21** L.S. Ayres and Company department store
- **23** Marott's Department Store

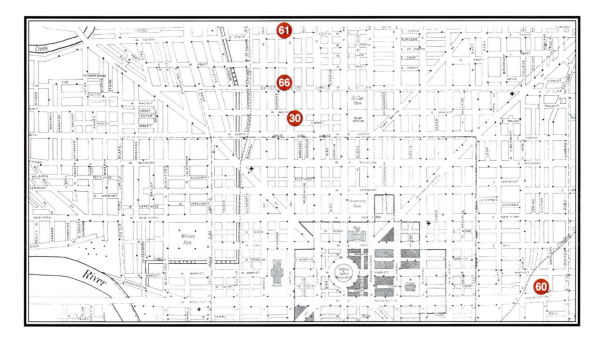

Map 1.2

Buildings from Chapter 1 plotted on 1914 Sanborn Insurance Map (Vol. 1) of area north, west, and east of Mile Square (numbers drawn from figure numbers)

- **30** Williams Building
- **60** Cole Motor Car Company factory building
- **61** Stutz Motor Car Company factory buildings
- **66** Kahn Tailoring Company factory building

| *Map 1.1 key continued*

- **25** William H. Block Company department store
- **26** + Aeolian, Gibson Automotive, and Wulschner-Stewart Buildings
- **27** Geiger Building
- **29** + Globe Realty Company garages
- **31** + Fisher Automotive Company Building
- **32** + Claypool Hotel
- **36** Hotel Washington
- **38** Hotel Severin
- **40** + Majestic Theater
- **41** + Colonial Hotel and Theater
- **42** Murat Temple and Theater
- **45** + Alhambra Theater
- **46** Circle Theater
- **49** Union Station Concourse and Train Shed
- **53** KO-WE-BA Building
- **54** Hibben, Hollweg and Company Building
- **56** Century Building
- **57** John W. Murphy Building

2 | PUBLIC, SOCIAL, AND CHARITABLE ARCHITECTURE

1900–1920

While commercial and industrial buildings dominated the nonresidential architectural scene in Indianapolis between 1900 and 1920, all levels of government and many nonprofit organizations also responded to the period of prosperity and growth by constructing major buildings for public purposes and private social and charitable organizations. A new federal courthouse and post office, a new state school for the deaf, Fort Benjamin Harrison, a city hall, a new fire headquarters, and a new central public library commanded much attention. The Indianapolis Public Schools board constructed additional elementary schools and opened a new high school, Arsenal Technical. Fraternal orders constructed major buildings downtown, both standalone fraternal structures and combined fraternal and office buildings. Fundraising efforts during the period focused on constructing a new YMCA and a new YWCA for white residents and a new YMCA for African American youth and men. And five new hospitals rose around the city in response to the increase in population and growth in city boundaries.

Architectural competitions played a significant role in the selection of designers for public buildings, and several architects with national reputations obtained commissions in the state capital through that procedure. With respect to style, architects tended to rely on the Italian Renaissance as a reliable source for compositions and detailing while also increasingly incorporating the new taste for direct Roman and Greek sources.

The white majority continued to impose racial discrimination and segregation on the African American minority in the population. Deeply rooted in the histories of the city and state, discrimination and segregation pervaded the local culture during the 1900–1920 era. Discrimination against African Americans resulted in Black citizens being restricted in nearly all their activities to a handful of neighborhoods and commercial districts. Segregation of African Americans forced them to create separate social and fraternal organizations, churches, public schools, hospitals, and entertainment options for Black citizens. The principal African American community centered on Indiana Avenue and the adjacent areas north and west of the avenue. Few, if any, Black architects practiced in Indianapolis. A few African American contractors found work. White architects frequently designed buildings commissioned by African American organizations.[1]

PUBLIC BUILDINGS

During the nineteenth century (see vol. 1), Indianapolis had enjoyed high standards of design, decoration, and materials for its public buildings. The first federal courthouse and post office building of 1857–61, the Marion County Courthouse of 1869–76, the Indiana Statehouse of 1878–88, and the Indianapolis Public Library of 1892–93—each imposing and monumental—had added to the civic character and reputation of the state capital. As the twentieth century opened, the federal, state, and city governments erected a new generation of public structures that reached new heights in design, materials, and craftsmanship.

US Courthouse and Post Office

The federal government made the first contribution with an elegant and lavishly appointed new US Courthouse and Post Office. Despite making two additions to the original federal building at Market and Pennsylvania Streets, the national government found that it had outgrown the structure by the late 1890s. In 1898, the US Department of the Treasury announced that it would build a much larger new building in Indianapolis. In the spring of 1899, James Knox Taylor, supervising architect of the Treasury, visited the state capital and inspected several potential sites. Civic boosters especially promoted Square 36 of the 1821 Ralston plan: the block bounded by Ohio, Meridian, New York, and Pennsylvania Streets. It fronted on University Park and was judged to be removed from the bustle and noise of the business district. The secretary of the Treasury did choose that site, and the federal government set into motion the first clearance of a city block in Indianapolis for a civic purpose.[2]

Much additional public discussion centered on the next decision to be made. Local architects and civic leaders urged the Treasury to hold a competition for selecting the architect of the new courthouse and post office and to open such a contest to Indianapolis firms. They urged the secretary of the Treasury not to delegate responsibility for the design and supervision of the project to James Taylor and the staff architects of the Treasury. The *Indianapolis Journal* editorialized that "Indianapolis has some high-class architects, men undoubtedly competent to do the work in question, and it would be a gratification to local pride if one of them should be chosen to draw the plans and superintend the work."[3]

In 1900, the Department of the Treasury decided to hold a national architectural competition in which both out-of-town and local architects would be invited to participate. Four Indianapolis firms competed—Adolph Scherrer, Vonnegut and Bohn, P. C. Rubush and Company, and Andrews and Martindale. The department sent the competitors detailed instructions on the program, dimensions, and site for the project and appointed H. Langford Warren of Boston, Daniel H. Burnham of Chicago, Edward B. Green of Buffalo, and J. R. Marshall as judges. James Knox Taylor served on the panel ex officio. Early in 1901, the department announced that the judges had recommended the design of two young architects from Philadelphia—John Hall Rankin and Thomas M. Kellogg—and the department had accepted the recommendation. Only one of the local firms was chosen for one of the top three places in the competition—Vonnegut and Bohn shared a three-way tie for third place.[4]

The winning submission called for a facade inspired by the Greek Ionic colonnade of the US Treasury Building in Washington, designed by architect Robert Mills in the 1830s. Supervisory Architect Taylor later explained that he and his staff had studied which styles from the past were best suited for buildings of the federal government. They had concluded that Romanesque suggested churches and Gothic indicated churches or educational institutions. In contrast, the Classical style of the Greeks and Romans was associated in the public mind with some of the principal buildings in Washington—the Treasury Building, the US Capitol, the White House, and the US Patent Office—and connoted dignity, impressiveness, and stability. The public would associate the Classical style with the national capital if it were used for federal buildings around the country. In light of these comments, it seems quite possible that the judges chose the Rankin and Kellogg design at least in part because of its style linked to Washington.[5]

Figure 2.1. US Courthouse and Post Office, 46 East Ohio Street, built in 1903–5 and designed by John Hall Rankin and Thomas M. Kellogg of Philadelphia with an Ionic colonnade based on the Greek Revival US Treasury Building in Washington designed by Robert Mills. View of south elevation in 2021. James Glass.

The design of Rankin and Kellogg called for a U-shaped building facing Ohio Street. As finally sited, the building occupied the center of the block. The architects reserved the southern portion of the site for a lawn and open court to enable passersby, in the words of Rankin, "not to have to strain their necks to get a full view of the structure." A recessed site on the north side would provide a similar view of the building.[6]

Between 1901 and 1903, the Department of the Treasury negotiated the purchase of all the privately and publicly owned parcels in Square 36 and demolished the buildings standing in the block. Several notable structures—the 1864–70 First Presbyterian Church and 1883–84 Plymouth Congregational Church—came down, as did a public school and several residences.

Between 1903 and 1905, Rankin and Kellogg, together with James Taylor and the Office of the Supervising Architect, supervised the construction of the new courthouse and post office. They constructed the final building with a fireproof steel structure and brick exterior walls, faced with Indiana Bedford limestone.[7] The main facade on Ohio consists of a long colonnade of eighteen Ionic semicolumns at the center (fig. 2.1). At the east and west ends, pavilions containing the four principal entrances to the building project forward of the colonnade. At the east and west entries, paired Ionic semicolumns flank each entrance. The entries themselves are marked by projecting pediments supported by consoles. The two southern entrances are contained in two-story rectangular cavities. Full Ionic columns standing in antis flank the southern entries. Along the Meridian Street and Pennsylvania Street elevations, the rhythm of the Ionic colonnade continues with Ionic pilasters. On the south, east, and west elevations, the architects gave the columns and pilasters the same scale. Both support the same Ionic frieze and entablature. In planning the location of the four entrances, Rankin and Kellogg followed the French Beaux Arts system of planning. They employed a logical circulation pattern within the building and clearly articulated the exterior entries and stairways that gave access to the interior.

Inside, Beaux Arts principles further guided the planning. Postal patrons or participants in federal court proceedings who entered each of the four entrances passed through a barrel-vaulted corridor and entered one of two octagonal-shaped vestibules. One side of each vestibule led into a long corridor running east and west that contained the postal windows and post rental boxes. The north side of each vestibule led into a courts lobby containing elevators and a grand stairway providing access to the federal courts and other federal offices. Each visitor could clearly see the paths leading to the post office or the courts. At the southwest and southeast corners of the second floor, the architects placed the courtrooms for the federal district court of Indiana and the Indiana circuit court judges. In between, they located the court library, chambers for the judges, and offices for the clerks and the staff of the US Department of Justice. On the third floor, the designers placed offices for federal pension employees, the US Marshals Service, the Secret Service, and collectors of revenues and customs. The fourth floor contained quarters for the railway mail clerks.[8]

The interior decorative scheme and materials dazzled visitors. Rankin and Kellogg drew principally from Roman imperial architecture for their themes. Barrel vaults with Roman-style limestone coffers cover the entry corridors, which are lined by Tuscan columns of Italian marble standing in antis. The architects covered the two octagonal vestibules with groin vaults shimmering with Roman-style

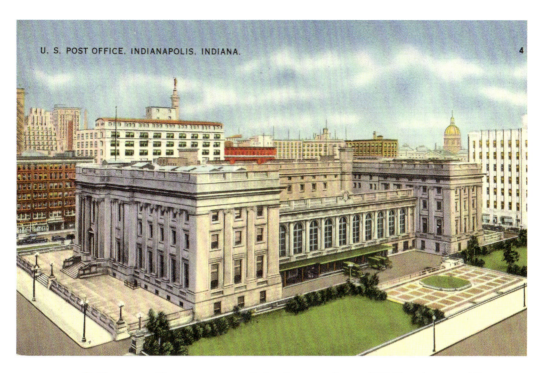

Figure 2.2. Circa 1925 postcard view from northeast of US Courthouse and Post Office showing Renaissance-style screen fronting mail-sorting room in the courtyard. Postcard from author's collection.

glass mosaics in deep hues of green, blue, and gold. They covered the vestibule walls with varieties of colored marble from around the world and placed niches flanked by Tuscan columns on each of the four diagonal sides. Marble also covers the walls, ceiling, and floors of the long post office corridor.[9]

The pièce de résistance of Rankin and Kellogg's interior appears in the two lobbies north of the vestibules. The visitor passes through bronze gates into lofty chambers in which the eye is drawn up to more groin vaults adorned with Roman-style mosaics depicting symbols of justice (fig. 2.3). White marble walls provide contrast. On the west and east sides of the two lobbies, grand, self-supporting stairways of marble sweep upward in spiral curves (fig. 2.4). Screens of columns—Ionic on the second floor and Corinthian on the third floor—line the corridors along the three-story stairwells. Large stained glass windows grace the outer walls of the stairways, while plaster semidomes with fish-scale, stained glass skylights cap each stairwell.[10]

PUBLIC, SOCIAL, AND CHARITABLE ARCHITECTURE | 115

Above, **Figure 2.3.** East courts lobby, US Courthouse and Post Office, with Roman groin vaults covered by mosaics, marble wall panels, and terrazzo floors. Carol M. Highsmith for US General Services Administration, c. 2009, Carol M. Highsmith Archive, Library of Congress.

Facing, **Figure 2.4.** Self-supporting spiral stairway, half plaster dome, art glass, and screens of columns, east stair hall, US Courthouse and Post Office. David Sundberg Photography, courtesy of the US District Court for the Southern District of Indiana.

Figure 2.5. Original district court courtroom, US Courthouse and Post Office, with Italian Renaissance Corinthian pilasters of marble and Baroque geometric patterns in the plaster ceiling. David Sundberg Photography, courtesy of the US District Court for the Southern District of Indiana.

The two original courtrooms effectively represent the majesty of justice. The architects lined the two-story rectangular rooms using Italian Renaissance–style Corinthian pilasters with gray and white marble shafts and gilded capitals (fig. 2.5). The plaster ceilings with raised beams in geometric patterns contain skylights at their centers. Along the longer outside walls, the designers placed stained glass windows made by the New York firm of Heinigke and Bowen. An aedicule with Corinthian columns looks down over the bench in the southwest courtroom and contains a painting, *Appeal to Justice* by Philadelphia artist W. B. Van Ingen. Local sculptor Alexander Sangernebo carried out the plaster ornamentation and sculpted details.[11]

A final touch of artistic excellence and symbolic meaning came in 1908 with the installation of four statues executed by American sculptor John Massey Rhind flanking the two southern entrances. The limestone female figures represent "Industry," "Agriculture," "Literature," and "Justice."[12]

Rankin regretted that the design program did not allow the courthouse and post office to face University Park. The large mail-sorting workroom of the Indianapolis post office occupied the first three stories of the U-shaped courtyard of the building, and mail was brought in from the north side. Therefore, the mail operation dominated the design of the north elevation. The architects compensated somewhat by designing a two-and-a-half-story screen of limestone to mask the mail-sorting room. The screen contained tall arched windows flanked by Ionic pilasters (fig. 2.2).[13]

The first-class character of the US Courthouse and Post Office is indicated by the costs: $375,000 for the interior finishes, materials, and artwork, and a total cost of $2 million, more than spent on any Indianapolis building to that date except the Indiana Statehouse.[14]

Fort Benjamin Harrison

Soon after completion of the courthouse and post office, the federal government undertook an even larger-scale building project about nine miles northeast of downtown Indianapolis. In 1902, Congress authorized the establishment of a post suitable for a regular US Army regiment in Indianapolis. Lieutenant Colonel Russell B. Harrison, son of former president Benjamin Harrison, campaigned first to redesign the US Arsenal on East Michigan Street for the post, but after objections from surrounding residents, he shifted his focus to persuading the US army and Congress to build a post near the little town of Lawrence in northeastern Marion County. Harrison's lobbying proved successful: the army spent $279,000 to purchase 2,415 acres in a wooded tract with both hilly and level topography, suitable for operating an up-to-date army post and conducting regimental maneuvers and other training. The post-to-be was named Fort Benjamin Harrison in honor of the Civil War general and president.[15]

After Congress appropriated funds, construction began on the fort in 1906 and continued until 1910. As the focus of the post plan, the Quartermaster General's Office of the US Army chose a level portion of the tract and laid out a curvilinear loop drive that ran around the perimeter of a spacious parade ground. The loop and parade ground followed the lines of the topography. The Quartermaster General's Office planners located the commissioned officer quarters along the north

ARCHITECT PROFILES

Rankin and Kellogg

John Hall Rankin (*at left*) and Thomas M. Kellogg (*at right*) posing with an Ionic capital from the US Courthouse and Post Office of Indianapolis, c. 1904–5.

John Hall Rankin (1868–1952) and Thomas M. Kellogg (1862–1935) headed one of the most successful architectural firms in Philadelphia during the first three decades of the twentieth century.

Rankin was born in Lock Haven, Pennsylvania, and graduated from Lock Haven High School in 1885. Conceiving an interest in architecture, he entered a two-year course of architectural studies at the Massachusetts Institute of Technology (MIT) and graduated in 1889. After moving to Philadelphia, Rankin gained architectural experience first in the office of James H. Windom and then in that of Wilson Brothers and Company. He then worked for New York architects Boring and Tilton. Returning to Philadelphia, in 1891, Rankin formed an architectural partnership with a fellow alumnus of the two-year MIT course of study, Thomas M. Kellogg.

Kellogg was born in Washington, DC. He graduated from Laurel High School in Maryland and then spent one year at Baltimore City College. With an interest in architecture, he worked as an apprentice/draftsman for Baltimore architect Charles L. Carson. Next, Kellogg decided to enter the MIT program. In 1884, he moved to New York and obtained work as a draftsman in the office of McKim, Mead, and White, one of the largest and most prestigious architectural firms in the country. While there, Kellogg mastered the elements of the Beaux Arts method of planning and designing.

It is not known which of the partners in the firm took the lead in design. Rankin appears to have been the spokesperson for the firm on the Indianapolis US Courthouse and Post Office project, but both he and Kellogg had substantial academic and professional education and experience in design and construction. Kellogg had the benefit of working for McKim, Mead, and White, with its substantial corpus of outstanding buildings with Classical and Italian Renaissance compositions.

In its first decades, the firm participated in several national architectural competitions, receiving second place in the contest for the design of the New York City Hall and first place for their 1901 design of the US Courthouse and Post Office in Indianapolis.

In 1903, architect Edward A. Crane, another MIT alumnus, joined the partnership. Rankin, Kellogg, and Crane expanded their practice to include commissions for all types of buildings in the Philadelphia area. One of their largest public structures was the US Post Office at Thirtieth and Market Streets in Philadelphia (1930).

After Crane left the practice, Rankin and Kellogg continued the firm until Kellogg's death in 1935. In 1943, the firm became Rankin, Kellogg, and Doe.

Sources: Sandra L. Tatman, "Rankin and Kellogg," "Rankin, John Hall (1868–1952)," "Kellogg, Thomas M," and "Projects, Rankin and Kellogg," Philadelphia Architects and Their Buildings, n.d. https://www.philadelphiabuildings.org/pab/app/ar_display.cfm/26268, accessed June 26, 2024. Source for photo: Bass Photo Co. Collection, Indiana Historical Society (image cropped).

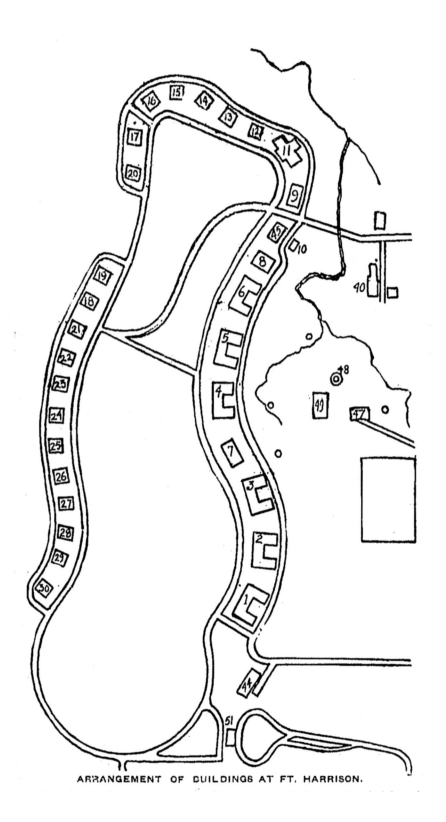

ARRANGEMENT OF BUILDINGS AT FT. HARRISON.

Facing, **Figure 2.6.** Plan of Lawton Loop, Fort Benjamin Harrison, 1907, designed by the US Quartermaster General's Office, US Army. The barracks are shown on the right (east) side of the loop, and the officer quarters are on the north and west sides. "Detail Marks Army Post Completion," *Indianapolis Star*, July 14, 1907, 25.

and west sides of the Lawton Loop drive and the barracks for enlisted men, the administrative building, and support buildings along the east side (fig. 2.6). The planners located the hospital building a short distance east of the north edge of the loop to facilitate the isolation of contagious patients.[16]

The Quartermaster General's Office planned all army posts and designed the buildings for each. It developed a series of standardized plans for the principal building types required. The floor plans, architectural style, materials, and interior finishes of a new officer quarters or barracks at Fort Harrison would be identical to comparable structures at other posts, such as Fort Leavenworth in Kansas. Major George H. Penrose, the constructing quartermaster for Fort Harrison, obtained blueprint copies of the standardized plans selected at headquarters in Washington and oversaw the construction of the buildings by contractors. The total number of structures built in the new post by 1910 was forty-nine. Nearly all were constructed with steel frames, foundations of rock-faced limestone, and exterior brick walls.[17]

During the first decade of the twentieth century, the Quartermaster General's Office preferred the Georgian style for officer quarters, noting its increasing popularity as a residential style and its association with the architecture of the thirteen original colonies and the early American republic (see chap. 4 of this volume). A modern perspective might see a mixture of Georgian, Federal, and Greek Revival features in the officer quarter designs selected for Fort Harrison. The designs of eighteen of the twenty officer quarters built along the Lawton Loop followed three standardized plans from the quartermaster. Eight followed Plan 142-F, for a duplex; six followed Plan 120-F, also for a duplex; and four followed Plan 145-D, for a single-family house.[18]

Those duplexes following Plan 142-F have an oblong shape, a facade six bays wide, full pediments in lieu of gables on the side elevations, and expansive frame verandas with Tuscan columns (fig. 2.7). The verandas wrap around the corners on either side of the facade, providing access to the two duplex entrances. In the front slopes of the gable roof, two dormers framed with pilasters and overhead pediments project out. The red brick exterior walls, six-over-six window sashes, flat brick lintels with keystones, and careful symmetry all suggest the Georgian and

PUBLIC, SOCIAL, AND CHARITABLE ARCHITECTURE | 123

Above, **Figure 2.7.** Duplex officer quarters, 5873 and 5875 Lawton Loop, Fort Benjamin Harrison, built 1906–10. Constructed from standardized Plan 142-F, designed by the US Quartermaster General's Office. The style is a mixture of Georgian and Greek Revival. The army originally intended such duplexes for captains and lieutenants and their families. 2021 view. James Glass.

Facing top, **Figure 2.8.** Duplex officer quarters, 5768 and 5770 Lawton Loop, Fort Benjamin Harrison, constructed from standardized Plan 120-F, designed by the US Quartermaster General's Office. Greek Revival details include the pediment over the front pavilion and in-turning trim in the side gables. The flat arches over the windows and the use of symmetry are Georgian in style. 2021 view. James Glass.

Facing bottom, **Figure 2.9.** Single-family officer quarters, 5861 Lawton Loop, constructed from standardized Plan 145-D. The facade is asymmetrical but includes a similar mixture of Georgian and Greek Revival details. The army originally intended such quarters for the commanding colonel or majors. 2021 view. James Glass.

Federal styles, although there are six bays instead of the usual five in eighteenth-century houses. The multiple pediments and pilasters recall the Greek Revival.

The second group of duplexes, following Plan 120-F, project more of a Greek Revival theme than Georgian (fig. 2.8). They have a cruciform plan, with four arms projecting from the center. One of the arms projects forward to form the facade. The dominant feature of the facade is the pediment overhead. There are four bays across the first and second stories; the details of the fenestration are the same as in Plan 142-F. The gables of the side pavilions are styled in partial pediments with returning trim at the sides. Rectangular frame porches appear at the front of the side elevations.

The last group of quarters, following Plan 145-D for single-family residences, features an asymmetrical design, with a gable on one side of the facade and gables off-center in both side elevations (fig. 2.9). A rectangular veranda appears across the facade.

The hierarchical nature of the army structure dictated the type of accommodations received by each rank of commissioned officer. The colonel of the regiment posted at the fort received the largest and most elaborate of the four single-family residences. The lieutenant colonel and two majors received the other single-family quarters. The fourteen captains and thirty-two lieutenants qualified for the duplexes. The quartermaster general also reinforced the hierarchy more subtly by the amount of oak finish each of the quarters received: the colonel's house received six rooms finished in oak, while those of the majors received four such rooms.[19]

The Quartermaster General's Office architects specified six barracks for enlisted men along the eastern side of Lawton Loop, all following standard plan 75-G.[20] Each barrack has a U-shaped plan, with the base of the U forming a two-story facade facing the Lawton Loop parade ground (fig. 2.10). The standardized plans placed two gables symmetrically at either end of the facade wing. The cornice and in-turning trim along each gable suggest a Greek pediment. The dominant feature of each barrack facade originally was a two-story veranda with two floors that extended across the entire facade and afforded places for the enlisted men to cool off in the shade during the summers.[21] The plans called for two companies to occupy a barrack, each unit of men occupying an L-shaped section on either side. Major Penrose, the constructing quartermaster, provided baths, showers, and a boiler room in each basement. The second floor contained the mess room, the kitchen, a reading and living room, and two large sleeping rooms for the enlisted men.[22]

The quartermaster's architects placed a three-story building next to the northern row of officer quarters for the bachelor officer quarters. The unmarried officers

Figure 2.10. Enlisted men's barracks, 5757 Lawton Loop, constructed from standardized Plan 75-G. The simply detailed barracks buildings have in-turning Greek Revival trim on the facade gables and expansive verandas. The Quartermaster General's Office designed such barracks to house two companies of troops. 2021 view. James Glass.

each lived in a suite of rooms, and the standardized plan furnished a library, reception, room, and laundry.[23]

The Quartermaster General's Office planned for a self-contained community, with all the buildings required for daily life in an army post. On the east side of Lawton Loop, the quartermaster general's staff constructed a post exchange at the center of the row of barracks, an administration building, a guard house, and a fire engine house. Elsewhere they built a bakery, granary, ammunition magazine, commissary storehouse, band barracks, hospital, pumping station, and water tower. Between 1908 and 1917, Fort Harrison served as the home post for the Tenth and Twenty-Third US Army regiments and as a training center for the Indiana state militia.[24]

Indiana School for the Deaf

On a smaller scale, in 1906, the State of Indiana adopted plans to construct a new campus of buildings for the Indiana School for the Deaf. The previous campus, constructed in the early 1850s and 1880s (see chap. 3 of vol. 1), occupied a site at East Washington Street and State Avenue and had been engulfed by later residential neighborhoods and factories. The main building, designed by Joseph Willis in the Greek Revival style, was considered obsolete for the education of the deaf. Governor J. Frank Hanly appointed a commission to oversee the construction of the new campus, and the panel retained the up-and-coming architectural firm of Rubush and Hunter to design the buildings. The preliminary plans, announced in February 1906, called for as many as twenty-two structures on a twenty-six-acre tract located on the north side of East Forty-Second Street, immediately north of the Indiana State Fairgrounds (fig. 2.11). Just as the original campus had been located in the country in the 1850s, the new campus was situated north of most residential development in 1906.[25]

The architects laid out the principal buildings in a quadrangle plan, with the main building, containing classrooms and administration, situated along the south edge, a long dormitory building for girls along the west side, an identical dormitory for boys along the east side, and a combined dining hall and social hall building along the north side. The designers used a mixture of Roman and Italian Renaissance details as their architectural theme. They constructed the buildings all with buff-colored, load-bearing brick walls with limestone accents.[26]

Rubush and Hunter gave the main two-story building, presenting the face of the institution, an imposing Roman-style portico, consisting of six smooth-shafted Ionic columns in limestone supporting a pediment and standing on a podium (fig. 2.12). They used an E-shaped plan for the facade as a whole, with a central pavilion and side pavilions projecting forward at the end of east and west wings. The architects styled the piers on the facades of the two side pavilions as pilasters echoing the temple front of the portico at center. They faced the high basement with limestone. A Renaissance-style cornice with modillions appears above a plain frieze. Above it runs a brick parapet with limestone coping. Banks of three windows with eight-over-eight sashes impose countering horizontal lines across the facades of the wings. Behind the facade, three pavilions extend north, separated

Figure 2.11. Aerial view rendering of the Indiana School for the Deaf campus, prepared by architects Rubush and Hunter about 1906. The administration and classroom building is at the lower center, the girls' dormitory on the west (left) side of the central quadrangle, the boys' dormitory on the east side, and the dining and social hall at the north end. Max R. Hyman, ed., *Hyman's Handbook of Indianapolis* (Indianapolis: M. R. Hyman, 1909), 120.

by courtyards. In the center stands a wing containing the school gymnasium in the basement and first floor and a seven-hundred-seat auditorium on the second. The two side wings originally contained classrooms.[27]

The two dormitories each consisted of three two-story pavilions running north–south and linked by hyphens (fig. 2.13). The central pavilions projected slightly forward of the side pavilions, and the three pavilions presented long facades along the quadrangle. The architects used several Renaissance elements: a tall Palladian opening in each of the two central pavilions, an arcade in front of

PUBLIC, SOCIAL, AND CHARITABLE ARCHITECTURE | 129

Facing top, **Figure 2.12.** Facade, administration and classroom building, Indiana School for the Deaf, 1200 East Forty-Second Street, built in 1906–11 and designed by Rubush and Hunter with a handsome Ionic portico and buff brick exterior walls. 2021 view. James Glass.

Facing bottom, **Figure 2.13.** A + beside the name of a building indicates that it no longer exists. +One of the dormitory buildings after completion in 1911, Indiana School for the Deaf, designed by Rubush and Hunter with a Renaissance-style Palladian arch and columns at the center and a cornice with modillions. The state demolished the boys' dormitory (Beecher Hall) in 2002 and the girls' dormitory (Simpson Hall) in 2019. See "Decades-Long Effort to Save Simpson Hall Ends in Defeat," Indiana Landmarks, July 30, 2019, https://www.indianalandmarks.org/2019/07/simpson-hall-effort-ends-in-defeat/#:~:text=Lost%20Opportunity&text=In%20April%2C%20those%20efforts%20were,as%20the%20school's%20girls'%20dormitory. Bass Photo Co. Collection, Indiana Historical Society. (Image cropped)

each hyphen, and a tall arched window in the north and south end elevations. They used cornices and parapets to match those of the main building and limestone keystones over windows in the buff brick exteriors. The architects employed an E-shaped facade plan for the dining and social hall, giving it a slightly projecting frontispiece with limestone enframements and two side pavilions. For decorative elements, they used Renaissance-style arched windows on the first floor of the side pavilions and Georgian-style flat brick arches on the second story. Rubush and Hunter linked all the buildings in their campus plan with common materials and motifs: buff brick exteriors, Renaissance cornices, and plain parapets.[28]

Over 110 years later, the main building and the original powerhouse of the Indiana School for the Deaf continue in use, but the two dormitory buildings and the dining and social hall have been demolished.

Indianapolis City Hall

Mayor Charles A. Bookwalter conceived of the next major public building to be erected in Indianapolis and made it his passion. After taking office in January 1906, he attempted to remodel Tomlinson Hall (see chap. 8 of vol. 1) and build an extension to it on the site of the Indianapolis City Market along Market Street. He intended the much larger structure to serve as a combined city hall and civic colosseum. Legal challenges upended the colosseum–city hall scheme, so in 1908, the mayor announced plans for a new city hall alone on the northwest corner of Ohio and Alabama Streets. He then held an architectural competition for the best design. Five architectural firms submitted plans. Other firms complained about the shortness of time to prepare designs and the failure of the city to retain an architectural advisor to guide municipal officials in evaluating the submissions. A citizens' group, the Municipal Art Association, objected to the program for the competition and the site selected. Undeterred, Mayor Bookwalter proceeded with the competition, and in November 1908, he, the building committee, and the city board of public works selected the design submitted by Rubush and Hunter. Second place went to the firm of Nelson and Rigg (probably from out of town), third place to veteran architect Adolph Scherrer, and fourth place to local firm Foltz and Parker.[29]

The partnership of Preston Rubush and Edgar Hunter was only four years old but already had won the prestigious commissions for designing both the Indiana School for the Deaf (see previous) and the new Masonic Temple (see later in this chapter). They had also been finalists for designing the short-lived colosseum–city hall project.[30] They devised a design for the Indianapolis City Hall similar in composition and massing to the one they had created for the Masonic Temple.

In their winning city hall submission, Rubush and Hunter proposed a rectangular limestone building of four stories occupying nearly all of the 202-by-135-foot lot.[31] Engaged Doric columns standing in antis dominate the centers of the second and third stories of the eastern facade and south and north elevations (figs. 2.14 and 2.15). Like that of the Masonic Temple, the city hall facade composition is composed of three sections—a base story, a middle section made up of the second and third stories and articulated by the columns and broad pilasters at the corners, and a top section defined by an entablature and parapet. The architects anticipated a flow of citizens entering and exiting the building and designed a trio of entries at the center of the facade, each marked by a pediment overhead and a sculpture of bundled grain. Other decorative elements appearing in the exterior include disks in the main frieze, dentils below the main cornice, and cornices supported by consoles above the second-floor windows. The architects obtained a balance between vertical and horizontal in the facade with the projecting, fluted columns,

Facing top, **Figure 2.14.** Circa 1909 rendering by Rubush and Hunter of the design for the Indianapolis City Hall exterior. The city built the hall between 1909 and 1910, and the architects devised colossal Doric columns standing in antis on the second and third floors of the exterior and other details drawn from Roman imperial architecture. Jacob Piatt Dunn, *Greater Indianapolis* (Chicago: Lewis, 1910), vol. 1, frontispiece.

Facing bottom, **Figure 2.15.** Former Indianapolis City Hall, 202 North Alabama Street. The windows were filled with limestone panels in 1964 as part of the adaptation of the building for use as the Indiana State Museum. View in 2015. James Glass.

which direct the eye upward, while the rows of windows between the columns originally moved the eye from side to side.

The building was certainly monumental but perhaps too large for its site; the columns and other oversized details would have benefitted from a larger site in which the building could have been set back from the street and more perspective afforded.

In accord with Beaux Arts planning, the architects clearly indicated the circulation patterns of the building. The trio of entries leads into a vestibule and then into a four-story rotunda, the most impressive element of the Rubush and Hunter design (fig. 2.16). An oval stained glass skylight transmits colored light down through circular openings at the center of each floor to the base of the rotunda. Opposite the vestibule, visitors can see a marble stairway rising in stages to the second floor and descending to the basement. Elevators are also visible on either side of the ground floor of the rotunda. On the north and south sides of the first floor of the rotunda and subsequent floors, large archways lead into corridors along which city offices were located.[32]

The decorative program in the interior is another high point of the Rubush and Hunter design. Costly materials and design patterns define all the public spaces, beginning with the vestibule (fig. 2.17), in which marble Tuscan columns support a series of quadripartite ribbed vaults that lead to concentric marble arches and bronze light standards on the north and south ends. In the floor of the rotunda and the floors surrounding the atrium openings on each floor, the architects specified varieties of marbles with burgundy, gray, black, and white hues to fashion decorative patterns—a star at the center, a sunburst, diamonds imposed on squares, and a grid around the perimeter. One of the architects' models for polychromatic marble patterns in the floor of a rotunda may have been the Pantheon in Rome, constructed in the second century AD.

The architects lined the perimeter of each floor in the rotunda with pairs of Doric columns (fig. 2.18). Each column shaft, made of metal, is covered by imitation gray and white marble veining. The pairs of columns support elaborate plaster entablatures created by Alexander Sangernebo and composed of friezes with triglyphs, fret patterns, mutules, and egg and dart moldings. On several floors,

Facing, Figure 2.16. View of the rotunda, former Indianapolis City Hall. Note the stained glass skylight and the plaster moldings by sculptor Alexander Sangernebo, incorporating Roman and Renaissance details on each floor. View from 1996. James Glass.

Facing top, **Figure 2.17.** Marble Tuscan columns and ribbed vaults in vestibule. 1996 view. James Glass.

Facing bottom, **Figure 2.18.** West wall of rotunda, Indianapolis City Hall, showing Doric columns with metallic shafts with applied marble graining and a mural by painter and decorator William F. Behrens. 1996 view. James Glass.

William F. Behrens, the noted interior decorator, created gold-tinted murals depicting cherubs and other figures from Roman mythology.[33]

Rubush and Hunter placed the mayor's office in a suite on the second floor and the city council chamber on the fourth floor. The chamber ceiling was domed, and with its balcony, the room could seat two hundred. The building structure consisted of a steel interior frame, with hard-burned brick exterior walls, faced with dressed Bedford limestone. The architects used clay tile or brick for the interior partition walls. After several cost increases, the final expense for constructing the Indianapolis City Hall came to approximately $850,000.[34]

Fire Headquarters and Fire Stations

In 1910, the City of Indianapolis sold its 1873 fire headquarters building at the corner of New York Street and Massachusetts Avenue. Three years later, the fire department announced plans to build a new headquarters up the street, on the southeast corner of New York and Alabama Streets. The old building had been designed for horse-drawn fire engines and lacked sufficient space for a motorized fire force. Chief Charles E. Coots drew up a sketch of what he desired in a new building, and the city sold a $75,000 bond issue to pay for construction. Next, the board of public works retained the firm of D. A. Bohlen and Son as architects, who devised a design for a three-story steel-frame building with orange, glazed-brick exterior walls.[35]

Oscar Bohlen and his draftsmen developed a composition for the facade in which Italian Renaissance details set the overall tone (fig. 2.19). In keeping with Renaissance symmetry, two pavilions on either side project slightly forward of the main elevation at the center and create two vertical elements that balance the rows of windows that extend horizontally. A large Renaissance-style cornice caps the facade and the two side elevations; it is supported by modillions and lined with dentils. Above the cornice appears a simple brick parapet. Other Renaissance details command attention: the stone quoins on the corners of the pavilions and the limestone window surrounds, which contain keystones and partial quoins

Facing top, **Figure 2.19.** Former Fire Headquarters, 301 East New York Street, built in 1913–14 and designed by D. A. Bohlen and Son, with Italian Renaissance details, such as limestone quoins at the corners and a projecting cornice supported by modillions. 2023 view of the facade. James Glass.

Facing bottom, **Figure 2.20.** Detail of tablet with a cartouche containing the letters *IFD*. 2023 view. James Glass.

Above, **Figure 2.21.** Former Hose Company No. 28 Fire Station, 512 East Thirty-Eighth Street, built in 1911 and designed by Herbert L. Bass and Company, with distinctive California bungalow features adapted from residential versions of the bungalow. Note projecting gable supported by large brackets. 2021 view. James Glass.

along their sides. Two wide and high vehicle doors centered on the ground floor of the facade suggest the function of the building. At the center of the parapet, the architects provided a delight: an elaborate stone cartouche with the letters *IFD* sculpted (fig. 2.20).

Inside on the first floor, the architects provided space for storing the firefighting "apparatuses." On the second floor, they placed the dormitory for firefighters, three poles for the firefighters to use in sliding down to the fire engines, and

Chief Coots's office and quarters. The fire department intended to use the third floor for a drill and instruction room. Bohlen designed a "germ-proof" building in which the interior was lined with white enameled brick without square corners on which dust or dirt could accumulate. The architects also designed a one-story municipal garage building just east of the fire headquarters with similar glazed brick and limestone details.[36]

In 1911, several years before the completion of the headquarters, the City of Indianapolis had built several new downtown and neighborhood fire stations, including one at Kentucky Avenue and Maryland Street, another at New Jersey and South Streets, and the city's first "bungalow" fire engine station. The latter, designed by Herbert L. Bass and Company (fig. 2.21) for Hose Company No. 28, rose on the northwest corner of Thirty-Eighth and Ruckle Streets. Bass, who had developed an extensive residential practice (see chap. 5 of this volume), adapted the popular California bungalow house for use as a one-story fire station. He used a low-slung gable roof with steeply projecting eaves on the sides supported by horizontal brackets. On the facade, he marked the engine doorway with a gable projecting forward, supported by more substantial brackets. As he did in some of his residential commissions, Bass used stucco and timber for the gables and a dark-brown brick for the exterior walls.[37]

Carnegie Library Branches

Beginning about 1902, Indianapolis watched small towns and cities all over Indiana apply to philanthropist Andrew Carnegie for funds to build public libraries. Carnegie's usual arrangement: he made a grant to pay for the construction of a library, and the town or city agreed to staff and maintain it. Finally, in 1909, City Librarian Eliza Browning obtained a $120,000 grant from Carnegie to build six public library branches in Indianapolis. Ultimately, five were built, and two are still in use: the East Washington Branch at 2822 East Washington Street and the Spades Park Branch at 1801 Nowland Avenue.[38]

The Indianapolis Public Schools board, which operated the public library system, retained the Indianapolis firm of Foltz and Parker in 1909 to design the East Washington Branch.[39] The architects created a rectangular building with a principal story and high basement (fig. 2.22). They used a combination of Gothic and Tudor details for the facade composition. At the center, they placed a frontispiece consisting of a terra-cotta frame around the entry with an ogee arch overhead and stepped buttresses supporting brick pilasters on either side. At the top of the two pilasters, sculptor Alexander Sangernebo created delightful gargoyle statues

Figure 2.22. East Washington Branch, Indianapolis Public Library, 2822 East Washington Street, built in 1909 and designed by Foltz and Parker, drawing on architecture of English Tudor palaces for the ogee arch over the entry and the window surrounds with quoins and on Gothic architecture for the stepped buttresses and battlements. Artist Alexander Sangernebo created the crouching gnomes clutching books. 2021 view. James Glass.

of crouching gnomes clutching books.[40] The two principal windows of the facade have terra-cotta frames, quoins from Tudor palace architecture, and segmental arches. Above a modest cornice, the architects placed battlements with crenellations. They chose a distinctive Flemish bond for the brick exterior walls. Black headers alternate with orange stretchers.

Inside, they laid out two reading rooms symmetrically, connected at the center by space for a checkout desk. On each of the outside walls for each room, they placed a fireplace with a red-tile face and hearth and a wooden shelf supported by brackets. A meeting room in the basement provided space for lectures.

In 1911, the school board commissioned Wilson Parker alone to design the Carnegie branch on Nowland Avenue. Parker planned a two-story building with symmetrical, one-story wings on the sides. He chose an updated interpretation of

PUBLIC, SOCIAL, AND CHARITABLE ARCHITECTURE | 141

ARCHITECT PROFILES

Foltz and Parker

Herbert W. Foltz (1867–1946; *at left*) and Wilson B. Parker (1867–1937; *at right*) maintained a fruitful partnership between 1904 and 1911. Foltz was born in Indianapolis and received engineering training at the Rose Polytechnic Institute of Terre Haute, graduating in 1886. He also studied at the Art Institute of Chicago. In 1891, he launched a solo architectural practice in Indianapolis, specializing in residential designs, such as the Rustic-style Charles Donson House of 1895–96 (see chap. 10 of vol. 1).

Wilson Boyden Parker was born in Natick, Massachusetts, and graduated from the Peddle Institute and the Massachusetts Institute of Technology, presumably with a degree in architecture from the latter. Parker's MIT training opened the door to a position as a draftsman in the renowned firm of McKim, Mead, and White and also work with Tiffany Studios of New York. Sometime in the 1890s, he moved to South Bend, Indiana, and opened an architectural practice. He earned a reputation as "an expert interior architect" and made interior design his specialty. In 1902, he relocated to Indianapolis, and in 1904, he formed the partnership with Foltz.

For much of their seven years of practice, Foltz and Parker obtained commissions involving most building types. They designed Georgian-style residences for Meredith and Eugenie Nicholson and Henry R. and Margaret Bliss, English Tudor vernacular houses for Frank Darlington and Frank Elliott, and a feudal Italian-style house for William J. and Jeannie Reid (see chaps. 4 and 5 of this volume). They also served as architects for the Indianapolis Country Club, the Indianapolis Orphan Asylum, the main YMCA Building, and the East Washington Branch of the Indianapolis Public Library. In the realm of office buildings, they designed the Bobbs-Merrill Building. Outside Indianapolis, they designed the Southeastern Asylum for the Insane in Madison, Indiana, and the dormitory and hospital for the Indiana Boys' School in Plainfield.

After the partnership ended, each man practiced on his own, and each continued successfully. Foltz designed the Senate Avenue YMCA in Indianapolis, the Tudor Hall School for Girls, the 1925 Broadway Methodist Episcopal Church, the Irvington Methodist Episcopal Church, and the Meridian Heights Presbyterian Church. He also designed the Louisiana State Hospital for the Insane. Parker specialized in Carnegie public libraries in Indiana after 1911, designing the Spades Park Branch of the Indianapolis Public Library and libraries in Shoals, North Vernon, LaPorte County, Brookville, and Linden, Indiana.

During the 1930s, both Foltz and Parker worked for the Historic American Buildings Survey to document the historic and architectural landmarks of the state. Foltz served as state supervisor and Parker as a project architect documenting such early houses as the Macy House of Indianapolis.

Sources: "Architect Locates Here," *Indianapolis Journal*, December 7, 1902, 12, c. 4; "Herbert Willard Foltz," in Paul Donald Brown, ed., *Indianapolis Men of Affairs 1923* (Indianapolis: American Biographical Society, 1923), 199; "Herbert Foltz, Architect, Dies," *Indianapolis News*, July 6, 1946, Indiana Biography Series, 30:105, Indiana State Library; listings for "Foltz and Parker" in *R. L. Polk and Co.'s Indianapolis City Directories* for the years 1903 to 1911; "Wilson B. Parker, Architect, Dies; Resident for Many Years," *Indianapolis Star*, January 7, 1937, 14. Sources for photos: Foltz—Kate Milner Rabb and William Herschell, eds., *An Account of Indianapolis and Marion County* (Dayton: Dayton Historical Publishing Company, 1924), 4:654. Parker—Panoramic photo of architects and possibly some draftspersons at the 1920 Indiana Society of Architects convention in Indianapolis, taken in the Sunken Gardens at Garfield Park, Bass Photo Co. Collection, Indiana Historical Society (image cropped).

Figure 2.23. Spades Park Branch, Indianapolis Public Library, 1801 Nowland Avenue, built in 1911 and designed by Wilson B. Parker, using an updated version of the Italianate style, with arched windows, large brackets supporting the cornice, and a hipped roof. A highlight is the terra-cotta portico over the entry. 2021 view. James Glass.

the Italianate style for the exterior design, giving the building a vertical massing, lining the second story with arched windows, supporting the cornice with wooden brackets, and employing a hipped roof (fig. 2.23). The focal point of the facade composition is an Italian Renaissance–style portico for the entry, in which tall Tuscan columns in cream-colored terra-cotta frame the entrance and support an entablature and parapet. The architect used what was termed at the time oriental brick with multiple shades of brown for the exterior walls. He used varied patterns for the brick courses, interspersing vertical segments of stretchers or headers alone with regular running bond. Inside, a single large reading room runs north and south. Three broad arches separate the main room from another reading room at the rear. The focal point of the north room is a handsome fireplace with dark greenish-black marble surround and hearth and wooden mantel. On the second floor, Parker placed a spacious auditorium for lectures and meetings. He supported the ceiling with heavy wooden trusses.[41]

Central Library

In 1918, Ralph Adams Cram, one of the leading Gothic architects in the country, said of the newly completed Central Library in Indianapolis that it was "one of the most distinctive and admirable contributions to architecture that have [sic] been made in America." Cram's comment indicates that the design of the Central Library building was something extraordinary, certainly one of the best works of architecture produced in Indianapolis during its first century.[42]

Eliza Browning, the city librarian, had noted for some time that the 1893 public library building at Ohio and Meridian Streets (see chap. 8 of vol. 1) was overcrowded by patrons. She concluded that it would not serve future needs and persuaded the Indianapolis Public Schools board in 1908 to begin assembling a spacious site for a new building along the north side of St. Clair Street between Meridian and Pennsylvania Streets. Browning chose a location situated in the midst of the fashionable neighborhood north of the Mile Square. At its new site, the library would be following the shift of population north while still being accessible to the neighborhoods on the east, south, and west sides of town.[43]

In 1913, the school board decided to hold a national architectural competition to select a design and a supervising architect. Competitions had been used successfully elsewhere in the country for libraries and other public buildings, and Browning and the board were convinced that they would obtain a superior result by soliciting the best architectural proposals and selecting a winner through a blind, juried selection. In October of that year, they retained H. Van Buren Magonigle, a noted Philadelphia architect, as their architectural advisor.[44] Magonigle drew up a program for the building that drew many specifics from the competition program for the Detroit Public Library, a majestic Renaissance-style building ultimately designed by New York architect Cass Gilbert. To afford a full opportunity for local architects to compete in the contest, the board invited all those interested to submit a proposed design. Magonigle then recommended that three Indianapolis architects participate in the final competition based on their submissions: Adolph Scherrer, Herbert L. Bass and Company, and William Earl Russ.

Next, he recommended three nationally known architects to compete: Paul Philippe Cret and associated architects Borie, Zantzinger, and Medory of Philadelphia; Egerton Swarthwout of New York; and York and Sawyer of New York. Finally, the school board, in consultation with Magonigle, assembled a jury composed of architect Benno Janssen of Pittsburgh; Edwin Anderson, director of the New York Public Library; and architect H. Mills Day, former president of the School of Architecture of the American Institute of Architects.[45]

In April 1914, the jury chose the design submitted by thirty-seven-year-old Paul Philippe Cret and his associated architects. The winner, already known for his Italian Renaissance–style Pan American Union Building in Washington and his mastery of Classicism, created for Indianapolis a modern library building clothed in the garb of classical Greece (fig. 2.24).[46] He employed the language of the Parthenon for the rank of eight Doric columns that stand in antis across the central facade and for the delicately detailed Doric entablature, with its frieze, metopes, triglyphs, and mutules, that extends across the whole facade and along the east and west elevations. The columns are carefully studied and proportioned, evoking the height-width ratios of their Greek prototypes.[47]

The architect combined a knowledge of Classical precedents with the design philosophy of the École des Beaux-Arts in Paris, of which he was a graduate. As a professor of architecture at the University of Pennsylvania, he taught the Beaux

Facing, **Figure 2.24.** The Central Library of the Indianapolis Public Library, 40 East St. Clair Street, built in 1915–17 and designed by Paul Philippe Cret, using a design that draws on the language and proportions of the Parthenon and other temples of Classical Greece for the Doric columns of the facade and the entablature. Leading architect Ralph Adams Cram called Cret's design "one of the most distinctive and admirable contributions to architecture that have [*sic*] been made in America." View from southwest in 2021. James Glass.

Above, **Figure 2.25.** Looking west in the delivery room of the Central Library along the main east–west axis of the interior design. In keeping with the French Beaux Arts planning precepts, one can see at a glance the paths to each part of the library. 2021 view. James Glass.

Arts method of planning buildings, which involved the creation of a rational scheme for laying out the circulation patterns of a building.[48] The Beaux Arts approach is evident at the Central Library. Cret used a U-shaped plan for the facade. The central portion, marked by the columns and large windows located between

PUBLIC, SOCIAL, AND CHARITABLE ARCHITECTURE | 147

the columns, indicated the large delivery room within. The two side pavilions of the facade indicated the two principal reading rooms. A granite stairway drew the visitor to the main entrance, located at the center of the columns. Inside, Cret used the Beaux Arts system of axes and cross-axes to indicate the circulation paths. The visitor proceeded through a small vestibule into the majestic, two-story delivery room, running east and west. Straight ahead, the entry axis originally led to the circulation desk and the main stacks of the library. Looking east along an east–west axis, one could see a monumental marble stairway leading up to the periodical reading room, and looking west on the same axis, one could see an identical stairway leading up to the reference room.

Around three sides of the delivery room (fig. 2.25), Cret laid out lofty, one-and-a-half-story corridors lined with bookshelves. On the east and west sides, these corridors provided access to the two principal reading rooms. The third corridor, along the south side, connected the east and west corridors. To provide sufficient natural light to the delivery room, the architect designed rectangular openings in the south wall of the room that corresponded exactly in shape and scale to the south windows of the facade. Additional natural light came in from light wells through corresponding rectangular windows along the north side of the delivery room. For balance and symmetry, Cret cut identical openings in the west and east walls of the room, providing transparency between the inner and outer spaces of the interior.

A corridor led east of the vestibule down to a lower level, where a lecture room and children's room could be reached. Cret also provided access to the lower level via a secondary entrance at the center of the east elevation. On the floor beneath the west reference room, he placed a long room devoted to administration and cataloging.

In addition to the careful proportions and delicacy of sculpted detail of the exterior, the decorative program in the interior won high praise. Cret injected elements of antiquity and color into the delivery room, with its gray, Caen stone walls and immense ceiling, in which artist Gustav Ketterer painted polychromatic details on canvas, suggesting paintings of Roman Pompeii (figs. 2.26 and 2.27).[49] The architect complemented Ketterer's lunettes, temple fronts, and arabesques of Pompeii with bronze bas-relief panels depicting historical scenes. The artist

Facing, Figure 2.26. Ceiling of delivery room, showing paintings by Gustave Ketterer and bronze panels on historical subjects. 2021 view. James Glass.

continued the Pompeiian scheme in the coved ceilings of the ancillary corridors. High on the Caen stone walls, sculptors created medallions containing bas-relief figures from mythology and sculpted the names of great figures in world literature.

In the west reference room, Cret's associated architects, Borie, Zantzinger, and Medary, specified oak paneling for the walls and a coved plaster ceiling consisting of octagonal coffers. In the east periodical reading room (fig. 2.28), oak paneling with a projecting cornice covers the walls, while plaster beams augmented by consoles support the ceiling.[50] Decorative fireplaces adorn the north ends of the two reading rooms. In a niche on the south wall of the east reading room, noted sculptor Gutzon Borglum created a bas-relief sculpture in bronze of Dr. John S. Bobbs of Indianapolis.[51]

One of the reasons that the completed Central Library building exerted a powerful visual impact was Cret's use of Bedford limestone as the exterior material.

Facing, **Figure 2.27.** Detail of arabesques and Classical motifs created by Gustave Ketterer, inspired by paintings in Roman Pompeii. 2021 view. James Glass.

Above, **Figure 2.28.** Looking north in the east periodical room, showing plastered beams supporting the ceiling, adorned by consoles and oak paneling. 2021 view. James Glass.

The crisply sculpted capitals, shafts, entablatures, and rosettes in sparkling grayish-white stone all evoked the architecture of the Acropolis. The architects and consulting engineers used a fireproof steel structure and brick curtain walls for the exterior and the interior partitions.

World War I occasioned delays, as Paul Cret found himself serving in the French army and materials shortages and strikes slowed construction. Finally, the school board and city dedicated the library in October 1917. The final cost was slightly more than $501,000.[52]

PUBLIC, SOCIAL, AND CHARITABLE ARCHITECTURE | 151

ARCHITECT PROFILE

Paul Philippe Cret

Paul Philippe Cret (1876–1945) was born in Lyons, France, and enrolled in the prestigious École des Beaux-Arts in Paris, where he spent six years learning the famed Beaux Arts method of design. That technique emphasized proficiency in watercolors, charcoal studies, draftsmanship, and, above all, study of Classical Roman and Greek monuments, Renaissance works by Italian masters, and French Classical designs. Formality and rationality of planning were hallmarks of the Beaux Arts method. Cret's gifts as a designer led to an offer, at age twenty-seven, of a faculty position in architecture at the University of Pennsylvania, then one of the leading American academic programs teaching the Beaux Arts method. Cret taught architectural design from 1903 to 1937 at the university, with a four-year interruption when he served in the French army during World War I.

The young faculty member soon demonstrated his capacity to win major national architectural competitions, placing first in the competition for the design of the Pan American Union Building in Washington, DC (completed in 1910) and then in 1914 winning the Indianapolis Public Library competition.

After World War I, Cret designed the Detroit Institute of Arts in 1927 and the John Herron School of Art Building in Indianapolis in 1929. In Washington, he served as architect for the Folger Shakespeare Library, and in Philadelphia, he designed the Rodin Museum and the Barnes Foundation Gallery. In all, Cret employed the formality and rational planning of the Beaux Arts method, and in most, he combined Italian Renaissance and Classical details in articulating the exteriors.

He also was quite influential in the American architectural profession through his teaching of design to many University of Pennsylvania architecture graduates.

Sources: Mary Ellen Gadski, "Paul Philippe Cret," in *Stacks: A History of the Indianapolis-Marion County Public Library*, S. L. Berry and Mary Ellen Gadski (Indianapolis: Indianapolis-Marion County Public Library Foundation, 2011), 72; "Paul Philippe Cret 1876–1945," Penn University Archives and Records Center, Penn Libraries, n.d. https://archives.upenn.edu/exhibits/penn-people/biography/paul-philippe-cret, accessed June 26, 2024. Source for photo: Richard T. Dooner, courtesy of University Archives and Records Center, Penn Libraries.

SCHOOLS

With the largely unbroken period of prosperity between 1900 and 1917, the blue-collar and white-collar working populations and their families steadily increased. Public schools were soon bursting, and the years after 1900 showed almost constant construction of new, eight-grade elementary schools and additions to existing buildings. Several private schools or academies also constructed new structures.

Lincoln School 18

In 1901, for example, the board retained architect Clarence Martindale to design an eight-room brick building for elementary children—Abraham Lincoln School 18. The resulting two-story brick structure stands on Palmer Street between Rheingold and Barth Avenues in a working-class neighborhood south of Fountain Square (fig. 2.29). For the initial building, Martindale devised a main block with a gable roof, and at the center of the facade, he designed a projecting frontispiece, with a limestone surround for the first-floor entry. Above, Martindale lined the second story of the frontispiece with

Figure 2.29. Abraham Lincoln School 18, 1602 Barth Avenue, built in 1901 and designed by Clarence Martindale of Indianapolis, with Classical details in the entry pavilion and cornices supported by Renaissance-style modillions. The building is vacant and needs a new use. Bass Photo Co. Collection, Indiana Historical Society. (Image cropped)

engaged Ionic columns flanking arched windows. A limestone balustrade with substantial supporting brackets extends in front of the frontispiece windows. The architect styled the gables on the east and west sides of the main block as pediments lined with consoles. He employed orange, load-bearing bricks for the walls and incorporated limestone stringcourses and friezes below the simple cornices. Later additions to the east and west harmonized well with the initial design. Inside, four broad corridors intersect at the center. In each corner of the original building are rectangular schoolrooms.[53]

George W. Julian School 57

Two years later, the board sold a $300,000 bond issue and raised an additional $80,000, hoping to build three new elementary schools and construct additions to Shortridge High School and the Manual Training High School. Ultimately, they postponed the Shortridge addition and hired architects to design the rest. One of the largest of the new grade schools resulted from the recent annexation of the town of Irvington to the city. Architect Herbert W. Foltz designed the George W. Julian School 57 and supervised its construction at 5539 East Washington Street. Foltz used an L-shaped plan for the two-story red brick structure and employed a symmetrical composition for the facade involving two arched entries with stone frames on either side (figs. 2.30 and 2.31). He used Georgian-style lintels for the windows: brick flat arches on the first story and stone flat arches with keystones on the second. On the first story, to add interest, he fashioned a rusticated look in the bricks with deep joints. The Renaissance-style cornice—projecting and lined with modillions—terminated the facade. Inside, Foltz included twelve rooms and an assembly hall to serve a total student body of six hundred.[54]

Robert Gould Shaw School 40

On the near north side, within the principal neighborhood of African Americans, the school board constructed in 1903 what the *Indianapolis News* called "one of the best schools in the city." Previously, Black children living in the area just northwest of the Mile Square had attended a substandard segregated school on the same grounds as Shortridge High School. The school board demolished the former school and commissioned Indianapolis architect Thomas A. Winterrowd to design the Robert Gould Shaw School 40 at 702 North Senate Avenue. The architect laid out the two-story brick building with its long side along Senate Avenue and its facade on Walnut Street (fig. 2.32). He used simple Italian Renaissance details to define the facade. Limestone Tuscan columns with rusticated shafts flanked the entrance. They stood on brick plinths and supported a limestone frieze containing the name "Robert Gould Shaw School." Shaw had been commander of the famed African American regiment, the Fifty-Fourth Massachusetts, during the Civil War. Winterrowd carried a hint of the Renaissance further with brick quoins on the corners of the school. He provided manual training and physical exercise rooms in the basement and classrooms in the upper stories. The cost of the new building came to $30,000. The *News* further stated that the Shaw School would be "the only modern colored school in this city."[55]

Facing top, **Figure 2.30.** George W. Julian School 57, 5539 East Washington Street, Irvington, built in 1903 and designed by Herbert W. Foltz with a symmetrical facade incorporating Georgian and Renaissance details. View from c. 1905. Bass Photo Co. Collection, Indiana Historical Society. (Image cropped)

Facing bottom, **Figure 2.31.** School 57 as recently rehabilitated by the Indianapolis Public Schools. Note the rusticated brick voussoirs over the twin entries and the elegant limestone balconies supported by consoles. 2023 view. James Glass.

Above, **Figure 2.32.** +Robert Gould Shaw School 40, 702 North Senate Avenue, built in 1903 and designed by Thomas A. Winterrowd of Indianapolis, using Italian Renaissance details, such as the rusticated Tuscan columns flanking the entry and the brick quoins for ornamentation. Under segregation, African American children in the northwest section of downtown attended the school, which included rooms for manual training and physical exercise in the basement. When School 40 opened, the *Indianapolis News* called it "one of the best schools in the city." The building was closed in 1969–70 and stood vacant until its demolition in 1984–85. View in 1910. Bass Photo Co. Collection, Indiana Historical Society. (Image cropped)

George W. Sloan School 41

At the same time that the school board built the Julian and Shaw Schools, it erected one of its largest elementary buildings—George W. Sloan School 41, in North Indianapolis—to respond to overcrowding. The population of that factory suburb had grown swiftly (see chap. 7 of vol. 1). The board retained Clarence Martindale to design a substantial two-story building sufficient to accommodate a total of one thousand pupils. The site was located on the southwest corner of West Thirty-First and Rader Streets, northeast of an existing building. Martindale used an H-shaped plan, with a large central section joined at its east and west sides by wings running perpendicular to it (figs. 2.33 and 2.34). The facade faces south, originally looking over a schoolyard and in view of the previous building. The two side wings project forward from the central pavilion, which is recessed slightly along the first floor and more at the second-story level. Martindale used an appealing Italian Renaissance scheme for the main story of the central section of the facade—three arched windows flanked by arched entries with fan-shaped tympanums. He framed the entries with limestone Tuscan columns supporting entablatures and pediments. The Renaissance theme continued with a projecting cornice supported by modillions. As was becoming common in the new century, the architect employed a buff-colored pressed brick for the load-bearing exterior walls. He afforded further color and texture through a red-tile roof, which he capped with a cupola. The new building added fourteen classrooms and an assembly hall to School 41. The cost, one of the highest for new elementary schools, came to $65,000.[56]

Facing top, **Figure 2.33.** South facade of George W. Sloan School 41, southwest corner, West Thirty-First and Rader Streets, in the factory suburb of North Indianapolis. The board of the Indianapolis Public Schools constructed the 1903 structure as an addition to the original school buildings. It was designed by Clarence Martindale, drawing on Italian Renaissance details, such as arched entries and windows, porticos over entries, and cornices supported by modillions. The 1903 building included fourteen classrooms and an assembly room and was one of the largest elementary structures in the city's public school system. View in 1904. Bass Photo Co. Collection, Indiana Historical Society. (Image cropped)

Facing bottom, **Figure 2.34.** Former George W. Sloan School 41, showing south facade, with limestone porticos over the east and west entries and brick quoins. The whole is constructed with orange brick, newly popular in the first decade of the twentieth century. Adaptively used for apartments. 2023 view from the southeast. James Glass.

Schools 52, 3, and 60

Other neighborhoods also received new schools in the next decade. Rubush and Hunter designed a two-story brick building for School 52, at King Avenue and Michigan Street in 1905, addressing the needs of the largely immigrant population in Haughville. On the east side, also in 1905, Clarence Martindale designed Lucretia Mott School 3 at 27 North Rural Street. He used red brick for a Renaissance-inspired composition, with a limestone frontispiece for the entry, brick quoins at the corners of the building, and (originally) a projecting cornice with modillions (fig. 2.35). Elaborate consoles support a cornice with modillions in the entry frontispiece. Martindale provided manual training rooms in the basement and an auditorium on the second floor.

North of Fall Creek, the school board commissioned Foltz and Parker in 1907–8 to design the William A. Bell School 60 on the northwest corner of Thirty-Third and Pennsylvania Streets. The architects used the classic E-shaped plan for the facade of the two-story brick building (fig. 2.36). They incorporated a Renaissance-style arcade for the entry at the center and brick quoins at the corners of the building. The school structure included nine rooms and an assembly room seating five hundred people.[57]

St. Agnes Academy

Schools operated by the Catholic Church also continued to be built. For example, in 1908, the Sisters of Providence at Saint Mary-of-the-Woods constructed a new building for a girls' school on the southwest corner of Fourteenth and Meridian

Facing top, **Figure 2.35.** Former Lucretia Mott School 3, 27 North Rural Street, built in 1905. Architect Clarence Martindale drew on the Italian Renaissance for such details as consoles and modillions in the entry cornice, brick quoins at the corners of the main pavilions, and originally a projecting cornice for the building supported by modillions. Martindale provided manual training rooms in the basement and an assembly room on the second floor. This building has also been adapted for apartments. 2023 view. James Glass.

Facing bottom, **Figure 2.36.** +William A. Bell School 60, northwest corner of Thirty-Third and Pennsylvania Streets, built in 1907–8 and designed by Foltz and Parker, with standard Renaissance details for ornamentation: triple-arched entry, brick quoins on the corners of the three major pavilions, and a modillioned cornice. The building accommodated nine classrooms and an auditorium seating five hundred. Demolished in c. 1995–2000 after construction of a new building to the north. View in 1917. Bass Photo Co. Collection, Indiana Historical Society. (Image cropped)

ARCHITECT PROFILE

Clarence Martindale

Clarence Martindale (1866–1937) was born in Indianapolis, the fourth son of wealthy real estate investor and judge Elijah B. Martindale. His education and training as an architect are not known, but Martindale began a solo architectural practice in the state capital about 1886. He specialized in residences during the first two decades of his practice and then was able to expand into public buildings and some commercial and industrial work. Among the schools that Martindale designed were Abraham Lincoln School 18, George W. Sloan School 41, and Lucretia Mott School 3. In 1915 and 1916, he designed the National Motor Vehicle Company factory at Twenty-Second and Yandes Streets. A major public commission came with the design of the Classically styled Hendricks County Courthouse in Danville, Indiana.

In north-side Indianapolis neighborhoods, Martindale designed the English Tudor–style Samuel E. Rauh House, the English Tudor M. L. McMurray–J. W. Jenkins House, the Prairie-influenced Kleinschmidt House, and the Spanish Mission–style Louis Burckhardt House (see chap. 5 of this volume).

In 1921, Martindale retired from his architectural practice and studied sculpture in Paris. In 1926, he moved with his family to Nice. In 1936, the retired architect returned to Indianapolis.

Source for profile and photo: "Clarence Martindale Dies; Prominent State Architect," *Indianapolis Star*, January 22, 1937, 5, c. 6.

Figure 2.37. Former St. Agnes Academy, southwest corner, Fourteenth and Meridian Streets, built in 1908 and designed by Oscar Bohlen and D. A. Bohlen and Son, with a standard E-shaped plan and Romanesque, Renaissance, and Classical details. Bohlen used the newly popular orange brick for the exterior walls. The building constructed by the Catholic Sisters of Providence accommodated grade school and high school female students. 2019 view. James Glass.

Streets. The Sisters chose a site across from the newly built SS. Peter and Paul Cathedral and the bishop's residence, and construction of the St. Agnes Academy required the removal of several large homes in the prestigious residential district along Meridian south of Sixteenth Street. The Sisters retained D. A. Bohlen and Son as their architects. The Bohlens had served the order as the designers for a wide range of buildings in Indianapolis and the Saint Mary-of-the-Woods campus since the 1850s. Oscar Bohlen designed a large building with an E-shaped plan (fig. 2.37). A main wing at the center is joined on the sides by wings that extend west. At the rear of the central section, Bohlen designed a chapel. For the facade, he used the firm's usual formula of a secondary E shape in which a central pavilion and the wings on the sides project slightly from the central section. In articulating the facade, the architect used a mixture of Neoclassical, Romanesque, and Georgian

PUBLIC, SOCIAL, AND CHARITABLE ARCHITECTURE | 163

details. Classical pediments define the front gables, while a broad Romanesque arch frames the entrance. For most of the windows, he used Georgian flat brick arches with keystones. Somewhat unusually, he employed an orange brick for the exterior walls with stone trim. The $175,000 cost was higher than those of most new public schools, but the school provided classrooms for both elementary and high school students.[58]

COLLEGES AND UNIVERSITIES

At the beginning of the century, a new church-affiliated college took shape south of Indianapolis, and Butler College expanded its campus. Other, smaller collegiate institutions and professional schools also came into existence, but the 1900–1920 period did not see a major growth in postsecondary education.

Indiana Central University

In 1902, Indianapolis real estate dealer William L. Elder made a business proposition to several conferences of the United Brethren Church in Indiana and adjacent states. He proposed that if the conferences would sell 450 lots in his new University Heights Addition, Elder would donate an eight-acre site and a $40,000 building for a United Brethren college. Such trades of lots sales for university or college buildings were not unusual. In 1898, for example, real estate interests had constructed a building for a normal college in Muncie in exchange for leading citizens selling lots in an adjacent addition.[59]

The United Brethren Church leaders saw an opportunity to establish a college for young men and women in their congregations and readily accepted Elder's challenge. The Reverend John T. Roberts of Marion, the Reverend William Karstedt of Indianapolis, the Reverend John Simmons of Peru, and Morton Hobson of Richmond took the lead in selling lots to church members and others over a two-year

Facing top, **Figure 2.38.** Indiana Central University college building, 4001 Otterbein Avenue, was built in 1904–5 and designed by architect A. H. Ellwood with a monumental portico supported by Ionic columns and Classical and Renaissance details. The building, constructed by real estate dealer William L. Elder, included all the functions of the infant college founded by the United Brethren Church. View from c. 1905–10. Jacob Piett Dunn, *Greater Indianapolis* (Chicago: Lewis, 1910), 1:442.

Facing bottom, **Figure 2.39.** Original Indiana Central University building in 2023, now known as Good Hall, University of Indianapolis. James Glass.

period. Early in 1904, Elder decided enough lots had been sold to justify upholding his side of the bargain and proceeded to hire Indianapolis architect A. H. Ellwood to design the college building on the southeast corner of what is now Hanna and Otterbein Avenues. The adjacent University Heights Addition was situated about four miles southeast of downtown Indianapolis, and the Indianapolis, Columbus, and Southern electric interurban tracks ran just to the west, affording easy access for new residents to both downtown and Greenwood, Indiana, to the south.[60]

On a relatively modest budget, Ellwood designed an imposing building set back for maximum visual effect from Otterbein on an eight-acre setting (figs. 2.38 and 2.39). The architect devised a monumental Ionic portico as a key feature at the center of the facade. Two-story columns support an entablature in which consoles support the cornice and dentils appear above the frieze. Above the portico, Ellwood fronted the gable of a central wing running east and west with a pediment containing bas-relief sculptures in its tympanum. He thereby obtained the rest of the monumental impact he sought. In plan, the building consists of three pavilions running east and west. The one at the center, with its higher, gable roof, contains a third story; the other two flanking it rise two stories, and Ellwood gave them hipped roofs. He used concrete for the foundations and load-bearing red brick for the exterior walls. The interior structure probably consisted originally of slow-burning wooden beams and columns.[61]

Ellwood recessed slightly the central portion of the facade, below the portico, and marked the entry with story-and-a-half pilasters supporting a substantial frame entablature. The cornice and consoles above the latter match those of the portico. The architect used flat brick arches from Georgian architecture for the first-floor windows and a special molding over the second-floor windows that continues as a stringcourse around the rest of the building. To unify the composition, he continued the cornice and entablature of the portico around the rest of the structure. On the north elevation, Ellwood designed a smaller portico with two columns.

In the interior, Ellwood, under instructions from Elder and doubtless in consultation with the founders of the nascent college, provided for all the functions required of a university. The architect included twenty classrooms, an assembly hall with balconies seating eight hundred, a library, fraternity rooms, offices, and a gymnasium in the basement (fig. 2.40). The Reverend John Roberts and other United Brethren leaders chartered Indiana Central University in 1905, and the new institution opened in the fall of that year.[62]

Figure 2.40. Circa 1910 view of the library in the Indiana Central University building, including Ionic columns supporting the structural beams. Bass Photo Co. Collection, Indiana Historical Society. (Image cropped)

Bona Thompson Memorial Library, Butler College

In 1901, Mary and Edward Thompson donated $40,000 to Butler College for the construction of a library in Irvington. They made the gift in memory of their daughter, Bona, an 1899 graduate who had died shortly after. The Thompsons chose a site several blocks east of the Butler campus, at the southwest corner of Downey and University Avenues. They could observe the location, on a triangle, from their home across the street.[63]

The college retained Indianapolis architect Jesse T. Johnson to design the building, and he devised a facade composition and plan similar to those of many Carnegie libraries then under construction across the state (fig. 2.41). Following the lead of many of those buildings, Johnson employed a T-shaped plan and provided for a central foyer flanked by reading rooms and offices and stacks at the rear. His facade composition featured a central pavilion, complemented symmetrically by identical wings. Johnson employed a NeoClassical design for the limestone temple front at the center in which two Ionic columns stand in antis within a shallow porch framed by Doric pilasters. Both columns and pilasters support a frieze and pediment. Within the tympanum of the pediment, the architect specified a dramatic sculpture of a cartouche carrying the letters *BMT* superimposed on flowing tree branches. On either side of the central pavilion, Johnson employed tall windows with round arches for heads and linked the arches with impost blocks and stringcourses similar to those used by McKim, Mead, and White in the Boston Public Library facade ten years earlier (see chap. 8 of vol. 1). The impost blocks also function as capitals for pilasters separating the two windows on either side. The bases of the pilasters and the temple front rest on a high limestone foundation. The architect constructed the walls above of finely tooled brown face brick and capped the composition with a Renaissance-style limestone balustrade.[64]

The foyer inside originally was two stories high with a barrel-vaulted ceiling. To the north and south of the foyer, the architect situated the reading rooms, also two stories in height, which he covered with flat coffered ceilings. Johnson specified mosaic for the foyer floor and windows with Greek fret patterns in their muntins.[65]

JOHN HERRON ART INSTITUTE

The only museum in Indianapolis until the beginning of the twentieth century was the Indiana State Museum, a collection of natural history artifacts and other curiosities housed in a room of the statehouse. Finally, an act of philanthropy by

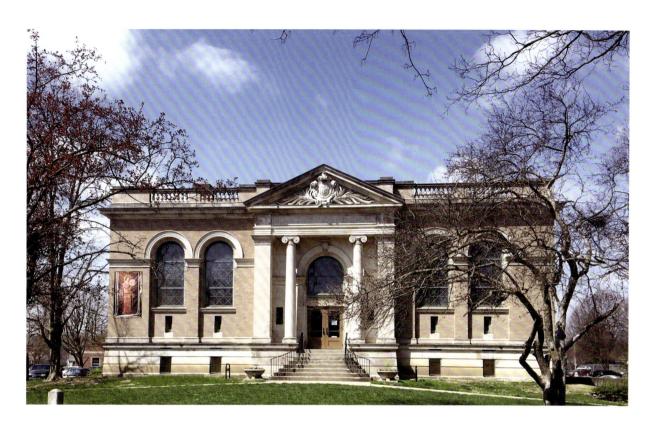

Figure 2.41. Bona Thompson Memorial Library, 5350 East University Avenue, Irvington, built by Butler College as its library in 1901–3 and designed by architect Jesse T. Johnson of Indianapolis, drawing partially on the design of the Boston Public Library with its arches and impost blocks and employing at the center a Classical portico with Ionic columns standing in antis. The Irvington Historical Society has restored it for its headquarters, galleries, and archives. 2020 view. James Glass.

a former city resident, John Herron, made possible the establishment of an art museum and art school. Herron's 1895 bequest left $240,000 to the Art Association of Indianapolis, founded in 1883, to educate students in art, buy paintings for an art museum, and construct a building for such an institution. The association purchased the Tinker-Talbott homestead on the north side of Sixteenth Street between Pennsylvania and Talbott Streets and, in 1903, retained the firm of Vonnegut and Bohn as architects for a new structure on the Tinker-Talbott site. It is unclear which of the partners in the firm—Bernard Vonnegut or Arthur Bohn—took the lead on design. Their initial proposal, for a rectangular building with an Ionic colonnade and limestone exterior, exceeded the budget of the art association.

Facing top, **Figure 2.42.** John Herron Art Institute facade, facing Sixteenth Street between Pennsylvania and Talbott Streets, built in 1905–6 and designed by Vonnegut and Bohn, drawing on Italian Renaissance and Classical sources for the details of a monumental building set back from the street. Below the cornice, note the sculptures created by Rudolph Schwarz of great Renaissance artists. View from 1908. *Art Work of Indianapolis*, Indiana (Chicago: Gravure Illustration, 1908).

Facing bottom, **Figure 2.43.** 2023 view of the facade of Herron High School, which has adaptively used the former John Herron Art Institute buildings. James Glass.

In 1905, after the architects made substantial revisions, reducing the budget to $85,000, their clients approved the design and let contracts for construction.[66]

The final design called for the building to face Sixteenth Street and be set back considerably from the street, allowing for the retention of some forest trees (figs. 2.42 and 2.43). The architects specified a steel structural frame and fireproof construction, with concrete floors and brick, load-bearing exterior walls. They projected the central pavilion slightly forward of the two end sections of the facade and, following an Italian Renaissance design theme, placed two-story brick pilasters with abstracted details at regular intervals across the front. The capitals, reduced to square abacuses, support a narrow limestone frieze, a course of dentils, and a projecting cornice. The focal point of the facade design is a series of panels below the frieze at the center. The architects commissioned sculptor Rudolph Schwarz to create, within the panels, terra-cotta busts of renowned artists in major periods of European art history. At the tops of the two end sections of the facade, two abstract stone sculptures composed of interconnected limestone blocks project outward. Otherwise, Vonnegut and Bohn's exterior design is simply detailed, with windows appearing only on the first floor. The architects used light-brown face brick for the walls and limestone for the trim and accents. They used limestone for a surround to encase the central entrance and gave the surround "ears" in the Classical fashion. The designers capped the entry with an entablature, above which they placed Greek antefixae. Defying the rules of Classical and Renaissance architectural grammar, they ran a limestone Ionic frieze of three horizontal bands across the shafts of the four brick pilasters.[67]

Vonnegut and Bohn devoted most of the interior space to galleries for exhibiting the art association's collection of works by European and Indiana artists. A front gallery on the first floor showcased the decorative arts. At the center, the architects created a large stair hall. On the second floor, visitors could walk

Figure 2.44. 1912 view of the Sculpture Court in the north-central portion of the John Herron Art Institute building. *Year Book of the Indiana Chapter A.I.A. and Catalog of the Third Annual Exhibition 1912* (Indianapolis: Indiana Chapter A.I.A., 1912).

through a long gallery south of the stair hall and enter four galleries, all of which exhibited paintings. Following the example of French art galleries, the architects lit the galleries through skylights in their ceilings. As a highlight of the interior, they devised a two-story sculpture court at the center of the north side of the building (fig. 2.44). In 1906, the art association opened the John Herron Art Institute, giving Indianapolis an essential cultural institution.[68]

SOCIAL, FRATERNAL, AND ATHLETIC BUILDINGS

Indianapolis, like cities across the country, had been a community of "joiners" from an early point. People of all classes and ethnic and racial backgrounds organized clubs and fraternal lodges to socialize, hold festivals, sponsor musical programs and cultural events, and host athletic activities. Some of these clubs and fraternal orders had already built meeting halls in the years before and after the Civil War. The explosive growth of the city's population and steady prosperity after 1900 produced a demand for more buildings to accommodate the activities of new organizations and larger facilities to meet the needs of existing groups.

[Old] Columbia Club

Stimulated by the example of men's private clubs in New York, Philadelphia, Boston, Chicago, and other major cities, Indianapolis businessmen, politicians, and professionals organized such clubs in the 1880s and 1890s. The typical pattern was to lease or buy a comfortable house north of the Circle and remodel it to accommodate dining, billiards, reading, and other social pursuits. One club was an outgrowth of President Benjamin Harrison's 1888 presidential campaign. Young men in the state capital formed a marching society to boost the hometown candidate and, after achieving success, decided to formalize their association through a permanent organization, the Columbia Club. Initially, they occupied the former home of William H. and Elizabeth Tinker Morrison on the northeast quadrant of the Circle (see chap. 6 of vol. 1). After only ten years, the club had grown so much that its leaders decided to build a substantial clubhouse on the same site.[69]

In 1899, the building committee retained Dayton architect Frank M. Andrews. Shortly afterward, Henry Lawrence engaged Andrews to design the Claypool Hotel (see chap. 1 of this volume). For the clubhouse, the Dayton architect doubtless studied designs for clubs by leading architects in architectural periodicals and may have also visited other cities for firsthand examination of highly regarded designs. The result was a sumptuous, five-story brick building with a limestone facade that compared favorably to clubhouses throughout the eastern United States (fig. 2.45). Andrews chose the Italian Renaissance for his overall theme, and his design for the facade owed much to clubhouses and private residences created by the top architectural firm McKim, Mead, and White of New York.

The lower four stories resembled the facades of several Boston houses designed by McKim, Mead, and White, such as 199 Commonwealth Avenue in the Back Bay neighborhood. In the latter house, twin bows project out on either side of the

Figure 2.45. +[Old] Columbia Club, 46 Monument Circle, built in 1900–1901 and designed by Frank M. Andrews of Dayton, drawing from sixteenth-century Italian Renaissance sources and the Boston Back Bay row houses of the 1890s for the details of the facade. View in 1908. Demolished in 1924 and replaced by the current Columbia Club building. Art Work of Indianapolis, Indiana (Chicago: Gravure Illustration, 1908).

Figure 2.46. +Ballroom, fifth floor of the 1900 Columbia Club, in c. 1910. The whole was a sumptuous Baroque feast for the eyes, designed by Frank Andrews and executed by decorator William F. Behrens. Bass Photo Co. Collection, Indiana Historical Society. (Image cropped)

facade and rise to a Renaissance-style balustrade across the parapet. In Andrews's composition, twin bows also projected out on the sides and incorporated a similar balustrade that ran across the base of the fifth story.[70]

At the center, a three-bay Renaissance arcade commanded attention, rising two stories and fronting a spacious porch. Across the first story, Andrews employed rusticated limestone blocks with deep joints from the Renaissance and rusticated shafts for the Ionic columns with which he flanked the central entry. On the fifth story, the architect used a Palladian motif at the center and Corinthian pilasters along the sides. Bull's-eye openings lined the frieze above, and foliated sculptures and festoons encrusted the whole of the fifth story. Andrews capped the composition with a second balustrade.

The club's directors desired elegance for their interior and were prepared to spend lavishly. On the first floor, Andrews laid out a grand lobby, library, men's café, and billiard room. On the second floor, he placed the principal banqueting room, general dining rooms, and private dining rooms. The architect employed different themes for each space—a Renaissance treatment with a plaster coffered ceiling for the grand lobby; a German rathskeller treatment for the café, with wooden paneling and wooden beamed ceiling; and wooden paneling adorned with Ionic columns and a French Baroque-style ceiling for one of the dining rooms. Andrews made the ballroom on the top floor the highlight of the whole club (fig. 2.46). He lined the walls with pairs of Corinthian columns, each set with its own entablature. The columns supported ribbed vaults that rose to a flat plaster ceiling detailed with Baroque-style moldings, geometric shapes, and a central medallion embellished with ribs. Foliated bas-relief sculptures filled every interstice, and incandescent bulbs placed throughout dazzled ballroom guests. The club hired William F. Behrens of the New York firm Neumann and Company to execute the plaster decorations of the ballroom and other areas of the building.[71]

Masonic Temple

As already seen in chapter 1 of this volume, some of the principal statewide fraternal orders, after the turn of the twentieth century, constructed tall office buildings that included auditoriums for their statewide meetings. The Indianapolis Shriners built a fraternal structure that also functioned as public theater. Other fraternal organizations, such as the Grand Lodge of Free and Accepted Masons of Indiana and most local Masonic lodges, desired to build structures totally devoted to their rituals, social occasions, and meetings.

Previously, the Grand Lodge of Masons had occupied a building erected in 1873–74 on the southeast corner of Washington Street and Capitol Avenue. A fire had damaged part of the former building in 1906, and the Grand Lodge joined forces with the Indianapolis Masonic Temple Association, made up of local lodges, to erect a new structure. The Masons retained the firm of Rubush and Hunter as their architects. Both Preston Rubush and Edgar Hunter were members of York Rite Masonic lodges in Indianapolis, which may have assisted them in obtaining the commission. The architects and directors of the Masonic Temple Association visited leading Masonic temples in cities across the country to obtain ideas for their building. In 1907, the Masons adopted final plans for a building on the southeast corner of North and Illinois Streets, the site of a house constructed by pioneer retailer Charles Mayer.[72]

Rubush and Hunter designed a massive rectangular building with Classical details (figs. 2.47 and 2.48), similar to their later design for the Indianapolis City Hall (see earlier in this chapter). The 110-foot-high temple measured 150 by 130 feet, with a slight setback on North Street and a yard to the south. The architects devised full compositions for the facade on Illinois Street and the north and south elevations. As the chief defining features of these Bedford limestone exteriors, they specified forty-foot-high Ionic columns standing in antis and engaged within rectangular cavities on each of the three elevations. The screens of columns extend across the third and fourth floors, while the architects used rusticated stone blocks with deep joints to cover the first and second floors, following ample precedents from Renaissance buildings. Large Doric pilasters cover the four corners of the building, and the pilasters and columns support an Ionic architrave and frieze adorned with disks. A substantial parapet rises above a projecting cornice lined with dentils. One of the peculiarities of the design involved the insertion of windows only in the first and second stories of the north and south elevations. On those two elevations, above the second story, architraves for window openings appear between the Ionic columns, but the windows are blind, covered with stone slabs. On the facade, the architects installed translucent stained glass panels in most of the window openings, but the Masons later removed the windows above the second story and covered the resulting openings with limestone slabs.[73]

The designers were sparing in ornamenting the exterior. They concentrated decorative elements on the Illinois Street entrance, giving it a surround lined with disks and sheltering it with a pediment supported by consoles. Above the pediment, sculptors created swags of grain hung from pegs. Similar pediments and consoles also appear above the third-floor faux windows.

Facing top, **Figure 2.47.** Masonic Temple, 525 North Illinois Street, built in 1907–8 and designed by Rubush and Hunter with a facade composition derived from Classical and Italian Renaissance sources that was similar to the one they used in 1909–10 for the Indianapolis City Hall. Note the colossal Ionic columns standing engaged on the third and fourth stories and the rusticated treatment of the first two stories. View in 1912. *Year Book of the Indiana Chapter A.I.A. and Catalog of the Third Annual Exhibition 1912* (Indianapolis: Indiana Chapter A.I.A., 1912).

Facing bottom, **Figure 2.48.** Masonic Temple in 2021. James Glass.

Above, **Figure 2.49.** Auditorium, first floor, Masonic Temple. View in 2016. James Glass.

Inside, the architects used varied architectural themes, high-quality materials, and abundant ornamentation in the principal rooms. Marble columns stand around the perimeter of the lobby, and the architects employed marble for the floor. On the east side of the first floor, the architects designed a 1,200-seat auditorium for Grand Lodge meetings (fig. 2.49). A stage and plaster ceiling with coffers

PUBLIC, SOCIAL, AND CHARITABLE ARCHITECTURE | 179

Facing, **Figure 2.50.** Ancient Egyptian motifs in the Red Cross Room, Masonic Temple. View in 2024. James Glass.

defines the lofty space. Rubush and Hunter arranged four lodge rooms on the second and third floors for the eight basic blue lodges of the city. In keeping with the architecture-related ritual of Masonry, they finished each lodge room with one of the four orders of Classical building: Doric, Ionic, Corinthian, and Composite. On the fourth and fifth floors, the architects situated lodge rooms for the York Rite. They gave the Red Cross Room an exotic design incorporating Ancient Egyptian motifs—columns with reed capitals, sphinxes, and two-dimensional paintings of Egyptian figures (fig. 2.50). Finally, Rubush and Hunter included several banqueting halls and social rooms.[74]

The architects devised a fireproof design for the building, with a steel structural skeleton and tile and concrete floors. When completed in 1910, the total cost of the Indianapolis Masonic Temple came to $1 million.[75]

African American Pythian Building

Because of pervasive discrimination by the majority white community, African Americans in Indianapolis found themselves barred from attending or participating in a variety of white-dominated social and fraternal organizations. Early in the nineteenth century, Black men in many northern cities organized their own fraternal lodges, using much the same ritual and nomenclature as the white organizations. As seen in chapter 8 of volume 1, the local lodges of the African American Grand United Order of Odd Fellows had constructed their meeting hall on Indiana Avenue in 1890. In 1908, the African American "Colored" Knights of Pythias lodges in Indianapolis purchased a lot for $4,000 on the northeast corner of Senate Avenue and Walnut Street. They began to hold benefits and sell stock in a Castle Fund to raise money for the construction of a Pythian building across the street from the new Robert Gould Shaw School Number 40 (see earlier in this chapter).[76]

The Pythians hired a white architect, Frank B. Hunter, to produce a design, and he produced a handsome composition based on English Tudor palaces of the sixteenth century, with gatehouse and turrets, red brick walls, and stone surrounds for the windows. The cost estimated by the architect was $40,000.[77]

Apparently the Pythians could not meet their building fund goal, and a delay of two years ensued while they cut the budget and revised the plans. It is not known

Facing top, **Figure 2.51.** Former African American Pythian Building, 244 West Walnut Street, built in 1910–11. The architect is not confirmed but may have been Frank B. Hunter. The simple exterior design uses reddish-brown brick with black bricks as occasional accents, brick rusticated blocks, hollow crosses, corbeled brick courses, and a parapet lined with terra-cotta coping as decorative elements. 2023 view. James Glass.

Facing bottom, **Figure 2.52.** The parapet above the entry with crosses and slightly corbeled brick stringcourses. 2021 view. James Glass.

if Hunter continued as the architect. Finally, in 1910, the Knights were ready to proceed, and a three-story brick building rose on the lot, filling the same footprint as the original design. The building as constructed was simply detailed but well planned to house a maximum number of functions (fig. 2.51). The architect used face brick colored mostly reddish orange, with occasional black bricks as accents. He divided the facade on Walnut Street and the west elevation on Senate into three sections: a street level containing seven retail store rooms for rental income and an entrance to the upper floors, a midsection covering the second and third stories, and a top section comprising a substantial parapet. Between each section, the designer employed a heavy stringcourse that he corbelled out. Above and below the windows of the second and third floors, minor stringcourses composed of a single corbeled brick course add horizontal lines to the composition. The architect provided a parapet containing recessed crosses at the top of all elevations. Above the entry and at the corners of the building, the architect raised the silhouette of the parapets (fig. 2.52). He gave the entrance a grooved limestone head and lined the sides with rusticated brick blocks.[78]

On the second and third floors, the architect placed the lodge meeting hall and smaller club rooms for the various Pythian lodges to use.[79]

Oriental Lodge

Although most of the lodges of the white Masonic order in Indianapolis drew members from throughout the city and met in the Masonic Temple at North and Illinois, a few felt ties to specific neighborhoods and met in their home areas. The largest of these, the Oriental Lodge, had leased space for meetings since being founded in 1874. The first decade of the twentieth century brought rapid growth, and in 1914, the lodge acquired a lot on the northeast corner of Twenty-Second Street and Central Avenue for a building of its own. In an unusual arrangement, three architectural firms whose principals were members of the Oriental Lodge

Facing top, Figure 2.53. The former Oriental Lodge, now the Prince Hall Masonic Temple, on the northeast corner of Twenty-Second and Central Avenue, was built in 1914–15 and probably designed by Rubush and Hunter, with assistance from Herbert L. Bass and Herbert W. Foltz. The design suggests Islamic architecture with the trio of horseshoe arches and the geometric details in terra-cotta. View in 2014. James Glass.

Facing bottom, Figure 2.54. Lodge room, Prince Hall Masonic Temple, showing the Greek Doric order. 2014 view. James Glass.

jointly designed the structure: Rubush and Hunter, Herbert L. Bass, and Herbert W. Foltz. It appears that Rubush and Hunter took the lead.[80]

The architects employed an unusual exterior design that was somewhat exotic (fig. 2.53). In keeping with the lodge name, the designers devised a composition that appeared Islamic and vaguely evocative of the Middle East. A newspaper of the time termed the style "of the Moorish school." The architects created a four-story, rectangular block with a reinforced concrete structure and exterior brick walls of reddish brown-gray color. The most Moorish feature appears at the center of the third floor on the facade: a three-bay terra-cotta arcade with horseshoe arches lined with cusps. A rectangular terra-cotta block frames the entrance and forms a second focal point. Interlocking geometric figures decorate the block, and the whole resembles entry treatments used in mausoleums and mosques in the Middle East, North Africa, and Spain. Pentagons and other geometric figures appear at the upper corners of the building and in the cornice. Incorporating a vaguely Middle Eastern motif, the architects designed a diaper pattern with red bricks across much of the west, south, and east elevations.[81]

Inside, the architects located a dining room and kitchen on a slightly depressed first floor, a social room and lounge on the second floor, and a two-story lodge room on the third floor. The Doric order appeared as a lead motif in the lodge room (fig. 2.54).[82]

In 1983, the Prince Hall Masons of Indianapolis, the local African American Masonic organization, acquired the former Oriental Lodge building for their meetings and social occasions.[83]

YMCA Building

Business and civic leaders had organized Young Men's Christian Associations (YMCAs) in cities across the country in the years after the Civil War. They constructed buildings in downtowns where young (white) men could maintain their physical fitness, take classes for self-advancement, attend lectures, and socialize

Figure 2.55. +Main YMCA Building, northwest corner, New York and Illinois Streets, built in 1908–9 and designed by Foltz and Parker of Indianapolis, employing a design drawing largely on Italian Renaissance details with a Classical frontispiece created by Alexander Sangernebo in terra-cotta above the main entrance. The interior included gymnasiums, a swimming pool, an auditorium, a dining room, classrooms, and dormitory rooms. View in 1912. Demolished in 1973–74 and replaced by a parking lot. *Year Book of the Indiana Chapter A.I.A. and Catalog of the Third Annual Exhibition 1912* (Indianapolis: Indiana Chapter A.I.A., 1912).

in a wholesome atmosphere. The first building constructed for the Indianapolis YMCA stood on Illinois Street just south of Market and was built in the 1880s (see chap. 8 of vol. 1). The initial building proved inadequate as the number of youth in the city grew. In 1907, the board of directors for the YMCA purchased a new site on the northwest corner of New York and Illinois Streets and retained the firm of Foltz and Parker to design a much larger structure. The building committee, chaired by banker J. F. Wild, traveled with the architects to visit some of the most recent and impressive YMCA buildings in other cities to note especially desirable features. The general secretary of the local YMCA, A. H. Godard, then obtained plans for some of the other buildings. The committee noted choice aspects of exterior designs or interior arrangements. The architects then produced preliminary plans, which the committee submitted to experts on YMCAs for final review.[84]

Foltz and Parker designed a five-story, rectangular block with a facade on Illinois Street and an L-shaped plan (fig. 2.55). They employed a reinforced concrete structure and fronted the exterior with impervious face brick.[85] The overall style drew from Classical and Renaissance sources. As focal points for the facade, the architects placed four terra-cotta pilasters created by Alexander Sangernebo at the center of the second and third stories; the pilasters supported an entablature with a sharply projecting cornice.[86] Below the second story, the designers created a setting for the entrance consisting of a segmental arch over the entry and three small windows set within a cartouche overhead. On either side, they placed trios of windows with transoms. At the top of the east and south elevations, the architects employed a Renaissance-style cornice with modillions and a balustrade above. Terra-cotta balconies added interest to the south elevation, while the designers gave most of the windows flat terra-cotta arches.

Inside, Foltz and Parker efficiently organized the functions desired. A bowling alley and laundry went into the basement. Senior and junior gymnasiums, parlors, and a billiard room appeared on the first floor. A dining room and classrooms occupied part of the second floor, while a six-hundred-seat auditorium could be found on the second and third floors. The architects arranged for dormitories on the third through fifth floors. At the northwest corner of the property, they incorporated a running track and swimming pool.[87]

The building committee, the board of directors, and other members mounted a determined and successful fundraising campaign and raised $126,000 for acquiring the site and $250,000 for constructing and furnishing the building.[88]

YWCA Building

Women of the city had organized a Young Women's Christian Association (YWCA) in 1895. The new association built a modest brick building for their activities at the back of a lot on the east side of Pennsylvania Street just south of Vermont. In 1906, the YWCA board and an associated committee of businessmen hired the firm of D. A. Bohlen and Son to design a new, much larger building on the front of the existing lot. The architects and the businessman committee studied scores of new YWCA buildings in other cities, and Oscar Bohlen and his draftsmen produced

Figure 2.56. +YWCA Building, 329 North Pennsylvania Street, built in 1907–8 and designed by D. A. Bohlen and Son, using Classical elements, including colossal Ionic columns in antis, an Ionic frieze, and a cornice with antefixae, as well as Georgian details, such as flat lintels with keystones over the windows. Sculptor Alexander Sangernebo created all the decorative elements in terra-cotta. The interior arrangement provided for all the functions in the main YMCA Building. View in 1909. Demolished in 1975 and replaced with an addition to the Indianapolis Star-News Building. Max R. Hyman, ed., *Hyman's Handbook of 1909* (Indianapolis: M. R. Hyman, 1909), 124.

a preliminary design for a four-story Renaissance-style building that featured an impressive limestone frontispiece. The sponsors delayed fundraising until the campaign for the new YMCA was completed in 1907. At that point, a campaign began to raise approximately $100,000 for the YWCA structure. Three different committees of male civic and business leaders took on lead roles in raising funds.

The board of directors of the YWCA, led by president Katherine Huntington Day, worked with the architects on a redesign of the building, made necessary probably because of higher-than-anticipated bids.[89]

Bohlen's final design presented a handsome NeoClassical composition in which he used the idea of colossal columns standing in antis and arranged them within a recessed section at the center of the facade (fig. 2.56). The architects used an orange-colored pressed brick for the facade material and specified terra-cotta for the Ionic columns and the Ionic architrave that the latter supported. Alexander Sangernebo modeled and executed the columns and architrave. The designers used the standard three-part division of the facade to provide horizontal lines to counter the verticality of the columns. The central entry formed the focal point for the lowest section, with its limestone surround and pediment supported by consoles. The architects faced the foundations of the high basement with limestone, which they also used to build a projecting cornice for the first story. In addition, the cornice served as a ledge on which the Ionic columns stood. Bohlen capped the upper windows on either side of the central recession with flat brick arches accented by stone keystones and outer voussoirs. In contrast, he used flat stone lintels for the first-story windows and those in the recession. For the two sections of the facade flanking the columns, the architect used chains of rusticated brick to continue the vertical lines of the columns in a more subdued fashion. Finally, above a brick frieze, Bohlen terminated the composition with an elegant terra-cotta cornice by Sangernebo, supported by modillions and topped by Greek antefixae.[90]

The architect employed fireproof construction for the building, which in this case involved concrete floors and roof and load-bearing exterior brick walls. He and his staff provided space for the typical functions of a YMCA or YWCA of the time. In the basement, they installed a swimming pool, and on the first floor, they provided offices and a lunchroom. On the second floor was an auditorium. More offices and classrooms filled the third floor, and the fourth floor provided space for a dormitory. The original building at the rear contained a schoolroom and the gymnasium. The YWCA completed their new home and opened it in 1908.[91]

The Senate Avenue YMCA

In the 1880s, several Black men had applied for membership in the city's YMCA and been denied admission. In 1902, a group of African Americans organized a separate YMCA and found quarters in a modest commercial and residential building at North and California Streets. Growth in membership was rapid, and by 1910, the need for expanded and modern facilities was obvious. At that point, philanthropist Julius Rosenwald, president of Sears, Roebuck, and Company of Chicago, announced that he would advance $25,000 to any city in the country that could raise $75,000 for the construction of a YMCA for African American men. The board of managers for the Black YMCA and other leaders in the Black community seized upon the opportunity. The board of the general YMCA of Indianapolis agreed to a joint fundraising campaign to meet Rosenwald's challenge, and two teams of campaign workers—one Black and the other white—organized their calls. Remarkably, the campaign met its goal in just ten days. The African American team raised over $20,000, a large sum given the impoverished circumstances of many in the community. Pioneering Black businesswoman Madam C. J. Walker gave a significant boost to the campaign with a $1,000 pledge.[92]

The general YMCA organization took responsibility for purchasing a site, hiring an architect, and overseeing construction. The site chosen, on the southwest corner of Senate Avenue and Michigan Street, was close to Indiana Avenue, the principal African American commercial street. The general board selected Herbert Foltz, who had taken the lead in designing the YMCA at New York and Illinois, as architect. They awarded the contract for construction to a firm headed by African Americans, Blankenship and Waymire.[93]

Foltz designed a three-story building with a 73-foot frontage on Senate Avenue and 140 feet along Michigan Street (fig. 2.57). He constructed the exterior walls with load-bearing brick and a semifireproof interior structure involving steel beams in the first floor. The architect used hard-burned brick with different shades as facing for the two principal elevations.[94] With a limited budget, Foltz was unable to employ limestone or terra-cotta for decorative details on the Senate Avenue facade. Instead, he used segmental arches for the central entrance and the trios of windows on either side, a transom window and sidelights for the entry, and rusticated brick piers on either side of the entrance. On the facade, Foltz employed stylized brick buttresses as vertical elements to balance the horizontal rows of windows in each story. He also crafted diaper patterns with dark, upraised bricks along the substantial parapet at the top of the facade and side elevation.

Inside, the architect fit many functions into the four floors. In the basement, he placed a twenty-by-forty-three-foot swimming pool, boys' and men's locker rooms, a barber shop and barber school, four boxball alleys, and an automobile and machine shop. On the first floor, he planned a large lobby; a two-story gymnasium, fifty by seventy feet, with a running track (fig. 2.58); a library; a lunchroom; a billiard room; and offices. On the second floor, Foltz arranged six classrooms for young men to learn varied trades and take school courses. He located dormitory rooms for one hundred men on part of the second and all of the third floor.[95]

Figure 2.57. +Senate Avenue YMCA Building, southwest corner, Senate Avenue and Michigan Street, built in 1912–13 and designed by Herbert W. Foltz with decorative detailing in brick, such as stylized brick buttresses on the facade and side elevation, rusticated piers flanking the entrance, and a diaper pattern below the parapet. Constructed for the use of African American men and youth, the building contained four floors and varied facilities: a gymnasium with a running track, a swimming pool, a library, a lunch room, classrooms, an automobile and machine shop, a barber school and shop, recreational rooms, and dormitory rooms. The building was demolished in 1968–69 and replaced by a parking lot. Undated view. Bass Photo Co. Collection, Indiana Historical Society. (Image cropped)

Figure 2.58. +1927 photo showing a workout class in the gymnasium, Senate Avenue YMCA. Courtesy YMCA Archives Photo Collection, Kautz Family YMCA Archives, Elmer L. Andersen Library, University of Minnesota.

The Senate Avenue YMCA reached the five-hundred-member mark in November 1912, making it the largest African American YMCA in the country. The dedication in July 1913 featured prominent educator Booker T. Washington as a speaker and drew a crowd of 1,200.[96]

Southside Turnverein

As the twentieth century opened, the German American population of Indianapolis continued to be one of the largest ethnic groups. It was a community that treasured the culture and language of its home country, as witnessed by the publication of at least three German newspapers in the city until World War I.

Most of the Germans on the south side originally belonged to the Socialer Turnverein that built Das Deutsche Haus in the 1890s (see chap. 8 of vol. 1). In 1893, the southsiders organized their own Southside Turnverein, and under the leadership of the charismatic Henry Victor, the new organization grew steadily in numbers. In keeping with the Turners' philosophy of physical fitness, Victor established physical training classes with five hundred pupils in rented quarters. He then launched a movement in 1899 to build a home for the turnverein. In 1900, the turnverein purchased a site at 306 Prospect Street, in the midst of a German neighborhood, and Victor sold shares in a stockholder's association to members and raised funds. With the help of a loan, the Turners reached their $45,000 goal and hired Vonnegut and Bohn as architects for their new building. Bernard Vonnegut, the senior partner, had designed Das Deutsche Haus and knew the needs of a turnverein quite well.[97]

On a modest budget, Vonnegut devised an imposing building that would quickly become a landmark. Like the west wing of Das Deutsche Haus, the Southside Turnverein has a tall hipped roof and red brick, load-bearing walls. For the facade on Prospect, the architect used a symmetrical composition with five arched bays at the center and two projecting pavilions on either side (fig. 2.59). He positioned the entrance off-center, at the base of the west pavilion. At the top of the side pavilions, Vonnegut incorporated large arches containing stucco and timber panels and twin windows at the center. On the west elevation, he incorporated the artistic highlight of the exterior—a stone sculpture in the gable honoring Father Friedrich Jahn, the father of the German Turner movement. Austrian-born sculptor Rudolph Schwarz depicted Jahn in a Baroque-style cartouche with male and female figures paying homage (fig. 2.60). Below the Jahn memorial, Vonnegut projected a bay with a faceted roof and a stucco and timber treatment in its upper story. Throughout the exterior, he used limestone effectively as an accent, using

Facing top, **Figure 2.59.** Former Southside Turnverein, 306 Prospect Street, built in 1900–1901 and designed by Bernard Vonnegut of Vonnegut and Bohn, drawing on German Renaissance *rathauses* of the sixteenth century, Romanesque architecture, and European stucco and timber structures for massing and details. Rehabilitated in 2018 by Point Comfort Underwriters. 2021 view. James Glass.

Facing bottom, **Figure 2.60.** Restored sculpture on west gable of Father Friedrich Jahn, founder of the German Turner movement, by sculptor Rudolph Schwarz. 2021 view. James Glass.

it in stone voussoirs above the arched openings and as a stringcourse across the exterior. As picturesque elements, he placed a small cupola on the roof ridge and a row of chimney-like stacks along the lower edge of the roof.[98]

Inside, the architect devoted much of the space to a combination gymnasium and auditorium on the main floor. At one end, he devised an elevated gallery that could seat two hundred people; at the other end, he designed a stage. In the basement, Vonnegut arranged several dining rooms and a set of bowling alleys.[99]

The Maennerchor

The Indianapolis Maennerchor was a singing society of German American men in the state capital whose founders had emigrated from Germany after the revolutions of 1848 failed in their homeland. In 1854, they formed the Maennerchor and performed in a variety of venues. Finally, in the first decade of the twentieth century, they were ready to build a substantial clubhouse and concert hall. The leaders followed the precedent of the Socialer Turnverein and the Southside Turnverein in raising funds by sale of stock shares and purchased the northwest corner of Illinois and Michigan Streets as their site in 1906. They chose a location one block north of the property that the main YMCA bought at almost the same time for its central building. Construction of the two institutional buildings marked the transition of Illinois from a residential street to a corridor with commercial and community structures.[100]

The Maennerchor retained senior Indianapolis architect Adolph Scherrer as their designer. Scherrer had been born in the German-speaking part of Switzerland and was familiar with the culture and traditions of Germany. The society raised a substantial budget for their clubhouse, and Scherrer designed an imposing building in which he used high-quality materials, sculptures, and decorations with great effect (fig. 2.61).[101]

Scherrer planned four main parts for the building: a principal, gable-roofed wing running east and west across the north part of the lot, two wings perpendicular to the main wing extending south from either end of the main section, and a central section running between the two wings to the south of the main wing. Scherrer constructed the exterior walls of the three-story building with reddish-brown brick. He used a steel frame for the structure and steel trusses to support the roofs.[102]

The architect designed two facades. He reserved the principal facade for the east end of the principal pavilion or wing. A trio of entries, framed in stone with Baroque details, appeared on the first story, above which Scherrer placed a stone frieze with more bas-relief sculptures. On the second-story level, he designed three

Facing, **Figure 2.61.** +Maennerchor Building, northwest corner, Michigan and Illinois Streets, built in 1906–7 for a German men's singing society and designed by Adolph Scherrer, drawing from the Italian Renaissance for details of the facade. Note the medieval-like tower with Renaissance motifs. View in c. 1912. Demolished in 1974 and replaced by a parking lot. Bass Photo Co. Collection, Indiana Historical Society. (Image cropped)

Above, **Figure 2.62.** +Concert hall on second floor, Maennerchor Building, with Italian Renaissance pilasters, columns, and arches. View in 1908. Bass Photo Co. Collection, Indiana Historical Society. (Image cropped)

arched windows separated by traditional Renaissance-style pilasters supporting an entablature, all in stone. At the third-story level, he incorporated four smaller rectangular windows flanking a blind window with segmental pediment overhead. A parapet with limestone coping lined the gable at the top of the principal pavilion. The architect capped the apex of the gable with an arched ornament. Immediately south of the principal facade on Illinois, for picturesque effect, he designed an octagonal tower with Renaissance-style stone details.

On the Michigan Street side, Scherrer used gables with similar parapets and coping for the two side wings and limestone surrounds for the first-floor windows that appeared on the wings and the central section. For the second story on the south elevation, he devised three-part stained glass windows with segmental arches and transom windows overhead. Between the third stories of the two wings, the architect created one of the first roof gardens in Indianapolis. He framed the off-center Michigan Street entry with stone pilasters and a frieze and pediment.[103]

Inside the Illinois Street entrance, the architect laid out a spacious lobby with a beamed ceiling supported by Tuscan columns and a tile floor. On either side, he ran marble stairways leading up to the second floor. In other parts of the first floor, Scherrer placed a ladies' dining room and a ladies' parlor. On the second floor, he located the principal feature of the whole building: the eighty-four-by-fifty-foot concert hall, which ran east–west within the principal wing (fig. 2.62). The architect lined the sides of the two-story hall with white Renaissance arches, pilasters, and clerestory windows. South of the concert hall, above the ladies' dining room, he planned another popular feature—the *kneipe* (drinking room). He styled it as a rathskeller, with dark paneling, stained glass windows, and a fireplace with grotesque herm figures and green tile. Elsewhere, Scherrer included a rehearsal room, library, and bowling alley.[104]

HOSPITALS

Indianapolis entered the twentieth century with two full-service hospitals—the Indianapolis City Hospital located at Locke Street and Fall Creek Boulevard, founded in the 1860s, and the St. Vincent's Infirmary at South and Delaware Streets, constructed by the Catholic Sisters of Charity in 1888–89 (see chap. 8 of vol. 1). As the city expanded in population after 1900, demand grew for more hospitals serving different constituencies. The German Protestants acted first, building a modest, Romanesque-style Protestant Deaconess Hospital on the northwest corner of Ohio Street and Senate Avenue.[105] It remained of limited size. Larger new hospitals came about through the actions of the Methodist Episcopal

Church, the Sisters of Charity, the Sisters of St. Francis, the City of Indianapolis, and the State of Indiana.

Methodist Hospital

In 1889, an international conference of the Epworth League, the young people's arm of the Methodist Episcopal Church, met in Indianapolis. The conferees decided to use leftover funds to launch a drive for a hospital and nurses' training school in the state capital. All three Methodist annual conferences in the state and the Women's Home Missionary Societies of Indiana pledged to support the effort and formed a corporation to oversee it. In 1902, all the Methodist churches in Indianapolis held a "hospital service" and raised $32,000. Subsequent pledges brought the total to $50,000, and the hospital corporation moved to plan the initial building of Methodist Hospital. They purchased a spacious site on the northwest corner of Sixteenth Street and Capitol Avenue, close to both the north-side residential district south of Fall Creek and the downtown area.[106]

The building committee hired the firm of Vonnegut and Bohn as architects, and in 1904, the firm designed a handsome three-story building set back from Capitol Avenue (fig. 2.63).[107] The architects used a yellow face brick for the exterior walls and a steel frame for fireproof construction. Bernard Vonnegut, the probable designer, employed a T-shaped plan—the main portion faced Capitol Avenue, and a wing projected from it at the rear and extended to the west. For the composition of the facade, Vonnegut designed a projecting pavilion at the center and embellished it with a porch supported by Corinthian columns. At the corners of the porch, rising, almost floating above it, were sculptures of two elongated angels, unusual in a Protestant-sponsored building. The figures seemed to symbolize the healing that would occur within. On either side of the central pavilion, wings extended to the north and south. Just below the cornice, the architect devised decorative cartouches. For contrast with the yellow brick walls, he employed a red clay tile covering on the hipped roof. Directly above the central pavilion and entrance, on the ridge of the roof, Vonnegut placed a cupola as a vertical accent.[108]

After completion of the initial building in 1905, the trustees of the hospital found considerable demand for additional facilities. In 1910 and 1911, another fundraising campaign raised $125,000 for a wing to the south of the original building. Vonnegut and Bohn (now headed by Arthur Bohn) prepared plans for both a south building and a matching north building.[109] The architects first designed a four-story structure that joined the south end of the 1905 building and projected

forward of the original facade (fig. 2.64). The exterior composition of the new wing harmonized with the original—yellow brick walls with a high limestone foundation, limestone lintels for the windows, and an extension of the same cornice, but without the sculptural embellishments of 1905.

Facing top, Figure 2.63. +Original pavilion of Methodist Hospital, 1602 North Capitol Avenue, built in 1904–5 and probably designed by Bernard Vonnegut of Vonnegut and Bohn, using a symmetrical plan and varied colors through buff-colored brick walls and green tile roof. Note the angel sculptures flanking the entrance, unusual in a Protestant-founded institution. View from c. 1905–6. The facade was removed and replaced by a new hospital wing in c. early 1960s. Postcard from author's collection.

Facing bottom, Figure 2.64. +South wing (*left*), original Methodist Hospital, constructed in 1911, and north wing (*right*), constructed in 1913. The designs of the two wings harmonized with the central wing, but Vonnegut and Bohn gave them a different treatment with multiple cornices. View in 1912. The south wing was demolished in the early 1960s and replaced with a lawn. Postcard from author's collection.

Inside, Vonnegut and Bohn provided for sixty-five patient rooms, a children's ward, and a sun parlor. Atop the wing, they devised a roof garden for patients. In 1913, the hospital raised sufficient funds to build the north wing, which the architects designed to match the appearance of the south wing and placed it so as also to project forward of the central building. The result was a shallow entry court and drive where ambulances could deliver emergency patients.[110]

St. Vincent's Hospital

The Sisters of Charity of St. Vincent de Paul concluded after 1900 that they had overgrown their infirmary downtown at South and Delaware Streets. In 1908, they purchased a large tract on the north bank of Fall Creek between Illinois Street and Capitol Avenue as the site for a much larger hospital in the fast-growing neighborhood north of the creek. The process for planning the new building proceeded slowly. Oscar Bohlen of the firm D. A. Bohlen and Son, who had designed the previous St. Vincent's Infirmary (see chap. 8 of vol. 1), won the commission to design the Fall Creek hospital. He spent two years visiting modern hospitals in the United States and Europe to note the best features and layouts and repeatedly revised the plans for St. Vincent's Hospital in Indianapolis. Bohlen finished preliminary plans early in 1909, but approval by the mother house of the Sisters of Charity in Maryland was slow to come. Then, at the end of 1909, the architect revised the plans to provide for a much more ambitious building than initially envisioned. He advertised for construction bids and sent those received for review by the mother house. In the spring of 1910, the Sisters solicited bids for just the foundation, and work began on the excavation and basement walls. The previous bids for the rest of the building from general contractors had been too high, so Bohlen revised the specifications. More delays pushed completion of the revisions and bidding into 1911. Construction required another year, and the new hospital finally opened for patients in January 1913. Over a two-year period, the budget for the largest hospital building constructed in the city to date increased from an initial estimate of $350,000 to a final cost of $800,000.[111]

Oscar Bohlen devised a five-story building with an E-shaped plan on the south (figs. 2.65 and 2.66), facing the new Fall Creek Parkway designed by landscape architect George E. Kessler. A large pavilion set back considerably from the parkway forms the centerpiece of the facade. A frontispiece at the center of the pavilion projects forward and contains the entrance. At the rear of the pavilion, wings extend east and west and then turn south, forming long wings that run nearly to the parkway. The result is a spacious courtyard bounded by the two lateral wings and the central pavilion. In composing the details of the simply ornamented exterior, Bohlen used materials effectively to provide a richness of texture and color. He used pressed, glazed bricks with a deep-brown hue for the outside walls. For the grand stairway leading up to the entrance, he employed Indiana limestone for its balustrade and the parapet of the brick porch sheltering the entry. At the top of the frontispiece, the architect used limestone for the frieze and the bas-relief sculptures within the tympanum of a culminating pediment. Stone also appears in the capitals on colossal pilasters arranged across the central pavilion and in keystones for the Georgian-style flat brick arches over all the windows. As a contrast, Bohlen used copper for all the cornice moldings and the edges of the pediment. To add interest to the south ends of the lateral wings, he used five-story bowed shapes. He articulated these bays with arched windows in the top story, a limestone stringcourse, and a rusticated treatment of the brick. Overall, for the exterior of St. Vincent's Hospital, Bohlen employed a creative mix of Classical, Georgian, and Renaissance motifs.[112]

Facing top, **Figure 2.65.** St. Vincent's Hospital, 132 West Fall Creek Parkway, North Drive, built in 1910–13 and designed by Oscar Bohlen and D. A. Bohlen and Son and based in part on numerous trips by Bohlen to view the latest hospitals and their layouts and equipment. The facade draws its details from Italian Renaissance, Classical, and Georgian architecture. View in c. 1915. Bass Photo Co. Collection, Indiana Historical Society. (Image cropped)

Facing bottom, **Figure 2.66.** Central facade and courtyard of former St. Vincent's Hospital, after rehabilitation of facade and side wings for Ivy Tech State College. View in 2023. James Glass.

With respect to functions, Bohlen placed administrative offices in the central east–west wing behind the entry pavilion. He devoted most of the first, second, and third floors in the lateral wings to 152 patient rooms. On the fourth floor, the architect located nine operating rooms, a laboratory, and doctors' scrub rooms. To the rear of the central wing, he designed a three-story chapel with Baroque details and stained glass windows. To the north of the west lateral wing of the facade, the architect ran a third major wing for patients. He arranged sun parlors and porches for patient recuperation. Inside the entry, a central stairway with marble steps and cast-iron balustrades leads up to the upper floors. Doric pilasters line the structure around the open stairwell. Terrazzo floors covered all the original corridors, and mosaic floors were used in the operating rooms.[113]

St. Francis Hospital, Beech Grove

In 1906, the Reverend Peter Killian, pastor of the Catholic Church of the Holy Sacrament in the infant town of Beech Grove, organized a movement to bring a hospital to the community. He persuaded Bishop Francis Silas Chatard to allow him to invite the Sisters of St. Francis of Lafayette, Indiana, to establish such a hospital. The Sisters were agreeable, but several years passed while the town of Beech Grove constructed a sewerage system adequate for a hospital operation. By 1912, the Sisters were ready to act and made plans to erect a four-story building on a five-acre tract that they acquired on the northeast corner of Albany Street and Seventeenth Avenue.[114] They hired a Louisville architect,[115] who designed a building with a fireproof steel structure and exterior walls of pressed, brown brick (fig. 2.67). The architect devised a central pavilion flanked by north and south wings. He made the facade of the pavilion the focal point of the composition, with a projecting limestone porch fronted by a temple front with Corinthian pilasters and pediment. Above the porch, he placed a limestone niche surmounted by a smaller pediment supported by consoles. The architect adorned the fourth story of the pavilion with brick pilasters and stone capitals. Above, he placed limestone bull's-eyes with keystones and, finally, a projecting cornice with modillions. He used no ornamentation for the two wings but employed an unusual device of unbroken rows of dormer windows imposed on a partial mansard roof.[116]

In the interior, the Louisville architect planned space on three floors for one hundred patients, to be accommodated in private rooms and wards. The Sisters of St. Francis occupied quarters in the fourth floor.[117]

Figure 2.67. +Original section of St. Francis's Hospital (*at center*), northeast corner, Albany Street and Seventeenth Avenue, Beech Grove, built in 1912–13 and designed by a Louisville architect with a symmetrical plan, glazed brick walls, and Italian Renaissance embellishments for the entry vestibule. At right is a 1930 wing designed by D. A. Bohlen and Son. The whole hospital was demolished in 2017 after St. Francis Hospital closed in Beech Grove. View in 2017. James Glass.

City Hospital

The City Hospital, which offered care to indigent patients who lived in Indianapolis, was housed at the beginning of the twentieth century in a collection of brick buildings that mostly dated from the 1860s and 1880s. By 1906, hospital administrators judged the original 1860s building to be grossly inadequate and in need of immediate replacement. The city board of works retained veteran architect Adolph Scherrer as architect for a potential $100,000 building but did not direct him to complete final plans. The board apparently shelved the matter until early 1912, when the administration of Mayor Samuel Lewis Shank finally decided to make a master plan for a new campus of City Hospital buildings. They invited four local architectural firms—Adolph Scherrer and Son, Brubaker and Stern, Vonnegut and Bohn, and Herbert W. Foltz—to enter a competition for selection of the architect of future hospital buildings. Each firm had experience designing hospitals. Under the rules adopted, each competitor submitted a plan for the hospital buildings and floor plans and an elevation for each building. The city board of works retained Warren P. Laird, head of the architecture program at the University of Pennsylvania, as umpire (judge) for the competition. Laird was a practicing architect who also directed the architectural degree program at one of the most prestigious universities in the country.[118]

In March 1912, Laird selected the campus and detailed plans submitted by Adolph Scherrer and his son, J. Anton Scherrer, as "the most suitable" of those entered in the competition. In their proposed master plan, the Scherrers sited the principal hospital buildings—administration building, superintendent's home, nurses' home, major medical building, and laboratory building—to face Fall Creek to the north. They placed the five anticipated ward buildings to the rear to obtain the southern exposure. The Scherrers designed attractive porticos with Doric columns for the administration and nurses' home structures (fig. 2.68). The board of works and Mayor Shank expected to construct all the buildings in the plan in the future, spending as much as $2 million.[119]

For immediate needs, the city council appropriated $105,000 raised through a bond issue, and the city board of health provided $225,000 bequeathed by

Facing top, **Figure 2.68.** Elevation drawing of nurses' home, physician's court, and administration building submitted by Adolph Scherrer and Son for the architectural competition held in 1912 to produce a new campus design for Indianapolis City Hospital. Note the Doric porticos proposed for the nurses' home and administration building. *Year Book of the Indiana Chapter A.I.A. and Catalog of the Third Annual Exhibition 1912* (Indianapolis: Indiana Chapter A.I.A., 1912).

Facing bottom, **Figure 2.69.** +West and east wings of the Burdsal Units, City (later Wishard) Hospital, 960 Locke Street, built in 1912–13 and designed with pavilions at the ends and ward floors between, with ornamentation concentrated in the copper cornices. For the children's and adult wards, Indianapolis artists painted murals and canvasses for the enjoyment of patients. Demolished in 2014–15 after the opening of Eskenazi Hospital. View in 2014. James Glass.

NURSES HOME　　PHYSICIANS COURT　　ADMINISTRATION

businessman Alfred Burdsal for hospital purposes. All parties decided to construct the first two ward buildings west of the existing hospital structures. The Scherrers prepared revised plans in May 1912 for what came to be called the Burdsal Units. The two parallel ward buildings, of identical exterior design (fig. 2.69), ran north and south a short distance south of Fall Creek Boulevard (now West Tenth Street). The architects gave them fireproof structures and exterior walls of buff-colored brick, which had become a popular material for hospitals and public school buildings in the first two decades of the new century. Each building consisted of a large rectangular pavilion with five stories at its north end and a smaller rectangular pavilion with four stories at its south end. Between the large and small pavilions of each unit ran a slightly recessed four-story wing. Originally, a one-story brick corridor, and below it a tunnel, linked the two north pavilions of the units.[120]

The architects articulated the exteriors of the north pavilions using brick pilasters without capitals. The pilasters served to divide pairs and trios of windows. A large primary copper cornice projected from the top of each pavilion, echoed by a smaller copper cornice below the fifth story. The Scherrers continued regular brick pilasters along the third and fourth stories of the two connecting wings. The architects gave the two south pavilions, which contained the solariums, broad windows on three sides of the second through fourth stories. A continuation of the lower cornice on the north pavilions ran along the top of the wings and south pavilions. The architects used ornament sparingly. They designed stamped fleurs-de-lis for the lower cornice and rosettes for the upper. Limestone appeared as stringcourses, lintels, and accents. The designers styled the first-story brick walls with deep rusticated joints. To balance the dominant buff color of the walls, they employed green copper for the cornices, red tile for the hipped roofs on the north pavilions, and gray-white limestone for details.

The Scherrers devised wards on three floors of the unit wings, and each ward accommodated twenty-four beds. The architects placed the men's wards on the two first floors, the women's wards on the second floors, and the children's wards on the third floors. After the completion of construction in 1914, St. Margaret's Guild, a women's volunteer organization, approached Dr. T. Victor Keene, the director of City Hospital, and offered to raise funds for decorating the interior of the Burdsal Units. Keene approached Indianapolis artists Clifton Wheeler and Wayman Adams about creating some paintings, and the artists proposed an ambitious plan for paintings and murals in all the wards. Twelve artists under the direction of William Forsyth ultimately participated in the art project, producing paintings of natural scenes and landscapes for the men's and women's wards and murals based on Mother Goose rhymes and folklore for the children's wards.[121]

Figure 2.70. Facades with Corinthian porticos of the nurses' home (*left*) and administration building, City Hospital, built 1922–23 and designed by Anton and Herman Scherrer. View in 2023. James Glass.

The execution of the hospital master plan halted in 1914 but resumed after World War I. In 1922, Adolph Scherrer's two sons, Anton and Herman, designed an administration building and nurses' residence on Locke Street, using the two porticos proposed originally (fig. 2.70).[122]

Robert W. Long Hospital

While City Hospital cared for residents of Indianapolis unable to pay for care, in the early twentieth century, no public hospitals existed for the indigent in rural counties and the small towns of the state. That situation changed between 1911 and 1914, when an act of philanthropy launched a campaign to construct a hospital in the state capital that would provide hospitalization for those outside Indianapolis who needed free care. Dr. Robert W. Long had practiced medicine on East Washington Street downtown for many years and noted that some of his patients could not afford to go to the hospital. In 1910, he approached Dr. William

Figure 2.71. Robert W. Long Hospital, 1102 West Michigan Street, built in 1912–14 and designed by Robert Frost Daggett and R. P. Daggett and Company, employing a symmetrical facade with Classical portico and Renaissance pilasters and rustication. Note the pergolas sheltering the roof gardens for patient convalescence on the top floor. View in c. 1915. Bass Photo Co. Collection, Indiana Historical Society. (Image cropped)

Lowe Bryan, president of Indiana University, and offered a $200,000 gift if the State of Indiana would construct a hospital for indigent patients to be operated by the Indiana University School of Medicine. The Indiana General Assembly promptly accepted the gift, and President Bryan agreed to manage the hospital. The university acquired a sixteen-acre site at 1080 West Michigan Street, in the midst of one of the oldest and poorest neighborhoods in the city.[123]

In 1912, the board of trustees for Indiana University retained the firm of R. P. Daggett and Company as architects, selecting it from eleven firms whom the board had interviewed. Robert Frost Daggett, the principal in the Daggett office, had recently designed the biology building at the main university campus in Bloomington and was known to the university.[124]

Daggett and his draftsmen designed an imposing building set back to advantage from Michigan Street on the south (fig. 2.71). They laid out three principal parts—a central rectangular pavilion, east and west wings, and a shorter northern wing. The architects used a reinforced concrete structure and brownish-gray, vitrified brick for the exterior walls. They effectively attracted the eye to the center with a monumental Doric portico standing on a podium with three arched entries, all in Indiana limestone. Above the portico, a large arched window marked the surgery department on the fourth floor. The archway broke through the cornice of the central pavilion for dramatic effect. On either side of the main pavilion, the architects used both colossal Doric pilasters and smaller secondary pilasters to define the second and third stories. For the first floor, they employed deep rusticated joints to suggest a Renaissance-style treatment for ground stories. At the ends of the two wings, the architects provided extensive windows to light sunporches for patients. On the fourth story, on either side of the enclosed surgery structure, Daggett designed an innovative open-roof garden covered by a decorative wooden pergola. The intent was for convalescents to speed their recovery in warm weather by resting in the open air.[125]

Inside, the architects planned for offices, reception rooms, and private patient rooms on the first floor. On the second and third floors, they planned patient wards. In all, the hospital provided eighty-eight free beds and sixteen private rooms. Each floor had a laboratory, nurses' rooms, and hydrotherapeutic rooms. The architects packed seaweed in the walls of the wards and patient rooms to keep the environment as quiet as possible.[126]

The Longs increased their gift to $250,000 as the structure was completed to pay for the equipment and furnishing of the hospital. The Long building marked the beginning of an extensive campus of hospital buildings operated by the Indiana University School of Medicine.[127]

CONCLUSION

The first two decades of the twentieth century saw Indianapolis complement its impressive array of tall office buildings, department stores, hotels, train terminals and concourses, and factories with imposing public buildings of all types and

ARCHITECT PROFILE

Robert Frost Daggett

Robert Frost Daggett (1875–1955) was born in Indianapolis, the son of prominent architect Robert Platt Daggett. The younger Robert graduated from Indianapolis High School and then attended the University of Pennsylvania, graduating with a degree in architecture in 1896. Next, he enrolled in the capstone institution for the Beaux Arts method of design, the École des Beaux-Arts itself in Paris. After several years of study in the École and work in the atelier of a master architect, Daggett received a diploma from the French government in 1901 and returned to Indianapolis, probably the first architect in the state of Indiana to graduate from the École des Beaux-Arts.

He joined the firm of R. P. Daggett and Company, assuming design and management responsibilities along with his father and R. P. Daggett's longtime partner, James B. Lizius. Among the major works on which Robert Frost Daggett undoubtedly worked in the first decade of the twentieth century was the Lemcke Annex office building on North Pennsylvania Street (1909). He also probably designed the Wulschner-Stewart retail building on North Pennsylvania Street (1909).

In 1910–11, Robert Platt Daggett retired from management of the firm and moved to Escalon, California. In 1911, James Lizius died, leaving Robert Frost solely in charge.

He continued the firm's mix of designing office buildings, retail structures, university buildings, and hospitals. He designed Hotel Washington in 1912 and the Robert W. Long Hospital of 1912–14 and continued the design of industrial buildings for Eli Lilly and Company that his father had begun. In his early years of practice, Robert Frost Daggett conducted Beaux Arts design competitions among younger architects to encourage education and practice following the Beaux Arts principles.

After service in World War I, Daggett returned to his Indianapolis practice and enjoyed a successful decade during the 1920s. Major buildings that he and his draftsmen designed in the city included the 1922 Italian Renaissance–style Indianapolis Athletic Club, the Renaissance-style Continental Bank Building (1924), the Gothic-derived Indianapolis Chamber of Commerce Building (1926), the Tudor-style original Riley Hospital, the Renaissance-style William H. Coleman Hospital for Women, and the Art Deco–style Third Church of Christ, Scientist. Together with architect Thomas E. Hibben, Daggett designed the monumental Gothic-style Jordan Hall at the new campus of Butler University. Outside

Indianapolis, he designed the Spanish Mission–style Greenfield Laboratories of Eli Lilly and Company and several buildings at the campuses of Indiana and Purdue Universities. In the early 1930s, Daggett designed residences in the Crow's Nest suburb of Indianapolis for Josiah K. Lilly Sr. and his older son, Eli Lilly. He also restored the 1823 William Conner House near Noblesville for Eli Lilly in 1934.

After World War II, Daggett took E. Harold Naegele and Robert Frost Daggett Jr. into the practice, and the office continued as Daggett, Naegele, and Daggett. Earlier, Robert Frost Sr. helped found the Construction League of Indianapolis.

Sources: "Well-Known Architect Dead," *Indianapolis News*, April 24, 1911, 16; "Architects Plan Contest," *Indianapolis Star*, October 3, 1913, 11; "Robert Frost Daggett," in Kate Milner Rabb and William Herschell, eds., *An Account of Indianapolis and Marion County* (Dayton: Dayton Historical Publishing Company, 1924), 4:293–94; "Robert Frost Daggett, Sr. Dies," *Construction News*, vol. 21, no. 37 (September 12, 1955), 8; Andrew R. Seager, "Daggett, Robert Frost," in *Encyclopedia of Indianapolis*, ed. David J. Bodenhamer and Robert G. Barrows (Indianapolis: Indiana University Press, 1994), 490. Source for photo: Paul Donald Brown, ed., *Indianapolis Men of Affairs 1923* (Indianapolis: American Biographical Society, 1923), 142.

structures devoted to social and charitable organizations. The new federal courthouse and post office, city hall, central public library, schools, fraternal lodges, clubs, athletic facilities, and hospitals compared favorably with those of any other major city of the Midwest.

Architectural competitions served as the vehicle for selecting architects of public buildings to a much larger degree than with commercial buildings. Despite some grumbling by local architects about the fairness of the process and the selection of out-of-town designers in several cases, the competitions resulted in a variety of imaginative conceptual designs being generated for each project and several notable designs being selected. In the case of the US Courthouse and Post Office and the Indianapolis Central Library, the final designs were outstanding on a national basis. Those two competitions also afforded opportunities for some top talents in the East to create designs in Indianapolis—Rankin and Kellogg and Paul Cret, both of Philadelphia. The two public competitions involving only local architects—for the Indianapolis City Hall and City Hospital—produced handsome buildings, but not perhaps of the aesthetic brilliance of Rankin and Kellogg or Cret.

In noncompetition projects, local architects produced fine results with all building types. Bernard Vonnegut, in several final projects involving the Southside Turnverein, Methodist Hospital, and possibly the Herron Art Institute, continued to approach creatively facade compositions with varied materials and interpretations of Renaissance and Classical details. All the while, he incorporated his trademark shields and cartouches. The new firm of Rubush and Hunter produced impressive Neoclassical facades and lavish interior designs for the Masonic Temple, the Indianapolis City Hall, and an imposing cluster of buildings for the new Indiana School for the Deaf. Adolph Scherrer, in the last decades of his career, crafted a richly and imaginatively detailed exterior for the Maennerchor Building and a compelling master plan for the projected City Hospital campus. Oscar Bohlen continued to show his mastery of design in his carefully studied plans and elevations for the YWCA Building and the new St. Vincent's Hospital. The new partnership of Foltz and Parker drew on the Renaissance and Classicism for their design of the main YMCA Building, and individually, Herbert Foltz responded to the Senate Avenue YMCA Building with a design that made use of color, texture, and patterns in brick to provide character for the exterior and efficiently planned varied functions in the interior. Wilson Parker achieved similar qualitative results with his updated Italianate design for the Spades Park Branch library building.

A recurring theme in the design of major public and nonprofit buildings of this period involves the research conducted by both architects and their clients before developing final plans. Oscar Bohlen, in particular, was known for his trips to other cities to study the latest designs for new building types, such as he did with the expansion of English's Opera House and Hotel (see vol. 1), the Murat Theater, the YWCA Building, and the new St. Vincent's Hospital. Foltz and Parker did the same in conjunction with the principal committee for the main YMCA building, and Eliza Browning, the city librarian, sought out the advice of other librarians on the design of the 1914–17 public library building.

Architects of the period relied principally on the Italian Renaissance and Classical sources for the overall compositions and detailing of most of the public and nonprofit buildings in Indianapolis. Renaissance elements continued to be staples for embellishing facades, such as the pilasters, cornice, and busts of artists in Vonnegut and Bohn's design for the John Herron Art Institute or the entry porticos, entablatures, and rusticated brick corners in Thomas Winterrowd's Robert Gould Shaw School 40 and Clarence Martindale's George E. Sloan School 41. The direct use of Greek or Roman Classical design elements can be seen after 1900 in the Greek Ionic columns and entablatures of Rankin and Kellogg's US Courthouse and Post Office, the evocation of the Parthenon in the Greek Doric colonnade in Paul Cret's public library, Rubush and Hunter's use of Classical columns and pilasters in their designs for the Masonic Temple and Indianapolis City Hall, and Oscar Bohlen's colossal Ionic columns in the facade of the YWCA building.

A final design theme derives from the German Renaissance that Bernard Vonnegut had evoked so successfully with Das Deutsche Haus in the 1890s and continued to draw on for the design of the Southside Turnverein in 1900. Adolph Scherrer relied on Italian and German Renaissance details for the entry and window treatments of the facade for the Maennerchor and for the arcade and pilasters in the concert hall within.

Several public, fraternal, and charitable buildings rose in the African American community along Indiana Avenue and adjacent streets during the 1900–1920 period. The Indianapolis Public Schools board constructed one elementary school for Black students—the Robert Gould Shaw School 40 on Senate Avenue. The African American Pythian lodges built a Pythian hall and commercial building on Walnut Street, and the African American YMCA pushed for and obtained a substantial YMCA building for young Black men on Senate Avenue. In none of these cases did African American architects design the buildings. In each case, a white architect obtained the commission.

Map 2.1

Buildings from Chapter 2 of Volume 2 plotted on 1914 Sanborn Insurance Map (Vol. 1) of Mile Square of Indianapolis (Vol. 1) (numbers drawn from figure numbers); + = demolished

- **1** 1903-05 U.S. Courthouse and Post Office
- **14** Indianapolis City Hall
- **19** 1913-14 Fire Headquarters
- **45** + 1900-01 Columbia Club
- **47** Masonic Temple
- **55** + 1908-09 Main Y.M.C.A. Building
- **56** + Y.W.C.A. Building
- **57** + Senate Avenue Y.M.C.A. Building
- **61** + Maennerchor Building

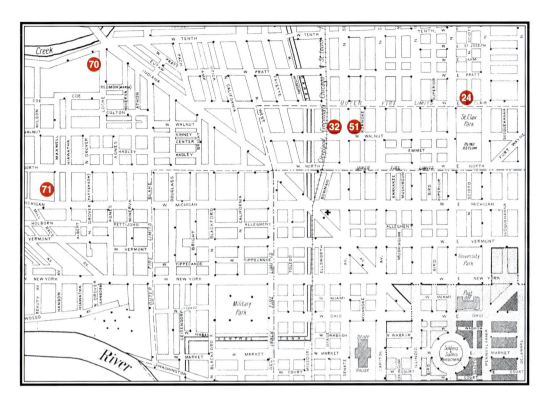

Map 2.2

Buildings from Chapter 2 plotted on 1914 Sanborn Insurance Map of area west and north of Mile Square (Vol. 1) (numbers drawn from figure numbers); + = demolished

- **24** Indianapolis (Central) Public Library
- **32** + Robert Gould Shaw School 40
- **51** African American Pythian Building
- **70** City Hospital
- **71** Robert W. Long Hospital

Map 2.3

Buildings from Chapter 2 plotted on 1915 Sanborn Insurance Map (Vol. 4) of area between 10th and 23rd Streets and between Capitol Avenue and Alvord Street (numbers drawn from figure numbers); + = demolished

- **23** Spades Park Carnegie Library Branch
- **37** St. Agnes Academy
- **42** John Herron Art Institute (now Herron High School)
- **53** Oriental Lodge (now Prince Hall Masonic Temple)
- **63** Methodist Episcopal Hospital

Map 2.4

Buildings from Chapter 2 plotted on 1915 Sanborn Insurance Map (Vol. 5) of area between Maple Road (38th Street) and 46th Street and between Illinois Street and the Indiana State Fairgrounds (numbers drawn from figure numbers)

12 Indiana School for the Deaf
21 Fire Hose Company Station 28

Map 2.5

Buildings from Chapter 2 plotted on 1915 Sanborn Insurance Map (Vol. 5) of area between Fall Creek and 35th Street and between Senate Avenue and College Avenue (numbers drawn from figure numbers); + = demolished

36 + William A. Bell School 60

65 1913 St. Vincent's Hospital

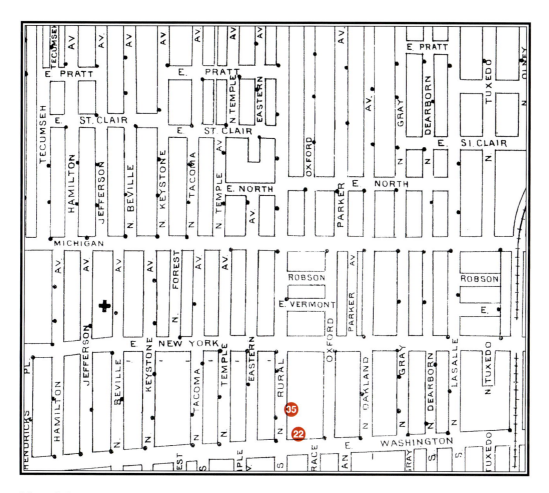

Map 2.6

Buildings from Chapter 2 plotted on 1915 Sanborn Insurance Map (Vol. 3) of area between Tecumseh and Tuxedo Streets and between East Washington Street and 10th Street (numbers drawn from figure numbers)

- 22 East Washington Street Carnegie Library Branch
- 35 Lucretia Mott School 3

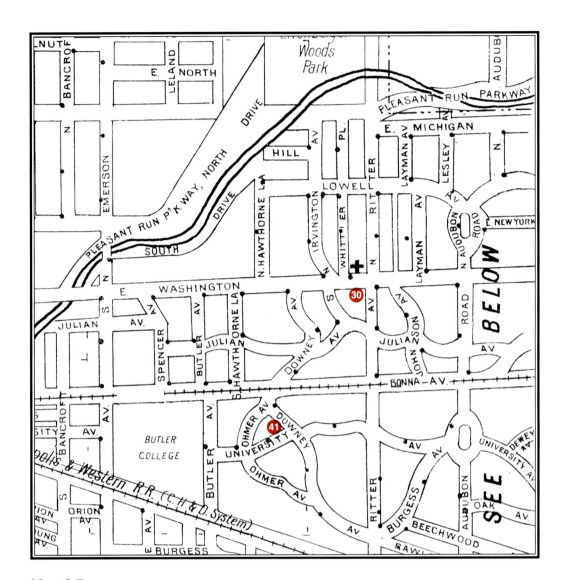

Map 2.7

Buildings from Chapter 2 plotted on 1915 Sanborn Insurance Map (Vol. 3) of Irvington (numbers drawn from figure numbers)

- **30** George W. Julian School 57
- **41** Bona Thompson Memorial Library, Butler College

3 | BUILDINGS OF WORSHIP
1900–1920

The growth in the population of Indianapolis between 1900 and 1920 served as a substantial spur for increasing the number of religious bodies in the city. The population increased by approximately 65 percent in those twenty years, rising from 204,518 to 314,194. Parallelling that increase, churches and synagogues increased in number from 168 in 1900 to 284 in 1920, a 69 percent rise. As the state capital increased in area to forty-two square miles in 1920, most of the established religious denominations organized mission chapels or new churches in additions and communities annexed by the city. Annexation also brought additional congregations into Indianapolis that had been previously established nearby in former towns, such as West Indianapolis, Brightwood, Haughville, and Irvington.[1]

The number of religious sects increased as well. In 1900, twenty-eight denominations were represented in the city. By 1920, that number had risen to thirty-eight, several of which were new.[2] The increase in sects reflected the growing diversity of the population, as immigrants from varied European countries arrived, bringing with them the faiths of their homelands. New Pentecostal and charismatic churches arose, with congregations made up of both white and Black members. Most congregations in the city, though, belonged to traditional Protestant denominations and the Catholic Church. Both the large Protestant churches and the Catholic diocese sought to expand the presence of their denominations by organizing and sponsoring mission chapels in areas without religious bodies. Most of the chapels swiftly grew into self-sustaining congregations.

By 1920, the largest denomination in Indianapolis was the Methodist Episcopal, a mostly white denomination with thirty-eight churches. The Disciples of Christ, especially strong in Indiana, had grown to twenty-nine. Next in size came the African American Baptist churches, with twenty-eight congregations, then the white Baptists, with twenty-one. The Presbyterians included nineteen congregations, followed by the Catholic Diocese of Indianapolis, which contained seventeen parishes within the city. Other familiar white denominations included the Lutheran, Congregational, Episcopal, Evangelical, Reformed, United Brethren, and Friends, with numbers ranging from two to eight congregations. The second-largest African American denominations were the African Methodist Episcopal (AME) and African American Episcopal Zion churches, numbering ten and seven congregations, respectively. Seven Hebrew congregations existed by 1920, mostly Orthodox bodies. Newly formed Christian denominations of the early twentieth century represented in Indianapolis included the Christian Scientist, Apostolic Faith, Pentecostal Bands, Seventh-day Adventist, and Spiritualist denominations. The Unitarians, long established in New England, also organized a congregation.[3]

The large increase in the number of congregations stimulated the construction of many buildings of worship between 1900 and 1920. In most Protestant denominations, the individual churches decided to build, hired an architect, raised the funds, and retained a contractor. In the Catholic Church, the bishop of Indianapolis and his close advisors made most decisions, in consultation with the local pastor.

Other impetuses for the construction of new buildings proved to be the destruction by fire of previous buildings, the need for larger edifices to serve growing congregations, and a desire to move to locations closer to most of the members.

The Romanesque style was probably the most popular style chosen by congregations for their buildings of worship between 1900 and 1905, popularized by architect Henry Hobson Richardson in the 1880s (see chaps. 7–10 in vol. 1 and chap. 1 of this volume). His type of Romanesque faded as a preferred architectural language by 1905, and Gothic emerged as a preferred style for many congregations. Classical designs inspired directly by the Romans and Greeks also became popular after about 1905 and kept pace with the number of Gothic designs. Some architects created churches that drew on both Classical and other European sources, such as Renaissance, Romanesque, and Gothic. A fully articulated Italian Renaissance style continued to be favored for a few churches, especially Catholic. Designers also embraced the English Arts and Crafts Movement and so-called English Tudor style in a few cases, and in at least one instance, the design details for a church came from the popular California bungalow style.

Architects designed nearly all the new buildings of worship between 1900 and 1920. A few designers specialized in church commissions, but most architects embraced church design as one of many building types covered in their practice. Architects from out of town readily obtained work and landed several choice commissions. In one case, that of the church complex constructed by the Pentecostal Bands of America, no designers or contractors were involved and no stylistic currents incorporated.

This chapter surveys examples of the churches built in this twenty-year period and considers them within the architectural styles or themes they represent.

ROMANESQUE

At the beginning of the 1900–1920 period, the designers of several large buildings of worship and some smaller church structures drew on the Romanesque treatment popularized by Richardson in his churches and other buildings. Large arches framing windows and entries, wedge-shaped stone voussoirs, stepped columns for entrances, rock-faced exteriors and foundations—all these had become staples of Romanesque facades.

Mayflower Congregational Church

The founders of Mayflower Congregational Church organized it in 1869 by recruiting residents of the neighborhood just north of the Mile Square. The congregation grew rapidly during the 1870s and 1880s, and in the early 1890s, it purchased a lot on the southwest corner of Sixteenth and Delaware Streets for a new building. As their architects, they retained Robert S. Stephenson and Ernest Greene of New York, known for their designs of church architecture. Initially, Stephenson and Greene designed a chapel in which the congregation could worship temporarily, and the church completed that structure in 1894. They sited the chapel at the west end of the lot and provided for a single, two-story room with a gable roof. Inside, the architects exposed the wooden ceiling and used hammer-beam trusses and collar beams from English architecture to support the roof and provide a pleasing decorative element.[4]

In 1901, the congregation again hired Stephenson and Greene to design the auditorium for the church, and the architects filled the eastern portion of the lot with a building constructed of load-bearing, pressed red brick. They specified Wisconsin red sandstone for the foundation and decorative details on the exterior.[5] Stephenson and Greene laid out a modified cruciform plan, in which the east,

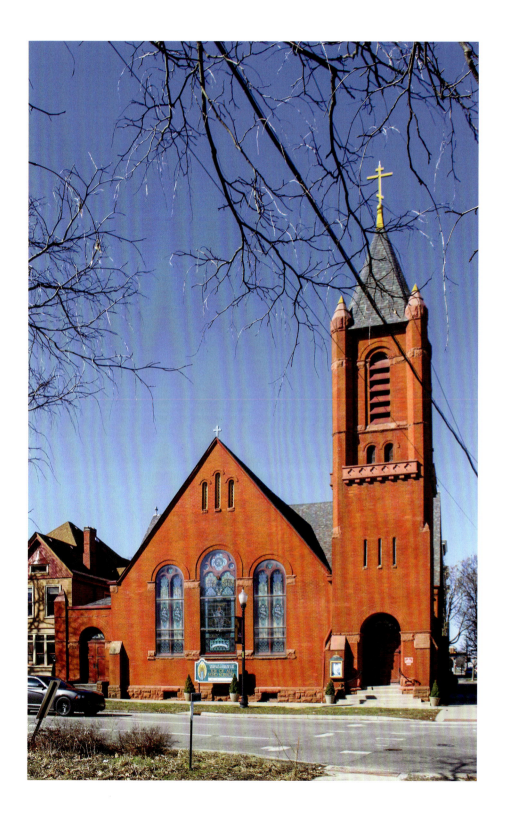

Facing, **Figure 3.1.** Former Mayflower Congregational Church (now Joy of All Who Sorrow Orthodox Church), 1526 North Delaware Street, built in 1894 and 1901 and designed by architects Robert S. Stephenson and Ernest Greene of New York, drawing from the Romanesque arches and massing of churches and other buildings designed by H. H. Richardson of Boston. 2020 view. James Glass.

Above, **Figure 3.2.** The auditorium of the former Mayflower Congregational Church, showing exposed wooden ceiling, English hammer-beam trusses, apse, and a rose window. 2021 view. James Glass.

north, and south arms were of equal length, and located a shorter apse on the west side of the crossing. At the northeast corner, they designed an imposing, three-story bell tower, providing a picturesque element to the facades on both Delaware and Sixteenth Streets (fig. 3.1). The architects generally drew from Richardson's Romanesque for the details of the exterior, using broad arches with brick voussoirs as heads for the trio of windows on the east elevation and the two Delaware Street entrances. They employed similar arches for the belfry in the tower and for the groups of slit windows that they installed in the gables of the Delaware

BUILDINGS OF WORSHIP | 227

and Sixteenth Street facades and at the base of the tower. Stephenson and Greene invoked one element of the Gothic—small stepped buttresses—and placed them at periodic intervals along the two facades.[6]

Inside, the architects created an auditorium with a lofty wooden ceiling supported by a system of hammer-beam trusses and arched braces adapted from English great halls and churches of the fifteenth and sixteenth centuries (fig. 3.2). They incorporated tracery consisting of rounded arches and trefoil and quatrefoil heads into the trio of windows in the east wall and inserted rose windows in the north and south walls. For all the windows, Stephenson and Greene specified stained glass, with several figural scenes included originally. An archway appears in the center of the west wall, outlining a shallow apse for the altar. The cost of the building, property, and furnishings came to approximately $35,000.[7]

First Baptist Church

In January 1904, fire destroyed the First Baptist Church building at New York and Pennsylvania Streets, constructed during the Civil War (see chap. 5 of vol. 1). The congregation sought a new location and built on what the *Indianapolis Journal* called "one of the most beautiful and most desirable church sites in the city." The new site, a lot on the northeast corner of Vermont and Meridian Streets, was located only about a block away from the ruins of the old building, but it was in the midst of the most prestigious residential district in the state capital and away from the disturbing rattle of streetcars moving down tracks along Pennsylvania Street.[9]

The building committee, led by businessman Arthur Jordan, interviewed architects who specialized in church design and planned to visit other cities to survey recent church architecture. In June 1904, the committee selected two firms—Brown and Davis of Cincinnati and Gillespie and Carrel of New York—as associated architects. William R. Brown had previously designed churches in Ohio and Kentucky and was moving to New York with his business partner, David Davis, when the First Baptist Church selected their firm. George G. Gillespie and his partner, Henry C. Carrel, had established reputations in New York for designing hotels, a warehouse, and a brewery. When they won the Indianapolis commission, the two firms were jointly designing a Methodist Episcopal church in Philadelphia.[10]

The architects prepared plans for the new First Baptist Church in July 1904[11] and created one of the most pleasing Romanesque designs, either secular or ecclesiastical, in Indianapolis. The sophistication of the composition and the boldness of the details spoke of an acquaintance with a range of Romanesque buildings, both medieval and contemporary (fig. 3.3).

Figure 3.3. A + beside the name of a building indicates that it no longer exists. +First Baptist Church, 401 North Meridian Street, built in 1904–6 and designed by associated architects Brown and Davis of Cincinnati and Gillespie and Carrel of New York, based on Romanesque details from medieval churches in southern France and inspired by the work of H. H. Richardson. Note the stepped entries with massive arches composed of voussoirs, the rose window, the rounded arcade at the corner, and the lantern with rounded openings and Gothic gables. Local sculptor Alexander Sangernebo created the Romanesque details. View from 1908. The church was demolished in 1960 to complete the landscape setting for the Indiana World War Memorial. *Art Work of Indianapolis and Vicinity* (Chicago: Gravure Illustration, 1908).

The architects filled most of the southern two-thirds of the lot with a rectangular limestone building that drew eyes immediately with a varied massing and picturesque silhouette. They placed a curvilinear pavilion resembling an apse at the southwest corner of the building. To the east of the pavilion, they designed a one-story vestibule faced with an immense Romanesque arch resting on dressed stone impost blocks, supported in turn by stepped Corinthian columns on either side. The stepped columns idea ultimately derived from the treatment of portals in medieval Romanesque churches of southern France and northern Spain. Richardson had popularized such entries through his design for Trinity Episcopal Church in Boston. The architects devised a similar treatment for the entrance on Meridian

BUILDINGS OF WORSHIP | 229

Street. In both cases, local artist Alexander Sangernebo probably sculpted the details. The designers contributed to the picturesqueness of the silhouette by designing intersecting gabled roofs over the auditorium. Above the intersection, the designers placed a hexagonal lantern in which they contrasted Romanesque arches over elongated windows with Gothic gables.[12]

The architects articulated the exterior with varied textures, giving the exterior walls a rock-faced treatment and using dressed limestone for sculpted elements and stringcourses. Along the exterior of the rounded pavilion, they devised an arcade of Romanesque arches, supported by narrow pilasters and sculpted by Sangernebo. In the west wall of the sanctuary, they inserted a large stained glass window divided into three vertical lights, with tracery at the top composed of circles. On the face of the gable projecting south of the lantern, over the south entry, the designers crafted a rose window encircled by 360 degrees of stone voussoirs. For added color and texture, they specified a tile roof.

Inside, Brown and Davis and Gillespie and Carrel laid out an unusual sanctuary plan with an oval shape. They placed the pulpit, altar, pipe organ, and choir loft within the rounded pavilion at the southwest corner of the building. They laid out the pews northeast of the chancel, followed by a gallery with a semicircular wall. To the north of the auditorium, the architects located meeting space for Sunday school classes; when the partition between the auditorium and Sunday school department was lifted, the combined space could seat 1,500 people. As was typical of the time, the architects designed a high basement that housed a dining room, kitchen, and assembly room.[13]

The congregation dedicated the new building in November 1906. The total cost of the building, organ, and furnishings came to $155,000, one of the costliest buildings of worship in the city to that date.

Hillside Christian Church

In 1892, the Disciples of Christ denomination sponsored a new congregation for residents of the near-east-side neighborhood of Oak Hill. The following year, the

> *Facing top,* **Figure 3.4.** Hillside Christian Church, 1737 Ingram Street, built in 1910–11 and designed with huge lunette windows incorporating Romanesque arches. Originally, a dome crowned the sanctuary. View of west and north elevations in c. 1911–12. Bass Photo Co. Collection, Indiana Historical Society. (Image cropped)

> *Facing bottom,* **Figure 3.5.** View of Hillside Christian Church—east and north elevations in 2021. James Glass.

Hillside Christian Church constructed a building on Hillside Avenue. After fourteen years, the congregation of "working people of the home-making class" had grown to three hundred and hired architect Louis H. Gibson to design a larger building. In 1907, Gibson planned a stucco church with a dome and a Classical portico for the site at Ingram and Nevada (now Nineteenth) Streets. The auditorium was to seat five hundred, and the architect estimated the cost at $12,000. Almost immediately after the announcement of the design, Gibson died, and the project was shelved until 1911, when the congregation hired another architect to redesign the church.[14]

The new architect produced a different design than Gibson's on the same site at 1737 Ingram Street. On a knoll above the street, the designer constructed a building with a brick exterior veneer on a high concrete foundation (figs. 3.4 and 3.5). He placed large, lunette-shaped windows with Romanesque arches at the center of the facade and the side elevations. The architect crowned the intersection of the gabled roofs over the auditorium with an octagonal dome topped by a faceted roof and lit by clerestory windows. In the facade, on either side of the large lunette window, the designer located two recessed entries with Romanesque arches. Originally, two flights of concrete steps led up to each entry. The architect used terra-cotta to line the arches of the north, east, and west elevations and for the stringcourse that linked windows and entries. The theme of arches continued in the east elevation of the Sunday school wing, which was larger than the auditorium. The high basement allowed for a social/dining room below the sanctuary.[15]

The auditorium seated four hundred, and the final design cost about $20,000.[16]

St. Catherine of Siena Catholic Church

As new neighborhoods filled with residents near Garfield Park on the south side, in 1909, five men from the Garfield area petitioned Catholic bishop Francis Chatard to create a parish to serve the southeast section of Indianapolis. Chatard appointed Father Cornelius Bosler as the first pastor of the new St. Catherine of Siena parish. Bosler acquired a site for a church building on the east side of Shelby Street, between Tabor and Kelly Streets, and the diocese and charter members of the parish raised funds for constructing a combined church and school structure. The diocese hired a Chicago architect, Henry Schlacks, who had developed a reputation as an ecclesiologist, a specialist in church design. The architect designed the church portion of the building with a Latin Cross plan, in which a long nave expanded at its east end into short transepts. East of the crossing, the fourth arm of the cross extended east, ending in a faceted apse (fig. 3.6).[17]

Figure 3.6. +St. Catherine of Siena Catholic Church, 2245 Shelby Street, built in 1909 and designed by Henry Schlacks of Chicago, drawing on details from the twelfth-century Italian Romanesque Church of San Zeno in Verona, Italy. View from the northwest in 1959. Demolished in c. 2000 after closure of the parish. "Golden Jubilee 1909–1959 St. Catherine of Siena Church," anniversary booklet in Indiana State Library, after page 9.

The facade resembled that of the twelfth-century church of San Zeno in Verona, Italy, with its large central rose window and entry composed of Romanesque arches supported by Corinthian columns and pointed gable overhead. Schlacks also drew the brick corbel tables with which he lined the gable of the facade and side elevations from Italian Romanesque antecedents. In a departure from the usual Catholic practice of building school buildings separately from the church structure, he constructed identical school wings on either side of the main facade. The architect lined the facades of the school wings and their side elevations with Italian Romanesque arcades, continuing the arch and Corinthian column motif of the church entry. When completed in 1910, the church and school cost $38,000.[18]

BUILDINGS OF WORSHIP | 233

GOTHIC

As Romanesque faded in Indianapolis as a preferred style for buildings of worship, Gothic grew stronger. Authors in architectural periodicals devoted much discussion to "archaeological Gothic" designs based on careful study of medieval cathedrals and churches and replication of plan and details. In Indianapolis, the architects of most Gothic designs drew on elements found in medieval structures but used them to articulate and ornament modern buildings.

First Presbyterian Church

In 1899, the federal government announced its intention to acquire the downtown block on which the 1864–70 building of the First Presbyterian Church stood as the site for the new US Courthouse and Post Office (see chap. 5 of vol. 1 and chap. 2 of this volume). The congregation then formed a committee to select a new location. In 1901, the committee purchased several lots on the southeast corner of Sixteenth and Delaware Streets and solicited proposals from architects. Twenty-three firms submitted designs, and the building committee, which included former president Benjamin Harrison, selected the proposal of Cincinnati firm Crapsey and Lamm. Charles Crapsey, the senior partner, had specialized in designs for Protestant churches in Ohio, Indiana, and Kentucky.[19]

The design of Crapsey and Lamm exemplified the ascendancy of the Gothic as a popular style for Indianapolis churches after the turn of the twentieth century. Unlike First Baptist Church, where Romanesque predominated but occasional Gothic elements appeared, First Presbyterian Church was articulated totally with Gothic details. At the same time, Crapsey and Lamm designed a modern church building tuned to the needs of Protestant worship and education. At the heart of the design, the architects designed the auditorium with three equal arms and a shallow fourth arm to the east, opposite the entrance, somewhat like Stephenson and Greene's plan for the Mayflower Congregational Church across the street. Each of the three arms extends out from its intersection at the center with a double-sloped gable roof and ends in a monitor-shaped facade. Between the double slopes, the architects installed ribbons of stained glass clerestory windows. Originally, above the intersection of the wings, a square lantern with a pyramidal roof added a crowning element, admitting light on the auditorium below through additional stained glass windows (fig. 3.7).[20]

In front of the main facade on the west arm of the church, the architects placed a rectangular vestibule in which three entries lead into the interior, framed

Figure 3.7. First Presbyterian Church, 1525 North Delaware Street, built in 1901–3 and designed by Crapsey and Lamm of Cincinnati, who created a modern church building with Gothic detailing and decoration. Three equal pavilions (arms) intersect at the center, originally crowned by a square lantern. View from southeast in 1915, before removal of the lantern. Bass Photo Co. Collection, Indiana Historical Society. (Image cropped)

by pointed arches (fig. 3.8). Decorative features from Gothic cathedrals provided models for the vestibule facade—gables with open tracery at their bases on either end, stepped buttresses capped by pinnacles with crocketed spires at regular intervals, and a frieze of blind tracery acting as a unifying horizontal element. The architects specified rock-faced Indiana limestone as a veneer for the exterior walls, which are constructed of brick. They incorporated large stained glass windows in the facades for the three arms. In each window, lights with simple shapes culminate in tracery with circles and quatrefoils. At the east end of the auditorium, the architects designed a rectangular Sunday school wing with a two-story central portion and one-story adjuncts to the north and south.

Above, **Figure 3.8.** Facade of First Presbyterian Church (now Redeemer Presbyterian Church), showing the rhythm of stepped buttresses capped by Gothic finials with sculpted crockets. The broad Gothic arch above frames the west stained glass window of the auditorium. 2021 view. James Glass.

Facing, **Figure 3.9.** Main-floor plan, First Presbyterian Church, as initially designed, 1901. Note the Sunday school room in the upper section of the diagram (east end), with classrooms opening to a stage for opening exercises, following the Akron plan. *Plan of the Proposed First Presbyterian Church to Be Erected at the Southeast Corner of Delaware and Sixteenth Street, Indianapolis,* c. 1901, Indiana State Library pamphlet collection.

Inside, the three arms define the 700-seat auditorium, each providing space for banks of pews (fig. 3.9). The worship platform stands at the center of the east wall, which originally contained a pipe organ. Also initially, a gallery seating 150 people occupied the upper level of the west arm.[21] Reflecting the swiftly changing practices of building construction, a system of exposed steel trusses supports

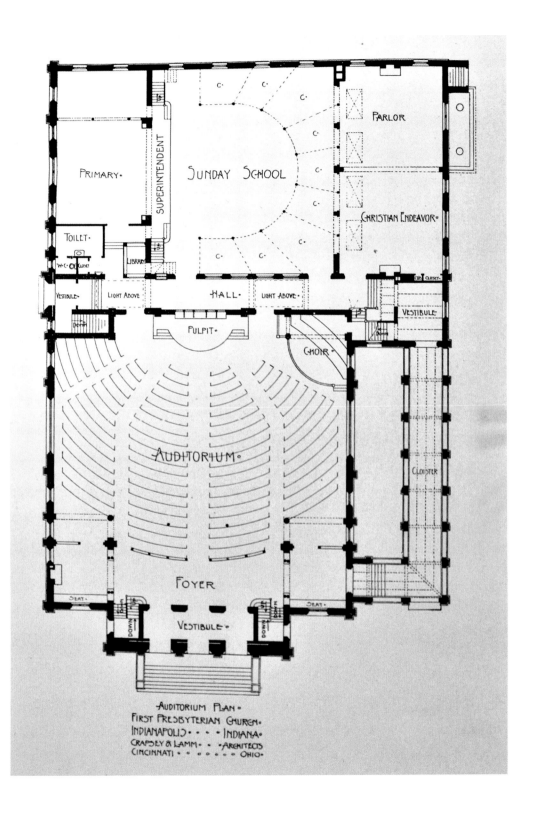

the wooden slopes of the auditorium ceiling and springs in part from four large wooden columns. In the north wall, the central window transmits colored rays from the bright hues of the stained glass panes, which depict foliated designs. Similar panes appear in the west window and smaller windows in the auditorium. The artistic focal point of the sanctuary originally was a large window in the south wall created by Tiffany Studios of New York depicting the archangel Michael. Benjamin Harrison had died during the early stages of the church design, and his widow, Mary Lord Harrison, donated funds for the window in his memory.[22]

Crapsey and Lamm designed a central Sunday school room in the east wing of the church that demonstrated the principles of the Akron plan, which was appearing in Protestant churches across the country. The plan placed a stage along one side of a two-story room and a horseshoe-shaped arrangement of classrooms on two levels along the rear and side walls. At the beginning or end of class sessions, glass partitions could be opened in each room, and the whole church body could engage in unified exercises. Crapsey was one of the first American architects to exploit the Akron plan in church designs. In the basements of the auditorium and Sunday school wing, the architects followed the standard practice of housing a large assembly hall, dining room, and kitchen.[23] The church raised the $108,321 cost of their new building through subscriptions and dedicated it in 1903.[24]

Meridian Street Methodist Episcopal Church (II)

Like the First Baptist congregation, the congregation of the Meridian Street Methodist Episcopal Church suffered the destruction of their building by fire. The conflagration in November 1904 forced the demolition of the Gothic-style structure at New York and Meridian Streets, completed in 1867–70 (see chap. 5 of vol. 1). The congregation resolved to rebuild and hired Oscar Bohlen of D. A. Bohlen and Son, experienced in church design, as their architect. In 1905, the church purchased a lot on the northwest corner of St. Clair and Meridian Streets, and Bohlen devised a Gothic design sure to capture attention along the still-residential Meridian Street (fig. 3.10).[25]

Facing, Figure 3.10. Meridian Street Methodist Episcopal Church (II), 802 North Meridian Street, built in 1905–6 and designed by Oscar D. Bohlen and D. A. Bohlen and Son, drawing on the traditional formula for Gothic cathedrals—twin spires, central Decorated Gothic window with elaborate rose tracery, three entries, and a rectangular nave. View c. 1925. Bass Photo Co. Collection, Indiana Historical Society. (Image cropped)

Figure 3.11. Former Meridian Street Methodist Episcopal Church in 2022. The congregation moved in 1952, and the Indiana Business College remodeled the building to serve as classrooms and meeting spaces. The structure was adapted for apartments through the intervention of Indiana Landmarks in 2007. James Glass.

The architect gave the facade monumentality by flanking it with symmetrical spires that rose 150 feet. He gave the towers supporting the spires octagonal shapes and reinforced them with stepped buttresses. Bohlen used lancet Gothic openings for the belfries, topped by pointed gables. Between the towers at ground level, he fashioned a trio of dressed limestone entries with pronounced Gothic gables. Above the entries and recessed between the towers, a large Decorated Gothic window with stained glass lights and tracery acted as a counterpoint to the spires. Along the sides of the rectangular auditorium, ten windows, twenty-five feet tall, provided daylight. Each window contained two lights with pointed arches and a quatrefoil head similar to those in English churches such as Westminster Abbey. Between the auditorium windows, Bohlen placed decorative stepped buttresses.[26]

The architect constructed the whole church building with brick walls and applied rock-faced limestone on most of the exterior and dressed stone for sculpted details, window architraves, and the water table. The auditorium with its gallery could seat one thousand congregants; the ceiling rose fifty feet overhead. Bohlen provided for a full basement finished in yellow pine that presumably was to serve as a social room and house a kitchen. In the rear Sunday school wing, Bohlen placed a rose window in the south gable, above an elaborate entrance to the wing. When the new church opened in 1906, the total cost came to about $90,000.[27]

All Saints Episcopal Cathedral

The Episcopal Diocese of Indianapolis invoked a different interpretation of Gothic in 1910 when it began construction of an Episcopal cathedral. In 1888, Bishop Davis Knickerbocker had bought a large tract along the east side of Central Avenue immediately south of Sixteenth Street as the site for a frame cathedral building and several other diocesan buildings. In 1909, under the leadership of Bishop Joseph Francis, the diocese and cathedral parish raised $40,000 to build a permanent cathedral at Sixteenth and Central. They hired English-born Alfred Grindle, an Indianapolis architect, to design it. Grindle devised a design that provided dignity and monumentality but exceeded the budget of the diocese for the project. He conceived of a red brick building with a cruciform plan, crowned at the crossing by a rectangular tower (fig. 3.12).[28]

The diocese decided to build Grindle's design in phases, and in 1910, the architect supervised construction of the nave proper and the transepts in their final, permanent state. The diocese deferred building the crossing tower, the apse intended by Grindle for the east side of the crossing, and a chapel adjoining the north transept. As a temporary substitute for the intended apse, the architect designed a T-shaped frame structure at the east end of the crossing containing a small, faceted apse, along with a choir room, sacristies, and vestry rooms.[29]

At the time, the *Indianapolis News* referred to the style of the new All Saints Cathedral as "Early English Gothic," and indeed, there are elements that hark back to the Early Gothic period in England, particularly the lancet windows in the west facade, along the nave, and in the transepts. Above the entrance in the west facade, Grindle devised a large, pointed arch of dressed limestone, within which he inserted a trio of lancet windows, similar to those that had been used in Gothic

Facing top, **Figure 3.12.** Drawing by architect Alfred Grindle of his initial design for All Saints Episcopal Cathedral, 1910. Note that an imposing square tower was originally intended for the crossing. Courtesy of All Saints Episcopal Church.

Facing bottom, **Figure 3.13.** All Saints Episcopal Cathedral (now Church) as built, 1559 Central Avenue. Notable features include early English Gothic lancet windows, Latin Cross plan, and stepped buttresses along the nave. 2020 view. James Glass.

Above, **Figure 3.14.** Looking from the crossing west through the nave, All Saints Cathedral, in 1911. Note the braces and collar beams that support the roof, drawn from English medieval parish churches. Bass Photo Co. Collection, Indiana Historical Society. (Image cropped)

ARCHITECT PROFILE

Alfred Grindle

Alfred Grindle (1863–1940) was a major architectural practitioner in Indiana from the 1890s through the 1920s. He was born near Sherwood Forest in England and trained in architecture at King Charles School and in art at the Manchester Institute of Art. While at King Charles School, young Grindle became proficient in drawing and became an authority on creating organic ornament pictured in the noted book *The Grammar of Ornament* by Owen Jones. After marriage, Grindle immigrated to the United States in 1888, stopping briefly in New Jersey. He made his way to Fort Wayne, Indiana, where he opened an office. His practice soon extended to Muncie, and he designed several notable residences there, such as the Suzanne Thomas House and later the Grace Episcopal Church.

In 1908, he moved to Indianapolis and expanded his practice. Two of his notable commissions in the state capital involved English architectural sources—All Saints Episcopal Cathedral and the Alfred M. and Minnie Stroup Glossbrenner House (see chaps. 3 and 4 of this volume). He also became active in the architectural profession in the city, serving in 1915 as president of the Architects' Association of Indianapolis. He developed particular proficiency in drawing colored perspectives in pen and ink and advised younger draftsmen on the Beaux Arts method of design for competitions held in Indianapolis.

In 1920, Grindle moved to Brown County for health reasons and opened an architectural office in Bloomington, where he designed numerous residences, civic buildings, and Trinity Episcopal Church.

His family estimated that he designed buildings and houses valued at more than $20 million during his career. He also served as choirmaster and organist at All Saints Episcopal Cathedral in Indianapolis.

Sources: "Alfred Grindle Services Today," *Indianapolis Star*, January 6, 1940, 12; "Architects Show Designs," *Indianapolis Star*, May 19, 1911, 13; "Architects Plan Contest," *Indianapolis Star*, October 3, 1913, 11; "Architects' Association Selects New President," *Indianapolis Star*, December 17, 1915, 3; "Alfred Grindle," Bloominpedia, 2024. https://www.bloomingpedia.org/w/index.php?title=Alfred_Grindle&action=history; City of Muncie, "Walking Tour #3—Historic Architecture in the Emily Kimbrough Historic District, Muncie, Indiana," c. 2000. https://www.muncie.in.gov/egov/documents/1621350220_4887.pdf. Source for photo: "Architects' Association Selects New President."

Episcopal churches in the United States since the 1850s (see chap. 3 of vol. 1).[30] He repeated the trio of lancets theme within the gables of the north and south transepts. Immediately above the ground-level entrance in the facade, Grindle designed a smaller limestone arch that encloses lancet arches with blind stone panels. He recessed the lancet windows along the north and south elevations of the nave in deep reveals and outlined the pointed arches with limestone moldings. He added rhythm to the side elevations by placing ornamental buttresses with limestone caps between the windows (fig. 3.13).[31]

In the interior, the architect turned the limited budget to an advantage by specifying bare brick walls in the nave and transepts, achieving an austere dignity unusual for churches of the period. He recalled the exposed timber truss tradition of medieval English parish churches by designing braces and collar beams to support the open roof structure (fig. 3.14).[32] In the late 1960s or early 1970s, All Saints Episcopal Church replaced Grindle's temporary frame apse with a permanent brick apse in the Modern style designed by architect Evans Woollen.[33]

St. Mary's Catholic Church

One of the most majestic expressions of Gothic architecture in Indianapolis came about when the German parish of St. Mary's Catholic Church decided to move. They had been housed in their Gothic-style brick church building on East Maryland Street since 1858 (see chap. 3 of vol. 1). Gradually, the downtown business district engulfed the church and its school, and its parishioners moved north and northeast to the Germantown neighborhood east of the Mile Square. The pastor of the church, Father Anthony Schiedeler, and the chief laymen in the parish desired a more spacious location closer to the residences of their members. They chose the southeast corner of Vermont and New Jersey Streets and purchased several lots in 1907. Providentially, Chicago architect Hermann Gaul provided plans for a new church without charge to repay Father Schiedeler for introducing him to the family of Gaul's future wife during a visit to Indianapolis.[34]

The architect had grown up in Cologne, Germany, near the historic cathedral and told the pastor that he had always wanted to build a church with "the stamp of [Cologne Cathedral's] beauty."[35] Accordingly, for the new St. Mary's Church, he drew elements from the cathedral design and adapted them for a much-smaller parish church. He gave St. Mary's a Latin Cross plan similar to that in Cologne, with a nave, transepts, and an apse, and clad the exterior with sparkling gray-white Indiana limestone (fig. 3.15).[36] He considered the facade of Cologne Cathedral (see fig. 3.16) and developed a composition for St. Mary's that took several essential elements—the twin spires, three entries, a central window, and a gable between the spires—and interpreted them at a scale appropriate for the church. The three entries are framed in pointed arches with deep reveals and stepped columns. Over each arch is a steeply pointed gable based on those in Cologne, but with blind tracery instead of the openwork of the original. Gaul adapted the stone tabernacles and pinnacles that flank the entries in Cologne for use on either side of each entrance in Indianapolis. In the St. Mary's facade, the architect made the central window above the entries the dominant feature of the second story. Within a broad, pointed arch, he crafted a rose window with Gothic tracery below.[37]

Gaul sent the spires of St. Mary's soaring, with their heights of 160 feet making them monumental elements in his composition.[38] He adorned the lower stories with pointed gables similar to Cologne. One of the most striking features of the Cologne facade—encrustations of tabernacles on the lower stages of the spires—Gaul incorporated in layers at the corners of the belfries and the first story of the spires of St. Mary's. He worked with sculptor Alexander Sangernebo in the creation of the Gothic details of the facade, including gargoyles.[39]

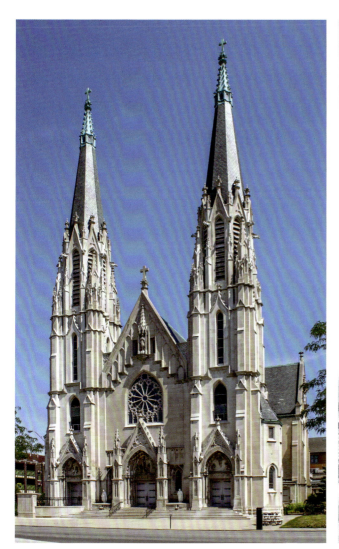 

Left, **Figure 3.15.** St. Mary's Catholic Church, 317 North New Jersey Street, built in 1911–12 and designed by Hermann Gaul of Chicago, who derived inspiration for the plan and many details from the medieval Gothic masterpiece Cologne Cathedral. Note the 160-foot-high twin spires encrusted with Gothic tabernacles, the elaborate three entries with sharply pointed gables, the central window with rose tracery, the central gable between the towers, and the profusion of sculpture, created by Alexander Sangernebo. View in 2013. James Glass.

Right, **Figure 3.16.** 1896 photo of the facade of Cologne Cathedral, Cologne, Germany, designed in c. 1320 and completed in the nineteenth century. Note the elements similar to St. Mary's: twin spires, encrustation of tabernacles on all sides of the towers and belfries, the central gable between the towers, and the three entries with pointed gables. Differing from St. Mary's, there are five large windows across the second story, gables with openwork sculpted detail, and a concentration of gables and tabernacles over every part of the facade. Courtesy of Schlesinger Library, Harvard Radcliffe Institute.

Facing, **Figure 3.17.** View of the nave of St. Mary's Church from the north aisle. Note the hall church plan, with nave and aisles of the same height, the cylindrical marble columns modeled on those in medieval Italian or German churches, and the quadripartite Gothic vaults. View in 2021. James Glass.

The architect used sculptures effectively to decorate the facade and interpret the Christian message. At the apex of the central gable, Gaul specified a statue of St. Mary, standing within a tabernacle. In the tympanums above the three entries, he incorporated bas-relief sculptures showing the Nativity, Crucifixion, and Ascension. And around the spires, he inserted gargoyles.[40]

Within the interior, Gaul used elements of the High Gothic in medieval cathedrals to complement the exterior design (fig. 3.17). He laid out a hall church plan in which the central nave and flanking aisles are of the same height. On either side of the crossing, he created shallow transepts. At the east end of the crossing, he designed a four-sided apse that originally contained the high altar from the Maryland Street church. The architect modeled the cylindrical marble columns and capitals between the nave and aisles on those in such medieval churches as Milan Cathedral, the Santa Croce church in Florence, and the Frauenkirche in Nuremberg.[41] Along the walls of the aisles and transepts, he employed piers adorned with colonnettes and capped by capitals with bas-relief sculptures of flowers. At the rear of the church, Gaul placed a loft for the choir and pipe organ. Overhead, he employed ribbed, quadripartite vaults of stone. Initially, the parish installed art glass windows from the Maryland Street building along the aisles.[42] In 1912, the final cost of this monumental and elaborately decorated church came to $250,000, one of the largest construction budgets of any church in the city to that point.[43]

German Evangelical Zion Church

One of the prime Indianapolis congregations from the Evangelical tradition of northern Germany had been founded in 1841. The German Evangelical Zion Church worshipped between 1867 and 1913 in a brick building with round-headed windows on the north side of Ohio Street between Meridian and Illinois Streets. In 1912, the congregation decided to erect a new edifice outside of what was then the downtown. The church acquired the northeast corner of North and New Jersey Streets, close to the concentration of German American residents east of the business district. They also hired Oscar Bohlen of D. A. Bohlen and Son as their architect.[44]

Above, **Figure 3.18.** German Evangelical Zion Church (now Zion Evangelical United Church of Christ), 603 North New Jersey Street, built in 1912–13 and designed by Oscar D. Bohlen of D. A. Bohlen and Son, employing a popular formula for churches of that period that involved a large rectangular tower on the corner, an echoing smaller tower on the other side of the facade, and, frequently, a vestibule in between. Note the Gothic details—pinnacles, stepped buttresses, and pointed arch windows. View in 2019. James Glass.

Facing, **Figure 3.19.** One of the art glass windows depicting scenes from the life of Jesus, created for the German Evangelical Zion Church by the Ford Brothers of Minneapolis, using opalescent glass and the rich hues popularized by Tiffany Studios. View in 2019. James Glass.

Bohlen developed an exterior design with Gothic details that, in its basics, had become a formula for many Protestant churches in Indiana and elsewhere. The formula called for a cruciform-shaped plan, with a tall, square tower on one side of the facade and a shorter tower echoing the larger one on the other. Sometimes the rear wall of the auditorium was recessed between the two towers; in other cases, it was flush with the tower facades. An early example of the formula appeared with the construction of the First Methodist Episcopal Church in the new town of Gary, Indiana, in 1907–8. That building was constructed of brick, the tall

tower appeared on the right side of the facade, and the rear auditorium wall was recessed between the towers. Several years later, in Indianapolis, the congregation of Broadway Methodist Episcopal Church constructed a larger version with a limestone exterior at Twenty-Second Street and Broadway. In that case, the tall tower appeared on the left side of the facade, and the sanctuary's rear wall was flush with the facade.[45]

For Zion, Bohlen produced an imposing version of the formula (fig. 3.18). He placed a hundred-foot-tall tower on the right side of the facade, sure to command attention on both New Jersey and North Streets, and devised a two-story tower with similar details on the left side. Between the two towers, Bohlen deeply recessed the rear sanctuary wall to accommodate a spacious rectangular narthex with its own crenellated roof. He constructed the exterior of the church with a reddish-orange, glazed brick and used limestone for details. The architect gave the corner tower added prominence by adding copper-roofed pinnacles on each corner of the top. In between, he specified crenellations. He decorated the second tower with similar buttresses and topped it with crenellations composed of square and pointed panels. Like many churches of the early twentieth century, Zion's design included a trio of entrances, symbolizing the Trinity. The architect visually reinforced the corners of the lower stories with simple buttresses.[46]

The auditorium inside Zion is dominated by superb art glass windows that depict scenes from the life and teachings of Jesus Christ. The Ford Brothers of Minneapolis created the windows, the largest of which resemble the brilliant landscape scenes created by Tiffany Studios for many of their church windows (fig. 3.19).[47] Bohlen gave the auditorium a polygonal shape. Overhead, he constructed a domed plaster ceiling in which eight ribs come together at the apex. At the east end, he created an apse for the chancel and a second "apse" for the organ. The congregation completed the building in 1913 at an approximate cost of $100,000.[48]

Central Universalist Church

The former building of the Central Universalist Church represents simplicity in the use of Gothic details and a modest construction budget. The Universalist denomination had been slow to establish itself in Indianapolis, but in 1884, a group of adherents organized the Central Universalist Church. Its first permanent home came in 1894 after John Herron and his wife, Electa Turrel Herron, donated a lot on the northwest corner of Fifteenth and New Jersey Streets. Fire gutted the initial frame building a couple of years later, and the congregation promptly rebuilt.

Figure 3.20. Former Central Universalist Church, 1502 North New Jersey Street, built in 1904, originally constructed with stucco and timbers on the outside. It retains its Gothic windows. Now a private residence. View from 2020. James Glass.

In 1904, a second fire badly damaged the new structure. Led by their pastor, Dr. Marion Crosley, the Central Universalist members again rebuilt.[49]

The third building features a central, gable-roofed section containing the auditorium (fig. 3.20). Immediately to the east, the designer placed a rectangular, one-story wing containing the vestibule and a small chapel. The exterior received a coat of stucco, with half-timbering in the south gable and in the parapet of the vestibule/chapel segment. The congregation chose lancet Gothic windows for the south wall of the auditorium and vestibule and pointed gable moldings for the windows on the east facade. They installed stained glass in all the windows. The designer used exposed timbers in the auditorium to support the roof. The building has been adapted for use as a residence and retains all the essential elements of its character, with some additions since its construction.[50]

BUILDINGS OF WORSHIP | 253

St. Anthony's Catholic Church

The industrial suburb of Haughville grew up in the 1880s on the west bank of White River. Benjamin Haugh and his partners developed the principal factory, an ironworks, and hired many workmen, who moved with their families into cottages on newly platted lots. Population growth led to incorporation as a town, and in 1897, the city of Indianapolis annexed Haughville. By 1914, the area's rough boundaries ran from White River west to the Central State Hospital for the Insane and from Washington Street north to Tenth.[51]

The workers in Haughville included immigrants from several European nationalities—Irish, Hungarian, Slavonian, and German—most of which were Catholic. Bishop Francis Chatard of Indianapolis moved to organize a parish at the heart of the community in 1886. Father Michael Collier purchased an acre of land on the southeast corner of Vermont and Warman Streets, and in 1891, the parish dedicated a church building and school. By 1903, the congregation had outgrown its building of worship, and Father Joseph F. Byrne led efforts to raise funds to construct a much-larger edifice. The diocese hired architect Cornelius Custin, who appears to have been from out of town, to design the new red brick structure. Custin drew on standard elements of church design at the time—a nave with a gable roof and a facade with a central window flanked by two towers—and embellished the facade with limestone details derived from Gothic architecture (fig. 3.21).[52]

Custin designed an unusual limestone vestibule that projects from the center of the facade, decorated by sculpted stepped buttresses, tabernacles, and a parapet with crenellations. Above the vestibule, a rose window dominates the facade proper. It is framed by an ogee arch with limestone voussoirs that rises to a pinnacle. The architect inserted another novel detail—slender, arched openings that contain two-light windows only in their top halves—into the west and north faces of the north tower. He capped each of these openings with a smaller ogee arch and pinnacle. At the top of the north tower, Custin constructed an octagonal belfry with crenellations, crowned by a truncated spire.[53] The south tower echoes the design of the north, but in the upper story, two rectangular windows with Tudor dripstone moldings appear in lieu of an arch and belfry.

Custin designed the nave of the church without transepts or a crossing but provided a generous apse at the east end for the high altar. The nave and gallery together could seat one thousand people. Originally the high altar incorporated Gothic spires, pinnacles, and tracery, as well as statues of St. Anthony and the Sacred Heart of Jesus. On either side of the apse are smaller altars of similar design

Figure 3.21. St. Anthony's Catholic Church, 377 North Warman Avenue, Haughville, built in 1903–4 and designed by architect Cornelius Custin, using the formula of two square towers on either side of the facade but a spire on top of a belfry on one side and a pyramidal roof on the other side. Note the Gothic details—pinnacles, stepped buttresses, and crenellations; a central rose window; and the Tudor-style dripstone and ogee arch on the facade. View in 2021. James Glass.

dedicated to St. Mary and another saint. Art glass windows in the nave depicted the patron saints of the principal four European nations represented by members of the parish: St. Elizabeth of Hungary, Saints Cyril and Methodius of Slavonia, St. Boniface of Germany, and St. Patrick of Ireland. The parish completed construction of the church in November 1904 for a total cost of $30,000.[54]

Holy Trinity Slovenian Catholic Church

By the beginning of the twentieth century, Haughville was attracting new immigrants, especially from eastern and southeastern Europe. A large colony of new arrivals from Slovenia and other parts of the Austro-Hungarian Empire established themselves in the residential neighborhood north and east of the Central State Hospital and near the large National Malleable Castings Company foundry. Bishop Chatard desired to organize a parish devoted to Slovenian Americans and at length persuaded Father Joseph Lavrie, a recent Austrian immigrant who spoke the Slovenian language, to move to Indianapolis and found the Holy Trinity Slovenian Catholic Church. Lavrie acquired a site for a church building on the northeast corner of Calvelage Street and Holmes Avenue, and the diocese and new parish retained Indianapolis architect George V. Bedell to design the church structure.[55]

At that point, Bedell was establishing himself as a designer of buildings for worship in the city. In consulting with the Holy Trinity parishioners, he found that some desired a building in "the Roman style." Therefore, he prepared plans showing a church structure with round-headed Romanesque arches above the windows, entry, and belfry openings. When he presented his initial drawings to the parish, many in the congregations told him that they desired Gothic pinnacles and a high, pointed spire. The architect patiently revised the design to incorporate several Gothic elements. The result was a hybrid blend of Romanesque and Gothic (fig. 3.22). The diocese and parish laid the cornerstone in 1906 and completed the building in 1907.[56]

In his initial design, Bedell provided for a nave and transepts. The final design eliminated the transepts and retained a nave with a gabled roof.[57] He constructed the building of red, load-bearing brick, with limestone trim. The focal point of the facade is the central tower, which rises four stories and culminates in a copper spire. Bedell incorporated four elements into the facade that catches the eye. At the center on the ground level, he placed the entrance, sheltered by a limestone Romanesque arch supported by Tuscan columns on either side. He crowned the arch with a pointed Gothic gable. Above the entry, he arranged a large rose window with limestone molding, echoed on either side of the tower by two smaller

Facing, Figure 3.22. Former Holy Trinity Slovenian Catholic Church, 901 North Holmes Avenue, Haughville, built in 1906 and designed by architect George V. Bedell of Indianapolis, using a mixture of Gothic and Romanesque details. Note the Gothic stepped buttresses and pinnacles and the Romanesque arches and rose windows. Closed as a parish in 2014. View in 2021. James Glass.

ARCHITECT PROFILE

George V. Bedell

George V. Bedell (1862–1948) was born in Madison, Indiana, and moved to Indianapolis as a child. He became proficient as a builder and obtained training and experience as an architect. About 1898, he began practice as an architect-builder and designed most building types, including schools, office buildings, houses, and neighborhood movie theaters. In the first and second decades of the twentieth century, Bedell developed church design as a specialty and served as the architect for Holy Trinity Slovenian Catholic Church, St. Francis de Sales Catholic Church, St. Philip Neri Catholic Church, and the Congregation Sharah Tessila. He also prepared the initial plans for Holy Rosary Catholic Church. Bedell expanded his business by obtaining the contracts to build some of the structures he designed.

Other Indianapolis buildings for which he served as architect include St. Mary's Academy and School, the Ritz Theater, Talbott Theater, and the Indianapolis Glove Company factory. Bedell retired in 1937.

Sources: "G. V. Bedell, Builder, Dies," *Indianapolis Star*, October 11, 1948, 1; "New Holy Rosary Catholic Church," *Indianapolis News*, May 31, 1910, 14. Source for photo: "G. V. Bedell, Builder, Dies."

rose windows. The tall, round-headed windows along the south and north sides of the nave resemble Italian Renaissance–style openings. To highlight them, Bedell used courses of brick headers to compose the arches, which rest on limestone impost blocks. To make the design more Gothic, he added stepped buttresses at the corners of the tower and facade and between the nave windows. Finally, he placed Gothic pinnacles above the fourth story of the tower.

CLASSICAL

As related in chapter 2 of this volume, during the 1890s, an interest in the architecture of imperial Rome and ancient Greece spread across the country, spurred by the monumental Classical-style buildings that dominated the Columbian Exposition of 1893 in Chicago. Such architectural firms as McKim, Mead, and White and D. H. Burnham and Company drew directly from the language of Roman buildings for public buildings and occasionally for buildings of worship. In such designs, these firms derived compositional ideas and details from the ancient originals, not as distilled and interpreted by the Italian Renaissance. Architectural journals published drawings and photographs of Roman and Greek landmarks, and architects across the country could easily produce buildings with Classical elements. As the twentieth century opened in Indianapolis, several congregations chose designs for their buildings that were based in part on Roman or Greek architecture. In these structures, the architects did not recreate the plans or elevations of ancient buildings; rather, they added Classical details to provide a unifying architectural theme to modern churches or synagogues.

First Church of Christ, Scientist

The Christian Science movement, founded by Mary Baker Eddy in 1879, rapidly gained adherents during the 1890s and the early twentieth century in the United States. During the years after the Columbian Exposition, Christian Science congregations increasingly favored buildings incorporating details from the architecture of ancient Greece or imperial Rome. Anna B. Dorland, a student of Eddy, organized the First Church of Christ, Scientist in Indianapolis about 1892. The congregation worshipped in the Propylaeum on North Street for several years and grew rapidly. In 1911, a building committee pursued the construction of a substantial church structure. They acquired two lots on Meridian Street south of

Facing top, **Figure 3.23.** First Church of Christ, Scientist, 2011 North Meridian Street, built in 1911–12 and designed by Rubush and Hunter with a Greek Doric portico modeled on temples of ancient Athens that includes a full entablature of triglyphs, metopes, and mutules. Photo c. 1911. *Year Book of the Indiana Chapter A.I.A. and Catalog of the Third Annual Exhibition 1912* (Indianapolis: Indiana Chapter A.I.A., 1912).

Facing bottom, **Figure 3.24.** Former First Church of Christ, Scientist (now the Julian Center), view from southeast, 2023. James Glass.

Twenty-First Street and hired Indianapolis architects Rubush and Hunter to design their building. The architects devised a rectangular brick structure and fronted it with a Classical portico (figs. 3.23 and 3.24).[58]

The *Indianapolis Star* said of the design, "The building is unique in that it is a radical departure from the design adopted by most congregations. It is quite monumental, the design being of Greek-Doric style."[59] And, in fact, Rubush and Hunter did design a tetrastyle portico consisting of four Doric columns fluted in the Greek manner and modeled on such Athenian monuments as the Parthenon and the Temple of Hephaestus. The limestone columns support an entablature and pediment similar to that of the Hephaestus temple, including an architrave and frieze with triglyphs. A stairway led up to the portico, much in the manner of a Greek or Roman temple, and the portico served as a porch to shield worshippers from inclement weather. The architects created three entries in the inner wall of the portico, with each entry corresponding to one of the three openings among the columns. Plain limestone surrounds frame the entries, which have simple, projecting cornices. The architects effectively contrasted the gray-white color of the facade with the red brick of the building proper.

The entries led to a vestibule, from which parishioners could enter the Sunday school room and committee rooms on the ground floor. The architects located the seven-hundred-seat auditorium on the second floor. It was a rectangular room with a coved, plaster ceiling supported by beams forming segmental arches. Art glass skylights provided additional natural light in panels between the beams. Along the sides of the auditorium, the architects provided simple six-over-six sash windows. At the east end, a rectangular apse contained the platform for reading texts during each service.[60]

The congregation dedicated its building at 2011 North Meridian in 1912. The total cost came to $75,000.[61]

Second Church of Christ, Scientist

Only eleven years after the First Church of Christ was organized, another Christian Scientist congregation came into being. The Second Church of Christ, Scientist constructed a small, one-story brick building for its initial needs in 1905 at Walnut and Meridian Street. The architect fronted the rectangular structure with a wooden portico supported by Tuscan columns. The congregation quickly outgrew the small Classical building and moved their meetings to the new Masonic Temple. Finally, in 1912, with their attendance grown to one thousand people, the Second Church of Christ planned a substantial, permanent building. They acquired the northeast corner of Twelfth and Delaware Streets for $30,000 and hired one of the principal architects of Christian Scientist churches in the country, Solon Spencer Beman of Chicago, to design their building. Beman believed that the architectural language of imperial Rome and ancient Greece, associated with the early Christian Church and its primitive ideals of healing, was the most appropriate for the emerging denomination. He and his son, Spencer Solon Beman, had designed several Christian Science churches around the country before the Indianapolis congregation approached them.[62]

The projected budget of $110,000 enabled the architects to design a substantial, even monumental, edifice that would dominate its corner.[63] They devised a rectangular building constructed of brick, with Bedford limestone cladding the exterior (fig. 3.25). As the focal point of the facade, the Bemans fashioned a pavilion projecting slightly forward at the center, approached by two flights of stairs, somewhat like a Roman temple. At the top of the stairs, parishioners passed through a screen of colossal Roman Tuscan columns standing in antis and entered an open vestibule. The columns support an entablature consisting of an architrave, frieze, and steeply projecting cornice. From Greek architecture, the architects derived triglyphs, the only ornamental detail along the entablature, which extends from the front pavilion around the remainder of the facade and along the side elevations. The central pavilion continues to the rear of the building, and the architects crowned it with a limestone attic story and a frame half story containing clerestory windows.

Three entries led from the vestibule into a spacious rectangular foyer, from which stairways ascended to the auditorium. To the east of the foyer, the architects located a reading room containing Christian Science literature and a Sunday school room seating 500. The auditorium seated 1,200 people, and the Bemans

Figure 3.25. Former Second Church of Christ, Scientist (now Traders Point Christian Church Downtown), 1201 North Delaware Street, built in 1912–13 and designed by architects Solon Spencer and Spencer Solon Beman of Chicago, creating a modern church building with a Roman Classical colonnade, frontal stairway, and absolute symmetry. The architects believed that the architecture of ancient Rome and ancient Greece were the most appropriate styles for Christian Science churches. View in 2021. James Glass.

designed it so that all congregants had a clear view of the reading desks in the front. The clerestory windows along the sides of the auditorium bathed it in light.[64]

One of the striking features of the finished building was the Bemans' use of translucent stained glass windows in which streaks of amber and green provide an attractive pattern without figural or geometric elements. The architects used lead cames fashioned into patterns of intersecting crosses and X's as frameworks for the windows. The congregation completed construction in 1913.

BUILDINGS OF WORSHIP | 263

Congregation Sharah Tessila

Other religious bodies besides Christian Scientists chose designs for new buildings with Classical features. In 1910, the Sharah Tessila congregation decided to leave their simple frame building in the 700 block of South Meridian Street and build an imposing brick structure on the southeast corner of Merrill and Meridian Streets. The members of Sharah Tessila, an Orthodox Jewish congregation organized in 1882, were largely Polish Jews who had emigrated to the United States after the Civil War.[65]

As their architect, the Sharah Tessila building committee chose George V. Bedell, who devised a handsome design incorporating Classical elements.[66] He created a rectangular building with a portico of Ionic limestone columns as the central feature of the facade (fig. 3.26). Two fluted columns stood on brick plinths flanking the central entrance. A stone pediment with a steep profile crowned the entry. Above, Bedell provided for a full entablature on the portico, the rest of the facade, and part of the side elevations. He ornamented the frieze with alternating circle and rectangle motifs in place of the metopes and triglyphs of a Classical Greek frieze. At the top of the portico, a pediment with a pronounced profile projected forward. The architect observed Classical/Renaissance symmetry in the facade and side elevations, placing side entries with pediments at ground level on either side of the frontal portico and matching entablatures supported by consoles above the side entries.

Although he used a rectangular footprint for the synagogue, Bedell suggested Christian-style transepts by designing a cross gable at the rear of the building. He topped the faces of the "transepts" with pediments and applied Doric pilasters. He also mixed in elements from medieval Christian churches, such as a rose window in the facade of the north "transept" and ornamental Gothic buttresses in the side elevations.[67]

Inside, the architect provided an auditorium and gallery seating six hundred people and finished both in oak, with tinted walls. He placed Sabbath classrooms, toilets, and the heating plant in the basement. The growing prosperity of the congregation is indicated by the $25,000 cost of the finished building, fully furnished and equipped.[68]

Figure 3.26. +Congregation Sharah Tessila, 601 South Meridian Street, built in 1910 and designed by George V. Bedell of Indianapolis using an Ionic temple front and other Classical details from the architecture of the Greeks and Romans as the language for the exterior. Note the rose window drawn from Christian medieval churches in the side elevation. View from 1929. Demolished in c. 1964, when Sharah Tessila merged with other Orthodox congregations on the south side and moved to the north side. Bass Photo Co. Collection, Indiana Historical Society. (Image cropped)

Third Christian Church

The third congregation of the Disciples of Christ denomination to be organized in Indianapolis was founded in 1863. The Third Christian Church met initially in the chapel of the North Western Christian University building at Thirteenth Street and College Avenue. In 1870, the congregation built a modest, story-and-a-half brick church at Thirteenth Street and Ashland Avenue. Having outgrown that building, they constructed a more substantial brick building in the Romanesque style at the same location in 1887. Further growth came rapidly, and the church launched a campaign in 1909 to erect a larger building further north. They purchased two lots on the southwest corner of Seventeenth Street and Broadway and hired the prominent firm of Rubush and Hunter as architects. The architects designed a basement to act as an assembly room for use by the congregation while the church raised funds for building the auditorium. The contractor finished the room in 1910. In 1912, the congregation called the Reverend Thomas W. Grafton as pastor to lead them in raising the funds necessary to complete the church. The following year, they were ready to resume construction.[69]

Rubush and Hunter did not design the Third Christian building above ground. The congregation instead turned to another local architect, Charles E. Bacon, to design their structure.[70] He planned a two-story brick building, rectangular in shape, and used Classical features as the predominant theme for the facade and side elevations (fig. 3.27). Bacon made a temple front the focal point of the facade. Two limestone Ionic columns stood in antis above a high stone foundation, flanked by brick Doric pilasters. The columns and pilasters supported a limestone entablature composed of an Ionic architrave, plain brick frieze, dentils, and projecting cornice. A pediment with plain tympanum and dentils completed the temple front. The entablature continued along the rest of the facade and along the side elevations, supported by brick Doric pilasters. Identical entrances framed in stone with Etruscan/Roman ears flanked the temple front. The recessed transom windows above the entry doors incorporated cames forming the pattern of crosses superimposed over X's often seen in buildings of the period with Classical features. Bacon devised tall, round-headed windows for the facade and side elevations, illustrating the mixture of stylistic elements found in many buildings of worship from the period. Each window contained Romanesque tracery consisting of two lights with round heads and a circular light at the top. The architect recessed the three windows on the facade between the Ionic columns. All windows contained stained glass with an amber hue.

Figure 3.27. +Third Christian Church, 1660 Broadway, built between 1910 and 1914 and designed above the basement by Charles E. Bacon of Indianapolis, using an Ionic temple front recessed into the facade, where the columns stand in antis. Other Classical elements include a full entablature and Doric pilasters along the side elevations. Note the Romanesque windows with round-headed arches incorporated into the design. The view is undated; from c. 1915–20. In 1963, the congregation moved to a new location on what is now Binford Boulevard. Their former building became the Broadway Christian Center until 1972, when it was demolished. The site is now part of Dr. Martin Luther King Jr. Memorial Park. Charles M. Fillmore, *History of Third Christian Church of Indianapolis, Indiana* (Indianapolis: Third Church Board, 1943), vol. 2.

Bacon devoted most of the space in the building to a two-story auditorium with a gallery at its rear. The auditorium seated 900 persons, and by combining the prayer meeting room under the gallery with the auditorium, 1,200 people could be accommodated. Twelve Sunday school rooms in the basement could be opened to create an assembly room seating 1,000. The basement also included a dining room and kitchen. The cost of the completed building came to approximately $90,000.[71]

BUILDINGS OF WORSHIP | 267

St. Paul Methodist Episcopal Church (now Christ Missionary Baptist Church)

A couple of years before the final construction of Third Christian Church, another congregation erected a building with a similar exterior design that incorporated Classical details. Laypeople residing in the industrial suburb of North Indianapolis had organized North Indianapolis Methodist Episcopal Church in 1884 and constructed a frame church building near Radar and Eugene Streets in 1885. Rapid growth among the mainly white working-class population of the suburb led the church to raise the funds needed to begin construction of a substantial brick building in 1910. Led by the Reverend Charles A. Parkin, the congregation took a new name, St. Paul Methodist Episcopal Church. They acquired a double lot on the southwest corner of Eugene and Radar. The unknown architect devised a three-story brick structure, rectangular in shape, in which simple double-hung sash windows containing stained glass lined each story (fig. 3.28).[72]

As at Third Christian, the designer placed a temple front at the center of the facade, above the first story, and pilasters between windows on the side elevations. With a smaller, $33,000 budget, he fashioned the temple front using brick Doric pilasters applied to the facade instead of recessing them in antis. Similarly to Third Christian Church, a full Classical entablature of brick and sheet metal extended around the east and west sides. The architect applied no ornamental details to the frieze. A pediment with a decorative circular motif in the tympanum completes the temple front. The designer located two recessed entries on the ground floor, to the east and west of the temple front, and rusticated the brick courses of the first story. As a non-Classical element, he used projecting vertical brick courses to outline and tie together the windows of the second and third floors. The congregation constructed a brick parsonage adjacent to the rear of the church building.[73]

Inside, the designer provided for a social room and kitchen on the first floor and a two-story auditorium on the second and third floors. A balcony offered additional space around the rear and sides of the auditorium. In 1955, the building became the home of Christ Missionary Baptist Church, an African American congregation.[74]

Westminster Presbyterian Church

A third example of a Classical temple front in the design of a brick church building came in 1916, when a new Presbyterian congregation on the east side raised funds to construct a sizeable building at 445 North State Avenue. The congregation

Figure 3.28. Former St. Paul Methodist Episcopal Church (now Christ Missionary Baptist Church), 1001 Eugene Street, North Indianapolis, built in 1910 and designed with a Classical temple front composed of brick Doric pilasters and full entablature and pediment on the facade and pilasters along the side elevations. The Christ Missionary Baptist Church, an African American congregation, was organized on West Seventeenth Street in 1919 and moved to this building in 1955. "About Christ Missionary [Baptist] Church, n.d., https://www.cmbcindy.org/cmbc-indy-history, accessed June 24, 2024. View in 2023. James Glass.

hired Indianapolis architect Lewis H. Sturges to design their structure. Sturges had been in the city since 1904 and had served initially as supervising architect for the Hetherington and Berner ironworks and more recently in private practice.[75]

The architect devised a rectangular brick building set on a knoll above State Avenue and used a couple of Classical elements similar to those employed by Bacon and the architect of St. Paul Methodist Episcopal Church (fig. 3.29). Unlike the other two architects, Sturges gave his structure two facades. On the south side,

Figure 3.29. Former Westminster Presbyterian Church, 445 North State Avenue, built in 1916 and designed by Lewis H. Sturges of Indianapolis, using a brick Classical temple front at the center of the south elevation and large Doric pilasters linked by Greek fretwork. View in 2023. Now the SOMA Downtown church. James Glass.

facing Sturm Avenue, he applied a temple front composed of abstracted Doric pilasters with brick shafts and limestone capitals, a brick architrave and frieze, and a projecting frame pediment. For the larger facade, facing State Avenue, he placed three entries at the center, each with limestone, eared architraves. Colossal Doric pilasters divided the west facade into three sections and continued with narrower shafts on the south elevation. Sturges continued the brick architrave/frieze and projecting cornice of the temple front along the rest of the south facade and along the west elevation, unifying the two fronts. As another horizontal element, he employed a limestone fret pattern along the heads of the third-floor windows on the south and west facades. The architect used large stained glass windows along the second and third stories as vertical elements, complementing the pilasters.

The Westminster building includes three stories, counting the basement. Sturges located the one-thousand-seat auditorium with a balcony on the second floor, together with a Sunday school assembly room, classrooms, a choir room, and the pastor's study. Following the familiar pattern, he placed a social room and kitchen on the first floor, supplemented by a gymnasium. The total cost to the congregation amounted to $35,000.[76]

Second Baptist Church

A final instance of a Classical temple front and pilasters incorporated into a brick church building came with the long and laborious campaign of the Second Baptist Church to construct a new home. The African American congregation, the second oldest in the Black community, had been founded in 1846 and, after a period of slow growth, began to flourish in the 1860s. In 1867, the church erected a two-story brick building at what is now 428 West Michigan Street and continued to worship there until 1911, when the city building inspector condemned the structure and ordered it torn down. The congregation hired a white architect, William O. Morck of Indianapolis, and, with optimism about the future, directed him to design a building with an imposing scale and character on the site of the former structure. Figure 3.30 shows Morck's sketch of a building that the *Indianapolis Star* said would be "the finest ever erected in Indianapolis by the negro [sic] race."[77]

Morck designed a large building with a seventy-foot frontage on Michigan Street.[78] Above a rusticated first story at the center would be a full Roman-inspired portico in which Corinthian columns would support a pediment ornamented by modillions. Over the portico would rise a Renaissance-style dome, resting on the ridge of the gable roof. The architect provided for a series of stained glass windows with round heads. A large window would appear within the portico and two others of matching size in the side elevations. Morck devised three entries: a central one, deeply recessed, below the portico and the other, smaller ones flanking the pavilion containing the portico. He used ogee-style arches derived from Tudor architecture over the entries.

Unfortunately, the congregation lacked funds to rebuild, and fundraising proved difficult. In the spring of 1912, the congregation under its pastor, the Reverend Boston J. Prince, formed fundraising teams and sought the assistance of white Baptist and other African American congregations in the city. The church set $10,000 as its goal for constructing the first story of their new building, and slowly, money came in. After raising about $5,000, the congregation decided to try and realize its vision in phases. In June 1912, they laid the cornerstone, intending initially to build the first story and provide immediate space to house the church. The contractor, Samuel Plato, was a well-known African American

Above, **Figure 3.30.** Drawing by Indianapolis architect William O. Morck showing his proposed design for a grand Classical and Renaissance-style building for Second Baptist Church, 1911. Note the Corinthian portico at the center, the Renaissance dome and drum above, and the rusticated first story. "Corner Stone Will Be Laid Sunday," *Indianapolis Star,* June 7, 1912, 7.

Facing top, **Figure 3.31.** Second Baptist Church, 428 West Michigan Street, as designed by an unknown architect and constructed in 1919–20, with a Classical temple front at the center and colossal Doric pilasters arranged symmetrically on either side. Note the Romanesque-style stained glass windows in the facade and along the side elevations. View in c. 1970. Courtesy, Indiana Landmarks.

Facing bottom, **Figure 3.32.** Facade of former Second Baptist Church. The congregation moved to a new location in 1993 and sold the Michigan Street property, which was subsequently converted to housing units. Part of the facade was retained. View in 2022. James Glass.

architect from Marion, Indiana. During the summer and through the following year, Plato slowly completed the first story as funds became available. Finally, in August 1913, Second Baptist Church dedicated the one-story structure, hoping to build more in the future.[79]

In 1919–20, under the pastorate of the Reverend Dr. B. J. F. Westbrook, the congregation constructed what appears to have been a new building on the site

of the 1912–13 structure.[80] The unknown architect whom the church selected devised plans that differed considerably from Morck's 1911 conception (fig. 3.31). The 1919 designer provided for a two-story brick building with basement that was considerably narrower than the footprint intended in 1911. The architect employed Classical elements similar to those used in the Disciples of Christ, Methodist, and Presbyterian churches discussed previously. At the center of the facade, he applied a temple front, but with elongated Doric brick pilasters that rose from plinths near the ground to the cornice. The pairs of pilasters in the portico supported a full entablature without ornament and a steeply projecting pediment. Identical Doric pilasters fronted shallow pavilions on either side of the facade. At regular intervals along the facade, the architect placed tall, Romanesque-style windows with rounded tracery and stained glass lights. On the side elevations, he used similarly scaled windows with truncated heads. The designer retained one feature of the 1911 design: the three entries with ogee arches overhead. The design effectively contrasted the orange-colored brick masonry with limestone details.[81]

Inside, the architect used fireproof construction, with reinforced concrete floors and roof. On the ground level, he provided for a meeting hall and Sunday school, kitchen, and pastor's study. On the second floor, the designer created an auditorium and constructed an unusual balcony on three sides with concrete Romanesque piers.[82]

ITALIAN RENAISSANCE

As seen in chapter 7 of volume 1 and chapter 1 of this volume, the Italian Renaissance style had found favor for the exteriors of multiple commercial office buildings during the 1890s and the first two decades of the twentieth century. It also appeared as the theme for the facades of some public buildings (chap. 7 of vol. 1 and chap. 2 of this volume) and for a handful of residences prior to 1900 (chap. 10 of vol. 1). But very few buildings of worship took shape in the Renaissance style before 1900. After 1900, a small number of religious congregations chose the Renaissance as their desired aesthetic theme.

SS. Peter and Paul Cathedral

The most ambitious building of worship to be constructed in the city with Italian Renaissance elements after 1900 came about through the decision of the Catholic Diocese of Indianapolis to erect a cathedral. In 1891, Bishop Francis Chatard had purchased a spacious site on the southeast corner of Fourteenth and Meridian

Streets and in the following year constructed a bishop's residence (see chap. 10 of vol. 1) and a chapel in which the congregation for the future SS. Peter and Paul Cathedral could worship. The bishop selected the New York architectural firms of Renwick, Aspinwall, and Russell and W. L. Coulter to design both buildings and prepare a preliminary design for the cathedral. William W. Renwick, head of the former firm, had made the design and decoration of ecclesiastical structures his specialty.[83]

Figure 3.33 shows an 1892 perspective view by Renwick, Aspinwall, and Russell of the proposed cathedral to be sited immediately south of the chapel. The architects envisioned a building with a basilican plan and a facade with twin towers. They drew on Roman imperial architecture for key details of the facade—an Ionic temple front framing the entrance and details on the second story drawn from the designs of Roman triumphal arches, including arches and engaged Corinthian columns with individual entablatures above the entry. For the three-story towers, they turned to the Renaissance and Baroque churches of the sixteenth, seventeenth, and eighteenth centuries for such features as arched openings for the belfries, twin columns projecting from the four corners of each tower, and domes atop the third stories. Above the temple front, niches contained statues of Saints Peter and Paul, and above the central parapet, two winged statues of angels stood guard.[84]

The diocese was financially unable to proceed immediately with the construction of the cathedral, but after rapid growth in the parish, Bishop Chatard turned to William W. Renwick to revise the 1892 plans. About 1899, the architect and his associates proceeded to redesign the facade and devise the details of the interior. The project then paused for about six years while the diocese raised funds.[85]

Finally, in 1905, excavations for the foundation began, and Renwick's new facade became public. The architect designed an elaborate, monumental facade that, like the treatment in 1892, incorporated elements from both imperial Roman architecture and the Italian Renaissance, but in different ways from the previous proposal. A plaster of paris model by Renwick (fig. 3.34) showed a three-story structure with the lower two stories drawn from triumphal arches of the Roman Empire. At the center, engaged Corinthian columns supported a monumental archway. On either side, statues of Saints Peter, Paul, and Joseph topped Corinthian columns with individual entablatures. Above the sides of the triumphal arch, Renwick proposed single-story Renaissance-style belfries with elaborate aediculae framing the belfry openings. Domes topped the belfries.

Insufficient funds prevented construction of the $100,000 facade, and the diocese proceeded to complete the rest of the cathedral.[86]

Figure 3.33. 1892 rendering of the original design proposed by architects Renwick, Aspinwall, and Russell of New York for the facade of the proposed SS. Peter and Paul Cathedral at 1347 North Meridian Street. The design featured a Roman temple front at ground level and Corinthian columns with individual entablatures and arches derived from Roman triumphal arches at the center of the second story. Above on either side appeared towers with belfries drawn from Italian Renaissance and Baroque sources. "Cathedral of St. Peter and St. Paul, Indianapolis, Ind.," *American Architect and Building News* 36 (April 9, 1892), between 24 and 25.

Figure 3.34. A plaster model prepared about 1905 by New York architect William W. Renwick showing a revised proposal for a Roman-Italian Renaissance-style facade for SS. Peter and Paul Cathedral. Renwick derived the lower stories of the design from Roman triumphal arches and the belfries from Renaissance and Baroque sources. "Façade of the SS. Peter and Paul Cathedral," *Indianapolis News*, November 18, 1905, 16.

Figure 3.35. SS. Peter and Paul Cathedral, 1347 North Meridian Street, as completed in 1906 with temporary facade, incorporating a lunette window and a porch of Tuscan columns. View in c. 1910–15. Bass Photo Co. Collection, Indiana Historical Society. (Image cropped)

For the building behind the facade, Renwick devised a monumental structure constructed of buff-colored brick exterior walls. He used steel framing to achieve fireproof construction and laid out the cathedral plan using the Latin Cross—with a long nave, transepts, and a large projection at the east for the apse. The brick masonry is largely devoid of ornamentation, with the exception of large brick quoins at the corners of the transepts and apse. More elaborate originally were the cornices of the side and front elevations, each with an Ionic frieze and modillions, and the brackets with acanthus leaves and volutes that support the pediments at the ends of the transepts. Renwick designed a temporary stucco facade for the building with a large lunette window at the center and a simple one-story portico of Tuscan columns to shelter parishioners arriving or departing (fig. 3.35).[87]

Figure 3.36. Nave of SS. Peter and Paul Cathedral as seen from the northwest corner in rear. Note the arcades along the sides of nave, colossal pilasters, flat coffered ceiling, and substantial apse, all based on sources in early Christian or Italian Renaissance churches. View in 1907. Bass Photo Co. Collection, Indiana Historical Society. (Image cropped)

Although the diocese lacked the funds to build Renwick's Roman-Renaissance facade, it fully carried out his design for the interior. He planned the Indianapolis cathedral drawing especially on Italian Renaissance details for the interior. The architect devised a ninety-foot-high nave with an eighty-foot width (fig. 3.36). Along the sides of the nave, Renwick created large arches leading to side chapels. The arches and colossal pilasters that adorn the piers between them resemble those used in the Italian Renaissance by such architects as Leon Battista Alberti for the Sant'Andrea church in Mantua and Michelangelo for the nave of St. Peter's Basilica in Rome.[88] Renwick employed a flat plaster ceiling with rectangular coffers for the nave and crossing, reminiscent of early Christian basilicas, such as Santa Maria Maggiore in Rome, and Renaissance churches, such as San Lorenzo in Florence.[89] The transepts are shallow on either side of the crossing. The capitals of each of the twenty pilasters lining the nave and crossing contain volutes and sculptures of human faces. Below each capital appears an elaborate cartouche. In 1905–6, the diocese ordered temporary art glass windows to be installed along the upper walls of the nave.

Renwick gave the apse at the center of the east wall a generous depth and placed within it a white marble high altar made in New York. Above, muralist and stained glass artist Louis Millet of Chicago created murals depicting Saints Peter and Paul, Jesus Christ, St. Mary, and others. The nave, filled with oak pews, could seat several hundred parishioners. At the rear of the nave, Renwick designed a loft for the choir and pipe organ.[90] When dedicated, the SS. Peter and Paul Cathedral cost approximately $140,000, with the facade deferred to a later date.[91]

St. Francis de Sales Catholic Church

In 1912–13, a church building with a design derived from other sources in the Italian Renaissance rose on the southeast corner of Twenty-Second Street and Avondale Place in the former town of Brightwood. St. Francis de Sales Catholic Church had begun in 1881 as a mission of the Catholic Diocese of Indianapolis in Brightwood, which had developed as a community for railroad workers after the Civil War. Rapid growth in the parish congregation, which at first worshipped

Facing, Figure 3.37. Drawing of facade for Sant'Atanasio dei Greci in Rome, designed by sixteenth-century Renaissance architect Giacomo della Porta and a possible model for George Bedell in designing the facade of St. Frances de Sales. Note especially the twin belfry towers with domes, use of symmetry, central pediment, and pilasters. Peter Murray, *The Architecture of the Italian Renaissance* (New York: Schocken Books, 1963), 211.

Figure 3.38. Former St. Francis de Sales Catholic Church, 2195 Avondale Place, built in 1912–13 and designed by George V. Bedell, drawing on the design of such Italian Renaissance churches as Sant'Atanasio in Rome. Note the symmetrical towers adorned by Classical pilasters and the belfries with Renaissance-style domes. Bedell contributed the central rose window and the entry vestibule with Tuscan columns. View in 2021. Now part of Martin University. James Glass.

in an existing building they had acquired, led to the construction of an imposing new structure west of the main rail yards in the community. As their architect, the diocese and parish hired George V. Bedell, who, as previously seen, was becoming known for his design of buildings for worship.[92]

Bedell created a design based on such Renaissance-era churches in Rome as Sant'Atanasio dei Greci, built by noted sixteenth-century architect Giacomo della Porta. The facade of Sant'Atanasio is a three-story brick structure with symmetrical towers on either side (fig. 3.37). Doric pilasters ornament the first story and Ionic the second. The entrance is at the center, and above it is a round-headed window. A pediment appears at the top of the facade. Small domes cap the two towers.[93]

Similarly, Bedell gave St. Francis de Sales a three-story facade with Doric pilasters adorning the second stories and twin towers with shallow domes flanking the central portion of the facade (fig. 3.38). As in the Roman church, he lined the belfries with Doric pilasters. At the center, Bedell made some modifications—he created an entry porch with Tuscan columns and inserted a Romanesque rose window at the center of the second story. But at the apex of the central portion of the facade, the architect placed a limestone pediment, as Della Porta had done at Sant' Atanasio. The St. Francis de Sales building sparkles with pressed orange brick walls and limestone details. The architect arranged large, round-headed Romanesque windows along the side elevations, each divided into two lights and bull's-eyes at the apexes. He ornamented the sides with narrow brick buttresses between the windows.

Inside, the nave could seat five hundred parishioners. Bedell fashioned a rectangular nave with an apse at the east end. The total cost amounted to about $25,000.[94]

ARTS AND CRAFTS/BUNGALOW STYLE

A few Indianapolis buildings of worship from the 1900–1920 period derived their designs in part from the English Arts and Crafts Movement and its disciples in the United States. English artist William Morris inspired the movement in England, and it caught fire in that country, continental Europe, and the United States. Morris advocated for the rejection of monotonous, machine-made furnishings and furniture for houses and the creation of such objects by designer-artisans, who would oversee all aspects of interior decoration, design, and production. He preferred the use of natural materials. Total handicraft production by master artists and artisans implied high costs, and Morris's ideals were realized chiefly in the homes of the wealthy and in other building types with construction budgets that would permit the custom design of interior features.[95] In designing structures with Arts and Crafts features, American architects frequently merged them with popular styles of the day. The design of All Souls Unitarian Church exemplifies this merger.

In the United States, the Arts and Crafts tenets regarding simple forms with natural materials found a proponent in furniture maker Gustav Stickley, who promoted affordable houses with the appearance of handcrafting (see chap. 5 of this volume). Through his magazine, *The Craftsman*, Stickley popularized "Craftsman" houses, some of which became known as California bungalows. Characteristics of the latter included horizontal massing; low-slung, projecting gable roofs; and large brackets supporting the eaves.[96] The Second Christian Church of Indianapolis, more than any other building of worship, exemplifies elements of Stickley's bungalow designs.

All Souls Unitarian Church

In 1903, the American Unitarian Society sent the Reverend E. E. Newbert to Indianapolis to organize a Unitarian congregation in the Indiana state capital. He met with success, and All Souls Unitarian Church took shape the following year. Horace McKay, a charter member, led efforts to acquire two lots and an existing building at 1455 North Alabama Street. The new congregation met in that structure until growth necessitated a new structure. Under the Reverend Frank S. C. Wicks, the church hired the well-known firm of Vonnegut and Bohn as their architects in 1910, and Arthur Bohn, Kurt Vonnegut Sr., and their draftsmen created what had the appearance of a comfortable home in terms of scale, style, and materials.[97] The architects designed a one-story, L-shaped building consisting of the principal structure running east and west with a gable roof and a wing at the rear extending to the south (fig. 3.39). Vonnegut and Bohn chose the so-called English Tudor style for many of the details, strengthening the connection to many contemporary houses being built in that style (see chap. 4 of this volume).

The design includes elements reflecting the vernacular tradition in houses and other buildings of sixteenth-century Tudor England, such as a stucco exterior and cypress wood timbers incorporated in the gable of the facade and in the lower framing. As with many houses built in the vernacular Tudor style, the architects combined the stucco and timber upper story with a brick basement story and chimneys. To vary the color palette, they specified green ceramic tiles for the roof. As horizontal elements, the designers inserted banks of art glass windows in the facade and side elevations, each consisting of lower lights with segmental arches and transoms above.[98]

Vonnegut and Bohn, somewhat unusually, located the main entrance to the church on the side. From the entry, the congregants passed into a rectangular foyer in which the influence of the Arts and Crafts Movement is obvious and striking. In

Facing top, **Figure 3.39.** Former All Souls Unitarian Church, 1455 North Alabama Street, built in 1910–11 and designed by Vonnegut and Bohn, drawing largely on the English Tudor vernacular style for the exterior, with stucco and timber structure. The architects designed the church to have a residential character. Most recently, the building has in fact served as a residence. View of facade in 2020. James Glass.

Facing bottom, **Figure 3.40.** Art glass windows in the foyer of All Souls Church, depicting the World Tree, Yggdrasill, from Norse mythology, designed by architect and artist Rembrandt Steele and a fine example of the Arts and Crafts Movement in Indianapolis. View in 2021. James Glass.

Figure 3.41. Auditorium of All Souls Church as seen from the rear. The beamed ceiling with slanted plaster panels on the sides and flat panels at the center resembles an interior in a ranch bungalow depicted in Gustav Stickley's *The Craftsman* magazine. View in 2021. James Glass.

the west and north walls are superb windows depicting the World Tree Yggdrasill, a giant ash tree that supported the universe in Norse mythology (fig. 3.40). Rembrandt (Brandt) Steele, the architect and artist son of painter T. C. Steele, designed the windows, which Ulysses Grant Cassady made.[99] At the center of the west wall is a large fireplace with a simple wooden mantel, beamed overmantel, and green tile hearth, all suggesting the center of life in a home. A partition composed in its upper half by a series of leaded windows separates the foyer from the rectangular auditorium. At the east end of the auditorium is an apse-like recession in which the speaking platform stands (fig. 3.41). Overhead, a beamed ceiling with slanted sides rising to a flat surface at the center is similar to that in a ranch bungalow illustrated in Gustav Stickley's *The Craftsman* magazine.[100] Along the sides of the auditorium, Brandt Steele designed simple leaded glass windows with small, colored insets depicting branches and leaves.

In the basement, Vonnegut and Bohn provided a social room in the eastern portion and a men's room with a fireplace at the west end. The final cost of the building came to $30,000.[101]

Second Christian Church

African Americans made up the second-oldest congregation of the Disciples of Christ denomination in Indianapolis, the Second Christian Church. In 1866, aided by the mother church of the Disciples in the city, the Christian Chapel (later Central Christian Church), a body of Black citizens organized the Second Christian congregation. Eventually, the church acquired a building at Thirteenth and Missouri Streets. As increasing numbers of African Americans from the South arrived in the city, the Second Christian Church grew. In 1910, under the Reverend Henry L. Herod, it acquired a lot on the northwest corner of Ninth and Camp Streets, in what is now Ransom Place. Together with white Disciple laymen, Second Christian members raised enough funds to excavate the foundation for a new building and complete the basement in 1910. They hired an unknown architect, who produced the design for a handsome brick and frame building with features drawn from the Arts and Crafts Movement and bungalow houses. The designer estimated the cost at about $10,000. The congregation was able to raise the remainder of the funds needed, and the church dedicated the completed building in 1911.[102]

The architect laid out a U-shaped plan for the story-and-a-half structure (fig. 3.42). An entry and a vestibule projected on either side of the facade from the bulk of the building. The designer specified brick for the first story and frame board-and-batten walls above. The bungalow aspect can be seen in the sweeping frontal slope of the roof that descends from the gable ridge at the top to projecting eaves supported by exposed rafters. The choice of brick and frame natural materials showed the influence of Arts and Crafts and the Craftsman designs. In the side

Figure 3.42. Former Second Christian Church, 702 West Ninth Street, Ransom Place, built by one of the oldest African American congregations in the city between 1910 and 1911 and designed by an unknown architect with a sweeping, sloping roof similar to those on California bungalows at the time. Saved by Indiana Landmarks, the building is now a residence. View in 2020. James Glass.

elevation, the designer interjected one Gothic element—a large window with a broad pointed arch enclosing three large lights and six upper lights contained in tracery. Originally, all the windows in the south facade and east side elevation contained stained glass. Inside, most of the building was devoted to a sanctuary for worship.[103]

PENTECOSTAL BANDS BUILDINGS

A very unusual Christian building complex from beginning of the twentieth century departed from all other practices in design and construction for church structures and from the stylistic currents of the time. The Pentecostal Bands of the World, founded in 1890, believed in the power of prayer and preaching in healing

Figure 3.43. +Church building and residence of the Pentecostal Bands of the World, 223 North New Jersey Street, built in 1901 largely by Pentecostal preachers using donated limestone and other contributed materials. There appears to have been no architect and no contractor involved. The bands constructed the exterior of rock-faced Indiana Bedford stone. View in c. 1910. Demolished in 1922 and replaced by the reinforced concrete Print Craft Building. Jacob Piatt Dunn, *Greater Indianapolis* (Chicago: Lewis, 1910), 1:623.

and providing for life's needs. By 1901, under the leadership of Thomas H. Nelson, the movement moved its headquarters to Indianapolis and started constructing a church and ministry building. They purchased a lot at 223 North New Jersey Street, and with no money raised, no bids, and no construction contracts, Nelson led the bands to erect multiple buildings. Pentecostal Bands preachers contributed much of the labor of construction, and members and friends of the congregation donated the stone for the walls and shipping costs. It is doubtful that the church solicited a design for their simple structures, but surely they had some basic floor plans and elevation drawings.[104]

In 1901, over nine months, the Pentecostal congregation constructed a one-story church structure, with a rectangular shape, gable roof, and pediment-like front gable (fig. 3.43). The members fashioned the exterior walls from rock-faced

Bedford limestone blocks and put on a slate roof. The upper floor contained a worship room, and the basement afforded quarters to house a printing press for the Pentecostal newspaper. At the rear of the church structure, the bands built a wing containing the residence of Thomas Nelson and his family and twenty-five missionaries. At the rear of the lot, the congregation constructed a four-story Free Shelter house for the destitute in 1908. The bands estimated the cost of the original two buildings at $10,000.[105]

CONCLUSION

Indianapolis began the 1900–1920 period with the construction of buildings of worship that represented several styles and themes that had previously found favor. The most popular architectural theme in the 1890s, the Romanesque, had found ready clients and architects since the early 1880s and continued in favor for some congregations until about 1905. The Gothic had first appeared in Indianapolis buildings of worship in the late 1850s and continued to appeal to particular congregations or parishes during the 1880s and 1890s. It entered a new period of popularity between 1900 and the entry of the United States into World War I in 1917.

The Classical style, derived directly from Roman and Greek sources, found ready acceptance in the early twentieth century for public buildings and eventually for buildings of worship. In the case of the two Christian Scientist churches, the Classicism of ancient Greece and Rome seemed to some, such as architect Solon Spencer Beman, to be most appropriate because of its association with early Christianity. For the Congregation Sharah Tessila, Third Christian Church, St. Paul Methodist Episcopal Church, and Second Baptist Church, the architects probably suggested designs with temple fronts and pilasters to their clients. Along with Gothic, the Classical style became the most widely favored architectural language for buildings of worship by 1910. The Italian Renaissance, although popular for commercial and public buildings since the 1850s, did not appear as an ecclesiastical style in the state capital until Bishop Chatard retained William W. Renwick and his associated New York architects to design a Catholic cathedral in 1892 and 1899.

The influence of the Arts and Crafts and bungalow movements on church design appears to have been much less than the other styles. The cultured All Souls Unitarian congregation sought out Brandt Steele to create the Yggdrasill tree windows and incorporated several hearths and natural materials in their home-like worship complex. The architect of the Second Christian Church designed a building with bungalow lines and materials. But most congregations desired traditional building styles.

Although local architects probably won the commissions for most buildings of worship in the early twentieth century, out-of-town firms designed a significant number of such structures. Of the fifteen structures discussed, out-of-towners designed eight. They obtained their commissions in several ways. Some of the firms—such as Crapsey and Lamm for First Presbyterian Church and the associated firms of Brown and Davis and Gillespie and Carrel for First Baptist Church—competed with several other firms for selection. Henry Schlacks of Chicago for the St. Catherine of Siena parish had designed several other Catholic churches in Chicago and may have been known to Bishop Chatard. Some of the remaining firms enjoyed a personal connection of some sort to a key decision-maker—such as Hermann Gaul with Father Scheideler at St. Mary's Catholic Church. Bishop Chatard may have known of William W. Renwick and his association with the decoration and design of St. Patrick's Cathedral in New York. Solon Spencer Beman likely won his commission at the Second Church of Christ, Scientist on the strength of his advocacy within the Christian Scientist movement for Classical designs.

Of the Indianapolis architects mentioned in this chapter, George Bedell designed three buildings of worship, more than any of the others. Compared to the major firms operating in the city, Bedell had a small practice, but he seems to have specialized in church work. Vonnegut and Bohn, Oscar Bohlen of D. A. Bohlen and Son, and Rubush and Hunter dominated commercial and public commissions but only designed a handful of worship buildings. Three of the other local architects mentioned—Alfred Grindle, Charles E. Bacon, and Lewis Sturges—may have designed only a single church. William O. Morck designed two church buildings for African American congregations, but neither was realized.[106]

More research is needed in the church archives of the African American congregations who built structures during this period regarding the identity of the architects of the buildings constructed. Some white architects, such as Morck, prepared the initial and possibly the final designs for churches. In the case of Second Baptist Church, Morck prepared the first design, but another architect may have conceived the design of the final building. We also do not know the architect of the bungalow-style Second Christian Church. The final designers of both buildings of worship may have been early African American architects, or they may have been white.

A word should be said about the sources of designs for Indianapolis buildings for worship. Although the ultimate sources in Europe have been cited for several structures, probably most local and out-of-town architects derived ideas and details from an abundance of photographs and drawings available in periodicals. Designers could find illustrations of medieval and Classical buildings and contemporary designs in the leading architectural periodicals of the era—the *Inland Architect* of Chicago, the *American Architect and Building News* of Boston, and the *Architectural Record* and *The Brickbuilder* of New York. In addition, every architect's library came to include books with photographs and sketches of historic and recently built buildings, including churches, in Europe and the eastern United States. That is not to say that individual architects did not add their own interpretation and refinement to overall compositions or details that they found in the periodicals. In the case of Hermann Gaul, he drew his interpretation of elements from Cologne Cathedral for the design of St. Mary's Catholic Church from his actual study of the original.

Also, architects in Indianapolis sometimes used formulas derived from published sources in shaping their buildings of worship. As seen, in several Protestant churches in which Gothic elements were to be used, architects such as Oscar Bohlen used the formula of a tall corner square tower with crenellations, balanced on the other side of the facade by a smaller tower echoing it. Another formula for Gothic designs involved flanking a gabled facade with two symmetrical spires and placing a large pointed arch window at the center, such as at the 1905–6 Meridian Street Methodist Episcopal Church and St. Mary's Catholic Church. With respect to those buildings discussed with Classical elements, the architects of Third Christian Church, St. Paul Methodist Episcopal Church, Westminster Presbyterian Church, and Second Baptist Church all applied Classical temple fronts to the second stories of brick buildings and extended pilasters along the sides. George Bedell designed a more fully developed Classical portico for the Congregation Sharah Tessila.

The buildings of worship from this period illustrate both the similarities of style that buildings of worship shared with commercial and public structures and their differences. Richardson's Romanesque and Roman and Greek Classical designs lent themselves readily to all building types except residential. Gothic, in contrast, lent itself almost exclusively to the design of buildings of worship. The Italian Renaissance found favor for all building types but not as much for the structures of religious bodies. Some of the most popular currents in residential design—American Foursquare, English Tudor, and Arts and Crafts/bungalow—had only a slight appeal for most congregations.

Map 3.1

Buildings from Chapter 3 of Volume 2 plotted on 1914 Sanborn Insurance Map of Mile Square of Indianapolis (Vol. 1) (numbers drawn from figure numbers); + = demolished

- **3** + 1904-05 First Baptist Church
- **15** 1911-12 St. Mary's Catholic Church
- **31** 1919-20 Second Baptist Church
- **43** + Church building and residence, Pentecostal Bands of the World

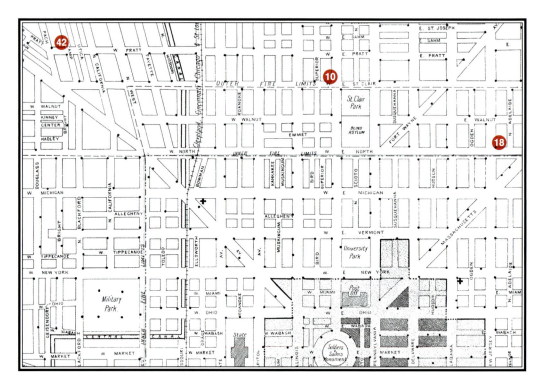

Map 3.2

Buildings from Chapter 3 plotted on 1914 Sanborn Insurance Map of area west and north of Mile Square (Vol. 1) (numbers drawn from figure numbers)

- **10** 1905-06 Meridian Street Methodist Episcopal Church
- **18** 1912-13 German Evangelical Zion Church
- **42** 1910-11 Second Christian Church

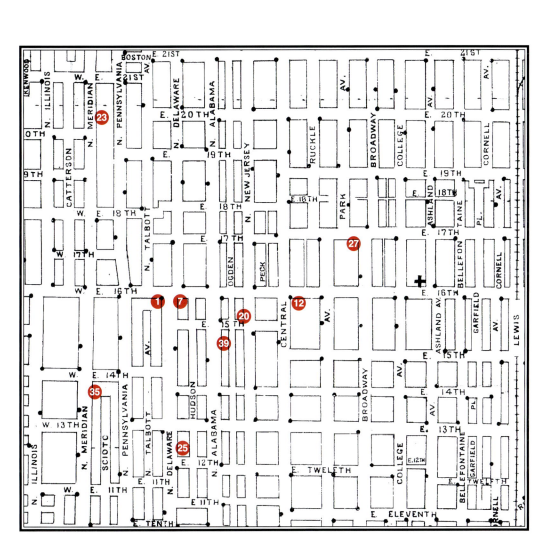

Map 3.3

Buildings from Chapter 3 plotted on 1915 Sanborn Insurance Map (Vol. 4) of area between 10th and 21st Streets and between Illinois and Lewis Streets (numbers drawn from figure numbers); + = demolished

- **1** Mayflower Congregational Church
- **7** 1901-03 First Presbyterian Church
- **12** All Saints Episcopal Cathedral (Church)
- **20** Central Universalist Church
- **23** First Church of Christ, Scientist
- **25** Second Church of Christ, Scientist
- **27** + 1910-14 Third Christian Church
- **35** Saints Peter and Paul Catholic Cathedral
- **39** 1910-11 All Souls Unitarian Church

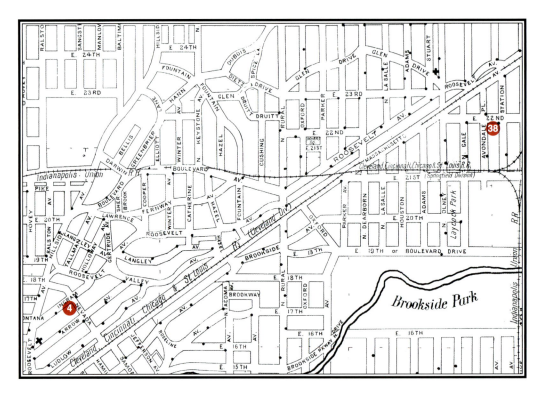

Map 3.4

Buildings from Chapter 3 plotted on 1915 Sanborn Insurance Map (Vol. 4) of area between Roosevelt Avenue and Station Streets and between Brookside Parkway and 24th Street (numbers drawn from figure numbers)

🔴 **4** Hillside Christian Church
🔴 **38** St. Francis de Sales Catholic Church

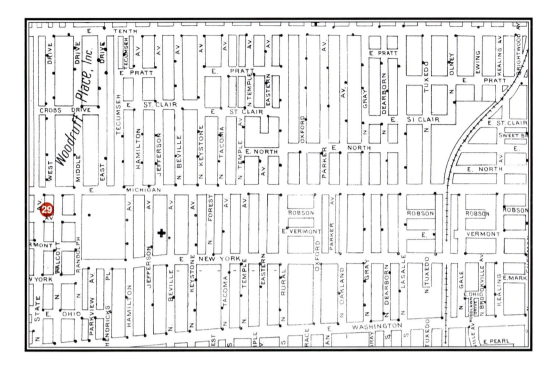

Map 3.5

Buildings from Chapter 3 plotted on 1915 Sanborn Insurance Map (Vol. 3) of area between West Drive, Woodruff Place, and Kealing Avenue and East Washington and 10th Streets (numbers drawn from figure numbers)

29 Westminster Presbyterian Church

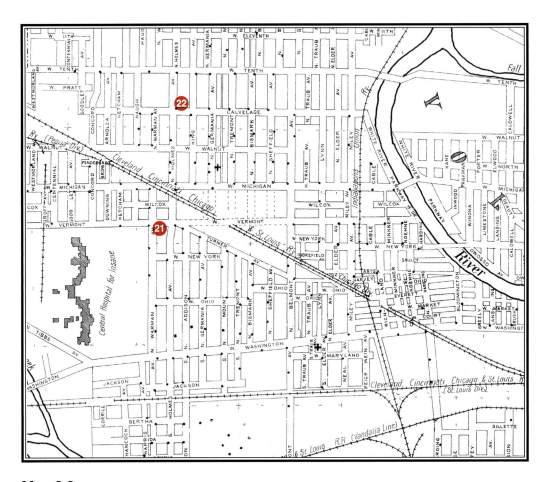

Map 3.6

Buildings from Chapter 3 plotted on 1915 Sanborn Insurance Map (Vol. 6) of Haughville, between West Washington and West 10th Street and between Central State Hospital and White River (numbers drawn from figure numbers)

- 21 St. Anthony's Catholic Church
- 22 Holy Trinity Slovenian Catholic Church

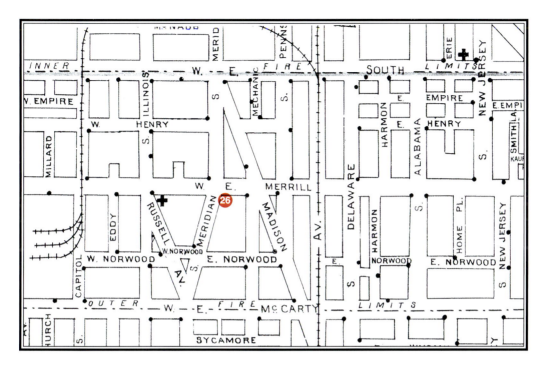

Map 3.7

Buildings from Chapter 3 plotted on 1915 Sanborn Insurance Map (Vol. 2) between McCarty and South Streets and between Capitol Avenue and New Jersey Street (numbers drawn from figure numbers); + = demolished

26 + Sharah Tessila Synagogue

4 | CITY MANSIONS AND COUNTRY ESTATES
1900–1920

As the old century closed in 1900 and the new one began, Indianapolis prided itself on being a "city of homes," in which most white citizens and some African American citizens could afford to be homeowners. The Commercial Club proclaimed in 1907 that the state capital ranked second in the whole country with respect to the number of working-class men who owned their homes. Three years later, the club reported that Indianapolis residents lived in a city that was not densely built; real estate additions were laid out with wide streets and alleys. Houses of all types and sizes received more air and sunshine than other communities as a result. The city also attracted and held residents by expanding its park system, which boasted twenty-six parks with three thousand acres by 1913, and constructing new schools as its territory expanded and its population increased. By 1916, city students attended seventy public schools and three high schools.[1]

As the population increased by about 65 percent between 1900 and 1920—from 204,518 to 314,194—the demand for housing of all types exploded. Real estate investors platted additions for new neighborhoods in all directions from the Mile Square.[2] Wealthy people, business and professional people, and middle-class homebuyers[3] constructed detached houses or purchased them from real estate firms or builders. Investors constructed cottages and bungalows for sale or rental to working-class families. Besides the many homeowners noted by the Commercial Club, a sizeable number of Indianapolis residents rented their dwellings.

Home building occurred both in the areas previously platted and in additions opened after 1900. The north side continued to appeal to wealthy homebuyers, business and professional people, and many middle-class purchasers. Meridian

Street retained its reputation as the most prestigious corridor for residences. The north–south streets on either side of it attracted a similar mixture of income levels. The neighborhood between Sixteenth Street and Fall Creek rapidly filled with rows of detached houses and doubles, while new additions extending north of the creek to the town of Mapleton and north of Maple Road (later Thirty-Eighth Street) attracted investors to build speculative houses. The larger east side, stretching from College Avenue all the way to Emerson Avenue and the town of Irvington, found its niche as a series of neighborhoods full of detached houses for the middle class and cottages and bungalows for working-class people. Irvington itself, annexed to Indianapolis in 1902, retained its character as a college community clustered around the Butler campus, but with annexation, some wealthy, business and professional-level, and upper-middle-class families bought properties and built houses near Pleasant Run.

Residential architecture in the city between 1900 and 1920 could be categorized according to the size and elaborateness of houses, the income levels of home buyers or renters, and the stylistic features used to define the residences. Wealthy families constructed additional mansions along Meridian Street and several other north–south streets. A few of them also built Rustic-style houses outside of town. A handful of the wealthiest constructed full estates in the country after 1900, seeking both retreats from the city and elaborate residences and landscape designs that proclaimed their status as the leaders in local society.

For most houses, style continued to be a matter of choice for the client and the architect. For large residences, designs frequently included details derived from historical sources, such as Italian Renaissance, Georgian, English Tudor palace, English Tudor vernacular, and Classical architecture, and from a contemporary prototype, the Foursquare.

Architects designed residences of every size and cost. Nearly every architect competed for at least some residential commissions, but many found niches within that market. The larger firms well known for their commercial and public buildings often obtained commissions for designing mansions and large-scale apartment buildings.

This chapter discusses a sampling of the houses built by the wealthy between 1900 and 1920. First, some of the mansions built in the city proper are discussed, especially those on Meridian Street and the other north–south streets north of downtown. Varied architectural themes appeared in the designs of these large urban houses. Second, five surviving large houses from the country estate era are examined. These houses and their surrounding estates exemplify multiple architectural themes and differing landscape treatments.

CITY MANSIONS

As already observed in chapters 6 and 10 of volume 1, Meridian Street became the principal residential street of Indianapolis early on. The pattern of the wealthiest families building pretentious residences on the street had become well established by the late 1860s. By the late 1890s, large houses had risen solidly along Meridian up to Sixteenth Street, and many had been built along the Meridian corridor to Fall Creek. A few had appeared north of the creek. During the first two decades of the twentieth century, well-to-do families filled the remainder of the vacant lots south of Fall Creek with a few grand houses and many more comfortably scaled and attractively detailed residences. Prosperous owners of factories and large businesses, along with their spouses, constructed additional mansions north of Fall Creek to Thirty-Fourth Street and a sprinkling further north, up to Forty-Second Street. Although most of the mansions appeared on Meridian Street, several wealthy families headed by top businessmen constructed houses of comparable scale on other north–south streets, Sutherland Avenue south of Fall Creek, and Fall Creek Parkway north of the creek. Over on the east side, large houses appeared in Woodruff Place, on Pleasant Run Parkway, and around Audubon Circle in Irvington. The city's parkways, designed by St. Louis landscape architect George Kessler, provided attractive drives along the principal creeks in the state capital and desirable locations for large houses.[4]

Schnull-Rauch House (Queen Anne/Medieval French)

The first substantial house built north of Fall Creek on Meridian probably was the one constructed by Gustav A. Schnull, heir to one of the principal businesses downtown, wholesale grocers Schnull and Company. Previously, Gustav and his wife, Matilda Mayer Schnull, had previously lived in a Civil War–era house at Michigan and Illinois Streets. In 1902, they decided they wanted to live in a spacious setting removed from the noise and rapid commercialization encroaching on their previous home. They found a country-like setting in the North Park Addition north of Thirtieth Street and acquired a double lot at 3050 North Meridian Street. The Schnulls retained Gustav's brother-in-law, Bernard Vonnegut, to design their house. As seen in chapter 9 of volume 1, Vonnegut had designed several large houses previously in the 1880s and 1890s, drawing on the English Queen Anne, Romanesque, and Italian Renaissance styles.[5]

For the Schnulls, the architect designed a rectangular, three-story house constructed of yellow brick (fig. 4.1).[6] For the facade, he drew on the 1890s Queen

Figure 4.1. Schnull-Rauch House, 3050 North Meridian Street, built between 1902 and 1904 and designed by Bernard Vonnegut of Vonnegut and Bohn, drawing on the 1890s Queen Anne formula of a rounded tower combined with a contrasting facade consisting of a bowed, projecting bay; a central entry porch; and an open terrace. The tower design derives from similar structures in medieval fortifications, and Vonnegut drew from Tudor palaces and Gothic churches for other details. Preserved by Indiana Landmarks, the Rauch family, and the Junior League of Indianapolis in 1979 and subsequently the headquarters of the Junior League. Now owned by the Children's Museum of Indianapolis. View of facade, 2019. James Glass.

Anne formula of a rounded tower on one side, combined with a contrasting treatment on the other and a central entrance (see chap. 10 of vol. 1). A large, round tower on the north side dominates the Schnull facade, crowned by a conical roof resembling the towers found along the perimeter walls of such French medieval castles as Pierrefonds or along medieval French town walls, such as those at Carcassonne. Vonnegut placed a substantial limestone porch over the entrance at the center. Continuing with the medieval theme, he lined the top of the porch with crenellations and augmented the piers with Gothic buttresses. On the south side

Figure 4.2. Stair hall, Schnull-Rauch House, showing use of oak for the Ionic column and pilaster at right, beams, newel post, balustrade, and trim. Note also the shield on the newel post; shields were a trademark of architect Bernard Vonnegut. View from 2013. James Glass.

of the facade, he balanced the tower with a two-story projecting bay with a slight curve. On the south elevation, the architect constructed a three-story rounded bay to capture the sunlight. A terrace with a roof wraps around the base of the bay and continues uncovered east along the side of the house and around the southeast corner to meet the entry porch. For detailing, Vonnegut employed a Tudor dripstone molding for the central second-story window on the facade, a Renaissance balustrade along the terrace, and flat stone lintels for the rest of the windows. He covered the main roof and that of the tower with red clay tiles and slightly upturned the corners of the main roof and the roofs on the dormer windows.

At the rear of the property, Vonnegut designed a combined carriage house and garage, with the eastern portion devoted to carriage storage and a stable and the rear section to storing an automobile. The front section harmonizes with the house—constructed of yellow brick laid in Flemish bond and covered by a red tile roof but with shed dormer windows.

Vonnegut collaborated with Matilda Schnull in deciding on the interior features and furnishings. On the first floor, he laid out a long central hall that intersected with a cross stair hall at the center (fig. 4.2). He specified golden oak, stained green, for the trim, the Ionic columns, and the overhead beams in the main stair hall and the principal stairway. For the drawing room in the northeast corner, the architect took advantage of the expansive curve of the tower to create a sunny space for entertaining. He incorporated a family heirloom mirror into the mahogany mantel he designed for the west wall and inserted a stained glass window in the north wall. Overhead, he specified low-relief Rococo plaster patterns on the ceiling. The dining room is another highlight, with cherry wood grained to resemble mahogany used for the large buffet, the fireplace mantel, and the beams supporting the ceiling. On the second floor, Vonnegut again used a central corridor to organize the plan and lined it with six bedrooms. The third floor he devoted to a ballroom.

On the corners of the exterior porch and throughout the first-floor corridor, the architect incorporated one of his trademarks—decorative shields. Work on the house ended in 1904, and the family moved in.[7]

Louis and Alice Reynolds Levey House (French Baroque/Renaissance)

While working on the Schnull House, Bernard Vonnegut obtained another choice Meridian Street commission. Louis H. Levey was president of Levey Brothers and Company, a large printing concern. In 1903, he and his wife, Alice Reynolds Levey, decided to build a mansion about a block south of the Schnull House. Previously, the Leveys had lived with their family in a frame Queen Anne–style house at 1730 North Meridian. Now the couple aspired to life in a much-larger home north of Fall Creek. They acquired a large lot at 2902 North Meridian Street.[8]

Vonnegut sited the Levey House at the summit of a ridge above the street and designed a residence very different from the Schnull House in style and aesthetics. He created a sparkling, white limestone block with a symmetrical facade and drew its details from French Baroque and Italian Renaissance architecture (see fig. 4.3). The focal point is the central entrance, with its overscaled, broken segmental pediment supported by elaborate consoles and decorated by a cartouche and festoons, all suggested by treatments of entries in late seventeenth-century French Baroque architecture.[9] From the Renaissance came shouldered architraves for the windows, a cornice supported by modillions and lined with dentils, and a balustrade above the cornice. As at the Schnull House, Vonnegut constructed a terrace south of the entrance and extended it around the southeast corner. At the southwest corner of

Figure 4.3. Louis H. and Alice Reynolds Levey House, 2902 North Meridian Street, built between 1903 and 1904 and designed by Bernard Vonnegut of Vonnegut and Bohn, drawing from late seventeenth-century French Baroque architecture for the treatment of the entry and the Italian Renaissance for the symmetry, entablature, and balustrades. Preserved and restored by the Indianapolis Life Insurance Company in the 1980s and 1990s. View in 2023. James Glass.

the house, he created a charming feature—a two-story cylindrical bow containing windows.

Vonnegut also adopted an interior layout that differed from that of the Schnull House: a central stair hall led west from the entry but ended in a grand stairway proceeding up to the second floor. The culmination of a visit to the Levey household was a concert in which an organist played the pipe organ that the family installed on the second floor.[10]

Frank W. and Emma Salter Lewis House (Renaissance/Classical)

Woodruff Place had been a prestigious residential suburb on the near east side since the 1870s, incorporated as a separate town from Indianapolis. As seen in

Figure 4.4. Frank W. and Emma Salter Lewis House, 720 West Drive, Woodruff Place, built in 1902–3 and designed with a mix of Italian Renaissance and Greek Classical details. Note the Ionic columns and entablature of the porch and the colossal Ionic column supporting the rear porch. View from 1908. *Art Work of Indianapolis, Ind.* (Chicago: Gravure Illustration, 1908).

chapter 6 of volume 1, James Woodruff had platted the enclave with spacious esplanades adorned with cast-iron statuary and fountains at the midpoints of East, Middle, and West Drives. The attractiveness of Woodruff Place for well-to-do families, business and professional people, and middle-class households continued to grow during the 1890s and the first two decades of the new century.

One of the largest houses to rise in the suburb resulted from the desire of Frank W. Lewis and his wife, Emma Salter Lewis, to move from the 1500 block of North Park Avenue to the refined setting of Woodruff. Frank Lewis was the president of the Indianapolis Foundry Company, an investor in oil extractions, and a board member of the American National Bank. In 1902, he and Emma purchased a

CITY MANSIONS AND COUNTRY ESTATES | 307

large lot on the west side of West Drive, just south of Cross Drive. They hired an unknown architect, who designed for them a substantial two-and-a-half-story frame residence with a rectangular facade and symmetrical features (fig. 4.4).[11]

From the Renaissance, the designer drew pilasters for the corners, a cornice with consoles and dentils, and a Palladian window for the front dormer. From Greek Classicism, he drew inspiration for the Ionic columns supporting a majestic veranda, which extended across the facade and around the southeast corner. The architect used a full-sized Ionic column to support a two-story porch on the south elevation. He also drew from early nineteenth-century American architecture for the fan light over the front entry and for the widow's walk with balustrade at the top of the steep roof. The architect designed a combined carriage house and garage at the rear.

Joseph A. and Caroline Pfau Rink House (Renaissance)

As the twentieth century opened, Joseph A. Rink was a rising star in the Indianapolis business community. He had previously founded a company that manufactured fine cloaks, suits, and furs and sold them in a retail store downtown. After 1900, he also invested in real estate and was about to build a substantial apartment building at Vermont and Illinois (see discussion of apartments in chap. 5 of this volume). Rink's wealth expanded, and in 1903, he and his wife, Caroline Pfau Rink, were ready to construct a large mansion at Twenty-First and Meridian Streets. They acquired one of the largest unbuilt tracts south of Fall Creek—a full quarter block—and hired local architect Thomas A. Winterrowd, who had previously designed several residences in the city (see chap. 10 of vol. 1). The designer prepared plans for an imposing three-story residence (fig. 4.5).[12]

The house is a massive, rectangular block constructed with a timber structure. A veneer of rock-faced limestone covers the exterior walls. The architect detailed the facade simply; dressed limestone slabs form lintels over the windows but without sculpted ornamentation. As a focal point, he designed a rectangular dormer at the center of the facade that cuts through the cornice. Renaissance elements include a Palladian window within the dormer, a cornice supported by consoles, and a balustrade along the front and side porches. Winterrowd used an asymmetrical composition for the facade, employing a bowed bay similar to that of the Schnull House on the south side and running the front porch across just the north portion. As Vonnegut had done with both the Schnull and Levey Houses, Winterrowd provided an open terrace across part of the facade. The Rinks also built a large, stone-faced auto garage to the rear of their property.

Figure 4.5. Joseph A. and Caroline Pfau Rink House, 2105 North Meridian Street, built in 1903–4 and designed by local architect Thomas A. Winterrowd with Renaissance details, such as a Palladian window, a cornice with consoles, Tuscan columns supporting the porches, and balustrades. The curved projecting bay on the facade also appeared in contemporary house designs by Bernard Vonnegut. Now offices. View in 2022. James Glass.

In the interior, the architect laid out an east–west corridor from the front entry to the rear of the first floor. About halfway through the house, the main hallway intersected with a cross corridor that gave access to a stone veranda on the south elevation and the porte cochere on the north elevation. Winterrowd used a Renaissance theme for decorative details in the north drawing room on the first floor, which also included a library with a large, open fireplace, a dining room, and a billiard room. On the second floor, the architect provided space for six bedrooms. He devoted the top floor to a ballroom.[13]

CITY MANSIONS AND COUNTRY ESTATES | 309

Henry A. and Ada Freeland Mansfield House (Renaissance)

The next large house to take shape on Meridian Street rose in 1905–6 on a substantial lot at 2550 North Meridian, just north of the bridge over Fall Creek. Henry A. Mansfield was a civil engineer who cofounded and headed a successful general contracting firm, the Moore-Mansfield Construction Company. He also conducted an engineering consulting practice with his chief business partner, DeWitt V. Moore. As his contracting company prospered, Mansfield and his wife, Ada Freeland Mansfield, aspired to a showy mansion. They had previously resided in a frame house at 2630 North Meridian.[14]

The Mansfields hired an architectural partnership that, during the first decade of the twentieth century, became one of the leading firms specializing in residential architecture. Herbert W. Foltz and Wilson B. Parker (see their profile in chap. 2 of this volume) obtained some notable commercial and public commissions but found their niche designing aesthetically pleasing houses for the well-to-do.[15] They situated the Mansfield House at the center of the lot and gave it a rectangular shape and two-and-a-half stories (fig. 4.6). The exterior was constructed of load-bearing Indiana limestone with a dressed finish. The architects made the facade asymmetrical, with one projecting bay emerging from the north side of the facade and a second, more substantial one on the south end of the facade. Classical and Renaissance details defined the exterior—entablatures with modillions and triglyphs for the main house and the porch that ran across the facade, balustrades above the main and porch cornices, and fluted Doric columns to support the porch. In terms of contrasting elements, Foltz and Parker included three dormers with Gothic-style gables above the center of the facade and covered the roof with red clay tiles.

Frank and Clarissa Lintner Van Camp House (Tudor Palace/Gothic)

While the Mansfield House was under construction, work began on what was probably the largest house ever built on Meridian Street. Frank Van Camp headed one of the top packing firms in the state, the Van Camp Packing Company, which produced canned pork and beans for a national market. Previously, he and his family had lived in a frame house at 1910 North Pennsylvania Street, but their growing wealth made possible a move to the North Park addition north of Fall Creek. In 1904, Frank Van Camp paid $18,000 for two lots in the addition, comprising six-tenths of an acre. He and his wife, Clarissa Lintner Van Camp, then commissioned one of the top residential architects in the eastern United States, William Price of Philadelphia, as their designer. As seen in his profile (chap. 1 of

Figure 4.6. A + beside the name of a building indicates that it no longer exists. +Henry A. and Ada Freeland Mansfield House, 2550 North Meridian Street, built in 1905–6 and designed by Foltz and Parker, who gave it an asymmetrical facade with Italian Renaissance details for the porch, cornice, and balustrades and Gothic-style dormer windows. Demolished in 1929 to make way for the former American Central Insurance Company headquarters building at Meridian and Fall Creek Parkway North Drive. View c. 1906–8. *Art Work of Indianapolis, Ind.* (Chicago: Gravure Illustration, 1908).

this volume), Price and his business partner, Martin Hawley McLanahan, designed houses for affluent clients in the East and Midwest and eventually many stations for the Pennsylvania Railroad, including the expansion of Union Station in Indianapolis (see chap. 1 of this volume).[16]

CITY MANSIONS AND COUNTRY ESTATES | 311

Facing top, **Figure 4.7.** +Frank and Clarissa Lintner Van Camp House, 2820 North Meridian Street, built in 1904–6 and designed by William Price of Price and McLanahan of Philadelphia, drawing on Tudor palace architecture of the sixteenth century, Gothic sources, and some Renaissance details for a picturesque ensemble of pavilions, gables, and arcades, all given texture by Price's use of rock-faced Indiana limestone. Demolished in 1963–64 and replaced with the Indianapolis Stouffer's Inn, which now houses the restaurant and hospitality programs of Ivy Tech State College. View in 1908. *Art Work of Indianapolis, Ind.* (Chicago: Gravure Illustration, 1908).

Facing bottom, **Figure 4.8.** Mexican mahogany overmantel with human figures and arabesques modeled by master craftsman A. Zettler and carved by local woodcarvers for the interior of the Van Camp mansion. Now on the top floor of the former Stouffer's Inn, in a restaurant operated by Ivy Tech. View in 2013. James Glass.

Price laid out a long, rectangular block that rose three stories on a north–south ridge above Meridian Street (fig. 4.7). He added multiple pavilions to the facade with varying silhouettes and details. The result was an asymmetrical, picturesque composition. He gave the pavilions bold profiles, avoiding any of them dominating the facade, and balanced the profiles and details harmoniously. The choice of rock-faced Indiana limestone for the exterior contributed to the sense of permanence and the fortress character that the architect sought. He marked the entry, slightly off-center, with a substantial, two-bay porch and employed slightly pointed arches in the porch, reinforcing the corners with Gothic buttresses. Price echoed the design of the porch in his approach to the porte cochere at the north end of the facade.

Directly above the porch, Price achieved a monumental effect by first placing a rectangular pavilion and then a more substantial pavilion to house the main stairway inside. Crenellated battlements capped the top pavilion, suggesting a medieval palace or castle. Adjoining the entry porch to the north and projecting from the main structure of the house, Price fashioned a pavilion with a Tudor gable. To the south of the stair hall pavilion, he constructed a one-story covered porch with an open terrace above, then another pavilion, echoing the northernmost pavilion. Finally, Price located a rectangular, two-story tower at the southeast corner of the facade.

The architect drew the details for the facade from several sources: dripstones, rectangular banks of windows and pointed gables from sixteenth-century Tudor palaces, buttresses from Gothic architecture, and an arcade of Doric columns adapted from the Italian Renaissance for the recessed porch, but with unusual elliptical arches. The designer enhanced the picturesque quality through the rock-faced stone on the walls, dressed limestone for details, and red clay tiles for the roofs. For entertaining, Price laid out a spacious terrace fronted by a balustrade along most of the facade.

The Van Camps spent lavishly on their interior. The C. C. Foster Lumber Company of Indianapolis supplied one million feet of Mexican mahogany wood, from which the architects selected the wood for the main stairway, paneling, and sculpted details. Price brought two master craftsmen, A. Zettler, originally from Germany, and Henry Chandler, of New York, to oversee the carving of the wood. Price or his draftsman would provide detailed sketches of desired details to Zettler, who would make a plaster model of each. Zettler would turn the models over to Chandler and several local wood-carvers, who would carve each feature by hand. On the stairway, they created newel posts and panels for the stair rails. In every room of the house, they carved either oak acorns or ivy and berries as ornaments. The artisans also created brackets, grotesques, and human heads for the cornices of rooms and arabesques for fireplace mantels (fig. 4.8).[17] By November 1906, when the family moved into their grand residence, they had spent approximately $100,000.[18]

Robert W. and Hannah Wright Furnas House (American Foursquare/Classical/Georgian)

As the first decade of the twentieth century advanced, more families of means left homes in the north-side neighborhoods south of Twenty-Second Street and built residences north of Fall Creek. In 1906–7, Robert W. Furnas, president of the R. W. Furnas Ice Cream Company, and his wife, Hannah Wright Furnas, purchased a double lot on the east side of Pennsylvania Street north of Thirty-Fourth Street and constructed a substantial house. They hired Foltz and Parker to design it for them, and the architects created a residence that showed the popularity of what has since been called the American Foursquare style.[19] The label has been applied by architectural historians to houses with square shapes, hipped roofs, a central dormer in the front slope of the roof, and, frequently, a rectangular porch

Facing top, **Figure 4.9.** Robert W. and Hannah Wright Furnas House, 3435 North Pennsylvania Street, built in 1906–7 and designed by Foltz and Parker, using elements of the Foursquare design formula—rectilinear shape, a hipped roof, and a front dormer. The architects drew the other details from Classical and Georgian architecture. View in 1908. *Art Work of Indianapolis, Ind.* (Chicago: Gravure Illustration, 1908).

Facing bottom, **Figure 4.10.** Furnas House in 2022. Now part of an apartment court. James Glass.

across the facade. Foursquare designs appeared on houses for all income levels and became sought after in Indianapolis following 1900.[20]

For the Furnas House, Foltz and Parker created an imposing version of the Foursquare while applying decorative elements from other sources (figs. 4.9 and 4.10). They designed a two-and-a-half-story, rectangular block that departed from the usual square shape and constructed its exterior walls of reddish-orange, load-bearing brick.[21] The architects specified a hipped roof from which they projected a central dormer with its own hipped roof and additional dormers on the slopes of the south and north elevations. As in most Foursquare houses, the Furnas House facade was symmetrical.

Foltz and Parker placed projecting bays with bowed curves on either side of the central entry. They sheltered the entry with a porch originally supported by stone Ionic columns from the Classical tradition standing in antis. At the corners of the porch, they employed substantial brick piers styled as pilasters. A porch on the south elevation echoed the design of the front porch. In the original design, the architects repeated the in antis columns motif on either side of the second-floor window directly above the entry. As seen in other houses, the architects laid out an open terrace to flank the entry porch. They ran a Renaissance-style balustrade along it and above the entry porch and specified flat Georgian arches made of stone for the windows of the exterior. Some alterations have been made to the details of the exterior, and the house is now part of a U-shaped apartment court.

Meredith and Eugenie Kountze Nicholson House (Georgian)

Several years earlier, Foltz and Parker had designed a house in the Georgian style that was to lead to a series of similar, elegant residences. By 1902, the author Meredith Nicholson had won renown and financial success with publication of his novel *The Main Chance*. He and his wife, Eugenie Kountze Nicholson, decided to build an imposing house on Delaware Street, still the most fashionable address

> *Facing top,* **Figure 4.11.** Meredith and Eugenie Kountze Nicholson House, 1500 North Delaware Street, built in 1902–3 and designed by Foltz and Parker, using Georgian house designs of the eighteenth-century English colonies as models. Note the symmetrical facade, five bays across the first story, cornice with modillions, flat stone arches over the windows, dormer windows with pediments, and gambrel roof. Restored and occupied by Indiana Humanities. View in 2021. James Glass.

> *Facing bottom,* **Figure 4.12.** McPhedris-Warner House, Portsmouth, New Hampshire, built in 1718–23 and a possible model for parts of the Nicholson House design. View from 1994. James Glass.

after Meridian. They retained Foltz and Parker, who had recently formed their partnership, and the architects created a design that evoked Georgian architecture in the American English colonies of the eighteenth century—particularly several houses in New England.[22]

The three-story red brick house that rose at 1500 North Delaware Street during 1903 (fig. 4.11) owed its massing and many of its details to such residences as the McPhedris-Warner House in Portsmouth, New Hampshire, of 1718–23 (fig. 4.12) and the John Hancock House in Boston of 1737–40. As in the eighteenth-century residences, the architects devised a symmetrical facade with five bays across the first floor, a central entry, a mansard-like roof rising to a platform screened by a balustrade,[23] a cornice supported by modillions, dormer windows with pediment caps, and double-hung window sashes with twelve panes in each sash. From the Hancock House may have come the idea to place brick quoins at the corners of the facade. The architects possibly gleaned the flat stone arches with keystones that appear over the windows from the 1761–62 Mount Pleasant house in Philadelphia. The remaining exterior details of the Nicholson House came from other sources. The gambrel-shaped gables derived ultimately from Dutch or Flemish Colonial houses in the Middle English colonies of the early eighteenth century. The elliptical fan light over the entrance and the side lights can be found in Federal-era houses after the Georgian period. The semicircular portico-porch that originally stood over the entrance, with its smooth-shafted Ionic columns, may have been inspired by late eighteenth-century European and American residences, such as the White House.[24]

The architects laid out the rectangular main block to face Delaware Street and extended a substantial wing to the rear. The Nicholsons suggested the layout of the first floor, which is unconventional. To the north of the central hall, in the northeast corner, is what the family called a "visitor's room," in lieu of a parlor or drawing room. Instead of sliding doors, the architects admitted visitors to the northeast room through a screen of Ionic columns. To the south of the hall is the highlight of the interior—a spacious library for the author that runs along the south side of the main block. The hall leads directly back to the dining room, which also adjoins the library. The designers chose dull mahogany for the columns and finished the library in weathered oak.[25]

Bliss-Vonnegut-Cummings House (Georgian)

Foltz and Parker evidently attracted favorable attention with their design for the Nicholson House. During the next five years, they found other clients who wished

Figure 4.13. Bliss-Vonnegut-Cummings House, 2850 North Meridian Street, built in 1905–6 by Henry R. and Margaret Bliss and designed by Foltz and Parker with Georgian features similar to those on the Nicholson House. Variations include a projecting central pavilion with pediment and oval windows as well as limestone and brick voussoirs over the windows. Now attorney's offices. View in 2019. James Glass.

to build very similar Georgian houses, and three of those residences rose in the 2800 and 2900 blocks of North Meridian Street. Henry R. Bliss constructed two of the houses. In 1902, he held the posts of secretary and treasurer at the Sinker-Davis Company, manufacturers of engines, boilers, and sawmill machinery, and also invested in real estate. Bliss constructed his first Georgian house at what is now 2850 North Meridian in 1902–3 and resided there with his family for three years. The Blisses then moved into a second house in the next block (see the following). Previously, Henry and his wife, Margaret Hooker Bliss, had lived in a frame house at 1817 North Meridian Street.[26]

A comparison of the Nicholson House and the first Bliss house shows marked similarities in the designs. For the Blisses, Foltz and Parker created a red brick, rectangular house with three stories, a gambrel roof, and dormer windows capped by pediments (fig. 4.13). Further, they composed the facade with five bays across

CITY MANSIONS AND COUNTRY ESTATES | 319

the first story, a central entrance, and a rounded portico with columns (since removed) over the entry. They placed brick quoins on the corners, attached a second porch to the south elevation, and fashioned the entry with a fan light and side lights. The architects also incorporated some variations: they added a pavilion to the center of the facade with a pediment at the top, very much like such eighteenth-century Georgian houses in the colonies as the Vassall-Longfellow House (1759) in Cambridge, Massachusetts. They flanked the central second-story window with vertical oval lights and used both limestone and brick voussoirs for the flat arches over the windows. For windows, the designers used six-over-one sash windows. In the side porch, they made use of columns in antis, much like they did with the Furnas House (see previous discussion).[27]

Henry and Margaret Bliss sold their new house to Clemens Vonnegut Jr., son of the founder of the Vonnegut Hardware Company, and Vonnegut and his family occupied the 2850 house briefly, succeeded by the family of lawyer Lawrence B. Cummings.[28]

Henry R. and Margaret Bliss House II (Georgian)

In 1906, Henry and Margaret Bliss commissioned Foltz and Parker to design a second Early Georgian house at 2905 North Meridian Street in the North Park Addition (fig. 4.14). The architects followed a similar formula: a three-story brick main block with five bays across the first story, a central entry with fan and side lights, a steep front roof slope with three dormers capped by pediments, flat arches composed of limestone voussoirs and keystones over the windows, and a rectangular side porch on the south elevation. Again, Foltz and Parker sought to provide some individuality to the design. They placed a simple porch over the entry composed of a flat-roofed entablature, supported by single Corinthian columns. A trio of shortened windows at the center of the second story replaced the oval light of the previous house. The architects used a gable roof, not a gambrel, and they capped the central dormer with a swan's neck pediment. They also used six-over-six sash windows—soon to become a standard in Georgian-style houses.[29]

John P. and Philippine Bennerscheidt Frenzel House (Georgian)

John P. Frenzel was one of the three Frenzel brothers who operated Merchants National Bank. John also headed the Indiana Trust Company, controlled by the family. In 1907, the Frenzels were beginning construction on the tallest skyscraper in the state—the Merchants National Bank tower (see chap. 1 of this volume)—and

Figure 4.14. +Henry R. and Margaret Bliss House II, 2905 North Meridian Street, built in 1906–7 and designed by Foltz and Parker using similar elements from eighteenth-century colonial Georgian houses. Note the single Corinthian columns supporting the entrance portico, a trio of shortened windows over the entry, and a fan light and side lights flanking the entrance door, from Federal architecture. Demolished in 1965–66 and its site used as a parking lot for an adjacent life insurance company. View in 1908. *Art Work of Indianapolis, Ind.* (Chicago: Gravure Illustration, 1908).

John Frenzel and his wife, Philippine Bennerscheidt Frenzel, decided to move from a modest house at 620 North East Street, near old Germantown, to an imposing residence in the North Park Addition. They purchased a lot and built a house in 1907–8 at 2908 North Meridian Street. There is no documentation of

CITY MANSIONS AND COUNTRY ESTATES | 321

Figure 4.15. +John P. and Philippine Bennerscheidt Frenzel House, 2908 North Meridian Street, built in 1907–8 and probably designed by Foltz and Parker, using a design that follows the Georgian formula seen in the Nicholson House, with a few variations, such as double columns supporting the entry portico and a trio of windows over the entrance. Demolished in 1973–74 after being vacant for seven years. View in 1908. *Art Work of Indianapolis, Ind.* (Chicago: Gravure Illustration, 1908).

the architects, but the marked similarities with the two Bliss houses point to Foltz and Parker.[30]

The Frenzel House (fig. 4.15), like its neighbors, consisted of a three-story block constructed of brick, with five bays across the first and second stories, a steep roof with three dormers, flat stone arches over the windows, a cornice with modillions, and a fan light and side lights for the entry. Variations included a porch for the entry with pairs of Corinthian columns flanking the passage instead of single columns; a trio of windows at the center of the second story, with narrow side lights; segmental pediments for all the dormers; and double chimneys interrupting the front and back slopes of the steep roof, similar to the treatment in the eighteenth-century Hancock House. A balustrade at the top of the front slope of the roof resembled the treatment on the Nicholson House.[31]

A final house that closely resembles this group of four homes, probably all designed by Foltz and Parker, stands at 4220 Central Avenue. Likely built between 1909 and 1910 by Edward C. Strathmann, general superintendent of the Bedford Stone and Construction Company, it is similar to both the second Bliss House and the Frenzel residence.[32]

Herman P. and Alma Bachman Lieber House (Sixteenth-Century English Tudor Vernacular/Arts and Crafts)

Although most of the large homes built in the city after 1905 rose north of Fall Creek, several well-to-do families constructed new houses in the well-established neighborhood bounded by Meridian Street, Sixteenth Street, College Avenue, and Tenth Street. Herman P. Lieber and his wife, Alma Bachman Lieber, headed one such family. Lieber was one of four brothers who operated the H. Lieber Company, known for its art gallery downtown and manufacture of picture frames. The Liebers purchased a double lot at what is now 1415 Central Avenue and, in 1908, hired as their architects Vonnegut and Bohn, whose varied residential designs had gained attention.[33]

Bernard Vonnegut may have had a hand in the design of the Lieber House; he died in August 1908, and the planning likely began before then. Vonnegut and his draftsmen created a rectangular block with exterior walls constructed of a reddish-brown brick. They used stucco and timber for the gables on the side elevations and the projecting bays on the facade and south side (fig. 4.16). The facade is picturesque in its asymmetry; Vonnegut and Bohn arranged dissimilar dormers on the roof and contrasting bay windows on the second story. The entry is at the center, but the architects provided access from a stairway and terrace located to the north. The designers also strove for varied texture and colors, using red clay tiles on the main roof and the porch to contrast with the deep-brown brick walls and rusticating the brick piers on the front porch and the lower courses of the south chimney. The architects drew the stucco and timber elements from vernacular buildings in England from the fifteenth and sixteenth centuries. The design for the garage at the east side of the property replicates the materials of the house—brick first story, stucco and timber front gable, and red tile roof.

Figure 4.16. Herman P. and Alma Bachman Lieber House, 1415 Central Avenue, built in 1908–9 and designed by Bernard Vonnegut and the firm of Vonnegut and Bohn, drawing on English Tudor vernacular sources for the stucco and timber gables and bay windows and the Arts and Crafts Movement for the asymmetrical and picturesque arrangement of features. Since 1942, the Psychic Scientist Spiritualist Church has occupied and preserved the house. View from 2020. James Glass.

Inside, Vonnegut and his draftsmen located the living room in the northwest corner of the first floor, the library in the southwest corner, and the dining room in the southeast. In keeping with the Arts and Crafts vogue (see later in this chapter), they placed wooden beams on the ceilings of the living and dining rooms. They designed a red brick fireplace with an oak mantel for the living room and one with a green hearth, mahogany mantel, and mirror for the library. As Vonnegut and Bohn had done at the All Souls Unitarian Church (see chap. 3 of this volume), they retained artist and architect Brandt Steele to design delightful art glass windows for the library, dining room, and north wall of the main stairway. In the west window of the library, Steele depicted a Classical folly reached by a long white stairway within a landscape setting, all in lustrous opalescent glass. In the dining room window, he showed three sailing ships with a deep-blue sea in the background.[34]

Henry and Sarah Lang Kahn House (English Tudor Vernacular)

In 1908, Henry Kahn and his wife, Sarah Lang Kahn, began construction on one of the largest city mansions of the period. Henry owned the Kahn Tailoring Company, a major manufacturer and retailer of men's and women's suits and other apparel (see chap. 1 of this volume), and the firm was growing. Previously, the Kahns had lived in a simple, two-story frame house at 1801 North Pennsylvania Street. Now they purchased a choice tract of land on the north bank of Fall Creek, a block east of Meridian, and hired as architects Foltz and Parker, who were just completing almost a decade of designing distinctive homes.[35]

The architects sited the Kahn House on the north side of the property and gave it two facades. One, containing the entrance and porte cochere, faced Twenty-Seventh Street (fig. 4.17), and the other faced south and overlooked the natural beauty of the creek.[36] Foltz and Parker's design featured a residential formula that became quite popular in Indianapolis over the next two decades. Often today called English Tudor, the style drew its elements from fifteenth- and sixteenth-century vernacular houses and commercial buildings of English cities and towns. The *Indianapolis Star* referred to the Kahn House in 1909 as being "of the pure English type of architecture."[37] An extant example in London of a sixteenth-century house that illustrates the formula that American architects employed stands within the precincts of the Tower of London. The so-called Queen's House of about 1530 is three and a half stories in height. Its first story is brick, its second and third stories are constructed of stucco and timber, and its attic story consists of gables faced with stucco and timber (see fig. 4.18).

Foltz and Parker constructed the first story of the Kahn House with brick and used stucco and timber for the second and third stories. They employed a long footprint for the residence. At the center of both facades, the architects placed three-story brick pavilions. They made the north, principal facade asymmetrical and picturesque in its arrangement. In front of the central north pavilion, they constructed a substantial porte cochere to shelter arriving and departing automobile

Facing top, **Figure 4.17.** +Henry and Sarah Lang Kahn House, 101 East Twenty-Seventh Street, built in 1908 and designed by Foltz and Parker, drawing on English Tudor vernacular houses of the sixteenth century for the stucco and timber upper stories, brick first story, and picturesque arrangement of pavilions, gables, and dormer windows. The house served as the governor's residence from 1921 to 1946 and as an office building for Indianapolis city parks department until 1959. It was demolished in 1959–60. View from c. 1920s. Bass Photo Company Collection, Indiana Historical Society. (Image cropped)

Facing bottom, **Figure 4.18.** Queen's House, Tower of London, c. 1530. Note brick first story, stucco and timber second story, and multiple gables, all elements incorporated in English Tudor vernacular houses in the United States. View in 2019. James Glass.

passengers. Broad, ogee arches defined the porte on three sides, and crenellations lined its top. West of the entry, the architects located a porch with a secondary entrance and dormer windows irregularly arranged. East of the entry, they placed another three-story pavilion with stucco and timber face. In the style of English vernacular houses, the north roof sloped down from a high ridge to the first story. The architects provided a more simply detailed south facade: two shallow pavilions with stucco and timber second stories flanked the central brick pavilion.

In their interior planning, Foltz and Parker used a long southern exterior terrace as the organizing element for the major rooms. The western living room, central main dining room, and eastern breakfast room all opened through French doors onto the terrace, which afforded vistas of the gardens to the south. At the west end of the living room, the architects interjected a key feature of the English Arts and Crafts Movement—an inglenook with a fireplace and flanking window seats. Overhead, they employed a Jacobean-style ceiling with geometric patterns formed by plaster moldings. They used wooden beams as decorative elements in the ceilings of the two dining rooms. The Kahns asked the architects to provide a separate suite of rooms for their servants in the northwest corner of the house. At the east end of the property, the architects designed a story-and-a-half brick garage; the transition from carriage houses to garages was well underway.[38]

Dellmore C. and Annie Hamilton Allison House (English Tudor Vernacular)

A short time after the Kahns completed their English Tudor residence, another house in the same style took shape on the south side of Fall Creek, east of College Avenue. Dellmore C. Allison was a member of the large Allison family that owned

Figure 4.19. Dellmore C. and Annie Hamilton Allison House, 2823 Sutherland Avenue, built in 1908–9 and designed by Herbert L. Bass and Company, architects, drawing on the English Tudor vernacular formula—brick first story, stucco and timber second story, shed dormer windows, and picturesque arrangement of features. Note porte cochere on right with second story. View in 2022. James Glass.

and operated the Allison Coupon Company in Indianapolis. Dellmore and his brother James (one of founders of the Indianapolis Motor Speedway) built houses next to each other on Sutherland Avenue. Dellmore and his wife, Annie Hamilton Allison, purchased two lots at 2823 Sutherland and retained Herbert L. Bass as their architect in 1908.[39]

One of the leading residential architects of the city, Bass followed the developing formula for houses in the English Tudor vernacular style: a brick first story, stucco and timber on the second story, and stucco and timber in the several gables at the third-story level (fig. 4.19). He laid out the house with an L-shaped footprint

ARCHITECT PROFILE

Charles H. Byfield

Charles H. Byfield (1873–1935) was born in Louisville and educated in the public schools of Madison, Indiana. He began his interest in architecture at a young age and started to work in the building trades at age fifteen. He spent four years as a woodworker in the 1890s and then found work as a draftsman in an architectural office about 1900. In 1907, Byfield opened his own office and quickly found clients. Much of his practice was in the residential sphere, and he designed large houses, such as the Hare-Tarkington House; doubles, such as the Gocke-King Double (see next chapter); and small bungalows for clients with modest incomes, such as the John F. and Louise Rentsch Bryan House (see next chapter) and the Anton Geiger House at 411 North College Avenue (1910).

He also designed commercial buildings, such as the Wulsin Building at 222 East Ohio Street; apartment buildings, such as the Davlan Apartments at 430 Massachusetts Avenue; and several public schools.

Sources: "Leading Architect, C. H. Byfield, Dies," *Indianapolis Star*, May 15, 1935, 3; "Charles Howard Byfield," Find a Grave, n.d. https://www.findagrave.com/memorial/45898698/charles-howard-byfield, accessed June 26, 2024; "How Others Have Built," *Indianapolis Sunday Star*, October 9, 1910, Women's Section, 4, c. 2. Source for photo: "Leading Architect, C. H. Byfield, Dies."

and attached an unusual two-story porte cochere to the west side, in which the second story is an extension of the second floor in the house.[40] The facade is asymmetrical, and Bass strove for a picturesque effect, with an off-center gable on the east side and a shed dormer on the main roof to the south. He projected forward the upper portions of the gables on the facade and side elevations, forming jetties similar to those found in seventeenth-century colonial houses of New England.[41] He attached a spacious covered porch to the facade and used red clay tiles for the main roof and the porch.

In the interior, Bass laid out a central stair hall, with a living room to the west and the music and dining rooms to the east. For both the living and dining rooms, the architect specified wooden beams for the ceiling, and in the living room, he included a fireplace incorporating Rookwood tile. In another novel touch, Bass incorporated the garage within the first floor of the house at the rear.[42]

Hare-Tarkington House (English Tudor Vernacular)

Maria Fletcher Hare, a member of the wealthy Fletcher family, decided in 1909 to build a house at what is now 4270 North Meridian Street, one of the first residences constructed north of Fortieth Street on Meridian. Previously, Hare and her late husband, Clinton, had lived at 950 North Pennsylvania Street.[43]

Maria Hare hired Charles H. Byfield of Indianapolis as her architect. He had established a practice that by 1909 emphasized residential design. Byfield chose a design (fig. 4.20) that was very close to that of Bass for the Dellmore C. and Annie Hamilton Allison House. The massing and facade composition match most of the details of the Allison residence, except the front elevation is reversed, with the front gable appearing on the left and the shed dormer on the right. In addition, instead of a covered porch, Byfield provided a spacious open terrace along the facade for entertaining and marked the entry with a simple shelter covered by a pyramidal roof. He laid out a rectangular footprint for the house running east and west, with a northern porte cochere, which, like the Allison House, includes a second story.[44]

Inside, the central first-floor corridor led to a cross stair hall and beyond to the dining room. On the south side of the corridor, Byfield devised a spacious living room with a central fireplace. Like Bass, he followed the trend for Tudor and Arts and Crafts houses in employing wood beams across the ceilings of the living and dining room.[45]

From 1923 to 1946, the house was the home of Pulitzer Prize–winning novelist Booth Tarkington and his wife, Susannah.[46]

Figure 4.20. Hare-Tarkington House, 4270 North Meridian Street, built in 1909–10 and designed by Charles H. Byfield of Indianapolis, using the English Tudor vernacular as the theme and replicating the arrangement of features and materials found in the Dellmore C. and Annie Hamilton Allison House, except the facade elements are reversed. Note the pyramidal roof over the small entry porch and the extension of the second story over the porte cochere. Later it became the home of novelist Booth Tarkington and his wife, Susannah. Restored by Doris Anne and Tim Sadler as their residence. View from 2023. James Glass.

Alfred M. and Minnie Stroup Glossbrenner House (Tudor Palace)

A small number of large houses built in Indianapolis between 1900 and 1920 derived from the architecture of English Tudor palaces and country houses of the sixteenth century. One of the best expositions of the style came from English-born architect Alfred Grindle (see profile in chap. 3 of this volume). His opportunity came when Alfred M. Glossbrenner, vice president of the printing firm Levey Brothers and Company, and his wife, Minnie Stroup Glossbrenner, decided to build a substantial residence on the northwest corner of Thirty-Second and Meridian Streets. Previously, they had lived in a modest frame residence at 10 East Thirty-Second Street. In 1910 or 1911, they purchased the corner lot and hired Grindle to design their new home.[47]

Grindle devised plans for a red brick house with limestone trim sited to advantage along the top of a ridge overlooking Meridian Street (fig. 4.21). The architect gave the residence an irregular, picturesque silhouette, with a rectangular block at its core, from which a pavilion projects from its east side and several one-story appendages extend from the south elevation. The core block has a hipped roof, and the east pavilion has a gable roof. Tudor-style gables with limestone coping are used at the top of the east pavilion and on several modest projections from the main roof. Grindle used the Tudor palace vocabulary for most details—dripstone moldings above most windows, limestone blocks as surrounds for the windows, and an oriel window above the entry. He made the entrance at the juncture of the main block and east wing a focal point of the facade, with limestone surround augmented by stepped buttresses, an ogee arch, and crenellations. Likewise, for the rectangular solarium running along the south elevation, Grindle used a series of limestone ogee arches from the Tudor period, crenellations, and Gothic buttresses.

Facing top, **Figure 4.21.** Alfred M. and Minnie Stroup Glossbrenner House, 3210 North Meridian Street, built in 1911–12 and designed by Alfred Grindle of Indianapolis, drawing from the details of sixteenth-century royal Tudor palaces, with gables lined by limestone coping, dripstones above the windows, oriels, and limestone surrounds for windows. Note also Gothic elements—stepped buttresses and crenellations and the overall picturesque arrangement of features. Saved by Indiana Landmarks and restored and adaptively used by R & B Architects for their offices. View in 2023. James Glass.

Facing bottom, **Figure 4.22.** Arts and Crafts design and furnishing of the Glossbrenner House dining room. Note the horizontal fireplace with tiles for hearth, wooden beams for ceiling, and Craftsman-style chandelier. View in 1912. *Year Book of the Indiana Chapter A.I.A. and Catalog of the Third Annual Exhibition 1912* (Indianapolis: Indiana Chapter A.I.A., 1912).

He located a porte cochere with similar detailing on the south side of the solarium, connecting with the side entry. In front of the main entry and along the east side of the east pavilion, the architect laid out an open terrace with a tile floor and brick and limestone parapet.[48]

Inside, the main entry communicates with the primary corridor. Immediately to the north is the principal stairway, with large leaded glass windows containing art glass insets at the landing. The dining room on the first floor bespeaks of Arts and Crafts influence, with polished wood paneling, a central fireplace with tile hearth, and an overmantel with art glass windows (fig. 4.22). A full ballroom with hardwood floors and wooden accents fills the third floor.[49] The Glossbrenners moved into their house in 1912.

Charles Warren and Cornelia Cole Fairbanks House (Italian Renaissance)

Former US vice president Charles W. Fairbanks and his wife, Cornelia Cole Fairbanks, had previously resided in a frame Queen Anne house at 1522 North Meridian Street (see chap. 10 of vol. 1). After completing a trip to Alaska, they began to plan a new residence north of Fall Creek in the midst of the fine houses of the North Park Addition. In 1911, they purchased more than an acre of land on the southwest corner of Thirtieth and Meridian Streets and hired one of the Midwest's top residential architects, Howard Van Doren Shaw of Chicago. Shaw's work had been introduced to Indianapolis a couple of years earlier, when Louis C. and Mary McDonald Huesmann had retained him to design a large brick house at 3148 North Pennsylvania Street. Shaw had crafted a residence for the Huesmanns with few decorative details and no references to historic architecture.[50]

For the Fairbanks residence, the Chicago architect designed a house that perhaps was the ultimate in elegance and fine proportions for an Indianapolis house of the period and clothed it with the fabric of the Italian Renaissance (fig. 4.23).

Facing top, **Figure 4.23.** Charles Warren and Cornelia Cole Fairbanks House, 2960 North Meridian Street, built in 1911–13 and designed by Howard Van Doren Shaw of Chicago in an updated interpretation of Italian Renaissance design: horizontal facade, hipped roof with dormers, and a carefully detailed and proportioned limestone screen consisting of paired Ionic pilasters supporting an entablature with Baroque urns. View in 2023. James Glass.

Facing bottom, **Figure 4.24.** View of the twin limestone porches on the south elevation of Fairbanks House, with Renaissance arches, Ionic pilasters, and entablature with modillions. View in 2022. James Glass.

ARCHITECT PROFILE

Howard Van Doren Shaw

Howard Van Doren Shaw (1869–1926) was born to wealthy parents and grew up in the Prairie Avenue neighborhood of Chicago. After graduation from Yale University and a year's intensive study in architecture at the Massachusetts Institute of Technology, Shaw entered the office of Jenney and Mundie, then among the top designers of Chicago skyscrapers. In 1892–93, he traveled extensively in Europe, visiting a range of architecture, both historic and contemporary. He returned to Jenney and Mundie briefly and then opened his own office in 1894. Shaw developed a practice centered on the design of large homes in Chicago and its suburbs, especially the newly developed community of Lake Forest. He was adept in a variety of architectural idioms, including Renaissance, English Tudor vernacular, Tudor palace, and abstracted English vernacular, exemplified by the work of English architect Edwin Lutyens.

He also designed the Market Square of Lake Forest in 1913, with Tudor vernacular storefronts and towers with abstracted medieval features.

In East Chicago, Indiana, Shaw obtained the commission to plan and design a company town for Clayton Mark, head of the Mark Manufacturing Company. In Marktown, Shaw showed his affinity for the work of English Arts and Crafts architect Charles Voysey, designing multiple buildings with twin gables and stucco facades without detailing.

In Indianapolis, Shaw is known to have designed two houses—the Louis C. and Mary McDonald Huesmann House at 3148 North Pennsylvania Street in an abstracted English vernacular and the Charles Warren and Cornelia Cole Fairbanks House in an elegant and original composition invoking Renaissance elements.

Sources: "Howard Shaw, Architect, Dies in Baltimore," *Chicago Tribune*, May 7, 1926, 1; Leland M. Roth, *A Concise History of American Architecture* (New York: Harper & Row, 1980), 236; "Howard Van Doren Shaw," Wikipedia, n.d. https://en.wikipedia.org/wiki/Howard_Van_Doren_Shaw, accessed June 26, 2024. Source for photo: "Howard Van Doren Shaw."

He sited the residence along the top of the ridge that ran through the west side of the North Park Addition, giving it prominence along the street. Shaw fashioned a rectangular main block with a plain hipped roof to face Meridian Street.[51] From the center of the main block, he ran a long wing to the west. He formed a U-shaped courtyard on the south side of the house with two symmetrical wings.

The architect used a new interpretation of Renaissance elements for the facade. He employed red brick for the exterior walls of the entire house and along the first story of the facade attached an engaged limestone screen in which paired Ionic pilasters support a continuous architrave and cornice. As a focal point of the screen, he designed a limestone frontispiece at the center, containing an arched entry with a wrought-iron gate, flanked by Ionic pilasters, niches, and additional pilasters. The pilasters occur at regular intervals across the facade, creating a rhythm. Between the paired pilasters outside the frontispiece are windows and blind limestone panels. Shaw lined the top of the first-story cornice with bulbous urns decorated by foliated sculpture. He used limestone pilasters, an architrave, and a cornice similar to those in the facade for the frontispiece that he fashioned around the north entrance to the house on Thirtieth Street. Shaw also employed Ionic pilasters at the corners of the two enclosed limestone porches on the south elevation. He filled the bays between the porch pilasters with large Renaissance-style arches capped by keystones (fig. 4.24).

The remaining designed landscape features are concentrated in the approach to the main entrance. A brick walkway approaches the house from Meridian Street and cuts through the hill on which the house stands, meeting a stairway on axis with the main entrance. A limestone balustrade flanks the stairway.[52]

The result of Shaw's labors on the exterior is a restful, serene Renaissance design, quite different from the picturesque, asymmetrical facades of the English Tudor and Arts and Crafts.

Inside, the architect laid out a central corridor that runs through the main block and extends back into the rear wing. South of the corridor, he located the living room, which connects in turn with one of the south porches. To the north, he designed a spacious library, paneled in dark wood. Shaw located the dining room and morning room in the western wing that extended to the south. On the second floor, he arranged six bedrooms.[53]

When completed in 1912, the house cost the Fairbanks couple approximately $100,000. Unfortunately, Cornelia was only able to enjoy it for a short time, dying within a year.[54] The house and landscape setting served Charles Fairbanks well in 1916 when he received there a delegation from the Republican National Convention, formally notifying him of his nomination a second time as their candidate for vice president.

Thomas and Eva Bryant Taggart House (Renaissance)

One of the great business and political figures in Indianapolis during the early twentieth century was Thomas Taggart, former mayor of the city, builder and owner of the French Lick Springs Hotel, and chairman of the Democratic National Committee. During his rise in politics and the hotel industry, Taggart and his family had lived at 810 North Capitol Avenue in the midst of a cluster of residences occupied by businessmen and their families. With growing hotel investments and revenue, Taggart and his wife, Eva Bryant Taggart, decided in 1912 to construct a new residence at 1331 North Delaware Street, along a corridor in which affluent families continued to build homes. The Taggarts' oldest daughter, Lucy, is credited with shaping much of the design. She was an artist with a growing reputation and had traveled in Italy. Upon her return, she decided the house should be Italian in

Figure 4.25. Thomas and Eva Bryant Taggart House, 1331 North Delaware Street, built in 1912–13 and designed by architect Frederick Wallick, consulting with artist Lucy Taggart. The result was an Italian Renaissance composition, including a symmetrical facade with horizontal massing, an Ionic portico, a balustrade over the entry, arched windows on the first story, and an entablature supported by consoles. Adaptively used as offices. View in 2021. James Glass.

style. Her parents hired Frederick Wallick, a New York–based architect with ties to Indianapolis, and Lucy consulted with him on the design.[55]

Wallick devised a rectangular block to face the street and wings on either end of the rear, forming a courtyard (fig. 4.25).[56] He incorporated several elements from the Italian Renaissance into the facade, to respond to Lucy Taggart's desires, and mixed them harmoniously with details from other sources. From the Renaissance came symmetry in the facade and a limestone entry porch supported by Ionic columns and decorated at the rear by Ionic pilasters. Wallick also employed a Renaissance-style cornice with consoles and dentils and an Italian balustrade

CITY MANSIONS AND COUNTRY ESTATES | 339

above the entry porch. He used matching stone balustrades to form balconies outside two second-story windows. In addition, he incorporated arched windows with lunette lights and French doors in the first story and a delicately wrought-iron grille to enclose the entry porch, all elements drawn from the Italian Renaissance. The architect used the contrasting colors and textures of the brick and limestone effectively, employing dark headers laid in Flemish bond and limestone surrounds for three of the second-story windows. The two dormer windows in the slope of the facade roof are unconventional—simple projections with Classical entablatures, but without details.

The entry leads into a rectangular hall with a marble floor. To the east of the hall, Wallick located the dining room, which overlooked a formal Italian garden in the courtyard to the rear. To the south of the entry hall, the architect created a living room that featured a large stone fireplace with a projecting shelf supported by carved brackets. Overhead, he lined the ceiling with wooden beams. At the east end of the living room, arched French doors gave access to a solarium. On the second floor, the architect arranged four bedrooms with private baths, and on the third floor, Lucy Taggart occupied a spacious studio for her painting. Wallick provided space for the kitchen and servants' quarters in the northeast corner of the first and second floors and in the northeast rear wing.[57] The Taggarts occupied their residence in 1914 and spent about $25,000 on the house proper.[58]

Florence Baxter and George D. Thornton House (Rustic/Arts and Crafts)

Popular interest in Rustic houses incorporating boulders or cobblestones into the construction and striving for harmony with nature began in Indianapolis with the 1893–96 "Lombardy" house designed by John H. Stem for John T. Brush (see chap. 10 of vol. 1). Enthusiasm grew stronger in the early twentieth century with the advent of the Arts and Crafts Movement and the publication of many Rustic designs in *The Craftsman* magazine (see the next chapter). One of the more striking large houses embodying the Rustic theme rose in 1911–12 on a large, irregular lot at the center of Irvington. According to a newspaper account, Florence Baxter Thornton hired local architect Marshall E. Van Arman to design a home for herself and her husband, George D. Thornton. George was secretary and treasurer of the Puritan Bed Springs Company of Indianapolis.[59] The Thorntons purchased the lot on the southeast corner of Audubon Road and Lowell Avenue; a corner of the property formed part of the Audubon Road oval. The north and northwest boundaries of the lot are curved and thus afford a sweeping vista of the oval and

Figure 4.26. Florence Baxter Thornton and George D. Thornton House, 75 North Audubon Road, Irvington, built in 1911–12 and designed by architect Marshall Van Arman of Indianapolis, drawing on the popularity of Rustic materials, such as fieldstones ("bowlders"), and the Arts and Crafts Movement. Note the asymmetrical yet picturesque arrangement of the facade and the dominance of the fieldstone porch. View in 2022. James Glass.

the houses on the north side of Lowell Avenue from the Thornton House. The elevated site also gives prominence to the house, which faces northwest.[60]

Van Arman designed a rectangular, two-story residence with an irregular, picturesque silhouette (fig. 4.26). He used cobblestone and stucco as the primary

CITY MANSIONS AND COUNTRY ESTATES | 341

materials. At the northwest corner, he appended a one-story, hexagonal sunporch, with cobblestone base and stucco walls. At the center of the facade, he designed a large cobblestone porch with curved parapets and irregular shaped arches for the entrance. An elevated, cobblestone terrace with a pergola overhead runs east from the entry. A central gable with stucco and timber surface offers a vertical accent to the facade, contrasting with the porch and terrace, and a smaller gable complements it to the east. The architect devised a large, sloping roof initially covered with stained shingles. On the west elevation, he used a jerkinhead gable, and on the east elevation, an unusual combination of pointed and jerkinhead gables. A couple of cobblestone chimneys add to the Rustic character of the exterior.

Inside the entry, Van Arman laid out a reception hall. On one side, he designated a living room that occupied all of the west side of the first floor. The room communicated with the sunporch at its northwest corner. East of the hall, the architect specified the dining room, with pantry and kitchen. On the second level, he configured four bedrooms around a central hall.[61]

RUSTIC COUNTRY RETREATS

When John T. Brush commissioned the Rustic-style house "Lombardy" in 1893, he not only launched a taste for Rustic dwellings locally but also a yen among some well-to-do Indianapolis businessmen for country retreats. Over the next fifteen years, several leading citizens purchased properties on wooded or rural tracts and constructed informal "suburban" houses either as their primary residences or as second homes for spending weekends or summers. For example, George A. Dickson, senior partner in the theater-operating firm Dickson and Talbott, constructed a rambling log house on a wooded bluff above White River and called it "Crow's Nest."[62] He had previously resided with his family at 1310 North Pennsylvania Street and now desired to live amid nature in the country. Unfortunately, Dickson died before he could enjoy his retreat.[63]

In 1904–5, banker Stoughton A. Fletcher II and his wife, May Henley Fletcher, who had previously lived in a frame Queen Anne–style house at 1526 North Meridian Street, decided to build a "suburban" residence outside the city. In 1905, they purchased a substantial tract of land on Bluff Road south of the then city limits and hired architect Clarence Martindale to design a roomy, informal house on the top of a hill (fig. 4.27). The architect drew on ideas from the Arts and Crafts and bungalow movements for the two-story residence, to which he gave horizontal massing and a massive roof that swept down to meet an expansive

Facing, **Figure 4.27.** +Stoughton A. Fletcher II and May Henley Fletcher "suburban" house, on Bluff Road, south of the then city limits, built in 1905 and designed by Clarence Martindale, who created a sprawling residence on a hilltop with a wraparound porch supported by rock-faced concrete piers and shingled upper story, all asymmetrical and informal, following the Rustic theme. Demolished after 1917. View in 1908. *Art Work of Indianapolis, Ind.* (Chicago: Gravure Illustration., 1908).

porch. The Fletchers desired such a porch, and Martindale made it the focal point of the design, wrapping it around the facade and continuing it along the sides of the house. He recalled the Shingle style (chap. 10 of vol. 1) with wooden shingles on the exterior and set large dormers into three slopes of the roof. The shingles and rock-faced concrete piers supporting the porch reinforced the Arts and Crafts Movement's emphasis on informality and connections to nature. To provide a sense of drama for visitors approaching the house, Martindale constructed six

Figure 4.28. +(unknown if extant) August Coburn Residence, on Cold Spring Road, built in 1907–8 and reflecting elements of the Adirondack cabins of upstate New York, with a large frame main house, the design of which was influenced by the Arts and Crafts Movement, with projecting eaves and shed dormers, two outbuildings, and a tower. All suggested a rustic retreat from the clamor and bustle of Indianapolis. View in 1909. The exact location is unclear; it may have stood on Cold Spring Road south of Thirtieth Street. *Art Work of Indianapolis, Ind.* (Chicago: Gravure Illustration., 1909).

flights of concrete stairs leading from the road up the hill to the residence. He also used hydraulic cement as the structural material for the house.[64]

In 1907–8, Augustus Coburn, owner of the Michigan Lumber Company, built as his primary residence a rambling frame structure on Cold Spring Road, which wound through a rolling landscape west of White River. The main house resembled an Adirondacks cabin of upstate New York—horizontal in its massing, covered with wood shingles, and asymmetrically laid out with large shed dormers of differing sizes cutting through the cornices (fig. 4.28).[65]

COUNTRY ESTATES

At the beginning of the twentieth century, American families of great wealth began to shift their residences from mansions in cities to estates in the country, modeled on the palaces and villas of royalty and nobility in Europe since the Renaissance. Such country estates became popular beginning in the 1890s. One of the most celebrated early estates, Biltmore, took shape in that decade near Ashville, North Carolina, as George Washington Vanderbilt built a palatial home based on the sixteenth-century royal château at Blois, France, and surrounded it with formal gardens and informal landscape designs. By the first decade of the twentieth century, the leading families of New York were building great estates on the north shore of Long Island, and the millionaires of Boston and Philadelphia were following suit in the countryside outside their cities.[66]

A primary motivation for such extravagant displays of wealth was to assume grand lifestyles that emulated those of the Old World's aristocrats. Estate owners asserted their claim to social primacy by entertaining lavishly with banquets and parties for others of the same income level. Tennis courts, polo grounds, and private golf courses afforded athletic pastimes and opportunities for husbands to cement business relationships with peers in the commercial world. The world of country estates depended on large staffs of servants, who occupied quarters in the main houses and maintained the properties, prepared and served the food at meals, cleaned and pressed clothes for the presiding family, and chauffeured the limousines that were replacing horses and carriages.

For architects fortunate enough to win commissions to design the houses, the country estate era offered an opportunity to create sumptuous residences with extensive decorative programs and very large budgets. It also created demand for the new profession of landscape architects, who, since the Civil War, had complemented the work of architects by designing both elaborate formal gardens and informal gardens that seemed to blend into the natural setting. Frederick Law Olmsted Sr. set high standards for estate planning and garden design in country properties such as Biltmore, and his son and stepson formed a firm, Olmsted Brothers, which designed several grandly scaled estates in Long Island and outside major cities across the country in the early twentieth century. Jens Jensen of Chicago provided his own brand of informal and formal landscapes in midwestern estates, including at least one in Indianapolis.[67]

Architects in cities like Indianapolis could readily obtain plans and photos of the estates in the East through architectural periodicals, such as the *American*

Architect and Building News and the *Architectural Record*. In the Midwest, architects could review designs produced in Chicago and Detroit by subscribing to the *Inland Architect*. Landscape architects followed the work of the premier landscape architecture firms, such as the Olmsted Brothers, in the periodical *Landscape Architecture*.

A handful of Indianapolis families built country estates during the two decades after 1900. The scale and budgets of these estates went far beyond what Dickson, Fletcher, and Coburn created in their informal retreats. A review of five of the largest surviving estates illustrates the design themes and lifestyles entailed by such commissions.

David McLean and Hessie Maxwell Parry Estate, "Golden Hill" (Rustic/English Tudor Vernacular)

David McLean Parry amassed his fortune building carts, carriages, and automobiles. The Parry Manufacturing Company became one of the largest carriage manufacturers in the country during the 1890s, and after 1900, like other companies producing horse-drawn vehicles, Parry's firm transitioned to making motorcars. As his wealth grew, David Parry acquired the elegant Bates-Allen-Parry-McGowan mansion for his family at 1305 North Delaware Street (see chap. 6 of vol. 1). After 1900, he purchased a large tract of land encompassing hills and ravines overlooking the Central Canal and White River and located west of Michigan Road and north of West Thirty-Sixth Street. Woods covered the tract, and it was secluded. Parry and his family moved into a large frame house already on the property but found it of insufficient size. Accordingly, in 1904, Parry and his wife, Hessie Maxwell Parry, hired the seasoned designer of Rustic-style houses in the city, John H. Stem, to create a large new house.[68]

Facing top, **Figure 4.29.** David McLean and Hessie Maxwell Parry estate ("Golden Hill"), 3650 Spring Hollow Road, built in 1904–5 and designed by Indianapolis architect John H. Stem, who continued his mastery of Rustic-type design by incorporating large "bowlders" and a Romanesque porch into the construction of the first story. View of the original appearance in c. 1905–25. Courtesy of Jerico Properties. Thanks to Sharon Butsch Freeland for posting the photo with her article "Hi Mailbag: Parry Mansion in Golden Hill," HistoricIndianapolis.com, March 5, 2013, https://historicindianapolis.com/hi-mailbag-parry-mansion-in-golden-hill/.

Facing bottom, **Figure 4.30.** The Parry House as it is today, showing the redesign of the exterior that occurred after 1915. 2022 photo. James Glass.

Stem, assisted by landscape architect George G. MacDougall, used "bowlders" from the surrounding property to give the house a special Rustic character. He constructed the foundation and first floor from these large fieldstones, some of which were so heavy that ten or twelve men and a team of horses were required to dig them out and haul them to the construction site. The house faced east, and the west elevation looked down on the canal and river. Stem built the upper walls of pressed brick and gave the rectilinear structure a hipped roof with dormers. He fashioned an entry porch out of especially large fieldstones along the south half of the facade. For openings in the porch, the architect created large Romanesque arches (fig. 4.29).[69]

Inside the house, Stem created a two-story central reception hall with marble floor and sixteenth-century French fireplace. The main stairway ascended to the second floor along one side of the hall. In a drawing room, Stem specified a mantel with Classical atlantes statues supporting the shelf. The plans of the architect also called for an auditorium in the basement, in which the Parrys could enjoy entertainments with guests, music rooms, and a billiard room.[70] A gatehouse to the estate, also constructed with "bowlders," controlled access from the south.

David Parry hired Scottish-born George G. MacDougall, who had recently started a landscape architecture practice in Indianapolis, to take charge of the landscape design on the estate, and MacDougall planted some sixteen thousand imported bulbs and other plants along the hills and ravines of Golden Hill, the Parry estate.[71]

After David Parry's death in 1915, the family platted most of the estate into spacious residential lots. The main elements of the original house still exist, but subsequent owners enlarged it and made some modifications (fig. 4.30). Jerico Properties rehabilitated and restored the house in 2014. The setting still includes 3.44 acres.[72]

Frank H. and Harriet Githens Wheeler Estate (Abstracted Modern)

In 1911, three business associates and friends—Carl G. Fisher, James A. Allison, and Frank H. Wheeler—all bought adjoining pieces of land for residences along the west side of Cold Spring Road north of Thirtieth Street.[73] The three men, along with Arthur C. Newby, had founded the Indianapolis Motor Speedway on West Sixteenth Street in 1909 and built the speedway track to showcase automobile capabilities. All four also were pioneers in the manufacture of automobiles and automobile parts.

Figure 4.31. Frank H. and Harriet Githens Wheeler House, 3200 Cold Spring Road, built between 1911 and 1914 and designed by William L. Price of Price and McLanahan, Philadelphia. Price strove for a picturesque massing of the facade, with pavilions and openings of varying sizes and detailing. He incorporated elements of the Romanesque, Gothic, and bungalow styles into the facade and other elevations but abstracted them for a Modern look, breaking with his previous use of explicit historical styles. Note the orange tile contrasting with the buff brick. Now offices for Marian University. View in 2022. James Glass.

After arriving in Indianapolis from California, Frank Wheeler had engaged first in making brass parts and fittings and then cofounded the Wheeler & Schebler works to manufacture one of the first successful carburetors for automobiles. The revenues poured in, and by 1911, Wheeler had amassed enough funds to build a costly estate.[74]

He may have been familiar with the Frank Van Camp House on Meridian Street and through that connection aware of the work of William Price of Price and McLanahan in Philadelphia. A restless and ambitious businessman, Wheeler retained the Philadelphia architects to design a Wheeler Heights real estate development in Indianapolis, a hotel for the downtown, and an estate on Cold Spring Road. Ultimately, the industrialist only built the estate.[75]

Wheeler asked Price to design a large house and an extended designed landscape for himself; his wife, Harriet Githens Wheeler; and their son, Douglas. After completing preliminary plans, Price estimated the house would cost approximately $80,000, and the outbuildings and landscape design would cost an additional $100,000, which, together with the $40,000 that the client had spent purchasing the property, pushed the total cost to $250,000—the most expensive residential property in the city or its environs to date.[76]

Price laid out an immense, L-shaped house set back from Cold Spring Road (fig. 4.31). As he was to do later with the Union Station concourse downtown (see chap. 1 of this volume), Price used buff-colored brick for the exterior walls and abstracted historical details. He also strove for a picturesque and varied massing that was asymmetrical yet harmoniously unfolded across the facade (on the east side) and along the south elevation, similar to how he had composed the facade for the Van Camp House. He devised a large open pavilion containing the entrance as the focal point of the Wheeler House facade. Three simplified Romanesque arches articulate the front of the pavilion; above the central arch, Price placed a balcony with a parapet above. He used brick buttresses of two different types to define the corners of the entry pavilion and abstracted their details. Two other pavilions with hipped roofs, differing in height and fenestration, project from the facade on either side of the entry vestibule. The main roof sweeps down from a high ridge to cover the entry pavilion, in the bungalow manner, and Price covered it with green clay tile to contrast with the buff brick below. He fashioned a covered terrace that ran around the southeast corner of the facade.

Emphasizing a break with the explicit historical elements of design seen earlier in the Van Camp House, Price minimized obvious decorative details on the exterior, preferring occasional insets of colored terra-cotta or varied patterns in the brick courses as accents.

Figure 4.32. South elevation of Wheeler House, showing (*from the right*) the terrace, the solarium with bank of windows, a projecting bay with crenellations, and a service wing. 2022 view. James Glass.

Figure 4.33. Reception hall, Wheeler House, showing the plaster-encased steel beams carrying the structure of the residence, stenciling on the undersides, and polished mahogany paneling on the walls and the stairway with divided flights. View in c. 1914. Frank H. Wheeler Estate Photographs, courtesy of Andrew R. Seager Archive of the Built Environment, Ball State University Libraries' Archives and Special Collections.

Figure 4.34a. Right half of a 1913 panoramic photo showing the Wheeler mansion and landscaped approach from Cold Spring Road. Bass Photo Co. Collection, Indiana Historical Society. (Image cropped)

On the south elevation, extending west along the rear wing, Price strove equally for picturesqueness and harmonious variety (fig. 4.32). He moved from the hipped roof terrace at the east end to a rectangular solarium with a flat roof, then to a three-story projecting bay with crenellations, and finally to a pavilion with a hipped roof.

Inside the entry, Price created a long rectangular reception room running north and south, two stories high, with a grand stairway rising two flights along the west side (fig. 4.33). He specified polished mahogany for the wainscoting on the walls. South of the reception hall, a drawing room led to the terrace, which was open along its sides. On the west side of the first floor, south of the stairway, the architect placed the dining room and breakfast room. He used steel beams and reinforced concrete for the interior structure of the house.[77]

Figure 4.34b. Left half of 1913 view (*from the right*) of the pergola walkway, eighty-foot-high water tower, and seven-car garage behind the Wheeler estate. Bass Photo Co. Collection, Indiana Historical Society. (Image cropped)

Price delegated the extensive landscape design to J. Fletcher Street, a landscape architect on his staff. That design included a large artificial lagoon southwest of the house and a series of islands surrounded by small pools of water west of the lagoon. The pools and islands led to a Japanese garden and teahouse. Directly behind the house, Price and Street designed a pergola-like walkway with buff brick walls and a green tiled roof that ran along the north side of the lagoon to one of the landmarks of the estate—an eighty-foot-high water tower intended to store 150,000 gallons of water for the property (fig. 4.34b). The architect constructed the tower of concrete; like the house, it bore a minimum of detail. Its chief defining features were massive, abstracted buttresses at the four corners. Wheeler asked Price to include a pool room and private office in the tower for the master of the estate.[78]

CITY MANSIONS AND COUNTRY ESTATES | 353

Behind the tower, Price located a nine-car garage and quarters for the servants. Near the Japanese garden, he designed a two-story guesthouse.[79]

Price made several trips between 1911 and completion of the estate in 1914 to meet with the client and inspect progress. One of his chief staff architects, Ralph Bencker, supervised the work on site. Afterward, Frank and Harriet Wheeler moved into the imposing house and extended setting.[80]

The Wheeler estate is now part of the campus of Marian University, which uses the main house and guesthouse and has restored the Japanese tea garden. The lagoon, tower, water garden, and garage are gone, but the long pergola remains.

Carl G. Fisher Estate ("Blossom Heath")

Immediately north of Wheeler's estate on Cold Spring Road, Carl Fisher purchased land for an estate and remodeled and enlarged an existing house, creating within it a sixty-foot living room for entertaining and business conferences.[81] On the estate, he built cottages and stables and grounds for playing polo. He also enclosed grass and clay tennis courts and constructed an enclosed swimming pool and greenhouses for fresh flowers in the winter. None of Fisher's buildings have survived.[82]

James A. and Sara Willis Cornelius Allison Estate (Prairie/Renaissance)

On the north side of the Fisher property, James A. Allison purchased sixty-four acres of land covering a bluff above Crooked Creek, the hillside below the bluff, and the flat-bottom terrain to the west. Allison had made a fortune along with Carl Fisher in founding and developing Prest-O-Lite, one of the first manufacturers of headlamps for automobiles. Allison and his first wife, Sara Willis Cornelius

Facing top, **Figure 4.35.** Winslow House, River Forest, Illinois, designed by Frank Lloyd Wright in 1893. Its rectangular massing, hipped roof, and regular arrangement of windows may have served as a model for the Allison mansion and also for elements of the Kleinschmidt House design (see next chapter). 2023 photo. James Glass.

Facing bottom, **Figure 4.36.** James A. and Sara Willis Cornelius Allison estate, 3200 Cold Spring Road, built in 1911–14 and designed by Herbert L. Bass (probably the exterior) and William L. Price (probably the interior and some elements of exterior). The rectangular, horizontal massing of the main block and hipped roof are similar to elements in the Winslow House, designed by Frank Lloyd Wright. Decorative highlights of the exterior are the limestone columns with intricate, foliated capitals. More subtle are varying patterns in brick and the use of terracotta insets. Also in common with the Prairie houses of Wright is the use of Roman brick. View in 2022. James Glass.

Allison, moved into an existing house on the tract and hired Indianapolis architect Herbert L. Bass to design a large mansion for an estate.[83] As seen in the next chapter, Bass had designed numerous houses for middle-class clients in the city, but this was one of his first commissions for a house of truly large scale.

The architect sited the house at the edge of the bluff, facing north and perpendicular to Cold Spring Road to the east. His design drew on the Prairie style that Frank Lloyd Wright and his circle had developed since the 1890s in Oak Park, Illinois, and the Chicago area. In particular, Bass's approach to the Allison House exterior resembled Wright's design for the facade of the 1893 Winslow House in River Forest, Illinois (see fig. 4.35), and later residences, such as the 1902 Heurtley House in Oak Park.[84] Like the Winslow House, the Allison design (fig. 4.36) features a two-story, rectangular brick structure with a hipped roof. Both houses spread out horizontally. Bass added a shallow pavilion to the facade, slightly off-center, to contain the entry and added red tile as roofing. He extended from the pavilion a porte cochere with a hipped roof and supported the latter with pairs of limestone columns capped by intricate, foliated capitals. Bass used the columns and capitals as unifying motifs for the exterior. He placed smaller versions at the corners of the entry pavilion, on either side of the windows overlooking the porte cochere, along the exterior of the aviary pavilion at the west end of the house, and on the outside of the sunporch adjoining the north side (fig. 4.37). A local sculptor, William A. Kriner, carved the columns.[85]

Sometime during the design and construction process, James Allison fired Bass and hired William Price of Price and McLanahan to take over the project. One of the stories that have come down from the period states that Allison saw the results of Price's work on the Wheeler House and decided he wanted the Philadelphian to transform the Allison House.[86] It is difficult to know where Bass's design ends and Price's begins. Probably Bass designed the essentials of the exterior and Price the interior. Nevertheless, the use of multicolored brick motifs in the upper story and the understated patterns achieved in brick across the exterior are elements that Price employed on the Wheeler House and may have been his.

Facing top, **Figure 4.37.** View from the west, showing the exterior of the aviary at left, lined by limestone columns and foliated capitals, and the main entry porte cochere on the right. 2022 view. James Glass.

Facing bottom, **Figure 4.38.** Reception hall, Allison House, in c. 1916, showing the stone fireplace with details from Loire Valley royal châteaus of the sixteenth century and stairway newel posts and balustrade of polished mahogany. Historic American Buildings Survey, Prints & Photographs Division, Library of Congress.

Figure 4.39. Hemicycle-shaped pergola constructed of rock-faced limestone "bricks" designed by famed Chicago landscape architect Jens Jensen for James and Sara Allison, c. 1911–14. View in 2022. James Glass.

The Allisons wished to have a splendid interior, and Price did not disappoint. Inside the entry, similar to the Wheeler House, he created a two-story reception hall with an imposing stairway opposite the entrance leading up to a second-story hall, with a balustrade lining the perimeter (fig. 4.38). The architect fashioned the stairway with intricate twin newel posts and balustrades of polished mahogany. At the west ends of the first-floor reception hall and the second-floor hall, Price designed stone fireplaces with tapered hoods based on sixteenth-century prototypes in châteaus of the French Loire Valley. He brought sculptors from Philadelphia to carve the fireplaces. Among the "wonders" that Price devised for the rest of the first floor were a music room with an $18,000 Aeolian pipe organ, a library with mahogany panels carved into elaborate patterns and a Rookwood tile fireplace, a French room decorated in the Louis XV style, and his pièce de résistance, the fifty-foot-long aviary. For the latter, Price devised a rectangular pavilion at the west end, in which he covered the floor and walls with marble imported from Italy. The coved plaster ceiling contains a stained glass skylight.

Along the north side of the first floor, Price attached a solarium with a tile floor. Nearby, he placed the dining room with fruit designs incorporated into the fireplace and walls. In the basement, the architect designed a sixty-foot tile swimming pool and a den with tooled leather walls and multicolored bottle glass windows.[87] As with the Wheeler House, Price employed reinforced concrete for the structure, supplemented by a steel frame.[88]

To complement the stupendous residence that Price was creating, Allison hired one of the top landscape architects in the Midwest, Jens Jensen of Chicago, to create formal and informal landscape design.[89] Immediately west of the house, on axis with the aviary, Jensen laid out a formal garden. At its end, he laid out a cross axis, at the north end of which, overlooking the flat terrain below the bluff, he designed a hemicycle-shaped pergola (fig. 4.39). Jensen constructed the pergola with columns composed of rock-faced limestone "bricks."

Below the bluff, Jensen composed an informal design that resulted in the construction of five ponds linked by trails and bridal paths that created a sprawling natural retreat for the Allisons and a limitless source of fishing for James Allison.[90]

The completion of the house and landscape design required three years. The total cost may never be known, although local lore holds that Allison spent $2 million. What is most likely is that the house cost hundreds of thousands of dollars while Jensen's designs for the estate required hundreds of thousands more. The Allisons called their estate "Riverdale Springs." Construction came to a close in 1914, three years after breaking ground.[91]

James Allison died in 1928, and in 1936, the Sisters of St. Francis of Oldenburg purchased the estate for the Marian College (now University) campus. The house now houses the president's office, and the informal landscape below is used as an Ecolab.

Hugh McKennan and Suzette Davis Landon Estate ("Oldfields")
(French Seventeenth Century/Renaissance)

While the Wheeler and Allison estates took shape, another major figure in Indianapolis business built an impressive property on a different bluff. Hugh McKennan Landon had been an officer since 1902 in the Indianapolis Water Company, controlled by the family of his wife, Suzette Davis Landon. Beginning in the 1890s, he and his family had lived in a Shingle-style house at 1315 North Alabama Street

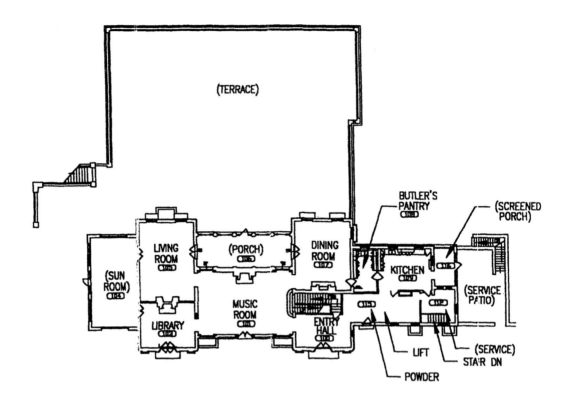

Above, Figure 4.40. Plan of ground (first) floor of Hugh McKennan and Suzette Davis Landon House (Oldfields) as completed in 1913. Carolyn Schleif, AIA, National Historic Landmark nomination for Oldfields, National Park Service, 2003, https://npgallery.nps.gov/NRHP/GetAsset/NHLS/03001041_text.

Facing, Figure 4.41. Facade of Oldfields, Landon-Lilly House, 4000 North Michigan Road, built in 1909–13 and designed by architect Lewis Ketcham Davis with the main block at the center and a wing on either side. Davis drew on French seventeenth-century architecture, such as the châteaus designed by Francois Mansart, for the steep, hipped roofs with dormer windows, and on the Italian Renaissance for the arched windows and pilasters of the facade. Now open to the public as part of Newfields, the arts and nature institution. View in 2013. James Glass.

(see chap. 10 of vol. 1). In 1907, Landon and a fellow officer in the Water Company, Linneas Boyd, purchased a tract of land west of Michigan Road, north of Maple Road (now Thirty-Eighth Street) and immediately east of the Central Canal and White River. Landon and Boyd divided the property, and Landon took the northern thirty acres, which included a sizeable area on the bluff above the canal and river, the hillside descending from the bluff, and some land below.[92]

The Landons hired Suzette's brother, Lewis Ketcham Davis, to design a grandly scaled house. Davis had training as an architect and possibly as an engineer but did not practice in Indianapolis. He may have lived out of town. Little is known of his experience as an architect, but the quality of the residence that he produced attested to his considerable abilities as a designer.[93]

Davis sited the house on the edge of the bluff to afford a pleasant vista of White River and its valley below. He laid out an H-shaped main block for the

CITY MANSIONS AND COUNTRY ESTATES | 361

Figure 4.42. View of grass-covered terrace along the north elevation of the Landon-Lilly House, lined with a Renaissance-style balustrade. Below the terrace, architect Davis designed a garage and arcaded porch. View in 2013. James Glass.

house along a north–south axis and extended a substantial service wing from the north end of the block. He set back the wing from the east facade of the block and attached a smaller secondary pavilion to the south end (fig. 4.40). Seen from the east, the facade reads as a series of substantial pavilions, each with a steeply pitched hipped roof (fig. 4.41). The main block, at the center, consists of the east half of the *H*, with two smaller pavilions projecting forward at either side of the central portion. The steep roofs over the various pavilions are clustered so as to indicate the primacy of the central block and the subordinate status of the side wings. The roofs themselves, with dormer windows, are similar to those designed by seventeenth-century master architect Francois Mansart for royal and noble châteaus in France.[94]

Davis drew on the Italian Renaissance for the articulation of the facade: tall arched openings along the ground story, each containing lunettes and French doors, and colossal Corinthian pilasters applied to the edges of the two projecting pavilions of the main block. He applied stucco to the exterior and painted it white to draw the eyes of those approaching to the house, contrasting it with the gray slates of the large roofs. On the west side, Davis constructed a grass-covered terrace (fig. 4.42), below which he designed a three-car garage and extension of the house basement.

The architect originally located the main entrance off-center in the facade, placing it in the north pavilion of the main block (fig. 4.40). The entry led into an entry hall. At the center of the first floor, he placed the music room, followed to the south by the library, sunporch, and living room. Northwest of the entry hall, he laid out the dining room. At the center of the west side on the main floor, Davis constructed a second enclosed sunporch, which opened onto the expansive grass terrace. In the second floor, he provided five bedrooms and a study. The architect gave over nearly all of the third floor to a ballroom.[95]

On axis with the center of the south pavilion, Davis or a landscape architect laid out a walk leading over a bridge to a small formal garden. Tennis courts lay east of the garden. The Landons operated part of the estate as a working farm, with livestock and barn.[96]

During the 1920s, Hugh Landon and his second wife, Jessie Spalding Landon, transformed the grounds by retaining the Olmsted Brothers firm to design a formal allée extending east from the house and an informal ravine garden leading down to the Central Canal. In 1933, Josiah K. Lilly Jr. and his wife, Ruth Brinkmeyer Lilly, purchased the estate and remodeled the house. It is now part of the arts and nature institution Newfields.[97]

Stoughton A. Fletcher II and May Henley Fletcher Estate, "Laurel Hall" (Tudor Palace/Elizabethan/Jacobean)

As already noted, in 1904–5, Stoughton A. Fletcher II and his wife, May, constructed a rambling house on a hill along Bluff Road, south of Indianapolis. In the years that followed, Stoughton became president of the family Fletcher National Bank and arranged a merger of it with the American National Bank. He also organized a merger of two trust companies to form the Fletcher Savings and

Trust Company (see chap. 1 of this volume). As his importance in the community increased and his wealth expanded, Fletcher aspired to a true country estate. In 1913 or 1914, he acquired as much as 1,500 acres of land along the east side of Fall Creek, near the country town of Millersville (northeast of Indianapolis). In anticipation of building a house, the banker made some improvements on the wooded portion of the estate, constructing winding drives and imposing wrought-iron gates. In 1915, the Fletchers retained Herbert L. Bass and Company as their architects.[98]

Despite losing the Riverdale commission to William Price, Bass retained his reputation for creating fine houses and sought to provide satisfaction to his new clients. He and his staff made a careful study of the landscape and decided to site the house at the crest of the ridge that runs above the east side of Fall Creek, providing an impressive vista of the creek valley and wooded land to the north, east, and south. Bass laid out an L-shaped, three-story brick house that extended two hundred feet from north to south and contained thirty rooms (figs. 4.43 and 4.44).[99] For its architectural language, he chose a mixture of massing and details that derived from early Tudor palaces of sixteenth-century England and late Elizabethan country houses. The architect devised two facades—one approached from the east and the other best seen from the west. As the focal point for the eastern facade, Bass placed a porte cochere at the intersection of the north–south main block and a wing running east from the block. He detailed the porte cochere with limestone Tudor dripstones and crenellations.

The architect obtained a picturesque silhouette by interrupting the cornice line of the gabled roofs with brick gables lined with limestone coping and dormer windows derived from late Elizabethan houses. He enhanced the effect by punctuating the roofline with tall chimney stacks with sculpted multiple flues and topped by

Facing top, **Figure 4.43.** Stoughton A. Fletcher II and May Henley Fletcher House ("Laurel Hall"), 5395 Emerson Way, built between 1915 and 1917 and designed by Herbert L. Bass and Company, architects, drawing from the architecture of Tudor palaces of the early sixteenth century and Elizabethan country houses. This view from 1916 or 1917 shows the east facade of the completed house. Note from the left a porch with Renaissance-style arcades, gables with limestone coping, Tudor dripstones over windows, oriels, the porte cochere over the entry with crenellations, and the multiple chimney stacks. Bass Photo Co. Collection, Indiana Historical Society. (Image cropped)

Facing bottom, **Figure 4.44.** View of east facade. Local sculptor Alexander Sangernebo probably created the stone details. The southern porch was later enclosed and a second story added. 2023 view. James Glass.

stone caps. Bass obtained more Tudor character by arranging three large oriels of stone asymmetrically on both the main block and the eastern wing and employing stone dripstones and stone surrounds around the window openings. Local sculptor Alexander Sangernebo probably created the stone ornamental details.[100] The gray-white limestone details contrasted with the buff brick of the walls. For more polychromy, the architect used green clay tile for the roofs. On the south end of the main block, Bass added a covered limestone porch with open arcades, in the Renaissance style. The porch led south down to a formal garden designed by landscape gardener Alex Tuschinsky (see discussion following).[101]

On the west side, Bass extended two pavilions with gables asymmetrically from the main block (fig. 4.45). He projected a two-story faceted bay from the face of the south pavilion and inserted banks of windows with art glass medallions and intervening stone tracery in the face of the north pavilion. In between, he arranged two large oriels on the second story like those on the east facade, gabled dormers above, and a row of arched doorways along the first story. The windows of the west side looked out on a long open terrace that ran along the entire west facade. Originally, Bass constructed a green tile floor and marble borders along the terrace and lined the perimeter with a Renaissance-style stone balustrade. On the north end of the main block, the architect attached a rectangular one-story solarium, similar in design to that of the porch on the south end, but enclosed.[102]

Entering the east entrance, one passes into a large reception hall leading to the main stairway, which rises to a landing and divides into two flights (fig. 4.46). Art glass windows contained in rectangular banks of openings over the stair landing shine colored light down on the hall. The balustrade on the stairway derives from Jacobean country houses. In the reception hall, the designers installed a white ceiling composed of geometric cells formed by plaster moldings, also Jacobean. The paneling in the hall is Circassian walnut. Adjoining the reception hall to the south is the spacious drawing room, with wooden beams dividing the ceiling into rectangular cells adorned with Jacobean-style strapwork in plaster. A central focal point is a limestone fireplace mantel with a segmental arch and foliated sculpted details. To the north of the reception hall, the dining room presents a quietly elegant space with walnut paneling, wooden beams overhead, and a stone fireplace with an ogee arch for the firebox and sculpted panels. For the library, also on the first floor, Bass used walnut paneling similar to the dining room, a Jacobean-style plaster ceiling, and a French sixteenth-century-style stone mantel with a hood. He decided on a Georgian theme for the music room and the bedrooms on the second floor. He devoted the third floor to the ballroom and gave it plaster quadripartite Gothic vaults and a parquet floor.[103]

Figure 4.45. West facade, overlooking Fall Creek. Note the two-story faceted bay at the right, twin oriels at the center, the projecting pavilion with art glass windows at the left, and the terrace with a balustrade. 2023 view. James Glass.

Stoughton Fletcher hired Alex Tuschinsky, a Polish-born landscape gardener, to design landscape features and plantings for the estate.[104] Below the western terrace, the Fletchers commissioned a stone fountain with sculptures of dancing nymphs. On a hillside across from the east facade of the house, probably Bass or his draftsman Merritt Harrison designed a circular stone folly with dome,

CITY MANSIONS AND COUNTRY ESTATES | 367

Figure 4.46. Reception hall and main stairway, first floor, Laurel Hall, c. 1920s. Note the Circassian walnut paneling on the walls and the geometric cells formed by plaster moldings on the ceiling, derived from Jacobean country houses. 2023 view. James Glass.

entablature, and Corinthian columns, below which a double stairway with a cascading fountain in between descended from the top of the hillside. The stairway ended in a limestone wall containing another fountain at the center and seats (fig. 4.47).[105]

Bass also designed a large, two-story garage and powerhouse, casting it in the Tudor style. The *Indianapolis Star* reported in 1915 that estimates made based on the completed plans for the house alone approximated $200,000. The landscape design could easily have added much more. The contractors finished all work in 1917, and the Fletchers took up residence, calling their estate Laurel Hall.[106]

Figure 4.47. On a hillside across from Laurel Hall, the architects or landscape gardener Alex Tuschinsky designed this combination of a Classical tholos at the top, composed of a circular pavilion supported by Corinthian columns, then a double stairway with a cascading fountain at the center and finally a wall fountain with limestone seats. Bass Photo Co. Collection, Indiana Historical Society. (Image cropped)

ARCHITECT PROFILE

Herbert L. Bass

Herbert L. Bass (1877–1926) was born in Indianapolis and obtained his architectural training from his uncle, W. H. Bass, a teacher at the Manual Training High School. At fifteen, Herbert became an office boy for architect Louis H. Gibson for a year and then entered other architectural offices, working as a draftsman. By age twenty-two, Bass had been promoted to head draftsman, showing his talent as a designer. About 1903, he formed his own office as Herbert L. Bass and Company and soon found work as a residential architect, both for well-to-do clients such as Dellmore Allison on Sutherland Avenue and middle-class homeowners, such as A. D. Hitz at 2108 North Park Avenue, H. B. Reynolds at 2305 Broadway, and George Arnold at 3358 Ruckle Street. In his domestic work through 1910, Bass made use of English Tudor vernacular and Foursquare for most of his designs. With his commission to design the James A. and Sara Willis Cornelius Allison House, Bass became the favored architect for the country estate residences of a group of wealthy Indianapolis businessmen, designing homes for Stoughton Fletcher, Charles B. Sommers, Gerry M. Sanborn, Niles Chapman, Allan A. Wilkinson, James I. Holcomb, and Lucius French. He also won some downtown commercial commissions, such as the design of the Cole Motor Car Company factory (see chap. 1 of this volume).

In the 1920s, Bass took on engineer Lynn O. Knowlton as a business partner, and the firm designed the Test Building on Monument Circle, the Ben Hur office building in Crawfordsville, and Citizens National Bank in Greensburg. They also served as the architects and engineers for the Highland Country Club in Indianapolis and numerous public schools. Bass died suddenly on a business trip to Washington, DC, in 1926.

Sources: "H. L. Bass, Local Architect, Dies at Washington," *Indianapolis Star*, April 9, 1926, Indiana Biography Series, 2:57, Indiana State Library; "Herbert Lawrence Bass," in Paul Donald Brown, ed., *Indianapolis Men of Affairs 1923* (Indianapolis: American Biographical Society, 1923), 49. Source for photo: Brown, *Indianapolis Men of Affairs 1923*, 48.

Financial ruin and personal tragedy faced Stoughton Fletcher after World War I, and the house and estate became a Catholic girl's school, Ladywood, in the 1920s. It is now the national headquarters of the Phi Kappa Psi Fraternity.[107]

CONCLUSION

With the great expansion of population that occurred in Indianapolis between 1900 and 1920, the demand for new houses and residential units grew at a rate not previously experienced. The number of all types of dwellings increased in response to this demand. Mansions for the wealthy filled the remaining vacant lots along Meridian Street south of Fall Creek and on other north–south streets, such as Delaware Street between Tenth and Sixteenth Street, and Pennsylvania Street and Washington Boulevard north of Fall Creek. This was the era of country estates, and a handful appeared on bluffs overlooking White River, along Cold Spring Road, and above Fall Creek near Millersville.

Architectural fashions shifted in residential architecture for the wealthy from the Queen Anne and Romanesque styles popular in the 1890s to the English Tudor vernacular, English Tudor palace, Georgian, Arts and Crafts, bungalow, and Prairie styles. Some themes of the previous period continued to find favor—Italian Renaissance, NeoClassical, and Rustic. Occasionally, as in the case of the Robert W. Hannah Wright Furnas House, elements of the new Foursquare—rectangular block, hipped roof, single front dormer, and porch across the facade—could be found. The Foursquare was more frequently chosen by middle-class home-building clients (see next chapter). More popular for homes of the well-to-do were houses cast in the English Tudor vernacular, known for their brick first story, stucco and timber upper stories, front and side gables, and shed dormers. The Tudor vernacular derived ultimately from houses and commercial buildings constructed of brick, stucco, and timber and built in England during the sixteenth and seventeenth centuries. The immediate antecedent for American architects seems to have been a revival in England of similar stucco and timber dwellings, which were constructed in such planned communities as Port Sunlight and Bournville beginning in the 1890s.[108]

Some substantial houses derived much of their details from English Tudor palaces and Elizabethan country houses of the sixteenth century. Stone dripstones, oriel windows, gables with stone coping, stone surrounds for windows, and quoins all appeared on Tudor palace mansions in Indianapolis, supplemented in the interiors with plaster ceilings composed of moldings forming irregular cells.

Although Georgian designs for residences became popular across the eastern United States, only an occasional Indianapolis owner chose designs based on the style. Foltz and Parker provided a cluster of fine Georgian houses for the Nicholsons, Blisses, and Frenzels.

The Italian Renaissance, a constant in Indianapolis architecture since before the Civil War, continued to attract the interest of some well-to-do clients, with newer interpretations stressing horizontality, a hipped roof, a cornice with consoles or brackets, a symmetrical facade, arches and arcades, and, occasionally, pilasters and entablatures. Almost no residences in the city were designed as full-scale Classical designs based on Greek or Roman architecture. Occasionally, an architect would incorporate elements of Classical monuments, such as the Ionic columns of the Lewis House of Woodruff Place, into a home design.

The Rustic style, closely related to Arts and Crafts, appeared independently of the English movement in Indianapolis during the 1890s, beginning with its use by John H. Stem in the "Lombardy" house of John T. Brush. The Rustic ideal involved crafting a dwelling made up of natural materials from the environs of the house. Boulders ("bowlders"), such as the immense stones used to build Golden Hill, were characteristic elements, found also in bungalows, such as the William D. Vogel House and the Joseph Hooser House (see next chapter).

Just as there were certain architects who specialized in commercial and public buildings or buildings of worship, a sizeable number of others practicing in the city between 1900 and 1920 devoted most of their time to residences. Foltz and Parker designed nine of the residences described in chapters 4 and 5 of this volume, more than any other architects. Herbert Foltz and Wilson Parker, although they served as architects for a few commercial and public buildings, found their niche, especially in designing homes for the wealthy or business and professional people. Two architects active in residential architecture during this era—Frank B. Hunter and Herbert L. Bass—specialized in houses both for the wealthy and for the middle class. In the two years between the beginning of 1909 and the end of 1910, Hunter and Bass designed the largest number of the local houses that the *Indianapolis Star* featured in their weekly "As Others Have Built" series. Hunter particularly emphasized Foursquare designs, epitomized by the modestly scaled George W. and Alberta Barthel June House on North Talbott Avenue (see next chapter). Bass designed Foursquare and Tudor vernacular houses for middle-class clients in the neighborhoods between Sixteenth Street and Mapleton. He also landed commissions for country estate houses, including the Prairie-style Allison mansion and the English Tudor palace–style Fletcher mansion.

A few of the major commercial architects in the city also occasionally designed houses. Bernard Vonnegut, as mentioned in chapter 10 of volume 1, preferred residential projects and created some of the most original designs between 1900 and his death in 1908. Rubush and Hunter occasionally worked on houses for businesspeople, such as the Fred and Catherine Cushman Hoke House (see next chapter), and their much-larger commercial and public building practice may have introduced them to residential clients. The same was probably true of Robert Frost Daggett and his associates in the firm of R. P. Daggett and Company. Other local architects of considerable talent, such as Alfred Grindle and Lewis Ketcham Davis, designed only a few houses.

A couple of architects from outside the city took on major residential commissions. William Price of Price and McLanahan of Philadelphia found three wealthy clients in Indianapolis for whom he created imposing residences of great originality and character. Francke H. Bosworth Jr. of New York came to town in response to an opportunity to create the first skyscraper apartment building for Ferdinand Winter (see next chapter).

Finally, the question of the sources for design comes up in the context of residential commissions as well as for commercial, public, and religious projects. Most Indianapolis architects in this period, as in previous eras, derived many of their compositional ideas and their vocabulary for details from architectural periodicals. The best of those practicing started with a premise from a published source and then modified the layout, massing, facade composition, or ornamentation in an original way. Only a handful traveled to the centers of the architectural profession in New York, Boston, Philadelphia, or Chicago to see the latest fashions first hand. Similarly, few took voyages to Europe to draw or photograph medieval, Renaissance, Baroque, or contemporary landmarks. Despite the similar sources used by architects, houses, doubles, and apartment buildings built between 1900 and 1920 showed considerable variety, and streetscapes conveyed a distinctive personality for the city.

Map 4.1

Buildings from Chapter 4 of Volume 2 plotted on 1915 Sanborn Insurance Map (Vol. 4) of area between 10th and 23rd Streets and between Capitol Avenue and Arsenal Avenue (numbers drawn from figure numbers)

5 Joseph A. and Caroline Pfau Rink House

11 Meredith and Eugenie Kountze Nicholson House

16 Herman P. and Alma Bachman Lieber House

25 Thomas and Eva Bryant Taggart House

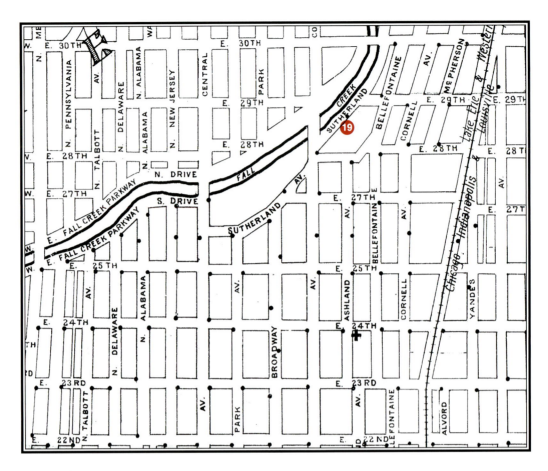

Map 4.2

Buildings from Chapter 4 plotted on 1915 Sanborn Insurance Map (Vol. 4) of area between 22nd Street and Fall Creek and between Meridian and Yandes Streets (numbers drawn from figure numbers)

19 Delmore C. and Annie Hamilton Allison House

Map 4.3

Buildings from Chapter 4 plotted on 1915 Sanborn Insurance Map (Vol. 5) of area between Fall Creek and 35th Street and between Boulevard Place and College Avenue (numbers drawn from figure numbers); + = demolished

- **1** Schnull-Rauch House
- **3** Louis H. and Alice Reynolds Levey House
- **6** + Henry A. and Ada Freeland Mansfield House
- **7** + Frank and Clarissa Lintner Van Camp House
- **9** Robert W. and Hannah Wright Furnas House
- **13** Bliss-Vonnegut-Cummings House
- **14** + Henry R. and Margaret Bliss House
- **15** + John P. and Philippine Bennerscheidt Frenzel House
- **17** + Henry and Sarah Lang Kahn House
- **21** Alfred M. and Minnie Stroup Glossbrenner House
- **23** Charles W. and Cornelia Cole Fairbanks House

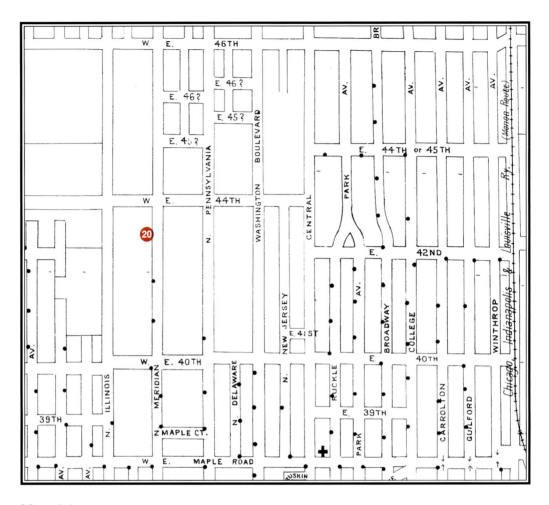

Map 4.4

Buildings from Chapter 4 plotted on 1915 Sanborn Insurance Map (Vol. 5) of area between Maple Road (38th Street) and 46th Street and between Illinois Street and Winthrop Avenue (numbers drawn from figure numbers)

20 Hare-Tarkington House

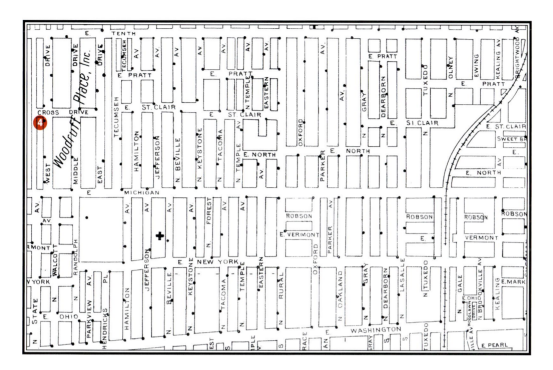

Map 4.5

Buildings from Chapter 4 plotted on 1915 Sanborn Insurance Map (Vol. 3) of area between West Drive, Woodruff Place, and Kealing Avenue and between East Washington and 10th Streets (numbers drawn from figure numbers)

④ Frank W. and Emma Salter Lewis House

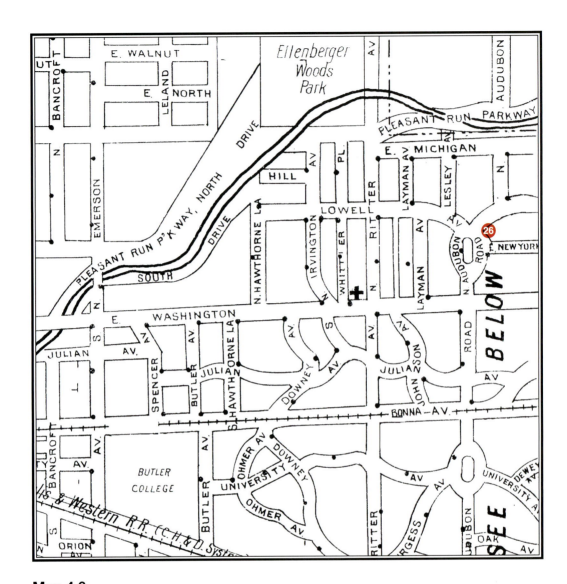

Map 4.6

Buildings from Chapter 4 plotted on 1915 Sanborn Insurance Map (Vol. 3) of Irvington (numbers drawn from figure numbers)

26 Florence Baxter Thornton and George D. Thornton House

5 | DETACHED HOMES, DOUBLES, AND APARTMENTS

1900–1920

Between 1900 and 1920, many prosperous business and professional men and their wives in Indianapolis built or purchased two-and-a-half story houses on narrow lots, as did sizeable numbers of middle-class homebuyers. Most working-class families continued to live in workers' cottages, constructed since the 1850s; shotgun houses, built since the 1870s and 1880s; and bungalows, a new architectural type that lent itself especially to modest-sized houses. Doubles (duplexes) emerged as a popular alternative to single-family dwellings for both middle-class and working-class families. The trend to apartment living begun in the early 1890s accelerated and became a major focus of real estate development and architectural design.

The large detached houses constructed by business and professional men and their wives were not as costly or pretentious as the city mansions discussed in chapter 4 of this volume. They rose on lots that averaged in size 46 feet by 195 feet and were thus spaced closely together.[1] The business- and professional-class houses of the early twentieth century were found primarily on the same north–south streets that had seen the construction of comparably sized residences in the post–Civil War era north of Tenth Street. In addition, they were seen in the midst of more recently platted additions between Sixteenth Street and Fall Creek and on new north–south streets north of Fall Creek to Forty-Sixth Street.

Middle-class heads of households and their wives constructed or purchased single-family houses of smaller scale than those of the business- and professional-class homebuyers. The middle-income families were headed by owners of small businesses, clerks, bookkeepers, teachers, architects, and members of the clergy. Detached middle-class houses could be found on most of the north–south streets, interspersed with those of higher-income households, and in newly planned additions to the city on the greater east side, between Arsenal and Emerson Avenues.

Working-class breadwinners in Indianapolis included not only factory workers but the host of laborers, janitors, carpenters, painters, streetcar conductors, coachmen, teamsters, charwomen, and so on who formed the foundation of the local economy.[2] In the south, west, northwest, and northeast sections of the city, new neighborhoods rapidly took shape for white working-class residents. On the south side, cottages and bungalows appeared in the area extending from Morris Street to Garfield Park and then in new additions south and east of the park. On the west side, the industrial communities of West Indianapolis and Haughville continued to attract factories and workers, and both began to fill with new immigrants from eastern and southeastern Europe. The unincorporated town of North Indianapolis, between Northwestern Avenue (now Dr. Martin Luther King Jr. Street) and White River, continued to attract workers for its factories. Northeast of downtown, the former town of Brightwood had become the home of workers employed in the large rail yards there.

Doubles became an established staple of home construction and architectural practice. Some investors built a double house in which they themselves could occupy one half and rent out the other half. Others built a double and sold each of the two halves or rented both halves. Doubles appealed, like apartments, to those who wished to shed some of the responsibilities and expenses of home ownership. Those living in large doubles often found themselves in three-bedroom residences. Doubles of all sizes were constructed in the midst of the single-family residences of most neighborhoods.

The range of accommodation for tenants of apartment buildings extended from full houses constructed together in rows to one- or two-bedroom flats in two-story buildings. Countless flats, or apartment buildings, rose in the downtown area and eventually in outlying neighborhoods.

For larger detached houses of business and professional families, style continued to be dictated by discussions between client and architect or builder, based on the principal styles of the period. Middle-class houses tended to be cast with Foursquare, Tudor vernacular, or Arts and Crafts/bungalow details, while a few displayed Spanish Mission or Dutch Colonial designs. For lower-middle-class or workers' families, the classic wood frame cottage continued its popularity at the beginning of the twentieth century but was soon superseded by the new bungalow. Doubles tended to be given Foursquare, bungalow, or Tudor features. Apartment building designs reflected several of the styles favored in houses—Renaissance, Tudor palace, Georgian, and Foursquare.

Given the large size of the residential market in this period, some architects worked almost exclusively designing houses, doubles, and apartments. Some real estate companies, such as the Burns Realty Company, built sizeable numbers of larger houses on particular tracts and retained an architect to design all the residences. Other real estate companies or builders obtained residential designs for middle-class or workers' bungalows from mail-order catalogs or magazines and constructed them on parcels. After 1900, customers could order plans or complete kits for assembling a modest-sized house from catalog companies such as Sears, Roebuck and Company or Montgomery Ward.

African American residents, restricted by rigid boundaries imposed by pervasive segregation and white prejudices, lived in a primary neighborhood along Indiana Avenue that extended northwest of downtown. Other clusters of Black families lived northeast of downtown, along Martindale (now Dr. Andrew J. Brown Street), Yandes, and Columbia Streets, and in the Norwood-Holbrook neighborhood southeast of downtown. A small number of Black professional men—physicians, attorneys, and clergymen—worked in offices and churches on and near Indiana Avenue and resided in modestly sized houses mostly in the northwest downtown neighborhood. Most of the rest of the breadwinners in the community worked as teachers, domestic servants, laborers, laundresses, and other low-income occupations. They resided in cottages, shotgun houses, and substandard rental shacks. Limited construction of new houses took place in the African American community.[3]

RESIDENCES OF BUSINESS OWNERS/MANAGERS AND PROFESSIONAL PEOPLE

After 1900, especially along the north–south streets of the Indianapolis north side, houses of business owners and professional people and their families filled many vacant lots as real estate agents and others platted new additions. The houses built by such persons often had some architectural distinction but were not mansions. Some owners could afford to hire architects to design their residences, and the designers afforded visual variety to the dwellings and streets on which these houses rose.

George G. and Kate Block Tanner House (English Queen Anne, Tudor Palace/Arts and Crafts/Baronial)

George Gordon Tanner offers a good example of a prosperous business owner who built a house of distinction along a residential street. He and his business partner, George R. Sullivan, operated a wholesale house on South Meridian Street dealing with tinner's supplies. Previously, Tanner and his family had resided in a house at 16 East Michigan Street, at the north edge of the Mile Square. In 1900, he and his wife, Kate Bock Tanner, purchased a lot at what became 1431 North Delaware Street in the midst of the prestigious section of that street.[4]

Their unknown architect designed for them an unusual residence in which varied elements from contemporary English architecture came together in a harmonious mix (fig. 5.1). The designer devised an L-shaped plan and combined features of dissimilar character in the facade.[5] A three-story baronial tower fronted with rock-faced limestone serves as a focal point next to the entrance, set back from a pavilion projecting forward at the north end. Rock-faced limestone functions as a unifying element for the first story of the facade and the south elevation. In part of the second story, white stucco provides contrast. A projecting bay with an overhead gable, drawn from English Queen Anne houses, attaches to the face of the front pavilion. Above the entrance on the south side of the façade is a large dormer window with a hipped roof. Drawing from the English Tudor palace tradition, the architect incorporated rectangular grids of casement windows into all the facade.

The tower draws additional attention with its bull's-eye window and crenellated battlements. Another remarkable feature dominates the south elevation: a broad gable filling two stories. The designer appears to have modeled it on similar broad gables with asymmetrical silhouettes created by English Arts and Crafts architect Charles F. Voysey.[6] Covered with rock-faced limestone, the gable is adjoined irregularly on the side by a chimney that merges into the face of the gable. The unusual ensemble of details ends with two parallel projections topped by arched gables at the rear.

Reid-Dickson House (Italian Romanesque/Medieval Castles)

A short distance north on Delaware Street, construction began in 1905–6 on another unusual house at what is now 1456 North Delaware. William J. Reid reputedly was a manager with Kingan and Company, an Irish-owned pork-packing company with a large plant in Indianapolis. He and his wife, Jeannie Lockard Reid, had the funds and leisure to travel in Europe and especially spent time in

Figure 5.1. George G. and Kate Block Tanner House, 1431 North Delaware Street, built in 1900–1901 and designed with a mixture of elements from the English Queen Anne style, Tudor palaces, the Arts and Crafts Movement, and motifs from the work of English architect Charles Voysey. Note the baronial tower with crenellations at the center, banks of casement windows, and expanded asymmetrical gable on the side similar to those used by Voysey in house designs. View in 2021. James Glass.

Italy, where they purchased antiques and art objects. When they returned in 1905, they hired Foltz and Parker to design a house that reminded them of Italy. The architects created a design that they described as "of the Italian style of the feudal period." An analysis of the design shows that indeed there are Italian elements and features from the medieval (feudal) period.[7]

Figure 5.2. Reid-Dickson House, 1456 North Delaware Street, built in 1905–6 by William J. and Jeannie Lockard Reid and designed by Foltz and Parker in "the Italian style of the feudal period." In practice, this meant multiple pavilions with medieval crenellations and machicolations, Romanesque arches, and pointed Gothic windows. View in 2021. James Glass.

Foltz and Parker devised a two-story red brick house with flat roofs (fig. 5.2). In lieu of cornices, they lined the roof edges with crenellations, supported by machicolations, both elements found in medieval castles in Italy and other countries in Europe. The architects strove for picturesque massing, devising a two-story main block at the rear and extending two wings from its east elevation—a two-story pavilion to the north and a one-story entry pavilion to the south. Foltz and Parker used Italian Romanesque arches for the main entrance and a secondary entry. They incorporated a similar arch for the main window in the east face of the north pavilion. Within the window, they employed a trio of leaded glass lights with pointed, Gothic heads and roundels at the top. The roof of the one-story entry pavilion served as a terrace for the Reids.[8]

Inside, Foltz and Parker continued the medieval theme, although with less reference to Italy. They gave the reception hall a seventeen-foot height and covered it

Figure 5.3. View from c. 1907 of the entry hall of the Reid-Dickson House, showing plaster groin vaults from Gothic architecture and simulated stone blocks on the walls composed of plaster. Bass Photo Co. Collection, Indiana Historical Society. (Image cropped)

with plaster groin vaults from Gothic architecture (fig. 5.3). They covered the walls with simulated stone blocks made of plaster. The designers also gave a vaulted ceiling to the spacious living room, which adjoined the dining room on the north side of the first floor. On the second floor, the architects included six bedrooms and three bathrooms. They used concrete for the main stairway and included a small "lift" for transit between stories.[9]

The Reids completed their house in 1906 and apparently lived there until 1911, when they sold it to theater manager and banker Fred C. Dickson and his wife, Hallie Terhune Dickson. The cost of construction was between $15,000 and $20,000.[10]

Willard W. and Josephine Niles Hubbard House (Foursquare/Renaissance)

Morton Place, which had attracted large city houses since its platting in the 1890s, continued to catch the attention of business and professional men and their wives who wanted to live nearer to downtown than the area north of Fall Creek. The largest houses rose along Delaware Street between Nineteenth and Twenty-Second Streets. One businessman who found the neighborhood appealing was Willard W. Hubbard, who had just organized the Commercial Trust Company and also served as secretary and treasurer of the Island Coal Company of Indianapolis. He and his wife, Josephine Niles Hubbard, had previously lived at 1002 North Delaware Street. In 1901–2, they purchased a lot on the southeast corner of Twentieth and Delaware Streets and hired an architect.[11]

The unknown designer drew from the still-new Foursquare fashion a rectangular massing,[12] a hipped roof, and attic dormer windows for the three-story house (figs. 5.4 and 5.5). A generous budget allowed him to construct the exterior walls

Facing top, **Figure 5.4.** Willard W. and Josephine Niles Hubbard House, 1941 North Delaware Street, Morton Place, built in 1902–3 and designed by an unknown architect with a rectangular block, hipped roof, and front dormer derived from the American Foursquare fashion but also with rounded turrets on each of the facade corners and Renaissance/Classical columns and balustrades on the front porch, terrace, and side porch. View from the south in 1908. *Art Work of Indianapolis, Ind.* (Chicago: Gravure Illustration, 1908).

Facing bottom, **Figure 5.5.** View in 2023 of the Hubbard House, showing the façade, rock-faced Indiana limestone walls, and minor alterations since construction. James Glass.

out of rock-faced limestone. The architect rounded the corners of the facade with towerlike curvatures similar to those of the Queen Anne style. Unlike Queen Anne turrets, these towers end below the expansive frame eaves of the roof. The designer employed Renaissance-style Ionic columns and an entablature on the porch with a projecting curve over the central entrance. Originally, a smaller, similar porch covered an entry in the south elevation and a Renaissance balustrade lined the main porch and adjacent terrace. A central door in the second story of the facade leads out onto the roof of the entry porch.[13]

Although the facade is symmetrical, the features of the side elevations are asymmetrical, with irregular projecting bays and a chimney with half of a stepped profile. The rock-faced limestone surface of the walls contrasted effectively with the smooth character of the Classical columns and entablature on the porches. The Hubbard family moved into their new residence in 1903.

Dr. John and Celeste Terrell Barnhill House (Foursquare/Georgian)

Immediately south of the Hubbards, the Barnhill family constructed a new residence in 1907–8. Dr. John F. Barnhill operated a practice downtown as one of the early specialists in the city examining the throat, nose, and ears. He and his family had previously resided in the Mile Square at 412 North Delaware Street and desired a larger house in a residential neighborhood away from the growing commercialization and congestion of downtown. Barnhill and his wife, Celeste Terrell Barnhill, hired the popular architectural firm of Foltz and Parker to design their dwelling, and the architects created a two-story brick residence with several similarities to the Hubbard House.[14]

As in the neighboring residence, Foltz and Parker gave the Barnhill House a rectangular footprint, a hipped roof, and dormer windows with hipped roofs (fig. 5.6).[15] They also extended the eaves out from the roof, supported by low-profile brackets, and gave the facade a symmetrical composition, a central entry porch, and an open terrace on either side. Otherwise, Foltz and Parker used different features in the Barnhill House: a red brick veneer for the exterior, an unorthodox version of the Georgian flat arch over the windows, and brick quoins from the Renaissance at the corners. The three dormers in the roof are Baroque-like with their pilasters, consoles, pediments, and S-curved panels projecting from the sides. The architects drew the fan transom and side lights in the entrance from Federal architecture and provided a vivid contrast with the red brick walls by employing green clay tiles on the roof.

Figure 5.6. Dr. John and Celeste Terrell Barnhill House, 1933 North Delaware Street, Morton Place, built in 1907–8 and designed by Foltz and Parker, drawing on Foursquare elements for the rectangular block, hipped roof, and central dormer and from Georgian colonial architecture for the symmetrical facade, quoins at the corners, and flat brick arches over the windows. The dormers are Baroque-like in use of curves and reverse curves and overscaled pilasters and pediments. View in 2023. James Glass.

Inside, the designers laid out a central hall with a Georgian-style stairway and used Arts and Crafts elements in the living room, such as a tile fireplace, contrasting with the Jacobean ceiling composed of undulating cells of plaster moldings.[16]

Dr. Louis and Adele Burckhardt House (Spanish Mission)

The Spanish Mission style became exceedingly popular in the American West and even east of the Mississippi during the first two decades of the twentieth century.

DETACHED HOMES, DOUBLES, AND APARTMENTS | 391

It derived from a popularization by writers and some architects in California of the architecture embodied in the mission churches constructed by the Spanish between 1769 and 1820. From the romantic fascination with the original mission structures, a demand ensued for contemporary buildings incorporating Spanish features. Mission-style buildings of all types appeared but particularly could be found in residences.[17]

In Indianapolis, only a handful of clients chose to build Mission-inspired houses. Dr. Louis Burckhardt and his wife, Adele Burckhardt, were among the few. Louis Burckhardt was a German-born physician with a downtown office. Previously, he and Adele had lived at 615 North Capitol Avenue in a neighborhood where commercial uses were taking over rapidly. In 1908, they purchased three lots on the east side of Pennsylvania Street south of Thirty-Second Street in Osgood's Meridian Park Addition. The Burckhardts hired local architect Clarence Martindale to design their residence.[18]

The architect took advantage of the descending topography of the three lots and sited the house at the apex of a hill on the north end (fig. 5.7). This position afforded the owners a pleasant vista through their southern garden and showed off the house to advantage from the south. Many Mission-style designs for houses and commercial enterprises appeared in architectural periodicals and books. An example of a well-known commercial design was the Mission Inn in Riverside, California (fig. 5.8). Most of the California designs incorporated multiple gables with parapets embellished by Baroque S curves and reverse curves, stucco exteriors and pastel colors, and often quatrefoils within the gables. All these features are found in the Burckhardt House.[19]

Martindale extended two pavilions from the core of the residence to the west and south and faced the pavilions with Mission gables in which moldings outlined the parapets with S curves and reverse curves. Within each gable, he inserted a quatrefoil window. On the north elevation, above the main entry, is a smaller

Facing top, **Figure 5.7.** Dr. Louis and Adele Burckhardt House, 3159 North Pennsylvania Street, in Historic Meridian Park, built in 1909–10 and designed by architect Clarence Martindale of Indianapolis in the Spanish Mission style. Note the two gables with Baroque curves and reverse curves along the parapet and the quatrefoil motifs, all elements drawn from the architecture of the California Spanish missions and from new houses and other buildings based on the style. At the corner are *canales* from Pueblo Native American architecture in New Mexico. View in 2022. James Glass.

Facing bottom, **Figure 5.8.** Entry arch and Mission-style parapet at the Mission Inn, Riverside, California, c. 1902. View in 2014. James Glass.

Mission gable. Adjoining the south pavilion, the architect located a one-story screened porch with large winged walls. At the southwest corner of the house, he placed a one-story enclosed porch with a flat roof resembling those on Pueblo-style houses in New Mexico, complete with *canales* (channels) for expelling water from the roof.[20] All along the western facade, a walled garden extends, with additional *canales*. Originally, Martindale designed a pergola supported by substantial piers at the center of the facade for the growth of English ivy. And as in the California prototypes, stucco applied over brick covers all the exterior surfaces. For a contrast to the pastel colors, the architect used red clay tile for the main roof.

The north entry led to a small reception hall, from which the library, living room, and kitchen could be reached. The dining room adjoined the living room, which offered access to the screened porch on the south. The Burckhardts took up residence in their distinctive house in 1909.[21]

Anthony F. Kleinschmidt House (Prairie Influence)

While the Burckhardts were building their house, their neighbor, Anthony F. Kleinschmidt, hired the same architect to design a very different residence at 3177 North Pennsylvania Street. Kleinschmidt headed the Builders' Supply Corporation of Indianapolis, which sold wholesale and retail hardware, wood mantels, tiles, and paints from two locations downtown. Previously, as a single person, Anthony had boarded in a house at 1417 North Delaware Street. In 1908, he decided that he (and possibly his family)[22] wanted to live in Osgood's Meridian Park Addition, where several fashionable houses were going up. He purchased a corner lot and retained Clarence Martindale.[23]

The architect created a design (fig. 5.9) that owes several of its essentials to the Prairie style created by Frank Lloyd Wright and his associates. Just as Herbert Bass was to do with the Allison mansion (see chap. 4 of this volume), Martindale drew on elements found in Wright's 1893 Winslow House in River Forest, Illinois (fig. 4.35).[24] He gave the Kleinschmidt House a horizontal orientation and a hipped roof and divided the first and second floors into separate zones by using different materials. Where Wright used brick for the first story and wood for the second, Martindale covered the first story of the Kleinschmidt House with white stucco and the upper story with dark-stained, board-and-batten wood. Otherwise, the Indianapolis architect freely composed the exterior of his house. Unlike Wright, who made his facade symmetrical, Martindale introduced asymmetry. On the south side of the facade, he placed a two-story projecting bay, while on the north side, he projected a trio of windows with a segmental arch on the first floor and

Figure 5.9. Anthony F. Kleinschmidt House, 3177 North Pennsylvania Street, in Historic Meridian Park, built in 1908–9 and designed by Clarence Martindale, drawing in part on the Prairie style of Frank Lloyd Wright, which can be seen in the horizontal massing, hipped roof, and use of different materials in the first and second stories. Other elements include an asymmetrical facade, a small pyramidal roof for the entry porch, and the use of board-and-batten. View in 2022. James Glass.

a flat bay window from the second story. He also ran an open terrace from the central entry porch along the north side of the facade only.

On the north elevation, which runs deep into the lot and fronts on Thirty-Second Street, the architect also employed asymmetry. He located a stucco-covered chimney with tapered edges on the west side and ran the stack through the roof eaves. On the east side of the elevation, he included no chimney and substituted a horizontal bank of windows, contrasting with vertically oriented windows on the west end. All the asymmetries on the north side are prevented from discord by the unifying effect of the bands of stucco along the first story and the dark-stained wood on the second. At the center, appearing above the side entry, an oversized board-and-batten dormer with a hipped roof dominates the north elevation.

The west entrance led into a stair hall, the south side of which offered access to the living room. There Martindale featured a beamed ceiling and large Rookwood tile fireplace. On the north side of the hall, he placed the dining room, with beams along the sides of the ceiling and another fireplace. The dining room communicated on the east with the breakfast room and kitchen.[25]

Fred and Katharine Cushman Hoke House (Italian Renaissance/Georgian)

About the time Anthony Kleinschmidt began to plan his house, Fred Hoke and his wife, Katharine Cushman Hoke, decided to build a home in a much more traditional spirit. Hoke was secretary and treasurer of the family business, the American Box Ball Company, dealers in bowling alleys. Previously, the Hokes had resided in a frame double at 2928 North Capitol Avenue. By 1908, Fred's business fortunes had improved sufficiently for them to acquire a lot in the Washington Park Addition, which featured large lots and some substantial houses. They bought a lot at 3445 Washington Boulevard and hired the firm of Rubush and Hunter to design their residence. In these years, Preston Rubush and Edgar Hunter were developing a practice that embraced all building types, including houses.[26]

The architects devised a composition that encompassed elements of both the Italian Renaissance and Georgian architecture (figs. 5.10 and 5.11). A new Renaissance formula was emerging, as seen a couple of years later with the Fairbanks mansion (see chap. 4 of this volume), for rectangular, two-story houses with a horizontal orientation, hipped roofs covered by tiles, and tall arched windows along the first floor of the facade. Rubush and Hunter used these ingredients for the Hoke facade, arranged them symmetrically, and added paired brackets to support the extended eaves. They incorporated a treatment for the entry drawn from

Facing top, **Figure 5.10.** Fred and Katharine Cushman Hoke House, 3445 Washington Boulevard, built in 1908–9 and designed by Rubush and Hunter, using the new formula for Renaissance-style houses: symmetrical facade, hipped roof, arched windows, and projecting cornice supported by brackets. Note also the recessed entry based on those of late eighteenth-century Georgian houses in the English colonies. The stucco exterior lent itself to light colors, contrasting effectively with the tile roof. *Year Book of the Indiana Chapter A.I.A. and Catalog of the Third Annual Exhibition 1912* (Indianapolis: Indiana Chapter A.I.A., 1912).

Facing bottom, **Figure 5.11.** View in 2023 showing modifications in windows and the enclosure of the south porch. James Glass.

late eighteenth-century Georgian houses in the American colonies.[27] A shallow portico made up of Tuscan columns and a pediment with partially returning trim precedes a recessed arch that introduces the entry, above which is a fan transom. On either side of the entry, the architects placed an arched window composed of many lights and topped by a fan-shaped head. On the south elevation, they devised an open porch with Tuscan columns and Doric pilasters. Rubush and Hunter chose to stucco all of the exterior of the frame house and painted it white, which contrasted harmoniously with the red clay tile roof.[28]

On the first floor, the entry led into a vestibule, then a reception hall. A music room lay to the left and a large living room to the right. The living room connected on the south with the porch, which in turn led to a terrace at the rear. The east end of the reception hall led to the dining room, which communicated with the kitchen and pantry in the northeast corner.[29]

Jacob Dorsey Forrest House (English Tudor Vernacular)

A couple of years earlier, in 1906–7, a Butler College professor constructed a variation on the English Tudor vernacular theme in Irvington. Jacob Dorsey Forrest had served as professor of sociology and economics at Butler since 1897 and took over management of the newly organized Citizens Gas Company of Indianapolis in 1907. Previously, he had resided in a house at 1115 North Park Avenue and commuted to Irvington. In 1906, he purchased the island at the center of the Audubon Road oval, one of the two original such configurations in the 1870 Irvington plan, and hired an architect to design a striking house at the south end of the island.[30]

The unknown architect proposed a composition that drew on the popular vernacular English Tudor formula already described in the designs of the Henry and Sarah Lang Kahn House, the Dellmore C. and Annie Hamilton Allison House, and the Hare-Tarkington House (see chap. 4 of this volume) but interpreted the theme differently in several respects. To the main block running east and west, the

Facing top, **Figure 5.12.** Jacob Dorsey Forrest House, south end of Audubon Road oval, Irvington, built 1906–7 and designed by its architect drawing on the English Tudor vernacular formula: brick veneer first story, exposed timbers in the upper story, prominent gables with bargeboards, and "jetties" whereby upper sections project slightly from the those below. A variation from the formula is seen in the use of orange brick, rather than stucco, between the timbers. View of facade in 1908. *Art Work of Indianapolis, Ind.* (Chicago: Gravure Illustration, 1908).

Facing bottom, **Figure 5.13.** The Forrest House, as remodeled and incorporated into the Irvington United Methodist Church today. View in 2023. James Glass.

designer added two pavilions that projected forward to form most of the facade (fig. 5.12). Like the more conventional English Tudor vernacular houses in the city, the Forrest House presented a facade in which timbers were exposed, the second story of the two pavilions projected over the first story through "jetties," and wooden bargeboards with decorative carvings and turned knobs at the center hung from the gables. Also like the other residences, the architect used a brick veneer for the first story and added a jetty between the apex of the two front gables and the second story.

The designer departed from the formula by using orange brick above the first story to fill the interstices between the timbers, in lieu of stucco. Originally, a vestibule filled the space between the two-facade pavilion, ornamented by a decorative wooden frieze and leaded glass windows.

In the 1920s, the Forrest House became part of the new Irvington Methodist Episcopal Church building, and the congregation made some modifications to it (fig. 5.13).

MIDDLE-CLASS DETACHED HOUSES

The homes of business owners and professional people tended to be found on streets and additions with larger lots and substantial houses. Most middle-class homebuyers commissioned or purchased houses that architects had designed, but were not extravagant in size, materials or decorative elements. These middle-class houses tended to be constructed on smaller lots than those of the business owners. Real estate companies built some middle-income residences in groups and sold them to homebuyers. The Burns Realty Company, for example, purchased tracts of land between Fall Creek and Maple Road (Thirty-Eighth Street) and others north of Thirty-Eighth and retained architect Herbert Foltz to design attractive and moderately priced dwellings. Company head Lee Burns then sold them to individuals.[31]

Brandt F. and Helen McKay Steele House
(English Tudor Vernacular Elements)

One of the most versatile artists practicing in Indianapolis during the early twentieth century was Rembrandt (Brandt) Steele, son of famed painter T. C. Steele. After study in Paris and Germany, Brandt found work as a potter, designer of art glass windows (such as at All Souls Unitarian Church), and architect. He worked as a designer for multiple mediums in a studio on East Market Street and, in 1904,

Figure 5.14. Brandt F. and Helen McKay Steele House, 811 East Drive, Woodruff Place, built in 1904–5 and designed by Brandt F. Steele, drawing on elements of the English Tudor vernacular style, such as stucco and timber exterior and prominent gables with bargeboards, but customizing the design by employing a central gable with curves and reverse curves and the central terrace. View in 2021. James Glass.

designed a house for himself and his wife, Helen McKay Steele, at what is now 811 East Drive, Woodruff Place.[32]

Steele created a one-and-a-half-story house with an I-shaped plan (fig. 5.14).[33] Like other houses drawn from English Tudor vernacular architecture, Steele's house featured pavilions projecting forward with gables and bargeboards and stucco and timber as primary exterior materials. Otherwise, the artist/architect departed from the Tudor vernacular formula. Steele did not build two stories or use brick for part of the exterior. He extended two similar pavilions forward from the main block to form the facade and between the pavilions located an open terrace, which preceded the central entrance. Above the entry, Steele devised an unusual

DETACHED HOMES, DOUBLES, AND APARTMENTS | 401

gable/dormer window with curves and reverse curves defining its edges and faced with stucco and timber. As in Clarence Martindale's design for the Kleinschmidt House, the Steele design achieves unity and harmony while injecting asymmetry. The two front pavilions, at first glance, appear to be symmetrical, but scrutiny reveals that the fenestration in each is different in size and arrangement. Also, a buff brick chimney rises along the center of the north pavilion only. Steele achieved unity by using the same materials and a consistent silhouette. The designer's other artistic skills are evident in the art glass features that he designed at the top of most of the first-floor windows in the facade.

Preston C. and Renah Wilcox Rubush House (English Tudor Vernacular/Bungalow/Medieval)

Although architects sometimes designed elaborate and costly houses for clients, many did not achieve the financial success necessary to design large residences for themselves. One architect who eventually became quite successful—Preston C. Rubush—designed a first house for himself and his wife, Renah Wilcox Rubush, that was modest in scale yet handsomely appointed in materials and original in composition. Rubush had formed his partnership with Edgar Hunter in 1904 and within a year acquired a lot on the southeast corner of Twenty-Eighth Street and College Avenue, just south of Fall Creek and adjacent to a row of large houses along Sutherland Avenue.[34]

Rubush made effective use of a narrow lot and designed a house with vertical massing (fig. 5.15). To create visual interest, he combined elements of a medieval castle, a bungalow, and English Tudor vernacular houses. As the focal point of the facade, he reached back to medieval castle turrets as the inspiration for a two-story tower on the south end with a crenellated battlement and balanced it with a sweeping roof similar to those in bungalows (see later in this chapter). The roof descends from the ridge high above to form a porch along the north side. Rubush inserted a small stucco and timber gable that interrupts the front slope and acts

Facing top, **Figure 5.15.** Preston C. and Renah Wilcox Rubush House, 2745 North College Avenue, built in 1905–6 and designed by Preston Rubush, combining a medieval-looking tower with crenellations and stucco and timber gables from the English Tudor vernacular. A sweeping roof inspired by bungalows comes down to cover the front porch. View in 2022. James Glass.

Facing bottom, **Figure 5.16.** First-floor plan of Preston C. and Renah Wilcox Rubush House. "Model Homes of Indianapolis," *Indianapolis Sunday Star,* June 17, 1906, 8.

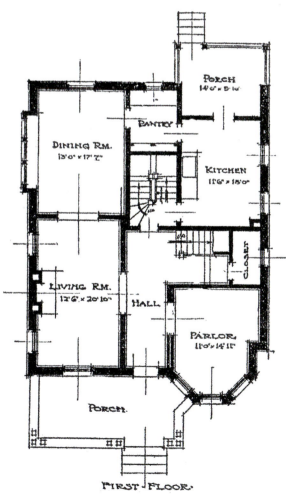

as a foil for the crenellated tower. He employed rock-faced limestone for the tower and the first story of the house. On the side elevations, he used stucco and timber for the second and attic stories.

In the interior, Preston and Renah Rubush desired both a traditional parlor and a spacious living room on the first floor, in keeping with new ideas of family living spaces (fig. 5.16). An entry hall led to the parlor in the southwest corner and the living room in the northwest corner. The living room connected at its east end to a dining room with a bay window. The kitchen and pantry occupied the southeast corner. The architect used Flemish oak for the wood trim in the entire house. In 1906, the *Indianapolis Star* described the decorative scheme in the living room as "art nouveau," in which wallpaper of a two-tone brown "with a slight tinge of green" was used. Upstairs, the house accommodated four bedrooms and a bathroom.[35] Although not a large house, the Rubush residence drew attention with its varied elements, contrasting materials, and different colors.

Herbert L. and Floria Logan Bass House (Bungalow/English Tudor Vernacular)

Another architect who designed and built his own house about the same time—Herbert L. Bass—had previously lived with his wife, Floria Logan Bass, in a cottage at 708 East Twentieth Street. By 1908, his practice had improved sufficiently for them to purchase a corner lot at 3301 North New Jersey Street, along a street on which many houses were being constructed. Herbert designed a residence with style and individuality but met their budget.[36]

For some of the design, Bass drew on elements of the Arts and Crafts and bungalow movements that were growing in popularity, popularized by Gustav Stickley and his *The Craftsman* magazine and other sources (see discussion of Stickley and bungalows later in this chapter). The architect gave the rectangular frame house a gable roof with a sweeping slope like those on some bungalows (fig. 5.17).[37] The roof came down from the ridge and hung over the second story with projecting eaves. Bass extended a second slope out from the second story to cover a spacious porch across the facade. While Arts and Crafts designs frequently featured shed dormers on the roof, Bass gave the dormer on the front slope a customized interpretation.

He projected the shed roof of the dormer above the main roof but merged the dormer window with the fenestration of the second story, interrupting the cornice. The architect also borrowed stucco and timber from the English Tudor vernacular

Figure 5.17. Herbert L. and Floria Logan Bass House, 3301 North New Jersey Street, built in 1909–10 and designed by Herbert L. Bass, with a mixture of bungalow elements, such as the sweeping roof with projecting eaves and shed dormer, and the English Tudor vernacular, with stucco and timber in the side gables. The way Bass pushed the dormer windows down to the second-floor level was a novel touch. View in 2022. James Glass.

formula but used the two materials in an understated manner for the second story and the side gables. For an unusual contrast, he used clapboards on the first story. The whole relied on various materials, colors, and forms for interest.

Inside, Bass used the traditional central hall to organize circulation. On the right, he placed the living room, with a large green tile fireplace, and on the left, the dining room. The dining room led to the kitchen at the northeast corner. The architect also designed a small garage with complementary features.[38]

William A. and Lahla Bond Walker House (Flemish/Classical)

Nearby, at Thirty-Fourth Street and Washington Boulevard, a chemist and his wife constructed a house in 1907–8 with a design drawn from an unusual theme in historic architecture. William A. Walker served as vice president of the McCoy-Howe Company, manufacturing chemists on Georgia Street downtown. Previously, he and his wife had resided in a frame double at 1527 Central Avenue. With growing income from his business, William and his wife, Lahla Bond Walker, were able to aspire to a brick single-family house with some special architectural character. The Walkers hired Rubush and Hunter as their architects, who proposed a house that drew equally from vernacular Flemish architecture of the sixteenth and seventeenth centuries and from Greek Doric architecture.[39]

Rubush and Hunter devised a rectangular block with gable roof running north and south (fig. 5.18). They specified brick laid in Flemish bond, with black headers alternating with red stretchers for the exterior walls. For the side elevations, the architects created Flemish gables, with parapets fashioned into convex curves interrupted by right angles. At the center of the north elevation, they ran a brick chimney up the center of the gable and above the roof line, much in the manner of Bacon's Castle, a 1650s brick house in colonial Virginia.[40]

At the center of the facade, the architects drew on Greek temples for a simple portico composed of Doric columns, an entablature with triglyphs, and a pediment. They continued the Greek element on the north elevation with a frame pergola supported by additional Doric columns. Rubush and Hunter used segmental arches for all the windows, which contain eight-over-eight sashes. Above, they extended the roof beyond the plane of the facade with elongated eaves. As a final accent on the front roof, the architects inserted a bank of windows within a shed dormer.

Carlos and Elizabeth Butler Recker House (Arts and Crafts/Bungalow)

The English Arts and Crafts movement spread to the United States in the 1890s and took root during the first decade of the twentieth century. Initially, the English movement stressed handicraft, as opposed to machine-made furniture, fabrics, and wall finishes for homes. Crossing the Atlantic, the Arts and Crafts ideas and aesthetic found an interpreter for the mass market in Gustav Stickley, who founded a popular magazine, *The Craftsman*. Stickley promoted his version of furniture and house designs rooted in the Arts and Crafts ideals of natural materials and spare details, with at least the appearance of being handmade. He publicized

Figure 5.18. William A. and Lahla Bond Walker House, 3363 Washington Boulevard, built in 1907–8 and designed by Rubush and Hunter with elements drawn from both Flemish architecture of the seventeenth and early eighteenth centuries and Greek Classical temples. The gables with their outline shaped into curves and reverse curves is Flemish; the idea of the chimney rising through the apex of the gables may have been inspired by a seventeenth-century Virginia house, Bacon's Castle. The entry porch is modeled on Greek Doric columns and entablatures; the side porch is covered by a pergola supported by Doric columns. View in 2023. James Glass.

Figure 5.19. Carlos and Elizabeth Butler Recker House, 59 North Hawthorne Lane, Irvington, built in 1907–8, based on a design that appeared in *The Craftsman* magazine of July 1905. Carlos Recker may have provided additional details. It is a classic Arts and Crafts bungalow, with a tall roof sweeping down to just above the first story, enclosing a porch on the south side of the facade. The three shed dormers parallel the roof slope and direct the eye downward to the porch. View in 2020. James Glass.

houses that derived from English vernacular dwellings and those reflecting a new fashion, the bungalow.[41]

One of Stickley's disciples in Indianapolis was Carlos Recker, who, with his brother Gustav Recker and Carl Sander, operated the Recker and Sander Furniture Company. Carlos and his wife, Elizabeth Butler Recker, had previously lived in a one-story frame house at 1635 North Delaware Street. In 1907, they acquired a lot on a newly platted street in Irvington, Hawthorne Lane, and decided to build a particular house design that had appeared in *The Craftsman* of July 1905. The couple finished construction in 1908. The perspective drawing in the magazine showed a two-story dwelling with a sweeping roof that descended from a high ridge and came down to the first story, enclosing a porch on the right side. Three long shed dormer windows projected from the roof slope. Carlos Recker adopted all these features but used wooden clapboards as the exterior material for the first story instead of the stone shown in *The Craftsman* (fig. 5.19). In the large side gables, he employed wood shingles. A 1909 *Indianapolis Star* article on the Recker House attributed its design to Gustav Stickley himself, but what probably happened is that Recker selected the 1905 prototype from the magazine and corresponded with Stickley.[42]

The veranda led inside to a stair hall at the center. To the south lay the living room, the chief feature of which was an inglenook, with a hearth at the center and built-in seats on either side, very much in the Arts and Crafts tradition. Adjoining the living room on the east was an enclosed "sun parlor," glassed in on one side to afford maximum daylight. The hall led to the dining room in the northwest corner of the first floor, with the kitchen in the northeast corner.[43]

Kin and Josephine Jackson Hubbard House (Arts and Crafts/Craftsman Bungalow)

The term *bungalow* came into general usage in the United States during the first decade of the twentieth century. It was an elastic word that people of the time used to describe varied types of houses. As can be seen in the discussion of working-class houses, in its most generic meaning, *bungalow* referred to a simple dwelling of moderate price, usually one story. In the Arts and Crafts realm, *bungalow* could mean any house designed with natural materials and following certain basic principles. Gustav Stickley and *The Craftsman* magazine depicted a range of houses that the publication sometimes termed bungalows. Often, the magazine also called such dwellings Craftsman.[44]

In 1908, Frank McKinney ("Kin") Hubbard, a cartoonist for the *Indianapolis News*, purchased a lot on the southwest corner of Emerson Avenue and New York Street in Irvington. Hubbard was soon to become famous for his depictions of Abe Martin and other fictional characters of Brown County, Indiana, and for the commentaries that he attributed to them on daily life. He and his wife, Josephine Jackson Hubbard, were ready to move from downtown to the artistic and literary atmosphere of Irvington. The lot they selected consisted largely of a knoll, ideal for a house overlooking Pleasant Run to the south. The Hubbards hired busy residential architect Frank B. Hunter as their architect.[45]

Figure 5.20. Kin and Josephine Jackson Hubbard House, 70 North Emerson Avenue, Irvington, built in 1908–9 and designed by Frank B. Hunter of Indianapolis, drawing on elements in bungalows published in Gustav Stickley's *The Craftsman* magazine. Note the broad bank of dormer windows set in the large sweeping roof and the jerkinhead gable at the east end. View of east and north elevations, 2023. James Glass.

Hunter devised a residence that the *Indianapolis Star* called a "craftsman house," and indeed, *The Craftsman* magazine published designs having some of the elements.[46] He created a rectangular footprint on which he placed a two-story house constructed with a high brick foundation and stucco and timber upper walls (fig. 5.20). The architect used a roof with a high ridge that swept down to eaves projecting out above the first story. At the east and west ends, he employed jerkinhead gables and exposed the timbers within the gables. At the centers of the north and south slopes of the roofs, he inserted large dormers containing banks of casement windows for the second floor. On the east elevation, the architect arranged an asymmetrical brick chimney with stepped, limestone coping on one side. Outside the east side, he laid out a terrace with a brick wall.[47]

Figure 5.21. Layton and Lelah Francis Allen House, 28 North Audubon Road, Irvington, built in 1912–13 and designed by local architect Layton Allen for himself and his wife, Lelah, drawing on themes in *The Craftsman* magazine, such as the sweeping roof descending to enclose the front porch, the picturesque arrangement of main dormer and smaller shed dormer, exposed timbers in the gables, and Rustic use of fieldstones in porch walls and chimney. View in 2023. James Glass.

The interior featured a spacious living room at the east end of the first floor with a beamed ceiling and a sizeable Arts and Crafts fireplace. Hunter situated the dining room to the west and gave it a southern exposure and a different pattern of beams overhead.[48]

Layton and Lelah Francis Allen House (Craftsman)

In 1912, Indianapolis architect Layton Allen provided a different interpretation of Craftsman home designs in the house he designed for himself and his wife, Lelah Francis Allen. The Allens had previously lived in a cottage at 107 South Ritter Avenue in Irvington. Evidently, Layton's practice had prospered, allowing them to

DETACHED HOMES, DOUBLES, AND APARTMENTS | 411

build a larger residence. They picked an advantageous site on the west side of the North Audubon Road oval, and Layton prepared the plans.[49]

He devised a frame rectangular structure with a long, sloping roof that descended east to enclose a front porch (fig. 5.21). As picturesque elements, he inserted both a shed dormer and a larger dormer with a triangular gable in the front slope. Allen used varied materials effectively to provide polychromy: he employed red brick with occasional fieldstone accents for the foundation of the porch, clapboards for the first story in the south and north elevations, and stucco and timber within the south and north gables. On the south elevation, the architect provided a splash of color and texture with a chimney composed of "bowlders" at its base and red brick and fieldstones for the stack. He extended the eaves of the roof on the north and south elevations and supported them with large brackets. Frame bay windows projected from the side elevations. In an eight-room interior, Allen included living and dining rooms, a library, a kitchen, three bedrooms, and a bathroom.[50]

George W. and Alberta Barthel June House (American Foursquare)

Several Indianapolis architects adopted the American Foursquare formula for designing houses of middle-class families. It was an original creation of American architects, beginning with houses designed in Colorado during the 1890s and then spreading across the country.[51] Although architectural historian Thomas Hanchett coined the *Foursquare* term assuming a square shape for such houses, in Indianapolis, many designs incorporating the basic Foursquare elements involved rectangular, rather than square, shapes. One of the most prolific architects of such houses in the state capital was Frank B. Hunter, who designed many Foursquare residences, both with square and rectangular footprints, between Sixteenth Street and Maple Road (Thirty-Eighth Street) during the first two decades of the twentieth century. George W. June and his wife, Alberta Barthel June, built one such house in 1909. June and his brother Homer operated a popular eatery downtown, June's "Pop" Shell Oysters, and found growing prosperity. Previously, the Junes had lived in an apartment over stores at 124 East Twenty-Second Street. They purchased a lot at 2021 North Talbott Avenue and hired Hunter, who devised a classic version of his approach to Foursquare houses.[52]

The essential ingredients that Hunter used included a rectilinear block with a hipped roof, a prominent dormer in the front slope with its own hipped roof, a rectangular porch across the facade, a brick veneer for the first story, and stucco and timber for the second story (fig. 5.22).[53] The architect arranged a brick

Figure 5.22. George W. and Alberta Barthel June House, 2021 North Talbott Avenue, built in 1908–9 and designed by Frank B. Hunter, using a formula he developed for middle-income, Foursquare houses—rectangular block, hipped roof, front dormer with hipped roof, a porch across the facade, brick first story, and stucco and timber second story. View in 2023. James Glass.

chimney on the south elevation with clean lines, no ornamentation, and no irregularities. Superimposed on the capitals of the piers on the porch, which was open originally, was an inverted keystone of concrete—one of his trademarks. On the second story of the facade, Hunter used trios of a window sash pattern growing in popularity—multiple panes over one.

Inside, he effectively used the limited space available to create a spacious reception hall, a living room with a fireplace, and the largest room in the house—the dining room—ornamented by beams in the ceiling. Upstairs, he provided three bedrooms and a bath.[54]

DETACHED HOMES, DOUBLES, AND APARTMENTS | 413

ARCHITECT PROFILE

Frank B. Hunter

Frank Baldwin Hunter (1883–1958) was born in Covington, Kentucky, but raised in Indianapolis. He attended the Classical Art School in the old Circle Hall on Monument Circle and the Manual Training High School. Interested in architecture and engineering, he entered the office of P. C. Rubush and Company as a draftsman for two years. Hunter then worked for J. W. Gaddis, an architect in Vincennes, and prepared the designs for the Huntington County and Putnam County courthouses. Returning to Indianapolis, he sought employment with a major architectural firm, R. P. Daggett and Company, and completed his stint as a draftsman there in 1907. Hunter then opened his own office, intending to specialize in "the creation of fine homes." He enjoyed immediate success in the residential field. Over a period of two years, 1909 through 1910, Hunter designed twelve houses featured in the "How Others Have Built" series of the *Indianapolis Star*. He especially obtained commissions for middle-class residences in those years and developed a formula for Foursquare houses that proved popular. Examples include the George W. and Alberta Barthel June House, the Albert T. and Elizabeth Gough Rapp House, the Lovel D. Millikan-Congresswoman Julia Carson House at 2540 North Park Avenue, the Frank A. Preston House at 3312 Ruckle Street, the George W. Stoner House at 3058 Washington Boulevard, and the Charles C. Miller House at 3250 North New Jersey Street. He also employed elements of the English Tudor vernacular and the Arts and Crafts style for middle-income residences, such as the Kin and Josephine Jackson Hubbard House.

In the 1920s, Hunter graduated to designing large homes along Meridian Street, Pennsylvania Street, and Washington Boulevard north of Fortieth Street. One such house, the Thompson-Trimble House, 4343 North Meridian Street, later became the governor's residence.

He also expanded his practice to commercial buildings, such as the Fountain Square Theater Building and Zaring's Egyptian Theater in Indianapolis, and designed the Ambassador Apartments. Hunter retired from architectural and engineering practice in the 1940s and moved to Nashville, Indiana, where he became part of the art colony there.

Sources: "Frank B. Hunter," in Paul Donald Brown, ed., *Indianapolis Men of Affairs 1923* (Indianapolis: American Biographical Society, 1923), 307; "Hunter, Frank B.," Citizens Historical Association Indianapolis, in Biographical clipping file "Hunter, A.–Hunter, M.," Indiana State Library; "Frank B. Hunter, Retired Architect," *Indianapolis Times*, January 5, 1958, 39, c. 1–2. Source for photo: Brown, *Indianapolis Men of Affairs 1923*, 306.

Alfred T. and Elizabeth Gough Rapp House (American Foursquare)

A bookkeeper named Alfred T. Rapp and his wife, Alberta Gough Rapp, hired Hunter about the same time to design a two-story frame house. Alfred operated a small office downtown. Previously, the Rapps had lived in half of a frame double at 608 East Nineteenth Street.[55]

Hunter devised a house at 3240 Broadway that was quite similar to the one he had designed for the Junes—a rectangular block, a hipped roof, a prominent

> *Above,* **Figure 5.23.** Alfred T. and Elizabeth Gough Rapp House, 3240 Broadway, built in 1909 and designed by Frank B. Hunter following his Foursquare formula but employing a small porch over the entry with a pyramidal roof, clapboards on the first story, and wood shakes on the second. View in 2023. James Glass.

> *Facing top,* **Figure 5.24.** Hunter used the incised arrow motif on the Rapp House and several of his other Foursquare houses. 2023 view. James Glass.

> *Facing bottom,* **Figure 5.25.** First- and second-floor plans, Rapp House. Note the placement of the living room across the front of the first floor and the dining room along the side, which became a standard layout. "How Others Have Built," *Indianapolis Sunday Star,* December 19, 1909, Women's Section, 4.

416 | ARCHITECTURE IN INDIANAPOLIS, 1900–1920

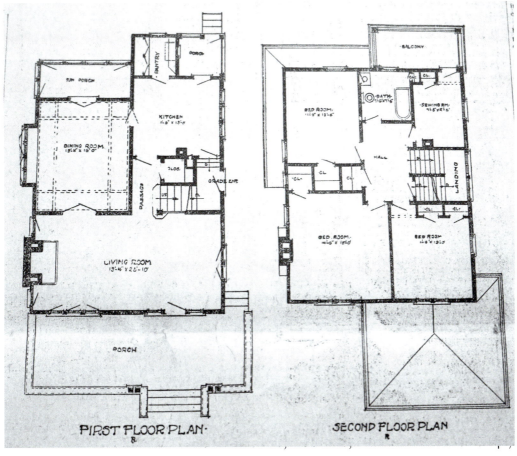

FIRST FLOOR PLAN · SECOND FLOOR PLAN

frontal dormer with hipped roof, and a rectangular porch along the facade (fig. 5.23).[56] He stretched out the Rapp House horizontally and clad its exterior with clapboards on the first story and wooden shakes on the second story. He also devised a novelty—a roof with a pyramidal shape covering just the north half of the front porch and supported by two sets of paired wooden columns. The columns contained another motif used frequently by Hunter—a stylized incised arrow (fig. 5.24). The brick foundation and wall around the porch contrasted with the frame texture of the house exterior.

For the interior, Hunter consulted Alberta Rapp, who asked for certain features (fig. 5.25), such as the large living room that extended across the east side of the first floor and included an imposing fireplace. Hunter placed the dining room along the south side of the house, west of the living room, and gave it a wooden beamed ceiling. The dining room led to a sunporch at the rear. To the north, it connected with a sizeable kitchen. On the second floor, the architect included three bedrooms and a sewing room.[57]

Madam C. J. Walker House (Foursquare)

American Foursquare designs could be found in all parts of the city by 1912. Madam C. J. Walker, a leading African American entrepreneur and manufacturer, moved to Indianapolis in 1910 and purchased a frame house at 640 North West Street (now Dr. Martin Luther King Jr. Street), near the center of the principal Black neighborhood. In 1911, Madam Walker added a two-story addition to the front of the existing residence, which had been built in the 1870s or 1880s. A photograph taken of her standing in front of the new structure (fig. 5.26) shows a

Facing top, **Figure 5.26.** A + beside the name of a building indicates that it no longer exists. +Madam C. J. Walker House, 640 North West (now Dr. Martin Luther King Jr.) Street, showing the facade and addition constructed by Madam Walker (who is standing in the center) in 1910–11. Her unknown architect added a new brick facade with Foursquare elements: rectangular facade, hipped roof, central dormer, and rectangular front porch. The facade appeared symmetrical, but the first floor was actually asymmetrical, with a projecting bay window on the left and a flat trio of windows on the right. View in c. 1912. Demolished in 1964–65 and replaced by a vacant lot or a parking lot. Madam C. J. Walker Collection, Indiana Historical Society.

Facing bottom, **Figure 5.27.** Detail of tablet incorporated into the design of the new facade for the Madam C. J. Walker House, reading, "Mme. C. J. Walker, Hair Culturist 640 N. West St." Madam C. J. Walker Collection, Indiana Historical Society.

rectangular brick house with the Foursquare features of a hipped roof, a central dormer containing two windows and capped by a hipped roof, and a spacious rectangular porch across the first story.[58]

Brick piers with square concrete abacuses supported the porch, the roof of which was lined by a frame balustrade. The facade appeared symmetrical, but the unknown architect introduced asymmetry on the first story, with a projecting bay window on the south side and a trio of flat windows on the north side. For the second story, the designer used simple detailing, such as flat brick arches above the windows. As part of the facade design, Madam Walker directed that a concrete or limestone tablet be incorporated into the brickwork of the second story. It read "Mme. C. J. Walker, Hair Culturist 640 N. West St" (fig. 5.27).

Also in 1910–11, Madam Walker constructed a two-story brick building to the rear of her lot for the manufacture of the hair-care products of the Mme. C. J. Walker Manufacturing Company. The building included space for a laboratory and a salon for hairdressing.[59]

Dr. Silas J. and Sarah McCullough Carr House (Dutch Colonial)

A type of house that appeared occasionally in the city during this period derived from the residential architecture of New England, Long Island, and New Jersey in the early eighteenth century.[60] Its essential feature was the gambrel roof, in which two slopes on each side form the gables. During the first decades of the twentieth century, houses with such roofs were widely called Dutch Colonial. An example in Irvington took shape between 1906 and 1907, the result of collaboration between a dentist, Dr. Silas J. Carr, and his architect-brother, Marrett Carr. Silas and Marrett had previously lived in their parents' house at 1220 East Washington Street. After Silas's marriage, he and his wife, Sarah McCullough Carr, decided to build a house in Irvington, where Silas maintained his practice. Marrett was working as a draftsman when he designed the residence for the Carrs.[61]

Given the limited budget of his clients, Marrett Carr's challenge was to create a house with individual character. He achieved his objective by encasing the second story of the rectangular house in two gambrel roofs that intersected at the center (fig. 5.28).[62] He used brick as a veneer for the first story and wood for the cornice and the three gables that project outward in the facade and in the north and south elevations. Within the facade gable, Carr inserted a double window with sunburst panel above and covered the gable surface with wood shingles. The descending slopes of the gambrel gable on the facade capture attention with their projecting eaves and the lower molding that projects out as part of the house cornice. The

Figure 5.28. Dr. Silas J. and Sarah McCullough Carr House, 76 Whittier Place, Irvington, built in 1909–10 and designed by Silas's architect-brother, Marrett L. Carr, drawing on the so-called Dutch Colonial style, which actually was based on houses with varied slopes of gambrel roofs constructed in New England, Long Island, and New Jersey from the early eighteenth century. Carr used three gambrel roofs intersecting at the center. The small entry porch is contained within the massing of the house as a whole. View in 2022. James Glass.

other two gables give personality to the sides of the house. The architect inserted a small porch at the northeast corner, within the mass of the house structure, and included a bay window in the south elevation.

Inside, he planned seven rooms—a reception hall, living room, dining room, and kitchen on the first floor and two bedrooms and a bath on the second. A single chimney served fireplaces in both the living room and dining room.[63]

DETACHED HOMES, DOUBLES, AND APARTMENTS | 421

LOWER-MIDDLE-CLASS/WORKERS' BUNGALOWS

The term *bungalow* originated in the Bengali section of eastern India, where it referred to temporary or seasonal frame dwellings with sweeping, low roofs and wide verandas. In the first decade of the twentieth century, the concept and word made their way to the United States, where they underwent some changes.[64] In this country, the bungalow became a permanent structure, often one story, with a sweeping gable roof that descended to eaves above the first story. Bungalows could be large and elaborate, but most provided housing for lower-middle-class and workers' families and were small and moderately priced. A generic worker's bungalow implied a one-story frame house, usually with a porch across the front. During the first decade of the century, the so-called California bungalow became popular, with many designs spread by *The Craftsman* magazine.[65]

Architects designed bungalows for all price ranges in Indianapolis. Some provided their services under contract with homebuyers, and others supplied designs to builders or real estate companies constructing groups of houses in new additions. An architect-designed bungalow could be purchased in 1913 for less than $3,000. Builders and homebuyers could also obtain bungalow plans from *The Craftsman* and other periodicals or order precut house materials from mail-order firms such as Sears, Roebuck and Company. Sears would ship the materials to the site to be assembled by a contractor or carpenter. A local firm, the Bungalow Company, offered a sixty-four-page book of bungalow plans for prospective homebuyers and would design and build bungalows for clients.[66]

John F. and Louise Rentsch Bryan House (Basic Bungalow)

In 1909, architect Charles Byfield designed a basic bungalow at 2829 North Pennsylvania Street for John K. Bryan and his wife, Louise Rentsch Bryan. Bryan worked as a bookkeeper for the Capital City Brewing Company, and the couple had previously lived in a frame cottage at 2627 North Capitol Avenue.

In his house for the Bryans, Byfield drew from the Foursquare ideas of a hipped roof, rectangular block, and porch across the facade and from the Prairie School notions of low-pitched roofs and horizontality. The one-story brick dwelling formed a rectangle that included the front porch in its mass (fig. 5.29). The hipped roof extended over the porch, which Byfield supported with square brick piers. The facade was symmetrical, and Byfield relied on the limestone trim to relieve the dark color and rough texture of the brick.[67]

Figure 5.29. +John F. and Louise Rentsch Bryan House, 2829 North Pennsylvania Street, built in 1909–10 and designed by Charles H. Byfield of Indianapolis as an expression of the basic bungalow plan: one story with a front porch. In this case, Byfield used elements of the Foursquare, such as a hipped roof and porch across the facade, but without the central dormer. He also included the space of the porch within the massing of the house as a whole. Demolished in 1969–70 for a parking lot. View in 1910. "How Others Have Built," *Indianapolis Sunday Star*, September 11, 1910, Women's Section, 4.

Inside, the architect provided six rooms. Adjacent to the porch, he located a spacious living room with a beamed ceiling and a central fireplace. Byfield adjoined the living room with the dining room, also adorned with wooden beams. In the rear, he situated the kitchen, two bedrooms, and a bath.[68]

Jacob F. and Abbie Gibbs Moyer House (Bungalow—Craftsman)

About the same time, dentist Jacob F. Moyer and his wife, Abbie Gibbs Moyer, decided to build a bungalow north of Maple Road (now Thirty-Eighth Street). Previously, the Moyers had lived in an apartment downtown, where Jacob had his dental office. They picked a lot at 3904 North Delaware Street and retained

Figure 5.30. Jacob F. and Abbie Gibbs Moyer House, 3904 North Delaware Street, built in 1910 and designed by architect George Ransdell of Franklin, Indiana, drawing on bungalow elements pictured in *The Craftsman*, such as projecting eaves supported by brackets, a shed dormer on the side, and a front porch across the front (originally open). View in 2023. James Glass.

George Ransdell, an architect from Franklin, Indiana, with a practice that covered Indianapolis. Ransdell suggested a design that may have been based in part on houses in *The Craftsman*. He devised a one-and-a-half story frame residence, rectangular in its footprint, with a gable roof running east and west and the east gable facing the street (fig. 5.30). Along the facade, the architect ran a brick porch (originally open) with its own roof. He included a couple of elements common to bungalows—wide, projecting eaves, supported by simple brackets, and shed dormers. In this case, Ransdell projected dormers from the north and south slopes of the main roof. He inserted a red brick chimney without ornament or details through the eaves on the north side.[69]

On the first floor, the architect included a reception hall, living room, dining room, kitchen, bath, and two bedrooms. On the small second floor, he provided a bedroom, sewing room, and two storerooms. Ransdell efficiently planned the interior to provide a maximum of specialized rooms in a modest-sized dwelling.[70]

Beville Avenue Workers' Bungalows

As had been true since at least the Civil War, the largest number of houses constructed each year between 1900 and 1920 were intended for skilled and unskilled (blue-collar) workers and their families. Many workers in the city purchased their houses, using financing provided through building and loan associations, builders, or real estate companies. As bungalows replaced cottages as the most popular home type for blue-collar residents, some home-building firms began to market groups of bungalows to workers. In 1912, one such entity—the Marion Home Building Company—advertised fifteen new bungalows for sale on both sides of Beville Avenue north of New York Street, southeast of Woodruff Place on the east side. The company had hired an unknown architect to design houses that had almost identical footprints but individual features. Prices ranged from $3,250 to $3,800 and could be paid in "easy monthly payments."[71]

Figure 5.31 shows four of the Beville Avenue bungalows. In 1914, Perman E. Linville and his family occupied the first, at 322 North Beville. Linville was a superintendent for the Otis Elevator Company. The architect gave the house a rectangular mass with a pyramidal roof. A gable projects from one side of the facade, supported by brackets. On the other side, the house mass encloses a small porch. The designer used clapboards on the exterior of the Linville House and, as was standard in the Marion Home bungalows, specified a concrete-block foundation with rock-faced surfaces. The advertisement stated that "every house has hardwood floors, beautifully papered and decorated walls, bath, furnace, basement and laundry room with hot and cold water, cistern, gas and electric lights, beautiful fixtures, closets, and china closets."[72]

In 1914, G. Frank Calvin, an ironworker, lived with his family at 326 North Beville, the next house.[73] In this case, the architect used a frequent device found in bungalows—extending a gable roof forward to enclose a front porch. Brackets support the eaves of the east gable, and clapboards cover the gable and the rest of the exterior. The architect covered the balustrade on the porch with clapboards.

Stanley F. Martin, a signwriter, occupied the next house, at 330 North Beville, with his family in 1914.[74] The designer gave it slightly different features: a gable roof facing forward but with shallow eaves, no brackets, and a front porch with its

Facing top, **Figure 5.31.** Four workers' bungalows on the west side of Beville Avenue north of New York Street, built in 1911–12 as part of a group of fifteen bungalows designed by an architect and constructed by the Marion Home Building Company. Pictured from the left are 322, 326, 330, and 334 North Beville, showing the variety of silhouettes, roof treatments, and porch designs used for the group. View in 2023. James Glass.

Facing bottom, **Figure 5.32.** Ernest L. Ethington House, 334 North Beville Avenue, showing the Foursquare treatment given by the Marion Home architect. View in 2023. James Glass.

own roof. Ernest L. Ethington, a clerk, resided in the fourth house of the group, at 334 North Beville (fig. 5.32).[75] Continuing the variety of silhouette and detailing, the architect used the basic formula of the Foursquare type, with a hipped roof and a front, central dormer. He hollowed out the south half of the facade to provide a porch and used brick for the corner pier and wall, to contrast with the clapboards of the rest of the exterior.

The Beville Avenue houses are intriguing because they present both individuality and architectural compatibility in a block of residences constructed by a single builder at the same time. The Marion Home Building Company obviously understood the psychology of appealing to homebuyers.

Overman-Arnold House (California Bungalow)

By 1910, a new variation on bungalow design began to appear in Indianapolis and across the country. Termed "California bungalows" by contemporaries, early examples in fact did appear on the West Coast. Spurred by publication in *The Craftsman*, the type became widely popular. The California bungalow can be discerned by its low-slung gable roofs, gable eaves that project considerably from the house, and simple, squared brackets that support the eaves.[76]

A classic example of a California bungalow designed for white-collar clients took shape at what is now 4329 North College Avenue in 1913–14 (fig. 5.33). It appears that a salesman, Thomas P. Overman, and a clerk, William V. B. Arnold, jointly hired the Bungalow Company to design the house and construct it. Under the supervision of manager Ralph W. Bauman, the company devised a one-story frame house in which steeply projecting gables extend from the facade and the north and south elevations.[77] The west gable covers the front porch. On the south elevation, a secondary gable projects below the primary one. Squared brackets supporting the eaves form the only exterior ornamentation. The designers chose

Facing top, **Figure 5.33.** Overman-Arnold House, 4329 North College Avenue, built in 1913–14 and designed and constructed by the Bungalow Company of Indianapolis, as a classic statement of the California bungalow. Note the steeply projecting gable eaves supported by elongated brackets on the facade and the gable within a gable on the side elevation. Also notice the chimney stack emerging through the side gable. View in 2021. James Glass.

Facing bottom, **Figure 5.34.** William D. Vogel House, 802 North Riley Avenue, Emerson Heights, built in 1914–15 and designed by architects Doeppers and Myers of Indianapolis, with a creative interpretation of the California bungalow. Note the two projecting eaves supported by brackets, the fieldstones used for the porch piers and walls, and the frame pergola over part of the porch. View in 2022. James Glass.

cedar for the clapboards and cypress for the fascia, brackets, and door and window surrounds. The porch foundations and walls are of brick. On the south side, a brick chimney penetrates the two gables and emerges from the roof with concrete pots.[78] Inside, the Bungalow Company provided a living room with fireplace, as well as a dining room, kitchen, and three bedrooms.[79]

William D. Vogel House (California Bungalow)

An even more striking design with California bungalow elements came from local architects Edwin C. Doeppers and Clarence Myers for a house they designed in the newly platted addition of Emerson Heights, just west of Irvington. The client, William D. Vogel, was a clerk in the Marion County Treasurer's Office and had previously lived with his parents at 2511 Bloyd Avenue on the near east side. His father was a contractor, and it is possible that the elder Vogel constructed the son's new house.[80]

Doeppers and Myers created a sophisticated California bungalow design for a modest-sized house and imparted their individual stamp (fig. 5.34). They took a rectangular frame dwelling and positioned the gable end to front the street.[81] The main gable eaves extend forward, supported by brackets in the conventional pattern. The architects gave the front porch individuality by using a secondary gable roof with projecting eaves to cover the north portion and extending a pergola-like structure of frame beams over the southern terrace section. They afforded vivid color and contrast in texture by employing "bowlders" (fieldstones) for the substantial piers supporting the porch roof and pergola and for the walls and foundations of the porch. On the north elevation, the designers used bowlders for a chimney that penetrated the eaves. Viewed from the street, the facade presents a pattern used repeatedly in California bungalows—a major projecting gable and, below it, a smaller, echoing gable set off-center.

Doeppers and Myers also incorporated a distinctive decorative element into the design of some of the beams and brackets, splitting them in the center and inserting squared pegs in the cracks so that the pegs project from the wooden member. Such attention to joinery may have been inspired by such masterpieces of the California bungalow as the Gamble House in Pasadena, designed by architects Greene and Greene.[82]

Inside, the architects departed from the conventional bungalow floor plan. Over the north end of the living room, which ran across the house, they fashioned a full Craftsman-style inglenook with a red matte tile floor, built-in seats, and bookcases. At the center of the north wall, Doeppers and Myers designed a bowlder fireplace with a fieldstone chimney breast extending to the ceiling. They divided the living room from the dining room with two columns. Fumed oak beams supported the ceilings of both rooms. A window seat projected from the south end of the dining room, to the west of which was the kitchen. Two bedrooms lay along the north side of the house.[83]

Joseph Hooser House (California Bungalow)

The Bungalow Company incorporated some of the same elements in the house they designed and built in 1913–14 at 5033 Broadway (fig. 5.35). According to the *Indianapolis Star*, the client was Joseph Hooser, a machine operator who had previously lived in an apartment at 1026 North College Avenue. The designers used fieldstones for the foundation and piers of a front porch (originally open) that projects from the west side of the house and for a chimney along the north elevation. The main block of the frame dwelling runs north and south. In keeping with the California bungalow formula, the Bungalow Company used projecting gables supported by brackets over the porch and along the north and south elevations. The architects applied clapboards above a horizontal wooden molding on the exterior of the house proper; below the molding, they covered the foundation with cypress skirts fashioned into a board-and-batten pattern.[84]

Like the Vogel House, the single-story Hooser House contains a fieldstone fireplace in its living room, which is reached through the porch. The dining room and kitchen lie to the east of the living room. Along the south side are two bedrooms and a bath.[85]

Figure 5.35. Joseph Hooser House, 5033 Broadway, built in 1913–14 and designed and constructed by the Bungalow Company of Indianapolis, drawing from California bungalow elements—projecting eaves and brackets, together with Rustic fieldstones for the piers and walls of the originally open porch and for the chimney. View in 2023. James Glass.

Edwin Wuensch House (Jerkinhead Gable Bungalow)

In 1914, Doeppers and Myers designed a very different bungalow from the Vogel House for Edwin Wuensch at 4323 Broadway. Wuensch worked in the bond department of the Fletcher-American National Bank downtown and previously had lived with his mother in a house at 217 North Gray on the east side. He may have been recently married and desired a home for setting up housekeeping.[86]

The architects created a residence with a rectangular footprint (fig. 5.36).[87] They constructed the exterior with matte brick as a veneer over a frame inner

DETACHED HOMES, DOUBLES, AND APARTMENTS | 431

Figure 5.36. Edwin Wuensch House, 4323 Broadway, built in 1914 and designed by Doeppers and Myers, departing from the usual formula for bungalows with an all-brick exterior, jerkinhead gables on the sides, and a large hipped roof dormer that cuts through the cornice of the facade. Note picturesque details, such as shed-roofed bay window on the side elevation and recessed brick panels on the porch piers. View in 2023. James Glass.

structure. The designers devised an unusual front porch that covers only the center of the facade; on either side, it continues as an open terrace. A hipped roof with jerkinhead gables on the north and south elevations covers the main block of the house. The designers gave the porch its own roof with a shed profile. Above the porch, they inserted a large dormer in the main roof that begins below the cornice level. There are four windows within the dormer, to which the architects gave a jerkinhead gable with a shallow pitch. For decorative elements, Doeppers and Myers employed recessed panels in the brick porch piers and wooden brackets above the porch openings. On the north and south elevations, they projected bay windows with rectangular shapes.

In the living room, the architects included Arts and Crafts elements shown in *The Craftsman*: an inglenook and fireplace, accompanied by built-in bookcases and seats. As in the Vogel House, they separated the living room from the dining room with oak columns and gave the living room a beamed ceiling. In the dining room, the projecting bay window outside in the south elevation is revealed to be a window seat. The designers situated the kitchen and pantry at the rear of the first floor. An oak stairway leads to the second floor, which in 1914 contained three bedrooms, a sewing room, and a bath. As in many homes of the period, the architects provided for a second-floor sleeping porch.[88]

DOUBLES

One residential type had existed in Indianapolis since at least the 1850s, but on a limited scale. Around 1900, the double, as it is usually called in Indiana, began to appear in large numbers in the city. A double contained two complete residences within a single structural envelope. It appealed especially to middle-class home seekers who wanted a full house but with less responsibility for maintenance. Doubles tended to be built as investments—either for sale of one or both sides to homebuyers or as rentals of one or both sides. In the spring of 1905, the *Indianapolis Star* predicted that there would be a great demand that building season for double houses. They would be constructed chiefly as investments, and the cost per structure would range between $4,000 and $8,000.[89]

The formula that developed involved a two-and-a-half story structure, frequently designed to resemble a single-family house, with the interior divided in the middle to produce two residences, with mirror-image floor plans and identical features. Many owners hired architects to design their doubles, and much variety of design ensued. The American Foursquare was a favorite style, but other arrangements of massing and detail also found favor. A sampling of doubles constructed north of downtown illustrates types of double design.

John S. Duncan Double (Eclectic)

In 1904, attorney John S. Duncan purchased a lot on the southeast corner of Fourteenth and New Jersey Streets and hired Indianapolis architect H. C. Hendrickson to design a double. Hendrickson devised a two-story, rectangular block with a brick veneer exterior (fig. 5.37). He gave the structure a rectilinear, symmetrical facade, austerely detailed, with plain stone lintels from the Federal style over the second story and attic windows and a simple, projecting cornice surmounted by a brick parapet. Hendrickson used the two porches—one for each house—to enliven the facade. He gave the porches hipped roofs and supported them with Tuscan

Figure 5.37. +John S. Duncan Double, 1335–39 North New Jersey Street, built in 1904–5 by John S. Duncan and designed by Indianapolis architect H. C. Hendrickson using an eclectic mixture—rectangular facade with simple cornice, Federal-style flat stone lintels over the windows, and two porches with hipped roofs—one for each side. View from 1905. Demolished in 1977–78 and replaced by a vacant lot. View in 1905. "The last few years has [sic] seen a great increase in the construction . . .," *Indianapolis Star*, August 14, 1905, 5.

columns. Inside (fig. 5.38), the architect provided amply for the needs of the new residents—each side included both a parlor and a living room, a dining room, and a kitchen on the first floor and four bedrooms on the second. He provided fireplaces for the two parlors, bay windows on the side elevations, and oak for the interior trim.[90]

The cost of construction for Duncan came to $9,500. It appears that he sold or rented both halves of the double to businessmen. In 1914, Hobart A. Boomer, general manager of the Lake Erie and Western Railroad, resided with his family in the 1335 North New Jersey half, and Don P. Hawkins, an independent broker, lived with his family at 1339.[91]

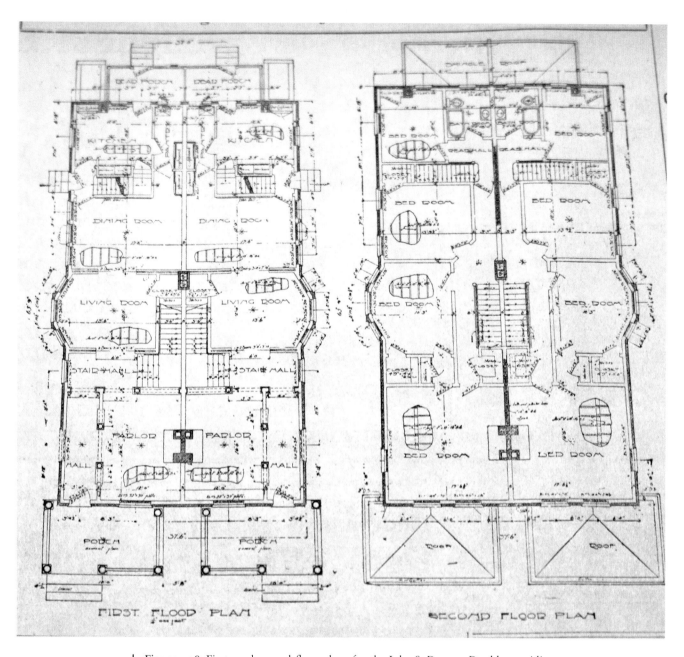

Figure 5.38. First- and second-floor plans for the John S. Duncan Double providing both a parlor and a living room for each side of the double, plus four bedrooms. "The last few years has [sic] seen a great increase in the construction . . .," *Indianapolis Star*, August 14, 1905, 5.

Gocke-King Double (Foursquare)

After 1910, increasing numbers of doubles appeared in Indianapolis neighborhoods—many in the area between Sixteenth Street and Maple Road (Thirty-Eighth Street). An example stands at 2156–2158 North Pennsylvania Street. O. Harry A. Gocke, a travel agent, constructed a substantial double both as an investment and as a home for himself and his family. In 1913, he and his wife, Winifred Shirtz Gocke, purchased a 129-by-40-foot lot in the Meridian Place Addition and retained Charles Byfield as their architect.[92]

Byfield used an exterior design that could easily have served for a single-family house, employing most of the features of a Foursquare residence (fig. 5.39). He devised a two-story, rectangular block, with a hipped roof, the trademark front dormer, and a rectilinear porch across the facade. As in English Tudor vernacular and other Foursquare houses, Byfield employed a dark-brown brick for the first story and porch and stucco for the second story. A single stairway at the center of the porch led to the twin entry doors for the two houses. The architect used squared piers to support the porch roof; instead of stone or concrete balusters along the front of the porch, he fashioned brick balusters with limestone sills. On the side elevations, he placed unusually tall chimney stacks to vary the silhouette of the whole.[93]

Inside, on each side, Byfield provided a living room with a fireplace, a dining room, a kitchen, three bedrooms, and a bath. Laundry rooms and furnaces occupied the basements. The first floors offered parquet hardwood patterns. The fireplace mantels were brick, with heavy wooden shelves.[94] When the contractor completed work, Gocke and his family moved into the 2158 North Pennsylvania half, and William F. King, assistant secretary of the Indiana Board of Health, and his family took up residence at 2156.[95]

Doubles on North New Jersey Street and Central Avenue (Varied Elements)

Investors built numerous doubles north of Fall Creek. Several structures in the 3200 block of North New Jersey Street and 3300 block of Central Avenue serve as illustrations.

On the southeast corner of Thirty-Third and New Jersey Streets, an investor constructed a double in about 1909 that departed from the Foursquare formula (fig. 5.40). The unknown architect designed a large rectangular block with an unusual hipped roof that included both dormers and gables.[96] He arranged the

Figure 5.39. Gocke-King Double, 2156–58 North Pennsylvania Street, built in 1913–14 and designed by Charles H. Byfield, using a similar Foursquare formula to that employed by Frank B. Hunter—rectangular block, hipped roof, central dormer, rectangular porch across the facade, brick first story, and stucco second story. Many Indianapolis doubles were designed to appear to be single-family dwellings. View in 2022. James Glass.

windows on the facade and north elevation asymmetrically. Departing from most porch layouts, the individual porches for each side of the double were placed without regard for symmetry—the south porch projects from the facade, while the north one wraps around the corner. The designer constructed the porches of rock-faced concrete block, called "artificial stone" at the time—including the foundations, columns and balustrades.

The investor either rented or sold the two sides of the double. The initial residents of the 3267 North New Jersey address were Edwin W. Thomas, an inspector, and his family. Omer Hunt, another travel agent, and his family occupied 3269 North New Jersey in 1913.[97]

In the same block, an investor—Georgiana Carter—constructed a double at 3241–3243 North New Jersey Street in 1913. She rented the two halves to brothers

DETACHED HOMES, DOUBLES, AND APARTMENTS | 437

Facing top, **Figure 5.40.** Thomas-Hunt Double, 3267–69 North New Jersey Street, built about 1909 and designed with an unorthodox composition of features—two porches placed asymmetrically on the facade and two types of dormer windows, gable roofed and hipped, with the windows also placed asymmetrically. Note use of concrete blocks on the porches and foundations, cast to resemble stone blocks. View in 2023. James Glass.

Facing bottom, **Figure 5.41.** Haskell L. and Herbert T. Conner Double, 3241–3243 North New Jersey Street, built probably in 1912 and cast in a Foursquare design, with a variation in the treatment of the porch and entrances—the two porches share a common roof, and the entries are located at the north and south ends of the facade. Note use of brick for the first story, wood shakes on the second, and the twenty-five-over-one sash windows harking back to the Queen Anne style. View in 2023. James Glass.

Above, **Figure 5.42.** Mead-Donavin Double, 3330–32 Central Avenue, built in 1914 with an original design for the facade: bay windows with shed roofs projecting from the second story, a porch that extends beyond the north and south edges of the house, and a large gable/pediment over the center of the porch. The architect employed varied materials for texture and color—clapboards on the first and second stories, wood shakes in the front gable, and concrete for the foundation and bases of the porch columns. View in 2022. James Glass.

Haskett L. and Herbert T. Conner, who lived in the double with their families. Haskett was a physician and surgeon, with offices in the Newton Claypool Building, and Herbert operated the Walk-Over Boot Shop downtown. The unknown architect devised a conventional Foursquare design—rectangular block, hipped roof, front dormer, and front porch across the facade (fig. 5.41).[98] He chose brick for the first story and front porch and frame for the second story, which he covered with stained wood shingles. The porch appears to be a single structure, but there are actually two porches with a gap in between, all under a single roof. The architect employed brick piers with concrete abacuses to support the porch. He used twenty-five-over-one sashes for the windows.

Over on Central Avenue, another double rose in 1914 that conveyed originality in its design. One of the original residents—Thorret R. Mead—was superintendent of the contracting firm Dunn-McCarty Company, and it is possible that he and his wife, Agenoria Sears Mead, built the double at 3330–3332 Central Avenue as an investment. The first tenant or buyer of 3330 Central, James F. Donavin, was president of the Donavin Shoe Company on Georgia Street downtown.[99]

The unknown architect devised a long rectangular block with a gable roof running east and west and attached to its facade a rectilinear porch that extended beyond the north and south walls of the house (fig. 5.42).[100] At the center of the porch roof, he incorporated a pediment. He used stone for the foundation of the porch and for pedestals supporting the wooden columns. Above the porch, the designer created two unusual bay windows with shed roofs. The whole of the facade is carefully symmetrical. The architect sought to exploit differences in texture with clapboards on the first story and wooden shingles in the front gable. On the north and south slopes of the house, he projected out shed dormers for the attic.

APARTMENTS

One of the most startling developments in Indianapolis real estate and building between 1900 and 1920 involved the tremendous growth in demand for apartments, or flats, as they were frequently called. A perusal of the lists of public buildings, halls, and flats appearing in the Indianapolis city directories reveals that the number of apartment/flat structures increased from 23 buildings in 1900 to 275 in 1910 and a staggering 539 in 1920. The trend already noted (see chap. 10 of vol. 1) of couples, families, and single people shifting from single-family dwellings or boardinghouses to comfortable apartments without the expenses and responsibilities of ownership exerted a powerful pull toward rental units in buildings especially designed for tenants. As demand rose, many local citizens saw an opportunity to make money by constructing apartment structures, and most hired architects to design attractive buildings and units with amenities especially oriented to flat dwellers.[101]

Construction of apartment buildings began in the northern half of the Mile Square and spread rapidly to neighborhoods throughout the city. The *Indianapolis Journal* reported in 1901 that the great demand for flats previously observed continued to be strong. Owners rented new apartments as soon as the architects finished the plans.[102] Many of the new buildings provided affordable housing for white-collar workers, widows, and people on fixed incomes. A smaller number provided luxury units for prosperous businessmen and those with higher incomes. Some attracted a mixture of white-collar workers and middle-class tenants. A sampling of apartment buildings erected between 1900 and 1920 illustrates the range of building configurations, architectural styles, layouts of units, and occupants.

The Rink (Italian Renaissance)

In 1901, Joseph A. Rink, owner of Rink's Cloak House downtown, made a major investment in response to the interest in rental flats. He purchased a large corner parcel at 401 North Illinois Street, next to the Romanesque-style Savoy apartments, built two years earlier. At the east end of the block stood the finely appointed Blacherne apartment building (see chap. 10 of vol. 1). Because of the high cost of real estate at this location, Rink decided to erect a seven-story building and maximize the number of units. His choice as architect, W. Scott Moore, had designed the Central Christian Church and codesigned the Propylaeum building during the previous decade.[103]

Moore planned a fireproof building, with a steel skeleton, brick exterior walls, and hollow clay tile incorporated into the floors. He gave it an L-shaped configuration to allow for a light court at the northeast corner.[104]

The architect chose Italian Renaissance details to impart an imposing character on the Illinois and Vermont Street facades. He used the three-part skyscraper formula for organizing the facades (see chap. 1 of this volume), cladding the base—the first two stories and the basement—with rusticated Indiana limestone blocks and a dressed limestone frieze (fig. 5.43). He clad the shaft—fourth through sixth stories—in yellow brick, and at the beveled southwest corner, where the two facades meet, he incorporated colossal brick pilasters with limestone Ionic capitals. For the capital section (top story), Moore used brick fashioned into rusticated

Facing top, **Figure 5.43.** The Rink Flats, 401 North Illinois Street, built in 1901–2 by Joseph A. Rink and designed by W. Scott Moore of Indianapolis, drawing on the three-part skyscraper formula for the facade—base section on the first and second floors with rusticated limestone blocks, brick shaft section for the fourth through seventh floors, and a capital section with rusticated brick on the eighth floor, all styled with Italian Renaissance details. Note the flat limestone portico over the corner entry, the tall Ionic pilasters and projecting bays in the shaft stories, and the Renaissance-style cornice. View in 2022. James Glass.

Facing bottom, **Figure 5.44.** Detail of Illinois Street facade, showing finely modeled sculptures of American eagles along the cornice of the base section and the rusticated blocks and brick patterns of the shaft section. View in 2022. James Glass.

blocks. Above, a copper cornice projects out, with dentils below, surmounted finally by a brick parapet.

At the central entrance, in the beveled zone of the first story, Moore designed a Renaissance-inspired flat portico composed of Ionic pilasters supporting an entablature. Arches with keystones appear between the pilasters, and a balustrade appears above the entablature. He added further interest to the west and south elevations by projecting rounded bay windows from the shaft section. As an artistic tour de force, the architect designed and commissioned the sculpture of four American eagles in limestone, crouched in a posture of imminent flight along the frieze at the top of the base section of the two facades (fig. 5.44).

Inside the entrance, the visitor passed into a reception hall appointed in marble and proceeded to passenger elevators at the center of the building. Rink decided to offer differently sized flat units on each floor, costing varied rents. On each floor, Moore therefore planned one five-room flat, one four-room flat, a two-room apartment suite, and a three-room apartment suite. This layout produced a total of fourteen flats and fourteen suites. An article about the building announced that the floors of each hallway in the building would be laid with marble or tile and the wainscotings would be marble. The floors of the units would be hardwood, and windows would have high-quality plate glass. Rink promised that the flats and suites would all have electric lights, steam heat, closets in every room, refrigerators, stove ranges, and butler and kitchen pantries.[105]

Among the tenants in 1914 were Frank Cutshaw, a retail manager; Mary K. Alexander, a cashier; John A. Moriarty, a manager with the Indianapolis Telephone Company and the New Long Distance Telephone Company; Joseph Livingston, a travel agent; and Helene LaReve, operator of a millinery business. Joseph Rink spent approximately $80,000 on the building.[106]

DETACHED HOMES, DOUBLES, AND APARTMENTS | 443

Coulter Flats (Renaissance/Mission)

In 1907, David A. Coulter, president of the Home Building and Realty Company, and a co-investor, Edgar G. Spink,[107] made plans to build a smaller flats building more typical in scale to the hundreds being constructed in the city. Coulter and Spink also wished to appeal to a well-heeled market and decided to provide extras in construction and amenities. They purchased a large, 58-by-126.75-foot lot in the Meridian Place Addition, just south of Twenty-Second Street, and hired the Indianapolis firm of George V. Bedell and Paul H. G. Lieske as their architects.[108]

Bedell and Lieske devised a three-story building with features drawn from the Italian Renaissance, Spanish missions, Jacobean architecture, and Georgian houses (fig. 5.45). In keeping with one of the chief fears of the era, the architects specified a fireproof building with a reinforced concrete structure, tile floors, and a tile roof. They constructed the exterior walls of dark-brown Oriental brick and used cream-colored terra-cotta for decoration.[109] Bedell and Lieske composed the facade with two pavilions projecting forward on either side of a recessed central section. They gave the tops of the pavilions Spanish Mission–style parapets, with curves and reverse curves lined by terra-cotta tiles and quatrefoil panels in the gables. Initially, faceted oriels from the Jacobean period projected unobstructed from the faces of the pavilions and complemented the gable treatments.

In the recessed center (fig. 5.46), terra-cotta Tuscan columns from the Renaissance continue to flank the entry and support an entablature, while above, French doors at the second and third floors open onto balconies with wrought-iron balustrades. The architects set quoins in the terra-cotta surrounds of the doorways and devised an elaborate cartouche with keystones to appear above the third-floor balcony. They gave the windows on either side of the balconies flat arches and keystones in terra-cotta. The flat arches and keystones were similar to those in

Facing top, **Figure 5.45.** Coulter Flats, 2161 North Meridian Street, built in 1907–8 by David A. Coulter and Edgard G. Spink and designed by Indianapolis architects Bedell and Lieske, drawing on Italian Renaissance architecture for the entry portico, quoins along the second- and third-story door surrounds, and a cartouche at the center. They derived the flat arches with keystones over the central windows from Georgian houses and from the Spanish Mission style the curves and reverse curves of the twin gables and quatrefoil details below. The two-porch structure was added after completion of the original design. 2022 view. James Glass.

Facing bottom, **Figure 5.46.** Detail of the central facade, showing three tiers of terra-cotta decorative elements. View in 2022. James Glass.

Georgian-style houses. On the north and south elevations, bay windows provided more light for all three stories.

Coulter and Spink intended to foster privacy by placing only two flats on each floor, for a total of six. By way of reinforced concrete and hollow tile in the floors, the architects provided extra soundproofing in the floors and walls. They also put cinders below the hardwood floors in the units to deaden the sound. Each of the flats contained a reception room and large living and dining rooms. Each also included a rear porch that could be closed off by shuttering windows. Coulter and Spink spent about $50,000 on the Coulter Flats at 2161 North Meridian Street.[110] Sometime during the following twenty years, the present three-tiered porches were added to the facade.

Perhaps to convey his confidence in the building, David Coulter took one of the flats himself. Among the other tenants in 1914 were Ada Lehman, a widow; Glenn W. Harkradar, a dealer in wholesale confections; and Frank G. Herman, an insurance salesman.[111]

Berrick Apartments (Mixture)

In 1911, as an investment, Frederick M. Bachman decided to construct a flats building that contained substantial apartments but bore a minimum of exterior detail. Bachman's principal business involved the F. M. Bachman Company, dealers in hardwoods, veneers, yellow pine lumber, and sash, doors, and shingles. He hired R. P. Daggett and Company to serve as architects for the Berrick, a two-story brick structure at 1323–1329 Central Avenue. Immediately north of the site stood another flats building, the Bronx, constructed a year earlier, probably also by Bachman. The two buildings are so similar in layout and elevations that it is likely that Robert Frost Daggett and his staff designed both.[112]

Daggett devised the Berrick, like the Bronx, to contain four seven-room flats—two on each floor (fig. 5.47). He designed a long, rectangular block running east and west for the Berrick and faced it with a two-story brick structure that provided spacious porches for each of the four units.[113] The architects applied little detail to the north and south elevations but included high parapets incorporating terra-cotta squares, projecting brick courses, and corbeling. They employed brick piers to support the two tiers of porches and brick balustrades. A frame roof covers the second level porches, with wooden brackets supporting the eaves.

Each of the seven-room flats also included a bathroom and quarters for a servant. In 1914, tenants occupied three of the Berrick flats: Wilson R. Warfield and William R. Hunter, both travel agents, and Barbara Cohn, a widow.[114]

Figure 5.47. Berrick Apartments, 1323–29 Central Avenue, built in 1911 by Frederick M. Bachman and designed by R. P. Daggett and Company, architects of Indianapolis, with a mixture of elements. The whole is sparingly detailed, with brackets and extended cornice suggesting the Italian Renaissance. Daggett applied two-tiered brick porches across the facade—a popular element in those years. Note also the pieces of terra-cotta in the parapet and the brick balusters on the porch. View in 2020. James Glass.

Audubon Court Apartments (Arts and Crafts/Bungalow)

In addition to buildings in which apartments occupied all or part of a floor, some investors sought to convey a homelike quality to each unit by arranging it on two floors, like a single-family dwelling or one side of a double. Such was the intention of Theodore Layman, member of a prominent Irvington family. Layman's main occupation involved Layman and Carey, the family wholesale hardware business. In 1914, he acquired the southeast corner of Washington Street and Audubon Road in Irvington, just north of the historic Julian-Layman House, where he lived. He hired Marrett L. Carr as his architect.[115]

Carr laid out three rows of two-story apartments, with courtyards between each row (fig. 5.48). The first range faced Audubon Road to the west, and the next

DETACHED HOMES, DOUBLES, AND APARTMENTS | 447

Figure 5.48. Audubon Court apartments, 5701–19 East Washington Street, Irvington, built in 1914–15 by Theodore Layman and designed by architect Marrett L. Carr with three rows of apartment houses and two courtyards. View of the east courtyard from the north, showing the individualized character that Carr gave each of the apartment houses, varying the porch designs and shape of the gables. View in 2023. James Glass.

faced east, with its back to the first courtyard. Then came the second courtyard, followed by the third row, which faced west. Carr strove for a picturesque variety of massing and silhouettes along each range and drew materials and details from the Arts and Crafts and bungalow movements.[116] He varied the facades by employing pavilions with alternating pointed and jerkinhead gables and in between the pavilions drew out the main roof, as in a bungalow, and inserted shed dormers. For the facades, the architect used a dark-colored brick, with a "Persian tapestry finish." For the side gables, he used stucco. Carr also varied the treatments of the porches. At the center of each row, porches with square parapets alternate with ones with hipped roofs. At the end of each row, the porches are enclosed within a pavilion that projects out further than the ones at the center. Carr provided individual walks to each of the eighteen apartments. A central furnace provided heat to all the dwellings.[117]

The apartments included suites of five, six, or seven rooms.[118] Although the 1914 city directory provides no listing for the tenants, presumably Audubon Court attracted white-collar workers, widows, and others on limited incomes.

Winter Apartments (Italian Renaissance)

A market also existed for apartments designed for the well-to-do, and in 1914, attorney Ferdinand Winter decided to respond to that market. He chose a location in the midst of what was still a prestigious stretch of Meridian Street residences. On the site stood his own home at 1321 North Meridian Street, built before 1900. Winter desired to erect a tall building, a "skyscraper" apartment structure, with nine stories and thirty-six apartments. The attorney retained a prominent New York architect to design his building. Francke H. Bosworth Jr. had been in practice with business partner Frank H. Holden since 1902 and had studied architecture at the famed École des Beaux-Arts in Paris.[119]

Bosworth devised an H-shaped plan for the Winter Apartments and achieved a fireproof structure by specifying a reinforced concrete frame, hollow tile partition walls, and exterior curtain walls of light-brown brick. The main block of the building faces Meridian Street, paralleled at the rear by a secondary north–south block (fig. 5.49). An east–west range connects the two blocks.[120]

The facade is an Italian Renaissance composition drawn from elements in fifteenth-century Florentine palazzos (palaces). The main entrance (fig. 5.50) draws attention with a large arch lined with rusticated limestone voussoirs, modeled on the Palazzo Gondi in Florence.[121] On either side of the entry, an arcade echoes rows of arches in Renaissance buildings. At the top of the facade, a boldly scaled cornice projects out, supported by long brackets, similar to several fifteenth-century palazzos. Just below the cornice, at the center, the architect placed an elaborate stone cartouche, similar to those on some sixteenth-century Italian palazzos. Otherwise, Bosworth brought elements of his own design into the composition, such as a dressed limestone apron at the base of the facade, blind brick tympanums within the arches of the first-story arcade, brick swags underneath a limestone entablature appearing below the third story, and arched windows with

Above, **Figure 5.49.** Winter Apartments, 1321 North Meridian Street, built in 1914–15 by Ferdinand Winter and designed by Francke H. Bosworth Jr., an architect from New York, using a modified skyscraper composition of four sections for the exterior and drawing from the Italian Renaissance for the details: an entry archway with large stone voussoirs, projecting cornice supported by brackets, and stone cartouche below the top, ninth story. Rehabilitated in c. 1970s for continued use as apartments. View from the southwest in 2022. James Glass.

Facing, **Figure 5.50.** Detail of facade, showing rusticated stone voussoirs around the entry arch, modeled on the entry of the Palazzo Gondi in Florence. Note also Renaissance arches in brick flanking the entrance. 2022 view. James Glass.

brick tympanums and alternating stone consoles and blind panels at either end of the third and sixth stories.

Bosworth varied the sizes and configurations of apartments on each floor, offering units with six, seven, eight, or ten rooms. He also included servants' rooms. Each apartment received natural light from three sides. Passenger elevators

provided service day and night (with attendants operating them). Steam radiators afforded heat, and a central artificial refrigeration system connected with refrigerators in each unit.[122]

A list of tenants in 1916 indicates that Winter succeeded in attracting those with higher incomes. He occupied an apartment, as did his brother William, also an attorney. Samuel Reid, manager of the large Kingan and Company pork-packing concern, rented an eighth-floor apartment, while Charles P. Rockwood, assistant secretary of his family's Rockwood Manufacturing Company, occupied a unit on the sixth floor. Finally, a wealthy widow, Hannah A. Mansur, resided in a top-floor apartment.[123]

Balmoral Court Apartments (Georgian)

About the time that construction of the Winter Apartments was coming to a close, another investor, Clarence Stanley, planned an apartment court also aimed at higher-income tenants. He formed a firm to undertake the project, the Balmoral Court Company, and acquired two lots each one hundred feet wide in Osgood's Meridian Park Addition, on the east side of the 3000 block of North Meridian Street. Stanley retained the Builders' Real Estate Company to design and construct his apartment structure and possibly to assist with the financing. The real estate company, headed by architect Lawrence W. George, engaged, in turn, the local architecture firm of George, MacLucas, and Fitton. George and Harry R. Fitton served as officers or partners in both companies. William H. MacLucas served as the primary designer.[124]

Facing top, **Figure 5.51.** Balmoral Court Apartments, 3055 North Meridian Street, built in 1915–16 by Clarence Stanley and designed by Indianapolis architect William H. MacLucas, of the firm George, MacLucas, and Fitton. MacLucas laid out a court bounded on three sides by ranges of three-story rental houses and used eighteenth-century houses from English and American colonial Georgian architecture as his model for massing and details. Note the large temple front/portico at the center of the east range, the focal point of the whole court, and the individualized treatments of each apartment house. View from the west in 2022. James Glass.

Facing bottom, **Figure 5.52.** The west end of the east range of apartments at Balmoral; here, MacLucas styled the end as the facade of an early eighteenth-century American Georgian house, including a central entry with pilasters and pediment, red brick contrasting with limestone quoins, and a trio of dormers with pointed gables/pediments. 2022 view. James Glass.

ARCHITECT PROFILES

George, MacLucas, and Fitton

The Indianapolis architecture firm of George, MacLucas, and Fitton was formed about 1911 by Lawrence W. George (1871–1936), William H. MacLucas (1881–1925; *at left*), and Harry F. Fitton (1884–1931; *at right*). Little is known of George's education or training as an architect. He evidently had some experience as a contractor. MacLucas was born in Bristol, England. He attended Heriot-Watt College and the Royal Institute in Edinburgh, Scotland, and served as apprentice for six years to George Craig, architect to the School Board of Edinburgh and Leith County. MacLucas became Craig's chief assistant and during his training specialized in "the Tudor style of architecture." In 1910, he and his wife immigrated to the United States, where he began practice as architect in Fond du Lac, Wisconsin. About 1911, he moved to Indianapolis and formed the architectural firm with George and Fitton. Harry Fitton was born in Evansville, Indiana, and educated at Culver Military Academy. He studied architecture and engineering for three years at Purdue University and moved to Indianapolis in 1905.

Of the partners in the firm, George appears to have been the primary figure in obtaining business, MacLucas the chief designer, and Fitton the construction supervisor. Prior to meeting MacLucas, George and Fitton had held positions in the Builders' Real Estate Company, which built homes, financed real estate developments, and sold fire insurance. After 1911, George and Fitton became the principals in the Builders' Real Estate Company. They worked out a collaboration between the two firms under which the realty company acted as general contractors and provided financing for projects designed by George, MacLucas, and Fitton.

Among the large apartment buildings designed and built by the two firms were the Balmoral, Hampton Court, the Haugh Hotel at 127 East Michigan Street, and the Seville Apartments at 1701–7 North Illinois Street. They also designed large houses during the 1910s and early 1920s, including those for Walter J. Goodall, Alexander Taggart, Sol Meyer, Frederick E. Matson, A. Kiefer Mayer, and George A. Buskirk. Fitton left the architectural firm in 1919–20, after which it became George and MacLucas.

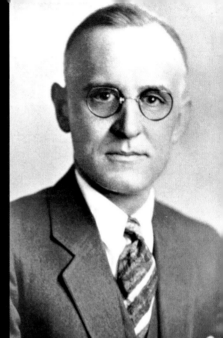

Sources: "Lawrence W. George, 65, Commits Suicide," *Indianapolis Star*, September 30, 1936, 12; "William Harold MacLucas," Find a Grave, n.d. https://www.findagrave.com/memorial/45962619/william-harold-maclucas, accessed June 26, 2024; "Wm. H. McLucas [*sic*]," in George S. Cottman, *Centennial History and Handbook* (Indianapolis: Max R. Hyman, 1915), 12; "Rites for W. H. MacLucas," *Indianapolis News*, January 30, 1925, 23; transcript of "Interview with George MacLucas, Son of William Harold MacLucas," conducted by Tracey Cox and Dan Kiernan, July 30, 1979, Indiana Historical Society Library Architectural Archives; "Harry F. Fitton," in Kin Hubbard, ed., *A Book of Indiana* (Indianapolis: Indiana Biographical Association, 1929), 333; "Death Believed Due to Heart Disease . . . ," *Indianapolis Star*, April 7, 1931, 2, c. 4; *R. L. Polk & Co.'s Indianapolis City Directory for 1919* (Indianapolis: R. L. Polk & Co., 1919), 106, 592; *R. L. Polk & Co.'s Indianapolis City Directory for 1920* (Indianapolis: R. L. Polk & Co., 1916), 672. Source for cartoon: Edward F. Schilder (ed.), "William H. MacLucas," *Club Men of Indianapolis in Caricature 1913* (East Aurora, NY: Roycrofters, 1913), 100. Source for photo: "Harry F. Fitton."

The architects laid out a U-shaped court of nineteen apartments styled like three-story row houses (fig. 5.51).[125] Two of the red brick ranges ran east–west and consisted of extended rectangular blocks; the third range ran north–south and connected the other two rows. Somewhat unusual for Indianapolis apartment buildings of the period, MacLucas based the design of the exteriors on early and mid-eighteenth-century Georgian houses in the English colonies.[126] He styled the western pavilions at the ends of the east–west ranges as if they were facades of Georgian houses, with a symmetrical arrangement of bays, a central entry sheltered by an elliptical projecting arch and pediment, and three dormers combining arches and pediments (fig. 5.52). On the north and south corners of the western pavilions, just as in Georgian houses, MacLucas applied limestone quoins. For each of the remaining units in the east–west ranges, he located the entrances off-center and gave one dormer to each apartment. Shallow porticos with varying designs sheltered these east–west entries. The designer projected a two-story portico supported by colossal Corinthian columns from the central pavilion of the north–south range, and the portico became the focal point of the entire court. The effect was similar to that resulting from the frontispieces used by Sir Christopher Wren along the U-shaped court at the Royal Hospital at Chelsea in London (1682–89).[127]

MacLucas set the west ends of the east–west ranges ninety feet from the sidewalk along the street and devoted the area between the ranges and walk to a lawn. A U-shaped drive originally provided automobile access to the Balmoral. A stone balustrade bounds the court at its west end; the court proper initially contained a hundred-foot-wide garden. For those tenants with motorcars, the architect provided garages along the rear of the north–south range, with chauffeurs' quarters furnished in the second story. At the south end of the center range, MacLucas constructed a one-story brick structure for the central furnace.[128]

Each apartment/house consisted of a vestibule, living room, dining room, kitchen, and pantry on the first floor, three bedrooms on the second floor, and two maid's rooms on the third floor. Laundries could be found in each basement. The total estimated cost to Clarence Stanley and his building company came to $100,000.[129]

The owner's expectation for high-income tenants appears not to have been entirely met, at least initially. The 1916 city directory shows as residents Henry H. Titsworth, president of the Clay Products Company; Fred A. Rogers, a sales manager; Thomas M. Kaufman, a loan company proprietor; and several people with no occupations indicated.[130]

Hampton Court Apartments (Tudor Palace)

After completing Balmoral Court, the partnership of the Builders' Real Estate Company and architects George, MacLucas, and Fitton turned to a very similar apartment project. Their client, Dr. Leon T. Leach, operated the Leach Sanatorium at 538 West New York Street. In 1914 or 1915, he had acquired the house and adjacent property that former vice president Charles W. Fairbanks and his wife, Cornelia Cole Fairbanks, had owned previously at 1522 North Meridian Street (see chap. 10 of vol. 1). The physician formed the Hampton Court Realty Company and retained the Builders' Company and its architectural firm to design and build another U-shaped apartment/house. Like the Balmoral, the new structure was to consist of two east–west ranges and a north–south range connecting the other two at the west end. Chief designer William H. MacLucas set the east–west ranges back from Meridian Street and laid out a circular drive and lawn between the street and the buildings. MacLucas linked the east ends of the two ranges with a balustrade and then plotted rectangular grass panels in the center of the court, with a central sunken garden.[131]

Leach admired the sixteenth-century Hampton Court Palace of Cardinal Wolsey and King Henry VIII outside London and chose to give his apartments the same name. MacLucas, who had studied Tudor architecture, in turn based the design of the twenty-nine apartments/row houses on elements of the Hampton Court Palace, the epitome of Tudor dynasty palace architecture (fig. 5.53). The designer constructed the row houses of brick and used cream-colored terra-cotta with Tudor-style quoins for the surrounds of the windows and plain terra-cotta for many of the entryways. He also varied the facades and silhouettes of the three-story houses in a picturesque fashion. Just as at Balmoral Court, MacLucas treated the east ends of the two east–west ranges as self-contained houses, in this case with central projecting pavilions that contained entries with terra-cotta surrounds and pediment-like panels overhead (fig. 5.54). Terra-cotta-framed windows flanked the entries, and leaded pane windows appeared in the second story with terra-cotta dripstones from the Tudor period. The architect capped the facades with pointed gables, dripstone moldings, and finials similar to those at the English Hampton Court.[132]

Along the east–west ranges, MacLucas employed Tudor-style projecting bays with crenellations as facades for some of the apartment houses, alternating with pavilions having gables and ones with hipped roofs. At the west end of the court, he cast the terminating structure as one large pavilion with two big gables on

Above, **Figure 5.53.** +Hampton Court apartments, 1512 North Meridian Street, built in 1916–17 by Dr. Leon Leach and designed by William H. MacLucas of George, MacLucas, and Fitton, architects, drawing on forms and details found in English Tudor palaces of the early sixteenth century, such as the Hampton Court Palace of Cardinal Wolsey and King Henry VIII outside London. View in c. 1920. Demolished in 1960–61 and replaced by a commercial building. Bass Photo Co. Collection, Indiana Historical Society. (Image cropped)

Facing, **Figure 5.54.** +Detail of the pavilion at the east end of one of the east–west ranges of Hampton Court, showing Tudor palace details: dripstones over windows, quoins in the window surrounds, gable with coping and finials, and brick construction. Note the use of terra-cotta in contrast with the brick. View in c. 1920. Bass Photo Co. Collection, Indiana Historical Society. (Image cropped)

either end and a sloping roof with three dormers at the center. As an added amenity, Leach instructed the architects to lay out a private garden and tennis court in a tract of land at the rear of the property that ran north to Sixteenth Street.[133]

Each house consisted of three floors. The first floor contained a reception hall, living room, dining room, kitchen, and pantry. The second floor included four

bedrooms and a bath, and the third floor provided a fifth bedroom and a maid's room. The houses fronting the court also offered a sun parlor in a projecting bay.[134]

A review of the city directory listings suggests that Leach was more successful than Clarence Stanley in attracting high-income tenants. In 1916, Shafer Zeigler, manager of the Park Theater downtown, lived in unit 20; Chester P. Wilson, president of the Interstate Public Service Company, resided in unit 19; Raymond P. Van Camp, vice president of Van Camp Hardware and Iron Company, occupied unit 30; and the Reverend Frank L. Loveland, pastor of the Meridian Street Methodist Episcopal Church, lived in unit 18. Widow Mary Leach, possibly Leach's mother, lived in unit 17. The owner ended up spending about $175,000 on this first-class apartment building.[135]

CONCLUSION

During the period of 1900 to 1920, homes of businessmen and professional people occupied lots primarily on north–south streets north of downtown and in the east-side suburbs of Woodruff Place and Irvington. Detached residences and doubles for middle-class homebuyers rose on some of the same streets as a mixture of income levels continued on many streets. Workers' cottages and bungalows appeared on the east and south sides and in the industrial suburbs located southwest, west, northwest, and northeast of downtown. Apartments—the new housing type—appeared all over the city, appealing to all income levels.

Architects designed all types of residential buildings, ranging from $3,400 workers' bungalows to great houses with estates costing $250,000. Real estate companies and builders commanded part of the market, constructing groups of houses and arranging financing. Often these concerns hired architects to design the houses. Magazines, such as *The Craftsman*, published photos, renderings, and floor plans for popular house types and styles and offered for purchase complete plans for construction. Some homebuyers even ordered disassembled whole houses from entities such as Sears, Roebuck and Company.

For houses built to serve business and professional clients, middle-class customers, and working-class families, architectural fashions after 1900 focused on the Foursquare, the English Tudor vernacular, Arts and Crafts, and different versions of bungalows. The Foursquare in particular became a favorite formula for architects such as Frank B. Hunter and Herbert L. Bass to use in creating single-family and double residences.

The Arts and Crafts Movement in architecture and furnishings began in England with the advocacy of artist William Morris for a return to handicrafts and natural materials. It crossed the Atlantic and became very popular for interior design and furniture in the United States. One of its chief exponents, Gustav Stickley, incorporated the aesthetic and specific design motifs into the house designs that he featured in his magazine, *The Craftsman*. Bungalows started with vernacular structures in East India and made their way to the western hemisphere. In the United States, the generic bungalow, with its simple one-story structure prefaced by a porch, found wide favor, succeeded by the California bungalow, featuring wide, projecting eaves on its gables, supported by brackets. Both types of bungalows could be found in *The Craftsman*. A few Indianapolis architects and their clients liked elements of the so-called Prairie style created by Frank Lloyd Wright in neighboring Illinois. In the cases of the Allison mansion (see chap. 4 of this volume) and the Kleinschmidt House, the architects used horizontal massing, a broad hipped roof, and at least some brick, invoking some of Wright's houses.

The Mission style, derived from the architecture of several Spanish mission churches in California and widely popular in the western United States, found only a few devotees in Indianapolis, such as the Burckhardts on North Pennsylvania Street.

A few of the major commercial architects in the city occasionally designed houses. Bernard Vonnegut, as mentioned in chapter 10 of volume 1, preferred residential projects and created some of the most original designs between 1885 and his death in 1908. Rubush and Hunter occasionally worked on large houses, such as the Fred and Katharine Cushman Hoke House, and their much-larger commercial and public building practice may have introduced them to residential clients. The same was probably true of Robert Frost Daggett and his associates in the firm of R. P. Daggett and Company. Other local architects of considerable talent, such as Alfred Grindle and Lewis Ketcham Davis, designed only a few houses. Still others, such as Charles H. Byfield and Clarence Martindale, focused almost exclusively on residential practice. George, MacLucas, and Fitton found a profitable practice designing apartment courts and apartment buildings. Most of the considerable number of other architects listed in the 1914 city directory, such as Doeppers and Myers, Marshall Van Arman, Marrett Carr, and Layton Allen, focused on smaller-budget residential commissions.

Nearly all of chapters 4 and 5 of this volume have dealt with houses/residential structures built by or for white citizens. What of African Americans? Much more research is needed regarding the purchase and sale of residential properties within the primary Black neighborhoods of the city. African American professionals and businesspeople undoubtedly constructed some houses during the 1898–1920 period, and some investors may have constructed houses or other residential structures for Black tenants. Research using African American newspapers, title records, US Census tracts, city directories, and Sanborn insurance maps could reveal the identities of Black residents at particular locations and whether houses were built by them or for them. Also, very little seems to have been recorded about African American architects in the white-owned newspapers of the early twentieth century. Further review of the Black-owned newspapers might uncover more information on who practiced and some of their commissions.

Map 5.1

Buildings from Chapter 5 of Volume 2 plotted on 1914 Sanborn Insurance Map of Mile Square of Indianapolis (Vol. 1) (numbers drawn from figure numbers)

43 Rink Flats

Map 5.2

Buildings from Chapter 5 plotted on 1914 Sanborn Insurance Map of area west and north of Mile Square (Vol. 1) (numbers drawn from figure numbers); + = demolished

26 + Madam C.J. Walker House

Map 5.3

Buildings from Chapter 5 plotted on 1915 Sanborn Insurance Map (Vol. 4) of area between 11th and 22nd Streets and between Capitol Avenue and Columbia Avenue (numbers drawn from figure numbers); + = demolished

- **1** George G. and Kate Block Tanner House
- **2** Reid-Dickson House
- **4** Willard and Josephine Niles Hubbard House
- **6** Dr. John and Celeste Terrell Barnhill House
- **22** George E. and Alberta Barthel June House
- **37** + John S. Duncan Double
- **39** Gocke-King Double
- **45** Coulter Flats
- **47** Berrick Apartments
- **49** Winter Apartments
- **53** + Hampton Court Apartments

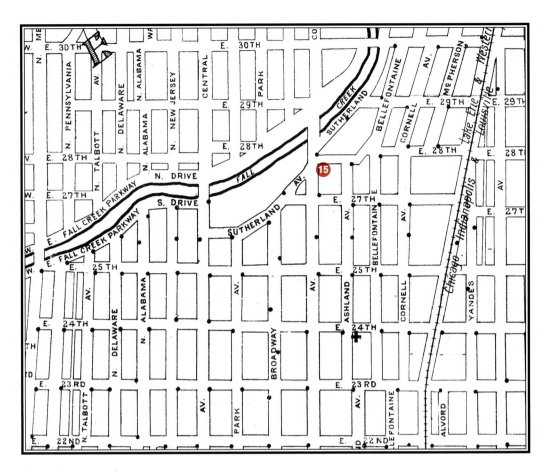

Map 5.4

Buildings from Chapter 5 plotted on 1915 Sanborn Insurance Map (Vol. 4) of area between 22nd Street and Fall Creek and between Meridian and Yandes Streets (numbers drawn from figure numbers)

15 Preston C. and Renah Wilcox Rubush House

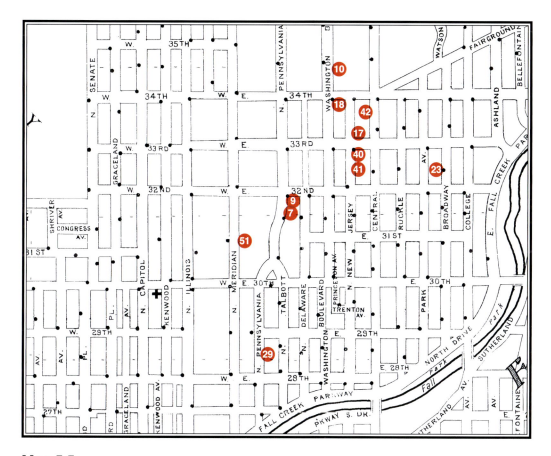

Map 5.5

Buildings from Chapter 5 plotted on 1915 Sanborn Insurance Map (Vol. 5) of area between Fall Creek and 37th Street and between Senate Avenue and College Avenue (numbers drawn from figure numbers);
+ = demolished

- **7** Dr. Louis and Adele Burckhardt House
- **9** Anthony F. Kleinschmidt House
- **10** Fred and Katharine Cushman Hoke House
- **17** Herbert L. and Floria Logan Bass House
- **18** William A. and Lahla Bond Walker House
- **23** Alfred T. and Elizabeth Gough Rapp House
- **29** + John G. and Louise Rentsch Bryan House
- **40** Thomas-Hunt Double
- **41** Haskell L. and Herbert T. Conner Double
- **42** Mead-Donavin Double
- **51** Balmoral Court Apartments

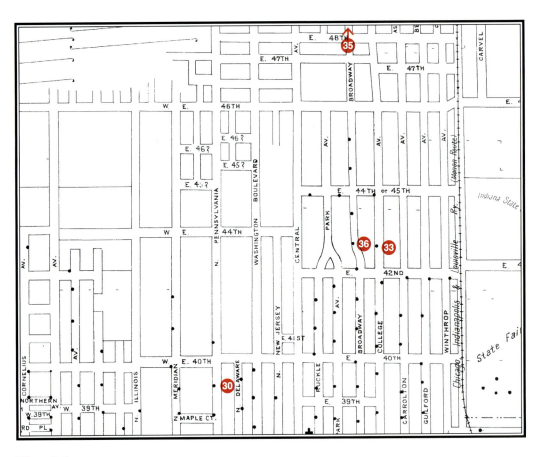

Map 5.6

Buildings from Chapter 5 plotted on 1915 Sanborn Insurance Map (Vol. 5) of area between 39th and 48th Streets and between Cornelius Avenue and Indiana State Fairgrounds (numbers drawn from figure numbers)

- 30 Jacob F. and Abbie Gibbs Moyer House
- 33 Overman-Arnold House
- 35 Joseph Hooser House (5033 Broadway)
- 36 Edwin Wuensch House

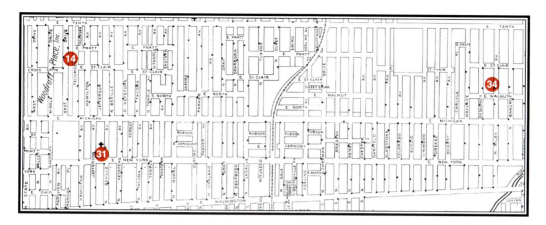

Map 5.7

Buildings from Chapter 5 plotted on 1915 Sanborn Insurance Map (Vol. 3) of area between west border of Woodruff Place and Bancroft Street and between Washington and 10th Streets (numbers drawn from figure numbers)

- **14** Brandt and Helen McKay Steele House
- **31** Four worker's bungalows on Beville Street
- **34** William D. Vogel House

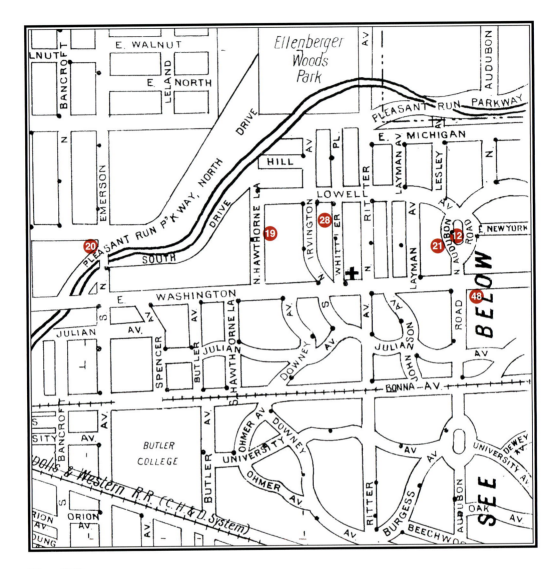

Map 5.8

Buildings from Chapter 5 plotted on 1915 Sanborn Insurance Map (Vol. 3) of western two-thirds of Irvington, between Emerson Avenue and Audubon Road (numbers drawn from figure numbers)

- **12** Jacob Dorsey Forrest House
- **19** Carlos and Elizabeth Butler Recker House
- **20** Kin and Josephine Jackson Hubbard House
- **21** Layton and Lela Francis Allen House
- **28** Dr. Silas J. and Sarah McCullough Carr House
- **48** Audubon Court Apartments

6 | THE DEVELOPMENT OF AN ARCHITECTURAL PROFESSION

1820–1920

This final chapter reviews the development of the architectural profession in Indianapolis during its first century. From a planned capital, in which builders and carpenters supplied designs for most buildings, to the beginnings of architectural practice with the canal boom and railroad era and then to the growth of a sizeable city during the late nineteenth century in which an architectural profession solidified, Indianapolis took its place as a major metropolis with a vocal and fully competent body of architects ready to design all manner of modern building types with any kind of stylistic features. The chapter also examines the growing role of formal education in architecture and the increasing influence of the Beaux Arts system of design and training on local architectural practice. The evolution of the architectural office is touched on, tracing the change from single architectural practitioners to large operations with draftsmen producing design and construction documents. The growth of the profession led to local architects making repeated efforts to organize themselves, finally reaching success in 1909 with the establishment of professional bodies in both Indianapolis and the state as a whole. The success enjoyed was limited to white male architects. African American men and women of all races were almost completely excluded from the architectural field.

When Indianapolis began in 1820–21, the architectural profession in the United States was in its infancy. A few architects, such as Benjamin Latrobe and

Charles Bullfinch, obtained commissions to design parts of the US Capitol or buildings in their home cities. Robert Mills, trained by Latrobe, had just designed a notable monument of the new Greek Revival architecture in Philadelphia, the 1818 Second Bank of the United States. Thomas Jefferson, a talented amateur architect, had recently designed the campus and Roman Classical buildings of the University of Virginia. Most of the commercial, public, religious, and residential architecture of the nation continued to be constructed either by gentleman amateurs like Jefferson or by builders. The latter assumed responsibility for the construction of most buildings in towns and cities by the 1820s. Builders typically learned construction while working as apprentice carpenters or masons. They obtained ideas for the designs of their commissions from clients and the host of builder's guides (also termed pattern books) that began to circulate throughout the eastern portion of the country during the first three decades of the nineteenth century.[1]

Two of the most popular building guide authors were Asher Benjamin and Minard Lafever. Benjamin (1773–1845) was born in Connecticut and learned about construction from a local builder. He then embarked on a career as a house constructor in New England. He published his first guide for carpenters and builders, *The Country Builder's Assistant*, in 1797. Eventually, Benjamin published seven different guides, the most popular of which were *The American Builder's Guide* (1806) and *The Practical House Carpenter* (1827). In his early editions, the author popularized designs created by Charles Bullfinch for his houses in Boston. These designs, similar to Georgian residences but with different detailing, became the basis for the Federal style that took hold in New England and spread west. As the years passed and fashions changed, Benjamin reproduced details from Roman and then Greek architecture. He took as his formula to provide instruction in geometry and drafting geometric forms and then furnish details of the Roman or Greek orders, cornices, window surrounds, doorways, fireplaces, interior trim, stairways, and ornamentation. A carpenter or builder could easily adapt the measured drawings in Benjamin's guides into polished details for a building in a midwestern community such as Indianapolis.[2]

Lafever (1798–1854) was younger but followed a similar path. He obtained training as a carpenter and settled in New York City, where he practiced architecture beginning in the late 1820s. He published *The Young Builders' General Instructor* in 1829, followed by the popular *Modern Builder's Guide* (1833). Authors like Benjamin and Lafever collected books by British architects on architecture and building, such as James Gibbs's *Book of Architecture* and Sir William Chambers's *Treatise on Civil Architecture*. They also likely had in their libraries the indispensable guide to the architecture of ancient Athens by British architects Stuart and Revett, *The Antiquities of Athens*. These works by master architects served as sources, in turn, for some of the text and plates in Benjamin's and Lafever's publications.[3]

Carpenters, masons, and builders were present in Indianapolis even before it was platted. Carpenter James B. Hall and brickmaker and mason Matthias Nowland arrived at the end of 1820 and soon found business constructing finished houses and other buildings (see chap. 1 of vol. 1). The potential for public buildings brought builders such as John E. Baker and James Paxton to the settlement, where they submitted a design for the first Marion County Courthouse in 1822 and proceeded to construct the brick Georgian-style building with a cupola. Baker and Paxton may have obtained the ideas for the plan and details from builder's guides. Another partnership of builders— Smith, Culbertson, Bishop, and Speaks—submitted plans in 1827 for the Governor's House on the Circle, probably drawing the plan, massing, and Georgian and Federal details from guides.

The design of commercial buildings, industrial structures, buildings of worship, and frame and brick residences continued to be supplied by carpenters, masons, and builders into the 1830s. The first architects to practice in Indianapolis came to the capital in response to the decision of the state to build a statehouse in 1831. New York architects Town and Davis won the commission in the first known architectural competition held in Indiana and presented a carefully studied design for a stately Greek temple with a Renaissance-style dome. The division of labor between the two architects foreshadowed the pattern followed in architectural partnerships for the next hundred years—Ithiel Town, the senior partner, coordinated the submission and marketing of the design and traveled to Indiana to deliver the firm's proposal personally to the Indiana General Assembly. He also had experience in designing and building bridges, which proved valuable in the structural aspects of designing a statehouse. Alexander Jackson Davis, the junior partner, provided an elegant design with fine draftsmanship, which helped persuade the building commissioners to select the firm's design.

After Town signed the contract to build the statehouse, he spent little time in Indianapolis, and Davis stayed in New York. Town sent a veteran draftsman, John Stirewalt, to serve as "chief architect" at the Indiana capital, overseeing construction. He also hired Edwin J. Peck of New Haven, Connecticut, to serve as superintendent of masonry for the capitol, in charge of constructing the stone foundation and brick structure. Peck later worked as an architect and builder in Indianapolis and Madison, Indiana. Thus, the design and construction of the

Indiana Statehouse brought the first architects to the city and acquainted the residents with the roles played by the architectural profession in the design and construction of major buildings.

The first architect to settle in Indianapolis and develop an architectural practice was John Elder, a builder from Harrisburg, Pennsylvania. He corresponded with James Blake about the statehouse competition and in 1833 moved to the Indiana capital. Like many others, Elder entered the architectural field after serving as a contractor—in his case, for a part of the Pennsylvania Canal. He evidently had studied Greek architectural designs and acquired an architectural library by 1831 because, in that year, he submitted a Grecian-inspired design for the competition held for the Indiana Statehouse.

With construction of the National Road to Indianapolis and the beginning of the canal boom in the late 1830s, Elder found abundant demand for architectural services and filled a void as virtually the only architect practicing in the city between 1836 and his departure for California in 1850. He designed and oversaw the construction of all building types—hotels, churches, banks, a hospital, county courthouses, and residences. In advertising his services, providing designs, advising clients on designs, and overseeing construction, Elder provided a model for the new architectural profession in a frontier city and state. Judging from the variety of designs he employed for his public buildings, churches, and commercial buildings, Elder owned a library of architectural books, as well as some builder's guides.[4] He also could customize a pattern book design to improve the design or please his clients, as he showed in his modifications of the stock church plan that Christ Episcopal Church gave him as the starting point for their 1838 building (see chap. 2 of vol. 1). Elder also allied himself with a contractor, Ephraim Colestock, in his business, and it appears that Colestock acted as the builder for several structures designed by Elder.

The railroad era inaugurated by the completion of the Indianapolis and Madison Railroad in 1847 brought a sustained boom in business activity to the state capital and the capacity to sustain more than one architect's practice. By 1850, when Elder left the scene, other architects had settled in Indianapolis. They came from varied locations, and most were experienced architectural practitioners. Joseph Willis, born near Philadelphia, came to Logansport, Indiana, in the 1840s and from there to Indianapolis, where he designed the Indiana Asylum for the Deaf and Dumb, a portion of the Indiana Hospital for the Insane, and the Masonic Temple. Edwin May, trained as a carpenter in Madison, Indiana, and Indianapolis, worked as a builder under John Elder in the 1840s and transitioned to architecture.[5] Joseph Curzon, born in Derbyshire, England, and raised in Harrisburg,

Pennsylvania, obtained architectural training and relocated to Indianapolis about 1850, showing his talent in the design of the original Indianapolis Union Depot of 1852–53. Francis Costigan, one of the most accomplished designers in the state between 1840 and 1865, obtained training as a carpenter's apprentice in his home city of Baltimore and then worked as a builder there. In the early 1840s, he moved to Madison, Indiana, and designed fine Greek Revival mansions, such as the Lanier and Shrewsbury Houses. When construction of the railroad shifted the economic focus to Indianapolis, Costigan moved to the state capital and became the architect for major commercial and public buildings, such as the Bates House hotel, the Indiana Blind Asylum, and the Odd Fellows Building.

Other architects attracted to Indianapolis during the 1850s immigrated to the United States from Europe. Two—Isaac Hodgson and William Tinsley—were born in Ireland, obtained apprenticeships in architect's offices, and practiced on their own there. Both made their way eventually to the Indiana state capital—Hodgson through Louisville and Tinsley through Cincinnati. Hodgson established himself as an architect of county courthouses in the 1850s, eventually designing the palatial second Marion County Courthouse in the 1870s. Tinsley found ready work as the architect of the original North Western Christian University building in Indianapolis and the 1855–56 main building for Indiana University in Bloomington. Based on these commissions, he obtained an appointment as the architect of Christ Episcopal Church on the Circle. Another gifted immigrant, Diedrich A. Bohlen, grew up in Hanover, Germany, and studied architecture at the University of Holzminden. He immigrated to the United States and made his way to Cincinnati, then to Indianapolis, where he briefly served as a draftsman in the office of Francis Costigan. Bohlen then opened his own practice and became one of the most successful architects in the city after the Civil War, designing major commercial buildings, public buildings, churches, charitable institutions, and residences.

The pattern of training for this first generation of architects after Elder was to engage in apprenticeships with either architects or builders. The apprenticeship system was firmly established in the British Isles, which tended to shape the United States culturally in the first half of the nineteenth century. After completing apprenticeships, architects-to-be usually worked for an established architect as a draftsman. This expanded their experience in an architect's office and their competence and confidence as designers. It provided their employer with capable assistants who could shoulder most of the burden of producing preliminary, presentation, and working drawings. Senior draftsmen could also assist in writing the specifications, which provided directions to the contractor for all aspects of the construction and decoration of the building.

Bohlen was the only one of this 1850s group of architects to have received training in a university or school of architecture, which had been the practice in France since the eighteenth century and was becoming the custom in Germany.

There were few civil or structural engineers practicing in Indianapolis. The architect and his drafting staff and possibly some of the contractors supplied the calculations involved in assuring a stable structure and mastered the theory and practical aspects of plumbing, heating, and ventilating the building. Most architects included in their services the oversight of construction, involving frequent visits to the construction site, where they conferred with the contractors over the intent of the drawings and specifications, the choice of materials, and the specifics of details.

The advertisements placed by four early architects in the 1857 Indianapolis city directory list the professional services they would offer clients. Joseph Curzon simply described himself as "Architect," while D. A. Bohlen advised that he would "furnish Designs & Specifications for Public and Private Buildings and Superintend the Erection of the same." Isaac Hodgson listed himself as "Architect and Superintendent," while William Tinsley sought to assure his clients that he could serve as both architect and civil engineer.[6] Of the four, Bohlen gave the most specific indication of what could be expected of an architect—draft designs (plans), write specifications, and supervise construction. We may assume that Curzon and Hodgson provided a like scope of services. Tinsley's reference to civil engineer suggests the growing importance of structural engineers or architects competent in the structural and mechanical design of large buildings.

By the 1850s, the reign of the Greek Revival as the preferred style for most buildings was coming to a close, replaced by a large assortment of styles drawn from Italian Renaissance, Romanesque, and Gothic architecture. New authors assembled plans, elevations, and perspective views of all the principal building types, clothed in the newest fashions, and published them for the benefit of clients, architects, and builders. For residences, a host of guides emerged, such as those issued by landscape gardener Andrew Jackson Downing, *Cottage Residences* (1842) and *The Architecture of Country Houses* (1850). He collaborated on the latter with the talented architect Alexander Jackson Davis, who earlier had published his own suggested designs, *Rural Residences* (1837). In Indianapolis, the unknown designer of the David and Mary Alvord Stevenson cottage drew much of its substance from a house in *Cottage Residences*, while the architect of the Maxwell-Tousey-Fitzgerald House based its design on a "Rural-Gothic" cottage in *The Architecture of Country Houses* (see chap. 3 of vol. 1). In the commercial realm, the advent of cast-iron facades for retail and wholesale buildings in the 1850s brought catalogs from the manufacturers, depicting varied designs for mass-produced facades that could be ordered by the owner or architect and shipped to the building sites.[7]

During the Civil War and the postwar boom that ended in the 1870s, a new factor came to bear on the competition among architects for business. Chicago was emerging as the great metropolis of the Midwest, and imposing and attractive buildings designed by its architects attracted attention in neighboring states. Among the first Chicago architects to obtain commissions in Indianapolis were William W. Boyington, designer of the Italian Romanesque First Baptist Church, and Theodore Wadskier, architect of the First Presbyterian Church in the Gothic style (see chap. 5 of vol. 1). The decision of the congregations to retain out-of-town architects suggests a growing awareness of the outside world, made much more accessible through the advent of the telegraph and railroad connections to Chicago and other large cities.

After the Civil War, one of the leading Chicago architects and engineers, William LeBaron Jenney, won multiple commercial and residential commissions in Indianapolis, setting a standard for the latest stylistic vocabulary and imaginative interpretations of the needs of his clients. The Fletcher and Sharpe Block at Washington and Pennsylvania Streets drew immediate attention to its grid of windows and limestone facade largely devoid of ornamentation at the height of the extravagant ornamentation found in the French Second Empire style. Jenney's Bates-McGowan mansion presented a contemporary interpretation of French Loire Valley châteaus and employed elements of the High Victorian Gothic style, alone among the residential designs of the boom. The presence of out-of-town architects likely encouraged the best out of the Indianapolis-based designers, as they competed with a larger pool of design ideas.

In fact, one of the noticeable changes in the architectural streetscape of Indianapolis during the 1860s and 1870s involved the high quality of the building designs produced by the city's own architects. Francis Costigan's well-proportioned and elegantly detailed Italian Renaissance design for the Lewis and Elizabeth Hasselman House, Diedrich Bohlen's exquisitely detailed Martindale-Atkins mansion in the Second Empire style, Enos and Huebner's unusual evocation of Gothic with slender spires at the Meridian Street Methodist Episcopal Church, Joseph Curzon's well-proportioned and finely detailed Gothic design for the Second Presbyterian Church, and, above all, Isaac Hodgson's superb second Marion County Courthouse drawn from Italian Renaissance and Second Empire sources—all these compared favorably with comparable building designs from across the eastern United States. The budding architectural profession of the Indiana state capital had matured by an important measure.

The 1876 city directory lists twenty single practitioners or partnerships in architecture, up from four in the 1857 directory, showing the growth of the profession amid the postwar boom. Several of the 1850s group—Diedrich Bohlen, Joseph Curzon, Edwin May, and Isaac Hodgson—were still in practice, and Bohlen, Hodgson, and May were reaching the height of their success as architects for major buildings and residences. Several newcomers—Robert Platt Daggett, James B. Lizius, John H. Stem, Louis H. Gibson, William H. Brown, and Charles A. Wallingford—put down roots in the community and established practices that lasted for as long as thirty years. Others listed—M. T. Allardt, Herman T. Brandt, Peter P. Cookingham, Benjamin V. Enos and Son, Henry Huebner, Edwin H. Ketcham, and Isaac Taylor—practiced alone or with partners for a few years and then left the city.[8]

As seen in chapter 7 of volume 1, the depression of the late 1870s lasted into the 1880s, and building slowly recovered. By 1897, after another depression, the pool of Indianapolis architects had expanded by almost 50 percent to thirty firms. A handful of 1876 practitioners—Robert P. Daggett, James Lizius, John H. Stem, and Louis H. Gibson—continued to prosper. One major firm of 1876, that of Diedrich Bohlen, had descended to the second generation in the person of Oscar D. Bohlen and become D. A. Bohlen and Son. Edwin May, who had developed a robust practice in the 1870s designing county courthouses, the Women's Department of the Indiana Hospital of the Insane, and the monumental second Indiana Statehouse, died in 1880 and left his practice to his chief draftsman, Adolph Scherrer. The latter, with the prestige of overseeing the construction of the statehouse as supervising architect, created his own expansive practice in the 1880s and 1890s. Others of a younger generation opened architectural offices in the 1880s and 1890s. The most successful of these was undoubtedly Vonnegut and Bohn, formed by two local men with deep roots in the German American community, Bernard Vonnegut and Arthur Bohn. Others opening new practices found niches in designing certain building types. Charles Edgar Bates, Herbert W. Foltz, W. Scott Moore, John G. Thurtle, Marion H. Traylor, and Thomas A. Winterrowd all concentrated on residential commissions, including the new apartment buildings of the 1890s. Samuel H. Brubaker focused on commercial, industrial, and wholesale buildings, while the new firm of Scharn and Rubush worked on a variety of building types.[9]

The number of out-of-town architects obtaining commissions in Indianapolis increased steadily during the 1880s and 1890s as the volume of construction increased and new building types appeared. J. B. McElfatrick and Son of New York came to town to design the original English's Opera House and Hotel, and Oscar Cobb of Chicago "landed" the commission for the Empire Theater. The

Pennsylvania Railroad drew on a consortium of architects and engineers from within its far-flung system to design Union Station, led by Thomas Rodd of Pittsburgh. The Pauly Company of St. Louis won the commission to design and build the new Marion County jail and sheriff's residence, based on their reputation for creating attractive jails, residences, and jail cells across the country.

Formal architectural education was becoming more common among Indianapolis architects and beginning to challenge the English-style apprenticeship system. The system of study promoted by the French École des Beaux-Arts had taken shape in the early nineteenth century. Students enrolled in lectures, learned design in ateliers (studios) under the tutelage of seasoned architects, and submitted designs to juries to evaluate in response to problems posed in competitions with other students. A small group of Americans—chief among them Richard Morris Hunt, Henry Hobson Richardson, and Charles F. McKim—enrolled in the École during the 1850s and 1860s and mastered the Beaux Arts approach to planning buildings and creating designs that met the requirements of programs (problems) posed through competitions. They also absorbed the rich vocabulary of the Roman, Renaissance, French NeoClassical, and medieval styles that they studied at the École.[10]

The eminence assumed by this initial group on the American architectural scene helped foster an interest in creating similar academic programs in architecture at American universities. The new Massachusetts Institute of Technology offered the first architectural courses in 1868, led by Professor William Robert Ware. The University of Illinois followed in 1870 and Cornell University in 1871.[11] In 1881, Ware moved to Columbia University and founded an architecture program there as well. He modeled the curriculums of the MIT and Columbia programs on the Beaux Arts system of instruction. During his tenure, MIT became the leader in architecture education, attracting students from across the country, including Indianapolis. Ware was at the height of his influence when he served as architectural advisor for the competitions involving the Indianapolis Commercial Club and the second Indianapolis Public Library in the early 1890s.

One of the first Indianapolis architects to obtain training in one of the new American programs was Louis Gibson, who attended MIT in 1873–74. In the 1880s, Bernard Vonnegut studied architecture at MIT and then took postgraduate coursework in architecture at the Polytechnic Institute of Hanover and a technical institute in Berlin. He may have been the first Indianapolis and Hoosier architect to enroll in graduate studies. His future business partner, Arthur Bohn, studied at the Royal Polytechnic Institute in Karlsruhe, Germany, and subsequently in an architectural atelier of Paris, where he learned the Beaux Arts method of design.

One of Vonnegut and Bohn's chief competitors, Oscar Bohlen, attended MIT in the early 1880s. Robert Frost Daggett, eventual successor to his father, Robert Platt Daggett, and James Lizius in practice, enjoyed the best kind of architectural education then available in the 1890s, first graduating from the University of Pennsylvania in 1896 and then spending five years in Paris studying at the École des Beaux-Arts itself and in an architectural atelier. Daggett was probably the first architect in the state to study at the École, and his return to Indianapolis presaged the dominance of the Beaux Art method of design in the state capital over the next thirty years.

Indianapolis architects of the 1880s and 1890s continued to acquire sizeable libraries of books containing plans, elevations, and renderings of Classical, medieval, Renaissance, and contemporary architecture in Europe.[12] They also subscribed to architectural periodicals—a new source of visual and written information about leading buildings proposed or just completed in American cities. Such publications connected local architects with the profession across the country, especially with designers practicing in the large cities of the Northeast and Midwest. One of the oldest of these periodicals was the *American Architect and Building News*, founded in 1876 and based in Boston. It was followed in 1883 by the chief midwestern periodical, the *Inland Architect and News Record*, based in Chicago. A New York journal, the *Architectural Record*, began publication in 1891, and the following year, *The Brickbuilder* appeared in Boston, "devoted to the advancement of brick architecture." The first three periodicals provided engravings and later photographs of current new buildings, plans and elevations, and articles discussing the work of the architects represented and describing the structures illustrated. *The Brickbuilder* initially provided drawings of brick buildings and their details, with articles, and gradually broadened to embrace general architectural topics, becoming the *Architectural Forum* in 1916. The popular periodical *Scientific American* began issuing its *Architects and Builders Edition* in 1885. The edition furnished colorized and black-and-white photographs of new houses and their floor plans. Indianapolis itself produced several building trade journals, such as the *Clay Worker* (1878–93), *Stone* (1888–1942), and *Wood-Worker* (1882–1960). City architects drew design ideas from the illustrations of all these sources.[13]

As the corpus of architects in the state capital increased after the Civil War, practitioners made several efforts to create an organization to represent their interests and improve the profession. The first-known effort occurred in 1869, when a group of architects established the Indiana Association of Architects. Local architect Joseph Curzon was elected president and Diedrich Bohlen secretary. The association apparently did not last for long because, less than twenty years later, another movement took shape to create a statewide organization. In 1886, architects from Indianapolis and other major Indiana cities formed the Indiana State Association of Architects and drew up a constitution and bylaws. The objects of the association were "to unite in fellowship the Architects of the State of Indiana, to combine their efforts so as to promote the artistic, scientific and practical efficiency of the profession, and to cultivate and encourage the study of kindred arts."[14]

The names of the committees indicated the chief concerns of the organizers: statutory revision, raising professional standards, competitions, and contracts. These were to continue to be major themes of Indiana architects over the next thirty years. Indianapolis architects dominated the committee memberships, although there was geographic balance among the officers.[15] There is no indication that the Indiana State Association lasted any longer than its predecessor. The next movement to organize at the state level came twenty-three years later.

Also in 1886, twelve Indianapolis architects formed a local group, the Indianapolis Architects' Society, with Diedrich Bohlen as president; Robert P. Daggett, vice president; James B. Lizius, secretary; and Oscar Bohlen, treasurer. The following year, the society applied for membership in the national American Institute of Architects (AIA) and became the Indianapolis Chapter of the AIA. This local organization also did not take root, and it discontinued its meetings in 1899.[16]

Some local architects also sought to form relationships with professional colleagues in other cities and states, joining regional architectural organizations. Isaac Hodgson and Bernard Vonnegut, for example, were elected members of the nascent Western Association of Architects in the 1880s. The association had been formed by some of the leading figures in Chicago architecture.[17]

The tempo of construction increased substantially between 1900 and 1920 as the population of Indianapolis grew rapidly and the economy boomed. In 1910, about midway through the period, the city directory showed a slight increase of four architectural firms over the thirty-two listed in 1900.[18] At this midpoint, five firms with large drafting staffs dominated the general-purpose market for architectural services. Four of these—D. A. Bohlen and Son, Vonnegut and Bohn, R. P. Daggett and Company, and Adolph Scherrer—were well established, and the fifth—Rubush and Hunter—had quickly risen to the top rank since its formation in 1904. These firms designed most of the office buildings, public buildings, charitable and nonprofit structures, buildings of worship, and apartments.

Oscar Bohlen won commissions to build one of the first city skyscrapers, the Majestic Building, two different St. Vincent's Hospital buildings, St. Agnes Academy, the Meridian Street Methodist Episcopal Church, and the German

Evangelical Zion Church. The Bohlen firm also designed a few large residences. Vonnegut and Bohn designed two buildings for the cultural and gymnastic activities of Indianapolis turnvereins, Das Deutsche Haus and the Southside Turnverein; office buildings such as the Commercial Club and the Fletcher Savings and Trust Building; two large department store buildings, L. S. Ayres and Company and the William H. Block Company; the John Herron Art Institute; the Indianapolis Hebrew Temple; All Souls Unitarian Church; and a host of fine residences. R. P. Daggett and Company designed the Lemcke Building skyscraper, the Eli Lilly and Company office building and plant, the Robert W. Long Hospital, and the Berrick Apartments. Adolph Scherrer and his sons, Anton and Herman, designed the Maennerchor Building and the Burdsal Units at City Hospital. And Rubush and Hunter designed some of the principal commercial, public, and fraternal buildings, such as the Hume-Mansur Building, the Indianapolis City Hall, the Independent Order of Odd Fellows Building, and the Masonic Temple, as well as an occasional building of worship and a handful of city mansions.

Two smaller firms—Herbert L. Bass and Company and Frank B. Hunter—designed many residences, such as Bass's Laurel Hall country house, varied middle-class houses south of Thirty-Eighth Street, and Hunter's mainly Foursquare houses for middle-income clients. Both firms also took on occasional commercial and industrial commissions. Foltz and Parker, with an office of about the same size, focused on upper-income residences but also designed an office building—the Bobbs-Merrill Building—and major public and nonprofit buildings, such as the main YMCA Building and the Indiana Hospital for the Insane in Madison, Indiana.

Four firms listed in 1910 specialized in buildings of worship but also served as residential architects. George Bedell created versatile designs for the Holy Trinity Slovenian Catholic Church in Haughville, the St. Frances de Sales Catholic Church in Brightwood, and the Congregation Sharah Tessila on South Meridian Street. Alfred Grindle designed the Alfred M. and Minnie Stroup Glossbrenner House on North Meridian and All Saints Episcopal Cathedral. William O. Morck provided designs for several African American congregations, including the Second Baptist Church and the Mt. Zion Baptist Church.[19] Lewis Sturges designed the Westminster Presbyterian Church and had served as supervising architect for the Hetherington and Berner ironworks; he probably supplemented his practice with residential commissions.[20]

A final group from the 1910 directory were small practitioners who probably operated alone and specialized in residences for middle-class and working-class clients. In his final years of practice, W. Scott Moore worked on residential buildings, such as The Rink apartments. Charles H. Byfield and Charles E. Bates designed a mixture of houses for well-to-do clients and workers. Doeppers and Myers, Layton Allen, and Marshall Van Arman focused on bungalows and Rustic-style houses. Thomas A. Winterrowd had worked on residences of various styles in the 1890s and resumed that practice after a stint as the Indianapolis building commissioner.[21]

The rapid continuing increase in construction raised the total number of architectural firms to fifty between 1910 and 1914. It stood at fifty-seven in 1916, the last full year before the United States entered World War I, but declined to forty-eight in 1920 as the war depressed civilian construction. A few new architects in the 1916 listing had previously served as draftsmen in established offices and entered practice on their own. This group included Fermor Cannon, Marrett Carr, J. Edwin Kopf, William E. Russ, probably Frederick Wallick, and Victor H. Winterrowd. Most of this group, at the beginning of their careers, worked on residential commissions, although Victor Winterrowd obtained work as the architect for the Alhambra Theater.[22]

Two other trends shaped the Indianapolis architectural profession between the late 1890s and 1920. One was the presence of out-of-town architects, who won important commissions. These particularly included Chicago practitioners, whose prestige from designing skyscraper office buildings and status as some of the top architectural firms in the country may have impressed Indianapolis clients. Henry Ives Cobb, head of one of the largest Chicago offices, won the commission to design the William L. Stevenson Building in 1896, while Daniel H. Burnham of Chicago, the driving force behind the influential Columbian Exposition of 1893, obtained two prestigious Indianapolis projects—the Traction Terminal office building and shed and the tallest office building in the state, the Merchants National Bank tower. Architects from other cities also designed important buildings. William L. Price of Price and McLanahan of Philadelphia made his presence felt by two imposing mansions—the Frank and Clarissa Lintner Van Camp House and the Frank H. and Harriet Githens Wheeler House—and his monumental Union Station concourse and train shed of 1916–22.

The second trend—holding architectural competitions to award commissions—brought additional out-of-state architects to the Indiana state capital. The 1900 competition held by the US Department of the Treasury for the architect of the new US Courthouse and Post Office awarded the commission to Philadelphia architects Rankin and Kellogg for their Ionic Greek Classical entry. In 1913–14, the Indianapolis Public Library's national competition selected the Greek Doric-style submission of Paul Philippe Cret of Philadelphia.

Formal competitions became a popular method of selecting an architect during the 1900–1920 period. Indianapolis architects tended to support them if the selection mechanism was truly blind and if a knowledgeable, objective architectural advisor was hired to guide the client organization. There was grumbling among some architects over the expectation of most competition sponsors that architects would prepare designs for entry without receiving any compensation.[23] The incentive to produce the best designs possible for competitions undoubtedly served to improve the work of local firms generally.

The rapid growth of the Indianapolis architectural profession between 1900 and 1920 finally gave it the necessary critical mass to organize itself and project a public voice. In December 1908, at the instigation of architect Wilson B. Parker, twenty leading architects of the city met at his office and agreed to establish the Architects' Association of Indianapolis. Officers elected were Arthur Bohn, president; Clarence Martindale, vice president; and Henry Dupont, secretary-treasurer.[24] The association adopted a constitution that defined the new organization's object as the "union in fellowship of the architects of Indianapolis and vicinity, and the combination of their efforts for the purpose of promoting the artistic, scientific and practical efficiency of the profession and fix the limits and rules of honorable practice; to the ultimate end that membership should be regarded by the public as a guaranty of the professional standing of the architect."[25]

The intent at the outset was for the association to affiliate with the AIA, the national professional organization of architects in the United States. The institute had been founded in 1857 with the object of promoting "the scientific and practical profession of its members" and elevating the standing of the architectural profession. The Indianapolis association hoped to become a state chapter of the AIA. They borrowed their definition of an architect from the constitution of the institute: "An architect is a professional person whose occupation consists of originating and supplying artistic and scientific data preliminary to and in connection with the construction of buildings, their appurtenances and decorations, in supervising the operations of contractors therefor, and in preparing contracts between the proprietors and contractors thereof."[26] At the end of 1909, the Indianapolis association invited architects from across the state to a meeting, at which Glenn Brown, secretary of the AIA, addressed the gathering and declared that "in union there is strength." He further asserted that a statewide chapter of the institute would improve the business interests of the profession. In January 1910, a statewide representation of architects formed a state organization and applied for a charter as the Indiana Chapter of the AIA. Indianapolis architect Oscar Bohlen was elected the first president.[27]

One of the chief interests of the new chapter was to monitor legislation relevant to architecture being considered by the Indiana General Assembly and advocate for bills that would improve the profession or the building and construction field. In 1913, the chapter supported a bill that would license all architects in the state, with the object of admitting to practice only those persons who passed examinations conducted by the state.[28] The chapter also lobbied for a state housing law, setting minimum standards for the construction of houses, and for a statewide building code. Also in 1913, the statewide organization adopted a code of professional ethics for its members.[29]

The Indiana chapter sponsored an exhibition of designs by Indiana architects in the spring of 1910 to acquaint the public with the capabilities of the architectural profession in the state. A strong response led to a second exhibition in the Sculpture Hall of the John Herron Art Institute of Indianapolis. In May of 1912, the chapter mounted its third exhibition and published the results. Exhibits of photographs, perspective views, and plans portrayed the work of both Indiana and out-of-state architectural firms.[30]

In 1911, draftsmen in Indianapolis formed the Indianapolis Architectural Club with the object of enhancing the education of the many draftsmen working in city architecture offices. The club launched a lecture series featuring some of the top architects in the country, including William Price of Philadelphia and Warren P. Laird, head of the architecture department at the University of Pennsylvania. Price admonished his audience to create "original" designs representing the United States, not the European past. He must have startled some in his audience when he described Pennsylvania Station in New York, designed by McKim, Mead, and White and modeled on the baths of imperial Rome, as "stupid" and "rotten." Price thought that the hope for originality lay in the Midwest, not in the East, which was too close to Europe. Laird asserted that the architectural profession had come into its own, finally recognized by the public as entailing far more than what a carpenter could provide. An architect now drew his training from both art and science and must carry out analyses involving structural, sanitary, electrical, and mechanical engineering. The architect worked under many limitations, chief among them cost. Laird invoked the Roman architect Vitruvius's admonition that a building must have stability, fulfillment of purpose, and beauty.[31]

The impulse toward enhanced education for neophyte designers continued to gain momentum. Increasing numbers of aspiring architects entered architectural degree programs at universities. Wilson Parker studied architecture at MIT, as did

Kurt Vonnegut Sr. and Jessie Gibson, one of the few women in the city or state to prepare for a career in architecture. Edgar O. Hunter graduated from the architecture program at the University of Pennsylvania. Herbert W. Foltz obtained a degree in engineering at Rose Polytechnic Institute, and Merritt Harrison obtained a degree in architecture from Cornell University.[32] Most of these university programs emphasized the Beaux Arts method, obtained through producing designs in response to a series of programs (problems) posed and learning design under the tutorship of a master architect or professor in an atelier. The growing adherence of the American architectural profession to the standards of Beaux Arts design made education in the techniques of the French program highly desirable for those obtaining their architectural experience as draftsmen.

Despite the apparent growth of interest by young designers in university programs, only one Indiana university or college started an architecture degree program between the Civil War and 1920: the University of Notre Dame on the north edge of the state. The university offered courses in architecture as early as 1869 and established a college of architecture with degrees in architecture and architectural engineering in 1906. It does not appear, though, that many Indianapolis architects engaged in studies at Notre Dame during the first two decades of the twentieth century.[33]

In response to the increasing dominance of the Beaux Arts method, the Indianapolis Architectural Club decided to affiliate with the Beaux Arts Society of New York and afford an opportunity for club members to participate in annual Beaux Arts architectural competitions sponsored by the society.[34] For the 1913 competition, Robert Frost Daggett, a graduate of the École des Beaux-Arts, agreed to conduct the proceedings, and Alfred Grindle, a gifted watercolorist and draftsman, hosted the participants at his home as they received the preliminary instructions. The club arranged for the competitors to work in a studio leased in the When Building at 36 North Pennsylvania Street downtown.[35]

Two years later, the popularity of participation in the competition led the club to form a Beaux Arts Society of Indianapolis, with Merritt Harrison as *massier* (president) and Walter Scholer as *sous-massier* (vice president). Daggett served as patron (mentor) of the Indianapolis atelier. For the 1915 competitions, the education committee of the parent society in New York prepared the problems to be posed, arranged for an impartial jury of leading architects in the United States, distributed the problems to both local societies and architecture programs in colleges, and oversaw the judging of competition entries. The competitions extended over ten to eleven months, from August to July. After the draftsmen or students received their problem, they prepared a sketch (*esquisse*) of their solution over a limited number of hours without the benefit of photographs or books. Based on the sketch, the entrants developed a final design over several months, with critiques by the patron. The jury made their judgments by rating the entries based on composition, draftsmanship, and general presentation. In 1915, in the Class B competition, local draftsman Walter Scholer was rated highest for his design presenting an infirmary for a small boys' school.[36]

In 1915 and 1916, the *Indianapolis Star* and the Indianapolis Architectural Club held competitions for the best house designs by local draftsmen. The *Star* offered one hundred dollars in prizes, and a three-person jury was impaneled for each competition, with one member chosen by the competitors, one by the club, and one by the *Star*. The entrants were to submit their designs for a house not costing more than $7,500. In the 1915 competition, Merritt Harrison's design for an old English manor house was selected for the first prize of forty-five dollars by the jury composed of architects Robert Frost Daggett and Anton Scherrer and local physician and city park board president Dr. Henry Jameson.[37]

Practicing architects and their drafting staffs continued to obtain many of their design ideas from national architectural periodicals such as the *Inland Architect*, the *American Architect and Building News*, the *Architectural Record*, and *The Brickbuilder/Architectural Forum*. In addition, many offices subscribed to magazines such as Gustav Stickley's *The Craftsman*, which provided an abundance of plans, renderings, and descriptions for architects with clients desiring bungalows of all types and Spanish Mission designs.

An analysis of the type of training or preparation possessed by architectural partnerships between 1900 and 1920 suggests something of the roles taken by the partners in the business of an architectural office. Often one partner had less formal training in architecture while the other had attended or graduated from university programs. This was true of the firms of Rubush and Hunter and Foltz and Parker; the firm of George, MacLucas, and Fitton; and the new firm of McGuire and Shook. Frequently, the partner with less architectural training served as the primary contact with clients and was charged with securing business. The other partner tended to develop designs or oversee the work of the drafting staff producing the construction documents. Writing specifications or overseeing the construction of a project might be done by either partner or by a third partner, such as the case of Harry Fitton and the firm of George, MacLucas, and Fitton. The clean division of labor did not always obtain, as with Bernard Vonnegut and Arthur Bohn and later Kurt Vonnegut Sr., wherein each partner had substantial design training and may have contributed to the solutions in certain projects. With single practitioners, the principal oversaw all aspects of the office, but in the larger operations, such as Edwin May's office of the 1870s and Herbert L. Bass's operation in the 1910s, a chief draftsman oversaw the production of construction documents.

Architectural firms also increasingly sought to increase their expertise in structural, mechanical, and electrical engineering. Traditionally, architects had mastered the fundamentals of design involving structure, heating, plumbing, ventilation, and electrical wiring and provided those elements as part of their services. This was more feasible in the pre-1880 world of masonry and wood structures, simple furnaces and chimneys, and limited indoor plumbing. As nonresidential buildings acquired steel skeletons, non-load-bearing masonry, central furnaces with ductwork, and electrical lights, larger architectural firms added engineers to their staffs and partnerships. The alliance of architect Henry Brubaker and engineer William K. Eldridge in 1905 to design the new Board of Trade Building with its reinforced concrete skeleton illustrates the trend. Vonnegut and Bohn added engineer Otto N. Mueller as a member of their firm in 1911.[38] Sometimes those trained as engineers, such Herbert W. Foltz, took on the additional function of architect.

Standardized, published specifications had appeared after the mid-nineteenth century, providing a sliding scale of percentages for the services of architects or engineers based on the total cost of building projects.[39] When Adolph Scherrer designed the Gothic gateway and office building at Crown Hill Cemetery in the 1880s, he was paid 4 percent of the project cost as his fee. By 1909, the fee in the United States generally had risen to 5 percent. For that fee, the architect consulted with the client about a desirable design, conducted additional research, produced a preliminary design, made revisions, produced final drawings and working drawings, wrote specifications, drew up contracts with contractors, and supervised construction. In 1908, the American Institute of Architects voted to establish 6 percent as the minimum fee to be charged by its members.[40] This increase helped underscore the identity of architects as a profession, comparable to engineers, attorneys, and physicians.

What of the roles of African American architects and women architects in the Indianapolis of 1820–1920? It appears that there were very few of either practicing in the state capital during its first century. In 1867, when the Bethel African Methodist Episcopal congregation sought to build the initial section of their building on West Vermont Street, they first hired a carpenter with a German surname, Adam Busch, apparently white, to design the structure and oversee construction. After difficulties arose with Busch's work, the congregation hired newly arrived white architect Robert Platt Daggett to revise and complete the drawings for the building (see chap. 5 of vol. 1).[41] One can infer that there were no carpenters, builders, or architects in the African American community at the time or the congregation would likely have awarded the commission to someone in their own community.

A search for the term *architect* in the search engines of Newspapers.com and the *Hoosier State Chronicle* between 1890 and 1920 only revealed one instance of a possible African American architect designing a building in the city. That person, M. H. Russell, designed the Grand United Order of Odd Fellows Building in 1890 at what was later 534–36 Indiana Avenue. He was not listed in the Indianapolis city directory at the time and so likely was from out of town. If he were a Black person, Russell was one of the first, perhaps the first, African American architect to practice in Indianapolis.

Circumstantial evidence points to an absence of Black architects practicing in the city from 1890 to 1920. None of the listings of architects in the business directory sections of the city directories from 1897, 1910, 1914, or 1916 appear to include any person with an address in the principal African American neighborhoods. In several instances, African American institutions hired white architects to design buildings for them. For example, the Mt. Zion Baptist Church selected white architect William O. Morck to prepare the initial plans for their building in 1908, and the Second Baptist Church hired him to prepare the preliminary design for their new building in 1912. The African American Knights of Pythias lodges in Indianapolis retained white architect Frank B. Hunter in 1908 to prepare the initial design for the Pythian meeting hall on Senate Avenue. The implication appears to be that few Black architects were practicing in the city. One nationally important African American architect, Samuel Plato of Marion, Indiana, served as the contractor for the construction of the initial structure of the Second Baptist Church building in 1912–13.[42]

A review of surviving issues from the three African American newspapers published in Indianapolis between 1890 and 1920 shows almost no articles on building, construction, laying of cornerstones, dedications of buildings, or architects. Much of the local news seems to have focused on personal events or church proceedings.[43] Therefore, it seems difficult to substantiate my supposition that few African American architects practiced in the city prior to 1920.[44] The reasons for the apparent absence of Black architects would seem to lie in the segregation enforced by the white majority and pervasive prejudice against African Americans serving in the professions. White clients were not inclined to hire African American architects or even contractors. The result was that potential Black designers were excluded from projects in all of the city except the small African American enclaves, where there were limited opportunities for new construction.

Women were excluded from the architectural profession in Indianapolis and elsewhere almost as much as Black citizens. The first woman to graduate from a university architecture program in the United States appears to have been Mary Hicks, who received a degree at Cornell University in 1880. The next year, Mary Whitford received an architecture degree from Syracuse University, followed in 1893 by Sophia Hayden, who graduated from the architecture program at MIT. As late as 1907, only one woman—Louise Bethune of Buffalo, New York—was a member of the American Institute of Architects. As the new century opened, a handful of women practiced architecture independently and frequently specialized in home design. One of the most successful was Lois L. Howe of Boston, who specialized in country houses.[45]

According to a 1900 article in the *Indianapolis News*, two young women in Indianapolis were then working in local architectural offices. Fanny Ayres had been working for H. V. Place for several years and was "able to originate plans and specifications for smaller buildings." A "Miss Richardson" was studying architecture with David Gibson.[46]

Architectural historian Amy Borland of the Indiana Division of Historic Preservation and Archaeology has researched and written about three women who obtained training in architecture or drafting and worked for Indianapolis architecture firms between 1900 and 1920. One of the most talented—Jessie Gibson Paine (1882–1959)—was the daughter of artistic architect Louis H. Gibson. She entered MIT and after four years of study graduated in 1903 with the highest academic record of her class of twenty. She was the only woman in the class. Upon returning to Indianapolis, Gibson worked as a partner in her father's practice for three years (fig. 6.1). She was one of the first women to practice architecture in Indiana and probably the first to become partner in an architectural office. At the end of the three years, Jessie Gibson married and left the profession, following a social convention that women in the professions or teaching should not be married. Edith Leonard (1883–1957) enrolled in the architecture program at the University of Illinois and graduated in 1906. Beginning in 1911, she worked successively in four Indianapolis architect's offices—Brubaker and Stern, Fermor S. Cannon, Herbert W. Foltz, and Rubush and Hunter (fig. 6.2). Presumably, she worked as a draftsperson. She had the distinction of being perhaps the first architect in Indiana to be licensed, passing the examinations set by the State of Illinois and receiving her certificate about 1911, eighteen years before the State of Indiana required licenses

Figs. 6.1 and 6.2. (*left to right*) Jessie Gibson Paine and Edith Leonard, early practicing Indianapolis women architects. For figure 6.1, family photo courtesy of Ellen Burnham Davis, granddaughter of Jessie Gibson Paine; for figure 6.2, from 1907 issue of *Illini Media Yearbook*.

Figure 6.3. Panoramic photo of architects and possibly some draftspersons at the 1920 Indiana Society of Architects convention in Indianapolis, taken in the Sunken Gardens at Garfield Park. Note three unidentified women at the center. Bass Photo Co. Collection, Indiana Historical Society. (Image cropped)

to practice. The third woman, Clara Maude Richardson Parry (1878–1971), followed a different path, graduating from the Industrial Technical High School and working as an architectural apprentice for the firms of Dupont and Johnson and David Gibson Jr. (the younger brother of Louis Gibson). Real progress in admitting women to the architecture field awaited the breakdown of barriers in many professional fields during the 1960s and 1970s.[47]

CONCLUSION

The end of World War I and the postwar adjustment to peacetime saw the firm establishment of a mature architectural profession in Indianapolis. Architecture in the state capital had evolved from a world in the 1820s of builders, carpenters, and masons designing and supervising construction of simple frame and brick structures to a confraternity in 1920 of architects capable of designing every type of modern building, regardless of its challenges aesthetically, functionally, and technically. From designs based largely on drawings and plans in builder's guides and pattern books, city architects added varied sources for inspiration—architectural periodicals, compendiums of designs by architects in other parts of the country, and travel to other cities. They also increasingly sought formal architectural training through new university programs or through practicing their craft through participation in Beaux Arts competitions after 1900.

The architects who found success worked out a formula of sharing the responsibilities of an architectural office with either a partner or draftsmen. The national trend toward large offices with many draftsmen and technicians took shape in Indianapolis, especially after 1900. Typically, one partner would take on the role of seeking business and client relations while the other would focus on design and supervising the production of drawings and specifications. Success was possible for white, male architects. As in most of the United States, African American men and women of all races found great difficulty in practicing in the Indiana state capital.

As the numbers of architects practicing in the Indiana state capital rose to thirty-six by 1910, members of the professions finally were able to organize the Architects' Association of Indianapolis and a statewide chapter of the AIA. These actions gave the growing profession a public voice and allowed it to lobby for desirable legislation in the Indiana General Assembly, such as licensure for architects, a state housing law, setting minimum standards for the construction of houses, and a statewide building code. Acceptance as a chapter of the American Institute of Architects gave the statewide organization national recognition and allowed its members to draw on the wisdom of other AIA members across the country.

The local architects increasingly competed with out-of-town firms for the largest and most prestigious commissions. Many of the decisions on such projects after 1880 came through architectural competitions, in which an impartial jury, often guided by an architectural advisor, awarded the commission to what its members considered the best submission. Through competitions, such noted outside practitioners as Rankin and Kellogg and Paul Philippe Cret designed and carried out outstanding designs for civic monuments such as the US Courthouse and Post Office and the Indianapolis Public Library, respectively. Other national figures in architecture, such as Daniel H. Burnham and William Price, obtained notable commissions through their prestige or relationships with clients. Chicago architects regularly gained local commissions due to the growing business and cultural influence of the Great Lakes metropolis. Early examples included William Boyington and Theodore Wadskier, followed later by talented William LeBaron Jenney, Reinhold W. Hellgren, Henry Ives Cobb, Jarvis Hunt, and, of course, Burnham.

The local architectural firms who enjoyed the most commissions and sustained practices were multitalented, and the principal or the partners were able to manage all the aspects of a successful architectural business—marketing their skills and designs, producing designs that pleased and satisfied their clients, communicating well with clients, supervising the construction of finished buildings to the clients' liking, supervising draftsmen to produce the best work and meet deadlines, and managing the finances of the office to produce a profit.

The Indianapolis firms that most met these criteria between 1833 and 1920 included John Elder, Joseph Curzon, Francis Costigan, Isaac Hodgson, D. A. Bohlen and Son, Edwin May, R. P. Daggett and Company, Louis H. Gibson, Adolph Scherrer, Vonnegut and Bohn, Rubush and Hunter, Foltz and Parker, H. L. Bass and Company, and Frank B. Hunter. Their work comprised some of the most impressive architecture of Indianapolis's first century, and they, as practitioners, especially shaped the development of the profession.

EPILOGUE

As Indianapolis emerged from materials shortages and a short depression after World War I, its architectural profession was poised to enjoy a decade of considerable business and artistic successes. The 1920s saw new firms enter the local market, and some of them, together with well-established offices, obtained commissions for a host of office buildings, fraternal structures, university edifices, buildings of worship, apartment buildings, single-family houses, and double residences. The 1920s were the last decade to feature designs for most building types drawn from the history of architecture. Some of the best architecture in the Gothic style came from the drawing boards of new architect George F. Schreiber for the Scottish Rite Cathedral (called "one of the world's most beautiful buildings" by the American Institute of Architects), Cleveland architect John W. Cresswell Corbusier for the new Tabernacle Presbyterian Church, Atlanta architect Charles Hopson for the North Methodist Episcopal Church, and veteran local architect Herbert W. Foltz for the new, cathedral-like Broadway Methodist Episcopal Church. Henry Schlacks of Chicago created a monumental and elegant interpretation of the Italian Romanesque with his design of St. Joan of Arc Catholic Church.

Rubush and Hunter dominated much of the office building market with Italian Renaissance compositions for the facades of the Guaranty, Illinois, and American Central Life Insurance Company Buildings. They devised a design adapted from English Tudor palaces for the new Columbia Club and a Spanish Churrigueresque facade for the Indiana Theater. Robert Frost Daggett and associate Thomas Hibben designed an imposing Italian Renaissance building for the Indianapolis Athletic Club and abstracted Gothic edifices for the Indianapolis Chamber of Commerce and Jordan Hall, the main structure for the new Butler University campus in Fairview Park. The most monumental of the historically inspired designs of the decade came with Cleveland architects Walker and Weeks' design for the five-block-long Indiana World War Memorial Plaza, which centered on the war memorial hall, based on the Tomb of Mausolus at Halicarnassus.

The 1920s also saw the advent of the Art Deco style, in which traditional forms were transformed into abstractions and fanciful organic and geometric details adorned facades. Two of the most memorable Art Deco creations of the period came from the office of Rubush and Hunter and chief draftsman Philip A. Weisenburgh: Circle Tower of 1929–30 and the initial Coca-Cola Bottling Plant of 1931.

Residential designs of the decade followed some of the same themes of the previous era. Architects of mansions on Meridian Street north of Fortieth and on adjacent streets continued to draw from the Italian Renaissance, American Foursquare, English Tudor vernacular, and Tudor palaces for much of their designs. The Foursquare also continued to dominate middle-class residences, some apartment buildings, and doubles, while the bungalow maintained its sway as the preferred form for workers' houses and small doubles.

The first century of architecture in Indianapolis prepared the way for all this production, developing a profession that followed national trends but customized their application to local conditions and the desires of clients. Growing sophistication in design and engineering came from increased training and education and contributed to the city's architectural profession a visible public profile, standards for practice, and the confidence to take on challenges of any size or complexity.

APPENDIX A

ARCHITECTURAL GLOSSARY[1]

Abacus. The flat slab on top of a capital in Greek and Roman architecture; in Greek Doric columns, the abacus is a thick, square slab.

Aedicule. The framing of a window, door, or other opening on a building with two columns, piers, or pilasters supporting a gable, lintel, or entablature and a pediment.

Anta. In Greek architecture, a pilaster with capital and base located along the cella of a temple or at the ends of the projecting walls of a temple portico.

Antefix (plural antefixae). An upright ornament in Greek, Roman, or Renaissance architecture that projects above the apex of a pediment or at the edge of a cornice.

Anthemion. An ornament of floral or foliated forms arranged in a radiating cluster, flat in character, as in bas-relief sculptures or painting.

Apse. A semicircular or polygonal structure usually terminating a chancel or choir in a church.

Arabesques. Ornamentations consisting of fanciful interlacing patterns of flowers, foliage, or fruit, sometimes geometric in nature, sometimes flowing.

Arcade. A range of arches carried on columns or piers, either freestanding or attached to a wall.

Architrave. 1. The lowest part of the entablature in Greek, Roman, and Renaissance architecture. 2. A molded frame surrounding a door or window.

Arts and Crafts. A movement that began in England during the late nineteenth century, spurred by the writings and practice of William Morris, who stressed simplicity, honest use of natural materials, and a minimum of ornament. The Arts and Crafts aesthetic crossed the Atlantic and became closely associated with Rustic and bungalow design.

Ashlar. Refers to hewn blocks of stone masonry with even faces and square edges, laid in horizontal courses with vertical joints.

Astragal. Generally in architecture, a small, convex molding of rounded surface. In the case of the Indiana Soldiers' and Sailors' Monument, the bronze works of sculpture that girdle the limestone shaft.

Axis. An imaginary straight line to which the different parts of an architectural design are referred.

Balustrade. A rail and supporting upright elements that line the perimeter of a stairway, balcony, or the ridge or edge of a roof.

Bargeboard. A series of boards hanging from the fascia of a gable, usually in a house, that covers the fascia and is often decorated with turned decorative wooden elements or cut in decorative patterns.

Baroque style. A style of European and Spanish colonial architecture of the seventeenth and eighteenth centuries derived from Renaissance details but transformed by exuberant decoration, curvilinear forms, and dematerialized surfaces.

Basilican plan. A plan derived from the layout of Roman imperial basilicas in which a central nave is flanked by aisles with lower heights. Early Christian churches evolved from Roman basilicas, and the basilican plan has been a staple of the architecture of Christian churches ever since.

Bas-relief. Used to refer to sculptures with low reliefs.

Bay. An opening in the facade or other elevation of a building, usually corresponding to a window or arch in an arcade.

Bay window. A projection from the exterior of house or other building containing windows with an angular or curved shape.

Beaux Arts method of architectural design. The approach to design developed by the École des Beaux-Arts in Paris between 1830 and about 1940. The method involved studying monuments of ancient Greece, Rome, the Italian Renaissance, and the Classical tradition in France; making studies in watercolor and charcoal; and perfecting drawing of buildings. The Beaux Arts method relied on rational planning of buildings and cities, with primary and secondary axes linking each part of a structure or portion of an urban plan.

Blind arch. An arch applied to the wall of a building within which is a solid surface without an opening.

Block. A rectangular or oblong portion of a building.

Board and batten. A system of exterior construction in which the walls of a wooden frame building are formed by alternating wide boards and narrow wood strips, called battens.

Boss. An ornamental knob or projection covering the intersections of ribs in a vault or ceiling.

Bracket. A piece of stone, wood, or metal, usually in the form of scrolls or volutes, that supports a projecting feature, such as a cornice. Associated especially with the Italianate style.

Broach spire. A tall structure on a medieval English church, usually octagonal in plan, that rises from a square tower. The four angles of the tower not covered by the base of the spire are covered with broaches—masonry or frame structures that have facets and are carried up to a point.

Buttress. A mass of stone masonry or brickwork projecting from or built against a wall to give additional strength, usually to counteract the lateral thrust of an arch, roof, or vault. Buttresses constructed adjacent to walls often have steps (stepped buttresses).

Caen stone. Plaster treated and scored to resemble Caen limestone from France.

Campidoglio. The piazza and palaces that Michelangelo designed in the sixteenth century for the top of the Capitoline Hill in Rome

Campanile. Italian word for bell tower, usually separate from the main building of a church or other structure.

Capital. The head or crowning feature of a column.

Cartouche. An ornamental panel in the form of a scroll or flat with curled edges.

Cast iron. A hard alloy of carbon and iron that can be cast in a mold. Cast-iron columns or building fronts have considerable compressive strength.

Cella. The main portion of a Greek or Roman temple, containing the cult statue of the deity to which the temple was dedicated. The cella was oblong and surrounded in a Greek temple by columns on all sides (peripteral); in a Roman temple, it typically was preceded by a portico and stood on a podium.

Clapboard. A wooden siding commonly used as an exterior covering for buildings of frame construction, applied horizontally and overlapped.

Clerestory. That part of a church or other building that rises above the roofs of other parts and whose walls contain windows for lighting the interior.

Collar beam. A horizontal or transverse timber in a traditional English roof structure that connects a pair of rafters at a height between the apex of the roof and wall plate.

Colonnette. In medieval Gothic architecture, a thin, round shaft usually found in groups on a compound pier.

Console. A bracket-like element used to support a cornice or serve as ornament, usually with a scroll or S-curve.

Corbel. A projecting element, usually of stone or brick, that supports a weight above it.

Corbel table. A range of corbels running just below the parapet or top of an exterior wall.

Corbiestepped. Also called crow stepped. Refers to steps on the coping of a masonry gable; derived from commercial and domestic buildings in Flanders, Holland, and East Anglia in England.

Corinthian order. The order in Greek, Roman, and Renaissance architecture in which the capital of the column was bell-shaped and enveloped with acanthus leaves and small volutes at the four corners. The column shafts were typically fluted, and the bases consisted of torus moldings.

Cornice. A projecting molding along the top of a building, wall, or arch finishing or crowning it. In Greek and Roman architecture, the cornice was the top, projecting section of an entablature.

Crenellation. In medieval castles or fortresses, a parapet at the top of a wall with alternating square indentations and raised square portions (merlons).

Cresting. Ornamental projections along the ridge of a roof, especially in French Second Empire mansard roofs, usually of wrought iron, and often composed of filagree designs.

Crocket. A carved ornament, often resembling curved foliage, on the slope edges of a gable, pinnacle, or spire of a church.

Cruciform plan. A plan for a church or other building that forms a cross. In most churches, such plans form a Latin cross, in which the nave arm is longer than the other three (transepts and chancel).

Cupola. A small structure built on top of a building to finish a design.

Curtain wall. An exterior wall that does not carry any of the structural load of its building and only supports its own weight. In the 1890–1920 period, such walls were usually brick or stone.

Decorated Gothic. A style of architecture that dominated the design of English churches during the late thirteenth and much of the fourteenth centuries. In Decorated Gothic windows, multiple lancet windows were surmounted by circular or diamond shaped tracery units, often fashioned into quatrefoils. There also typically were rich sculptural details and the use of ogee arches.

Dentil. A small, rectangular block in a series projecting like teeth, typically found under a cornice.

Diaper pattern. A pattern formed on an architectural surface consisting of small, repeated geometric motifs, such as diamonds or squares.

Doric order. An order used in Greek, Roman, and Renaissance architecture in which the column capital consisted of a simple rectangular abacus supported by an echinus. In Greek temples, Doric column shafts were fluted but had no bases. In Roman and Renaissance buildings, Doric columns usually had bases with torus moldings.

Dormer or dormer window. A window placed vertically on a sloping roof and with a roof of its own.

Dressed stone. Stone worked to a finished face, either smooth or molded.

Dripstone molding. A projecting molding, usually of stone, to throw off rain above a window, doorway, or arch. In Tudor palace or college architecture, dripstones frequently were applied above rectangular windows, with the ends of the molding extending horizontally on the left and right.

Eastlake. A style of exterior decoration inspired by the English architect Charles Lock Eastlake, who published an influential book, *Hints on Household Taste*, in 1868 and 1872. Used with early Queen Anne houses of the 1870s and early 1880s, Eastlake elements consisted mainly of bargeboards with three-dimensional knobs, struts, and brackets and porches with turned posts.

Elevation. One of the external faces of a building.

Ell. An extension at right angles to a building, most frequently used with respect to the wing extending at right angles from the rear of an I-house.

Ell-shaped. A building, usually a house, in which the shape of the plan forms an *L*.

Encaustic tiles. Glazed and decorated tiles created by baking clays of different colors and used to create decorative patterns in medieval buildings and in floors of nineteenth-century buildings.

English Perpendicular Gothic. The style employed for English cathedrals, churches, chapels, and palaces between roughly 1335 and 1560, in which straight verticals and horizontals (perpendiculars) were stressed in walls and vaults and window surfaces were maximized.

English Tudor vernacular. An interpretation of fifteenth- and sixteenth-century vernacular frame buildings in England for contemporary houses begun by English architects Richard Norman Shaw and William Eden Nesfield in the 1860s and used in new English towns of the 1890s, such as Port Sunlight and Bournville. From there it came to the United States, where the basic elements of sixteenth-century houses became a popular formula: brick first story, stucco and timber second story, and multiple gables with bargeboards.

Entablature. In Greek and Roman temples, the horizontal elements of the building between the column capitals and the roof, consisting of the architrave, frieze, and cornice. The decorative features of entablatures varied among the Doric, Ionic, and Corinthian orders.

Faceted. Multiple sided.

Fan light. A window in Federal architecture, often semicircular over a door, with radiating glazing bars suggesting a fan.

Federal style. A style that derived from Late Georgian architecture in the United States and usually dated between about 1790 and 1830. In Indiana it continued in some areas up into the 1860s. As applied to Indiana houses and commercial buildings, the Federal style denotes regular bays with rectangular openings, flat stone lintels or flat arches over windows, and gabled or hipped roofs, with frequently twin chimneys on the ends of buildings. Most Federal houses and other buildings were constructed of brick.

Fenestration. The arrangement of windows in a building.

Festoon. A carved ornament in the form of a garland of fruit and flowers, tied with ribbons and suspended at both ends in a loop.

Finial. An ornament, often vertical in profile, placed at the top of a gable or cupola.

Flat arch. An arch used often over windows in Late Georgian and Federal architecture, in which the intrados, the under or inner face of the arch, is horizontal or nearly horizontal.

Flat iron. A building shape resembling that of a clothes iron, with two facades coming diagonally to a point.

Flemish bond. A method of laying bricks so that alternate headers (ends of bricks) and stretchers (long, horizontal sides) appear in each course of a wall.

Fluting. Shallow, concave grooves running vertically on the shaft of a column or pilaster in Greek, Roman, and Renaissance architecture.

Foliated. Presenting, in sculptural detail, leaves, flowers, and branches.

Folly. A small tower or open structure without practical function sited in a landscape design to enhance a picturesque effect.

French Second Empire style. A term coined by American architectural historians for buildings constructed in the United States during the 1850s through 1870s that derived in part from the palatial architecture of the French Second Empire under Emperor Napoleon III (1852–70). The trademark elements involved a mansard roof with regular dormer windows encasing the top story and convex-shaped roof pavilions.

Frieze. The middle portion of an entablature in Greek, Roman, and Renaissance architecture, between the architrave and cornice. It may be decorated (in Doric and Corinthian orders) or plain (in Ionic). More generally, a frieze refers to a decorated band along the upper part of a wall, just below the cornice.

Frontispiece. A central pavilion, especially in a Renaissance-style facade, that usually contains the entry. Usually there are symmetrical wings on either side of the frontispiece, and sometimes subordinate pavilions project forward at the end of the wings.

Galvanized. Iron or steel covered with zinc, used in buildings to resist rust.

Gambrel roof. A roof in which there is a steep lower slope and flatter upper slope, used in Flemish colonial houses in the American colonies during the eighteenth century and adapted for barns in the United States during the nineteenth and early twentieth centuries.

Georgian style. In the original American colonies, architecture of especially houses built between about 1715 and 1790, during the reigns of British kings George I, George II, and George III. Classic elements included oblong shape, five bays across the facade with often a central entry, flat arches with sometimes keystones over the windows, a cornice with modillions, and a gabled or gambrel roof often with dormers. Georgian elements were revived in commercial buildings and especially residences in the United States after about 1885 and were popular in some areas until the late 1940s.

German Renaissance. A style popular in sixteenth-century Germany that used some of the orders and details of Italian Renaissance buildings but incorporated them into structures with expansive hipped roofs, stepped gables, and dormer windows.

Gothic architecture. A style that originated in France in the twelfth century and spread over all of western Europe between 1100 and 1550, ending in the late sixteenth century. Characterized by the pointed arch for windows and arcades, ribbed vaults, and stepped and flying buttresses.

Greek Revival architecture. A movement in architecture of Europe and the United States beginning in the late eighteenth century and lasting in the US until the 1850s that derived designs for contemporary buildings from temples and other buildings and monuments of Classical Greece and the Hellenistic period afterward.

Groin vault. A masonry vault produced in Roman, Byzantine, Romanesque, and Gothic architecture in which two tunnel or barrel vaults with identical shapes intersect at right angles.

Guastavino vault/tile. A type of vault invented by Spanish architect Rafael Guastavino in the late nineteenth century and brought by him to the United States. Guastavino vaults involve layers of terra-cotta tiles laid in a herringbone pattern and cured to form solid structures.

Hammerbeam truss. In traditional English construction, a truss in which a bracket projects at the level of the wall plate, carries at its end a vertical timber (hammer post), and supports braces reinforcing a collar beam.

Header. The exposed end of a brick.

Heads of windows. The upper horizontal member of a window (or door).

High Victorian Gothic architecture. Term for mid-nineteenth-century architecture preferred by English art critic John Ruskin, derived in part from medieval Gothic architecture in

Venice and characterized by inventive use of polychromy in materials, decoration, and texture.

Hipped roof. A roof that slopes upward on all four sides, rising either to a ridge or flat platform, typical of some Federal-style buildings and many Italianate-style houses and other buildings.

Hoods on windows. A projected molding over the head of a window.

Hyphen. A connecting link between two larger building elements.

I-house. A vernacular form of house originating in the eastern United States and brought by settlers to Indiana and other parts of the Midwest in the early nineteenth century. The term refers to two-story dwellings that are one-room deep and oblong shaped with gable roofs. Frequently an ell runs at a right angle from the rear of the main structure.

Imbricated. Laid so as to overlap, as with shingles or tiles, or conveying a decorative pattern resembling overlapping shingles or tiles.

Imposts. Blocks in a masonry building on either side of an arch that support and receive the thrust of the arch.

In antis. Refers in Greek and Roman architecture to a temple front or other facade in which the ends of the front consist of solid walls, sometimes covered with antae (pilasters). At the center is an opening in which full columns support an entablature.

Inglenook. A recess for bench or seat built beside a fireplace, frequently used in Arts and Crafts and bungalow designs published in *The Craftsman*.

Ionic order. The order in Greek, Roman, and Renaissance architecture in which the column capital consisted of two volutes (scrolls) above which was a thin abacus and below which typically was an egg and dart molding. The shafts of Ionic columns were usually fluted and rested on bases with torus moldings. The frieze in the entablature of an Ionic temple consisted of horizontal bands, without ornamentation, and the tympanum of Ionic temples were usually devoid of sculpture.

Italianate style. A style derived loosely from Renaissance-era villas of the Medicis in fifteenth-century Italy and developed in architecture guides and pattern books in England and the United States from about 1845 to 1880. Houses or commercial buildings with Italianate features typically have projecting cornices supported by ornamental brackets, arched windows and doorways, hipped roofs, asymmetrical plans, and occasionally towers.

Italian Renaissance style. Buildings of all types with designs that are modeled on palaces, churches, civic buildings, and villas in Italy during the fifteenth and sixteenth centuries. Such designs derived in part from a revival of interest in the architecture of ancient Rome.

Jacobean architecture. A continuation of some elements of Elizabethan architecture in palaces and great houses, with increased influence of Flemish free interpretations of the Renaissance orders for the facades and interiors and use of strap-work stucco decorations. Jacobean great houses tended to be constructed of brick, with stone quoins and surrounds for windows and tall projecting bays.

Jerkinhead gable. A gable that is truncated with a flat, triangular surface.

Jetty. In a traditional English heavy timber building or in seventeenth-century New England timber buildings, the projection of an upper story (or gable) beyond the story below.

Jigsaw. A sawing machine invented in the nineteenth century with a vertically reciprocating saw that can cut curved and irregular lines in wood. Much of the ornamental detail in Italianate, Stick style, and Queen Anne architecture was created using jigsaws.

Keystone. The central stone in an arch, sometimes carved.

King post. In late English architecture of the fourteenth through sixteenth centuries, the king post was part of an exposed structural system to support the roofs of great halls. It refers to a vertical timber standing at center on a tie or collar beam and rising to the apex of the roof, where it supported the ridge.

Kittanning brick. Brick produced in Kittanning, Armstrong County, Pennsylvania.

Lancet window. A narrow window, usually in a church, with an acutely pointed head and without tracery.

Lantern. A small cupola or towerlike feature crowning a larger one on the apex or ridge of a building roof. The lantern can serve as an ornament or to admit light.

Latin cross. A church plan in which there are three short arms and one long arm.

Light. A window or pane in a window that admits light to a building.

Lintel. A horizontal beam or stone bridging an opening, such as a window or door.

Loggia. A roofed open gallery, usually integrated into the face of a building or wall.

Louis XV style. Classical and Rococo design popular during the reign of French king Louis XV (1715–74). As used in American buildings such as the James Allison House, the Louis XV style denoted interiors with Rococo decorative designs.

Lunette. A semicircular opening in a building.

Luxfer light transoms. Transoms first produced by the Luxfer Prism Company of Chicago that, through a grid containing glass prisms, provided an abundance of daylight to the interiors of stores especially.

Machicolations. Parapets that project on brackets or corbels over the top of walls. In medieval castles, there would be openings between the corbels through which defenders could drop missiles or boiling oil on attackers.

Mansard roof. A roof that has a double slope, the lower being longer and steeper than the upper. Named after seventeenth-century French architect François Mansart and used in Second Empire–style architecture.

Matte tile. Tile with a dull finish.

Metope. The square space between two triglyphs in the frieze of a Doric temple or other building in Greek or Roman architecture.

Modillion. A horizontal bracket or console, usually in the form of a scroll with acanthus leaves but sometimes in the form of a plain block appearing directly below the cornice in a Greek, Roman, or Renaissance-style building.

Molding. An element of decoration treated to introduce varieties of outline or contour in edges or surfaces, both on projections and on cavities. A molding can appear on cornices, capitals, bases, door and window surrounds, and heads. It can be made of varied materials: stone, stucco, wood, or metal. Generally, a molding may be rectilinear or curved.

Monitor roof. A structure running above the ridge of a gable roof that contains along its long sides clerestory windows or louvers to light or ventilate the area within the building. Usually, the monitor has its own roof.

Mullions. A slender bar dividing the lights of a window or screen.

Narthex. In Roman and Byzantine churches, a vestibule at the west end that precedes the nave and aisles. In many American churches of the nineteenth and early twentieth centuries, a vestibule preceding the auditorium.

NeoBaroque style. In architecture, buildings or monuments of the nineteenth and early twentieth centuries inspired by churches, palaces, monuments, and civic spaces especially in Italy and France during the seventeenth and early eighteenth centuries. For civic squares, NeoBaroque often specified obelisks or colossal columns enriched by statuary and fountains that dominated the square, piazza, or circle.

Newel post. The principal post at the lower end of a flight of stairs, often carved or ornamented in nineteenth- and early twentieth-century stairways.

Oculus. A circular opening in a wall or at the apex of a dome.

Ogee arch. A pointed arch having on each side an S-shaped curve.

Oriel window. A large bay window, usually supported by a corbel or bracket.

Out-lot. A unit of land created in the 1820s when the area donated by the federal government as the site for the Indiana state capital and not taken for the Mile Square was subdivided.

Palladian/Venetian window. A window or archway with three openings, the central one arched, higher, and wider than the others, which are rectangular. The motif was popularized by the sixteenth-century Italian architect Andrea Palladio and is also known as a Serlian or Venetian window.

Parapet. Usually, a low wall at the edge of a roof.

Pavilion. A projecting subdivision of some larger building, usually square but sometimes curved. A pavilion often forms a feature of interest on a facade or terminates wings. A pavilion may also be an ornamental building, separately constructed, on the grounds of a larger property.

Pediment. In Greek, Roman, and Renaissance architecture, a triangular gable above the portico in a temple or other building. The outline of a pediment is generally lined by projecting moldings. The interior of a pediment may be empty or filled with sculpture. In Renaissance and nineteenth-century European and American architecture, pediments were also used as ornamental devices above doors and windows and could be triangular, curved, or broken.

Pendentive. A spherical triangle of masonry placed at each of the four corners below a dome that supports the dome and transfers the thrust down to the piers below.

Pergola. A frame structure, usually in a garden with an open, wood-framed roof, supported by regularly spaced posts or columns.

Permanent polychromy (constructive coloration). The use of clays of different colors to produce bricks or terra-cotta of multiple colors in order to create a decorative scheme in a building. Constructive coloration was first used in England with High Victorian Gothic churches of the 1850s and spread during the rest of the nineteenth century to varied building types involving different styles.

Picturesque. In architecture, the use of interesting, asymmetrical dispositions of forms and a variety of textures, seen especially in the Italianate, Stick, Romanesque, Queen Anne, Arts and Crafts, and Rustic styles.

Pier. A piece of wall between two openings or an extra mass of masonry or brick used to stiffen a wall.

Pilaster. A structural pier along a wall that is styled as a flat, rectangular version of a Greek or Roman column or an ornamental, purely decorative feature styled as a column with a rectangular profile.

Pinnacle. An upright feature, usually ending in a small spire, on a flying or stepped buttress in Gothic architecture.

Plinth. A block serving as the base for a column or statue.

Podium. In the architecture of the Roman Republic, a rectangular foundation that supported the cella and portico of a temple.

Porte cochere. A porch for carriages, usually attached to the side of a large nineteenth- or early twentieth-century house, next to a side entrance.

Portico. In Greek, Roman, and Renaissance architecture, a porch consisting of a roof supported by columns.

Proscenium. The arched framework that appears above the stage of many pre-1930 theaters.

Pyramidal. Having four triangular faces meeting at a point.

Quadripartite vault. A masonry vault in which each bay is divided into four quarters or cells.

Quatrefoil. An ornamental foliated (vegetative) motif having four lobes (foils).

Queen Anne style. An eclectic style first developed in England by Richard Norman Shaw and Eden Nesfield and based on architecture of the reigns of William and Mary and Queen Anne and on Elizabethan country houses and cottages. In the United States, during the style's later stage in the 1890s, Queen Anne houses drew freely from varied English sources and emphasized an asymmetrical silhouette, turrets with conical roofs, and expansive verandas.

Quoins. Dressed rectangular blocks, usually of stone, placed at the corners of a masonry building, especially in Italian Renaissance architecture and the Italianate style in the United States. The faces of the blocks usually alternate large and small in size.

Raking. Sloping, as in a raking floor.

Reinforced concrete. Concrete in which iron or steel bars are inserted to increase the tensile strength of the concrete.

Renaissance style. A style deriving from the revival of ancient Roman architecture in Italy and Western Europe between about 1500 and 1650 and again in Europe and the United States during the nineteenth and early twentieth centuries.

Reveal. The side of an opening for a window, doorway, etc., between the frame and the outer surface of the wall.

Richardsonian Romanesque. Designs reflecting the influence of Boston architect Henry Hobson Richardson (1838–86), who drew from the Romanesque architecture of southern France and northern Spain for many of his designs.

Rock-faced. Said of stone on the facade of a building that is dressed to resemble the natural appearance of stone.

Rococo style. A type of decorative interior design originating in France of the early eighteenth century in which shell- and coral-like forms and many S curves and C curves were used in a light, elegant manner in plaster on walls and ceilings.

Roman brick. Long, horizontal bricks with a short vertical dimension, first used in Roman architecture and later introduced in the United States by such architects as McKim, Mead, and White and Frank Lloyd Wright.

Romanesque style. A type of architecture that developed from late Roman imperial basilicas and reached its height in Italy and western Europe between about 800 and 1100. Characterized by round arches, barrel vaults, rounded piers, and use of arcades, Romanesque became popular in nineteenth-century Europe and in the United States from about 1850 to 1900. In its late stage, during the 1880s and 1890s, Romanesque in the United States was particularly influenced by the designs of Henry Hobson Richardson of Boston.

Rookwood tile. A type of ceramic pottery developed by the Rookwood Pottery Company of Cincinnati during the 1890s in which terra-cotta scenes in multiple colors for building interiors were produced by the company in a large client area in the Midwest and elsewhere.

Rosette. A sculptural ornament resembling a roundel with the shape of a rose.

Rose window. A circular window in Romanesque and Gothic architecture with foils (lobes) or patterned tracery arranged like spokes in a wheel.

Roundel. A circular panel, window, or niche.

Rusticated. Treatment of stone blocks, usually used for the foundation or ground story of a Renaissance-style building, in which smooth, dressed blocks are separated from each other by deep joints with chamfered edges.

Rustic style. Describing houses built between about 1880 and 1910 in which the design incorporates natural materials, such as fieldstones and boulders, and horizontal massing in an effort to blend in with a natural setting.

Scagliola. A material composed of cement or plaster and marble chips or coloring matter and finished to resemble marble. Frequently used for the shafts of columns in the early twentieth century but first used by the Romans in antiquity.

Screen. A partition wall of stone, brick, or wood.

Segmental arch. A circular arch in which the intrados (inner curve or underside) is less than a semicircle.

Segmental pediment. A pediment in which the upper sides form a segmental arch.

Shingle style. A term coined by architectural historian Vincent Scully to describe houses built between about 1875 and 1900 in which much of the exterior walls were covered with wooden shingles, inspired by seventeenth-century New England colonial residences.

Shotgun house. A narrow, gable-front frame house, one room wide, that is common in southern states and the Ohio River Valley, derived from the vernacular traditions of the South and possibly from folk architecture of the West Indies and ultimately from Africa. The term may derive from the Yoruba language word *togun*, referring to a house or gathering place.[2]

Side lights. A framed section of fixed glass appearing on either side of a door, especially in Federal and Greek Revival houses.

Spandrel. 1. The triangular surface between two arches in an arcade. 2. In a multistory office building, a wall panel filling the space between the top of the window in one story and the sill of the window in the story above.

Stepped buttress. A buttress in Gothic architecture in which the outside profile is of steps proceeding outward from the wall being reinforced to provide additional support for the thrust.

Stick style. A term coined by architectural historian Vincent Scully to describe asymmetrical wood frame houses built between about 1860 and 1880 in the United States in which the structure of the frame is exposed on the exterior and two-dimensional bargeboards hang from gables.

Stretcher. The long edge of a brick.

Stringcourse. A continuous horizontal band or molding running across the surface of an exterior wall or projecting from it.

Stucco and timber construction. Construction used in vernacular buildings of England and northern Europe of the fifteenth and sixteenth centuries especially, in which the structural timbers of the frame construction are exposed on the exterior and the intervening spaces filled with stucco or plaster on lath.

Swan's neck pediment. A broken pediment in which the two outer slopes of the pediment form S-curves and frequently end in volutes (scrolls). In the base of the pediment, often an urn or other device fills the open space between the two sides.

Tabernacle. A decorative stone niche on the exterior of especially Gothic-style churches, sometimes carrying a statue but often serving as a finial on a buttress.

Tensile strength. Resistance of a horizontal member or beam to longitudinal stress.

Terrace. In early twentieth-century American domestic architecture, a paved, open porch along the facade, side, or rear of a house.

Terra-cotta. Hard, unglazed, fired clay cast in molds and used for ornament, roof tiles, and floor tiles.

Tetrastyle. A portico with four frontal columns.

Tie beam. In English traditional construction, a horizontal timber that connects two opposite rafters at their lower ends to prevent them from spreading.

Tourelle. A turret corbelled out from a masonry wall.

Tracery. The curvilinear, openwork shapes of stone or wood that create patterns within the upper part of a Gothic window.

Transepts. The transverse (cross or side) arms of a cruciform plan in a cathedral or church, usually located between the nave and the chancel.

Transom window. Usually, a window appearing above the head of a door.

Transverse rib. A projecting band or molding following the line of an arch separating two bays of masonry vaults in a Gothic cathedral or church.

Triglyphs. In Greek Doric architecture, blocks separating the metopes in a temple frieze. Each triglyph block has two vertical grooves (glyphs) at the center and half grooves at the edge.

Tudor palace architecture. Architecture of palaces and college buildings in England during the reigns of the Tudor monarchs, 1485–1603, characterized by usually redbrick walls with stone trim, gatehouses with turrets, oriel windows, faceted bays, the beginnings of Italian Renaissance details, E-shaped or H-shaped plans, great halls with hammerbeam roofs, etc.

Turned post. A post rotated on a lathe to produce decorative forms, most often associated with Queen Anne houses and worker's cottages of the post–Civil War era in the United States.

Turret. A little tower, often merely ornamental, found at a corner or angle of a larger building; especially found in Richardsonian Romanesque buildings and Queen Anne–style houses.

Tuscan column. An order by tradition invented by the Etruscans but more probably invented by the Romans and adapted from the Doric order. Columns in the order have plain shafts, bases with torus moldings, and plain friezes.

Tympanum. The triangular or segmental space enclosed by the moldings of a pediment, derived from Greek and Roman architecture.

Veranda. An open, roofed porch, usually wood frame, that is attached to the first story of a house, particularly houses in the United States built between 1880 and 1900, and associated especially with Queen Anne architecture.

Vernacular architecture. Forms of building based on regional traditions and materials. In Indiana, vernacular architecture derived from building traditions in England and Scotland that crossed the Atlantic to the eastern seaboard and was brought by settlers to the state of Indiana.

Vitrified brick. Brick fired in the kiln to produce a glassy surface.

Volute. A spiral or scroll-like ornament used widely in Greek, Roman, and Renaissance architecture and later in revivals of such architecture in Europe and the United States.

Voussoir. A wedge-shaped stone forming part of an arch in a building.

Wrought iron. A form of iron that is highly malleable and can be worked into a variety of shapes. Wrought iron has high tensile strength, making it suitable for beams in structural systems in buildings.

APPENDIX B

ARCHITECTURAL STYLE GUIDE

Federal style. E. Sachse & Co., *View of Indianapolis* (Baltimore: J. T. Palmatary, 1854). Indiana Historical Society.

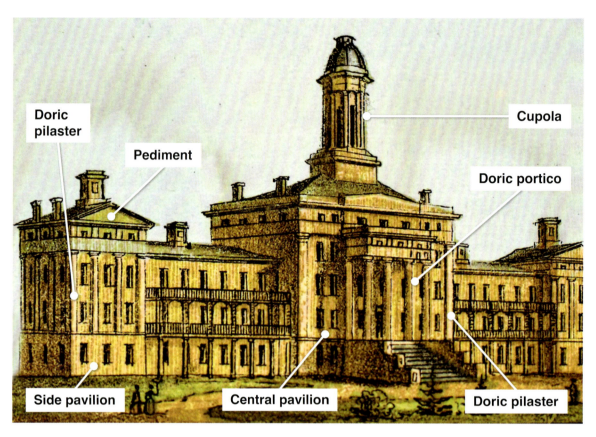

Greek Revival style. E. Sachse & Co., *View of Indianapolis* (Baltimore: J. T. Palmatary, 1854). Indiana Historical Society.

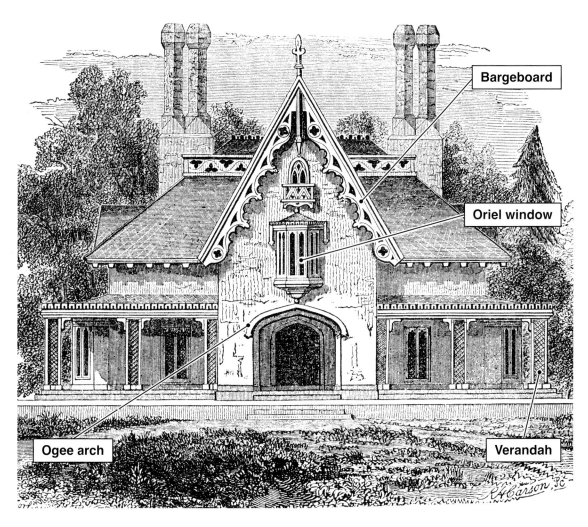

Gothic houses/cottages. A. J. Downing, *The Architecture of Country Houses*, first published in 1850 (New York: Dover, 1969), figure 128.

ARCHITECTURAL STYLE GUIDE | 513

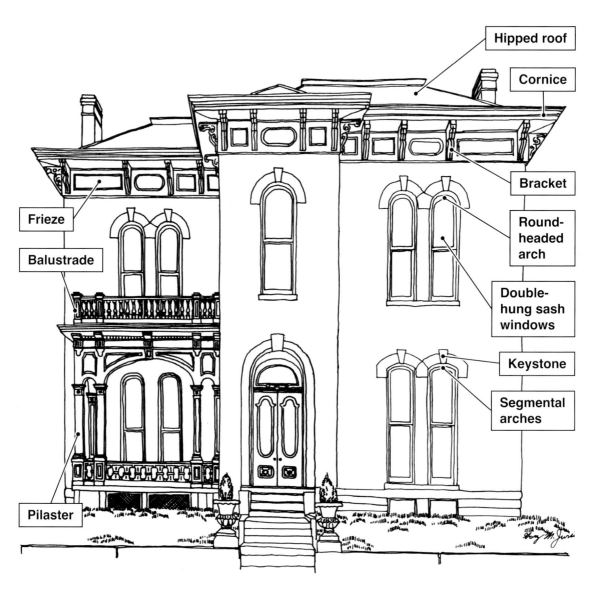

Italianate style. Drawing by Gary M. Jursik, *Historical Preservation Area Plan 1—Lockerbie Square* (Indianapolis: Department of Metropolitan Development and Indianapolis Historic Preservation Commission, 1978), 47.

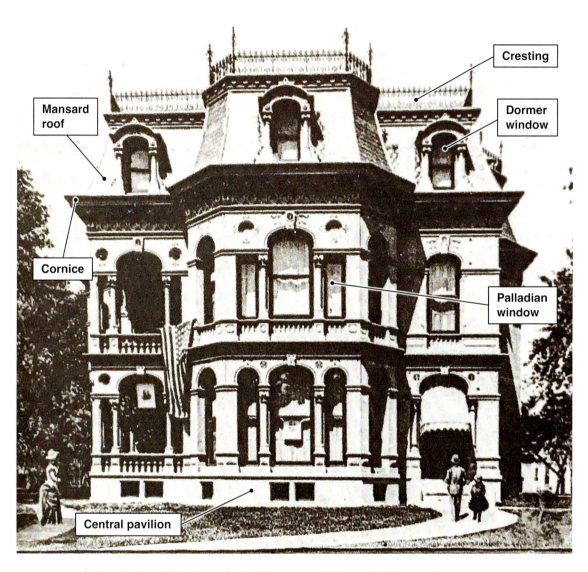

French Second Empire style. A. Wittemann, *Indianapolis Illustrated* (New York: Albertype, 1888).

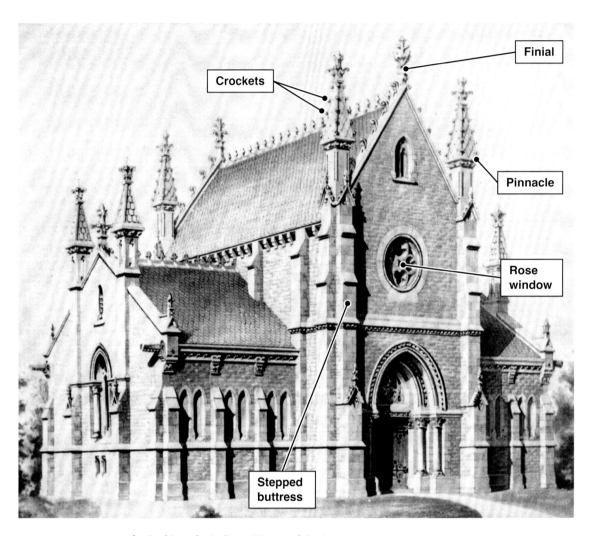

| **Gothic style.** Indiana Historical Society.

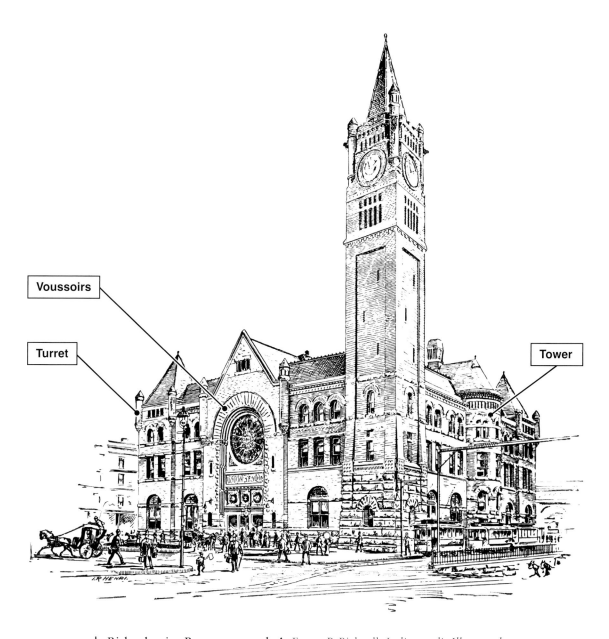

Richardsonian Romanesque style A. Ernest P. Bicknell, *Indianapolis Illustrated* (Indianapolis: Baker-Randolph Lith. & Eng. Co., 1893), 11.

ARCHITECTURAL STYLE GUIDE | 517

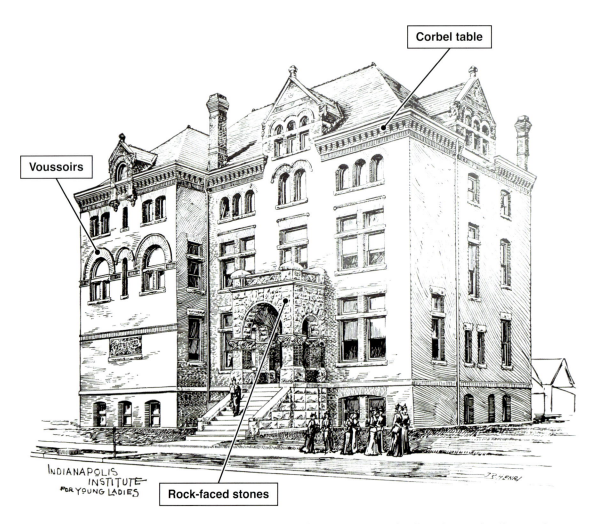

Richardsonian Romanesque style B. Ernest P. Bicknell, *Indianapolis Illustrated* (Indianapolis: Baker-Randolph Lith. & Eng. Co., 1893), 215.

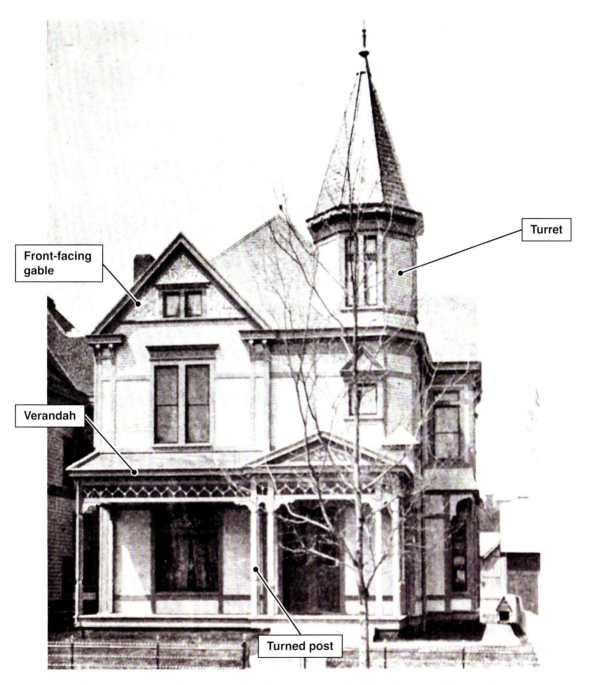

Queen Anne style—turret and gable. Ernest P. Bicknell, *Indianapolis Illustrated* (Indianapolis: Baker-Randolph Lith. & Eng. Co., 1893), 94.

ARCHITECTURAL STYLE GUIDE | 519

Queen Anne style—without turret. *Art Work of Indianapolis and Vicinity* (Chicago: Gravure Illustration, 1908).

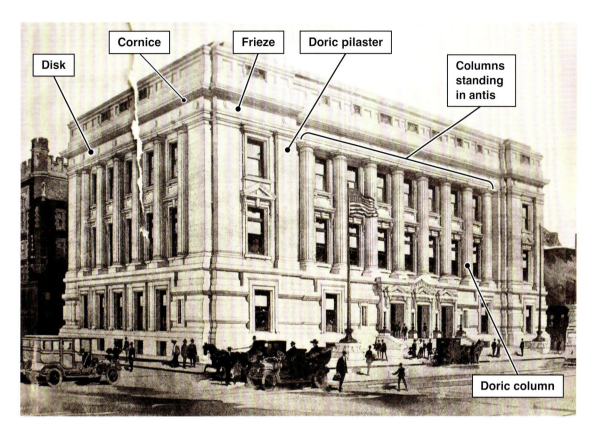

Classical style. Jacob Piatt Dunn, *Greater Indianapolis* (Chicago: Lewis, 1910), frontispiece.

ARCHITECTURAL STYLE GUIDE | 521

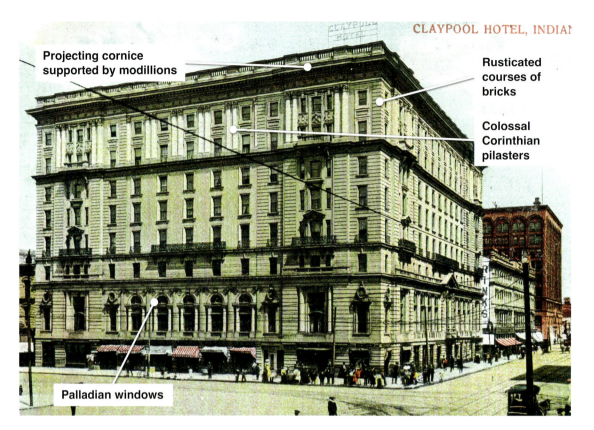

| **Italian Renaissance style.** Postcard, c. 1910, from author's collection.

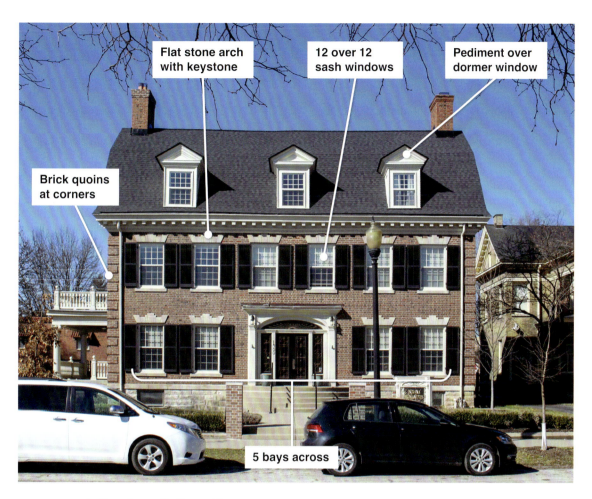

| **Georgian style.** James Glass, 2021.

ARCHITECTURAL STYLE GUIDE | 523

Chicago skyscraper three-part formula, based on a classical column. *Year Book of the Indiana Chapter A.I.A. and Catalog of the Third Annual Exhibition* (Indianapolis: Indiana Chapter A.I.A., 1912).

NOTES

INTRODUCTION

1. Jacob Piatt Dunn first quoted this statement in his *Greater Indianapolis: The History, the Industries, the Institutions, and the People of a City of Homes* (Chicago: Lewis, 1910), I:29.
2. See, for example, the *Center Township, Marion County Interim Report* (Indianapolis: Indiana Landmarks and Indiana Division of Historic Preservation and Archaeology, 1991).

1. COMMERCIAL AND INDUSTRIAL ARCHITECTURE, 1900-1920

1. "Introductory," in *R. L. Polk & Co.'s Indianapolis City Directory for 1907* (Indianapolis: R. L. Polk, 1907), 73. The "largest inland city" reference apparently related to Indianapolis being the most sizeable municipality not on a major body of water or major river.
2. Ibid.; "Introductory," in *R. L. Polk & Co.'s Indianapolis City Directory for 1913* (Indianapolis: R. L. Polk, 1913), 68.
3. "Introductory," in *R. L. Polk & Co.'s Indianapolis City Directory for 1900* (Indianapolis: R. L. Polk, 1900), [65]; "Introductory," in *R. L. Polk & Co.'s Indianapolis City Directory for 1913*, 68.
4. "Indianapolis of To-Day as Viewed by the Commercial Club," in *R. L. Polk & Co.'s Indianapolis City Directory for 1910* (Indianapolis: R. L. Polk, 1910), 74–75; "Introductory," in *R. L. Polk & Co.'s Indianapolis City Directory for 1900*, 65; "Indianapolis," in *R. L. Polk & Co.'s Indianapolis City Directory for 1916* (Indianapolis: R. L. Polk, 1916), 20.
5. "Indianapolis of To-Day as Viewed by the Commercial Club," 75; "Introductory," in *R. L. Polk & Co.'s Indianapolis City Directory for 1913*, 68; "Indianapolis," in *R. L. Polk & Co.'s Indianapolis City Directory for 1916*, 20; Clifton J. Phillips, *Indiana in Transition: The Emergence of an Industrial Commonwealth 1880–1920* (Indianapolis: Indiana Historical Bureau and Indiana Historical Society, 1968), 274, 315.
6. "Introductory," in *R. L. Polk & Co.'s Indianapolis City Directory for 1907*, 73; "Introductory," in *R. L. Polk & Co.'s Indianapolis City Directory for 1913*, 70.
7. "Indianapolis," in *R. L. Polk & Co.'s Indianapolis City Directory for 1916*, 20.
8. For discussion of each firm's contributions, see Carl W. Condit, *The Chicago School of Architecture: A History of Commercial and Public Building in the Chicago Area 1875–1925* (Chicago: University of Chicago Press, 1964), 79–142.

9. See previous discussion in chapter 7 of volume 1. For a sampling of both Chicago and New York skyscraper designs between 1880 and 1920, see Winston Weisman, "A New View of Skyscraper History," in *The Rise of an American Architecture*, ed. Edgar Kaufmann Jr. (New York: Praeger, 1970).

10. [Announcement of Newton Claypool Building], *Indianapolis Journal*, November 18, 1900, 7; Another Large Building," *Indianapolis News*, December 5, 1900, 11; *R. L. Polk & Co.'s Indianapolis City Directory for 1901* (Indianapolis: R. L. Polk, 1901), 285; *R. L. Polk & Co.'s Indianapolis City Directory for 1902* (Indianapolis: R. L. Polk, 1902), 144, 297; *Insurance Maps of Indianapolis, Indiana 1914* (New York: Sanborn Map Co., 1914), vol. 1, plan 38.

11. "Another Large Building," *Indianapolis News*, December 5, 1900, 11.

12. "Draft of Franchise; Conference on Interurban Terminal Question To-Morrow," *Indianapolis Journal*, July 27, 1902, 12, c. 2; Phillips, *Indiana in Transition*, 257.

13. "Draft of Franchise; Conference on Interurban Terminal Question To-Morrow"; "Will Open Terminal Station Bids Monday," *Indianapolis News*, June 12, 1903, 15, c. 3; Thomas S. Hines, *Burnham of Chicago: Architect and Planner* (Chicago: University of Chicago Press, 1979), 285.

14. *Insurance Maps of Indianapolis, Indiana 1914*, vol. 1, plan 36.

15. Ibid.; "Will Open Terminal Station Bids Monday"; Phillips, *Indiana in Transition*, 257.

16. "Will Build Home on Pyle House Site," *Indianapolis Star*, June 20, 1905, 1; "Board of Trade Plans," *Indianapolis News*, August 19, 1905, 14; *R. L. Polk & Co.'s Indianapolis City Directory for 1904* (Indianapolis: R. L. Polk, 1904), 264, 411; *R. L. Polk & Co.'s Indianapolis City Directory for 1905* (Indianapolis: R. L. Polk, 1905), 275, 436, and 1290.

17. "Board of Trade Plans"; "Ready for the Roof," *Indianapolis News*, September 11, 1906, 7; *Insurance Maps of Indianapolis, Indiana 1914*, vol. 1, plan 38.

18. "Fourteen Sets of Plans," *Indianapolis Star*, January 10, 1905, 7; "K. of P. Grand Lodge Building," *Indianapolis News*, July 21, 1905, 14; "Tenants of the New K. of P. Building," *Indianapolis Star*, April 14, 1907, 27; Quentin Robinson, "James F. Alexander," Tippecanoe County Historical Association, accessed August 11, 2021, https://tippecanoehistory.org/finding-aids/james-f-alexander/; Margaret M. Scott, "New Buildings Reflect City's Growth in Appreciation of Commercial Art," *Indianapolis Star*, September 11, 1927, 40.

19. *Insurance Maps of Indianapolis, Indiana 1914*, vol. 1, plan 52.

20. *R. L. Polk & Co.'s Indianapolis City Directory for 1908* (Indianapolis: R. L. Polk, 1908), 780; *R. L. Polk & Co.'s Indianapolis City Directory for 1914* (Indianapolis: R. L. Polk, 1914), 1722; *Insurance Maps of Indianapolis, Indiana 1914*, vol. 1, plan 52.

21. "New Home Planned," *Indianapolis Star*, November 23, 1906, 1.

22. Scott, "New Buildings Reflect City's Growth in Appreciation of Commercial Art."

23. Ibid.; *Insurance Maps of Indianapolis, Indiana 1914*, vol. 1, plan 52.

24. "To Consider Plan for Larger Building," *Indianapolis Star*, November 19, 1906, 3.

25. Ibid.; "Plans for New Structure," *Indianapolis Star*, November 22, 1906, 10; *Insurance Maps of Indianapolis, Indiana 1914*, vol. 1, plan 40.

26. "Plans for New Structure"; Scott, "New Buildings Reflect City's Growth in Appreciation of Commercial Art."

27. "Plans for New Structure"; *R. L. Polk & Co.'s Indianapolis City Directory for 1914*, 1788.

28. "Leases Hinder Bank's Plans," *Indianapolis Star*, January 22, 1907, 10; "Bank Building Under Way," *Indianapolis Star*, August 25, 1907, 13; "Merchants' National Bank to Have Reception To-Day, and to Begin Business in Its New Home on Monday," *Indianapolis News*, April 25, 1908, 8.

29. "Bank Building Under Way"; "Big Building Is to Be Ready by September 1, 1912," *Indianapolis News*, November 3, 1911, 7.

30. "Big Building Is to Be Ready by September 1, 1912."

31. "Merchants' National Bank to Have Reception To-Day, and to Begin Business in Its New Home on Monday."

32. "Big Building Is to Be Ready by September 1, 1912."

33. "New Buildings Are of Artistic Design," *Indianapolis Star*, March 21, 1909, 47.

34. Ibid.

35. "New Building of the Indianapolis News," *Indianapolis News*, September 11, 1909, 11; Phillips, *Indiana in Transition*, 53; Samuel A. Roberson & Associates, National Register of Historic Places Inventory-Nomination Form for Indianapolis News Building, November 18, 1983, SHAARD database, Indiana Division of Historic Preservation and Archaeology.

36. "New Building of the Indianapolis News."

37. Ibid.; *Insurance Maps of Indianapolis, Indiana 1914*, vol. 1, plan 37.

38. "Plans for New Bobbs-Merrill Building," *Indianapolis News*, January 29, 1910, 28; Jack O'Bar, "The Origins and History of the Bobbs-Merrill Company" (occasional paper 172, University of Illinois Graduate School of Library and Information Science, December 1985), 10, https://core.ac.uk/download/pdf/4814034.pdf.

39. "Plan for New Bobbs-Merrill Building"; "Herbert Willard Foltz," in *Indianapolis Men of Affairs 1923*, edited by Paul Donald Brown (Indianapolis: American Biographical Society, 1923), 199.

40. "Plan for New Bobbs-Merrill Building."

41. Ibid.; *Insurance Maps of Indianapolis, Indiana 1914*, vol. 1, plan 67.

42. "New Office Block Will Cost $500,000," *Indianapolis Star*, February 21, 1911, 1.

43. Ibid.; *Insurance Maps of Indianapolis, Indiana 1914*, vol. 1, plan 38.

44. "Crowns Property Worth $1,000,000," *Indianapolis Star*, December 17, 1911, 22; *Insurance Maps of Indianapolis, Indiana 1914*, vol. 1, plan 38.

45. "Steps Taken to Erect Building of Ten Stories," *Indianapolis Star*, January 15, 1915, 1; *R. L. Polk & Co.'s Indianapolis City Directory for 1916*, 1518; *R. L. Polk & Co.'s Indianapolis City Directory for 1917* (Indianapolis: R. L. Polk, 1917), 1559.

46. "Kahn Building Marks New Era," *Indianapolis Star*, December 9, 1915, 9; Scott, "New Buildings Reflect City's Growth in Appreciation of Commercial Art," 40.

47. "Kahn Building Marks New Era."

48. "Plans for 16-Story Bank Building Due Tomorrow," *Indianapolis Star*, November 24, 1912, 40; "New Fletcher Trust Building, One of Finest in Country, Is Partially Opened to Tenants," *Indianapolis Star*, September 30, 1914, 9; *R. L. Polk & Co.'s Indianapolis City Directory for 1914*, 544.

49. "Contest for Architects," *Indianapolis News*, December 2, 1912, 2; "Skyscraper Plans in Hands of Expert Jury," *Indianapolis News*, December 3, 1912, 4; "Fletcher Block Design Chosen," *Indianapolis Star*, December 5, 1912, 16.

50. "Fletcher Block Design Chosen."

51. "Architect of Fletcher Trust Building Is Here," *Indianapolis News*, December 17, 1912, 10; "New Fletcher Trust Building, One of Finest in Country, Is Partially Opened to Tenants"; "Fletcher Savings and Trust Company," *Indianapolis News*, January 23, 1915, 12; Anton Scherrer, "City Architecture of the Year Considered from Artistic Viewpoint," *Indianapolis Star*, December 31, 1914, 31.

52. "New Fletcher Trust Building, One of Finest in Country, Is Partially Opened to Tenants."

53. Ibid.; "Fletcher Savings and Trust Company."

54. "New Seven-Story Block," *Indianapolis News*, January 26, 1900, 8.

55. "Plans Ready for M'Ouat Block," *Indianapolis News*, April 17, 1901, 18; *R. L. Polk & Co.'s Indianapolis City Directory for 1901*, 1138, 1190; *R. L. Polk & Co.'s Indianapolis City Directory for 1903* (Indianapolis: R. L. Polk, 1903), 185; Max R. Hyman, ed., *The Journal Handbook of Indianapolis* (Indianapolis: Indianapolis Journal Newspaper, 1902), 370–71.

56. *R. L. Polk & Co.'s Indianapolis City Directory for 1903*, 185; Hyman, *The Journal Handbook of Indianapolis*, 370.

57. Elizabeth Periale, "Alexander Turney Stewart, Father of the Department Store," *Unbound* (blog), Smithsonian Libraries and Archives, September 14, 2010, https://blog.library.si.edu/blog/2010/09/14/alexander-turney-stewart/#.YRUq64hKg2w.

58. "Showing Progress to Date on the Ayres Building at Washington and Meridian Streets," *Indianapolis Star*, April 17, 1905, 2; *Insurance Maps of Indianapolis, Indiana 1914*, vol. 1, plan 21; "Sculptor's Work Graces Towering Edifices; Home Is Art and Love," *Indianapolis Sun*, October 8, 1911, 10.

59. "Showing Progress to Date on the Ayres Building at Washington and Meridian Streets."

60. Max R. Hyman, ed., *Hyman's Handbook of Indianapolis* (Indianapolis: M. R. Hyman, 1909), 226.

61. "Lets Building Contract," *Indianapolis Star*, September 20, 1910, 14.

62. Ibid.; *Insurance Maps of Indianapolis, Indiana 1914*, vol. 1, plan 36; Scott, "New Buildings Reflect City's Growth in Appreciation of Commercial Art."

63. "Lets Building Contract."

64. "Ayres Company Plans Addition," *Indianapolis Star*, July 11, 1914, 1, 3; "Every Convenience Is Planned in New Store," *Indianapolis News*, July 11, 1914, 7.

65. "New Buildings Are of Artistic Design," *Indianapolis Sunday Star*, March 21, 1909, 47; "Preston C. Rubush," biographical article in Jacob Piatt Dunn, *Indiana and Indianans* (Chicago: American Historical Society, 1919), V, 2241.

66. "Leonard Geiger Adds New Store," *Indianapolis Star*, March 11, 1917, 8.

67. "New Buildings Are of Artistic Design," *Indianapolis Sunday Star*, March 21, 1909, 47.

68. "Garage Buildings to Be Erected on Capitol Avenue," *Indianapolis Star*, March 27, 1911, 10.

69. "New Building for Automobile Row," *Indianapolis Star*, July 26, 1914, 10; *Insurance Maps of Indianapolis, Indiana Republished 1956* (New York: Sanborn Map Co., 1956), vol. 1, plan 81.

70. "$90,000 Building for Autos Begun," *Indianapolis Star*, March 24, 1917, 9.

71. "Plans for New Hotel," *Indianapolis Journal*, December 7, 1899, 8, c. 4; "Claypool Hotel Stock," *Indianapolis News*, April 11, 1900, 3, c. 2; "Hotels Examined," *Indianapolis Journal*, May 7, 1900, 8, c. 5; "Chicago Firm Wins," *Indianapolis Journal*, June 9, 1901, 8, c. 2; "Magnificent New Claypool Will Open To-Morrow," *Indianapolis Journal*, May 17, 1903, Edition 2, 1, c. 1.

72. "Magnificent New Claypool Will Open To-Morrow."

73. *Insurance Maps of Indianapolis, Indiana 1914*, vol. 1, plan 36.

74. Ibid.; "Magnificent New Claypool Will Open To-Morrow."

75. "Architect Tells of Big Changes," *Indianapolis Star*, March 28, 1915, 58.

76. "Work Is Begun on Skyscraper Hotel," *Indianapolis News*, February 5, 1912, 1; *Insurance Maps of Indianapolis, Indiana 1914*, vol. 1, plan 38.

77. "Work Is Begun on Skyscraper Hotel."

78. "New Company Signs Severin Hotel Lease," *Indianapolis Star*, May 22, 1912, 1; "New Hotel Ranks Among Greatest," *Indianapolis Star*, August 24, 1913, 1, 8; *R. L. Polk & Co.'s Indianapolis City Directory for 1913*, 1109, 1438.

79. "New Hotel Ranks among Greatest; *Insurance Maps of Indianapolis, Indiana 1914*, vol. 1, plan 6; Scott, "New Buildings Reflect City's Growth in Appreciation of Commercial Art," 40.

80. "New Company Signs Severin Hotel Lease"; "New Hotel Ranks among Greatest."

81. "Talks of Plans of New Majestic Theater," *Indianapolis News*, March 13, 1907, 3; Howard Caldwell, *Golden Age of Indianapolis Theaters* (Indianapolis: Quarry Books, 2010), 58–59; *Insurance Maps of Indianapolis, Indiana 1914*, vol. 1, plan 18.

82. "Morris Inspects Colonial Theater," *Indianapolis Star*, November 13, 1909, 3; Caldwell, *Golden Age of Indianapolis Theaters*, 68–69; *Insurance Maps of Indianapolis, Indiana 1914*, vol. 1, plan 50.

83. "Will Consult Shuberts Regarding New Theater," *Indianapolis Star*, June 13, 1909, 28; Caldwell, *Golden Age of Indianapolis Theaters*, 69, 72; J. E. Luebering, "Shubert Brothers: American Theatrical Managers," Encyclopedia Britannica, accessed August 16, 2021, https://www.britannica.com/biography/Shubert-Brothers#ref252539.

84. "Will Consult Shuberts Regarding New Theater"; "Shubert Stage to Turn," *Indianapolis Star*, June 23, 1909, 7.

85. Leigh Darbee, "Murat Temple," in *Encyclopedia of Indianapolis*, ed. David J. Bodenhamer and Robert G. Barrows, 1026–27 (Indianapolis: Indiana University Press, 1994); John D. Hoag, *Western Islamic Architecture* (New York: George Braziller, 1963), plates 90 and 92.

86. "Sculptor's Work Graces Towering Edifices; Home Is Art and Love."

87. "Crowd Sees Trusses Set," *Indianapolis Star*, November 15, 1909, 10; "Murat Theater in the Hands of Decorators," *Indianapolis News*, February 15, 1910, 7; "Murat Theater to Be Finest in West," *Indianapolis Star*, February 20, 1910, 22; *Insurance Maps of Indianapolis, Indiana 1914*, vol. 1, plan 69.

88. "Murat Theater to Be Finest in West."

89. "Shubert Fired by Murat Enthusiasm," *Indianapolis Star*, February 22, 1910, 3. For a summary of companies and artists performing at the Murat, see Caldwell, *Golden Age of Indianapolis Theaters*, 74–76.

90. "Will Build New Picture Theater," *Indianapolis Star*, January 31, 1912, 10.

91. "Theater with 3,000 Capacity Assured," *Indianapolis News*, November 6, 1915, 1.

92. Ibid.

93. Ibid.; *Insurance Maps of Indianapolis, Indiana Republished 1956*, vol. 1, plan 58.

94. "Circle Theater Plans Reveal Many Features," *Indianapolis News*, January 29, 1916, 1; "Grecian Friezes to Feature Circle Theater," *Indianapolis News*, May 2, 1916, 13.

95. "Theater with 3,000 Capacity Assured"; "Grecian Friezes to Feature Circle Theater"; "Circle Theater Plans Reveal Many Features."

96. "Circle Theater Plans Reveal Many Features."

97. "Classic Beauty Is Restored in Circle Theater," *Indianapolis Star*, December 22, 1933, 10. Henry Richard Behrens was the brother of William F. Behrens, who supplied the decorative features of the 1900 Columbia Club building, the 1914 addition to the Claypool Hotel, and murals in the new City Hall. Henry worked on the plaster decorative features of both the 1900 and 1924–25 Columbia Club buildings. See "Membership Roster Is More than 3,000," *Indianapolis Times*, August 10, 1925, 3.

98. "Introductory," in *R. L. Polk & Co.'s Indianapolis City Directory for 1894* (Indianapolis: R. L. Polk, 1894), 58; Jacob Piatt Dunn, *Greater Indianapolis: The History, the Industries, the Institutions, and the People of a City of Homes* (Chicago: Lewis, 1910), I, 263; Wesley I. Shank, "Part I—Historical Information," Historic American Buildings Survey, 4, August 1971, https://tile.loc.gov/storage-services/master/pnp/habshaer/in/in0000/in0069/data/in0069data.pdf.

99. Shank, "Part I—Historical Information," 4; "Proposed Union Station Track Elevation," *Indianapolis Star*, April 12, 1916, 18; "Track Elevation Work in Full Blast," *Indianapolis Star* Magazine Section, July 23, 1916, 63; George E. Thomas, *Arts and Crafts to Modern Design: William L. Price* (New York: Princeton Architectural Press, 2000), 150–51, 157–58, 222–25, 352.

100. *Insurance Maps of Indianapolis, Indiana Republished 1956*, vol. 1, plans 5, 6, 7, and 8.

101. Scott, "New Buildings Reflect City's Growth in Appreciation of Commercial Art."

102. Communication from George E. Thomas to the author, September 19, 2023.

103. Thomas, *Arts and Crafts to Modern Design*, 222; "Indianapolis' Modern Union Station, Built at Cost of $2,000,000, Nearing Completion," *Indianapolis Star*, October 8, 1922, 13, 21.

104. *Insurance Maps of Indianapolis, Indiana Republished 1956*, vol. 1, plans 5 and 6.

105. "Indianapolis' Modern Union Station, Built at Cost of $2,000,000, Nearing Completion."

106. *R. L. Polk & Co.'s Indianapolis City Directory for 1913*, 68.

107. *R. L. Polk & Co.'s Indianapolis City Directory for 1907* (Indianapolis: R. L. Polk, 1907), 790; Hyman, *Hyman's Handbook of Indianapolis*, 229; *Insurance Maps of Indianapolis, Indiana Republished 1956*, vol. 1, plan 23.

108. *R. L. Polk & Co.'s Indianapolis City Directory for 1914*, 695; Arthur Bohn, obituary, Indiana Biography Series, 21:42, Indiana Division, Indiana State Library; *Insurance Maps of Indianapolis, Indiana 1914*, vol. 1, plan 20.

109. Hyman, *The Journal Handbook of Indianapolis*, 248–50; *R. L. Polk & Co.'s Indianapolis City Directory for 1914*, 1794; *Insurance Maps of Indianapolis, Indiana 1914*, vol. 1, plan 22; information provided by Professor Michael Tomlan of Cornell University, June 30, 2023.

110. "Plans $400,000 Building," *Indianapolis Star*, September 16, 1909, 1; *Insurance Maps of Indianapolis, Indiana 1914*, vol. 1, plan 20.

111. "Beech Grove Mint for Indianapolis," *Indianapolis Star*, July 31, 1910, 17.

112. George W. Bunting Jr. was the son of George W. Bunting, who designed several county courthouses in Indiana during the post–Civil War period. During the 1890s, father and son worked together in the architectural firm of G. W. Bunting and Son. See "G. W. Bunting, 81, Architect, Dies," *Indianapolis Star*, March 1, 1941, 3; *R. L. Polk & Co.'s Indianapolis City Directory for 1890* (Indianapolis: R. L. Polk, 1890), 216.

113. "Beech Grove Mint for Indianapolis"; "G. W. Bunting, 81, Architect, Dies"; *Insurance Maps of Indianapolis, Indiana 1914*, vol. 3, plan 299.

114. "Beech Grove Mint for Indianapolis."

115. "Plans $80,000 Building," *Indianapolis Star*, July 20, 1911, 11; "Tell of Roof Collapse," *Indianapolis News*, April 17, 1912, 3; *Insurance Maps of Indianapolis, Indiana 1914*, vol. 1, plan 46.

116. "Big Addition for Cole Auto Plant," *Indianapolis Star*, April 13, 1913, 41; "New Cole Factory Finished in Spring," *Indianapolis Star*, January 18, 1914, 42; "New Cole Plant Opens This Week," *Indianapolis Star*, May 24, 1914, 58; *Insurance Maps of Indianapolis, Indiana 1914*, vol. 1, plan 46.

117. Wesley I. Shank, "Cole Motor Car Company Factory: Part I. Historical Information," Historic American Buildings Survey, December 1971, https://tile.loc.gov/storage-services/master/pnp/habshaer/in/in0000/in0047/data/in0047data.pdf.

118. "Front and Side View of New Home for National Company and Scene of Building Being Erected," *Indianapolis Star*, August 29, 1915, 18; *R. L. Polk & Co.'s Indianapolis City Directory for 1915* (Indianapolis: R. L. Polk, 1915), 1040; *Insurance Maps of Indianapolis, Indiana 1915* (New York: Sanborn Map Co., 1915), vol. 4, plan 421; *Insurance Maps of Indianapolis, Indiana 1915* (New York: Sanborn Map Co., 1915, corrected to 1951), vol. 4, plan 421.

119. "Henry F. Campbell," in *Indianapolis Men of Affairs 1923*, edited by Paul Donald Brown (Indianapolis: American Biographical Society, 1923), 101; "Harry C. Stutz," in *Indianapolis Men of Affairs 1923*, edited by Paul Donald Brown (Indianapolis: American

Biographical Society, 1923), 593; *Insurance Maps of Indianapolis, Indiana 1915*, vol. 4, plan 356; "Stutz Auto Company Will Add to Plant," *Indianapolis Star*, January 26, 1916, 11; *Insurance Maps of Indianapolis, Indiana Republished 1956*, vol. 4, plan 356; M1212, Job #417, box 6, folder 11, Rubush and Hunter Collection, Indiana Historical Society Library; M1212, Job #433, box 7, folder 2, Rubush and Hunter Collection, Indiana Historical Society Library.

120. "Takes Over Tailoring Company," *Indianapolis News*, January 14, 1913, 8; "Contract for New Kahn Tailoring Company Building Awarded to Bedford Company," *Indianapolis Star*, March 6, 1913, 15; "Indianapolis Firm Rushing Out Uniforms," *Indianapolis Times*, February 28, 1918, 1, c. 3; *Insurance Maps of Indianapolis, Indiana 1914*, vol. 1, plan 92.

121. *Insurance Maps of Indianapolis, Indiana 1914*, vol. 1, plan 92.

122. See chapter 12.

123. S. L. Berry and Mary Ellen Gadski, *Stacks: A History of the Indianapolis-Marion County Public Library* (Indianapolis: Indianapolis-Marion County Public Library Foundation, 2011), 77; Phillips, *Indiana in Transition*, 596; Jare R. Cardinal and David R. Bush, National Register of Historic Places Registration Form for Fort Benjamin Harrison, March 10, 1989, Section 8, 3.

124. James H. Madison, *Indiana through Tradition and Change: A History of the Hoosier State and Its People 1920–1945* (Indianapolis: Indiana Historical Society, 1982), 204, 211.

2. PUBLIC, SOCIAL, AND CHARITABLE ARCHITECTURE, 1900–1920

1. For a review of the consequences of discrimination and segregation for the African Americans of Indianapolis and Indiana in the early twentieth century, see Emma Lou Thornbrough, *Indiana Blacks in the Twentieth Century* (Bloomington: Indiana University Press, 2001), 4–32; see also James H. Madison, *Hoosiers: A New History of Indiana* (Indianapolis: Indiana University Press and Indiana Historical Society Press, 2014), 191–96, and A'Lelia Bundles, *On Her Own Ground: The Life and Times of Madam C. J. Walker* (New York: Washington Square Press, 2001), 104.

2. "To Choose Site," *Indianapolis Journal*, March 9, 1899, 1, c. 1; "Mr. Taylor on the Sites," *Indianapolis Journal*, April 26, 1899, 8, c. 2; "John H. Rankin Here," *Indianapolis Journal*, June 5, 1901, 8, c. 3; "Indianapolis Will Change Her Postoffice Address to the Beautiful New Federal Building within the Next Two Weeks," *Indianapolis News*, September 2, 1905, 13.

3. "The Post Office Plans," *Indianapolis Journal*, November 24, 1899, 4, c. 2; "Plans by Competition," *Indianapolis News*, February 21, 1900, 3, c. 1.

4. "Local Men Lose," *Indianapolis News*, January 17, 1901, 1, c. 8.

5. "Local Men Lose"; "Federal Buildings in Indiana," *Indianapolis Journal*, October 25, 1903, Part 2, 13, c. 1.

6. "John H. Rankin Here."

7. Ibid.; *Insurance Maps of Indianapolis, Indiana 1914* (New York: Sanborn Map Co., 1914), vol. 1, plan 51.

8. "Indianapolis Will Change Her Postoffice Address to the Beautiful New Federal Building within the Next Two Weeks."

9. Ibid.; *Visitor's Guide to the Birch Bayh Federal Building and United States Courthouse* (United States District Court for the Southern District of Indiana, n.d.).

10. *Visitor's Guide to the Birch Bayh Federal Building.*

11. Ibid; Margaret M. Scott, "New Buildings Reflect City's Growth in Appreciation of Commercial Art," *Indianapolis Star*, September 11, 1927, 40.

12. Scott, "New Buildings Reflect City's Growth in Appreciation of Commercial Art."

13. "John H. Rankin Here"; "Indianapolis Will Change Her Postoffice Address to the Beautiful New Federal Building within the Next Two Weeks."

14. "Indianapolis Will Change Her Postoffice Address to the Beautiful New Federal Building within the Next Two Weeks."

15. Jare R. Cardinal and David R. Bush, National Register of Historic Places Registration Form for Fort Benjamin Harrison, March 10, 1989, Section 8, 1.

16. Ibid., Section 7, 1, and Section 8, 2.

17. Ibid., Section 7, 1, and Section 8, 2; "Detail Marks Army Post Completion," *Indianapolis Star*, July 14, 1907, 25.

18. Cardinal and Bush, National Register of Historic Places Registration Form, Section 7, 1.

19. "Detail Marks Army Post Completion."

20. Cardinal and Bush, National Register of Historic Places Registration Form, Section 7, 1.

21. The veranda of one of the barrack buildings has been removed.

22. "Detail Marks Army Post Completion."

23. "Detail Marks Army Post Completion."

24. Ibid.; Cardinal and Bush, National Register of Historic Places Registration Form, Section 8, 2.

25. "Tentative Plans for Deaf School," *Indianapolis Star*, February 6, 1906, 4.

26. Max R. Hyman, ed., *Hyman's Handbook of Indianapolis* (Indianapolis: M. R. Hyman, 1909), 120; *Insurance Maps of Indianapolis, Indiana 1914*, vol. 5, plan 587. Not all of the twenty-two buildings projected were constructed.

27. "Tentative Plans for Deaf School."

28. Photos of buildings at the Indiana School for the Deaf, c. 1910–15, Bass Photo Co. Collection, Indiana Historical Society Library.

29. Jacob Piatt Dunn, *Greater Indianapolis: The History, the Industries, the Institutions, and the People of a City of Homes* (Chicago: Lewis, 1910), I:431–32; "Architects of City Invited to Compete," *Indianapolis Star*, August 22, 1906, 14; "No Time to Draw Colosseum Plans," *Indianapolis News*, September 14, 1906, 1; "City Hall Plans Will Be Submitted Monday," *Indianapolis News*, October 30, 1908, 26; "Plans for Proposed City Hall Submitted," *Indianapolis News*, November 2, 1908, 18; "Choose City Hall Plans," *Indianapolis Star*, November 3, 1908, 1.

30. "No Time to Draw Colosseum Plans."

31. "City Hall Plans Will Be Submitted Monday."

32. *Insurance Maps of Indianapolis, Indiana 1914*, vol. 1, plan 53.

33. "Seeks to Assist Behrens," *Indianapolis Star*, January 12, 1910, 4; "Signs Away Chances for 'Little Angels,'" *Indianapolis News*, December 9, 1910, 20; Scott, "New Buildings Reflect City's Growth in Appreciation of Commercial Art," 40.

34. "Choose City Hall Plans"; "To Complete the New City Hall Building," *Indianapolis News*, November 5, 1909, 23.

35. William Herschell, "Passing of Old Fire Houses Recalls Early Days When the Volunteer Fighter Was a Social and Political Force in the Life of Indianapolis," *Indianapolis News*, November 26, 1910, 15; "Architects for Fire Headquarters Named," *Indianapolis News*, February 19, 1913, 2; "How Indianapolis New Fire Headquarters Building Will Appear," *Indianapolis Star*, May 4, 1913, 28; *Insurance Maps of Indianapolis, Indiana 1914*, vol. 1, plan 54.

36. "Architects for Fire Headquarters Named"; "How Indianapolis New Fire Headquarters Building Will Appear."

37. "Favor New Fire House Plans," *Indianapolis Star*, June 27, 1913, 14; "Bids on Engine Houses Far under Estimates," *Indianapolis News*, July 24, 1911, 4; *Insurance Maps of Indianapolis, Indiana 1915* (New York: Sanborn Map Co., 1915, corrected to 1941), vol. 5A, plan 583.

38. S. L. Berry and Mary Ellen Gadski, *Stacks: A History of the Indianapolis-Marion County Public Library* (Indianapolis: Indianapolis-Marion County Public Library Foundation, 2011), 56–59.

39. *Year Book of the Indiana Chapter A.I.A. and Catalog of the Third Annual Exhibition 1912* (Indianapolis: Indiana Chapter A.I.A., 1912), 81, copy at Indiana State Library.

40. "Sculptor's Work Graces Towering Edifices; Home Is Art and Love," *Indianapolis Sun*, October 8, 1911, 10.

41. "New Spades Park Library Follows Italian Style," *Indianapolis Star*, August 2, 1911, 7.

42. Ralph Adams Cram, "The Indianapolis Public Library," *Architectural Forum*, vol. XXIX, no. 3 (September 1918), 68.

43. Berry and Gadski, *Stacks*, 67.

44. Shortly before, Magonigle had served as one of the judges for the competition held by the Fletcher Savings and Trust Company for its downtown office building. See chapter 10 of volume 1.

45. "Noted Designer May Judge Plans," *Indianapolis Star*, October 15, 1913, 13; "25 Enter Library Contest," *Indianapolis Star*, December 11, 1913, 11; "Architects Chosen in Library Contest," *Indianapolis Star*, February 5, 1914, 1; "Library Contest Drawing to Close," *Indianapolis Star*, April 3, 1914, 15; "Judging Plans for New Library Here," *Indianapolis Star*, April 10, 1914, 6; Berry and Gadski, *Stacks*, 67–68.

46. Berry and Gadski, *Stacks*, 72.

47. Cret may have drawn the idea of a facade in which a rank of Doric columns stands in antis from the design of the Festival Hall at the Columbian Exposition of 1893. See article on "Music and Choral Halls" on the Chicagology website, n.d. https://chicagology.com/columbiaexpo/fair028/, accessed June 26, 2024.

48. Berry and Gadski, *Stacks*, 72.

49. These "stone" walls were composed of a plaster treated and scored to resemble Caen limestone in France.

50. Ibid., 70, 78.

51. Ibid., 73. The Bobbs sculpture has been removed and now is located at the Indiana University School of Medicine.

52. Ibid., 76–77.

53. "New School Buildings," *Indianapolis News*, March 22, 1901, 5, c. 3.

54. "Situation a Surprise," *Indianapolis Journal*, May 13, 1903, 7, c. 2; "Public Schools Will Open September 14," *Indianapolis News*, August 22, 1903, 14, c. 1.

55. "Public Schools Will Open September 14."

56. Ibid.; *Insurance Maps of Indianapolis, Indiana 1915* (corrected to 1941), vol. 5, plan 551.

57. "Notice to Contractors," *Indianapolis News*, March 14, 1905, 8; "Notice to Contractors," *Indianapolis Star*, April 17, 1905, 10; *Insurance Maps of Indianapolis, Indiana 1915* (New York: Sanborn Map Co., 1915, corrected to 1951), vol. 5, plan 229; "New School Will Have First Branch Library," *Indianapolis Star*, February 2, 1908, 6; *Insurance Maps of Indianapolis, Indiana 1915* (corrected to 1941), vol. 5A, plan 582.

58. "Sisters Get School Permit," *Indianapolis Star*, August 13, 1908, 3; *Insurance Maps of Indianapolis, Indiana 1915* (corrected to 1951), vol. 4, plan 367.

59. "College Building Almost Finished," *Indianapolis Star*, October 25, 1904, 2.

60. Ibid.; "New College Building of United Brethren," *Indianapolis News*, December 10, 1904, 4.

61. "College Building Almost Finished"; "New College Building of United Brethren"; *Insurance Maps of Indianapolis, Indiana 1915* (corrected to 1941), vol. 3A, plan 303.

62. "New College Building of United Brethren."

63. Paul Diebold, *Greater Irvington: Architecture, People, and Places on the Indianapolis Eastside* (Indianapolis: Irvington Historical Society, 1997), 137.

64. Ibid., 138–39; *Insurance Maps of Indianapolis, Indiana 1915* (corrected to 1951), vol. 3, plan 293.

65. Diebold, *Greater Irvington*, 139.

66. "Herron Art Institute to Be Formally Opened Next Tuesday Evening," *Indianapolis Sentinel*, March 1, 1902, 7, c. 6; "Plans Accepted for Herron Art Institute," *Indianapolis News*, July 1, 1903, 1, c. 3; "Contract Is Let for Art Institute Building," *Indianapolis News*, September 20, 1905, 16, c. 3; "Herron Institute Corner Stone Laid," *Indianapolis News*, November 25, 1905, 4.

67. "Contract Is Let for Art Institute Building"; "John Herron Art Institute Building Will Be Ready for Dedication About Middle of May," *Indianapolis News*, December 11, 1905, 4, c. 3; *Insurance Maps of Indianapolis, Indiana 1915*, vol. 4, plan 394.

68. "Contract Is Let for Art Institute Building"; "John Herron Art Institute Building Will Be Ready for Dedication About Middle of May"; "Herron Home of Art Marked by Simplicity," *Indianapolis News*, November 16, 1906, 28.

69. Max R. Hyman, ed., *Hyman's Handbook of Indianapolis* (Indianapolis: M. R. Hyman, 1897), 41.

70. "New Columbia Club," *Indianapolis Journal*, November 5, 1899, 8, c. 2; "Will Be City's Pride," *Indianapolis Journal*, June 16, 1900, 5, c. 6; See Bainbridge Bunting, *Houses of Boston's Back Bay* (Cambridge, MA: Belknap Press of Harvard University, 1967), 327. An example of a house facade with a single bowed front in the Back Bay, also designed by McKim, Mead, and White, stands at 303 Commonwealth Avenue. See Bunting, *Houses of Boston's Back Bay*, 314.

71. "Will Be City's Pride"; See Bass photos of the café (#C510), the dining rooms (PO 130, box 23, folder 1, 6410), and the ballroom (PO 130, box 23, folder 2, C519), Bass Photo Co. Collection, Indiana Historical Society.

72. Dunn, *Greater Indianapolis*, I:375–76; "Temple to Be Built by the Indianapolis Masonic Lodges," *Indianapolis News*, March 3, 1906, 24; "Plans Revised for the New Masonic Temple," *Indianapolis News*, April 20, 1907, 7.

73. See original appearance in Bass photo #48077F, Bass Photo Co. Collection, Indiana Historical Society.

74. "Army at Work in Masonic Temple," *Indianapolis News*, May 22, 1909, 12.

75. Ibid.; *Insurance Maps of Indianapolis, Indiana 1914*, vol. 1, plan 67.

76. "Colored Pythians Are to Hold a Jubilee," *Indianapolis News*, May 23, 1908, 23; Dunn, *Greater Indianapolis*, I:381–82.

77. "Colored Pythians Are to Hold Jubilee."

78. Dunn, *Greater Indianapolis*, I:382; *R. L. Polk & Co.'s Indianapolis City Directory for 1910* (Indianapolis: R. L. Polk, 1910), 377; *R. L. Polk & Co.'s Indianapolis City Directory for 1911* (Indianapolis: R. L. Polk, 1911), 399; *Insurance Maps of Indianapolis, Indiana 1914*, vol. 1, plan 80.

79. *Insurance Maps of Indianapolis, Indiana 1914*, vol. 1, plan 80.

80. "Contract Is Awarded for Oriental Temple," *Indianapolis News*, April 13, 1915, 17; James A. Glass, National Register of Historic Places Registration Form for Oriental Lodge 500/Prince Hall Masonic Temple, June 18, 2014, Section 8, 32–33, 36.

81. "Contract Is Awarded for Oriental Temple"; Glass, National Register of Historic Places Registration Form, Section 8, 37–38; *Insurance Maps of Indianapolis, Indiana 1915*, vol. 4, plan 433.

82. "Contract Is Awarded for Oriental Temple."

83. Glass, National Register of Historic Places Registration Form, Section 8, 40.

84. "Lay Corner Stone of Y.M.C.A. Today," *Indianapolis Star*, July 26, 1908, 21; "How Y.M.C.A. Spent Building Fund Money," *Indianapolis News*, January 11, 1909, 11.

85. "Lay Corner Stone of Y.M.C.A. Today"; *Insurance Maps of Indianapolis, Indiana 1914*, vol. 1, plan 50.

86. Scott, "New Buildings Reflect City's Growth in Appreciation of Commercial Art," 40.

87. "Lay Corner Stone of Y.M.C.A. Today."

88. Ibid.

89. "Proposed Home for Indianapolis Y.W.C.A.," *Indianapolis News*, April 21, 1906, 23; "Now Then, Everybody Pull for the Y.W.C.A.," *Indianapolis News*, March 2, 1907, 5; "Y.W.C.A. Building to Be Started This Fall," *Indianapolis News*, August 23, 1907, 7; "Historical Sketch," collection guide for "Indianapolis Young Women's Christian Association

Records, 1896–1986," Indiana Historical Society Library, accessed August 18, 2021, https://indianahistory.org/wp-content/uploads/indianapolis-young-womens-christian-association-records.pdf.

90. Scott, "New Buildings Reflect City's Growth in Appreciation of Commercial Art."

91. *Insurance Maps of Indianapolis, Indiana 1914*, vol. 1, plan 52; "Now Then, Everybody Pull for the Y.W.C.A."

92. Stanley Warren, *The Senate Avenue YMCA for African American Men and Boys* (Virginia Beach, VA: Donning, 2005), 1–38; Lindsey Beckley, "Monster Meetings at the Senate Avenue YMCA," *Indiana History Blog*, Indiana Historical Bureau, May 11, 2018, https://blog.history.in.gov/monster-meetings-at-the-senate-avenue-ymca/; Bundles, *On Her Own Ground*, 112–20.

93. "Lot Bought for Colored Branch of the Y.M.C.A.," *Indianapolis News*, January 25, 1912, 13; "Contract Is Awarded for New Y.M.C.A. Building," *Indianapolis News*, July 23, 1912, 4.

94. "Accept Colored Y.M.C.A. Plans," *Indianapolis Star*, May 7, 1912, 1; "Lot Bought for Colored Branch of the Y.M.C.A."; *Insurance Maps of Indianapolis, Indiana 1914*, vol. 1, plan 64.

95. "Accept Colored Y.M.C.A. Plans"; Warren, *The Senate Avenue YMCA for African American Men and Boys*, 40.

96. Warren, *The Senate Avenue YMCA for African American Men and Boys*, 39–40.

97. Max R. Hyman, ed., *The Journal Handbook of Indianapolis* (Indianapolis: Indianapolis Journal Newspaper, 1902), 180; "South Side Germans," *Indianapolis Journal*, January 21, 1901, 3; "South Side Turnverein at Floodtide in History," *Indianapolis Journal*, April 21, 1904, 6; "City News Notes," *Indianapolis Journal*, April 4, 1900, 6.

98. William L. Selm, "Southside Turnverein Hall, 306 East Prospect Street," typed summary on history of the Southside Turnverein, January 19, 1986, Indianapolis Historic Preservation Commission.

99. "South Side Germans"; *Insurance Maps of Indianapolis, Indiana 1914*, vol. 2, plan 139.

100. Mort Karp and Drusilla Null, "Maennerchor Building: Part I. Historical Information," Historic American Buildings Survey, 1–2, August 1974 and July 1984, https://tile.loc.gov/storage-services/master/pnp/habshaer/in/in0100/in0148/data/in0148data.pdf.

101. Karp and Null, "Maennerchor Building," 1–2; "Plans for the New Maennerchor Hall to Be Built at Illinois and Michigan Streets," *Indianapolis News*, February 21, 1906, 3.

102. Karp and Null, "Maennerchor Building," 3; *Insurance Maps of Indianapolis, Indiana 1914*, vol. 1, plan 66.

103. "Plans for the New Maennerchor Hall to Be Built at Illinois and Michigan Streets."

104. Karp and Null, "Maennerchor Building," 5–6; "Plans for the New Maennerchor Hall to Be Built at Illinois and Michigan Streets"; Bass photos of the interior, from the Photo Co. Collection, Indiana Historical Society Library: concert hall (#C102), rathskeller (#C106), foyer (#46984F), and dining room (#C103).

105. Hyman, *Hyman's Handbook of Indianapolis* (1909), 90–91.

106. Dunn, *Greater Indianapolis*, I:552–53.

107. "Bernard Vonnegut Dies after Year's Illness," *Indianapolis News*, August 8, 1908, 4.

108. *Insurance Maps of Indianapolis, Indiana 1915*, vol. 4, plan 392.

109. "Hospital Addition to Provide for 70 Beds," *Indianapolis News*, January 22, 1910, 28; "Hospital Pavilion Plans," *Indianapolis News*, June 10, 1910, 2; "Contracts for Hospital Addition to Be Let Soon," *Indianapolis Star*, September 19, 1910, 4; "M. E. Hospital Fund Sought," *Indianapolis Star*, April 18, 1911, 14.

110. "Committee Approves Plans," *Indianapolis Star*, April 20, 1911, 9; "M. E. Hospital Fund Sought"; *Insurance Maps of Indianapolis, Indiana 1915*, vol. 4, plan 392.

111. "Hospital Plans Finished," *Indianapolis Star*, February 26, 1909, 14; "New St. Vincent's Hospital," *Indianapolis News*, September 25, 1909, 4; "New Hospital, $800,000," *Indianapolis News*, December 23, 1909, 7; "Sisters Break Ground," *Indianapolis Star*, May 24, 1910, 14; "Hospital Bid Received," *Indianapolis Star*, January 26, 1911, 12; "St. Vincent's Hospital to Be Ready in Fall," *Indianapolis Star*, July 22, 1912, 18; "St. Vincent's Hospital, Result of Many Year's Work by Sisters of Charity, Now Rapidly Nearing Completion," *Indianapolis News*, October 5, 1912, 27.

112. *Insurance Maps of Indianapolis, Indiana 1915*, vol. 5, plan 522.

113. "St. Vincent's Hospital to Be Ready in Fall."

114. "Hospital Erection to Be Begun Today," *Indianapolis Star*, November 9, 1912, 3.

115. The architect's name is unknown. The November 9, 1912, *Indianapolis Star* article cited in the prior note simply refers to "a Louisville architect" as the designer. D. A. Bohlen and Son designed later wings.

116. *Insurance Maps of Indianapolis, Indiana 1915*, vol. 3, plan 297.

117. "Hospital Erection to Be Begun Today."

118. "Plans for Hospital Changes," *Indianapolis Star*, May 18, 1906, 11; "Extensive Changes for City Hospital," *Indianapolis Star*, May 20, 1906, 23; "Named Hospital Plans Judge," *Indianapolis Star*, February 20, 1912, 3; "Eastern Architect to Be Hospital Umpire," *Indianapolis News*, February 19, 1912, 14. Later in 1912, Warren Laird was chosen by the Fletcher Savings and Trust Company to assume a similar role in its competition (see chap. 1 of this volume).

119. "Eastern Architect to Be Hospital Umpire"; "Adolph Scherrer Gets Hospital Plans Award," *Indianapolis News*, March 16, 1912, 1; "City Hospital Architects and Judge," *Indianapolis Star*, March 18, 1912, 5.

120. "Adolph Scherrer Gets Hospital Plans Award"; "Revised Plan for Hospital Ward Building," *Indianapolis Star*, May 1, 1912, 4; *Insurance Maps of Indianapolis, Indiana 1914*, vol. 1, plan 87.

121. "Revised Plan for Hospital Ward Building"; "City Hospital to Have Rare Beauty," *Indianapolis News*, July 4, 1914, 1, c. 6; "New Burdsal Buildings of the City Hospital with Their Splendid Mural Decorations by Indiana Artists to Be Shown to the Public Tonight," *Indianapolis News*, November 28, 1914, 14; Cinnamon Catlin-Legutko, *The Art of Healing: The Wishard Art Collection* (Indianapolis: Indiana Historical Society Press and Wishard Memorial Foundation, 2004), 2, 4–7; *Insurance Maps of Indianapolis, Indiana 1914*, vol. 1, plan 87.

122. "Plans for City Hospital's New Buildings," *Indianapolis News*, February 10, 1922, 21, c. 3.

123. William Herschell, "New Robert W. Long Hospital, Attached to I.U. School of Medicine, Will Afford Medical and Surgical Facilities for the State's Neediest," *Indianapolis News*, August 17, 1912, 13.

124. "Name Hospital Architects," *Indianapolis News*, February 23, 1912, 19.

125. Herschell, "New Robert W. Long Hospital, Attached to I.U. School of Medicine, Will Afford Medical and Surgical Facilities for the State's Neediest"; "Long Memorial Hospital to Be Pride of State," *Indianapolis Star*, May 10, 1914, 44; *Insurance Maps of Indianapolis, Indiana 1914*, vol. 1, plan 75.

126. "Long Memorial Hospital to Be Pride of State."

127. Ibid.

3. BUILDINGS OF WORSHIP, 1900–1920

1. *R. L. Polk & Co.'s Indianapolis City Directory for 1900* (Indianapolis: R. L. Polk, 1900), 65, 111–115; *R. L. Polk & Co.'s Indianapolis City Directory for 1920* (Indianapolis: R. L. Polk, 1920), 8, 9, 22–27.

2. *R. L. Polk & Co.'s Indianapolis City Directory for 1900*, 111–15; *R. L. Polk & Co.'s Indianapolis City Directory for 1920*, 22–27.

3. *R. L. Polk & Co.'s Indianapolis City Directory for 1920*, 22–27.

4. "New Mayflower Church," *Indianapolis News*, May 25, 1895, 8; "Mayflower Congregational Church," *Indianapolis News*, April 1, 1901, 1; "New Mayflower Church," *Indianapolis Journal*, October 20, 1901, 3; Ethel A. Wynne, "Congregationalists Active in City Long Before Their Formal Organization," *Indianapolis News*, n.d., in clipping file "Indianapolis Churches—Congregationalists," Indiana State Library; "Ernest Greene Dies; Retired Architect," *New York Times*, November 21, 1936, 17.

5. "New Mayflower Church."

6. *Insurance Maps of Indianapolis, Indiana 1915* (New York: Sanborn Map Co., 1915), vol. 4, plan 381.

7. Ibid.

8. "Wynne, "Congregationalists Active in City Long Before Their Formal Organization."

9. "Site for New Baptist Church Is Selected," *Indianapolis Journal*, April 13, 1904, 1; "Baptists Are Pleased with New Church Site," *Indianapolis News*, April 16, 1904, 9.

10. "Site for New Baptist Church Is Selected"; "Baptists Are Pleased with New Church Site"; "First Baptist Building," *Indianapolis News*, June 18, 1904, 11; Walter E. Langsam, "William R. Brown" and "David D. Davis," *Biographical Dictionary of Cincinnati Architects, 1788–1940*, Architectural Foundation of Cincinnati, n.d., obtained from defunct website and hard copy in the possession of the author; Michael Lewis, "A Review of the Building History of the Calvary Methodist Church," prepared for Calvary United Methodist Church, n.d., copy downloaded from defunct website in 2023 and in the possession of the author.

11. "Plans for New Church Will Be Received Soon," *Indianapolis Star*, July 2, 1904, 10.

12. "$100,000 Church of Stone," *Indianapolis News*, September 30, 1904, 14; *Insurance Maps of Indianapolis, Indiana 1914* (New York: Sanborn Map Co., 1914), vol. 1, plan 67;

Margaret M. Scott, "New Buildings Reflect City's Growth in Appreciation of Commercial Art," *Indianapolis Star*, September 11, 1927, 40.

13. "$100,000 Church of Stone." At the time, a "high basement" referred to a basement that was only partially below ground level, especially if it contained windows above grade.

14. "Plans Drawn for New Hillside Ave. Church," *Indianapolis News*, October 5, 1907, 24; "Hillside Christian Sets Attendance Goal at 1,000 for 50th Anniversary," *Indianapolis Star*, May 9, 1942, in clipping file "Disciples of Christ," Indiana State Library.

15. *Insurance Maps of Indianapolis, Indiana 1915*, vol. 4, plan 403.

16. "New Churches Here Will Exceed Half Million in Cost," *Indianapolis Star*, October 29, 1911, 29.

17. *Golden Jubilee 1909–1959 St. Catherine of Siena Church*, 6–9, anniversary booklet in Indiana State Library; *The Work of Henry John Schlacks, Ecclesiologist* (Chicago, 1903), https://books.google.com/books?id=oZs_AAAAYAAJ&q=mark&pg=PA5#v=onepage&q=mark.&f=false; *Insurance Maps of Indianapolis, Indiana 1915*, vol. 3, plan 287.

18. For a photo of the Church of San Zeno, see Kenneth John Conant, *Carolingian and Romanesque Architecture, 800–1200* (New York: Penguin Books, 1979), 400; for other possible Italian Romanesque sources, see Conant, *Carolingian and Romanesque Architecture*, 389, 397; *Golden Jubilee 1909–1959 St. Catherine of Siena Church*, 6.

19. *Centennial Memorial: First Presbyterian Church Indianapolis, Ind., 1823–1923* (Greenfield, Indiana: W. M. Mitchell Printing Co., 1925), 178–79, copy at Indiana State Library; *Plan of the Proposed First Presbyterian Church to Be Erected at the Southeast Corner of Delaware and Sixteenth Street, Indianapolis*, n.d., [1], Indiana State Library pamphlet collection; Walter E. Langsam, "Charles (C.) Crapsey," *Biographical Dictionary of Cincinnati Architects, 1788–1940*, n.d., Architectural Foundation of Cincinnati, in possession of the author. E. N. Lamm appears to have been a builder based in Winchester, Kentucky, early in his career.

20. *Plan of the Proposed First Presbyterian Church*, renderings and first floor plan; *Insurance Maps of Indianapolis, Indiana 1915*, vol. 4, plan 381.

21. *Plan of the Proposed First Presbyterian Church*, text; *Centennial Memorial: First Presbyterian Church Indianapolis, Ind.*, photo of auditorium, 178; "Tiffany Window Sent to Museum of Art," *Indianapolis News*, October 6, 1972, 3, c. 4.

22. The lantern over the auditorium, the west gallery, and the Harrison window all have been removed. The window is now on display at the Indianapolis Museum of Art, Newfields.

23. "Charles (C.) Crapsey"; *Plan of the Proposed First Presbyterian Church*, gallery and basement plans.

24. *Plan of the Proposed First Presbyterian Church*, text; *Centennial Memorial: First Presbyterian Church Indianapolis, Ind.*, 179.

25. Jacob Piatt Dunn, *Greater Indianapolis: The History, the Industries, the Institutions, and the People of a City of Homes* (Chicago: Lewis, 1910), I:594; "Front Like Old Church," *Indianapolis News*, January 5, 1905, 4.

26. *Insurance Maps of Indianapolis, Indiana 1914*, vol. 1, plan 93; "Contracts Let for the Meridian-Street Church," *Indianapolis News*, November 14, 1905, 12.

27. "Contracts Let for the Meridian-Street Church."

28. "Will Begin Work on New Cathedral Soon," *Indianapolis News*, March 4, 1910, 4; Ethel A. Wynne, "All Saints Cathedral Had Beginning in Indianapolis at Close of Civil War," *Indianapolis News*, April 15, 1931, in clipping file "Indianapolis—Churches Episcopal," Indiana State Library.

29. "Will Begin Work on New Cathedral Soon"; Wynne, "All Saints Cathedral Had Beginning in Indianapolis at Close of Civil War." See also *Insurance Maps of Indianapolis, Indiana 1915*, vol. 4, plan 383.

30. See discussion of Christ Episcopal Church in chapter 3 of volume 1.

31. "Will Begin Work on New Cathedral Soon."

32. For examples of exposed timber trusses in English medieval parish churches, see Edwin Smith, *English Parish Churches* (New York: Thames and Hudson, 1979), plates 117–19.

33. The crossing tower designed by Grindle was not added.

34. "Romance in Plans for New St. Mary's Church," *Indianapolis News*, January 1, 1909, 14; William Herschell, "After Twenty Years Hermann Gaul Makes Good His Wedding Day Pledge to Plan for the St. Mary's Parish a Miniature Cathedral of Cologne," *Indianapolis News*, July 6, 1912, 13.

35. Herschell, "After Twenty Years Hermann Gaul Makes Good His Wedding Day Pledge."

36. *Insurance Maps of Indianapolis, Indiana 1914*, vol. 1, plan 54.

37. Compare St. Mary's facade in figure 3.15 to photo of facade of Cologne Cathedral in figure 3.16.

38. *Insurance Maps of Indianapolis, Indiana 1914*, vol. 1, plan 54.

39. Scott, "New Buildings Reflect City's Growth in Appreciation of Commercial Art," 40.

40. "Noted Men Here for Dedication," *Indianapolis Star*, September 8, 1912, 49.

41. For photos of the naves of the three medieval churches, see Paul Frankl, *Gothic Architecture* (Baltimore: Penguin Books, 1962), plates 94, 118, and 122.

42. In 1928, the parish replaced the original windows with windows designed by artist Emil Frie and made in Munich. See "Church to Celebrate Silver Jubilee," *Indianapolis News*, August 14, 1937, in clipping file "Indianapolis—Churches, –1949," Indiana Division, Indiana State Library.

43. Herschell, "After Twenty Years Hermann Gaul Makes Good His Wedding Day Pledge."

44. "Downtown Church Sold for $104,000," *Indianapolis Star*, May 3, 1912, p 1.

45. For photo of the First Methodist Episcopal Church of Gary, see *Gary, America's Magic Industrial City* (Gary[?], 1913), 9, copy at Indiana State Library. For a perspective drawing of the Broadway Methodist Episcopal Church at Twenty-Second and Broadway, see Broadway Methodist Episcopal Church bulletin, June 7, 1925, in clipping file "Methodist Churches," Indiana State Library.

46. *Insurance Maps of Indianapolis, Indiana 1914*, vol. 1, plan 84.

47. For more on the Ford Brothers, see Paul Clifford Larsen, "A Centennial History of the Municipal Building Serving Minneapolis and Hennepin County, Minnesota," Sanford Berman Website, 1991, https://www.sanfordberman.org/hist/emer/sglass.htm.

48. "Downtown Church Sold for $100,000."

49. [Ethel A. Wynne], "Universalist Congregation First Appeared in Indianapolis in 1844; Second in 1853," *Indianapolis News*, February 21, 1931, in clipping file "Universalists,

Unitarian," Indiana State Library; "Universalist Anniversary Today," *Indianapolis Star*, September 30, 1934, in clipping file "Universalists, Unitarian," Indiana State Library.

50. [Wynne], "Universalist Congregation First Appeared in Indianapolis"; *Insurance Maps of Indianapolis, Indiana 1915*, vol. 4, plan 382.

51. *St. Anthony [sic] Church, Indianapolis, Indiana* (South Hackensack, NJ: Custombook, 1966), Indiana State Library pamphlet collection.

52. Ibid.; "St. Anthony's Church Ready for Dedication," *Indianapolis News*, November 12, 1904, 22.

53. The belfry and spire on the north tower were removed between 2021 and 2023.

54. *St. Anthony Church, Indianapolis, Indiana*; "St. Anthony's Church Ready for Dedication"; *Insurance Maps of Indianapolis, Indiana 1915*, vol. 6, plan 625.

55. "Church Planned for Slavonians," *Indianapolis Star*, May 27, 1906, 30.

56. Ibid.

57. *Insurance Maps of Indianapolis, Indiana 1915*, vol. 6, plan 616.

58. Paul Eli Ivey, "American Christian Science Architecture and Its Influence," Mary Baker Eddy Library, n.d. https://www.marybakereddylibrary.org/research/american-christian-science-architecture-and-its-influence/, accessed June 26, 2024; "Scientists Open Church Easter," *Indianapolis Star*, March 31, 1912, 30.

59. "Scientists Open Church Easter."

60. *Insurance Maps of Indianapolis, Indiana 1915*, vol. 4, plan 412.

61. "Scientists Open Church Easter."

62. "Announces Plans for a New $110,000 Home," *Indianapolis News*, April 26, 1912, 1; Ivey, "American Christian Science Architecture and Its Influence"; "Solon S. Beman and Spencer S. Beman Collection," Art Institute of Chicago, https://www.artic.edu/artworks/262151/solon-s-beman-and-spencer-s-beman-collection, accessed June 29, 2024.

63. "Announces Plans for a New $110,000 Home."

64. Ibid.; *Insurance Maps of Indianapolis, Indiana 1915*, vol. 4, plan 368.

65. Mabel Wheeler Shideler, "Half a Century Ago the Congregation Sharah Tefilla Had Its Inception; Anniversary Will Be Marked Sunday with Jubilee Program and Banquet," *Indianapolis News*, March 12, 1932, in clipping file "Indianapolis—Churches—Hebrew," Indiana State Library; Carolyn S. Blackwell, "Jews," in *Encyclopedia of Indianapolis*, ed. David J. Bodenhamer and Robert G. Barrows (Indianapolis: Indiana University Press, 1994), 847.

66. "Plans for New Sharah Tessila Synagogue Ready," *Indianapolis Star*, May 16, 1910, 10.

67. *Insurance Maps of Indianapolis, Indiana 1914*, vol. 2, plan 118.

68. "Finishing touches were put on the Sharah Tessila Synagogue . . . ," *Indianapolis Star*, December 18, 1910, 48.

69. Ethel A. Wynne, "Third Christian Church Traditions Are Entwined with Those of Butler," *Indianapolis News*, April 3, 1931, clipping file "Indianapolis Churches—Disciples of Christ," Indiana State Library; Charles M. Fillmore, *History of Third Christian Church of Indianapolis, Indiana* (Indianapolis: Third Church Board, 1943), 2:83–84; "Architects Selected to Plan New Third Church," *Indianapolis Star*, April 22, 1909, 3; "Church Edifice Dedicated Today," *Indianapolis Star*, February 3, 1914, 16.

70. Fillmore, *History of Third Christian Church of Indianapolis, Indiana*, 84; *R. L. Polk & Co.'s Indianapolis City Directory for 1914* (Indianapolis: R. L. Polk, 1914), 1917.

71. "Church Edifice Dedicated Today"; *Insurance Maps of Indianapolis, Indiana 1915*, vol. 4, plan 397.

72. "Corner Stone Is Laid," *Indianapolis Star*, October 21, 1910, 7; "Short History of the North Indianapolis Methodist Episcopal Church, Later the St. Paul Methodist Episcopal," in *Services and Program in the Dedication of the St. Paul Methodist Episcopal Church*, [1911?], 18–20, Indiana State Library pamphlet collection.

73. "Corner Stone Is Laid"; *Insurance Maps of Indianapolis, Indiana 1915*, vol. 5, plan 533.

74. "About Christ Missionary [Baptist] Church, n.d., https://www.cmbcindy.org/cmbc-indy-history, accessed June 24, 2024.

75. "Corner Stone to Be Laid Sunday," *Indianapolis News*, May 27, 1916, 26; "Louis [*sic*] Sturges Is Dead at 37 [*sic*]," *Indianapolis News*, January 24, 1941, 11.

76. "George L. Robinson to Give Principal Sermon," *Indianapolis News*, December 9, 1916, 18; *Insurance Maps of Indianapolis, Indiana 1915*, vol. 3, plan 212.

77. "A Brief History of Second Baptist Church, Indianapolis, Indiana," n.d., [1–3], Collection SC 1889, Indiana Historical Society Library; "Plans New $35,000 Church," *Indianapolis Star*, April 12, 1911, 13; "Campaign for Building Fund," *Indianapolis News*, March 16, 1912, 17; "Corner Stone Will Be Laid Sunday," *Indianapolis Star*, June 7, 1912, 7.

78. "Corner Stone Will Be Laid Sunday."

79. "The members and friends of the Second Baptist Church . . . ," *Indianapolis Star*, February 4, 1912, 46; "Campaign for Building Fund," *Indianapolis News*, March 16, 1912, 17; "Aid Will Be Given a Colored Congregation," *Indianapolis News*, March 30, 1912, p 16; "Decide to Extend Campaign," *Indianapolis Star*, April 30, 1912, 3; "Corner Stone Will Be Laid Sunday," *Indianapolis Star*, June 7, 1912, 7; "A special rally will be held today . . . ," *Indianapolis Star*, August 11, 1912, 16; "Jubilee Work," *Indianapolis News*, August 2, 1913, 23.

80. Parts of the 1912–13 first story, including the cornerstone, may have been incorporated into the 1919–20 building.

81. *Insurance Maps of Indianapolis, Indiana 1914*, vol. 1, plan 67; *Insurance Maps of Indianapolis, Indiana 1914* (New York: Sanborn Map Co., corrected to 1950), vol. 1, plan 67; Alan Goebes, "Second Baptist Church," 5–6, in Collection SC 1889, Indiana Historical Society Library.

82. "A Brief History of Second Baptist Church"; "A Brief History of Second Baptist Church, Indianapolis, Indiana," n.d., 8, Collection M0524, Second Baptist Church Records, 1912–1985, Indiana Historical Society Library. The second history, written by one of the members, states that construction of the 1919–20 building cost $160,000 and that the congregation equipped it with a $10,000 pipe organ and a $6,000 heating plant. In light of the previous financial challenges faced by the congregation and the size of the structure and its materials, the construction figure seems high. Much of the building has been removed, but part of the facade has been retained.

83. "W. W. Renwick Dies; Church Architect," *New York Times*, March 16, 1933, 20.

84. "Cathedral of St. Peter and St. Paul, Indianapolis, Ind.," *American Architect and Building News* (April 9, 1892), vol. XXXVI, between 24 and 25.

85. "Catholic Cathedral Near Bishop's House," *Indianapolis News*, November 1, 1902, 24, c. 2; "W. W. Renwick Dies; Church Architect," 20.

86. "Façade of the SS. Peter and Paul Cathedral to Be Executed in North Meridian Street," *Indianapolis News*, November 18, 1905, 16; "Big Cathedral to Be Opened Dec. 15," *Indianapolis Star*, December 2, 1906, 26.

87. *Insurance Maps of Indianapolis, Indiana 1915*, vol. 4, plan 367; "Big Cathedral to Be Opened Dec. 15."

88. See illustration of Sant'Andrea of Mantua in Ludwig Heidenreich, *Architecture in Italy 1400–1500* (New Haven: Yale University Press, 1996), 42, and illustrations of St. Peter's nave in Wolfgang Lotz, *Architecture in Italy, 1500–1600* (New Haven: Yale University Press, 1995), 99–100.

89. For an illustration of Santa Maria Maggiore, see Richard Krautheimer, *Early Christian and Byzantine Architecture* (New York: Penguin Books, 1981), plate 46; for illustration of San Lorenzo nave, see Peter Murray, *The Architecture of the Italian Renaissance* (New York: Schocken Books, 1970), fig. 19.

90. "Big Cathedral to Be Opened Dec. 15."

91. Ibid. A facade based on Roman temple fronts, designed by August C. Bohlen, was finally added to the cathedral in 1936, and the diocese remodeled the interior, installing new windows. See "New Façade for SS. Peter and Paul Cathedral," *Indianapolis Star*, April 12, 1936, in clipping file "Indianapolis Churches—Catholic," Indiana State Library.

92. Dunn, I:619; "Clear Parish Church Site," *Indianapolis Star*, July 2, 1912, 5.

93. For an illustration of Sant'Atanasio, see Murray, *The Architecture of the Italian Renaissance*, fig. 142.

94. "Clear Parish Church Site"; *Insurance Maps of Indianapolis, Indiana 1915* (New York: Sanborn Map Co., 1915, corrected to 1950), vol. 4, plan 456.

95. "The Arts and Crafts Movement—History and Concepts," The Art Story, n.d. https://www.theartstory.org/movement/arts-and-crafts/history-and-concepts/, accessed June 26, 2024.

96. Ibid.; see also Gustav Stickley, ed., *Craftsman Bungalows: 59 Homes from "The Craftsman"* (Mineola, NY: Dover, 1988).

97. Ethel A. Wynne, "First Unitarian Society in the City Formed Shortly after Civil War End," *Indianapolis News*, n.d., in clipping file "Indianapolis Churches—Unitarian," Indiana State Library; "Unitarians Adopt New Church Plans," *Indianapolis Star*, May 25, 1910, 25.

98. "All Souls Unitarian Church's New Home," *Indianapolis News*, July 16, 1910, 24.

99. Wynne, "First Unitarian Society in the City"; John M. Cunningham, "Yggdrasill," Encyclopedia Britannica, http://www.britannica.com/topic/Yggdrasill; "Family Resemblance," *Indiana Preservation* (November/December 2021), 3.

100. See photo of bungalow living room with similar ceiling treatment in Stickley, *Craftsman Bungalows*, 69.

101. "All Souls Unitarian Church's New Home"; "Latest Idea in Churches," *Indianapolis News*, January 7, 1911, 15; *Insurance Maps of Indianapolis, Indiana 1915*, vol. 4, plan 382.

102. *A History of Second Christian Church 1866 to 1966 Indianapolis Indiana*, pamphlet produced by church, 1966, 3–9, 23, copy at Indiana State Library; "A financial campaign is being conducted by the members and friends of the Second Christian Church . . . ," *Indianapolis Star*, March 20, 1910, 38; "The cornerstone of the new Second Christian Church building . . . ," *Indianapolis Star*, April 24, 1910, 41; "Second Christian Church Dedicatory Exercises," *Indianapolis Recorder*, February 11, 1911, 2.

103. *Insurance Maps of Indianapolis, Indiana 1914*, vol. 1, plan 90.

104. See "Pentecost Bands Building," *Indianapolis News*, December 26, 1901, 10; Jacob Piatt Dunn, I:525.

105. Dunn, I:525; "Pentecost Bands Church," *Indianapolis News*, April 3, 1901, 10; *Insurance Maps of Indianapolis, Indiana 1914*, vol. 1, plan 54.

106. Beside the initial design of Second Baptist Church, in 1908, Morck designed a frame building with Gothic details for the Zion Baptist Church at Twelfth and Fayette Streets, but only the basement was built. See "Proposed Mt. Zion Church," *Indianapolis News*, June 6, 1908, 9; "Mt. Zion Church," *Indianapolis News*, June 12, 1908, 9.

4. CITY MANSIONS AND COUNTRY ESTATES, 1900–1920

1. *R. L. Polk & Co.'s Indianapolis City Directory for 1907* (Indianapolis: R. L. Polk, 1907), 78–79; *R. L. Polk & Co.'s Indianapolis City Directory for 1910* (Indianapolis: R. L. Polk, 1910), 75; *R. L. Polk & Co.'s Indianapolis City Directory for 1913* (Indianapolis: R. L. Polk, 1913), 68; *R. L. Polk & Co.'s Indianapolis City Directory for 1916* (Indianapolis: R. L. Polk, 1916), 21.

2. *R. L. Polk & Co.'s Indianapolis City Directory for 1898* (Indianapolis: R. L. Polk, 1898), 67; *R. L. Polk & Co.'s Indianapolis City Directory for 1920* (Indianapolis: R. L. Polk, 1920), 7. For an indication of the growth of the city in these years, compare the key maps for the Sanborn fire insurance atlases of 1898 and 1914: *Insurance Maps of Indianapolis, Indiana 1898* (New York: Sanborn-Perris Map Co., 1898) and *Insurance Maps of Indianapolis, Indiana 1914* (New York: Sanborn Map Co., 1914).

3. For definitions of business and professional people and middle-class persons buying houses in Indianapolis, see the introductory paragraphs of chap. 5.

4. "Architect Submits a Boulevard System Plan," *Indianapolis News*, February 26, 1909, 19.

5. James A. Glass, "I Can't Sell Nails," paper presented to Indianapolis Literary Club, May 5, 2014, 11–12; "Oral History Conversation #3—Mrs. John G. (Gertrude Schnull) Rauch," transcript of recorded interview with Mrs. Rauch by James A. Glass, November 24, 1976, Gertrude Schnull Rauch File, Indiana Historical Society Library; Irma Vonnegut Lindener, transcript of taped interview by James A. Glass, January 4, 1978, Irma Vonnegut Lindener Interview File, Indiana Historical Society Library.

6. *Insurance Maps of Indianapolis, Indiana 1915* (New York: Sanborn Map Co., 1915), vol. 5, plan 560.

7. Lindener, interview.

8. Lindener, interview; Connie J. Zeigler, "Vonnegut and Bohn," in *Encyclopedia of Indianapolis*, ed. David J. Bodenhamer and Robert G. Barrows (Indianapolis: Indiana University Press, 1994), 1389; *R. L. Polk & Co.'s Indianapolis City Directory for 1903* (Indianapolis: R. L. Polk, 1903), 686; *R. L. Polk & Co.'s Indianapolis City Directory for 1904* (Indianapolis: R. L. Polk, 1904), 696; *Insurance Maps of Indianapolis, Indiana 1915*, vol. 4, plan 394; *Insurance Maps of Indianapolis, Indiana 1898*, vol. 1, plan 38; *Insurance Maps of Indianapolis, Indiana 1915*, vol. 5, plan 560.

9. See, for example, the facade of the Hall of Marchands-Drapiers, Paris, c. 1655–60, designed by Jacques Bruant, and an entry to the Town Hall of Toulon, 1656, designed by Pierre Puget, in Anthony Blunt, *Art and Architecture in France 1500–1700* (New York: Penguin Books, 1981), 239, 373.

10. *Indianapolis Architecture* (Indianapolis: Indiana Architectural Foundation, 1975), 100–101.

11. *R. L. Polk & Co.'s Indianapolis City Directory for 1902* (Indianapolis: R. L. Polk, 1902), 647; *R. L. Polk & Co.'s Indianapolis City Directory for 1903*, 688; *Insurance Maps of Indianapolis, Indiana 1915*, vol. 3, plan 211.

12. *R. L. Polk & Co.'s Indianapolis City Directory for 1903*, 910; *R. L. Polk & Co.'s Indianapolis City Directory for 1904*, 921; *Insurance Maps of Indianapolis, Indiana 1915*, vol. 4, plan 411; "Beauty and Strength Combined in New Home of Joseph Rink," *Indianapolis Morning Star*, December 7, 1903, 10.

13. "Beauty and Strength Combined in New Home of Joseph Rink."

14. *R. L. Polk & Co.'s Indianapolis City Directory for 1905*, 807; *R. L. Polk & Co.'s Indianapolis City Directory for 1906*, 849, 906; *Insurance Maps of Indianapolis, Indiana 1915*, vol. 5, plan 522.

15. *Brochure Containing Selections from the Recent Work of Herbert W. Foltz and Wilson B. Parker, Associate Architects* (Indianapolis: Foltz and Parker, 1908), [32], Indiana Landmarks Library and Archive, Indianapolis.

16. *R. L. Polk & Co.'s Indianapolis City Directory for 1906*, 1256; *R. L. Polk & Co.'s Indianapolis City Directory for 1907*, 1258; *Insurance Maps of Indianapolis, Indiana 1915*, vol. 5, plan 412; *Insurance Maps of Indianapolis, Indiana 1915*, vol. 5, plan 511; "High Price for Lot," *Indianapolis Star*, July 2, 1904, 3; George E. Thomas, *William L. Price: Arts and Crafts to Modern Design* (New York: Princeton Architectural Press, 2000), 67, 127, 156–57.

17. Some of the carved ornament can be seen in the top floor of the former Stouffer's Inn (now Ivy Tech Community College), on the site of the Van Camp mansion. See "Carvers at Work on Staircase of Frank Van Camp's $100,000 Home," *Indianapolis News*, January 30, 1906, 7.

18. Ibid.

19. *R. L. Polk & Co.'s Indianapolis City Directory for 1906*, 511, 530; *R. L. Polk & Co.'s Indianapolis City Directory for 1907*, 512; *Brochure Containing Selections from the Recent Work of Herbert W. Foltz and Wilson B. Parker*, [37].

20. Thomas Walter Hanchett, "The Four Square House in the United States" (Master's thesis, University of Chicago, 1986), 3–4, 17–60, 21–29, 33–70, 83–87; Renee Kahn, "The American Foursquare," *Old-House Journal* (February 1982), 29–32.

21. *Insurance Maps of Indianapolis, Indiana 1915*, vol. 5, plan 582.

22. *Brochure Containing Selections from the Recent Work of Herbert W. Foltz and Wilson B. Parker*, [22]; "Livable House Is Nicholson's," *Indianapolis Star*, November 15, 1903, 12, c.1; Ralph D. Gray, *Meredith Nicholson: A Writing Life* (Indianapolis: Indiana Historical Society Press, 2007), 94.

23. The balustrade of the Nicholson House has been removed since construction.

24. See Hugh Morrison, *Early American Architecture: From the First Colonial Settlements to the National Period* (New York: Dover, 1987), 123–24, 479–81, 526; Leland Roth, *A Concise History of American Architecture* (New York: Harper & Row, 1980), 58–59; *R. L. Polk & Co.'s Indianapolis City Directory for 1903*, 817; *R. L. Polk & Co.'s Indianapolis City Directory for 1904*, 828.

25. "Livable House Is Nicholson's"; *Insurance Maps of Indianapolis, Indiana 1915*, vol. 4, plan 381.

26. *Brochure Containing Selections from the Recent Work of Herbert W. Foltz and Wilson B. Parker*, [23]; *R. L. Polk & Co.'s Indianapolis City Directory for 1902*, 221; *R. L. Polk & Co.'s Indianapolis City Directory for 1903*, 227; *R. L. Polk & Co.'s Indianapolis City Directory for 1906*, 241, 1143; *R. L. Polk & Co.'s Indianapolis City Directory for 1907*, 239; *Insurance Maps of Indianapolis, Indiana 1915*, vol. 4, plan 412.

27. *Insurance Maps of Indianapolis, Indiana 1915*, vol. 5, plan 541; Morrison, *Early American Architecture*, 493–94.

28. *R. L. Polk & Co.'s Indianapolis City Directory for 1906*, 1265; *R. L. Polk & Co.'s Indianapolis City Directory for 1907*, 1268; *R. L. Polk & Co.'s Indianapolis City Directory for 1910*, 413.

29. *Brochure Containing Selections from the Recent Work of Herbert W. Foltz and Wilson B. Parker*, [29]; *Insurance Maps of Indianapolis, Indiana 1915*, vol. 5, plan 543.

30. *R. L. Polk & Co.'s Indianapolis City Directory for 1907*, 506; *R. L. Polk & Co.'s Indianapolis City Directory for 1908*, 524; *Insurance Maps of Indianapolis, Indiana 1914*, vol. 1, plan 84.

31. *Insurance Maps of Indianapolis, Indiana 1915*, vol. 5, plan 541.

32. *R. L. Polk & Co.'s Indianapolis City Directory for 1909*, 1255; *R. L. Polk & Co.'s Indianapolis City Directory for 1910*, 1330; *Insurance Maps of Indianapolis, Indiana 1915* (New York: Sanborn Map Co., 1915, corrected to 1950), vol. 5A, plan 599.

33. "How Others Have Built," *Indianapolis Sunday Star*, July 4, 1909, Women's Section, 4; *R. L. Polk & Co.'s Indianapolis City Directory for 1908*, 823; *R. L. Polk & Co.'s Indianapolis City Directory for 1909*, 828; *Insurance Maps of Indianapolis, Indiana 1915*, vol. 4, plan 383.

34. "How Others Have Built," July 4, 1909; *Insurance Maps of Indianapolis, Indiana 1915*, vol. 4, plan 383; Herbert Ray Worth, *Psychic Science Spiritualist Church—Church Building History*, brochure available at church, n.d.

35. "How Others Have Built—No. 2—An English Type," *Indianapolis Sunday Star*, January 24, 1909, Women's Section, [4]; *R. L. Polk & Co.'s Indianapolis City Directory for 1908*, 743; *Insurance Maps of Indianapolis, Indiana 1915*, vol. 4, plan 412.

36. *Insurance Maps of Indianapolis, Indiana 1915*, vol. 5, plan 544.

37. "How Others Have Built—No. 2—An English Type."

38. Ibid.

39. "How Others Have Built," *Indianapolis Sunday Star*, May 9, 1909, Women's Section, 4; *R. L. Polk & Co.'s Indianapolis City Directory for 1909*, 170.

40. *Insurance Maps of Indianapolis, Indiana 1915*, vol. 4, plan 436.

41. See, for example, the Whitman House in Farmington, Connecticut (1664), in Morrison, *Early American Architecture*, 57.

42. "How Others Have Built," May 9, 1909.

43. *R. L. Polk & Co.'s Indianapolis City Directory for 1909*, 610, 1486; *R. L. Polk & Co.'s Indianapolis City Directory for 1910*, 639.

44. "How Others Have Built," *Indianapolis Sunday Star*, October 23, 1910, Women's Section, 4, c. 3; *Insurance Maps of Indianapolis, Indiana 1915* (corrected to 1950), vol. 5A, plan 599J.

45. "How Others Have Built," *Indianapolis Sunday Star*, October 23, 1910.

46. "Author Is Negotiating for C. L. Hare Property," *Indianapolis News*, January 12, 1923, 18, c. 1.

47. *R. L. Polk & Co.'s Indianapolis City Directory for 1911*, 629; *R. L. Polk & Co.'s Indianapolis City Directory for 1912*, 647; photo of Glossbrenner House and caption listing Alfred Grindle as its architect, in *Year Book of the Indiana Chapter AIA and Catalog of the Third Annual Exhibition 1912* (Indianapolis: Indiana Chapter A.I.A., 1912), copy at Indiana State Library; *Insurance Maps of Indianapolis, Indiana 1915*, vol. 5, plan 561.

48. *Insurance Maps of Indianapolis, Indiana 1915*, vol. 5, plan 559.

49. Photo of dining room in Glossbrenner House, in *Year Book of the Indiana Chapter AIA and Catalog of the Third Annual Exhibition 1912*

50. "Fairbanks Awards Contract," *Indianapolis Star*, May 5, 1911, 16; "How Others Have Built—No. 2—Modern American Domestic," *Indianapolis Sunday Star*, January 31, 1909, Women's Section, 3.

51. *Insurance Maps of Indianapolis, Indiana 1915*, vol. 5, plan 541.

52. Shaw worked with noted Chicago landscape architect Jens Jensen on some of his residential commissions. I was unable to find documentation of Jensen's involvement with the landscape design for the Fairbanks mansion, but it is a possibility.

53. "Fairbanks Awards Contract."

54. "Prominent among the residences erected in this locality . . . ," *Indianapolis Star*, January 1, 1912, 9.

55. "Taggart Will Build," *Indianapolis Star*, January 13, 1913, 10; "New Residence Embodiment of Artistic Talent," *Indianapolis Star*, April 19, 1914, 51; *R. L. Polk & Co.'s Indianapolis City Directory for 1912*, 1523; *R. L. Polk & Co.'s Indianapolis City Directory for 1913*, 1563; *R. L. Polk & Co.'s Indianapolis City Directory for 1914*, 1369.

56. *Insurance Maps of Indianapolis, Indiana 1915*, vol. 4, plan 368.

57. "New Residence Embodiment of Artistic Talent."

58. "Taggart Will Build."

59. "Attractive Home Just Built in Irvington," *Indianapolis Star*, April 12, 1914, 47. The 1911 through 1913 Indianapolis city directories list George D. Thornton as residing at 75 N. Audubon beginning in 1911, two years before construction began on the present house.

60. "Attractive Home Just Built in Irvington"; *R. L. Polk & Co.'s Indianapolis City Directory for 1911*, 1494; *R. L. Polk & Co.'s Indianapolis City Directory for 1912*, 1550; *R. L. Polk & Co.'s Indianapolis City Directory for 1914*, 1343, 1421; *Insurance Maps of Indianapolis, Indiana 1915*, vol. 3, plan 295.

61. "Attractive Home Just Built in Irvington."

62. Dickson's tract later became an exclusive residential enclave south of Kessler Boulevard on Sunset Lane.

63. "At Crow's Nest," *Indianapolis News*, April 29, 1905, 15; *R. L. Polk & Co.'s Indianapolis City Directory for 1903*, 374; *R. L. Polk & Co.'s Indianapolis City Directory for 1904*, 378.

64. "Fletcher Home on Bluff Road," *Indianapolis News*, April 29, 1905, 15; *R. L. Polk & Co.'s Indianapolis City Directory for 1904*, 443; *R. L. Polk & Co.'s Indianapolis City Directory for 1905*, 471; *R. L. Polk & Co.'s Indianapolis City Directory for 1906*, 489; *Insurance Maps of Indianapolis, Indiana 1915*, vol. 4, plan 380.

65. *R. L. Polk & Co.'s Indianapolis City Directory for 1907*, 344; *R. L. Polk & Co.'s Indianapolis City Directory for 1908*, 355.

66. See Norman T. Newton, *Design on the Land: The Development of Landscape Architecture* (Cambridge, MA: Belknap Press of Harvard University, 1981), 427–46.

67. Ibid., 427–35.

68. Richard D. Feldman, "What Might Have Been," paper presented to the Indianapolis Literary Club, October 1, 2012, 2–4; "The New Parry Home," *Indianapolis News*, April 29, 1905, 15; Sharon Butsch Freeland, "Hi Mailbag: Parry Mansion in Golden Hill," Historic Indianapolis.com, March 5, 2013, https://historicindianapolis.com/hi-mailbag-parry-mansion-in-golden-hill/.

69. "The New Parry Home"; *Insurance Maps of Indianapolis, Indiana 1915*, vol. 5, plan 575. Dr. Richard Feldman, an authority on Golden Hill, has uncovered MacDougall's involvement in the landscape design of the Parry estate through interviews with members of the Parry family and with John MacDougall, a nephew of George MacDougall. Email communication from Dr. Richard Feldman, June 18, 2024.

70. "The New Parry Home." Also see Brody Patterson, "Sumptuous Golden Hill Estate in Indianapolis, Indiana," Luxatic, August 31, 2017, https://luxatic.com/sumptuous-golden-hill-estate-indianapolis-indiana/golden-hill-estate-5/.

71. "The New Parry Home;" Email communication from Dr. Richard Felman; *R. L. Polk & Co.'s Indianapolis City Directory for 1907*, 826.

72. *Insurance Maps of Indianapolis, Indiana 1915* (corrected to 1950), vol. 5, plan 575; "Tour Will Open Newly Restored Golden Hill Mansion," Naptown Buzz, June 9, 2014, https://naptownbuzz.com/2014/06/tour-will-open-newly-restored-golden-hill-mansion/; "Sumptuous Golden Hill Estate in Indianapolis, Indiana."

73. "Acquires Six-Acre Tract," *Indianapolis Star*, March 29, 1911, 13.

74. *R. L. Polk & Co.'s Indianapolis City Directory for 1911*, 1581; *R. L. Polk & Co.'s Indianapolis City Directory for 1913*, 1685; *R. L. Polk & Co.'s Indianapolis City Directory for 1914*, 1475, 1476; Matthew C. Morris, "Frank H. Wheeler," in *Encyclopedia of Indianapolis*, ed. David J. Bodenhamer and Robert G. Barrows (Indianapolis: Indiana University Press, 1994), 1423–24.

75. Thomas, *William L. Price*, 157.

76. "Wheeler House Contract Let," *Indianapolis Star*, May 28, 1911, 39.

77. "To Build $80,000 Residence Near Riverside Park," *Indianapolis News*, June 21, 1911, 13; Thomas, *William L. Price*, 158–59.

78. Thomas, *William L. Price*, 158; "To Build $80,000 Residence Near Riverside Park."

79. "To Build $80,000 Residence Near Riverside Park."

80. Thomas, *William L. Price*, 158–61.

81. No photos depicting Fisher's house appear to be available.

82. "To Build $80,000 Residence Near Riverside Park"; Betty Blythe, "Beautiful Home Overlooking Riverside Park Notable for Architectural Simplicity and Livable Interior," *Indianapolis Sunday Star*, February 2, 1913, Women's Section, 1; Jane Fisher, *Fabulous Hoosier* (New York: Robert M. McBride, 1947), 31–32.

83. "James Allison Mansion," National Park Service, https://www.nps.gov/nr/travel/indianapolis/allisonmansion.htm; *R. L. Polk & Co.'s Indianapolis City Directory for 1910*, 172; *R. L. Polk & Co.'s Indianapolis City Directory for 1911*, 174.

84. See Henry-Russell Hitchcock, *In the Nature of Materials: The Buildings of Frank Lloyd Wright, 1887–1941* (New York: DaCapo Press, 1982), plates 25 and 71.

85. Russell E. Campbell, "Allison 'House of Wonders' Now Open to Public, Becoming Catholic School," *Indianapolis Star*, August 22, 1937, part 1, 5, c. 3.

86. "James Allison Mansion," National Park Service; Steve Tinker and Clio Admin. "James Allison Mansion." Clio: Your Guide to History. February 22, 2017. https://theclio.com/entry/32486, accessed June 26, 2024.

87. Campbell, "Allison 'House of Wonders' Now Open to Public, Becoming Catholic School."

88. "Sisters of St. Francis Buy Allison Estate," *Indianapolis News*, October 17, 1936, 1.

89. "Allison Mansion: Landscape Information," Cultural Landscape Foundation, n.d. https://www.tclf.org/allison-mansion, accessed June 26, 2024.

90. "Bulletin Boards at Hatchery," *Indianapolis Star*, February 15, 1914, 50; "Sisters of St. Francis Buy Allison Estate," *Indianapolis News*, October 17, 1936, 1; Campbell, "Allison 'House of Wonders' Now Open to Public, Becoming Catholic School."

91. Campbell, "Allison 'House of Wonders' Now Open to Public, Becoming Catholic School"; "Mrs. James A. Allison opened her pretty new country home . . . ," *Indianapolis News*, March 25, 1911, 17.

92. *R. L. Polk & Co.'s Indianapolis City Directory for 1912*, 945; *R. L. Polk & Co.'s Indianapolis City Directory for 1913*, 967; *R. L. Polk & Co.'s Indianapolis City Directory for 1914*, 858; Carolyn Schleif, AIA, National Historic Landmark nomination for Oldfields,

National Park Service, 2003, 4, https://npgallery.nps.gov/NRHP/GetAsset/NHLS/03001041_text.

93. Schleif, National Historic Landmark nomination, 4; *R. L. Polk & Co.'s Indianapolis City Directory for 1911,* 457; *R. L. Polk & Co.'s Indianapolis City Directory for 1912,* 470; *R. L. Polk & Co.'s Indianapolis City Directory for 1913,* 478.

94. See Mansart's design for the Chateau of Maisons-Laffitte, built in 1642–46, in Blunt, *Art and Architecture in France, 1500 to 1700,* 215.

95. Schleif, National Historic Landmark nomination, 5–6.

96. Ibid., 6–7.

97. Ibid., 7–9.

98. *R. L. Polk & Co.'s Indianapolis City Directory for 1916,* 539; *R. L. Polk & Co.'s Indianapolis City Directory for 1917,* 537; Paul Donald Brown, ed., "Stoughton A. Fletcher," in *Indianapolis Men of Affairs 1923* (Indianapolis: American Biographical Society, 1923), 193; "Stoughton A. Fletcher Awards Contract for Magnificent New Country Residence," *Indianapolis Star,* May 7, 1915, 1. Architect Merritt Harrison as a draftsman assisted Bass in preparing the plans for the Fletcher residence. See *Indianapolis Star,* May 8, 1915, 18.

99. "Stoughton A. Fletcher Awards Contract for Magnificent New Country Residence."

100. Margaret M. Scott, "New Buildings Reflect City's Growth in Appreciation of Commercial Art," *Indianapolis Star,* September 11, 1927, 40.

101. Scott, "New Buildings Reflect City's Growth in Appreciation of Commercial Art"; Kate Lenkowsky, *The Herman Kahn Center of the Hudson Institute* (Indianapolis: Hudson Institute, 1991), [10], copy available from Phi Kappa Psi Fraternity National Headquarters, Indianapolis.

102. Ibid.

103. Lenkowsky, *The Herman Kahn Center of the Hudson Institute,* [10].

104. Lenkowsky, *The Herman Kahn Center of the Hudson Institute,* [10]; *R. L. Polk & Co.'s Indianapolis City Directory for 1915* (Indianapolis: R.L. Polk, 1915), 1402, 2021; *R. L. Polk & Co.'s Indianapolis City Directory for 1917,* 159, 669, 1255. According to research by Kate Lenkowsky, Alex Tuschinsky was born in Poland and worked as an apprentice on gardens of European nobility before emigrating to the United States. By 1915, when Fletcher hired him, he was employed as a landscape gardener in Indianapolis. With the income gained by his work on the Laurel Hall estate, Tuschinsky was able to open the Hillsdale Landscape Company and styled himself henceforth as a "landscape architect and gardener."

105. See photos in the Bass Photo Company Collection, Indiana Historical Society, of the Fletcher estate when it was occupied by Ladywood School, https://images.indianahistory.org/digital/collection/dc012/search/searchterm/Ladywood, accessed June 29, 2024.

106. "Stoughton A. Fletcher Awards Contract for Magnificent New Country Residence."

107. "The History of Laurel Hall," *Shield of Phi Kappa Psi* (Fall 2005), vol. 126, no. 3, 9, http://www.phikappapsiarchive.com/wp-content/uploads/2020/04/Shield-Fall-2005.pdf.

108. See photos of half-timber houses at Port Sunlight in A. R. Sennett, *Garden Cities in Theory and Practice* (London: Bemrose and Sons, 1905), 1:245B, 245D.

5. DETACHED HOMES, DOUBLES, AND APARTMENTS, 1900-1920

1. *Baist's Property Atlas City of Indianapolis* (Philadelphia: G. Wm. Baist, 1908), plan 8.

2. *R. L. Polk & Co.'s Indianapolis City Directory for 1900* (Indianapolis: R. L. Polk, 1900), 145–49.

3. Emma Lou Thornbrough, *Indiana Blacks in the Twentieth Century* (Indianapolis: Indiana University Press, 2001), 5; A'Lelia Bundles, *On Her Own Ground: The Life and Times of Madam C. J. Walker* (New York: Washington Square Press, 2001), 104; James H. Madison, *Hoosiers: A New History of Indiana* (Indianapolis: Indiana University Press and Indiana Historical Society Press, 2014), 191–96 and Brandon Drenon and Ko Lyn Cheang, "'We've Lost So Much,' Residents Defend Area from City Encroachment and Gentrification," *Indianapolis Star*, March 20, 2022, 1A.

4. *R. L. Polk & Co.'s Indianapolis City Directory for 1901* (Indianapolis: R. L. Polk, 1901), 1006; *R. L. Polk & Co.'s Indianapolis City Directory for 1902* (Indianapolis: R. L. Polk, 1902), 975, 976.

5. *Insurance Maps of Indianapolis, Indiana 1915* (New York: Sanborn Map Co., 1915), vol. 4, plan 381.

6. See Henry-Russell Hitchcock, *Architecture: Nineteenth and Twentieth Centuries* (New York: Penguin Books, 1977), 378.

7. "Novel House Is Planned," *Indianapolis Star*, January 30, 1906, 14.

8. *Insurance Maps of Indianapolis, Indiana 1915*, vol. 4, plan 381.

9. "Novel House Is Planned."

10. *R. L. Polk & Co.'s Indianapolis City Directory for 1908* (Indianapolis: R. L. Polk, 1908), 1081; *R. L. Polk & Co.'s Indianapolis City Directory for 1910* (Indianapolis: R. L. Polk, 1910), 1147; *R. L. Polk & Co.'s Indianapolis City Directory for 1911* (Indianapolis: R. L. Polk, 1911), 478, 1247; "Novel House Is Planned."

11. *R. L. Polk & Co.'s Indianapolis City Directory for 1902*, 547; *R. L. Polk & Co.'s Indianapolis City Directory for 1903* (Indianapolis: R. L. Polk, 1903), 580.

12. Architectural historian Thomas Hanchett was one of the first to use the term *American Foursquare* and define its characteristics. One of those was a square shape. However, in Indianapolis between 1900 and 1930, designers often used rectangular shapes together with the hipped roof, central front dormer, and rectangular porch across the facade associated with the Foursquare style by Hanchett and others. See Thomas Walter Hanchett, "The Four Square House in the United States" (Master's thesis, University of Chicago, 1986), 17–60, and Renee Kahn, "The American Foursquare," *Old-House Journal* (February 1982), 29–32.

13. *Insurance Maps of Indianapolis, Indiana 1915*, vol. 4, plan 414.

14. *R. L. Polk & Co.'s Indianapolis City Directory for 1907* (Indianapolis: R. L. Polk, 1907), 204; *R. L. Polk & Co.'s Indianapolis City Directory for 1908*, 208; *Brochure Containing Selections from the Recent Work of Herbert W. Foltz and Wilson B. Parker, Associate Architects* (Indianapolis: Foltz and Parker, 1908), [25], Indiana Landmarks Library and Archive, Indianapolis.

15. *Insurance Maps of Indianapolis, Indiana 1915*, vol. 4, plan 414.

16. *Brochure Containing Selections from the Recent Work of Herbert W. Foltz and Wilson B. Parker.*

17. See Karen J. Weitze, *California's Mission Revival* (Los Angeles: Hennessey & Ingalls, 1984).

18. "How Others Have Built," *Indianapolis Sunday Star*, August 15, 1909, Women's Section, 4; *R. L. Polk & Co.'s Indianapolis City Directory for 1909* (Indianapolis: R. L. Polk, 1909), 299; *R. L. Polk & Co.'s Indianapolis City Directory for 1910*, 306; *Insurance Maps of Indianapolis, Indiana 1915*, vol. 5, plan 561; *Baist's Property Atlas of the City of Indianapolis and Suburbs*, plan 20.

19. For a description of the Mission Inn, see Weitze, *California's Mission Revival*, 93–94.

20. See Hugh Morrison, *Early American Architecture: From the First Colonial Settlements to the National Period* (New York: Dover, 1987) 185.

21. "How Others Have Built," August 15, 1909.

22. A search of marriage and death records in Marion County produced no evidence of Anthony Kleinschmidt being married.

23. "How Others Have Built," *Indianapolis Sunday Star*, March 14, 1909, Women's Section, 4; *R. L. Polk & Co.'s Indianapolis City Directory for 1908*, 776; *R. L. Polk & Co.'s Indianapolis City Directory for 1909*, 297, 781; *Baist's Property Atlas of the City of Indianapolis and Suburbs*, plan 20.

24. See Henry-Russell Hitchcock, *In the Nature of Materials: The Buildings of Frank Lloyd Wright, 1887–1941* (New York: Da Capo Press, 1982), plate 25.

25. "How Others Have Built," March 14, 1909.

26. "How Others Have Built," *Indianapolis Sunday Star*, August 1, 1909, Women's Section, 4; *R. L. Polk & Co.'s Indianapolis City Directory for 1909*, 172, 668; *R. L. Polk & Co.'s Indianapolis City Directory for 1910*, 702; *Insurance Maps of Indianapolis, Indiana 1915*, vol. 5, plan 539; *Baist's Property Atlas of the City of Indianapolis and Suburbs*, plan 20.

27. See, for example, the William Corbit House, built in 1772–74 in Odessa, Delaware, depicted in Morrison, *Early American Architecture*, 531.

28. *Insurance Maps of Indianapolis, Indiana 1915*, vol. 5, plan 582.

29. "How Others Have Built," August 1, 1909.

30. *R. L. Polk & Co.'s Indianapolis City Directory for 1906* (Indianapolis: R. L. Polk, 1906), 495; *R. L. Polk & Co.'s Indianapolis City Directory for 1907*, 496; "J. Dorsey Forest," in Jacob Piatt Dunn, ed., *Indiana and Indianans* (Chicago: American Historical Society, 1919), V:2225–2226.

31. "Burns Company Buys Ground Valued at $30,000, Planning $200,000 Improvement," *Indianapolis Star*, February 11, 1913, 15.

32. Barry L. Shipman, "Rembrandt (Brandt) Steele," in *Encyclopedia of Indianapolis*, edited by David J. Bodenhamer and Robert G. Barrows (Indianapolis: Indiana University Press, 1994), 1293–94; *R. L. Polk & Co.'s Indianapolis City Directory for 1904* (Indianapolis: R. L. Polk, 1904), 1030; *R. L. Polk & Co.'s Indianapolis City Directory for 1905* (Indianapolis: R. L. Polk, 1905), 1115.

33. *Insurance Maps of Indianapolis, Indiana 1915*, vol. 3, plan 211.

34. *R. L. Polk & Co.'s Indianapolis City Directory for 1904*, 940; *R. L. Polk & Co.'s Indianapolis City Directory for 1905*, 1016, 1115; *R. L. Polk & Co.'s Indianapolis City Directory for 1906*, 1074; *Insurance Maps of Indianapolis, Indiana 1915*, vol. 4, plan 436; "Model Homes of Indianapolis," *Indianapolis Sunday Star*, June 17, 1906, 8.

35. "Model Homes of Indianapolis."

36. *R. L. Polk & Co.'s Indianapolis City Directory for 1909*, 213; *R. L. Polk & Co.'s Indianapolis City Directory for 1910*, 216; *Insurance Maps of Indianapolis, Indiana 1915*, vol. 4, plan 418.

37. *Insurance Maps of Indianapolis, Indiana 1915*, vol. 5, plan 582.

38. "How Others Have Built," *Indianapolis Sunday Star*, October 24, 1909, Women's Section, 4.

39. *R. L. Polk & Co.'s Indianapolis City Directory for 1907*, 822, 1275; *R. L. Polk & Co.'s Indianapolis City Directory for 1908*, 1330; *Insurance Maps of Indianapolis, Indiana 1915*, vol. 4, plan 383; Patricia J. Casler, "The Architecture of Rubush and Hunter" (Master's thesis, Graduate School of Architecture and Planning, Columbia University, 1985), 15.

40. *Insurance Maps of Indianapolis, Indiana 1915*, vol. 5, plan 582; Morrison, *Early American Architecture*, 146–49.

41. Leland Roth, *A Concise History of American Architecture* (New York: Harper & Row, 1980), 198; for examples of houses and interiors influenced by the Arts and Crafts that Gustav Stickley illustrated in *The Craftsman*, see Gustav Stickley, *Craftsman Homes: Architecture and Furnishings of the American Arts and Crafts Movement* (New York: Dover, 1979).

42. Architectural historian Paul C. Diebold has done detailed research and analysis regarding the Recker House and the relationship of its design to Gustav Stickley and *The Craftsman*. He also found the prototype design in the July 1905 issue of the magazine. See Paul Diebold, *Greater Irvington: Architecture, People, and Places on the Indianapolis Eastside* (Indianapolis: Irvington Historical Society, 1997), 67–69; *R. L. Polk & Co.'s Indianapolis City Directory for 1907*, 1031; *R. L. Polk & Co.'s Indianapolis City Directory for 1908*, 1075, 1136; *Insurance Maps of Indianapolis, Indiana 1915*, vol. 4, plan 395; *Insurance Maps of Indianapolis, Indiana 1915*, vol. 3, plan 290.

43. "As Others Have Built—No. 1—A Craftsman's House," *Indianapolis Sunday Star*, January 17, 1909, Women's Section, 4.

44. For a discussion of the origins and common elements found in American bungalows, see Diebold, *Greater Irvington*, 65–66. See also an assortment of California bungalow designs in Gustav Stickley, ed., *Craftsman Bungalows: 59 Homes from "The Craftsman"* (New York: Dover, 1988).

45. *R. L. Polk & Co.'s Indianapolis City Directory for 1909*, 687; *R. L. Polk & Co.'s Indianapolis City Directory for 1910*, 722; "How Others Have Built," *Indianapolis Sunday Star*, September 26, 1909, Women's Section, 4.

46. See, in particular, a house designed by William F. Freeman in Michigan, pictured in *The Craftsman*. It is included in Stickley, *Craftsman Bungalows*, 114–15.

47. "How Others Have Built," September 26, 1909; *Insurance Maps of Indianapolis, Indiana 1915*, vol. 3, plan 234.

48. "How Others Have Built," September 26, 1909.

49. "This Home Embodies Owner's Every Desire," *Indianapolis Star*, August 10, 1913, 43; *Insurance Maps of Indianapolis, Indiana 1915*, vol. 3, plans 292 and 294; *R. L. Polk & Co.'s Indianapolis City Directory for 1912* (Indianapolis: R. L. Polk, 1912), 172; *R. L. Polk & Co.'s Indianapolis City Directory for 1913* (Indianapolis: R. L. Polk, 1913), 173.

50. "This Home Embodies Owner's Every Desire."

51. See Hanchett, "The Four Square House in the United States," 3–4, 17–60, 21–29, 33–70, 83–87; Kahn, "The American Foursquare," 29–32.

52. *R. L. Polk & Co.'s Indianapolis City Directory for 1909*, 746; *R. L. Polk & Co.'s Indianapolis City Directory for 1910*, 784; *Insurance Maps of Indianapolis, Indiana 1915*, vol. 4, plan 432; "How Others Have Built," *Indianapolis Sunday Star*, October 31, 1909, Women's Section, 4.

53. *Insurance Maps of Indianapolis, Indiana 1915*, vol. 4, plan 413. Despite the use of *square* in the term by architectural historians, many houses in Indianapolis with all the other elements of Foursquare were rectangular rather than square in shape.

54. "How Others Have Built," October 31, 1909.

55. *R. L. Polk & Co.'s Indianapolis City Directory for 1909*, 1074; *R. L. Polk & Co.'s Indianapolis City Directory for 1910*, 1136; *Insurance Maps of Indianapolis, Indiana 1915*, vol. 4, plan 418; "How Others Have Built," *Indianapolis Sunday Star*, December 19, 1909, Women's Section, 4.

56. *Insurance Maps of Indianapolis, Indiana 1915*, vol. 5, plan 565.

57. "How Others Have Built," December 19, 1909.

58. See Bundles, *On Her Own Ground*, 105; Out Lot Tract Book 3, 5th Series, Out Lots 121 to 161, [p.]151, Indianapolis real estate title tract books, in offices of First America Title Company, Greenfield, IN; *R. L. Polk & Co.'s Indianapolis City Directory for 1910*, 1415; *R. L. Polk & Co.'s Indianapolis City Directory for 1911*, 1542, 1544; *Insurance Maps of Indianapolis, Indiana 1914* (New York: Sanborn Map Co., 1914), vol. 1, plan 79; "Mrs. C. J. Walker to Go to New York to Live," *Indianapolis News*, December 10, 1915, 21, c. 3.

59. Bundles, *On Her Own Ground*, 105; *Insurance Maps of Indianapolis, Indiana 1914*, vol. 1, plan 79.

60. See Morrison, *Early American Architecture*, 123–32.

61. *R. L. Polk & Co.'s Indianapolis City Directory for 1906*, 313, 314, 984; *R. L. Polk & Co.'s Indianapolis City Directory for 1907*, 313; "How Others Have Built," *Indianapolis Sunday Star*, April 6, 1910, Women's Section, 4.

62. *Insurance Maps of Indianapolis, Indiana 1915*, vol. 3, plan 291.

63. "How Others Have Built," April 6, 1910.

64. "The Bungalow," *Indianapolis News*, November 15, 1909, 6; Alan Weissman, "Introduction to the Dover Edition," in *Craftsman Bungalows: 59 Homes from "The Craftsman,"* ed. Gustav Stickley (New York: Dover, 1988), vi.

65. See a variety of California bungalow designs in Stickley, *Craftsman Bungalows*.

66. "Bungalow Contest Planned," *Indianapolis Star*, February 27, 1913, 16; Kate Cole Stevenson and H. Ward Jandl, Introduction to *Houses by Mail: A Guide to Houses from Sears, Roebuck and Company* (New York: John Wiley & Sons, 1986), 19–21; *R. L. Polk & Co.'s Indianapolis City Directory for 1914* (Indianapolis: R. L. Polk, 1914), 1918.

67. *R. L. Polk & Co.'s Indianapolis City Directory for 1910*, 300; *R. L. Polk & Co.'s Indianapolis City Directory for 1911*, 314; "How Others Have Built," *Indianapolis Sunday Star*, September 11, 1910, Women's Section, 4; *Insurance Maps of Indianapolis, Indiana 1915*, vol. 5, plan 539; *Insurance Maps of Indianapolis, Indiana 1915*, vol. 5, plan 543.

68. "How Others Have Built," September 11, 1910.

69. *R. L. Polk & Co.'s Indianapolis City Directory for 1909*, 964; *R. L. Polk & Co.'s Indianapolis City Directory for 1910*, 1017; *Insurance Maps of Indianapolis, Indiana 1915*, vol. 5, plan 581; "How Others Have Built," *Indianapolis Sunday Star*, December 18, 1910, Women's Section, 4.

70. "How Others Have Built," December 18, 1910.

71. "15 New Bungalows. Beville Avenue and New York Street," *Indianapolis News*, September 21, 1912, 11.

72. *R. L. Polk & Co.'s Indianapolis City Directory for 1914*, 890; "15 New Bungalows"; *Insurance Maps of Indianapolis, Indiana 1915*, vol. 3, plan 220.

73. *R. L. Polk & Co.'s Indianapolis City Directory for 1914*, 330.

74. Ibid., 966.

75. Ibid., 515.

76. See "Architect Explains Real California Type Bungalow," *Indianapolis Star*, April 8, 1912, 10; For examples of California bungalows depicted in *The Craftsman*, see Stickley, *Craftsman Bungalows*, 87, 112–13.

77. *R. L. Polk & Co.'s Indianapolis City Directory for 1913*, 193, 1234; *R. L. Polk & Co.'s Indianapolis City Directory for 1914*, 189, 311, 1088, 1212, 1606; "Attractive House of Bungalow Type," *Indianapolis Star*, March 1, 1914, 31. Paul Diebold first identified the house as a product of the Bungalow Company in his *The History and Architecture of Meridian-Kessler* (Indianapolis: Meridian-Kessler Neighborhood Association, 2005), 79.

78. *Insurance Maps of Indianapolis, Indiana 1915*, vol. 5, plan 586.

79. "Attractive House of Bungalow Type."

80. *R. L. Polk & Co.'s Indianapolis City Directory for 1913*, 1633; *R. L. Polk & Co.'s Indianapolis City Directory for 1914*, 466, 1431, 1807; *R. L. Polk & Co.'s Indianapolis City Directory for 1915* (Indianapolis: R. L. Polk, 1915), 1811, 1420; "Pretty New Home on Riley Avenue," *Indianapolis Star*, January 11, 1914, 19.

81. *Insurance Maps of Indianapolis, Indiana 1915*, vol. 3, plan 218.

82. Roth, *A Concise History of American Architecture*, 211–12.

83. "Pretty New Home on Riley Avenue."

84. "Attractive Bungalow on North Side," *Indianapolis Star*, April 5, 1914, 50. The *Star* article identifies the house as that of Joseph Hooser in 1914, but the 1914 and 1915 city directories do not list him at the 5033 Broadway location. See *R. L. Polk & Co.'s Indianapolis City Directory for 1914*, 721, and *R. L. Polk & Co.'s Indianapolis City Directory for 1915*,

717, 1572. See also *Insurance Maps of Indianapolis, Indiana 1915* (New York: Sanborn Map Co., 1915, corrected to 1950), vol. 5A, plan 594.

85. "Attractive Bungalow on North Side."

86. *R. L. Polk & Co.'s Indianapolis City Directory for 1914*, 1528; *R. L. Polk & Co.'s Indianapolis City Directory for 1915*, 1517; "Beautiful North Side Residence," *Indianapolis Star*, November 1, 1914, 18.

87. *Insurance Maps of Indianapolis, Indiana 1915*, vol. 5, plan 586.

88. "Beautiful North Side Residence."

89. "Many Plan New Houses," *Indianapolis Star*, March 26, 1905, 18.

90. *R. L. Polk & Co.'s Indianapolis City Directory for 1905*, 420, 1087; *R. L. Polk & Co.'s Indianapolis City Directory for 1906*, 436; "The last few years has [*sic*] seen a great increase in the construction . . . ," *Indianapolis Star*, August 14, 1905, 5; *Insurance Maps of Indianapolis, Indiana 1915*, vol. 4, plan 369.

91. "The last few years has [*sic*] seen a great increase in the construction . . ."; *R. L. Polk & Co.'s Indianapolis City Directory for 1914*, 264, 670, 1754.

92. *R. L. Polk & Co.'s Indianapolis City Directory for 1914*, 597, 826, 1792; "New Double House of Semi-English Style," *Indianapolis Sunday Star*, March 15, 1914, 24; *Baist's Property Atlas of the City of Indianapolis and Suburbs*, plan 9.

93. *Insurance Maps of Indianapolis, Indiana 1915*, vol. 4, plan 411.

94. "New Double House of Semi-English Style."

95. *R. L. Polk & Co.'s Indianapolis City Directory for 1914*, 1792.

96. *R. L. Polk & Co.'s Indianapolis City Directory for 1909*, 1294; *R. L. Polk & Co.'s Indianapolis City Directory for 1910*, 1360; *R. L. Polk & Co.'s Indianapolis City Directory for 1914*, 1756; *Insurance Maps of Indianapolis, Indiana 1915*, vol. 5, plan 563.

97. *R. L. Polk & Co.'s Indianapolis City Directory for 1910*, 1360; *R. L. Polk & Co.'s Indianapolis City Directory for 1913*, 833.

98. Addition Tract Book A 30, 1st Series, [p.] 65, Indianapolis real estate tract books, First America Title Company, Greenfield, IN; *R. L. Polk & Co.'s Indianapolis City Directory for 1913*, 423; *R. L. Polk & Co.'s Indianapolis City Directory for 1914*, 391, 1756; *Insurance Maps of Indianapolis, Indiana 1915*, vol. 5, plan 563.

99. *R. L. Polk & Co.'s Indianapolis City Directory for 1914*, 1596; *R. L. Polk & Co.'s Indianapolis City Directory for 1915*, 463, 480, 969.

100. *Insurance Maps of Indianapolis, Indiana 1915*, vol. 5, plan 582.

101. "The Building of Flats—Great Demand for Them Shows No Sign of Failing," *Indianapolis Journal*, March 3, 1901, 6, c. 4; "Real Estate Market: It Contained Some Surprises for Close Students—Apartment Houses Contemplated on a Big Scale," *Indianapolis Journal*, March 31, 1901, 6, c. 1; "Public Buildings, Halls, Etc.," in *R. L. Polk & Co.'s Indianapolis City Directory for 1900* (Indianapolis: R. L. Polk, 1900), 126–29; "Public Buildings, Halls, Flats, Etc.," in *R. L. Polk & Co.'s Indianapolis City Directory for 1910* (Indianapolis: R. L. Polk, 1910), 138–43; "Public Buildings, Halls, Flats, Etc.," in *R. L. Polk & Co.'s Indianapolis City Directory for 1920* (Indianapolis: R. L. Polk, 1920), 38–42.

102. "The Building of Flats—Great Demand for Them Shows No Sign of Failing."

103. "A new flat and apartment building . . .," *Indianapolis Journal*, April 21, 1901, 6, c. 1.

104. Ibid.; *Insurance Maps of Indianapolis, Indiana 1915*, vol. 1, plan 67.

105. "A new flat and apartment building . . ."

106. *R. L. Polk & Co.'s Indianapolis City Directory for 1914*, 168, 802, 892, 1027, 1676.

107. Edgar G. Spink left the Home Building and Realty Company partnership in 1912 and became one of the principal builders of apartments in Indianapolis. Between 1914 and 1923, through the E. G. Spink Company, he constructed more than sixty apartment buildings in the city. See "Edgar George Spink," in Paul Donald Brown, ed., *Indianapolis Men of Affairs 1923* (Indianapolis: American Biographical Society, 1923), 573.

108. "New Idea in Flat Building," *Indianapolis News*, May 11, 1907, 14; *Baist's Property Atlas of the City of Indianapolis and Suburbs* (Philadelphia: G. Wm. Baist, 1916), plan 9; *R. L. Polk & Co.'s Indianapolis City Directory for 1908*, 823.

109. *Insurance Maps of Indianapolis, Indiana 1915*, vol. 4, plan 411; "New Idea in Flat Building."

110. "New Idea in Flat Building."

111. *R. L. Polk & Co.'s Indianapolis City Directory for 1914*, 405, 653, 690, 875, 1730.

112. "Excavation work for the erection of a two-story flat . . . ," *Indianapolis Star*, March 12, 1911, 47; *R. L. Polk & Co.'s Indianapolis City Directory for 1910*, 139; *R. L. Polk & Co.'s Indianapolis City Directory for 1911*, 139, 200.

113. *Insurance Maps of Indianapolis, Indiana 1915*, vol. 4, plan 370.

114. *R. L. Polk & Co.'s Indianapolis City Directory for 1914*, 380, 742, 1449, 1594.

115. "Audubon Court will be the name of a new residential community . . .," *Indianapolis Star*, March 23, 1914, 10; *R. L. Polk & Co.'s Indianapolis City Directory for 1914*, 869.

116. *Insurance Maps of Indianapolis, Indiana 1915*, vol. 3, plan 296.

117. "Audubon Court will be the name of a new residential community . . ."

118. Ibid.

119. "Real Estate News," *Indianapolis Star*, April 8, 1914, 9; "New Dean of Architecture: F. H. Bosworth, Jr. Assumes New Duties in September," *Cornell Alumni News*, vol. XXI, no. 39 (July 1919), 482; "Francke Huntington Bosworth, Jr.," Find a Grave, n.d. https://www.findagrave.com/memorial/151229427/francke-huntington-bosworth, accessed June 26, 2024.

120. *Insurance Maps of Indianapolis, Indiana 1915*, vol. 4, plan 367.

121. See photo of Palazzo Gondi in Peter Murray, *The Architecture of the Italian Renaissance* (New York: Schocken Books, 1970), 73.

122. See advertisement for Winter Apartments: "First Inspection of These 36 Homes Wednesday, Sept. 8," *Indianapolis Star*, September 5, 1915, 23.

123. *R. L. Polk & Co.'s Indianapolis City Directory for 1916* (Indianapolis: R. L. Polk, 1916), 866, 1032, 1057, 1300, 1321.

124. "New Apartments Are Under Construction," *Indianapolis Star*, May 6, 1915, 14; *R. L. Polk & Co.'s Indianapolis City Directory for 1915*, 534, 578, 938, 1318.

125. *Insurance Maps of Indianapolis, Indiana 1915*, vol. 5, plan 562.

126. See, for example, the McPhedris-Warner House, Portsmouth, New Hampshire, built 1718–23, in Morrison, *Early American Architecture*, 479.

127. See illustrations of the Royal Naval Hospital in John Summerson, *Architecture in Britain, 1530–1830* (New York: Penguin Books, 1979), 240–41.

128. *Insurance Maps of Indianapolis, Indiana 1915*, vol. 5, plan 562; "New Apartments Are Under Construction."

129. "New Apartments Are Under Construction."

130. *R. L. Polk & Co.'s Indianapolis City Directory for 1916*, 747, 1059, 1215.

131. "'Hampton Court to Be Up to Minute," *Indianapolis Star*, January 2, 1916, 33; "Hampton Court Is Completed," *Indianapolis Star*, June 25, 1916, 31; *R. L. Polk & Co.'s Indianapolis City Directory for 1916*, 801; *Insurance Maps of Indianapolis, Indiana 1915* (corrected to 1950), vol. 4, plan 380.

132. "'Hampton Court to Be Up to Minute"; *Insurance Maps of Indianapolis, Indiana 1915* (corrected to 1950), vol. 4, plan 380.

133. "'Hampton Court to Be Up to Minute."

134. "Hampton Court Is Completed."

135. *R. L. Polk & Co.'s Indianapolis City Directory for 1916*, 808, 834, 1263, 1329, 1357; "Hampton Court Is Completed."

6. THE DEVELOPMENT OF AN ARCHITECTURAL PROFESSION, 1820-1920

1. Leland M. Roth, *A Concise History of American Architecture* (New York: Harper & Row, 1979), 59–71, 73–79.

2. Ibid., 64–66; William Morgan, "Introduction to the Dover Edition," in *The American Builder's Companion*, 6th ed., by Asher Benjamin (New York: Dover, 1969), v–ix; see also Benjamin's text and illustrations in the 1969 Dover edition; Asher Benjamin, *The Architect, or Practical House Carpenter*, 1830 ed. (New York: Dover, 1988), see text and illustrations; "Asher Benjamin: American Architect," Encyclopedia Britannica, n.d. https://www.britannica.com/biography/Asher-Benjamin, June 26, 2024.

3. Roth, *A Concise History of American Architecture*, 29, 98–99; Hugh Morrison, *Early American Architecture: From the First Colonial Settlements to the National Period* (New York: Dover, 1987), 568–69; John Summerson, *Architecture in Britain 1530–1830* (New York: Penguin Books, 1979), 416, 443.

4. Among the books that Elder acquired for his library was one containing measured drawings of architect Isaiah Roger's Greek Revival design for the Tremont House hotel in Boston. He also owned *A Book of Prices of the House Carpenters and Joiners of the Town of Indianapolis*, published in 1836. See Lee Burns, *Early Architects and Builders of Indiana* (Indianapolis: Indiana Historical Society, 1935), 194.

5. James DeGrazia, phone conversation with the author, August 18, 2022.

6. *A. C. Howard's Directory for the City of Indianapolis* (Indianapolis: A. C. Howard, 1857), 68, 70, 76.

7. Roth, *A Concise History of American Architecture*, 100–102; "Alexander Jackson Davis," History of American Landscape Design, National Gallery of Art, https://heald.nga.gov/mediawiki/index.php/Alexander_Jackson_Davis, accessed June 30, 2024; A. J. Downing, *The Architecture of Country Houses* (New York: Dover, 1869), fig. 128.

8. *Swartz & Co.'s Indianapolis City Directory 1876* (Indianapolis: Swartz & Co., 1876), 524.

9. *R. L. Polk & Co's Indianapolis City Directory for 1897* (Indianapolis: R. L. Polk, 1897), 942–43.

10. See David Van Zanten, "Architectural Composition at the École des Beaux-Arts from Charles Percier to Charles Garnier," in *The Architecture of the École des Beaux-Arts*, ed. Arthur Drexler (New York: Museum of Modern Art, distributed by MIT Press, 1977), 111–290; Roth, *A Concise History of American Architecture*, 135, 164; Henry-Russell Hitchcock, *Architecture: Nineteenth and Twentieth Centuries* (New York: Penguin Books, 1977), 207; "Charles Follen McKim," National Park Service, n.d. https://www.nps.gov/people/charles-follen-mckim.htm, accessed June 26, 2024.

11. "History of the Department of Architecture," Cornell University, n.d. https://aap.cornell.edu/academics/architecture/about/history, accessed June 26, 2024; "History," University of Illinois, n.d. Urbana-Champaign School of Architecture, https://arch.illinois.edu/about/history-of-the-school-of-architecture/, accessed June 26, 2024.

12. In 1880, the *Indianapolis News* reported that an auction would be held of items in the office of Edwin May, recently deceased. The items included "a large lot of architectural books." "Auction Sale," *Indianapolis News*, April 14, 1880, 1.

13. John Mark Ockerbloom, "The Online Books Page . . . The American Architect," University of Pennsylvania Library, n.d., https://onlinebooks.library.upenn.edu/webbin/serial?id=amarch, accessed June 26, 2024; John Mark Ockerbloom, "The Online Books Page . . . The Brickbuilder," University of Pennsylvania Library, n.d., https://onlinebooks.library.upenn.edu/webbin/serial?id=brickbuilder, accessed June 26, 2024; "The Inland Architect and News Record, 1883–1908," Internet Archive, https://archive.org/details/sim_inland-architect-and-news-record_1883-08_2_1_0, accessed June 26, 2024; "Architectural Record Archives," *Architectural Record*, https://www.architecturalrecord.com/articles/13598-architectural-record-archives, accessed June 30, 2024 ; *The Brickbuilder*, vol. I, no. 1, 1, https://babel.hathitrust.org/cgi/pt?id=iau.31858033436340&view=1up&seq=1&skin=2021, accessed June 30, 2024; "Scientific American: Architects and Builders Edition," Internet Archive, https://archive.org/details/bplsaaabe, accessed June 30, 2024; Professor Michael A. Tomlan of Cornell University, communication to the author, June 30, 2023.

14. "Constitution and By-Laws, Indiana State Association of Architects" (Indianapolis: A. R. Baker, 1886), 3, copy at Indiana State Library.

15. Ibid., 2.

16. "Historical Sketch of the Indiana Chapter of the American Institute of Architects," in *Year Book of the Indiana Chapter A.I.A. and Catalog of the Third Annual Exhibition 1912*, copy at Indiana State Library.

17. Tomlan communication; James DeGrazia, presentation on Isaac Hodgson, Indianapolis Propylaeum, October 25, 2023; "Bernard Vonnegut," *Brief Biographies of American Architects Who Died between 1897 and 1947*, n.d., https://www.sah.org/docs/misc-resources/brief-biographies-of-american-architects-who-died-between-1897-and-1947.pdf, accessed June 26, 2024.

18. *R. L. Polk & Co's Indianapolis City Directory for 1900* (Indianapolis: R. L. Polk, 1900), 1115–17; *R. L. Polk & Co's Indianapolis City Directory for 1910* (Indianapolis: R. L. Polk, 1910), 1558–59.

19. "Proposed Mt. Zion Church," *Indianapolis News*, June 6, 1908, 9.

20. *R. L. Polk & Co's Indianapolis City Directory for 1910*, 1558–59.

21. Ibid.; "New Building Code Is Ready for City Council," *Indianapolis News*, March 16, 1912, 27.

22. *R. L. Polk & Co's Indianapolis City Directory for 1916* (Indianapolis: R. L. Polk, 1916), 1718; *R. L. Polk & Co's Indianapolis City Directory for 1920* (Indianapolis: R. L. Polk, 1920), 1933–34.

23. "Architects Propose to Drop Competition," *Indianapolis News*, February 10, 1913, 16.

24. See "Historical Sketch of the Indiana Chapter of the American Institute of Architects"; "Architects Now Have an Organization Here," *Indianapolis News*, February 27, 1909, 17. Directors elected were Wilson Parker and Anton Scherrer. The rest of the charter members included Adolph Scherrer, Herman Scherrer, Robert P. Daggett, James B. Lizius, Oscar D. Bohlen, W. Scott Moore, Henry C. Brubaker, Philip N. Stern, Elmer E. Dunlap, Charles G. Mueller, Herbert L. Bass, Herbert Foltz, G.A.F. Riggs, Charles A. Wallingford, and Charles H. Byfield.

25. "Architects Now Have an Organization Here."

26. Ibid.

27. "Indiana Architects in First State Association," *Indianapolis Star*, December 19, 1909, 12; "Architects of Indiana Elect State Officials," *Indianapolis Star*, January 7, 1910, 14.

28. It took many years of patient advocacy, but finally the Indiana General Assembly adopted the Indiana Architectural Act in 1929, requiring licenses of all practicing Indiana architects. See "Registered Architects," in *Bulletin No. 2 of State of Indiana Board of Registration for Architects*, 11, copy at Indiana State Library.

29. "Consider State Building Code," *Indianapolis News*, February 10, 1913, 16; "Discuss Housing Law and Present Conditions," *Indianapolis News*, September 13, 1910, 3; "Tells Engineers of Housing Need," *Indianapolis Star*, January 24, 1913, 3; "Architects Prepare to Adopt New Ethical Code," *Indianapolis News*, June 16, 1913, 8.

30. "Architects Show Designs," *Indianapolis Star*, May 19, 1911, 13; "Historical Sketch of the Indiana Chapter of the American Institute of Architects."

31. "Indiana Architects Favor Competition," *Indianapolis Star*, November 5, 1911, 27; "Eastern Architect Holds Americans Influenced Too Much by Old World," *Indianapolis Star*, February 14, 1912, 4; "Explains Problems Facing Architects," *Indianapolis Star*, March 17, 1912, 35.

32. "First Prize Won by I. M. Harrison," *Indianapolis Star*, May 8, 1915, 18.

33. Illustrating this observation, of the architects profiled in the architect biographical summaries of this book, none studied at the University of Notre Dame. For a historical summary of the Notre Dame architecture program, see National Architectural Accreditation Board. *Architecture Program Report, University of Notre Dame School of Architecture*, Fall 2009, 6, https://architecture.nd.edu/assets/225445/2009_nd_soa_architecture_program

_report.pdf. The second architecture degree program in the state opened at Ball State University in 1965.

34. The society had held such competitions since 1890. See "Architects Plan Contest," *Indianapolis Star*, October 3, 1913, 11.

35. Ibid.

36. "Architects Have Beaux Arts Club," *Indianapolis Star*, January 31, 1915, 7.

37. "Contest Opened for Architects," *Indianapolis Star*, April 4, 1915, 1; "First Prize Won by I. M. Harrison"; "Winner Named in Star House Plan Contest," *Indianapolis Star*, March 5, 1916, 27.

38. "Admitted to Firm," *Indianapolis Star*, January 7, 1911, 9.

39. Tomlan communication.

40. Wesley I. Shank, "Written Historical and Descriptive Data," Crown Hill Cemetery Office Building, Historic American Buildings Survey, 1, June 1971, https://tile.loc.gov/storage-services/master/pnp/habshaer/in/in0000/in0050/data/in0050data.pdf; "Architects Now Have an Organization Here."

41. "New Buildings: Church Edifices in Progress," *Indianapolis Journal*, March 13, 1869, 4; Frances C. Stout, "A Brief History of Bethel African Methodist Episcopal Church, Indianapolis, Indiana," manuscript, n.d., copy at Indiana Landmarks Library and Archive, Indianapolis; Stanley Warren, "The Bethel African Methodist Episcopal Church," in *Traces of Indiana and Midwestern History*, vol. 19, no. 3 (Summer 2007), 34.

42. See chapters 2 and 3 of this volume and "Bro. Samuel Plato." Biographical summary on website of Phi Beta Sigma Fraternity, Louisville, n.d., https://phibetasigmalouisville.org/sample-page/the-chapter, accessed June 24, 2024.

43. The three principal African American newspapers of Indianapolis during the 1890–1920 period were *The Freeman*, the *Indianapolis World*, and the *Indianapolis Recorder*. All three were weeklies. Copies of most issues are available on microfilm at the Indiana State Library.

44. It is possible that a review of US Census data from 1900 and 1910 would turn up evidence of architects residing in the principal African American neighborhood along Indiana Avenue and north and west of downtown Indianapolis. The manuscript census lists residents for each street and provides the occupation of each person.

45. "Architecture for Women," *New York Tribune*, reproduced in *Indianapolis Journal*, August 31, 1901, 7, c. 2; "Women Architects and Builders," *Indianapolis Star*, April 14, 1907, 44.

46. The author is indebted to Pam Peirce for sharing the article about these two women: "Women in Architecture," *Indianapolis News*, August 18, 1900, 9.

47. Amy Borland, "That Exceptional One: Indiana's Early Female Architects and Builders," Indiana Department of Natural Resources, May 2022, https://www.in.gov/dnr/historic-preservation/files/hp-That-Exceptional-One.pdf; for a poster with photos and biographical sketches of early Indiana female architects and builders, see Indiana DNR Division of Historic Preservation & Archaeology, "2022 Historic Preservation Month Poster," Facebook, March 15, 2022, https://www.facebook.com/profile/100064571926998/search/?q=That

%20Exceptional%20One%3A%20Indiana%27s%20Early%20Female%20Architects%20%26%20Builders; "First Woman Architect," *Indianapolis Journal*, June 10, 1903, 8, c. 4.

APPENDIX A

1. The glossary is based on definitions found in the following: John Fleming, Hugh Honour, and Nikolaus Pevsner, *The Penguin Dictionary of Architecture* (New York: Penguin Books, 1983); Cyrill M. Harris, ed., *Illustrated Dictionary of Historic Architecture* (New York: Dover, 1983); *Webster's Collegiate Dictionary*, 5th ed. (Springfield, MA: G. & C. Merriam, 1948); Virginia McAlester and Lee McAlester, *A Field Guide to American Houses* (New York: Alfred A. Knopf, 1985); and Marcus Whiffen, *American Architecture since 1780: A Guide to the Styles* (Boston: MIT Press, 1969).

2. See article on "Shotgun House," Encyclopedia Britannica, accessed January 29, 2024, https://www.britannica.com/technology/shotgun-house.

BIBLIOGRAPHY

ARCHITECTURAL DRAWINGS AND SPECIFICATIONS

Designs and photos of buildings designed by Vonnegut and Bohn. Ryerson and Burnham Archives, Art Institute of Chicago. https://digital-libraries.artic.edu/digital/collection/mqc/id/9257.

BOOKS AND CHAPTERS IN BOOKS

Account of Indianapolis and Marion County, Indiana. Dayton: Dayton Historical Publishing, 1924.
Art Work of Indianapolis and Vicinity. Chicago: Gravure Illustration, 1908.
Art Work of Indianapolis and Vicinity. Chicago: Gravure Illustration, 1909.
Baist's Property Atlas City of Indianapolis. Philadelphia: G. Wm. Baist, 1908.
Baist's Property Atlas City of Indianapolis. Philadelphia: G. Wm. Baist, 1916.
Benjamin, Asher. *The Architect, or Practical House Carpenter,* 1830 ed. New York: Dover, 1988.
Berry, S. L., and Mary Ellen Gadski. *Stacks: A History of the Indianapolis-Marion County Public Library.* Indianapolis: Indianapolis-Marion County Public Library Foundation, 2011.
Blackwell, Carolyn S. "Jews." In *Encyclopedia of Indianapolis*, edited by David J. Bodenhamer and Robert G. Barrows, 847. Indianapolis: Indiana University Press, 1994.
Blunt, Anthony. *Art and Architecture in France 1500–1700.* New York: Penguin Books, 1977.
Bodenhamer, David J., and Robert G. Barrows, eds. *Encyclopedia of Indianapolis.* Indianapolis: Indiana University Press, 1994.
Bodenhamer, David J., Lamont Hulse, and Elizabeth B. Monroe. *The Main Stem: The History and Architecture of North Meridian Street.* Indianapolis: Historic Landmarks Foundation of Indiana, 1992.

Brochure Containing Selections from the Recent Work of Herbert W. Foltz and Wilson B. Parker, Associate Architects. Indianapolis: Foltz and Parker, 1908. Copy at Indiana Landmarks Library and Archive, Indianapolis.

Brown, Paul Donald, ed. *Indianapolis Men of Affairs 1923.* Indianapolis: American Biographical Society, 1923.

Bundles, A'Lelia. *On Her Own Ground: The Life and Times of Madam C. J. Walker.* New York: Washington Square Press, 2001.

Bunting, Bainbridge. *Houses of Boston's Back Bay.* Cambridge, MA: Belknap Press of Harvard University, 1967.

Burns, Lee. *Early Architects and Builders of Indiana.* Indianapolis: Indiana Historical Society, 1935.

Caldwell, Howard. *Golden Age of Indianapolis Theaters.* Indianapolis: Quarry Books, 2010.

Casler, Patricia J. "The Architecture of Rubush and Hunter." Master's thesis, Graduate School of Architecture and Planning, Columbia University, 1985.

Catlin-Legutko, Cinnamon. *The Art of Healing: The Wishard Art Collection.* Indianapolis: Indiana Historical Society Press and Wishard Memorial Foundation, 2004.

Centennial Memorial: First Presbyterian Church Indianapolis, Ind., 1823–1923. Greenfield, Indiana: W. M. Mitchell Printing Co., 1925.

Conant, Kenneth J. *Carolingian and Romanesque Architecture 800–1200.* New York: Penguin Books, 1979.

Condit, Carl W. *The Chicago School of Architecture: A History of Commercial and Public Building in the Chicago Area 1875–1925.* Chicago: University of Chicago Press, 1964.

Cottman, George S. *Centennial History and Handbook.* Indianapolis: Max R. Hyman, 1915.

Cunningham, Joan. "Stem, John H." In Bodenhamer and Barrows, *Encyclopedia of Indianapolis*, 1296.

Darbee, Leigh. "Murat Temple." In Bodenhamer and Barrows, *Encyclopedia of Indianapolis*, 1026–27.

Downing, A. J. *The Architecture of Country Houses.* New York: Dover, 1869.

Diebold, Paul C. "Gibson, Louis Henry." In Bodenhamer and Barrows, *Encyclopedia of Indianapolis*, 623.

———. *Greater Irvington: Architecture, People, and Places on the Indianapolis Eastside.* Indianapolis: Irvington Historical Society, 1997.

———. *The History and Architecture of Meridian-Kessler.* Indianapolis: Meridian-Kessler Neighborhood Association, 2005.

Drexler, Arthur, ed. *The Architecture of the École des Beaux-Arts.* New York: Museum of Modern Art, distributed by MIT Press, 1977.

Dunn, Jacob Piatt. *Greater Indianapolis: The History, the Industries, the Institutions, and the People of a City of Homes.* 2 vols. Chicago: Lewis, 1910.

———. *Indiana and Indianans.* 5 vols. Chicago: American Historical Society, 1919.

———, ed. *Memorial Record of Distinguished Men of Indianapolis and Indiana.* Chicago: Lewis, 1912.

Feldman, Richard D. "What Might Have Been." Paper presented to the Indianapolis Literary Club, October 1, 2012. https://www.literaryclub.org/presentations/.

Fillmore, Charles M. *History of Third Christian Church of Indianapolis, Indiana*. Vol. 2. Indianapolis: Third Church Board, 1943. Copy at Indiana State Library.

Fisher, Jane. *Fabulous Hoosier*. New York: Robert M. McBride, 1947.

Fleming, John, Hugh Honour, and Nikolaus Pevsner. *The Penguin Dictionary of Architecture*. New York: Penguin Books, 1983.

Frankl, Paul. *Gothic Architecture*. Baltimore: Penguin Books, 1962.

Gadski, Mary Ellen. "Paul Philippe Cret." in S. L. Berry and Mary Ellen Gadski, *Stacks: A History of the Indianapolis-Marion County Public Library*. Indianapolis: Indianapolis-Marion County Public Library Foundation, 2011, 72.

Gary, America's Magic Industrial City. Gary[?], 1913. Copy at Indiana State Library.

Glass, James A. "I Can't Sell Nails," paper presented to Indianapolis Literary Club, May 5, 2014. https://www.literaryclub.org/presentations/

Golden Jubilee 1909–1959 St. Catherine of Siena Church. Anniversary booklet in Indiana State Library.

Gray, Ralph D. *Meredith Nicholson: A Writing Life*. Indianapolis: Indiana Historical Society Press, 2007.

Greiff, Glory-June. *Remembrance, Faith, and Fancy*. Indianapolis: Indiana Historical Society Press, 2005.

———. "Rubush and Hunter." In Bodenhamer and Barrows, *Encyclopedia of Indianapolis*, 1208–9.

Hacker, Louis M., and Benjamin B. Kendrick. *The United States Since 1865*. New York: F. S. Crofts, 1947.

Hanchett, Thomas Walter. "The Four Square House in the United States." Master's thesis, University of Chicago, 1986.

Harris, Cyrill M. ed. *Illustrated Dictionary of Historic Architecture*. New York: Dover, 1983.

Heidenreich, Ludwig. *Architecture in Italy 1400–1500*. New Haven, CT: Yale University Press, 1996.

Hines, Thomas S. *Burnham of Chicago: Architect and Planner*. Chicago: University of Chicago Press, 1979.

"Historical Sketch of the Indiana Chapter of the American Institute of Architects." In *Year Book of the Indiana Chapter A.I.A. and Catalog of the Third Annual Exhibition 1912*. n.p. Copy at Indiana State Library.

A History of Second Christian Church 1866 to 1966 Indianapolis Indiana. Pamphlet produced by church, 1966. Copy at Indiana State Library.

Hitchcock, Henry-Russell. *Architecture: Nineteenth and Twentieth Centuries*. New York: Penguin Books, 1977.

———. *The Architecture of H. H. Richardson and His Times*. Cambridge, MA: MIT Press, 1975.

———. *In the Nature of Materials: The Buildings of Frank Lloyd Wright, 1887–1941*. New York: DaCapo Press, 1982.

Hoag, John D. *Western Islamic Architecture*. New York: George Braziller, 1963.

Hoyt, Giles R. "Germans." In Bodenhamer and Barrows, *Encyclopedia of Indianapolis*, 618.

Hubbard, Kin, ed. *A Book of Indiana*. Indianapolis: Indiana Biographical Association, 1929.

Hyman, Max R., ed. *Hyman's Handbook of Indianapolis*. Indianapolis: M. R. Hyman, 1897.

———. *Hyman's Handbook of Indianapolis*. Indianapolis: M. R. Hyman, 1907.

———. *Hyman's Handbook of Indianapolis*. Indianapolis: M. R. Hyman, 1909.

———. *The Journal Handbook of Indianapolis*. Indianapolis: Indianapolis Journal Newspaper, 1902.

Indianapolis Architecture. Indianapolis: Indiana Architectural Foundation, 1975.

Insurance Maps of Indianapolis, Indiana 1898. New York: Sanborn-Perris Map Co., 1898; corrected to 1907.

Insurance Maps of Indianapolis, Indiana 1914. New York: Sanborn Map Co., 1914.

Insurance Maps of Indianapolis, Indiana 1915. New York: Sanborn Map Co., 1915.

Insurance Maps of Indianapolis, Indiana 1915. New York: Sanborn Map Co., 1915; corrected to December 1941.

Insurance Maps of Indianapolis, Indiana 1914. New York: Sanborn Map Co., 1914; corrected to 1950.

Insurance Maps of Indianapolis, Indiana 1915. New York: Sanborn Map Co., 1915; corrected to 1950.

Insurance Maps of Indianapolis, Indiana 1915. New York: Sanborn Map Co., 1915; corrected to 1951.

Insurance Maps of Indianapolis, Indiana Republished 1956. Pelham, NY: Sanborn Map Co., 1956.

Krautheimer, Richard. *Early Christian Architecture and Byzantine Architecture*. New York: Penguin Books, 1981.

Lenkowsky, Kate. *The Herman Kahn Center of the Hudson Institute*. Indianapolis: Hudson Institute, 1991.

Lotz, Wolfgang. *Architecture in Italy, 1500–1600*. New Haven: Yale University Press, 1995.

"MacLucas, William H." In Edward F. Schilder (ed.), *Club Men of Indianapolis in Caricature*, 100. East Aurora, NY: Roycrofters, 1913.

Madison, James H. *Indiana through Tradition and Change: A History of the Hoosier State and Its People 1920–1945*. Indianapolis: Indiana Historical Society, 1982.

———. *A New History of Indiana*. Indianapolis: Indiana University Press and Indiana Historical Society Press, 2014.

McAlester, Virginia, and Lee McAlester. *A Field Guide to American Houses*. New York: Alfred A. Knopf, 1985.

McCarty, C. Walter, ed. *Indiana Today*. New Orleans: James O. Jones Company, 1942.

Men of Indiana in Nineteen Hundred and One. Indianapolis: Benesch Publishing Co., 1901.

Morgan, William. "Introduction to the Dover Edition," in *The American Builder's Companion*, 6th ed., by Asher Benjamin. New York: Dover, 1969, v–ix.

Morris, Matthew C. "Frank H. Wheeler." In Bodenhamer and Barrows, *Encyclopedia of Indianapolis*, 1423–24.

Morrison, Hugh. *Early American Architecture: From the First Colonial Settlements to the National Period*. New York: Dover, 1987.

Murray, Peter. *The Architecture of the Italian Renaissance*. New York: Schocken Books, 1970.

Newton, Norman T. *Design on the Land: The Development of Landscape Architecture*. Cambridge, MA: Belknap Press of Harvard University, 1981.

Phillips, Clifton J. *Indiana in Transition: The Emergence of an Industrial Commonwealth 1880–1920*. Indianapolis: Indiana Historical Bureau and Indiana Historical Society, 1968.

Plan of the Proposed First Presbyterian Church to Be Erected at the Southeast Corner of Delaware and Sixteenth Street, Indianapolis. n.d. Indiana State Library pamphlet collection.

Rabb, Kate Milner, and William Herschell, eds. *An Account of Indianapolis and Marion County*. Dayton: Dayton Historical Publishing Company, 1924.

Roll, Charles, ed. *Indiana: One Hundred and Fifty Years of American Development*. Chicago: Lewis, 1931.

Roth, Leland M. *A Concise History of American Architecture*. New York: Harper & Row, 1980.

Seager, Andrew R. "Daggett, Robert Frost." In Bodenhamer and Barrows, *Encyclopedia of Indianapolis*, 490.

———. "Daggett, Robert Platt." In Bodenhamer and Barrows, *Encyclopedia of Indianapolis*, 490–91.

Sennett, A. R. *Garden Cities in Theory and Practice*. London: Bemrose and Sons, 1905.

Shipman, Barry L. "Rembrandt (Brandt) Steele." In Bodenhamer and Barrows, *Encyclopedia of Indianapolis*, 1293 94.

"Short History of the North Indianapolis Methodist Episcopal Church, Later the St. Paul Methodist Episcopal." In *Services and Program in the Dedication of the St. Paul Methodist Episcopal Church*, 18–20. [1911?]. Indiana State Library pamphlet collection.

"Shotgun House," Encyclopedia Britannica. https://www.britannica.com/technology/shotgun house, accessed January 29, 2024.

Smith, Edwin. *English Parish Churches*. New York: Thames and Hudson, 1979.

Smith, Richard W. "Bohlen, Meyer, Gibson and Associates." In Bodenhamer and Barrows, *Encyclopedia of Indianapolis*, 334.

St. Anthony Church, Indianapolis, Indiana. South Hackensack, NJ: Custombook, 1966. Indiana State Library pamphlet collection.

Stevenson, Kate Cole, and H. Ward Jandl. Introduction to *Houses by Mail: A Guide to Houses from Sears, Roebuck and Company*, 19–21. New York: John Wiley & Sons, 1986.

Stickley, Gustav, ed. *Craftsman Bungalows: 59 Homes from "The Craftsman."* Mineola, NY: Dover, 1988.

———. *Craftsman Homes: Architecture and Furnishings of the American Arts and Crafts Movement*. New York: Dover, 1979.

Summerson, John. *Architecture in Britain, 1530–1830*. New York: Penguin Books, 1979.

Thomas, George E. *Arts and Crafts to Modern Design: William L. Price*. New York: Princeton Architectural Press, 2000.

Thornbrough, Emma Lou. *Indiana Blacks in the Twentieth Century*. Bloomington: Indiana University Press, 2001.

———. *The Negro in Indiana before 1900*. Indianapolis: Indiana University Press, 1992.

Tomlan, Mary Raddant, and Michael A. Tomlan. *Richmond, Indiana: The Physical Development and Aesthetic Heritage to 1920*. Indianapolis: Indiana Historical Society Press, 2003.

Tomlan, Michael A. "Popular and Professional American Architectural Literature in the Late Nineteenth Century." PhD diss., Cornell University, 1983.

Van Rensselaer, Mariana Griswold. *Henry Hobson Richardson and His Works*. New York: Dover, 1969.

Van Zanten, David. "Architectural Composition at the École des Beaux-Arts from Charles Percier to Charles Garnier." In *The Architecture of the École des Beaux-Arts*, edited by Arthur Drexler, 111–290. New York: Museum of Modern Art, distributed by MIT Press, 1977.

Warren, Stanley. *The Senate Avenue YMCA for African American Men and Boys*. Virginia Beach, VA: Donning, 2005.

Webster's Collegiate Dictionary, 5th ed. Springfield, MA: G. & C. Merriam, 1948.

Weisman, Winston. "A New View of Skyscraper History." In *The Rise of an American Architecture*, edited by Edgar Kaufmann Jr., 115–48. New York: Praeger, 1970.

Weissman, Alan. "Introduction to the Dover Edition." In *Craftsman Bungalows: 59 Homes from "The Craftsman,"* edited by Gustav Stickley, vi. New York: Dover, 1988.

Weitze, Karen J. *California's Mission Revival*. Los Angeles: Hennessey & Ingalls, 1984.

Whiffen, Marcus. *American Architecture since 1780: A Guide to the Styles*. Boston: MIT Press, 1969.

Wolner, Edward W. *Henry Ives Cobb's Chicago: Architecture, Institutions, and the Making of a Modern Metropolis*. Chicago: University of Chicago Press, 2011.

The Work of Henry John Schlacks, Ecclesiologist. Chicago, 1903. https://books.google.com/books?id=oZs_AAAAYAAJ&q=mark&pg=PA5#v=onepage&q=mark&f=false.

Wynn, Frank B. "Church History." In *Meridian Street Methodist Episcopal Church Centennial Memorial 1821–1921*, n.p. Indianapolis: William B. Burford, 1921.

Year Book of the Indiana Chapter A.I.A. and Catalog of the Third Annual Exhibition 1912. Indianapolis: Indiana Chapter A.I.A., 1912. Copy at Indiana State Library.

Zeigler, Connie J. "Vonnegut and Bohn." In Bodenhamer and Barrows, *Encyclopedia of Indianapolis*, 1389.

CITY DIRECTORIES

Architectural advertisements in *A. C. Howard's Directory for the City of Indianapolis*. Indianapolis: A. C. Howard, 1857.

"Indianapolis." In *R. L. Polk & Co.'s Indianapolis City Directory for 1916*, 20. Indianapolis: R. L. Polk, 1916.

"Introductory." In *R. L. Polk & Co.'s Indianapolis City Directory for 1894*, 58. Indianapolis: R. L. Polk, 1894.

"Introductory." In *R. L. Polk & Co.'s Indianapolis City Directory for 1900*, 65. Indianapolis: R. L. Polk, 1900.

"Introductory." In *R. L. Polk & Co.'s Indianapolis City Directory for 1907*, 73. Indianapolis: R. L. Polk, 1907.

"Introductory." In. *R. L. Polk & Co.'s Indianapolis City Directory for 1913*, 68. Indianapolis: R. L. Polk, 1913.

"Miscellaneous Schools." In *R. L. Polk & Co.'s Indianapolis City Directory for 1897*, 132. Indianapolis: R. L. Polk, 1897.

"Primary Grammar Schools." In *R. L. Polk & Co.'s Indianapolis City Directory for 1897*, 133. Indianapolis: R. L. Polk, 1897.

"Public Buildings, Halls, Etc." In *R. L. Polk & Co.'s Indianapolis City Directory for 1897*, 128–30. Indianapolis: R. L. Polk, 1897.

"Public Buildings, Halls, Flats, Etc." In *R. L. Polk & Co.'s Indianapolis City Directory for 1910*, 138–43. Indianapolis: R. L. Polk, 1910.

"Public Buildings, Halls, Flats, Etc." In *R. L. Polk & Co.'s Indianapolis City Directory for 1920*, 38–42. Indianapolis: R. L. Polk, 1920.

R. L. Polk & Co.'s Indianapolis City Directory for 1890. Indianapolis: R. L. Polk, 1890.

R. L. Polk & Co.'s Indianapolis City Directory for 1897. Indianapolis: R. L. Polk, 1897.

R. L. Polk & Co.'s Indianapolis City Directory for 1898. Indianapolis: R. L. Polk, 1898.

R. L. Polk & Co.'s Indianapolis City Directory for 1901. Indianapolis: R. L. Polk, 1901.

R. L. Polk & Co.'s Indianapolis City Directory for 1902. Indianapolis: R. L. Polk, 1902.

R. L. Polk & Co.'s Indianapolis City Directory for 1903. Indianapolis: R. L. Polk, 1903.

R. L. Polk & Co.'s Indianapolis City Directory for 1904. Indianapolis: R. L. Polk, 1904.

R. L. Polk & Co.'s Indianapolis City Directory for 1905. Indianapolis: R. L. Polk, 1905.

R. L. Polk & Co.'s Indianapolis City Directory for 1906. Indianapolis: R. L. Polk, 1906.

R. L. Polk & Co.'s Indianapolis City Directory for 1907. Indianapolis: R. L. Polk, 1907.

R. L. Polk & Co.'s Indianapolis City Directory for 1908. Indianapolis: R. L. Polk, 1908.

R. L. Polk & Co.'s Indianapolis City Directory for 1909. Indianapolis: R. L. Polk, 1909.

R. L. Polk & Co.'s Indianapolis City Directory for 1910. Indianapolis: R. L. Polk, 1910.

R. L. Polk & Co.'s Indianapolis City Directory for 1911. Indianapolis: R. L. Polk, 1911.

R. L. Polk & Co.'s Indianapolis City Directory for 1912. Indianapolis: R. L. Polk, 1912.

R. L. Polk & Co.'s Indianapolis City Directory for 1913. Indianapolis: R. L. Polk, 1913.

R. L. Polk & Co.'s Indianapolis City Directory for 1914. Indianapolis: R. L. Polk, 1914.

R. L. Polk & Co.'s Indianapolis City Directory for 1915. Indianapolis: R. L. Polk, 1915.

R. L. Polk & Co.'s Indianapolis City Directory for 1916. Indianapolis: R. L. Polk, 1916.

R. L. Polk & Co.'s Indianapolis City Directory for 1917. Indianapolis: R. L. Polk, 1917.

R. L. Polk & Co.'s Indianapolis City Directory for 1919. Indianapolis: R. L. Polk, 1919.

R. L. Polk & Co.'s Indianapolis City Directory for 1920. Indianapolis: R. L. Polk, 1920.

R. L. Polk & Co.'s Indianapolis City Directory for 1933. Indianapolis: R. L. Polk, 1933.

Swartz & Co.'s Indianapolis City Directory 1876. Indianapolis: Swartz & Co., 1876.

COMMUNICATIONS BY EMAIL

Email from Danita Davis, February 9, 2021.
Email from George E. Thomas, September 19, 2023.
Email from Professor Michael A. Tomlan of Cornell University, June 30, 2023.

GOVERNMENT REPORTS AND DOCUMENTS

Indiana Board of Registration for Architects

"Registered Architects." In *Bulletin No. 2 of State of Indiana Board of Registration for Architects*, 11. Copy at Indiana State Library.

Indianapolis Historic Preservation Commission

Glass, James A., compiler. "List of Buildings in Indianapolis Designed by Vonnegut and Bohn." July 10, 1982, Vonnegut Family File, Indianapolis Historic Preservation Commission.
Historic Area Conservation Plan Herron-Morton Place HA-19. Indianapolis: Indianapolis Historic Preservation Commission, 1986.
Selm, William L. "Southside Turnverein Hall, 306 East Prospect Street." Typed summary on history of the Southside Turnverein, January 19, 1986, Indianapolis Historic Preservation Commission.
Wholesale District Historic Area Plan. Indianapolis: Indianapolis Historic Preservation Commission, 1990.

Miscellaneous

Center Township, Marion County Interim Report. Indianapolis: Indiana Landmarks and Indiana Division of Historic Preservation and Archaeology, 1991.
Visitor's Guide to the Birch Bayh Federal Building and United States Courthouse. United States District Court for the Southern District of Indiana, n.d.

National Register/National Historic Landmark Nominations

Cardinal, Jare R., and David R. Bush. National Register of Historic Places Registration Form for Fort Benjamin Harrison, March 10, 1989, Section 8, 3.
Glass, James A. National Register of Historic Places Registration Form for Oriental Lodge 500/Prince Hall Masonic Temple, June 18, 2014, Section 8, 32–33, 36.
Glass, James A., and Mary Ellen Gadski. "Indianapolis Wholesale District." National Register Nomination, January 18, 1982. https://secure.in.gov/apps/dnr/shaard/r/1e6a5/N/Indianapolis_Wholesale_District_Marion_CO_Nom.pdf.

Samuel A. Roberson & Associates. National Register of Historic Places Inventory-Nomination Form for Indianapolis News Building, November 18, 1983. SHAARD database, Indiana Division of Historic Preservation and Archaeology. https://secure.in.gov/apps/dnr/shaard/r/1f3d1/N/Indianapolis_News_Bldg_Marion_CO_Nom.pdf accessed June 25, 2024.

Schleif, Carolyn, AIA. National Historic Landmark nomination for Oldfields, National Park Service, 2003. https://npgallery.nps.gov/NRHP/GetAsset/NHLS/03001041_text.

INTERVIEWS BY JAMES GLASS

DeGrazia, James. May 17, 2019.

———. December 14, 2019.

———. August 18, 2022.

Lindener, Irma Vonnegut. Transcript of taped interview by James A. Glass, January 4, 1978, Irma Vonnegut Lindener Interview File, Indiana Historical Society Library.

"Oral History Conversation #3—Mrs. John G. (Gertrude Schnull) Rauch." Transcript of recorded interview with Mrs. Rauch by James A. Glass, November 24, 1976, Gertrude Schnull Rauch File, Indiana Historical Society Library.

LECTURES/PRESENTATIONS

Davis, Danita L. "Prolific but Little-Known Indy Architect Subject of March 22 Talk." Presentation at Indiana Landmarks, February 16, 2018. https://www.indianalandmarks.org/2018/02/prolific-little-known-indy-architect-subject-march-22-talk/.

DeGrazia, James. Presentation on Isaac Hodgson, Indianapolis Propylaeum, October 25, 2023.

MANUSCRIPTS AND HISTORICAL PHOTOGRAPHS

Allison Mansion historical photos, Historic American Buildings Survey. https://www.loc.gov/pictures/item/in0045.photos.065136p/resource.

Bass Photo Company Collection, Indiana Historical Society Library.

"Bohlen, A. C." Citizens Historical Association, Indianapolis, November 18, 1944, in Biography clipping file "Boh-Boi," Indiana State Library.

"A Brief History of Second Baptist Church, Indianapolis, Indiana," n.d., Collection SC 1889, Indiana Historical Society Library.

"A Brief History of Second Baptist Church, Indianapolis, Indiana," n.d., 8. Collection M0524, Second Baptist Church Records, 1912–1985, Indiana Historical Society Library.

Broadway Methodist Episcopal Church bulletin, June 7, 1925, in clipping file "Methodist Churches," Indiana State Library.

Carol M. Highsmith Archive, Library of Congress.

"Constitution and By-Laws, Indiana State Association of Architects." Indianapolis: A. R. Baker, 1886, 3. Copy at Indiana State Library.

Goebes, Alan. "Second Baptist Church," 5–6, Collection SC 1889, Indiana Historical Society Library.
Historic American Buildings Survey, Prints and Photographs Division, Library of Congress.
"Hunter, Frank B." Citizens Historical Association Indianapolis, in Biographical clipping file "Hunter, A.–Hunter M.," Indiana State Library.
Jungclaus-Campbell Family Archive, Indianapolis.
Letter from David Gibson to Florence Venn, Librarian. William Henry Smith Library, October 6, 1937, Indiana Biography Series, 17:13, Indiana Division, Indiana State Library.
MacLucas, George. Transcript of "Interview with George MacLucas, Son of William Harold MacLucas," conducted by Tracey Cox and Dan Kiernan, July 30, 1979. Indiana Historical Society Library Architectural Archives.
Rubush and Hunter Collection, Indiana Historical Society Library.
"Solon S. Beman and Spencer S. Beman Collection." Art Institute of Chicago. https://www.artic.edu/artworks/262151/solon-s-beman-and-spencer-s-beman-collection, accessed July 1, 2024.
Stout, Frances C. "A Brief History of Bethel African Methodist Episcopal Church, Indianapolis, Indiana," manuscript, n.d., copy at Indiana Landmarks Library and Archive, Indianapolis.
Title tract books for Indianapolis and Marion County real estate transactions. First American Title Insurance Company, Greenfield, IN.
Worth, Herbert Ray. *Psychic Science Spiritualist Church—Church Building History.* n.d. Brochure available at church.
YMCA Archives Photo Collection, Kautz Family YMCA Archives, Elmer L. Andersen Library, University of Minnesota.

NEWSPAPER ARTICLES

"A new flat and apartment building . . ." *Indianapolis Journal*, April 21, 1901, 6, c. 1.
"Accept Colored Y.M.C.A. Plans." *Indianapolis Star*, May 7, 1912, 1.
"Acquires Six-Acre Tract." *Indianapolis Star*, March 29, 1911, 13.
"Admitted to Firm." *Indianapolis Star*, January 7, 1911, 9.
"Adolph Scherrer Gets Hospital Plans Award." *Indianapolis News*, March 16, 1912, 1.
"Aid Will Be Given a Colored Congregation." *Indianapolis News*, March 30, 1912, 16.
"Alfred Grindle Services Today." *Indianapolis Star*, January 6, 1940, 12.
"All Souls Unitarian Church's New Home." *Indianapolis News*, July 16, 1910, 24.
Announcement of Newton Claypool Building. *Indianapolis Journal*, November 18, 1900, 7.
"Announces Plans for a New $110,000 Home." *Indianapolis News*, April 26, 1912, 1.
"Another Large Building." *Indianapolis News*, December 5, 1900, 11.
"Architect Explains Real California Type Bungalow." *Indianapolis Star*, April 8, 1912, 10.
"Architect Locates Here." *Indianapolis Journal*, December 7, 1902, 12, c. 4.
"Architect of Fletcher Trust Building Is Here." *Indianapolis News*, December 17, 1912, 10.
"Architect Tells of Big Changes." *Indianapolis Star*, March 28, 1915, 58.
"Architects' Association Selects New President." *Indianapolis Star*, December 17, 1915, 3.

"Architects Chosen in Library Contest." *Indianapolis Star*, February 5, 1914, 1.
"Architects for Fire Headquarters Named." *Indianapolis News*, February 19, 1913, 2.
"Architects Have Beaux Arts Club." *Indianapolis Star*, January 31, 1915, 7.
"Architects Now Have an Organization Here." *Indianapolis News*, February 27, 1909, 17.
"Architects of City Invited to Compete." *Indianapolis Star*, August 22, 1906, 14.
"Architects of Indiana Elect State Officials." *Indianapolis Star*, January 7, 1910, 14.
"Architects Plan Contest." *Indianapolis Star*, October 3, 1913, 11.
"Architects Prepare to Adopt New Ethical Code." *Indianapolis News*, June 16, 1913, 8.
"Architects Propose to Drop Competition." *Indianapolis News*, February 10, 1913, 16.
"Architects Selected to Plan New Third Church." *Indianapolis Star*, April 22, 1909, 3.
"Architects Show Designs." *Indianapolis Star*, May 19, 1911, 13.
"Architect Submits a Boulevard System Plan." *Indianapolis News*, February 26, 1909, 19.
"Architecture for Women." *New York Tribune*, reproduced in *Indianapolis Journal*, August 31, 1901, 7, c. 2.
"Army at Work in Masonic Temple." *Indianapolis News*, May 22, 1909, 12.
"Arthur Bohn." *Indianapolis News*, February 24, 1941. Indiana Biography Series, 21:42, Indiana Division, Indiana State Library.
"Arthur Bohn." *Indianapolis Times*, January 14, 1948, 4, c. 2.
Arthur Bohn, obituary. Indiana Biography Series, 21:42, Indiana Division, Indiana State Library.
"As Others Have Built—No. 1—A Craftsman's House." *Indianapolis Sunday Star*, January 17, 1909, Women's Section, 4.
"At Crow's Nest." *Indianapolis News*, April 29, 1905, 15.
"Attractive Bungalow on North Side." *Indianapolis Star*, April 5, 1914, 50.
"Attractive Home Just Built in Irvington." *Indianapolis Star*, April 12, 1914, 47.
"Attractive House of Bungalow Type." *Indianapolis Star*, March 1, 1914, 31.
"Audubon Court will be the name of a new residential community . . ." *Indianapolis Star*, March 23, 1914, 10.
"Author Is Negotiating for C. L. Hare Property." *Indianapolis News*, January 12, 1923, 18, c.1.
"Ayres Company Plans Addition." *Indianapolis Star*, July 11, 1914, 1, 3.
"Bank Building Under Way." *Indianapolis Star*, August 25, 1907, 13.
"Baptists Are Pleased with New Church Site." *Indianapolis News*, April 16, 1904, 9.
"Beautiful North Side Residence." *Indianapolis Star*, November 1, 1914, 18.
"Beauty and Strength Combined in New Home of Joseph Rink." *Indianapolis Morning Star*, December 7, 1903, 10.
"Beech Grove Mint for Indianapolis." *Indianapolis Star*, July 31, 1910, 17.
"Bernard Vonnegut Dies after Year's Illness." *Indianapolis News*, August 8, 1908, 4.
"Bids on Engine Houses Far under Estimates." *Indianapolis News*, July 24, 1911, 4.
"Big Addition for Cole Auto Plant." *Indianapolis Star*, April 13, 1913, 41.
"Big Building Is to Be Ready by September 1, 1912." *Indianapolis News*, November 3, 1911, 7.
"Big Cathedral to Be Opened Dec. 15." *Indianapolis Star*, December 2, 1906, 26.

Blythe, Betty. "Beautiful Home Overlooking Riverside Park Notable for Architectural Simplicity and Livable Interior." *Indianapolis Sunday Star*, February 2, 1913, Women's Section, 1.

"Board of Trade Plans." *Indianapolis News*, August 19, 1905, 14.

"The Building of Flats—Great Demand for Them Shows No Sign of Failing." *Indianapolis Journal*, March 3, 1901, 6, c. 4.

"Bulletin Boards at Hatchery." *Indianapolis Star*, February 15, 1914, 50.

"Bungalow Contest Planned." *Indianapolis Star*, February 27, 1913, 16.

"The Bungalow." *Indianapolis News*, November 15, 1909, 6.

"Burns Company Buys Ground Valued at $30,000, Planning $200,000 Improvement." *Indianapolis Star*, February 11, 1913, 15.

"Campaign for Building Fund." *Indianapolis News*, March 16, 1912, 17.

Campbell, Russell E. "Allison 'House of Wonders' Now Open to Public, Becoming Catholic School." *Indianapolis Star*, August 22, 1937, part 1, 5, c. 3.

"Carvers at Work on Staircase of Frank Van Camp's $100,000 Home." *Indianapolis News*, January 30, 1906, 7.

"Catholic Cathedral Near Bishop's House." *Indianapolis News*, November 1, 1902, 24, c. 2.

"Central Avenue Methodist Marks 110 Years." *Indianapolis Times*, September 7, 1963, 7, c. 1.

"Chicago Firm Wins." *Indianapolis Journal*, June 9, 1901, 8, c. 2.

"Choose City Hall Plans." *Indianapolis Star*, November 3, 1908, 1.

"Church Edifice Dedicated Today." *Indianapolis Star*, February 3, 1914, 16.

"Church Planned for Slavonians." *Indianapolis Star*, May 27, 1906, 30.

"Church to Celebrate Silver Jubilee." *Indianapolis News*, August 14, 1937, in clipping file "Indianapolis—Churches, –1949," Indiana Division, Indiana State Library.

"Circle Theater Plans Reveal Many Features." *Indianapolis News*, January 29, 1916, 1.

"City Hall Plans Will Be Submitted Monday." *Indianapolis News*, October 30, 1908, 26.

"City Hospital Architects and Judge." *Indianapolis Star*, March 18, 1912, 5.

"City Hospital to Have Rare Beauty." *Indianapolis News*, July 4, 1914, 1, c. 6.

"City News Notes." *Indianapolis Journal*, April 4, 1900, 6.

"Clarence Martindale Dies; Prominent State Architect." *Indianapolis Star*, January 22, 1937, 5, c. 6.

"Classic Beauty Is Restored in Circle Theater." *Indianapolis Star*, December 22, 1933, 10.

"Claypool Hotel Stock." *Indianapolis News*, April 11, 1900, 3, c. 2.

"Clear Parish Church Site." *Indianapolis Star*, July 2, 1912, 5.

"College Building Almost Finished." *Indianapolis Star*, October 25, 1904, 2.

"Colored Pythians Are to Hold a Jubilee." *Indianapolis News*, May 23, 1908, 23.

"Committee Approves Plans." *Indianapolis Star*, April 20, 1911, 9.

"Consider State Building Code." *Indianapolis News*, February 10, 1913, 16.

"The Construction." *Indianapolis Journal*, May 15, 1902, 9, c. 1.

"Contest for Architects." *Indianapolis News*, December 2, 1912, 2.

"Contest Opened for Architects." *Indianapolis Star*, April 4, 1915, 1.

"Contract for New Kahn Tailoring Company Building Awarded to Bedford Company." *Indianapolis Star*, March 6, 1913, 15.

"Contract Is Awarded for New Y.M.C.A. Building." *Indianapolis News*, July 23, 1912, 4.

"Contract Is Awarded for Oriental Temple." *Indianapolis News*, April 13, 1915, 17.

"Contract Is Let for Art Institute Building." *Indianapolis News*, September 20, 1905, 16, c. 3.

"Contracts for Hospital Addition to Be Let Soon." *Indianapolis Star*, September 19, 1910, 4.

"Contracts Let for the Meridian-Street Church." *Indianapolis News*, November 14, 1905, 12.

"The Corner Stone Is Laid." *Indianapolis Star*, October 21, 1910, 7.

"Cornerstone of the new Second Christian Church building . . ." *Indianapolis Star*, April 24, 1910, 41.

"Corner Stone to Be Laid Sunday." *Indianapolis News*, May 27, 1916, 26.

"Corner Stone Will Be Laid Sunday." *Indianapolis Star*, June 7, 1912, 7.

"Crowd Sees Trusses Set." *Indianapolis Star*, November 15, 1909, 10.

"Crowns Property Worth $1,000,000." *Indianapolis Star*, December 17, 1911, 22.

"Death Believed Due to Heart Disease . . ." *Indianapolis Star*, April 7, 1931, 2, c. 4.

"Decide to Extend Campaign." *Indianapolis Star*, April 30, 1912, 3.

"Detail Marks Army Post Completion." *Indianapolis Star*, July 14, 1907, 25.

"Discuss Housing Law and Present Conditions." *Indianapolis News*, September 13, 1910, 3.

"Downtown Church Sold for $104,000." *Indianapolis Star*, May 3, 1912, 1.

"Draft of Franchise; Conference on Interurban Terminal Question To-Morrow." *Indianapolis Journal*, July 27, 1902, 12, c. 2.

Drenon, Brandon, and Ko Lyn Cheang. "'We've Lost So Much,' Residents Defend Area from City Encroachment and Gentrification." *Indianapolis Star*, March 20, 2022, 1A.

"Eastern Architect Holds Americans Influenced Too Much by Old World." *Indianapolis Star*, February 14, 1912, 4.

"Eastern Architect to Be Hospital Umpire." *Indianapolis News*, February 19, 1912, 14.

"Edgar O. Hunter." Indiana Biography Series, 34:91, Indiana Division, Indiana State Library.

"Edwin Hazen Ketcham Dead." *Indianapolis News*, December 19, 1916, 24, c. 8.

"Ernest Greene Dies; Retired Architect." *New York Times*, November 21, 1936, 17.

"Excavation work for the erection of a two-story flat . . ." *Indianapolis Star*, March 12, 1911, 47.

"Explains Problems Facing Architects." *Indianapolis Star*, March 17, 1912, 35.

"Extensive Changes for City Hospital." *Indianapolis Star*, May 20, 1906, 23.

"Every Convenience Is Planned in New Store." *Indianapolis News*, July 11, 1914, 7.

"Façade of the SS. Peter and Paul Cathedral to Be Executed in North Meridian Street." *Indianapolis News*, November 18, 1905, 16.

"Fairbanks Awards Contract." *Indianapolis Star*, May 5, 1911, 16.

"Favor New Fire House Plans." *Indianapolis Star*, June 27, 1913, 14.

"Federal Buildings in Indiana." *Indianapolis Journal*, October 25, 1903, part 2, 13, c. 1.

"15 New Bungalows. Beville Avenue and New York Street." *Indianapolis News*, September 21, 1912, 11.

"A Financial Campaign Is Being Conducted by the Members and Friends of the Second Christian Church." *Indianapolis Star*, March 20, 1910, 38.

"Finishing Touches Were Put on the Sharah Tessila Synagogue." *Indianapolis Star*, December 18, 1910, 48.

"First Baptist Building." *Indianapolis News*, June 18, 1904, 11.

"First Prize Won by I. M. Harrison." *Indianapolis Star*, May 8, 1915, 18.

"First Woman Architect." *Indianapolis Journal*, June 10, 1903, 8, c. 4.

"Fletcher Block Design Chosen." *Indianapolis Star*, December 5, 1912, 16.

"Fletcher Home on Bluff Road." *Indianapolis News*, April 29, 1905, 15.

"Fletcher Savings and Trust Company." *Indianapolis News*, January 23, 1915, 12.

"Fourteen Sets of Plans." *Indianapolis Star*, January 10, 1905, 7.

"Frank B. Hunter, Retired Architect." *Indianapolis Times*, January 5, 1958, 39, c. 1–2.

The Freeman: A National Illustrated Colored Newspaper. Indianapolis, 1884–1926 [incomplete collection at Indiana State Library].

"Front and Side View of New Home for National Company and Scene of Building Being Erected." *Indianapolis Star*, August 29, 1915, 18.

"Front Like Old Church." *Indianapolis News*, January 5, 1905, 4.

"Garage Buildings to Be Erected on Capitol Avenue." *Indianapolis Star*, March 27, 1911, 10.

"George F. McCulloch Buys the Handsome Schmidt Home." *Indianapolis News*, June 6, 1903, 2, c. 4.

"George L. Robinson to Give Principal Sermon." *Indianapolis News*, December 9, 1916, 18.

Glass, James. "Church Survives Flood, Urban Flight." *Indianapolis Star*, March 2, 2013, A15.

"Grecian Friezes to Feature Circle Theater." *Indianapolis News*, May 2, 1916, 13.

"G. V. Bedell, Builder, Dies." *Indianapolis Star*, October 11, 1948, 1.

"G. W. Bunting, 81, Architect, Dies." *Indianapolis Star*, March 1, 1941, 3.

"H. L. Bass, Local Architect, Dies at Washington." *Indianapolis Star*, April 9, 1926. Indiana Biography Series, 2:57, Indiana State Library.

"Hampton Court Is Completed." *Indianapolis Star*, June 25, 1916, 31.

"'Hampton Court to Be up to Minute." *Indianapolis Star*, January 2, 1916, 33.

"Handsome Suburban and Country Homes Are Springing Up around the City's Edge." *Indianapolis News*, April 29, 1905, 15.

"Herbert Foltz, Architect, Dies." *Indianapolis News*, July 6, 1946. Indiana Biography Series, 30:105, Indiana State Library.

"Herron Art Institute to Be Formally Opened Next Tuesday Evening." *Indianapolis Sentinel*, March 1, 1902, 7, c. 6.

"Herron Institute Corner Stone Laid." *Indianapolis News*, November 25, 1905, 4.

"Herron Home of Art Marked by Simplicity." *Indianapolis News*, November 16, 1906, 28.

Herschell, William. "After Twenty Years Hermann Gaul Makes Good His Wedding Day Pledge to Plan for the St. Mary's Parish a Miniature Cathedral of Cologne." *Indianapolis News*, July 6, 1912, 13.

———. "Crosstown Journeys of Large Brick Apartment House and Hotel Give Evidence of Demand for Living Quarters in the City's Central Area." *Indianapolis News*, November 27, 1926, 19, c.1.

———. "New Robert W. Long Hospital, Attached to I.U. School of Medicine, Will Afford Medical and Surgical Facilities for the State's Neediest." *Indianapolis News*, August 17, 1912, 13.

———. "Passing of Old Fire Houses Recalls Early Days When the Volunteer Fighter Was a Social and Political Force in the Life of Indianapolis." *Indianapolis News*, November 26, 1910, 15.

"High Price for Lot." *Indianapolis Star*, July 2, 1904, 3.

"Hillside Christian Sets Attendance Goal at 1,000 for 50th Anniversary." *Indianapolis Star*, May 9, 1942, in clipping file "Disciples of Christ," Indiana State Library.

"Hold Funeral for Architect W. Scott Moore." *Indianapolis Times*, June 1, 1922, 7, c. 7.

"Hospital Addition to Provide for 70 Beds." *Indianapolis News*, January 22, 1910, 28.

"Hospital Bid Received." *Indianapolis Star*, January 26, 1911, 12.

"Hospital Erection to Be Begun Today." *Indianapolis Star*, November 9, 1912, 3.

"Hospital Pavilion Plans." *Indianapolis News*, June 10, 1910, 2.

"Hospital Plans Finished." *Indianapolis Star*, February 26, 1909, 14.

"Hotels Examined." *Indianapolis Journal*, May 7, 1900, 8, c. 5.

"How Indianapolis New Fire Headquarters Building Will Appear." *Indianapolis Star*, May 4, 1913, 28.

"How Others Have Built." *Indianapolis Sunday Star*, March 14, 1909, Women's Section, 4.

"How Others Have Built." *Indianapolis Sunday Star*, May 9, 1909, Women's Section, 4.

"How Others Have Built." *Indianapolis Sunday Star*, July 4, 1909, Women's Section, 4.

"How Others Have Built." *Indianapolis Sunday Star*, August 1, 1909, Women's Section, 4.

"How Others Have Built." *Indianapolis Sunday Star*, August 15, 1909, Women's Section, 4.

"How Others Have Built." *Indianapolis Sunday Star*, September 26, 1909, Women's Section, 4.

"How Others Have Built." *Indianapolis Sunday Star*, October 24, 1909, Women's Section, 4.

"How Others Have Built." *Indianapolis Sunday Star*, October 31, 1909, Women's Section, 4.

"How Others Have Built." *Indianapolis Sunday Star*, December 19, 1909, Women's Section, 4.

"How Others Have Built." *Indianapolis Sunday Star*, April 6, 1910, Women's Section, 4.

"How Others Have Built." *Indianapolis Sunday Star*, September 11, 1910, Women's Section, 4.

"How Others Have Built." *Indianapolis Sunday Star*, October 9, 1910, Women's Section, 4, c. 2.

"How Others Have Built." *Indianapolis Sunday Star*, October 23, 1910, Women's Section, 4, c. 3.

"How Others Have Built." *Indianapolis Sunday Star*, December 18, 1910, Women's Section, 4.

"How Others Have Built—No. 2—An English Type." *Indianapolis Sunday Star*, January 24, 1909, Women's Section, [4].

"How Others Have Built—No. 2—Modern American Domestic." *Indianapolis Sunday Star*, January 31, 1909, Women's Section, 3.

"How Y.M.C.A. Spent Building Fund Money." *Indianapolis News*, January 11, 1909, 11.

"Howard Shaw, Architect, Dies in Baltimore." *Chicago Tribune*, May 7, 1926, 1.

"Indiana Architects Favor Competition." *Indianapolis Star*, November 5, 1911, 27.

"Indiana Architects in First State Association." *Indianapolis Star*, December 19, 1909, 12.

"Indianapolis Firm Rushing Out Uniforms." *Indianapolis Times*, February 28, 1918, 1, c. 3.

"Indianapolis' Modern Union Station, Built at Cost of $2,000,000, Nearing Completion." *Indianapolis Star*, October 8, 1922, 13, 21.

The Indianapolis Recorder: A Negro Newspaper Devoted to the Best Interest of the Colored People of Indiana, 1897 to present [partial collection at Indiana State Library].

"Indianapolis Will Change Her Postoffice Address to the Beautiful New Federal Building within the Next Two Weeks." *Indianapolis News*, September 2, 1905, 13.

The Indianapolis World [newspaper], 188?–19? [some issues at Indiana State Library].

Information documenting the role of Merritt Harrison as a draftsman assisting H. L. Bass in preparing the plans for the Fletcher residence. See *Indianapolis Star*, May 8, 1915, 18.

"John Herron Art Institute Building Will Be Ready for Dedication About Middle of May." *Indianapolis News*, December 11, 1905, 4, c. 3.

"John H. Rankin Here." *Indianapolis Journal*, June 5, 1901, 8, c. 3.

"John H. Stem Dies at Home of a Sister." *Indianapolis News*, August 31, 1910, 1.

"Jubilee Work." *Indianapolis News*, August 2, 1913, 23.

"Judging Plans for New Library Here." *Indianapolis Star*, April 10, 1914, 6.

"Kahn Building Marks New Era." *Indianapolis Star*, December 9, 1915, 9.

"K. of P. Grand Lodge Building." *Indianapolis News*, July 21, 1905, 14.

"Kurt Vonnegut." *Indianapolis Star*, October 2, 1956, 20.

"The last few years has [sic] seen a great increase in the construction . . ." *Indianapolis Star*, August 14, 1905, 5.

"Latest Idea in Churches." *Indianapolis News*, January 7, 1911, 15.

"Lawrence W. George, 65, Commits Suicide." *Indianapolis Star*, September 30, 1936, 12.

"Lay Corner Stone of Y.M.C.A. Today." *Indianapolis Star*, July 26, 1908, 21.

"Leading Architect, C. H. Byfield, Dies." *Indianapolis Star*, May 15, 1935, 3.

"Leases Hinder Bank's Plans." *Indianapolis Star*, January 22, 1907, 10.

"Leonard Geiger Adds New Store." *Indianapolis Star*, March 11, 1917, 8.

"Lets Building Contract." *Indianapolis Star*, September 20, 1910, 14.

"Library Contest Drawing to Close." *Indianapolis Star*, April 3, 1914, 15.

"Livable House is Nicholson's." *Indianapolis Star*, November 15, 1903, 12, c. 1.

"Local Men Lose." *Indianapolis News*, January 17, 1901, 1, c. 8.

"Long Memorial Hospital to Be Pride of State." *Indianapolis Star*, May 10, 1914, 44.

"Lot Bought for Colored Branch of the Y.M.C.A." *Indianapolis News*, January 25, 1912, 13.

"Louis [sic] Sturges Is Dead at 37 [sic]." *Indianapolis News*, January 24, 1941, 11.

"Magnificent New Claypool Will Open To-Morrow." *Indianapolis Journal*, May 17, 1903, Edition 2, 1, c. 1.

"Many Plan New Houses." *Indianapolis Star*, March 26, 1905, 18.

"Mayflower Congregational Church." *Indianapolis News*, April 1, 1901, 1.

"M'Culloch Home Is Sold." *Indianapolis News*, October 18, 1904, 5.

"M. E. Hospital Fund Sought." *Indianapolis Star*, April 18, 1911, 14.

"The members and friends of the Second Baptist Church . . ." *Indianapolis Star*, February 4, 1912, 46.

"Membership Roster Is More than 3,000," *Indianapolis Times*, August 10, 1925, 3.

"Merchants' National Bank to Have Reception To-Day, and to Begin Business in Its New Home on Monday." *Indianapolis News*, April 25, 1908, 8.
"Model Homes of Indianapolis." *Indianapolis Sunday Star*, June 17, 1906, 8.
"Morris Inspects Colonial Theater." *Indianapolis Star*, November 13, 1909, 3.
"Mrs. C. J. Walker to Go to New York to Live." *Indianapolis News*, December 10, 1915, 21, c. 3.
"Mrs. James A. Allison opened her pretty new country home . . ." *Indianapolis News*, March 25, 1911, 17.
"Mr. Taylor on the Sites." *Indianapolis Journal*, April 26, 1899, 8, c. 2.
"Mt. Zion Church." *Indianapolis News*, June 12, 1908, 9.
"Murat Theater in the Hands of Decorators." *Indianapolis News*, February 15, 1910, 7.
"Murat Theater to Be Finest in West." *Indianapolis Star*, February 20, 1910, 22.
"Name Hospital Architects." *Indianapolis News*, February 23, 1912, 19.
"Named Hospital Plans Judge." *Indianapolis Star*, February 20, 1912, 3.
"New Apartments Are Under Construction." *Indianapolis Star*, May 6, 1915, 14.
"New Building Code Is Ready for City Council." *Indianapolis News*, March 16, 1912, 27.
"New Building for Automobile Row." *Indianapolis Star*, July 26, 1914, 10.
"New Building of the Indianapolis News." *Indianapolis News*, September 11, 1909, 11.
"New Buildings Are of Artistic Design." *Indianapolis Star*, March 21, 1909, 47.
"New Buildings: Church Edifices in Progress." *Indianapolis Journal*, March 13, 1869, 4.
"New Burdsal Buildings of the City Hospital with Their Splendid Mural Decorations by Indiana Artists to Be Shown to the Public Tonight." *Indianapolis News*, November 28, 1914, 14.
"New Churches Here Will Exceed Half Million in Cost." *Indianapolis Star*, October 29, 1911, 29.
"New Cole Factory Finished in Spring." *Indianapolis Star*, January 18, 1914, 42;
"New Cole Plant Opens This Week." *Indianapolis Star*, May 24, 1914, 58.
"New College Building of United Brethren." *Indianapolis News*, December 10, 1904, 4.
"New Columbia Club." *Indianapolis Journal*, November 5, 1899, 8, c. 2.
"New Company Signs Severin Hotel Lease." *Indianapolis Star*, May 22, 1912, 1;
"New Double House of Semi-English Style." *Indianapolis Sunday Star*, March 15, 1914, 24.
"New Façade for SS. Peter and Paul Cathedral." *Indianapolis Star*, April 12, 1936, in clipping file "Indianapolis Churches—Catholic," Indiana State Library.
"New Fletcher Trust Building, One of Finest in Country, Is Partially Opened to Tenants." *Indianapolis Star*, September 30, 1914, 9.
"New Holy Rosary Catholic Church." *Indianapolis News*, May 31, 1910, 14.
"New Home Planned." *Indianapolis Star*, November 23, 1906, 1.
"New Hospital, $800,000." *Indianapolis News*, December 23, 1909, 7.
"New Hotel Ranks among Greatest." *Indianapolis Star*, August 24, 1913, 1, 8.
"New Idea in Flat Building." *Indianapolis News*, May 11, 1907, 14.
"New Mayflower Church." *Indianapolis Journal*, October 20, 1901, 3.
"New Mayflower Church." *Indianapolis News*, May 25, 1895.
"New Office Block Will Cost $500,000." *Indianapolis Star*, February 21, 1911, 1.

"The New Parry Home." *Indianapolis News*, April 29, 1905, 15.
"New Residence Embodiment of Artistic Talent." *Indianapolis Star*, April 19, 1914, 51.
"New School Buildings." *Indianapolis News*, March 22, 1901, 5, c. 3.
"New School Will Have First Branch Library." *Indianapolis Star*, February 2, 1908, 6.
"New Seven-Story Block." *Indianapolis News*, January 26, 1900, 8.
"New Spades Park Library Follows Italian Style." *Indianapolis Star*, August 2, 1911, 7.
"New St. Vincent's Hospital." *Indianapolis News*, September 25, 1909, 4.
"$90,000 Building for Autos Begun." *Indianapolis Star*, March 24, 1917, 9.
"Noted Designer May Judge Plans." *Indianapolis Star*, October 15, 1913, 13.
"Noted Men Here for Dedication." *Indianapolis Star*, September 8, 1912, 49.
"Notice to Contractors." *Indianapolis News*, March 14, 1905, 8.
"Notice to Contractors." *Indianapolis Star*, April 17, 1905, 10.
"No Time to Draw Colosseum Plans." *Indianapolis News*, September 14, 1906, 1.
"Novel House Is Planned." *Indianapolis Star*, January 30, 1906, 14.
"Now Then, Everybody Pull for the Y.W.C.A." *Indianapolis News*, March 2, 1907, 5.
"$100,000 Church of Stone." *Indianapolis News*, September 30, 1904, 14.
"P. C. Rubush Dies in Florida." Indiana Biography Series, 32:7, Indiana State Library.
"Pentecost Bands Building." *Indianapolis News*, December 26, 1901, 10.
"Pentecost Bands Church." *Indianapolis News*, April 3, 1901, 10.
"Pioneer Architect of City Is Dead." *Indianapolis Star*, February 14, 1925, 1, c. 7.
"Plans Accepted for Herron Art Institute." *Indianapolis News*, July 1, 1903, 1, c. 3.
"Plans by Competition." *Indianapolis News*, February 21, 1900, 3, c. 1.
"Plans Drawn for New Hillside Ave. Church." *Indianapolis News*, October 5, 1907, 24.
"Plans $80,000 Building." *Indianapolis Star*, July 20, 1911, 11.
"Plans for City Hospital's New Buildings." *Indianapolis News*, February 10, 1922, 21, c. 3.
"Plans for Hospital Changes." *Indianapolis Star*, May 18, 1906, 11.
"Plans for New Bobbs-Merrill Building." *Indianapolis News*, January 29, 1910, 28.
"Plans for New Church Will Be Received Soon." *Indianapolis Star*, July 2, 1904, 10.
"Plans for New Hotel." *Indianapolis Journal*, December 7, 1899, 8, c. 4.
"Plans for New Sharah Tessila Synagogue Ready." *Indianapolis Star*, May 16, 1910, 10.
"Plans for New Structure." *Indianapolis Star*, November 22, 1906, 10.
"Plans for Proposed City Hall Submitted." *Indianapolis News*, November 2, 1908, 18.
"Plans for 16-Story Bank Building Due Tomorrow." *Indianapolis Star*, November 24, 1912, 40.
"Plans for the New Maennerchor Hall to Be Built at Illinois and Michigan Streets." *Indianapolis News*, February 21, 1906, 3.
"Plans $400,000 Building." *Indianapolis Star*, September 16, 1909, 1.
"Plans New $35,000 Church." *Indianapolis Star*, April 12, 1911, 13.
"Plans Ready for M'Ouat Block." *Indianapolis News*, April 17, 1901, 18.
"Plans Revised for the New Masonic Temple." *Indianapolis News*, April 20, 1907, 7.
"The Post Office Plans." *Indianapolis Journal*, November 24, 1899, 4, c. 2.
"Pretty New Home on Riley Avenue." *Indianapolis Star*, January 11, 1914, 19.

"Prominent among the residences erected in this locality . . ." *Indianapolis Star*, January 1, 1912, 9.
"Proposed Home for Indianapolis Y.W.C.A." *Indianapolis News*, April 21, 1906, 23.
"Proposed Mt. Zion Church." *Indianapolis News*, June 6, 1908, 9.
"Proposed Union Station Track Elevation." *Indianapolis Star*, April 12, 1916, 18.
"Public Schools Will Open September 14." *Indianapolis News*, August 22, 1903, 14, c. 1.
"Ready for the Roof." *Indianapolis News*, September 11, 1906, 7.
"Real Estate Market: It Contained Some Surprises for Close Students—Apartment Houses Contemplated on a Big Scale." *Indianapolis Journal*, March 31, 1901, 6, c. 1.
"Real Estate News." *Indianapolis Star*, April 8, 1914, 9.
"Revised Plan for Hospital Ward Building." *Indianapolis Star*, May 1, 1912, 4.
"Rites for W. H. MacLucas." *Indianapolis News*, January 30, 1925, 23.
"Romance in Plans for New St. Mary's Church." *Indianapolis News*, January 1, 1909, 14.
Scherrer, Anton. "City Architecture of the Year Considered from Artistic Viewpoint." *Indianapolis Star*, December 31, 1914, 31.
———. "Our Town." *Indianapolis Times*, May 22, 1937, 9, c. 7.
"Scientists Open Church Easter." *Indianapolis Star*, March 31, 1912, 30.
"Second Christian Church Dedicatory Exercises." *Indianapolis Recorder*, February 11, 1911, 2.
"Seeks to Assist Behrens." *Indianapolis Star*, January 12, 1910, 4.
Shideler, Mabel Wheeler. "Half a Century Ago the Congregation Sharah Tefilla Had Its Inception; Anniversary Will Be Marked Sunday with Jubilee Program and Banquet." *Indianapolis News*, March 12, 1932, in clipping file "Indianapolis—Churches—Hebrew," Indiana State Library.
"Showing Progress to Date on the Ayres Building at Washington and Meridian Streets." *Indianapolis Star*, April 17, 1905, 2.
"Shubert Fired by Murat Enthusiasm." *Indianapolis Star*, February 22, 1910, 3.
"Shubert Stage to Turn." *Indianapolis Star*, June 23, 1909, 7.
"Signs Away Chances for 'Little Angels.'" *Indianapolis News*, December 9, 1910, 20.
"Sisters Break Ground." *Indianapolis Star*, May 24, 1910, 14.
"Sisters Get School Permit." *Indianapolis Star*, August 13, 1908, 3.
"Sisters of St. Francis Buy Allison Estate." *Indianapolis News*, October 17, 1936, 1.
"Site for New Baptist Church Is Selected." *Indianapolis Journal*, April 13, 1904, 1.
"Situation a Surprise." *Indianapolis Journal*, May 13, 1903, 7, c. 2.
"Skyscraper Plans in Hands of Expert Jury." *Indianapolis News*, December 3, 1912, 4.
"South Side Germans." *Indianapolis Journal*, January 21, 1901, 3.
"South Side Turnverein at Floodtide in History." *Indianapolis Journal*, April 21, 1904, 6.
"A special rally will be held today . . ." *Indianapolis Star*, August 11, 1912, 16.
"St. Anthony's Church Ready for Dedication." *Indianapolis News*, November 12, 1904, 22.
"Steps Taken to Erect Building of Ten Stories." *Indianapolis Star*, January 15, 1915, 1.
"Stoughton A. Fletcher Awards Contract for Magnificent New Country Residence." *Indianapolis Star*, May 7, 1915, 1.
"Stutz Auto Company Will Add to Plant." *Indianapolis Star*, January 26, 1916, 11.

"St. Vincent's Hospital, Result of Many Years' Work by Sisters of Charity, Now Rapidly Nearing Completion." *Indianapolis News*, October 5, 1912, 27.
"St. Vincent's Hospital to Be Ready in Fall." *Indianapolis Star*, July 22, 1912, 18.
"Taggart Will Build." *Indianapolis Star*, January 13, 1913, 10.
"Takes Over Tailoring Company." *Indianapolis News*, January 14, 1913, 8.
"Talks of Plans of New Majestic Theater." *Indianapolis News*, March 13, 1907, 3.
"Tell of Roof Collapse." *Indianapolis News*, April 17, 1912, 3.
"Tells Engineers of Housing Need." *Indianapolis Star*, January 24, 1913, 3.
"Temple to Be Built by the Indianapolis Masonic Lodges." *Indianapolis News*, March 3, 1906, 24.
"Tenants of the New K. of P. Building." *Indianapolis Star*, April 14, 1907, 27.
"Tentative Plans for Deaf School." *Indianapolis Star*, February 6, 1906, 4.
"Theater with 3,000 Capacity Assured." *Indianapolis News*, November 6, 1915, 1.
"This Home Embodies Owner's Every Desire." *Indianapolis Star*, August 10, 1913, 43.
"Tiffany Window Sent to Museum of Art." *Indianapolis News*, October 6, 1972, 3, c. 4.
"To Build $80,000 Residence Near Riverside Park." *Indianapolis News*, June 21, 1911, 13.
"To Choose Site." *Indianapolis Journal*, March 9, 1899, 1, c. 1.
"To Complete the New City Hall Building." *Indianapolis News*, November 5, 1909, 23.
"To Consider Plan for Larger Building." *Indianapolis Star*, November 19, 1906, 3.
"Track Elevation Work in Full Blast." *Indianapolis Star Magazine Section*, July 23, 1916, 63.
"25 Enter Library Contest." *Indianapolis Star*, December 11, 1913, 11.
"Unitarians Adopt New Church Plans." *Indianapolis Star*, May 25, 1910, 25.
"Universalist Anniversary Today." *Indianapolis Star*, September 30, 1934, in clipping file "Universalists, Unitarian," Indiana State Library.
Walton, Lloyd B. "Past Masters of Mortar." *Indianapolis Star Magazine*, June 11, 1978, 42–44.
"Well-Known Architect Dead." *Indianapolis News*, April 24, 1911, 16.
"W. E. Stevenson & Co . . . Made Possible the New Hotel Severin" [advertisement]. *Indianapolis Sunday Star*, August 24, 1913, 8.
"Wheeler House Contract Let." *Indianapolis Star*, May 28, 1911, 39.
White, Allen A. "Indiana's Network of Canals Was Merely a Dream." *Indianapolis Star*, June 10, 1934, part 5, 1.
"Will Be City's Pride." *Indianapolis Journal*, June 16, 1900, 5, c. 6.
"Will Begin Work on New Cathedral Soon." *Indianapolis News*, March 4, 1910, 4.
"Will Build Home on Pyle House Site." *Indianapolis Star*, June 20, 1905, 1.
"Will Build New Picture Theater." *Indianapolis Star*, January 31, 1912, 10.
"Will Consult Shuberts Regarding New Theater." *Indianapolis Star*, June 13, 1909, 28.
"Will Open Terminal Station Bids Monday." *Indianapolis News*, June 12, 1903, 15, c. 3.
"Wilson B. Parker, Architect, Dies; Resident for Many Years." *Indianapolis Star*, January 7, 1937, 14.
"Winner Named in Star House Plan Contest." *Indianapolis Star*, March 5, 1916, 27.
Winter Apartments advertisement in "First Inspection of These 36 Homes Wednesday, Sept. 8." *Indianapolis Star*, September 5, 1915, 23.

"Women Architects and Builders." *Indianapolis Star*, April 14, 1907, 44.

"Women in Architecture." *Indianapolis News*, August 18, 1900, 9.

"Work Is Begun on Skyscraper Hotel." *Indianapolis News*, February 5, 1912, 1.

"W. W. Renwick Dies; Church Architect." *New York Times*, March 16, 1933, 20.

Wynne, Ethel A. "All Saints Cathedral Had Beginning in Indianapolis at Close of Civil War." *Indianapolis News*, April 15, 1931, in clipping file "Indianapolis—Churches Episcopal," Indiana State Library.

———. "Congregationalists Active in City Long Before Their Formal Organization." *Indianapolis News*, n.d., in clipping file "Indianapolis Churches—Congregationalists," Indiana State Library.

———. "First Hebrew Congregation Formed by Early Residents of Indianapolis." *Indianapolis News*, January 10, 1931, in clipping file "Indianapolis Churches—Hebrew," Indiana State Library.

———. "First Unitarian Society in the City Formed Shortly after Civil War End." *Indianapolis News*, n.d., in clipping file "Indianapolis Churches—Unitarian," Indiana State Library.

———. "Inspiration from John O'Kane Factor in Forming Disciples Denomination." *Indianapolis News*, c. 1930, in clipping file "Indianapolis Churches—Disciples of Christ of Indianapolis Churches," Indiana Division, Indiana State Library.

———. "Third Christian Church Traditions Are Entwined with Those of Butler." *Indianapolis News*, April 3, 1931, in clipping file "Indianapolis Churches—Disciples of Christ," Indiana State Library.

[Wynne, Ethel A.] "Universalist Congregation First Appeared in Indianapolis in 1844; Second in 1853." *Indianapolis News*, February 21, 1931, in clipping file "Universalists, Unitarian," Indiana State Library.

"Y.W.C.A. Building to Be Started This Fall." *Indianapolis News*, August 23, 1907, 7.

PERIODICALS

"*The Architectural Record* Archives." *Architectural Record*. https://www.architecturalrecord.com/articles/13598-architectural-record-archives, accessed June 26, 2024.

The Brickbuilder, vol. I, no. 1 (1892). https://babel.hathitrust.org/cgi/pt?id=iau.31858033436340&view=1up&seq=1&skin=2021, accessed July 1, 2024.

"Cathedral of St. Peter and St. Paul, Indianapolis, Ind." *American Architect and Building News*, April 9, 1892, between 24 and 25.

Cram, Ralph Adams. "The Indianapolis Public Library." *Architectural Forum*, vol. XXIX, no. 3 (September 1918), 68.

"Family Resemblance." *Indiana Preservation* (November/December 2021), 3.

Glass, James A. "It Would Make a Beautiful City: The Planning of Indianapolis." *Traces of Indiana and Midwestern History* (Fall 2020), 4–19.

The History of Laurel Hall." *Shield of Phi Kappa Psi*, vol. 126, no. 3 (Fall 2005), 9. http://www.phikappapsiarchive.com/wp-content/uploads/2020/04/Shield-Fall-2005.pdf.

"The Inland Architect and News Record, 1883–1908." Internet Archive. https://archive.org/details/sim_inland-architect-and-news-record_1883-08_2_1_0, accessed June 30, 2024.

Kahn, Renee. "The American Foursquare." *Old-House Journal* (February 1982), 29–32.

"Kurt Vonnegut League Member Dies." *Construction News*, vol. 22, no. 41 (1956), 8.

"New Dean of Architecture: F. H. Bosworth, Jr. Assumes New Duties in September." *Cornell Alumni News*, vol. XXI, no. 39 (July 1919), 482.

O'Bar, Jack. "The Origins and History of the Bobbs-Merrill Company." Occasional paper 172, University of Illinois Graduate School of Library and Information Science, December 1985, https://www. https://files.eric.ed.gov/fulltext/ED266787.pdf.

"Robert Frost Daggett, Sr. Dies." *Construction News*, vol. 21, no. 37 (September 12, 1955), 8.

"Scientific American: Architects and Builders Edition." Internet Archives, 1891– https://archive.org/details/scientificameric1891unse/page/n5/mode/2up, accessed June 26, 2024.

Warren, Stanley. "The Bethel African Methodist Episcopal Church." In *Traces of Indiana and Midwestern History*, vol. 19, no. 3 (Summer 2007), 34.

WEBSITES

"Alexander Jackson Davis." History of American Landscape Design, National Gallery of Art, n.d., https://heald.nga.gov/mediawiki/index.php/Alexander_Jackson_Davis, accessed June 25, 2024.

"Alfred Grindle." Bloominpedia, 2024. .https://www.bloomingpedia.org/w/index.php?title=Alfred_Grindle&action=history.

"Allison Mansion: Landscape Information." Cultural Landscape Foundation, n.d., https://www.tclf.org/allison-mansion, accessed June 26, 2024.

"The Arts and Crafts Movement—History and Concepts." The Art Story, n.d., https://www.theartstory.org/movement/arts-and-crafts/history-and-concepts/, accessed June 26, 2024.

"Asher Benjamin: American Architect." Encyclopedia Britannica, n.d., https://www.britannica.com/biography/Asher-Benjamin, accessed June 26, 2024.

Beckley, Lindsey. "Monster Meetings at the Senate Avenue YMCA." *Indiana History Blog*. Indiana Historical Bureau, May 11, 2018. https://blog.history.in.gov/monster-meetings-at-the-senate-avenue-ymca/.

"Bernard Vonnegut." Brief Biographies of American Architects Who Died Between 1897 and 1947, n.d. https://www.sah.org/docs/misc-resources/brief-biographies-of-american-architects-who-died-between-1897-and-1947.pdf, accessed June 26, 2024.

Borland, Amy. "That Exceptional One: Indiana's Early Female Architects and Builders." Indiana Department of Natural Resources, May 2022. https://www.in.gov/dnr/historic-preservation/files/hp-That-Exceptional-One.pdf

"Bro. Samuel Plato." Biographical summary on website of Phi Beta Sigma Fraternity, Louisville, n.d. https://phibetasigmalouisville.org/sample-page/the-chapter, accessed June 24, 2024.

"Charles Follen McKim." National Park Service, n.d., https://www.nps.gov/people/charles-follen-mckim.htm, accessed June 26, 2024.

"Charles Howard Byfield." Find a Grave. n.d., https://www.findagrave.com/memorial/45898698/charles-howard-byfield., accessed June 26, 2024.

City of Muncie. "Walking Tour #3—Historic Architecture in the Emily Kimbrough Historic District, Muncie, Indiana," c. 2000. https://www.muncie.in.gov/egov/documents/1621350220_4887.pdf, accessed June 26, 2024.

Cunningham, John M. "Yggdrasill." Encyclopedia Britannica, May 20, 2024. http://www.britannica.com/topic/Yggdrasill.

"Decades-Long Effort to Save Simpson Hall Ends in Defeat." Indiana Landmarks, July 30, 2019. https://www.indianalandmarks.org/2019/07/simpson-hall-effort-ends-in-defeat/#:~:text=Lost%20Opportunity&text=In%20April%2C%20those%20efforts%20were,as%20the%20school's%20girls'%20dormitory.

"Francke Huntington Bosworth, Jr." Find a Grave, n.d. https://www.findagrave.com/memorial/151229427/francke-huntington-bosworth, accessed June 26, 2024.

Frank H. Wheeler Estate Photographs. Andrew R. Seager Archive of the Built Environment, Ball State University Libraries' Archives and Special Collections.

Freeland, Sharon Butsch. "Hi Mailbag: Parry Mansion in Golden Hill." HistoricIndianapolis.com, March 5, 2013. https://historicindianapolis.com/hi-mailbag-parry-mansion-in-golden-hill/.

"Henry Ives Cobb." Art Institute of Chicago, n.d. https://www.artic.edu/archival-collections/digital-resources/henry-ives-cobb, accessed June 26, 2024.

"Historic Area Preservation Plan—Wholesale District Historic Area." Indianapolis Historic Preservation Commission, 1990. https://citybase-cms-prod.s3.amazonaws.com/3/5/74ba24/24c92a559ee8562c51eb6.pdf.

"Historical Sketch." Collection guide for "Indianapolis Young Women's Christian Association Records, 1896–1986," Indiana Historical Society Library, n.d. https://indianahistory.org/wp-content/uploads/indianapolis-young-womens-christian-association-records.pdf, accessed August 18, 2021.

"History." University of Illinois Urbana-Champaign School of Architecture, n.d. https://arch.illinois.edu/about/history-of-the-school-of-architecture/, accessed June 26, 2024.

"History of the Department of Architecture." Cornell University. n.d. https://aap.cornell.edu/academics/architecture/about/history, accessed June 26, 2024.

"Housing." Lower East Side Tenement Museum, 2005. https://www.tenement.org/encyclopedia/housing_tenements.htm, accessed February 23, 2009.

"Howard Van Doren Shaw." Wikipedia., n.d. https://en.wikipedia.org/wiki/Howard_Van_Doren_Shaw, accessed June 26, 2024.

Indiana DNR Division of Historic Preservation & Archaeology. "2022 Historic Preservation Month Poster." Facebook, March 15, 2022. https://www.facebook.com/profile/100064571926998/search/?q=That%20Exceptional%20One%3A%20Indiana%27s%20Early%20Female%20Architects%20%26%20Builders.

Ivey, Paul Eli. "American Christian Science Architecture and Its Influence." Mary Baker Eddy Library, n.d. https://www.marybakereddylibrary.org/research/american-christian-science-architecture-and-its-influence/, accessed June 26, 2024.

Karp, Mort, and Drusilla Null. "Maennerchor Building: Part I. Historical Information." Historic American Buildings Survey, August 1974 and July 1984. https://tile.loc.gov/storage-services/master/pnp/habshaer/in/in0100/in0148/data/in0148data.pdf.

Langsam, Walter E. "Charles (C.) Crapsey." *Biographical Dictionary of Cincinnati Architects, 1788–1940.* Architectural Foundation of Cincinnati. Obtained from defunct website and hard copy in the possession of the author.

———. "William R. Brown" and "David D. Davis." *Biographical Dictionary of Cincinnati Architects, 1788–1940.* Architectural Foundation of Cincinnati. n.d. Obtained from defunct website and hard copy in the possession of the author.

Larsen, Paul Clifford. "A Centennial History of the Municipal Building Serving Minneapolis and Hennepin County, Minnesota." Sanford Berman Website, 1991. https://sanfordberman.org/hist/emer/sglass.htm.

Lewis, Michael, Clio Group. "A Review of the Building History of the Calvary Methodist Church," prepared for Calvary United Methodist Church, Philadelphia, n.d. Copy downloaded from defunct website in 2023 and in the possession of the author.

"Louis J. Millet (1853–1923) American." Architectural Antiques, n.d. https://archantiques.tumblr.com/post/92544053759/the-name-of-decorative-designer-louis-j-millet, accessed June 26, 2024.

Luebering, J. E. "Shubert Brothers: American Theatrical Managers." Encyclopedia Britannica. https://www.britannica.com/biography/Shubert-Brothers#ref252539, accessed August 16, 2021.

"Music and Choral Halls." Article on the Chicagology website. https://chicagology.com/columbiaexpo/fair028/, accessed June 26, 2024.

National Architectural Accreditation Board. *Architecture Program Report*, University of Notre Dame School of Architecture, Fall 2009. https://architecture.nd.edu/assets/225445/2009_nd_soa_architecture_program_report.pdf.

Ockerbloom, John Mark. "The Online Books Page . . . The American Architect." University of Pennsylvania Library, n.d. https://onlinebooks.library.upenn.edu/webbin/serial?id=amarch, accessed June 26, 2024.

———. "The Online Books Page . . . The Brickbuilder." University of Pennsylvania Library, n.d. https://onlinebooks.library.upenn.edu/webbin/serial?id=brickbuilder, accessed June 26, 2024.

"Oldfields." National Park Service, n.p. https://www.nps.gov/nr/travel/indianapolis/oldfields.htm, accessed June 26, 2024.

Patterson, Brody. "Sumptuous Golden Hill Estate in Indianapolis, Indiana." Luxatic, August 31, 2017. https://luxatic.com/sumptuous-golden-hill-estate-indianapolis-indiana/.

"Paul Philippe Cret 1876–1945." University Archives and Records Center, Penn Libraries, n.d. https://archives.upenn.edu/exhibits/penn-people/biography/paul-philippe-cret, accessed June 26, 2024.

Periale, Elizabeth. "Alexander Turney Stewart, Father of the Department Store." *Unbound* (blog). Smithsonian Libraries and Archives, September 14, 2010. https://blog.library.si.edu/blog/2010/09/14/alexander-turney-stewart/#.YRUq64hKg2w.

Richardson, Gary, and Tim Sablik. "Banking Panics of the Gilded Age, 1863–1913." Federal Reserve History, December 4, 2015. https://brewminate.com/banking-panics-of-the-gilded-age-1863-1913.

Robinson, Quentin. "James F. Alexander." Tippecanoe County Historical Association. https://tippecanoehistory.org/finding-aids/james-f-alexander/, accessed August 11, 2021.

"Samuel Plato" [text of the State Historical Marker in Marion]. Indiana Historical Bureau, 2014. https://www.in.gov/history/state-historical-markers/find-a-marker/find-historical-markers-by-county/indiana-historical-markers-by-county/samuel-plato/, accessed June 2024.

"Scottish Rite Cathedral." *Chicago.designslinger* (blog), February 19, 2015. https://chicagodesignslinger.blogspot.com/2015/02/scottish-rite-cathedral-chicago-chicago.html.

Shank, Wesley I. "Cole Motor Car Company Factory: Part I. Historical Information." Historic American Buildings Survey, December 1971. https://tile.loc.gov/storage-services/master/pnp/habshaer/in/in0000/in0047/data/in0047data.pdf.

———. "Union Station: Part I. Historical Information." Historic American Buildings Survey, 1, August 1971. https://cdn.loc.gov/master/pnp/habshaer/in/in0000/in0069/data/in0069data.pdf.

Smith, Jon-Charles. "The Architecture of Samuel M. Plato; The Marion Years, Grant County Projects, 1902–1921." Abstract for Master's thesis, Ball State University, 1998. https://cardinalscholar.bsu.edu/browse/author?scope=a775b6a3-ef4d-42bf-952b-8aaa0fcbeed3&value=Smith,%20Jon%20Charles&bbm.return=2, accessed June 26, 2024.

"Solon S. Beman and Spencer S. Beman Collection." Art Institute of Chicago. https://www.artic.edu/artworks/262151/solon-s-beman-and-spencer-s-beman-collection, accessed June 29, 2024.

Tatman, Sandra. "Kellogg, Thomas M." Philadelphia Architects and Their Buildings, n.d. https://www.philadelphiabuildings.org/pab/app/ar_display.cfm/26268, accessed June 26, 2024.

———. "Rankin and Kellogg." Philadelphia Architects and Their Buildings., n.d. https://www.philadelphiabuildings.org/pab/app/ar_display.cfm/26268, accessed June 26, 2024.

———. "Rankin, John Hall (1868–1952)." Philadelphia Architects and Their Buildings, n.d. https://www.philadelphiabuildings.org/pab/app/ar_display.cfm/26268, accessed June 26, 2024.

Tinker, Steve, and Clio Admin. "James Allison Mansion." Clio: Your Guide to History. February 22, 2017. https://theclio.com/entry/32486.

"Tour Will Open Newly Restored Golden Hill Mansion." Naptown Buzz, June 9, 2014. https://naptownbuzz.com/2014/06/tour-will-open-newly-restored-golden-hill-mansion/.

"The Unknown Architect: Frank Mills Andrews." Calvary Cemetery, Dayton, n.d. http://calvarycemeterydayton.org/the-unknown-architect/, accessed September 21, 2021.

INDEX

Page numbers in *italics* refer to illustrations.
Buildings are located in Indianapolis unless otherwise noted.

Abraham Lincoln School 18, 153–54, *154*
abstracted Modern style. *See* Modern style
Acropolis, influence, 151
Adam, Robert, influence, 81–82
Adams, Wayman, 208
Adler and Sullivan, 9
Adolph Scherrer and Son: City Hospital, 205–9, *207, 209*. *See also* Scherrer, Adolph
advertisements, architects', 476
Aeolian Building, 52, *53*
African American Pythian Building, 181–83, *182,* 489
African Americans: neighborhoods, 111, 215, 383; population growth, 287; religious denominations, 224; segregation imposed on, 111, 189–90, 383, 489–90; working as architects or contractors, 190, 271, 489; working as architects or contractors, lack of, 111, 215, 291, 471, 488–90
African Americans, buildings of, 5–6, 215; African American Pythian Building, 181–83, *182,* 489; Christ Missionary Baptist Church, 268, *269*; Grand United Order of Odd Fellows Building, 181, 489; Madam C. J. Walker House, 418–20, *419*; Mt. Zion Baptist Church, 482, 489; residences, 383, 418–20, *419,* 461–62; Robert Gould Shaw School 40, 155, *157*; Second Baptist Church, 271–74, *272, 273,* 489, 543n82; Second Christian Church, 287–88, *288*; Senate Avenue YMCA Building, 189–93, *191, 192*
Agriculture (Rhind), 119
Alberti, Leon Battista, 280
Alexander, James F., 36. *See also* J. F. Alexander and Son
Alexander, Mary K., 443
Alhambra Theater, 77, *78,* 79
Allardt, M. T., 478
Allen, Layton: about, 482; Allen (Layton and Lelah Francis) House, 411, *411*–12
Allen, Lelah Francis, 411
Allen (Layton and Lelah Francis) House, 411, *411*–12
Allison, Annie Hamilton, 328
Allison, Dellmore C., 327–28
Allison, James A., 55, 68, 348, 354, 359
Allison, Sara Willis Cornelius, 354, 356
Allison (James A. and Sara Willis Cornelius) Estate, 354–59, *355, 357, 358*

591

Allison (Dellmore C. and Annie Hamilton) House, 327–28, *328*, *330*
All Saints Episcopal Cathedral, 241–45, *242*, *243*, 482
All Souls Unitarian Church, 284–87, *285*, *286*, 482
American Architect and Building News, 106, 292, 345–46, 480, 487
American Box Ball Company, 396
American Builder's Guide, The (Benjamin), 472
American Central Life Insurance Company Building (1929–30), 37, 495
American Foursquare style: defined, 314, 316, 372, 412, 552n12; Barnhill (Dr. John and Celeste Terrell) House, 390–91, *391*; Conner (Haskell L. and Herbert T.) Double, 437–40, *438*; Furnas (Robert W. and Hannah Wright) House, 314–16, *315*; Gocke-King Double, 436, *437*; Hubbard (Willard W. and Josephine Niles) House, 388–90, *389*; June (George W. and Alberta Barthel) House, 412–13, *413*; Rapp (Alfred T. and Elizabeth Gough) House, 416, 416–18, *417*; Walker (Madam C. J.) House, 418–20, *419*
American Institute of Architects (AIA): chapters and affiliations, 481, 484–85; competitions advocated by, 40, 106; fees set by, 488; first woman as a member of, 490
American National Bank, 363
American Unitarian Society, 284
Ancient Arabic Order of the Nobles of the Mystic Shrine, 72
Anderson, Edwin, 145
Andrews, Frank M.: about, 64, *65* (portrait); Claypool Hotel, 58–63, 64, *59*, *60*, *61*, *62*, *65*; Columbia Club (1900–1901), 64, 173–76, *174*, *175*; Conover Building (Dayton), 64; Dayton Arcade, 64; George Washington Hotel (New York), 64; Hotel McAlpine (New York), 64; Hotel Seelbach (Louisville), 64; Hotels Sinclair and Taft (Cincinnati), 64; Kentucky State Capitol, 64
Andrews and Martindale, 112
annexation of towns, 223, 254
Antiquities of Athens, The (Stuart and Revett), 473
apartments, 381, 382, 440–60; Audubon Court Apartments, 447–49, *448*; Balmoral Court Apartments, 452–56, *453*; Berrick Apartments, 446, *447*; Coulter Flats, 444–46, *445*; Hampton Court Apartments, 457–60, *458*, *459*; The Rink Flats, 441–43, *442*; Winter Apartments, 449–52, *450*, *451*
Appeal to Justice (Van Ingen), 118
Architects' and Builders' Building, 37
Architects' Association of Indianapolis, 244, 484–85, 493
architects' travels, 374
architectural and building guides and manuals, 19th century, 474–80. *See also* architectural periodicals, as design sources
architectural apprenticeship system, 475–76, 492
architectural apprenticeships, 475–76
architectural competitions: in Beaux Arts and house designs, 486–87; City Hospital, 206; Fletcher Savings and Trust Building, 39–40; Indianapolis City Hall, 131–32; Indianapolis Commercial Club, 479; Indianapolis Public Library, Central Library, 145–46, 479, 484; Indiana Statehouse (1835), 473–74; trend of holding, 106, 110, 214, 483–84; US Courthouse and Post Office, 112, 483
architectural education: academic programs, 479–81, 485–86, 487; apprenticeship system, 475–76, 492; Beaux-Arts method in, 152, 479, 486, 498; École des Beaux-Arts, 146, 152, 212, 449, 479, 480; in Indiana, 486, 561n33; of women, 490, 492

592 | INDEX

architectural exhibitions, 485
Architectural Forum, 480, 487
architectural glossary, 497–509
Architectural Heritage of Evansville (Wooden), 3
architectural inventories, 2–4
architectural periodicals, as design sources, 106, 292, 345–46, 373–74, 480, 487
architectural profession: early 19th century, builders and carpenters, 471–74; early to mid-19th century, first architects in Indianapolis, 473–77; mid to late 19th century, development of Indianapolis architects, 477–81; early 20th century growth, 481–94; post–World War I, 495–96; advertising, 476; African Americans' absence from, 111, 215, 291, 471, 488–89; building type specialization, 373, 383, 478–79, 481–83; education and training (*see* architectural education); engineering services, 488; exhibitions and lectures, 485; fees, 488; formation of associations and clubs, 480–81, 484–85; legislation and licensing, 485, 490, 561n28; out-of-town architects, 483–84 (*see also* Chicago architects; New York architects; *and names of individuals and firms*); partners' roles, 487–88; women's limited participation in, 471, 488, 490–92
Architectural Record, 106, 292, 346, 480
architectural style guide, 510–24
Architectural Styles in Marshall County (Wythongan Valley Preservation Council), 3
Architecture of Country Houses, The (Downing), 476
Arnold, William V. B., 427
Art Association of Indianapolis, 169
Art Deco style: Circle Tower, 496; Coca-Cola Bottling Plant (1931), 496
art glass windows, 238, 250, 251, 284, 285, 286, 540n22
Art Institute of Chicago, 142

Art Nouveau movement, 85
Arts and Crafts/bungalow style: Allen (Layton and Lelah Francis) House, 411, 411–12; All Souls Unitarian Church, 284–87, 285, 286; Audubon Court Apartments, 447–49, 448; Bass (Herbert L. and Floria Logan) House, 404–5, 405; Coburn (August) Residence, 344, 344; Hubbard (Kin and Josephine Jackson) House, 409–11, 410; Recker (Carlos and Elizabeth Butler) House, 406, 408, 408–9, 554n42; Rubush (Preston C. and Renah Wilcox) House, 402–4, 403; Second Christian Church, 287–88, 288. *See also* Arts and Crafts style; bungalows; California bungalow style
Arts and Crafts Movement, 283, 340, 384, 406, 461, 497
Arts and Crafts style: Fletcher (Stoughton A., II, and May Henley) "suburban" house, 342–44, 343; Lieber (Herman P. and Alma Bachman) House, 323–25, 324; Tanner (George G. and Kate Block) House, 384, 385; Thornton (Florence Baxter and George D.) House, 340–42, 341. *See also* Arts and Crafts/bungalow style; bungalows; California bungalow style
Association of Architects, Indiana State 483
athletic buildings. *See* social, fraternal, and athletic buildings
Atwood, Charles, 14
Audubon Court Apartments, 447–49, 448
automobile factories, 95–103; Cole Motor Car Company Factory, 97–99, 98, 104; National Motor Vehicle Company Factory, 99–100, 101; Stutz Motor Car Company Factory, 100, 102, 103, 104
automobile production, rise of, 9, 95, 99, 104
automotive showrooms and service buildings, 54–58; Fisher Automobile Company Building, 55, 57, 58; Gibson Automotive Building, 53, 55; Globe Realty Company

garages, 55, 56, 57; Williams Building, 55, 56, 57
Auto Row, 55, 56
Ayres, Fanny, 490
Ayres, Frederic M., 44, 52

Bachman, Frederick M., 446
Bacon, Charles E.: Third Christian Church, 266–67, 267
Badger Furniture Company, 44
Baker, John E., 473
Balmoral Court Apartments, 452–56, 453
bank buildings: Fletcher Savings and Trust Building, 39–42, 41; Merchants National Bank Building, 24–27, 25, 26
Baptists, 224
Barksdale, David, 3
Barnhill, Celeste Terrell, 390
Barnhill, John F., 390
Barnhill (Dr. John and Celeste Terrell) House, 390–91, 391
baronial towers, 384, 385
Bass, Floria Logan, 404
Bass, Herbert L.: about, 370, 371 (portrait); Allison (James A. and Sara Willis Cornelius) Estate (with Price), 354–59, 355, 357, 358, 370; Allison (Dellmore C. and Annie Hamilton) House, 327–28, 328, 330; Arnold (George) House, 370; Bass (Herbert L. and Floria Logan) House, 404–6, 405; Fletcher (Stoughton A., II, and May Henley) Estate ("Laurel Hall"), 363–71, 365, 367, 368, 369; French (Lucius) Estate, 370; Hitz (A. D.) House, 370; Holcomb (James I.) Estate, 370; Reynolds (H. B.) House, 370; Sanborn (Gerry) Estate, 370; Sommers (Charles B.) Estate, 370; Wilkinson (Allan A.) Estate, 370. See also Bass, Knowlton and Company; Herbert L. Bass and Company
Bass, Knowlton and Company: Ben Hur Office Building (Crawfordsville), 370; Citizens National Bank (Greensburg), 370; Highland Country Club, 370; Test Building, 370
Bass, W. H., 370
Bass (Herbert L. and Floria Logan) House, 404–6, 405
Bates, Charles Edgar, 478, 482
Bates-Allen-Parry-McGowan House, 346, 477
Bates House (hotel), 475
Bauman, Ralph W., 427
Beaux Arts design: academic programs based on, 479, 486 (see also École des Beaux-Arts); defined, 152, 498; in public buildings, 114, 134, 135, 146–48; societies and competitions, 486–87
Beaux Arts Society of Indianapolis, 486
Beaux Arts Society of New York, 486
Bedell, George V.: about, 258, 258 (portrait), 482; Congregation Sharah Tessila, 258, 264, 265, 482; Holy Rosary Catholic Church (preliminary design), 258; Holy Trinity Slovenian Catholic Church, 256–59, 257, 482; Indianapolis Glove Factory, 258; Ritz Theater, 258; St. Francis de Sales Catholic Church, 258, 280–83, 282, 482; St. Mary's Academy and School, 258; St. Philip Neri Catholic Church, 258; Talbott Theater, 258. See also Bedell and Lieske
Bedell and Lieske: Coulter Flats, 444–46, 445
Bedford limestone, 40, 63, 68, 114, 137, 150, 177, 262, 290
Beech Grove: Big Four Shops, 95, 96, 97
Beech Grove, IN: St. Francis Hospital, 204, 205
Behrens, Henry Richard, 81, 81, 530n97
Behrens, William F., 63, 137, 176, 530n97
Beman, Solon Spencer: Second Church of Christ, Scientist (with Spencer Solon Beman), 262–63, 263
Beman, Spencer Solon: Second Church of Christ, Scientist (with Solon Spencer Beman), 262–63, 263
Bencker, Ralph, 353
Benjamin, Asher, 472, 473

Benjamin V. Enos and Son, 478
Berrick Apartments, 446, 447, 482
Bethel African Methodist Episcopal Church, 488–89
Bethune, Louise, 490
Beville Avenue workers' bungalows, 425–27, 426
Big Four Shops, Beech Grove, 95, 96, 97
Biltmore, Ashville, NC, 345
Bishop (19th century builder), 473
Blake, James, 474
Blankenship and Waymire, 190
Bliss, Henry R., 319, 320
Bliss, Margaret Hooker, 319, 320
Bliss (Henry R. and Margaret) House II, 320, 321
Bliss-Vonnegut-Cummings House, 318–20, 319
Block, A. L., 77
Block, William H., 48
Blois, France, Royal château, 345
"Blossom Heath" (Fisher Estate), 354
Bobbs, John S., 150
Bobbs, William C., 31
Bobbs-Merrill Building, 31–33, 32, 482
Bodenhamer, David J., 3
Bohlen, August C., 544n91
Bohlen, Diedrich A., 475, 476, 477, 478, 480, 481. See also D. A. Bohlen and Son
Bohlen, Oscar D.: about, 215, 480, 481–82, 485; German Evangelical Zion Church, 249–52, 250, 251, 481–82; Meridian Street Methodist Episcopal Church (1905–6), 238–41, 239, 240, 481; Murat Temple and Theater, 72–76, 73, 74, 75; St. Agnes Academy, 160, 163, 163–64; St. Vincent's Hospital, 201–4, 203; YWCA Building, 187–89, 188. See also D. A. Bohlen and Son
Bohn, Arthur C.: about, 50–51, 51 (portrait), 479–80, 484, 487; All Souls Unitarian Church, 284–87, 285, 286; All Souls Unitarian Church, 284–87, 285, 286; Fletcher Savings and Trust Building, 39–42, 41, 50, 482; Hibben, Hollweg, and Company Building, 90–91, 92, 93; Hotel Severin, 65, 67, 68, 68–69; Indianapolis Star Building, 20, 21. Kahn Office Building, 35, 38, 39, 48, 50; Kahn Tailoring Company Factory, 50, 103, 104; William H. Block Company Department Store, 48, 49, 50, 482. See also Vonnegut and Bohn
Bona Thompson Memorial Library, Butler College, 168, 169
Book of Architecture (Gibbs), 472
Bookwalter, Charles A., 131–32
Boomer, Hobart A., 434
Borglum, Gutzon, 150
Borie, Zantzinger, and Medory: Indianapolis Public Library, Central Library (1915–17; with Cret), 145, 150
Boring and Tilton (New York), 120
Borland, Amy, 490
Bosler, Cornelius, 232
Boston Public Library, 168
Bosworth, Francke H., Jr.: Winter Apartments, 449–52, 450, 451
Boyd, Linneas, 361
Boyington, William W., 477
Brandt, Herman T., 478
Brickbuilder, 292, 480, 487
brickmakers, 19th century, 473
Brightwood, IN, 223
British architecture books, 472–73
Broadway Methodist Episcopal Church (building at 22nd Street and Broadway), 252
Broadway Methodist Episcopal Church (building on Fall Creek Parkway), 495
Brown, Glenn, 484
Brown, William R., 228, 478. See also Brown and Davis
Brown and Davis: First Baptist Church (1904–6; with Gillespie and Carrel), 228–30, 229
Browning, Eliza, 140, 145, 215
Bruant, Jacques, influence, 546n9

Brubaker, Henry C., 16
Brubaker, Samuel H., 478
Brubaker and Eldridge: Indianapolis Board of Trade Building, 16, *17*, 107
Brubaker and Stern, 206, 490
Brush, John T., 340, 342, 372
Bryan, John K., 422
Bryan, Louise Rentsch, 422
Bryan, William Lowe, 209–10
builders and carpenters, 19th century, 3, 471–74
Builders' Real Estate Company, 452, 454, 457
Builders' Supply Corporation of Indianapolis, 394
building and architectural guides and manuals, 19th century, 474–80. *See also* architectural periodicals, as design sources
Buildings of the United States (Society of Architectural Historians), 2
buildings of worship, 223–98; Arts and Crafts/bungalow style, 283–88; Classical style, 259–74; Gothic style, 234–59; Italian Renaissance style, 274–83; maps, 293–99; Pentecostal Bands buildings, 288–90; religious denominations, 223–24; Romanesque style, 225–33; stylistic trends and influences, 224, 290–92. *See also* churches; synagogues *for individual buildings, and under specific architectural styles*
Bullfinch, Charles, 472
Bungalow Company, 422, 427, 429, 430
bungalows: Beville Avenue workers' bungalows, 425–27, *426*; Bryan (John F. and Louise Rentsch) House, 422–23, *423*; Hooser (Joseph) House, 430, *431*; lower-middle and working-class, 422–33; Moyer (Jacob F. and Abbie Gibbs) House, 423–25, *424*; Overman-Arnold House, 427–29, *428*; usage and definition, 409, 422; Vogel (William D.) House, *428*, 429–30; Wuensch (Edwin) House, 431–33, *432*. *See also* Arts and Crafts/bungalow style; Arts and Crafts style; California bungalow style

Bunting, George W., Jr.: about, 531n112; Big Four Shops, Beech Grove, 95, 96, 97
Bunting, George W., Sr., 531n112
Burckhardt, Adele, 392
Burckhardt, Louis, 392
Burckhardt (Dr. Louis and Adele) House, 391–94, *393*
Burdsal, Alfred, 208
Burnham, Daniel H., 14, *15* (portrait), 112, 483. *See also* D. H. Burnham and Company
Burnham and Root, 9
Burns, Lee, 3, 400
Burns Realty Company, 383, 400
Busch, Adam, 488
business and professional classes, 382, 383. *See also* detached houses (business and professional classes)
Butler College: Bona Thompson Memorial Library, 168, *169*; Jordan Hall, 495
Byfield, Charles H.: about, 329, *329* (portrait), 482; Bryan (John F. and Louise Rentsch) House, 329, 422–23, *423*; Davlon Apartments, 329; Geiger (Anton) House, 329; Gocke-King Double, 329, 436, *437*; Hare-Tarkington House, 329, 330, *331*; Wulsin Building, 329
Byrne, Joseph F., 254

California bungalow style: defined, 427; Hose Company No. 28 Fire Station (1911), *139*, 140; Hooser (Joseph) House, 430, *431*; Overman-Arnold House, 427–29, *428*; Second Christian Church, 287–88, *288*; Vogel (William D.) House, *428*, 429–30. *See also* Arts and Crafts/bungalow style; Arts and Crafts style; bungalows
Calvin, Frank, 425
Cannon, Fermor S., 490
Carcassonne, France, 303
Carnegie, Andrew, 140
Carnegie libraries, 140–44, *141*, *144*, 168
carpenters and builders, 19th century, 471–74

Carr (Dr. Silas J. and Sarah McCullough) House, 420–21, *421*

Carr, Marrett L.: Audubon Court Apartments, 447–49, *448*; Carr (Dr. Silas J. and Sarah McCullough) House, 420–21, *421*

Carr, Sarah McCullough, 420

Carr, Silas J., 420

Carrel, Henry C. *See* Gillespie and Carrel

Carson, Charles L. (Baltimore), 120

Carter, Georgiana, 437

cartouches: defined, 499; on churches, 280; on commercial and industrial buildings, 18, 23, 29, 35, 39, 46, 100; on public buildings, 139, 168, 187, 193, 199, 214; on residences, 305, 444, 449, 450

Cassady, Ulysses Grant, 286

cast-iron facades, 42, *43*

Catholic Diocese of Indianapolis, 254, 256, 274, 280

Catholic Sisters of Charity, 198, 201

Catholic Sisters of Providence at Saint Mary-of-the-Woods, 160, 163

C. C. Foster Lumber Company, 314

Central Universalist Church, 252–53, *253*

Century Building, 91, *93*

Chambers, Sir William, 472

Chandler, Henry, 314

Chatard, Francis Silas, 204, 232, 254, 256, 274–75

Chicago architects working in Indianapolis, 105–6, 477, 478, 483. *See also names of individuals and firms*

Chicago-style windows, 23, 39, 42

Christ Episcopal Church (1838), 474

Christ Episcopal Church (1857–61), 475

Christian Chapel (later Central Christian Church), 287

Christian Scientist congregations, 259, 262

Christ Missionary Baptist Church, 268, *269*

churches: All Saints Episcopal Cathedral, 241–45, *242*, *243*; All Souls Unitarian Church, 284–87, *285*, *286*; Central Universalist Church, 252–53, *253*; First Baptist Church (1904–6), 228–30, *229*; First Church of Christ, Scientist, 259–61, *260*; First Presbyterian Church (1901–3), 234–38, *235*, *236*, *237*; German Evangelical Zion Church, 249–52, *250*, *251*; Hillside Christian Church, 230–32, *231*; Holy Trinity Slovenian Catholic Church, 256–59, *257*; Mayflower Congregational Church, 225–28, *226*, *227*; Meridian Street Methodist Episcopal Church (1905–6), 238–41, *239*, *240*; Pentecostal Bands buildings, 288–90, *289*; Second Baptist Church, 271–74, *272*, *273*, 543n82; Second Christian Church, 287–88, *288*; Second Church of Christ, Scientist, 262–63, *263*; SS. Peter and Paul Cathedral, 274–80, *276*, *277*, *278*, *279*; St. Anthony's Catholic Church, 254–55, *255*; St. Catherine of Siena Catholic Church, 232–34, *233*; St. Francis de Sales Catholic Church, 280–83, *282*; St. Mary's Catholic Church (1911–12), 246–49, *247*, *248*; St. Paul Methodist Episcopal Church (now Christ Missionary Baptist Church), 268, *269*; Third Christian Church, 266–67, *267*; Westminster Presbyterian Church, 268–71, *270*

Circle Theater, 77–82, *79*, *80*, *81*

Circle Tower, 37, 496

Citizens Gas Company of Indianapolis, 398

City Hospital, 205–9, *207*, *209*

city mansions, 302–42; Allison (Dellmore C. and Annie Hamilton) House, 327–28, *328*, *330*; Bliss (Henry R. and Margaret) House II, 320, *321*; Bliss-Vonnegut-Cummings House, 318–20, *319*; Fairbanks (Charles Warren and Cornelia Cole) House, 334–38, *335*, 396, 548n52; Frenzel (John P. and Philippine Bennerscheidt) House, 320–23, *322*; Furnas (Robert W. and Hannah Wright) House, 314–16, *315*; Glossbrenner (Alfred M. and Minnie Stroup) House, 332–34, *333*; Hare-Tarkington House, 329, *330*, *331*; Kahn

(Henry and Sarah Lang) House, 325–27, *326*; Levey (Louis and Alice Reynolds) House, 305–6, *306*; Lewis (Frank W. and Emma Salter) House, 306–8, *307*; Lieber (Herman P. and Alma Bachman) House, 323–25, *324*; Mansfield (Henry A. and Ada Freeland) House, 310, *311*; Nicholson (Meredith and Eugenie Kountze) House, 316–18, *317*; Rink (Joseph A. and Caroline Pfau) House, 308–9, *309*; Schnull-Rauch House, 302–5, *303*, *304*; Taggart (Thomas and Eva Bryant) House, 338–40, *339*; Thornton (Florence Baxter and George D.) House, 340–42, *341*; Van Camp (Frank and Clarissa Lintner) House, 310–14, *312*, 349, *350*

City of Indianapolis: City Hospital, 205–9, *207*, *209*; fire headquarters building (1913–14) and fire stations (1911), 137–40, *138*, *139*; Haughville annexed by, 254; Indianapolis City Hall, 131–37, *133*, *135*, *136*; Indianapolis Public Library, branches, 140–44, *141*, *144*; Indianapolis Public Library, Central Library (1915–17), 145–52, *146*, *147*, *149*, *150*, *151*; Union Station, track elevation program, 82

civil engineers, 19th century, 476

Classical Art School, 414

Classical style: illustrated, *521*; sources for, 472–73; trends in, 106, 110, 215. *See also* Greek Revival style; NeoClassicism; Roman Republic and Roman Empire, influence on architecture

Classical style (buildings): Bona Thompson Memorial Library, Butler College, 168, *169*; Circle Theater, 77–82, *78*, *79*, *80*, *81*; Indiana Central University, 164–67, *165*; Indianapolis City Hall, 131–37, *133*, *135*, *136*; Indianapolis Public Library, Central Library (1915–17), 145–52, *146*, *147*, *149*, *150*, *151*; John Herron Art Institute, 168–73, *170*, *172*; Main YMCA Building (1908–9), 186–87; Masonic Temple, 176–81, *178*, *179*, *180*; Merchants National Bank Building, 24–27, *25*, *26*; Robert W. Long Hospital, 209–11, *212*; St. Vincent's Hospital, 201–4, *203*; YWCA Building, 187–89, *188*

Classical style (buildings of worship): Congregation Sharah Tessila, 264, *265*; First Church of Christ, Scientist, 259–61, *260*; Second Baptist Church, 271–74, *272*, *273*, 543n82; Second Church of Christ, Scientist, 262–63, *263*; St. Paul Methodist Episcopal Church (now Christ Missionary Baptist Church), 268, *269*; Third Christian Church, 266–67, *267*; Westminster Presbyterian Church, 268–71, *270*

Classical style (residences): Furnas (Robert W. and Hannah Wright) House, 314–16, *315*; Lewis (Frank W. and Emma Salter) House, 306–8, *307*; Walker (William A. and Lahla Bond) House, 406, *407*

Claypool, Edward Fay, 10, 58

Claypool, Newton, 10

Claypool Hotel, 58–63, *59*, *60*, *61*, *62*, 65

Clay Worker, 480

Cobb, Henry Ives, 105, 483

Coburn (August) Residence, 344, *344*

Coca-Cola Bottling Plant (1931), 37, 496

Cohn, Barbara, 446

Cohn, M., 77

Cole, Joseph J., 97, 99

Cole Motor Car Company Factory, 97–99, *98*

Colestock, Ephraim, 474

college and university buildings: Butler College, Bona Thompson Memorial Library, 168, *169*; Butler University, Jordan Hall, 595; Indiana Central University, 164–67, *165*

Collier, Michael, 254

Cologne Cathedral, Germany, influence, 246, *247*, 292

Colonial Theater, 70–72, *71*

Columbia Club (1900–1901), 173–76, *174*, *175*, 482

Columbia Club (1924–25), 37, 495
Columbian Exposition of 1893, 14, 64, 483
Columbia University, 479
commercial buildings, 7–95; hotels, 58–69; maps, *108, 109*; movie theaters, 77–82; office buildings, 9–42; railroad buildings, 82–87; retail buildings, 42–58; theaters, 69–76; wholesale buildings, 87–95. *See also under specific building types and names of individual buildings*
Commercial Trust Company, 388
company towns, 95
competitions. *See* architectural competitions
Conner, Haskett L., 440
Conner, Herbert T., 440
Conner (Haskell L. and Herbert T.) Double, 437–40, *438*
Construction League of Indianapolis, 213
contractors, 190, 271, 476
Cook, Walter, 40
Cookingham, Peter P., 478
Coots, Charles E., 137
Corbusier, John W. Cresswell: Tabernacle Presbyterian Church (1922–24), 495
Cornell University, 64, 479, 486, 490
Costigan, Francis, 475, 477; Indiana Grand Lodge of the Independent Order of Odd Fellows (Odd Fellows Building; 1854–55), 20–21, 475
Cottage Residences (Downing), 476
Coulter, David A., 444
Coulter, W. L: SS. Peter and Paul Cathedral (with Renwick, Aspinwall, and Russell), 274–80, *276, 277, 278, 279*
Coulter Flats, 444–46, *445*
Country Builder's Assistant, The (Benjamin), 472
country estates, 345–71; about, 345–46; Allison (James A. and Sara Willis Cornelius) Estate, 354–59, *355, 357, 358*; Fisher (Carl G.) Estate ("Blossom Heath"), 354; Fletcher (Stoughton A., II, and May Henley) Estate ("Laurel Hall"), 363–71, *365, 367, 368, 369*; Landon-Lilly House ("Oldfields"), 359–63, *360, 361, 362*; Parry (David McLean and Hessie Maxwell) Estate ("Golden Hill"), 346–48, *347*, 549n69; Wheeler (Frank H. and Harriet Githens) Estate, 348–54, *349, 351, 352, 353*, 356
country retreats, Rustic: Coburn (August) Residence, 344, *344*; Fletcher (Stoughton A., II, and May Henley) "suburban" house, 342–44, *343*
Craftsman (magazine): bungalows from prototypes in, 406, 408–12, 422, 424, 554n42; influence, 287, 340, 404, 427, 432–33, 460
Craig, George (Scotland), 454
Cram, Ralph Adams, 145
Crane, Edward A., 121
Crapsey, Charles, 234. *See also* Crapsey and Lamm
Crapsey and Lamm: First Presbyterian Church (1901–3), 234–38, *235, 236, 237*
Cret, Paul Philippe: about, 152, *153* (portrait), Barnes Foundation Gallery (Philadelphia), 152; Detroit Institute of Fine Arts, 152; Folger Shakespeare Library, 152; Herron School of Art (Indianapolis) 152; Indianapolis Public Library, Central Library (1915–17; with Borie, Zantzinger, and Medary), 145–52, *146, 147, 149, 150, 151*, 484; Pan American Union Building, 146, 152; Rodin Museum (Philadelphia), 152
Crosley, Marion, 253
Crown Hill Cemetery, 488
"Crow's Nest," 342
Cummings, Lawrence B., 320
Curtis, John J., 31
Curzon, Joseph, 474–75, 476, 477, 478
Custin, Cornelius: St. Anthony's Catholic Church, 254–55, *255*
Cutshaw, Frank, 443

D. A. Bohlen and Son: about, 478, 481; fire headquarters building (1913–14), 137–40,

138; Fisher Automobile Company Building, 55, *57, 58*; Majestic Theater, 69, *70*; Meridian Street Methodist Episcopal Church (1905–6), 238–41, *239, 240*; Pennway Building, 27–29, *28*; St. Agnes Academy, 160, *163*, 163–64; Stutz Motor Car Company Factory (with Rubush and Hunter), 100, *102*, 103; St. Vincent's Hospital, 201–4, *203*; YWCA Building, 187–89, *188*. *See also* Bohlen, Oscar D.

Daggett, Naegele, and Daggett, 213

Daggett, Robert Frost, Jr., 213

Daggett, Robert Frost, Sr: about, 212–13, *213* (portrait), 480, 486, 487; Continental Bank Building, 212; Greenfield Laboratories, Eli Lilly and Company, 213; Eli Lilly and Company Indianapolis buildings, 212; Eli Lilly House, 213; Indianapolis Athletic Club (with Hibben), 212, 495; Indianapolis Chamber of Commerce Building (with Hibben), 212, 495; James Whitcomb Riley Hospital, 212; Jordan Hall, Butler University (with Hibben), 212, 495; Josiah K. Lilly, Sr. House, 213; Robert W. Long Hospital, 209–11, 212, *212*; Third Church of Christ, Scientist, 212; William Conner House (Noblesville), 213; William H. Coleman Hospital for Women, 212. *See also* R. P. Daggett and Company

Daggett, Robert Platt, 212, 478, 480, 481, 489

Davis, Alexander Jackson, 473, 476. *See also* Town and Davis

Davis, David. *See* Brown and Davis

Davis, Lewis Ketcham: Landon-Lilly House ("Oldfields"), 359–63, *360, 361, 362*

Day, H. Mills, 145

Day, Katherine Huntington, 189

Delano and Aldrich, 39, 40

della Porta, Giacomo: Sant'Atanasio dei Greci, Rome, *281*, 282

demolished buildings, 5

department stores: first in Indianapolis, 44; L. S. Ayres and Company Department Store (1905), 44–46, *45*; L. S. Ayres and Company Department Store, 1914 addition, *45*, 52; Marott Department Store, 46, *47*; rise of, 8, 44; William H. Block Company Department Store, 48, *49*

design research and sources: for 19th century builders and architects, 472, 474–80; for 20th century architects, 106, 215, 291–92, 345–46, 373–74, 487

detached houses (business and professional classes), 381–400; Barnhill (Dr. John and Celeste Terrell) House, 390–91, *391*; Burckhardt (Dr. Louis and Adele) House, 391–94, *393*; Forrest (Jacob Dorsey) House, 398–400, *399*; Hoke (Fred and Katharine Cushman) House, 396–98, *397*; Hubbard (Willard W. and Josephine Niles) House, 388–90, *389*; Kleinschmidt (Anthony F.) House, 394–96, *395*; Reid-Dickson House, 384–88, *386, 387*; Tanner (George G. and Kate Block) House, 384, *385*

detached houses (middle-class): Allen (Layton and Lelah Francis) House, *411*, 411–12; Bass (Herbert L. and Floria Logan) House, 404–5, *405*; Bryan (John F. and Louise Rentsch) House, 422–23, *423*; Carr (Dr. Silas J. and Sarah McCullough) House, 420–21, *421*; Hooser (Joseph) House, 430, *431*; Hubbard (Kin and Josephine Jackson) House, 409–11, *410*; June (George W. and Alberta Barthel) House, 412–13, *413*; Moyer (Jacob F. and Abbie Gibbs) House, 423–25, *424*; Overman-Arnold House, 427–29, *428*; Rapp (Alfred T. and Elizabeth Gough) House, *416*, 416–18, *417*; Recker (Carlos and Elizabeth Butler) House, 406, *408*, 408–9, 554n42; Rubush (Preston C. and Renah Wilcox) House, 402–4, *403*; Steele (Brandt F. and Helen McKay) House, 400–402, *401*; Vogel (William D.) House, 428, 429–30; Walker (Madam C. J.) House, 418–20,

419; Walker (William A. and Lahla Bond) House, 406, *407*; Wuensch (Edwin) House, 431–33, *432*

Detroit Public Library, 145

Das Deutsche Haus, 482

D. H. Burnham and Company: Indianapolis Traction Terminal office building and shed, 10–15, *12, 13*, 483; Marshall Field and Company (Chicago), 44, 52; Merchants National Bank Building, 24–27, *25, 26*, 483; Pennsylvania Railroad station, Richmond, Indiana, 14; Union Station, Washington, D.C., 14. *See also* Burnham, Daniel H.

Dickson, Fred C., 77, 388

Dickson, George A., 342

Dickson, Hallie Terhune, 388

Diebold, Paul C., 3, 554n42

Disciples of Christ, 224, 230–32, 266, 287

Doeppers, Edwin C. *See* Doeppers and Myers

Doeppers and Myers: about, 482; Vogel (William D.) House, *428*, 429–30; Wuensch (Edwin) House, 431–33, *432*

Donavin, James F., 440

Donavin Shoe Company, 440

Dorland, Anna B., 259

doubles, 381, 382, 433–40; Conner (Haskell L. and Herbert T.) Double, 437–40, *438*; defined, 433; Duncan (John S) Double, 433–34, *434, 435*; Gocke-King Double, *436*, 437; Mead-Donavin Double, *439*, 440; Thomas-Hunt Double, 436–37, *438, 439*

Downing, Andrew Jackson, 476

draftsmen, roles of, 471, 475, 483, 485–87, 493, 494

Duncan, John S., 433

Duncan (John S) Double, 433–34, *434, 435*

Dunn-McCarty Company, 440

duplex homes. *See* doubles

Dupont, Henry, 484

Dupont and Johnson, 492

Dutch Colonial style: Carr (Dr. Silas J. and Sarah McCullough) House, 420–21, *421*

Early Architects and Builders of Indiana (Burns), 3

Early Architecture of Madison, Indiana, The (Windle and Taylor, Jr.), 3

École des Beaux-Arts, 146, 152, 212, 449, 479, 480. *See also* Beaux Arts design

economic trends: depressions and recoveries, 1870s to 1890s, 478; Panic of 1907, 8; working families' increased prosperity, 153

Eddy, Mary Baker, 259

educational buildings: Indiana School for the Deaf (1906–11), 128–31, *129, 130*; St. Agnes Academy, 163, 160, 163–64. *See also* college and university buildings; public school buildings

Efroymson, Meyer, 77

E. G. Spink Company, 558n107

Egyptian, Ancient, motifs, *180*, 181

Elder, John, 474, 559n4

Elder, William L., 164, 166

Eldridge, William K., 16. *See also* Brubaker and Eldridge

Eli Lilly and Company office building and plant, 482

Elizabethan style: Fletcher (Stoughton A., II, and May Henley) Estate ("Laurel Hall"), 363–71, *365, 367, 368, 369*

Ellwood, A. H.: Indiana Central University, 164–67, *165*

Empire Theater, 478

engineering, 476, 488

English Arts and Crafts Movement, 283, 340, 384, 406, 461, 497

English Queen Anne style. *See* Queen Anne style

English's Opera House and Hotel, 478

English Tudor palace style: explained, 332; African American Pythian Building, 181–83, *182*; Columbia Club (1924–25), 495; Fletcher (Stoughton A., II, and May Henley) Estate ("Laurel Hall"), 363–71, *365, 367, 368, 369*; Glossbrenner (Alfred M. and Minnie Stroup) House, 332–34,

333; Hampton Court Apartments, 457–60, *458*, *459*; Indianapolis Public Library, East Washington Branch, 140–41, *141*; Tanner (George G. and Kate Block) House, 384, *385*; Van Camp (Frank and Clarissa Lintner) House, 310–14, *312*, 349, 350

English Tudor vernacular style: defined, 372, 500; Allison (Dellmore C. and Annie Hamilton) House, 327–28, *328*, *330*; All Souls Unitarian Church, 284–87, *285*, *286*; Bass (Herbert L. and Floria Logan) House, 404–5, *405*; Forrest (Jacob Dorsey) House, 398–400, *399*; Hare-Tarkington House, 329, *330*, *331*; Kahn (Henry and Sarah Lang) House, 325–27, *326*; Lieber (Herman P. and Alma Bachman) House, 323–25, *324*; Parry (David McLean and Hessie Maxwell) Estate ("Golden Hill"), 346–48, *347*, 549n69; Rubush (Preston C. and Renah Wilcox) House, 402–4, *403*; Steele (Brandt F. and Helen McKay) House, 400–402, *401*

Enos and Huebner, 477

Episcopal Diocese of Indianapolis, 241

Epworth League, 199

Ethington, Ernest L., 427

Fairbanks, Charles W., 29, 334, 457

Fairbanks, Cornelia Cole, 334, 457

Fairbanks (Charles Warren and Cornelia Cole) House, 334–38, *335*, 396, 548n52

Fall Creek, IN: Rink (Joseph A. and Caroline Pfau) House, 308–9, *309*

Fidelity Trust Building, 36

Federal style: defined, 501, *511*; Fort Benjamin Harrison, 119, *122*, *123*, *124*, *125*, *126*–28, *127*; sources for, 472

Feibleman, Isidore, 77

Feldman, Dr. Richard, 549n69

fire headquarters building (1913–14) and fire stations (1911), 137–40, *138*, *139*

fireproofing: apartment buildings, 441, 444, 449; churches, 274, 278; hotels, 60, 63, 70–71; national trends in, 106–7; office buildings, 10, 15, 18, 23, 24, 31, 33, 35; public buildings, 114; retail buildings, 48; social and fraternal buildings, 181, 189

First Baptist Church (1862–64), 20, 228

First Baptist Church (1904–6), 228–30, *229*

First Church of Christ, Scientist, 259–61, *260*

First Methodist Episcopal Church, Gary, IN, 250, *252*

First Presbyterian Church (1864–70), 113, 234, 477

First Presbyterian Church (1901–3), 234–38, *235*, *236*, *237*, 540n22

"firsts": African American architect in Indianapolis (possibly), 489; Akron plan used in churches by an American architect, 238; architect in Indiana to be licensed, 490; architects working in Indianapolis, 473–74; architectural competition, 473; architectural courses offered, 479; department store in Indianapolis, 44; École des Beaux-Arts graduate in Indiana, 212, 480; Indianapolis architect trained in an American architectural program, 479; movie theaters in Indianapolis, 77; reinforced concrete buildings, 97, 107; roof garden, 35, 198; skyscraper hotel in Indiana, 63; skyscraper in Indianapolis, 481; terra-cotta facades, 27, 43; woman architect practicing in Indiana, 490

Fisher, Carl G., 55, 68, 348, 354

Fisher Automobile Company Building, 55, *57*, 58

Fisher (Carl G.) Estate ("Blossom Heath"), 354

Fitton, Harry R., about, 454, *452*, 454–55, *455* (portrait), 487. *See also* George, MacLucas, and Fitton

flat-iron buildings, 18, 501

flats. *See* apartments

Fletcher, May Henley, 342, 363

Fletcher, Stoughton A., II, 342, 363–64, 367, 371

602 | INDEX

Fletcher (Stoughton A., II, and May Henley) Estate ("Laurel Hall"), 363–71, *365, 367, 368, 369,* 482

Fletcher (Stoughton A., II, and May Henley) "suburban" house, 342–44, *343*

Fletcher and Sharpe Block, 477

Fletcher National Bank, 363

Fletcher Savings and Trust Building, 39–42, *41,* 482

Fletcher Savings and Trust Company, 39, 363–64

F. M. Bachman Company, 446

Foltz, Herbert W.: about, 31, 142–43, *143* (portrait), 478, 486, 490; Broadway Methodist Episcopal Church (1925), 142, 495; Burns Realty dwellings, 400; City Hospital competition, 206; George W. Julian School 57, 155, *156, 157;* Globe Realty Company garages, 55, *56, 57;* Irvington Methodist Episcopal Church, 142; Louisiana State Hospital for the Insane, 142; Meridian Heights Presbyterian Church, 142; Oriental Lodge (with Rubush and Hunter and Herbert L. Bass), 183–85, *184;* Senate Avenue YMCA Building (1912–13), 142, 189–93, *191, 192;* Tudor School for Girls, 142. *See also* Foltz and Parker

Foltz and Parker: about, 132, 142–43, *143* (portraits), 215, 373, 482, 487; Barnhill (Dr. John and Celeste Terrell) House, 390–91, *391;* Bliss (Henry R. and Margaret) House II, 320, *321;* Bliss-Vonnegut-Cummings House, 318–20, *319;* Bobbs-Merrill Building, 31–33, *32,* 482; Darlington (Frank) House, 142; Elliott (Frank) House, 142; Frenzel (John P. and Philippine Bennerscheidt) House (attributed), 320–23, *322;* Furnas (Robert W. and Hannah Wright) House, 314–16, *315;* Historic American Buildings Survey, service of both in, 142; Indianapolis Country Club, 142; Indianapolis Orphan Asylum, 142; Indianapolis Public Library, East Washington Branch, 140–41, *141,* 142; Kahn (Henry and Sarah Lang) House, 325–27, *326;* Main YMCA Building (1908–9), 142, 185–87, *186,* 482; Mansfield (Henry A. and Ada Freeland) House, 310, *311;* Nicholson (Meredith and Eugenie Kountze) House, 316–18, *317;* Reid-Dickson House, 384–88, *386, 387;* Southeast Asylum for the Insane (Madison, Indiana), 142; William A. Bell School 60, 160, *161*

Ford Brothers, 250, *251*

Forrest, Jacob Dorsey, 398

Forrest (Jacob Dorsey) House, 398–400, *399*

Forsyth, William, 208

Fort Benjamin Harrison, 119, 122, *123, 124, 125,* 126–28, *127*

Foursquare style. *See* American Foursquare style

Francis, Joseph, 241

fraternal buildings. *See* social, fraternal, and athletic buildings

Frauenkirche, Nuremberg, influence, 249

French Baroque style: Levey (Louis and Alice Reynolds) House, 305–6, *306,* 546n9

French Lick Springs Hotel, 338

French medieval style: Schnull-Rauch House, 302–5, *303, 304*

French seventeenth century style: Landon-Lilly House ("Oldfields"), 359–63, *360, 361, 362*

Frenzel, John P., 320, *321*

Frenzel, Philippine Bennerscheidt, 321

Frenzel brothers (John P., Otto N., and Oscar F.), 24

Frenzel (John P. and Philippine Bennerscheidt) House, 320–23, *322*

Frie, Emil, 541n42

friezes, 79–80, 501–2

Furnas, Hannah Wright, 314

Furnas, Robert W., 314

Furnas (Robert W. and Hannah Wright) House, 314–16, *315*

Furness, Frank, 88

Gaddis, J. W., 414
Gamble House, Pasadena, CA, 430
gardens. *See* landscape architecture and design
gas boom, 8
Gates-McClellan Hotel Company, 68
Gaul, Hermann: St. Mary's Catholic Church (1911–12), 246–49, *247*, *248*, 292
Geiger, Nicholas, 52
Geiger Building, 52–53, *54*
George, Lawrence W., 452, 454–55. *See also* George, MacLucas, and Fitton
George, MacLucas, and Fitton: about, 454–55, *455* (portraits), 487; Balmoral Court Apartments, 452–56, *453*; Buskirk (George) House, 454; Goodall (Walter J.) House, 454; Hampton Court Apartments, 454, 457–60, *458*, *459*; Haugh Hotel, 454; Matson (Frederick C.) House, 454; Mayer (A. Kiefer) House, 454; Meyer (Sol) House, 454; Seville Apartments, 454; Taggart (Alexander) House, 454;
George B. Swift and Company, 58
George W. Julian School 57, 155, *156*, *157*
George W. Sloan School 41, 158, *159*
Georgian style: defined, 502, 523; Balmoral Court Apartments, 452–56, *453*; Barnhill (Dr. John and Celeste Terrell) House, 390–91, *391*; Bliss (Henry R. and Margaret) House II, 320, *321*; Bliss-Vonnegut-Cummings House, 318–20, *319*; Bobbs-Merrill Building, 31–33, *32*; Fort Benjamin Harrison, 119, 122, *123*, *124*, *125*, 126–28, *127*; Frenzel (John P. and Philippine Bennerscheidt) House, 320–23, *322*; Furnas (Robert W. and Hannah Wright) House, 314–16, *315*; Hoke (Fred and Katharine Cushman) House, 396–98, *397*; Nicholson (Meredith and Eugenie Kountze) House, 316–18, *317*; St. Vincent's Hospital, 201–4, *203*
German-American Trust Company, 39

German Evangelical Zion Church, 249–52, *250*, *251*, 481–82
German immigrants and German Americans: Das Deutsche Haus, 193; Deaconess Hospital, 198; German Evangelical Zion Church, 249–52, *250*, *251*; in Haughville, 254; Maennerchor Building, 195–98, *196*, *197*; Southside Turnverein, 193–95, *194*
German Renaissance style: defined, 215, 502; Maennerchor Building, 195–98, *196*, *197*; Southside Turnverein, 193–95, *194*
Gibbs, James, 472
Gibson, David, 490
Gibson, David, Jr, 492
Gibson, Jessie, 486, 490, *491* (portrait)
Gibson, Louis H.: about, 478, 479, 490; Hillside Christian Church, 232
Gibson Automotive Building, 53, *55*
Gilbert, Cass, 39, 145
Gillespie, George G. *See* Gillespie and Carrel
Gillespie and Carrel: First Baptist Church (1904–6; with Brown and Davis), 228–30, *229*
Globe Realty Company garages, 55, *56*, *57*
glossary of terms, 497–509
Glossbrenner, Alfred M., 332
Glossbrenner, Minnie Stroup, 332
Glossbrenner (Alfred M. and Minnie Stroup) House, 332–34, *333*, 482
Gocke, O. Harry A., 436
Gocke, Winifred Shirtz, 436
Gocke-King Double, 436, *437*
Godard, A. H., 187
"Golden Hill" (Parry Estate), 346–48, *347*, 549n69
Gothic architecture, defined, 502, 513, 516
Gothic style (buildings): Indianapolis Chamber of Commerce Building, 495; Indianapolis News Building, 29–31, *30*; Indianapolis Public Library, East Washington Branch, 140–41, *141*; Jordan Hall, Butler

University, 495; Union Station Concourse and Train Shed, 83–84, *83*, 106

Gothic style (churches): illustrated, *516*; All Saints Episcopal Cathedral, 241–45, *242*, *243*; Broadway Methodist Episcopal Church (1925), 495; Central Universalist Church, 252–53, *253*; First Presbyterian Church (1901–3), 234–38, *235*, *236*, *237*; German Evangelical Zion Church, 249–52, *250*, *251*; Holy Trinity Slovenian Catholic Church, 256–59, *257*; Meridian Street Methodist Episcopal Church (1905–6), 238–41, *239*, *240*; North Methodist Episcopal Church, 495; Scottish Rite Cathedral, 495; St. Anthony's Catholic Church, 254–55, *255*; St. Mary's Catholic Church (1911–12), 246–49, *247*, *248*; Tabernacle Presbyterian Church (1922–24), 495

Gothic style (residences): illustrated, *513*; Van Camp (Frank and Clarissa Lintner) House, 310–14, *312*, *349*, *350*

government buildings: 19th century, 473; Carnegie library branches, 140–41, *141*, 144, *144*; fire headquarters building (1913–14) and fire stations (1911), 137–40, *138*, *139*; Fort Benjamin Harrison, 119, *122*, 123, *124*, 125, 126–28, *127*; Indianapolis City Hall, 131–37, *133*, *135*, *136*; Indianapolis Public Library, Central Library, 145–51, *146*, *147*, *149*, *150*, *151*; Indiana School for the Deaf, 128–31, *129*, *130*; public schools, 153–61, *154*, *156*, *157*, *159*, *161*; US Courthouse and Post Office (1903–5), 111–19, *113*, *115–18*

Governor's House on the Circle, 473

Grafton, Thomas W., 266

Grammar of Ornament, The (Jones), 244

Grand Lodge of Free and Accepted Masons of Indiana, 176–77

Grand United Order of Odd Fellows Building, 181, 489

Greater Irvington (Diebold), 3

Greek Revival style: defined, 502, 512; Fort Benjamin Harrison, 119, *122*, 123, *124*, 125, 126–28, *127*; preferences for, 110, 476; US Courthouse and Post Office (1903–5), 111–19, *113*, *115*, *116*, *117*, *118*; US Treasury Building, Washington, DC, 112. *See also* Classical style

Green, Edward B., 112

Greene, Ernest: Mayflower Congregational Church (with Stephenson), 225–28, *226*, *227*

Greene and Greene, influence, 430

Grindle, Alfred: about, 244, 245 (portrait), 482, 486; All Saints Episcopal Cathedral, 241–45, *242*, *243*, 482; Glossbrenner (Alfred M. and Minnie Stroup) House, 244, 332–34, *333*, 482; Grace Episcopal Church (Muncie), 244; Thomas (Suzanne) House (Muncie), 244; Trinity Episcopal Church (Bloomington), 244

Guaranty Building, 37, 495

G. W. Bunting and Son, 531n112. *See also* Bunting, George W., Jr.

Hall, James B., 473

Hall of Marchands-Drapiers, Paris, influence, 546n9

Hampton Court Apartments, 457–60, *458*, *459*

Hampton Court Palace, England, influence, 457

Hampton Court Realty Company, 457

Hanchett, Thomas, 412, 552n12

Hanly, J. Frank, 128

Hare, Maria Fletcher, 330

Hare-Tarkington House, 329, 330, *331*

Harkradar, Glenn W., 446

Harrison, Benjamin, 173, 234, 238

Harrison, Mary Lord, 238

Harrison, Merritt, 367, 486, 487

Harrison, Russell B., 119

Hasselman-Fahnley House, 477

Haugh, Benjamin, 254
Haughville, IN, 223; Holy Trinity Slovenian Catholic Church, 256–59, 257; St. Anthony's Catholic Church, 254–55, 255
Hawkins, Don P., 434
Hayden, Sophia, 490
Heinigke and Bowen, 118
Hendrickson, H. C.: Duncan (John S) Double, 433–34, 434, 435
Herbert L. Bass and Company: about, 488; Allison (Dellmore C. and Annie Hamilton) House, 327–28, 328, 330; Cole Motor Car Company Factory, 97–99, 98, 370; competition entry for Central Public Library, 145; Hose Company No. 28 fire station (1911), 139, 140; Fletcher (Stoughton A., II, and May Henley) Estate ("Laurel Hall"), 363–71, 365, 367, 368, 369, 482; Geiger Building, 52–53, 54, 370; Oriental Lodge (with Rubush and Hunter and Herbert W. Foltz), 183–85, 184. See also Bass, Herbert L.
Herman, Frank G., 446
Herod, Henry L., 287
Herron, Electa Turrel, 252
Herron, John, 169, 252
Hetherington and Berner ironworks, 482
Heurtley House, Oak Park, IL, influence, 356
Hibben, Harold B., 90
Hibben, Hollweg, and Company Building, 90–91, 92, 93
Hibben, Thomas: Indianapolis Athletic Club (with Daggett), 495; Indianapolis Chamber of Commerce Building (with Daggett), 495; Jordan Hall, Butler University (with Daggett), 495
Hicks, Mary, 490
Hillsdale Landscape Company, 551n104
Hillside Christian Church, 230–32, 231
Historic American Buildings Survey, 143
Historic Architecture of Lafayette, Indiana (Parrish), 3
Historic Homes of New Albany, Indiana (Barksdale and Sekula), 3

historic preservation movement, 3
Historic Washington Park (Waller and Vanderstel), 3
History and Architecture of Meridian-Kessler, The (Diebold), 3
History and Architecture of North Meridian Street, The (Bodenhamer and others), 3
Hobson, Morton, 164
Hodgson, Isaac, 475, 476, 477, 478, 481
Hoke, Fred, 396
Hoke, Katharine Cushman, 396
Hoke (Fred and Katharine Cushman) House, 396–98, 397
Holabird and Roche, 9
Holden, Frank H., 449
Hollweg, Louis, 90
Hollywood Beach Hotel, Florida
Holy Trinity Slovenian Catholic Church, 256–59, 257, 482
Home Building and Realty Company, 444, 558n107
Hooser, Joseph, 430
Hooser (Joseph) House, 430, 431
Hoosier State Chronicle, 489
Hopson, Charles: North Methodist Episcopal Church, 495
hospitals, 110, 198–211; City Hospital, 205–9, 207, 209; Methodist Hospital, 199–201, 200; Robert W. Long Hospital, 209–11, 212; St. Francis Hospital, Beech Grove, 204, 205; St. Vincent's Hospital, 201–4, 203
Hotel Lincoln, 36
hotels, 58–69; Claypool Hotel, 58–63, 59, 60, 61, 62, 65; Hotel Lincoln, 36; Hotel Severin, 65, 67, 68, 68–69; Hotel Washington, 63, 65, 66; and theaters combined with, 69, 70
Hotel Severin, 65, 67, 68, 68–69
Hotel Washington, 63, 65, 66
Howe, Lois L., 490
Hubbard, Frank McKinney ("Kin"), 409
Hubbard, Josephine Jackson, 409

Hubbard, Josephine Niles, 388
Hubbard, Willard W., 388
Hubbard Block, 44
Hubbard (Kin and Josephine Jackson) House, 409–11, *410*
Hubbard (Willard W. and Josephine Niles) House, 388–90, *389*
Huebner, Henry, 478
Huesmann, Louis C., 334
Huesmann (Louis C. and Mary McDonald) House, 334
Huesmann, Mary McDonald, 334
Hume, Mary E., 34
Hume-Mansur Building, 33–35, *34*, 482
Hungarian immigrants, 254
Hunt, Jarvis: Indianapolis News Building, 29–31, *30*
Hunt, Richard Morris, 29, 479
Hunter, Edgar Otis: about, 36, 23, 36–37, *37* (portrait), 177, 486. *See also* Rubush and Hunter
Hunter, Frank B.: about, 414–15, *415* (portrait), 482; design for African American Pythian Building, 181–83, *182*, 489; Fountain Square Theater Building, 414; Gibson Automotive Building, *53*, 55; Hubbard (Kin and Josephine Jackson) House, 409–11, *410*, 414; Huntington County Courthouse, 414; June (George W. and Alberta Barthel) House, 412–13, *413*, 414; Miller (Charles C.) House, 414; Millikan-Carson House, 414; Preston (Frank A.) House, 414; Putnam County Courthouse, 414; Rapp (Alfred T. and Elizabeth Gough) House, *416*, 414, 416–18, *417*; Stoner (George W.) House, 414; Thompson-Trimble House, 414; Zaring's Egyptian Theater, 414
Hunter, William R., 446

Illinois Building, 36, 495
Independent Order of Odd Fellows buildings. *See* Indiana Grand Lodge of the Independent Order of Odd Fellows

Indiana Architectural Act, 561n28
Indiana Architectural Foundation, 2–3
Indiana Association of Architects, 480–81
Indiana Bedford limestone, 40, 63, 68, 114, 137, 150, 177, 262, 290
Indiana Blind Asylum, 475
Indiana Central University, 164–67, *165*
Indiana Chapter of the AIA, 485
Indiana Division of Historic Preservation and Archaeology, 3, 490
Indiana General Assembly, 210, 485, 561n28
Indiana Grand Lodge of the Independent Order of Odd Fellows (Odd Fellows Building; 1854–55), 20–21, 475
Indiana Grand Lodge of the Independent Order of Odd Fellows (Odd Fellows Building; 1907–8), 20–24, *22*, 482
Indiana Hospital for the Insane, 474, 482
Indiana Hospital for the Insane, Women's Department Building, 478
Indiana Hotel Company, 58
Indiana Houses of the Nineteenth Century (Peat), 3
Indiana Landmarks, 3
Indianapolis Architects' Society, 481
Indianapolis Architectural Club, 485, 486–87
Indianapolis Architecture (Indiana Architectural Foundation), 2
Indianapolis Architecture: Transformations since 1975 (Indiana Architectural Foundation), 2–3
Indianapolis Athletic Club, 495
Indianapolis Board of Trade Building, 16, *17*
Indianapolis Chapter of the AIA, 481
Indianapolis City Hall, 131–37, *133*, *135*, *136*, 482
Indianapolis City Market, 131
Indianapolis Foundry Company, 307
Indianapolis Hebrew Temple (1899), 482
Indianapolis Journal, 112, 228, 441
Indianapolis Masonic Temple Association, 177
Indianapolis Motor Speedway, 348

INDEX | 607

Indianapolis News, 29, 31, 155, 241, 409, 490
Indianapolis News Building, 29–31, *30*
Indianapolis Public Library: 1892–93 Library, 111, 145; Central Library (1915–17), 145–52, *146, 147, 149, 150, 151*; East Washington Branch, 140–41, *141*; Spades Park Branch, 141, 144, *144*
Indianapolis Public Schools board: library commissions, 140, 141, 145. *See also* public school buildings
Indianapolis Shriners, 72, 74, 176
Indianapolis Star, 20, 261, 271, 325, 368, 404, 409, 430, 433, 487
Indianapolis Star Building, 20, *21*
Indianapolis Traction Terminal office building and shed, 10–15, *12, 13*, 483
Indianapolis Union Passenger Depot, 475
Indianapolis Union Railway Company, 82
Indianapolis Union Railway Station, 479
Indianapolis Water Company, 359, 361
Indiana School for the Deaf, 128–31, *129, 130*
Indiana Society of Architects convention, Indianapolis, 492 (group portrait)
Indiana State Association of Architects, 481, 483
Indiana State Asylum for the Deaf and Dumb, 474
Indiana Statehouse (1831–35), 473–74
Indiana Statehouse (1878–88), 111, 119, 478
Indiana State Museum, 168
Indiana Theater, 37
Indiana Trust Company, 320
Indiana University, Bloomington, 475
Indiana University School of Medicine, 210, 211
Indiana World War Memorial Plaza, 496
industrial buildings, 7–9, 95–107; automobile factories, 95–103; Big Four Shops, Beech Grove, 95, 96, *97*; Cole Motor Car Company Factory, 97–99, *98*; Kahn Tailoring Company Factory, 103, *104*; map, *109*; National Motor Vehicle Company Factory, 99–100, *101*; Stutz Motor Car Company Factory, 100, *102, 103*
Industrial Technical High School, 492
Industry (Rhind), 119
Inland Architect and News Record, 106, 292, 346, 480, 487
interurbans: accessibility of, 166; growth of, 5, 7–8, 9, 46; Indianapolis Traction Terminal Office Building and Shed, 10–15, *12, 13*
inventories, architectural, 2–4
Iowa State College, 64
Irish immigrants, 254
Irvington, IN: annexation to Indianapolis, 155, 223; Bona Thompson Memorial Library, Butler College, 168, *169*
Irvington Methodist Episcopal Church, 399, 400
Islamic architectural style: Murat Temple and Theater, 72–76, *73, 74, 75*; Oriental Lodge, 183–85, *184*
Italianate style: defined, 503, 514; Indianapolis Public Library, Spades Park Branch, 141, *144*
Italian Renaissance style: defined, 503, 522
Italian Renaissance style (apartments): Coulter Flats, 444–46, *445*; The Rink Flats, 441–43, *442*; Winter Apartments, 449–52, *450, 451*
Italian Renaissance style (churches): Holy Trinity Slovenian Catholic Church, 256–59, *257*; SS. Peter and Paul Cathedral, 274–80, *276, 277, 278, 279*; St. Francis de Sales Catholic Church, 280–83, *282*
Italian Renaissance style (commercial buildings): American Central Life Insurance Company Building, 495; Bobbs-Merrill Building, 31–33, *32*; Claypool Hotel, 58–63, *59, 60, 61, 62*; Fletcher Savings and Trust Building, 39–42, *41*; Guaranty Building, 495; Hotel Severin, 65, *67, 68*, 68–69; Illinois Building, 495; Indiana Grand Lodge of the Independent Order of Odd Fellows (Odd Fellows Building;

1907–8), 20–24, 22; Indianapolis Board of Trade Building, 16, 17; Indianapolis Star Building, 20, 21; Knights of Pythias Office Building, 18–20, 19; Merchants National Bank Building, 24–27, 25, 26

Italian Renaissance style (houses): Fairbanks (Charles Warren and Cornelia Cole) House, 334–38, 335, 396, 548n52; Hoke (Fred and Katharine Cushman) House, 396–98, 397; Hubbard (Willard W. and Josephine Niles) House, 388–90, 389; Landon-Lilly House ("Oldfields"), 359–63, 360, 361, 362; Levey (Louis and Alice Reynolds) House, 305–6, 306; Lewis (Frank W. and Emma Salter) House, 306–8, 307; Mansfield (Henry A. and Ada Freeland) House, 310, 311; Rink (Joseph A. and Caroline Pfau) House, 308–9, 309; Taggart (Thomas and Eva Bryant) House, 338–40, 339

Italian Renaissance style (public and nonprofit buildings): Columbia Club (1900–1901), 173–76, 174, 175; fire headquarters building (1913–14), 137–40, 138; George W. Sloan School 41, 158, 159; Indianapolis Athletic Club, 495; Indiana School for the Deaf, 128–31, 129, 130; John Herron Art Institute, 168–73, 170, 172; Maennerchor Building, 195–98, 196, 197; Main YMCA Building (1908–9), 185–87, 186; Methodist Hospital, 199–201, 200; preferences for, 106, 110, 215; Robert Gould Shaw School 40, 155, 157; Robert W. Long Hospital, 209–11, 212; St. Vincent's Hospital, 201–4, 203

Italian Romanesque style: Reid-Dickson House, 384–88, 386, 387; St. Catherine of Siena Catholic Church, 232–34, 233; St. Joan of Arc Catholic Church, 495

Jacobean style: defined, 503; Fletcher (Stoughton A., II, and May Henley) Estate ("Laurel Hall"), 363–71, 365, 367, 368, 369

Jahn, Friedrich, 193, 194
Jameson, Dr. Henry, 487
Janssen, Benno, 145
J. B. McElfatrick and Son, 478
Jefferson, Thomas, 472
Jenney, William LeBaron, 9, 14, 105, 106, 477
Jenney and Mundie, 64, 336
Jensen, Jens, 345, 358, 359, 548n52
J. F. Alexander and Son: Knights of Pythias Office Building, 18–20, 19
John Hancock House, Boston, influence, 318
John Herron Art Institute, 168–73, 170, 172, 482; Sculpture Hall, architectural exhibits, 485
Johnson, Jesse T.: Bona Thompson Memorial Library, Butler College, 168, 169
John W. Murphy Building, 91, 94
Jones, Owen, 244
Jordan, Arthur, 228
Julian-Layman House, 447
June, Alberta Barthel, 412
June, George W., 412
June, Homer, 412
June (George W. and Alberta Barthel) House, 412–13, 413
Justice (Rhind), 119

Kahn, Henry, 35, 103, 325
Kahn, Sarah Lang, 325
Kahn (Henry and Sarah Lang) House, 325–27, 326
Kahn Office Building, 35, 38, 39, 48
Kahn Tailoring Company, 35, 325
Kahn Tailoring Company Factory, 103, 104
Kaufman, Thomas M., 456
Keene, T. Victor, 208
Kellogg, Thomas M.: about, 120–21, 121 (portrait); US Courthouse and Post Office (1903–5; with Rankin): 111–19, 113, 115, 116, 117, 118
Kessler, George E., 202, 302
Ketcham, Edwin H., 478
Ketterer, Gustav, 148–50, 149, 150

INDEX | 609

Killian, Peter, 204
King, William F., 436
Kitchen, John M., 27
Kleinschmidt, Anthony F., 394
Kleinschmidt (Anthony F.) House, 394–96, *395*
Knickerbocker, Davis, 241
Knights of Pythias Office Building, 18–20, *19*
Knowlton, Lynn O., 370
Kopf, J. Edwin: Williams Building, 55, *56*, 57
Kothe, Wells, and Bauer Company, 87
KO-WE-BA Building, 87, 90, *90*
Krauss, J. Edward, 63, 65
Kriner, William A., 356

Ladywood (school), 371
Lafever, Minard, 472, 473
Laird, Warren P., 39, 40, 106, 206, 485
Lake Forest, Illinois, 336
Landon, Hugh McKennan, 359, 361, 363
Landon, Suzette Davis, 359
Landon-Lilly House ("Oldfields"), 359–63, *360*, *361*, *362*
Landscape Architecture, 346
landscape architecture and design: of city mansions, 325, 338; of country estates, 348, 353, *358*, 359, 363, 366–68, *369*; demand for new profession of, 301, 302, 345; source guides for, 346, 476
Lanier House, 475
LaReve, Helene, 443
Latrobe, Benjamin, 471, 472
"Laurel Hall" (Fletcher Estate), 363–71, *365*, *367*, *368*, *369*, 482
Lavrie, Joseph, 256
Lawrence, Henry W., 58, 63, 173
Lawton Loop. *See* Fort Benjamin Harrison
Layman, Theodore, 447
Layman and Carey, 447
Leach, Leon T., 457, 460
Leach, Mary, 460
Leach Sanatorium, 457
Lehman, Ada, 446
Lemcke Building, 482

Leonard, Edith, 490–92, *491*
Levey, Alice Reynolds, 305
Levey, Louis H., 305
Levey Brothers and Company, 332
Levey (Louis and Alice Reynolds) House, 305–6, *306*
Lewis (Frank W. and Emma Salter) House, 306–8, *307*
library buildings: Bona Thompson Memorial Library, Butler College, 168, *169*; Indianapolis Public Library, Central Library (1915–17), 145–52, *146*, *147*, *149*, *150*, *151*; Indianapolis Public Library branches, 140–44, *141*, *144*
Lieber, Alma Bachman, 323
Lieber, Herman P., 323
Lieber, Robert, 77
Lieber (Herman P. and Alma Bachman) House, 323–25, *324*
Lieske, Paul H. G., 444. *See also* Bedell and Lieske
Lilly, Josiah K., Jr., 363
Lilly, Ruth Brinkmeyer, 363
Linville, Perman E., 425
Litchfield, Electus D., 39; Fletcher Savings and Trust Building, 40, *41*
Literature (Rhind), 119
Livingston, Joseph, 443
Lizius, James B., 212, 478, 480, 481. *See also* R. P. Daggett and Company
Loire Valley, châteaus, influence, 358
"Lombardy" house, influence, 340, 342, 372
Long, Robert W., 209–11
Louis XIV period, 62, 63
Loveland, Frank L., 460
L. S. Ayres and Company Department Store, 44, 44–46, *45*, 52, 482
Lucretia Mott School 3, 160, *161*
Lutyens, Edwin, 336

MacDougall, George G., 348, 549n69
MacLucas, William H.: about, 454–55, *455* (portrait); Balmoral Court Apartments,

452–56, *453*; Hampton Court Apartments, 457–60, *458, 459*. *See also* George, MacLucas, and Fitton
Madam C. J. Walker House, 418–20, *419*
Maennerchor Building, 195–98, *196, 197*, 482
Magonigle, H. Van Buren, 145
Magonigle, H. Warren, 40
Majestic Building, 481
Majestic Theater, 69, *70*
Malott, Volney T., 69, *70*
Manchester Institute of Art (England), 244
Mansart, Francois, influence, 362
Mansfield, Ada Freeland, 310
Mansfield, Henry A., 310
Mansfield (Henry A. and Ada Freeland) House, 310, *311*
Mansur, Hannah A., 34, 452
manufacturers' catalogs, 476–77
manufacturing boom, 9
maps (building locations): buildings of worship, 293–99; commercial and industrial buildings, *108–9*; public, social and charitable buildings, *216–22*, residences (detached homes, doubles, and apartments), *463–70*; residences (mansions and estates), *375–80*
Marian University, 354, 359
Marion County Courthouse (1823–24), 473
Marion County Courthouse (1869–76), 111, 475, 477
Marion County Jail and Sheriff's Residence, 479
Marion Home Building Company, 425, 427
Marion Trust Company, 39
Marott Department Store, 46, *47*
Marott's Shoes Building, 42–44, *43*
Marshall Field and Company, 44, 52, 105–6
Martin, Stanley F., 425
Martindale, Clarence: about, 162, *162* (portrait), 484; Abraham Lincoln School 18, 153–54, *154*, 162; Burckhardt (Dr. Louis and Adele) House, 162, 391–94, *393*; Fletcher (Stoughton A., II, and May Henley) "suburban" house, 342–44, *343*; George W. Sloan School 41, 158, *159*, 162; Hendricks County Courthouse, 162; Kleinschmidt (Anthony F.) House, 162, 394–96, *395*; McMurray-Jenkins House, 162; Lucretia Mott School 3, 160, *161*, 162; National Motor Vehicle Company Factory, 99–100, *101*; Rauh (Samuel E.) House, 162
Martindale-Atkins House, 477
Martindale, Elijah B., 162
Masonic Lodge Temple, 474, 482
masons, 19th century, 473
Massachusetts Institute of Technology (MIT), 50, 142, 336, 479, 480, 485–86, 490
Maxwell-Tousey-Fitzgerald House, 476
May, Edwin, 474, 478, 488
Mayer, Charles, 177
Mayflower Congregational Church, 225–28, *226, 227, 234*
McCoy-Howe Company, 406
McCulloch, George, 20
McGowan, Hugh J., 11, 13
McGuire and Shook, 487
McKay, Horace, 284
McKim, Charles F., 479
McKim, Mead, and White: 120, 142; criticism of, 485; influence, 59, 168, 173
McLanahan, Martin Hawley, 88, 311
McLanahan, M. Hawley, 88. *See also* Price and McLanahan
McOuat, Eugenia B., 42
McOuat Building, 42–44, *43*
McPhedris-Warner House, Portsmouth, NH, influence, 317, *318*
Mead, Agenoria Sears, 440
Mead, Thorret R., 440
Mead-Donavin Double, *439*, 440
medieval castles, influence, 384–88, *386, 387*, 402–4, *403*
Merchants National Bank, 320
Merchants National Bank Building, 24–27, *25, 26*, 483
Meridian Street mansions. *See* city mansions

Meridian Street Methodist Episcopal Church (1867–70), 238
Meridian Street Methodist Episcopal Church (1905–6), 238–41, *239*, *240*, *481*
Merrill, Charles W., 31
Methodist Episcopal Church, 199, 224
Methodist Hospital, 199–201, *200*
Metzger, Albert E., 39
Michelangelo, influence, 280
Michigan Lumber Company, 344
middle-class residents, 381–83. *See also* detached houses (middle-class)
Middle Eastern architectural style: Oriental Lodge, 183–85, *184*
Milan Cathedral, influence, 249
Millet, Louis, 280
Mills, Robert, 112, 472
minarets, 74, 76
Mission Inn, Riverside, CA, influence, *392*, *393*
Mme. C. J. Walker Manufacturing Company, 420
Modern Builder's Guide (Lafeve), 472
Modern style: Wheeler (Frank H. and Harriet Githens) Estate, 348–54, *349*, *351*, *352*, *353*, *356*
Montgomery Ward catalog, 383
Monument Realty Company, 77
Moore, DeWitt V., 310
Moore, W. Scott: about, 478, 483; The Rink Flats, 441–43, *442*, *483*
Moore-Mansfield Construction Company, 310
Morck, William O.: Mt. Zion Baptist Church, 482, 489; Second Baptist Church, 271, *272*, *274*, 482, 489, 543n82
Moriarty, John A., 443
Morris, William, 71, 283, 461
Morrison, Elizabeth Tinker, 173
Morrison, William H, 173
Morrison (William H. and Elizabeth Tinker) House, 173
Morton, Oliver P., 27

movie theaters: Alhambra Theater, 77, *78*, *79*; Circle Theater, 77–82, *78*, *79*, *80*, *81*
Moyer, Abbie Gibbs, 423
Moyer, Jacob F., 423
Moyer (Jacob F. and Abbie Gibbs) House, 423–25, *424*
Mt. Zion Baptist Church, 482, 489
Mueller, Otto N., 50. *See also* Vonnegut, Bohn and Mueller; Vonnegut and Bohn
Municipal Art Association, 132
Murat Temple and Theater, 72–76, *73*, *74*, *75*
Murphy, John W., 91
Murphy (John W.) Building, 91, *94*
museums: *John Herron Art Institute*, 168–73, *170*, *172*
Myers, Clarence. *See* Doeppers and Myers

Naegele, E. Harold, 213
National Cash Register Company, 64
National Motor Vehicle Company Factory, 99–100, *101*
Nelson, Thomas H., 289, *290*
Nelson and Rigg, 132
NeoClassicism, 9, 20, 163, 168, 189, 214, 372, 479
Newbert, E. E., 284
Newby, Arthur C., 100, 348
Newfields (arts and nature institution), 360, 363
Newton Claypool Building, 10, *11*
New York architects, 9–10, 39, 40, 59, 473, 478. *See also names of individuals and firms*
New York Central Railroad, 95
Nicholson, Eugenie Kountze, 316
Nicholson, Meredith, 316
Nicholson (Meredith and Eugenie Kountze) House, 316–18, *317*
99 Historic Homes of Indiana (Indiana Landmarks), 3
North Indianapolis, IN: George W. Sloan School 41, 158, *159*

North Indianapolis Methodist Episcopal Church, 268
North Methodist Episcopal Church, 495
North Western Christian University, 475
Norwood, Ralph, 77
Nowland, Matthias, 473

office buildings, 7–42; Bobbs-Merrill Building, 31–33, *32*; Fletcher Savings and Trust Building, 39–42, *41*; Hume-Mansur Building, 33–35, *34*; Indiana Grand Lodge of the Independent Order of Odd Fellows (Odd Fellows Building; 1907–8), 20–24, *22*; Indianapolis Board of Trade Building, 16, *17*; Indianapolis News Building, 29–31, *30*; Indianapolis Star Building, 20, *21*; Indianapolis Traction Terminal office building and shed, 10–15, *12*, *13*; Kahn Office Building, 35, *38*, 39, 48; Knights of Pythias Office Building, 18–20, *19*; Merchants National Bank Building, 24–27, *25*, *26*; Newton Claypool Building, 10, *11*; Pennway Building, 27–29, *28*
"Oldfields" (Landon-Lilly House), 359–63, *360*, *361*, *362*
Olmsted, Frederick Law, Sr., 345
Olmsted Brothers, 345, 363
opera, 76
Order of Odd Fellows buildings. *See headings starting with* Indiana Grand Lodge of the Independent Order of Odd Fellows
Oriental Lodge, 183–85, *184*
Orpheum Amusement Company, 77
Overman, Thomas P., 427
Overman-Arnold House, 427–29, *428*

Paine, Jessie Gibson. *See* Gibson, Jessie
Palazzo Gondi, Florence, influence, 449
Palladian windows, 59, 505
Pan American Union Building, Washington, DC, 146
Pantheon, Rome, influence, 134
Paquette, C. A., 83
Parker, Wilson B.: about, 31, 142, *143* (portrait), 484, 485; Indianapolis Public Library, Spades Park Branch, 141, 142, 144, *144*; Libraries in Brookville, LaPorte County, Linden, North Vernon, and Shoals, 142. *See also* Foltz and Parker
Parkin, Charles A., 268
Parrish, David, 3
Parry, Clara Maude Richardson, 492
Parry, David McLean, 346
Parry, Hessie Maxwell, 346
Parry (David McLean and Hessie Maxwell) Estate ("Golden Hill"), 346–48, *347*, 549n69
Parry Manufacturing Company, 346
Parthenon, Athens, influence, 80, 146, 261
Patterson, John, 64
Pauly Company, 479
Paxton, James, 473
P. C. Rubush and Company, 112
Peat, Wilbur D., 3
Peck, Edwin J., 473
Peddle Institute, 142
Pennsylvania Railroad, 82, 479
Pennsylvania Railroad station, Richmond, IN, 14
Pennsylvania Station, New York, 485
Pennway Building, 27–29, *28*
Penrose, George H., 123, 126
Pentecostal Bands buildings, 288–90, *289*
Phi Kappa Psi Fraternity headquarters, 371
Pierrefonds castle, France, 303
Place, H. V., 490
Plato, Samuel, 271–72, 489
Plymouth Congregational Church, demolition of, 113
Polytechnic Institute of Hanover, 479
Pompeii, paintings of, influence, 148–50, *149*, *150*
population growth: and construction rates, 8, 223, 254, 280, 287; and housing, 300–301, 371–72
Post, George B., 64

INDEX | 613

powerhouses, 91, 95; Century and John W. Murphy Buildings, 91, 93, 94
Practical House Carpenter, The (Benjamin), 472
Prairie style, 461; Allison (James A. and Sara Willis Cornelius) Estate, 354–59, *355, 357, 358*; Kleinschmidt (Anthony F.) House, 394–96, *395*
Presbyterian congregations, 224, 234, 268
Prest-O-Lite, 354
Preston C. Rubush, 23
Price, William L.: about, 88–89, 89 (portrait), 483, 485; Allison (James A. and Sara Willis Cornelius) Estate (with Bass), 354–59, *355, 357, 358*; Union Station Concourse and Train Shed, 82–87, *83, 85, 86,* 106, 350; Van Camp (Frank and Clarissa Lintner) House, 310–14, *312,* 349, 350, 483; Wheeler (Frank H. and Harriet Githens) Estate, 84, 89, 348–54, *349, 351, 352, 353, 356,* 483
Price and McLanahan: Blenheim and Traymore Hotels, Atlantic City, NJ, 88; Pennsylvania Railroad stations in Converse, Hartford City, Ridgeville, Dunkirk, and Fort Wayne, Indiana, 88; Union Station Concourse and Train Shed, 82–87, *83, 85, 86,* 106, 350; Van Camp (Frank and Clarissa Lintner) House, 310–14, *312,* 349, 350; Wheeler (Frank H. and Harriet Githens) Estate, 84, 89. 348–54, *349, 351, 352, 353,* 356
Prince, Boston J., 271
Prince Hall Masons of Indianapolis, 185
professional and business classes, 382, 383. *See also* detached houses (business and professional classes)
public architecture, 110–52; 19th-century, 111; fire headquarters building (1913–14) and fire stations (1911), 137–40, *138, 139*; Fort Benjamin Harrison, 119, *122, 123, 124, 125,* 126–28, *127*; Indianapolis City Hall, 131–37, *133, 135, 136*; Indianapolis Public Library, branches, 140–44, *141, 144*; Indianapolis Public Library, Central Library (1915–17), 145–52, *146, 147, 149, 150, 151*; Indiana School for the Deaf, 128–31, *129, 130*; US Courthouse and Post Office (1903–5), 111–19, *113, 115, 116, 117, 118. See also* public school buildings
public school buildings: Abraham Lincoln School 18, 153–54, *154*; George W. Julian School 57, 155, *156, 157*; George W. Sloan School 41, 158, *159*; Lucretia Mott School 3, 160, *161*; Robert Gould Shaw School 40, 155, *157*; School 52, 160; William A. Bell School 60, 160, *161*
Puget, Pierre, influence, 546n9
Puritan Bed Springs Company, 340

Queen Anne style: defined, 506, 520; Schnull-Rauch House, 302–5, *303, 304*; Tanner (George G. and Kate Block) House, 384, *385*

racial segregation, 111, 189–90, 383, 489–90
railroad buildings: Big Four Shops, Beech Grove, 95, *96, 97*; Indianapolis Traction Terminal office building and shed, 10–15, *12, 13*; Union Station Concourse and Train Shed, 82–87, *83, 85, 86*
railroads: and growth of Indianapolis, 7–8, 9, 82, 105, 474–75; Indianapolis Union Railway Company, 82; railroad era, 474–75. *See also* interurbans
Ralston, Alexander, 2
Rankin, John Hall: about, 120–21, *121* (portrait); US Courthouse and Post Office (1903–5; with Kellogg), *115, 116,* 111–19, *113, 117, 118*
Rankin and Kellogg: about, 120–21; US Courthouse and Post Office (1903–5), *115, 116,* 111–19, *113, 117, 118,* 483
Ransdell, George: Moyer (Jacob F. and Abbie Gibbs) House, 423–25, *424*
Rapp, Alberta Gough, 416, *418*

Rapp, Alfred T., 416
Rapp (Alfred T. and Elizabeth Gough) House, *416*, 416–18, *417*
real estate: apartment building construction and expansion, 440–41; commercial and industrial development, 8–9; home building and investment, 300–301, 371, 383, 400; increases in all building types, 8; trades of lot sales, 164, 166
Recker, Carlos, 408–9
Recker, Elizabeth Butler, 408
Recker, Gustav, 408
Recker and Sander Furniture Company, 408
Recker (Carlos and Elizabeth Butler) House, 406, *408*, 408–9, 554n42
Reid, Jeannie Lockard, 384–85
Reid, Samuel, 452
Reid, William J., 384–85
Reid-Dickson House, 142, 384–88, *386*, *387*
reinforced concrete design: early buildings using, 9, 97, 107; and fireproofing, 107; Indianapolis Board of Trade Building's use of, 16, *17*, 107; Price's use of, 88
religious architecture. *See* buildings of worship; churches; synagogues
religious sects in Indianapolis, 223–24
Renaissance style. *See* German Renaissance style; Italian Renaissance style
Renwick, Aspinwall, and Russell: SS. Peter and Paul Cathedral (with Coulter), 274–80, *276*, *277*, *278*, *279*
Renwick, James, Jr.: Indiana Grand Lodge of the Independent Order of Odd Fellows (Odd Fellows Building; 1854–55), 21
Renwick, William W.: SS. Peter and Paul Cathedral (with Coulter), 274–80, *276*, *277*, *278*, *279*
residential architecture (detached homes, doubles, and apartments), 381–470; American Foursquare style, 388–91, 412–20, 437–40, 552n12; Arts and Crafts style, 384, 406, 408–11, 423–24, 447–49; bungalow style, 402–11, 422–27, 431–33, 447–49; California bungalow style, 427–30, *428*, *431*; Classical style, 406, *407*; Dutch Colonial style, 420–22, *421*; eclectic, 433–34, *435*; English Tudor palace style, 384, *385*, 457–60, *458*; English Tudor vernacular style, 398–406, *399*, *401*, *403*, *405*; Flemish style, 406, *407*; Georgian style, 390–91, *391*, 396–98, *397*, 452–56, *453*; Italian Renaissance style, 388–90, *389*, 396–98, *397*, 441–46, *442*, *445*, 449–52, *450*, *451*; Italian Romanesque style, 384–88, *386*, *387*; maps, 463–70; Prairie style, 394–96, *395*; Spanish mission style, 391–94, *393*, 444–46, *445*; stylistic trends, 382–83, 496. *See also under* apartments; bungalows; detached houses, *and* doubles *for individual residences*
residential architecture (mansions and estates), 300–380; American Foursquare style, 314–16, *315*, 372, 552n12; Arts and Crafts style, 323–25, *324*, 340–44, *341*, *343*, *344*; Classical style, 306–8, *307*, 314–16, *315*; Elizabethan style, 363–71, *365*, *367*, *368*, *369*; English Tudor palace style, 332–34, *333*; English Tudor vernacular style, 310–14, 323–31, 346–48, 372; French Baroque style, 305–6, *306*; French medieval, 302–5, *303*, *304*; Georgian style, 314–23, *315*, *317*, *319*, *321*, *322*; Gothic style, 310–14, *312*; Italian Renaissance style, 305–11, 334–40, 359–71; Jacobean style, 363–71, *365*, *367*–69; maps, 375–80; Modern style, 348–54, *349*, *351*, *352*, *353*; and population growth, 300, 371; Prairie style, 354–59, *355*, *357*, *358*; Queen Anne style, 302–5, *303*, *304*; Rustic style, 340–48, *341*, *343*, *344*, *347*, 372; Shingle style, 342–44, *343*; stylistic trends, 301, 371–72, 496. *See also under* city mansions; country retreats, Rustic, *and* country estates *for individual homes*
retail buildings, 42–58; Aeolian Building, *52*, *53*; automotive showrooms and service

INDEX | 615

buildings, 54–58; department stores, 44–52; Geiger Building, 52–53, 54; Gibson Automotive Building, 53, 55; L. S. Ayres and Company Department Store, 44–46, 45, 52; Marott Department Store, 46, 47; Marott's Shoes Building, 42–44, 43; McOuat Building, 42–44, 43; William H. Block Company Department Store, 48, 49; Wulschner-Stewart Building, 52, 53

Revett, Nicholas, 473

Rhind, John Massey, 119

Richardson, Henry Hobson: about, 224, 479; Trinity Episcopal Church, Boston, 229. *See also* Richardsonian Romanesque style

Richardson, Miss (early 20th century architecture student), 490

Richardsonian Romanesque style: defined, 507, 518; Century Building, 91, 93; First Baptist Church (1904–6), 228–30, 229; Hillside Christian Church, 230–32, 231; Indianapolis Traction Terminal office building and shed, 12, 13, 13, 15; Mayflower Congregational Church, 225–28, 226, 227; St. Catherine of Siena Catholic Church, 232–34, 233

Richmond, Indiana (Tomlan and Tomlan), 3

Rink, Caroline Pfau, 308

Rink, Joseph A., 308, 441, 443

Rink Flats, The, 441–43, 442, 483

Rink (Joseph A. and Caroline Pfau) House, 308–9, 309

Rink's Cloak House, 441

"Riverdale Springs" (Allison Estate), 354–59, 355, 357, 358

Robert Gould Shaw School 40, 155, 157

Roberts, John T., 164, 166

Robert W. Long Hospital, 209–11, 212, 482

Rockwood, Charles P., 452

Rodd, Thomas, 479

Rogers, Fred A., 456

Rogers, James Gamble, 39, 40

Romanesque style. *See* Italian Romanesque style; Richardsonian Romanesque style

Roman Republic and Roman Empire, influence on architecture: increased taste for, 110; Indianapolis City Hall, 134, 137; Indiana School for the Deaf, 128; Merchants National Bank Building, 24–27, 25, 26; sources on, 472; SS. Peter and Paul Cathedral, 274–80, 276, 277, 278, 279; Union Station Concourse and Train Shed, 83, 84; US Courthouse and Post Office (1903–5), 114–15, 116, 117. *See also* Classical style

roof gardens, 35, 69

Root, John Wellborn, 13, 14

Rosenwald, Julius, 190

Rose Polytechnic Institute, 142, 486

rotundas, 134, 135

Royal Hospital at Chelsea, London, influence, 456

Royal Institute, Edinburgh, 454

Royal Polytechnic Institute in Karlsruhe, 50, 479

R. P. Daggett and Company: about, 481; Berrick Apartments, 446, 447, 482; Hotel Washington, 63, 65, 66, 212; Lemcke Annex office building, 212; McOuat Building, 42–44, 43; Robert W. Long Hospital, 209–11, 212, 482; Wulschner-Stewart Building, 52, 53, 212

Rubush, Preston C.: about, 36–37, 37 (portrait), 177 (*See also* Rubush and Hunter); Rubush (Preston C. and Renah Wilcox) House, 402–4, 403

Rubush, Renah Wilcox, 402

Rubush and Hunter: about, 36–37, 39, 37 (portraits), 481, 487, 490; Architects' and Builders' Building, 37; Circle Theater, 36, 77–82, 78, 79, 80, 81; Circle Tower, 37, 496; Coca-Cola Bottling Plant (1931), 37, 496; Colonial Theater, 70–72, 71; Columbia Club (1924–25), 37, 495; First Church of Christ, Scientist, 259–61, 260; Guaranty, Illinois, and American Central Life Insurance Company Buildings, 37, 495; Hoke (Fred and Katharine Cushman)

House, 396–98, *397*; Hollywood Beach Hotel, 37; Hume-Mansur Building, 33–35, *34*, *36*, 482; Indiana Grand Lodge of the Independent Order of Odd Fellows (Odd Fellows Building; 1907–8), 20–24, *22*, *36*, 482; Indianapolis City Hall, 132–37, *133*, *135*, *136*, 482; Indiana School for the Deaf, 128–31, *129*, *130*, *132*; Indiana Theater, 37, 495; KO-WE-BA Building, 87, 90, *90*; Marott Department Store, 46, *47*; Masonic Temple, 132, 176–81, *178*, *179*, *180*, 482; Oriental Lodge (with Herbert L. Bass and Herbert W. Foltz), 183–85, *184*; School 52, 160; Stutz Motor Car Company Factory (with D. A. Bohlen and Son), 100, *102*, *103*; Third Christian Church, basement, 266; Walker (William A. and Lahla Bond) House, 406, *407*; Walker Theater, 37; Wasson, H. P. and Company department store redesign, 37

Rubush (Preston C. and Renah Wilcox) House, 402–4, *403*

Rural Residences (Davis), 476

Russ, William Earl: Claypool Hotel, addition, 63; competition entry, 145

Russell, M. H., 489

Rustic style, 372; Coburn (August) Residence, 344, *344*; Fletcher (Stoughton A., II, and May Henley) "suburban" house, 342–44, *343*; Parry (David McLean and Hessie Maxwell) Estate ("Golden Hill"), 346–48, *347*, 549n69; Thornton (Florence Baxter and George D.) House, 340–42, *341*

Samuel H. Brubaker and Company: Century and John W. Murphy Buildings, 91, *93*, *94*

Sander, Carl, 408

Sangernebo, Alexander: commercial building designs, 18, 20, 23, 39, 46, 48, 68, 74, 76, 84, 85; ecclesiastical designs, 230, 246; public building designs, 118, 140–41, 187, 189; residential designs, 364, 365

San Lorenzo church, Florence, influence, 280
Santa Croce church, Florence, influence, 249
Santa Maria Maggiore, Rome, influence, 280
Sant'Andrea church, Mantua, influence, 280
Sant'Atanasio dei Greci, Rome, influence, 281, *282*
San Zeno church, Verona, Italy, 233
Scharn, John H., 36
Scharn and Rubush, 478
Scherrer, Adolph: about, 478, 481, 488; City Hospital, 205–9, *207*, *209*; competition entries, 112, 132, 145; Maennerchor Building, 195–98, *196*, *197*, 482. *See also* Adolph Scherrer and Son
Scherrer, Herman: City Hospital, administration building, 209, *209*
Scherrer, J. Anton: about, 206, 487; City Hospital, administration building, 209, *209* (*See also* Adolph Scherrer and Son)
Schiedeler, Anthony, 246
Schlacks, Henry: St. Catherine of Siena Catholic Church, 232–34, *233*; St. Joan of Arc Catholic Church, 495
Schnull, Gustav A., 302
Schnull, Matilda Mayer, 302, 305
Schnull-Rauch House, 302–5, *303*, *304*
Schoepf-McGowan syndicate, 10–13
Scholer, Walter, 486, 487
school buildings. *See* college and university buildings; educational buildings; public school buildings
Schreiber, George F.: Scottish Rite Cathedral, 495
Schuyler, Montgomery, 10
Schwarz, Rudolph, 171, 193, *194*
Scientific American, Architects and Builders Edition, 480
Scottish Rite Cathedral, 495
Sears, Roebuck and Company, 383, 422, 460
Second Bank of the United States, 472
Second Baptist Church, 271–74, *272*, *273*, 482, 489, 543n82
Second Christian Church, 287–88, *288*

INDEX | 617

Second Church of Christ, Scientist, 262–63, *263*
Second Presbyterian Church (1864–70), 477
Sekula, Gregory A., 3
Senate Avenue YMCA Building (1912–13), 189–93, *191*, *192*
Severin, Henry, 65
Shank, Samuel Lewis, 206
Sharah Tessila, Congregation, 264, *265*, 482
Shaw, Howard Van Doren: about, 336, *337* (portrait); Fairbanks (Charles Warren and Cornelia Cole) House, 334–38, *335*, 548n52; Huesmann (Louis and Mary McDonald) House, 334, 336; Marktown (Indiana), 336
Shaw, Robert Gould, 155
Shingle style: Fletcher (Stoughton A., II, and May Henley) "suburban" house, 342–44, *343*
showrooms. *See* automotive showrooms and service buildings
Shrewsbury House, 475
Shubert, Jacob, 72, 76
Shubert, Lee, 72
Shubert Theatrical Company, 72
Simmons, John, 164
Sisters of Charity of St. Vincent de Paul, 198, 201
Sisters of Providence at Saint Mary-of-the-Woods, 160, 163
Sisters of St. Francis of Lafayette, 204
Sisters of St. Francis of Oldenburg, 359
skyscrapers: Chicago's and New York's influence on, 9–10, 13, 104–5; Hotel Washington, 63, 65, *66*. *See also* office buildings; tripartite column formula
Slavonian immigrants, 254, 256
Slovenian immigrants and Slovenian Americans, 256
Smith (19th century builder), 473
Smith, Delavan, 29
social, fraternal, and athletic buildings, 110; African American Pythian Building, 181–83, *182*; Columbia Club (1900–1901), 173–76, *174*, *175*; Columbia Club (1924–25), 495; Indiana Grand Lodge of the Independent Order of Odd Fellows (Odd Fellows Building; 1907–8), 20–24, *22*; Indianapolis Athletic Club, 495; Maennerchor Building, 195–98, *196*, *197*; Main YMCA Building (1908–9), 185–87, *186*; Masonic Temple, 176–81, *178*, *179*, *180*; Oriental Lodge, 183–85, *184*; Senate Avenue YMCA Building (1912–13), 189–93, *191*, *192*; Southside Turnverein, 193–95, *194*; YWCA Building, 187–89, *188*
Society of Architectural Historians, 2
Southside Turnverein, 193–95, *194*, 482
Spanish Churrigueresque style: Indiana Theater, 495
Spanish Mission style: Burckhardt (Dr. Louis and Adele) House, 391–94, *393*; Coulter Flats, 444–46, *445*
Speaks (19th century builder), 473
Spink, Edgar G., 444, 558n107
SS. Peter and Paul Cathedral, 274–80, *276*, *277*, *278*, *279*
St. Agnes Academy, 163, *160*, 163–64, 481
Stanley, Clarence, 452, 456
St. Anthony's Catholic Church, 254–55, *255*
State of Indiana: architectural licenses required by, 485, 490, 561n28; Indiana School for the Deaf, 128–31, *129*, *130*; Robert W. Long Hospital, 209–11, *210*
St. Catherine of Siena Catholic Church, 232–34, *233*
Steele, Rembrandt (Brandt): art glass windows, 285, *286*, *287*, 325; Steele (Brandt F. and Helen McKay) House, 400–402, *401*
Steele, T. C., 400
Steele (Brandt F. and Helen McKay) House, 400–402, *401*
steel structural frames, 106–7
Stem, John H., 478; "Lombardy," influence, 340, 342, 372; Newton Claypool Building, 10, *11*; Parry (David McLean and Hessie

Maxwell) Estate ("Golden Hill"), 346–48, *347*, 549n69
Stephenson, Robert S.: Mayflower Congregational Church (with Greene), 225–28, *226, 227*
Stevenson (David and Mary Alvord) House, 476
St. Francis de Sales Catholic Church, 280–83, *282*, 482
St. Francis Hospital, Beech Grove, 204, *205*
Stickley, Gustav, influence, 287, 404, 406, 409, 461, 487. *See also Craftsman* (magazine)
Stirewalt, John, 473
St. Joan of Arc Catholic Church, 495
St. Margaret's Guild, 208
St. Mary's Catholic Church (1857–58), 246
St. Mary's Catholic Church (1911–12), 246–49, *247, 248*
Stone (trade journal), 480
St. Paul Methodist Episcopal Church (now Christ Missionary Baptist Church), 268, *269*
St. Peter's Basilica, nave, Rome, influence, 280
Strathmann, Edward C., 323
Street, J. Fletcher, 353
streetcars, 46
structural engineers, 19th century, 476
Stuart, James, 473
Sturges, Lewis H.: about, 482; Westminster Presbyterian Church, 268–71, *270*, 482
Stutz Motor Car Company Factory, 100, *102, 103*
St. Vincent's Hospital, 201–4, *203*
St. Vincent's Infirmary, 198
Sullivan, George R., 384
Sullivan, Louis, 88
Swarthwout, Egerton, 145
synagogues: Congregation Sharah Tessila, 264, *265*
Syracuse University, 490

Tabernacle Presbyterian Church (1922–24), 495
Taggart, Eva Bryant, 338
Taggart, Lucy: Taggart (Thomas and Eva Bryant) House (with Wallick), 338–40, *339*
Taggart, Thomas, 338
Taggart (Thomas and Eva Bryant) House, 338–40, *339*
Talbot, Ona, 35
Talbott, Henry M., 77
Tanner, George Gordon, 384
Tanner (George G. and Kate Block) House, 384, *385*
Tarkington, Booth, 330
Tarkington, Susannah, 330
Taylor, Isaac, 478
Taylor, James Knox, 111, 112, 114
Taylor, Robert M., Jr., 3
Technical Institute of Berlin, 50
Temple of Hephaestus, Athens, influence, 261
terra-cotta facades: Alhambra Theater, 77, *78, 79*; Hume-Mansur Building, 33–35, *34*, 107; Indianapolis News Building, 29–31, *30*; Kahn Office Building, 39, 48, 107; Marott's Shoes Building, 42–44, *43*; Pennway Building as an early example of, 27–29, *28*; retail buildings, 52; William H. Block Company Department Store, 48, *49*, 107
theaters, 69–76; Colonial Theater, 70–72, *71*; and hotels combined with, 69, *70*; Majestic Theater, 69, *70*; Murat Temple and Theater, 72–76, *73, 74, 75*; revolving stages, 72. *See also* movie theaters
Third Christian Church, 266–67, *267*
Thomas, Edwin W., 437
Thomas-Hunt Double, 436–37, *438, 439*
Thompson, Bona, 168
Thompson, Edward, 168
Thompson, Mary, 168
Thornton, Florence Baxter, 340
Thornton, George D., 340
Thornton (Florence Baxter and George D.) House, 340–42, *341*
three-part compositional formula. *See* tripartite column formula

INDEX | 619

Thurtle, John G., 478
Tiffany Studios, 142
Tinsley, William, 475, 476
Titsworth, Henry H., 456
Tomb of Mausolus at Halicarnassus, influence, 496
Tomlan, Mary Raddant, 3
Tomlan, Michael A., 3
Tomlinson Hall, 131
Tower of London (Queen's House), influence, 325, 326
Town, Ithiel, 473. *See also* Town and Davis
Town and Davis: Indiana Statehouse (1831–35), 473–74
Town Hall of Toulon, France, influence, 546n9
Traylor, Marion H., 478
Treatise on Civil Architecture (Chambers), 472
Trinity Episcopal Church, Boston, 229
tripartite column formula: in apartment buildings, 441; hotels, 63, 66; illustrated, 524; in office buildings, 9–10, 12, 16, 18, 23, 24, 34, 35, 40; powerhouses, 93; in retail buildings, 46; term coined by Montgomery Schyler, 10
Tudor style. *See* English Tudor palace style; English Tudor vernacular style
Turners *(turnverein)*, 193
Tuschinsky, Alex, 366, 367, 551n104

Union Station Concourse and Train Shed, Indianapolis, 82–87, *83, 85, 86,* 106, 350; centrality and importance of, 7
Union Station, Washington, D. C., 14
United Brethren Church, 164, 166
university buildings. *See* college and university buildings
University Heights Addition, 164, 166
University of Illinois, 479, 490
University of Notre Dame, 486, 561n33
University of Pennsylvania, 39, 106, 152, 206, 212, 480, 485, 486
University of Virginia, 472

US Army, US Quartermaster General's Office: Fort Benjamin Harrison, 119, *122, 123, 124, 125,* 126–28, *127*
US Capitol, 472
US Department of the Treasury: competition, 112, 483; US Courthouse and Post Office (1857–61), 111; US Courthouse and Post Office (1903–5), 111–19, *113, 115–18,* 483

Van Arman, Marshall E.: about, 483; Thornton (Florence Baxter and George D.) House, 340–42, *341*
Van Camp, Clarissa Lintner, 310, 314
Van Camp, Frank, 310, 314
Van Camp, Raymond P., 460
Van Camp (Frank and Clarissa Lintner) House, 310–14, *312,* 349, 350, 483
Vanderbilt, George Washington, 345
Vanderstel, Sheryl, 3
Van Ingen, W. B., 118
Vassall-Longfellow House, Cambridge, MA, influence, 320
vaudeville, 69, 70, 71–72
Vitruvius, 485
Vogel, William D., 429
Vogel (William D.) House, 428, 429–30
Von Hake, Carl, 42
Vonnegut, Arthur C., 50–51, *51* (portrait)
Vonnegut, Bernard: about, 50, 91, 461, 478, 479, 481, 487; Indianapolis Star Building, 20, 21; Levey (Louis and Alice Reynolds) House, 305–6, *306;* Lieber (Herman P. and Alma Bachman) House, 323–25, *324;* L. S. Ayres and Company Department Store, 44–46, *45;* Methodist Hospital, 199–200, *201;* Schnull-Rauch House, 302–5, *303, 304;* Southside Turnverein, 193–95, *194. See also* Vonnegut and Bohn
Vonnegut, Bohn and Mueller, 50–51
Vonnegut, Clemens, Jr., 320
Vonnegut, Kurt, Sr.: about, 50–51, *51* (portrait), 486, 487; All Souls Unitarian Church, 284–87, *285, 286;* Fletcher

620 | INDEX

Savings and Trust Building, 39–42, *41*, 482; Hibben, Hollweg, and Company Building, 90–91, *92*, *93*; Hotel Severin, 65, *67*, *68*, 68–69;; Kahn Office Building, 35, *38*, 39, 48; Kahn Tailoring Company Factory, 103, *104*; William H. Block Company Department Store, 48, *49*, 482

Vonnegut and Bohn: about, 50, *51* (portraits), 478, 481; All Souls Unitarian Church, 284–87, *285*, *286*, 482; City Hospital competition, 206; competition entries, 39, 112; Fletcher Savings and Trust Building, 39–42, *41*, 482; George Washington High School, 50; Hibben, Hollweg, and Company Building, 90–91, *92*, *93*; Hotel Severin, 65, *67*, *68*, 68–69; Indiana Bell Telephone downtown buildings, 50; Indianapolis Star Building, *20*, *21*; John Herron Art Institute, 168–73, *170*, *172*, 482; Kahn Office Building, 35, *38*, 39, 48; Kahn Tailoring Company Factory, 103, *104*; Lieber (Herman P. and Alma Bachman) House, 323–25, *324*; L. S. Ayres and Company Department Store, 44–46, *45*, *52*, 482; Marott's Shoes Building, 42–44, *43*; Methodist Hospital, 199–201, *200*; Meyer-Kiser Bank, 50; Public Schools 10, 15, 35, 45; Roosevelt Building, 50; Southside Turnverein, 193–95, *194*, 482; William H. Block Company Department Store, 48, *49*, 50, 482

Voysey, Charles F., influence, 336, 384

Walker, Lahla Bond, 406
Walker, Madam C. J., 190, 418–20, *419* (portrait)
Walker, William A., 406
Walker and Weeks: Indiana World War Memorial Plaza, 496
Walker (Madam C. J.) House, 418–20, *419*
Walker (William A. and Lahla Bond) House, 406, *407*
Walker Theater, 37

Walk-Over Boot Shop, 440
Waller, Bret, 3
Wallick, Frederick: Taggart (Thomas and Eva Bryant) House (with Lucy Taggart), 338–40, *339*
Wallingford, Charles A., 478
Ware, William Robert, 479
Warfield, Wilson R., 446
Warren, H. Langford, 112
Washington, Booker T., 193
Wasson, H.P. and Company department store redesign (1934–36), 37
wealthy residents: 300–301 (*See also* city mansions; country estates; country retreats, Rustic; residential architecture (mansions and estates))
Weisenburgh, Philip A., 37, 496
Werner, Ernest, 37
Westbrook, B. J. F., 272
Western Association of Architects, 481
West Indianapolis, IN, 223
Westminster Presbyterian Church, 268–71, *270*
Wheeler, C. A., 52
Wheeler, Clifton, 208
Wheeler, Douglas, 350
Wheeler, Frank H., 348–50, 354
Wheeler, Harriet Githens, 350, 354
Wheeler (Frank H. and Harriet Githens) Estate, 84, 89, 348–54, *349*, *351*, *352*, *353*, *356*, 483
Wheeler & Schebler, 349
When Building, 486
White, Howard, 14
White House, Washington, DC, influence, 318
White, Howard J., 24. *See also* D. H. Burnham and Company
Whitford, Mary, 490
wholesale buildings, 87–95; Hibben, Hollweg, and Company Building, 90–91, *92*, *93*; KO-WE-BA Building, 87, 90, *90*
Wicks, S. C., 284
Wight, Peter B. 14

Wild, J. F., 186
William A. Bell School 60, 160, *161*
William H. Block Company Department Store, 48, *49*, 482
William L. Stevenson Building, 483
Williams, Oliver, 55
Williams Building, 55, *56*, *57*
Williamson, Fred C., 14, 24. *See also* D.H. Burnham and Company
Willis, Joseph, 474; Indiana State Asylum for the Education of the Deaf and Dumb, 128
Wilson Brothers and Company (Philadelphia), 120
Wilson, Chester P., 460
Windle, John T., 3
Windom, James H. (Philadelphia), 120
Winslow House, River Forest, IL, influence, 354, *355*, 356, 394
Winter, Ferdinand, 449, 452
Winter, William, 452
Winter Apartments, 449–52, *450*, *451*
Winterrowd, Thomas A.: about, 478, 483; Rink (Joseph A. and Caroline Pfau) House, 308–9, *309*; Robert Gould Shaw School 40, 155, *157*
Winterrowd, Victor E.: Alhambra Theater, 77, *78*, *79*
women architects, 471, 486, 488, 490–92
Women's Home Missionary Societies of Indiana, 199
Wooden, Howard E., 3
Wood Livery Stable, 77

Woodruff, James O., 307
Woodruff Place, IN: Lewis (Frank W. and Emma Salter) House, 306–8, *307*
Wood-Worker, 480
Woollen, Evans, III, 245
Woollen, Evans, Sr., 39
working-class residents, 381–83, 425–27. *See also* apartments; bungalows; doubles
World War I, 8, 104–5, 151, 495
Wren, Sir Christopher, influence: Royal Hospital at Chelsea, London, 456
Wright, Frank Lloyd, influence: Heurtley House, Oak Park, IL, 356; Winslow House, River Forest, IL, 354, *355*, 356, 394
Wuensch (Edwin) House, 431–33, *432*
Wulschner-Stewart Building, 52, *53*
Wythongan Valley Preservation Council, 3

Yale University architecture program, 336
YMCA Building (1886–87), 186
YMCA Building, Main (1908–9), 185–87, *186*, 482
YMCA Building (1912–13; Senate Avenue), 189–93, *191*, *192*
York and Sawyer, 39, 40, 145
York Rite Masonic lodges, 177, 181
Young Builders' General Instructor, The (Lafever), 472
YWCA Building, 187–89, *188*

Zeigler, Shafer, 460
Zettler, A., *312*, 313, 314

JAMES A. GLASS is an Indianapolis-based historic preservation and heritage consultant with over forty-five years of experience as a historian, deputy state historic preservation officer, and professor in the preservation field. He holds a PhD in the history of architecture and historic preservation planning from Cornell University and lectures regularly on the architectural history of other countries and Indianapolis.

FOR INDIANA UNIVERSITY PRESS

Tony Brewer *Artist and Book Designer*
Dan Crissman *Acquisitions Editor and Editorial Director*
Anna Francis *Assistant Acquisitions Editor*
Anna Garnai *Production Coordinator*
Samantha Heffner *Marketing and Publicity Manager*
Katie Huggins *Production Manager*
Darja Malcom-Clarke *Project Manager/Editor*
Dan Pyle *Online Publishing Manager*
Michael Regoli *Director of Publishing Operations*
Stephen Williams *Assistant Director of Marketing*
Jennifer Witzke *Senior Artist and Book Designer*